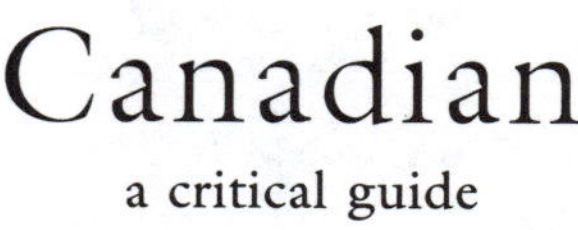

Canadian
a critical guide
Children's
to authors
Books
and illustrators

Raymond E. Jones
& Jon C. Stott

OXFORD
UNIVERSITY PRESS

OXFORD
UNIVERSITY PRESS

70 Wynford Drive, Don Mills, Ontario M3C 1J9
www.oupcan.com

Oxford University Press is a department of the University of Oxford.
It furthers the University's objective of excellence in research, scholarship,
and education by publishing worldwide in

Oxford New York

Athens Auckland Bangkok Bogotá Buenos Aires Calcutta
Cape Town Chennai Dar es Salaam Delhi Florence Hong Kong Istanbul
Karachi Kuala Lumpur Madrid Melbourne Mexico City Mumbai
Nairobi Paris São Paulo Singapore Taipei Tokyo Toronto Warsaw

with associated companies in Berlin Ibadan

Oxford is a trade mark of Oxford University Press
in the UK and in certain other countries

Published in Canada
by Oxford University Press

First published 2000

Canadian Cataloguing in Publication Data

Jones, Raymond E.
Canadian children's books : a critical guide to authors and illustrators

Authors in reverse order on first ed.
First ed. published under title: Canadian books for children.
Includes index.
ISBN 0-19-541222-2

1. Children's literature, Canadian – Bio-bibliography. 2. Illustrated children's books – Canada – Bio-bibliography. 3. Authors, Canadian. 4. Illustrators – Canada. 5. Children's literature, Canadian. I. Stott, Jon C., 1939– . Canadian books for children. II. Title.

PS8081.S86 2000 C810.9'9282 C00-930610-2
PR9186.2.S86 2000

Cover illustration from *Last Leaf First Snowflake to Fall*. Text and illustrations copyright © 1993 by Leo Yerxa. First published in Canada by Groundwood Books/Douglas & McIntyre. Reprinted by permission of the publisher.

Cover & Text Design: Tearney McMurtry

1 2 3 4 – 03 02 01 00

This book is printed on permanent (acid-free) paper ∞
Printed in Canada

Contents

In memory of my father, Edgar R. Jones,
who shared his love of words.
R.E.J.

For my children, Clare and Andrew,
who always gave support and inspiration.
J.C.S.

Acknowledgements

Like all books, this one has come into print only because many people have assisted the authors. First of all, we must thank the writers, illustrators, and publishers who have spoken to us over the years, sharing with us their experiences and helping us to gain a better appreciation of Canadian children's books and the conditions under which they are produced. Next we owe a debt of gratitude to Euan White, Laura Macleod, and Phyllis Wilson of Oxford University Press, Toronto, who believed in our project and were unflagging in their support. A number of people helped us during its composition. Graham Murphy, Leslie Helper, Karen Clark, and Carolyn Ives assisted us in compiling the bibliographies and lists of reviews. The staffs at the Herbert T. Coutts Library at the University of Alberta and the Southgate Branch of the Edmonton Public Library were gracious and efficient in obtaining many of the books and journals we needed. Roderick McGillis, University of Calgary, and Karen Day, University College of the Cariboo, deserve special thanks for reading major portions of the manuscript and for offering perceptive, helpful comments. Finally, we are grateful to our extraordinary copy editors, Laurna and Richard Tallman: they showed a flawless attention to detail, impeccable taste, and admirable tact while preparing the manuscript for the press.

Introduction

About 15 years ago, one of the authors of this book introduced himself to a new university faculty member who was moving into the office next door. When this new colleague, a Scots lady, learned that she was speaking to someone who specialized in children's literature, she was dismayed, declaring that the subject 'nae belongs in the academy'. Although she then defended her own specialty, Zane Grey and cowboy stories, as a serious academic pursuit that explored popular mythology and the American psyche, she refused to acknowledge that children's literature had any similar merit, that it could, for example, be studied as a way of understanding both adult attitudes to children and the values adults wanted children to accept or to challenge. Furthermore, when she learned that her neighbour had a particular interest in Canadian children's literature, she declared that the only Canadian book for children that she had ever heard of was *Anne of Green Gables*, which she immediately waved aside as fit only for sentimental girls. She then issued a challenge: 'Tell me, what other Canadian books for kids are worth studying?'

For most of this country's history, this question would have given pause to the most ardent literary nationalist. Even if such a person believed that children's literature is an important cultural enterprise that both reflects and shapes national identity, he or she would have had to apologize for Canadian children's literature as 'a poor thing, but mine own'. Simply put, up until about 20 years ago, books for Canadian children were neither numerous nor of the highest quality. For instance, it became so difficult to find worthy recipients that the Governor-General's Literary Awards for Juvenile Literature were suspended in 1959. Furthermore, Canadians themselves ignored most Canadian books for children, except for L.M. Montgomery's ubiquitous *Anne* series and the animal stories of Charles G.D. Roberts and Ernest Thompson Seton. (Ironically, these staples of Canadian libraries were initially published in the United States.)

The reasons for the paucity of Canadian children's books are similar to those that limited development of a Canadian literature for adults. Canada's small population and the vast distances between centres long made book publishing an expensive and risky undertaking. During the nineteenth century and the early part of the twentieth century, pioneering communities often regarded books, except for the Bible, religious tracts, and educational texts, as luxuries. Besides, British and American books were readily available and relatively more affordable than native products. Books from elsewhere had another attraction: they had already achieved approval in centres of intellect or fashion, making them highly desirable to a people sometimes afflicted with the national disease of many colonial cultures: the feeling that other cultures are superior.

Although hymns and religious works for children were printed earlier, Canadian children's literature in English probably begins with Mrs H. Bayley, the first resident of Canada to write a work of fiction for children. Her *Improvement; or, A Visit to Grandmama* (1832) is, as its title implies, a didactic tale designed to teach morality and to impart factual information. The first important children's novel written by a Canadian resident appeared 20 years later. Catharine Parr Traill's *The Canadian Crusoes* (1852) is a survival tale that set the pattern for the use of the Canadian wilderness as the testing ground of character. It was R.M. Ballantyne, however, who wrote the first widely popular children's books exploiting Canadian settings, *Snowflakes and Sunbeams* (1856) and *Ungava* (1858). A few years later, James De Mille showed that Canada could be a setting for more than wilderness survival tales. With *B.O.W.C.: A Book for Boys* (1869), the opening volume of 'The Brethren of the White Cross' series of school stories, he launched the first juvenile series written by a Canadian-born author.

If Canadian children's literature did not flourish, it still produced several notable books before World War I. Margaret Marshall Saunders became a best-selling author in the United States with *Beautiful Joe* (1894), the sentimental autobiography of an abused dog. More significantly, such works as Ernest Thompson Seton's *Wild Animals I Have Known* (1898) and Charles G.D. Roberts's *The Kindred of the Wild* (1902) established a new literary genre, the realistic animal story. The most famous of Canadian novels, however, was Montgomery's *Anne of Green Gables* (1907), which made both its author and its Prince Edward Island setting internationally famous.

The most significant Canadian children's book to appear between the two world wars was Grey Owl's *The Adventures of Sajo and Her Beaver People* (1935), an animal story expressing respect for nature. During World War II, Roderick Haig-Brown injected life into the formulaic wilderness adventure with *Starbuck Valley Winter* (1943). Shortly after the war, Catherine Anthony Clark added a new dimension to Canadian children's literature by writing the first true fantasy to employ Canadian materials, *The Golden Pine Cone* (1950). The wilderness continued to exert its hold during the 1950s, Farley Mowat writing a quintessential Arctic survival story, *Lost in the Barrens* (1956). Mowat also pioneered in another area, showing that animal tales did not have to be of either the anthropomorphic kind presented by Margaret Marshall Saunders or the 'red in tooth and red in claw' kind favoured by Seton and Roberts. In such books as *The Dog Who Wouldn't Be* (1957) and *Owls in the Family* (1961), Mowat made the relationships between people and animals both comical and touching.

The real upsurge in publishing for Canadian children came in the wake of the nationalism that developed as a result of the Centennial celebrations in 1967. During that celebratory year, there were three major events important to the growth of children's literature. First, Sheila Egoff published the first history of Canadian children's books, *The Republic of Childhood: A Critical Guide to Children's Literature in English*, drawing attention to an area of the national culture that had previously been shamefully ignored. Second, *In Review*, the first journal dedicated to reviewing Canadian children's books and to providing profiles of their authors, made its debut. Third, Tundra Books, the first small publishing firm devoted exclusively to producing Canadian children's books as works of art, was founded. Together, these three events suggested that the country was now mature enough and confident enough to produce its own literature for children.

Over the next few years, a number of other factors helped to change the climate for Canadian children's books. Dennis Lee's *Alligator Pie,* published in 1974, became a best seller, showing that there was a profitable market for Canadian children's books. In 1975, Elizabeth Waterston, Mary Rubio, and John Sorfleet founded *Canadian Children's Literature*, the first academic journal devoted to the subject, and the Canada Council began giving out prizes that honoured significant achievements. Such awards not only encouraged authors to write works of high quality, but they publicized literary achievements, making the public aware of and responsive to the idea that excellent books could be written in Canada. In the following year, Irma McDonough, long the editor of *In Review*, saw another of her dreams realized with the founding of the Canadian Children's Book Centre, which helps publishers to promote interest in their wares through such activities as Young Canada Book Week and its annual *Our Choice* compilations of good books. Federal and provincial government agencies also played a major role. The Canadian Book Publishing Development Program was established in 1976 to provide funding that would ensure profitable publication of Canadian books. The Canada Council and various provincial arts programs also began giving grants to both publishers and writers, creating a healthy climate for the book industry. Such programs made possible the creation of Vancouver's Groundwood Books, Edmonton's Tree Frog Press, and Toronto's Kids Can Press and Annick Press, which began as small firms specializing in the production of children's books. (All but Tree Frog have since grown into major forces in children's publishing.)

These factors produced a climate conducive to writers, illustrators, and publishers, so strong imaginative talents began devoting themselves to books for children. Since the late 1970s, they have produced an unparalleled abundance of high-quality literature of all kinds. For example, novelists such as Kevin Major, Brian Doyle, and Cora Taylor have depicted their own regions in ways that make them accessible and entertaining to children all over the country. Monica Hughes developed science fiction that stands as a touchstone for all juvenile works in that genre. Welwyn Katz and Michael Bedard began pushing the boundaries, giving fantasy a darker symbolic edge. Historical novelists like Janet Lunn, Kit Pearson, Karleen Bradford, and, more recently, Janet McNaughton have provided highly entertaining and informative works that do not blink at the rougher areas of social experience. The picture book writer Robert Munsch and the author-illustrator Ian Wallace have produced books for younger readers that have proved to be equally popular with readers in other countries. Canadian books gained such acceptance that it became possible for Canadian writers to thrive by providing 'recreational reading', books that are unabashedly 'escapist'. Gordon Korman thus created a following in Canada and the US for his antic school stories, Eric Wilson became popular for his mysteries set in various Canadian regions, and Martyn Godfrey and Paul Kropp churned out 'high-interest, low-vocabulary' books that they hoped would eventually lure reluctant readers on to more substantial works.

With the proliferation and acceptance of Canadian books, it is not surprising that an increasing number of them not only reflect but emanate from minority and Aboriginal communities. Barbara Smucker's Mennonite stories, Paul Yee's books about the Chinese-Canadian population, and Tololwa Mollel's retellings of African tales are just a few of the books that touch on Canada's ethnic diversity. The books of Maria Campbell, C.J. Taylor, Michael Kusugak, and Beatrice Culleton (now Beatrice Mosionier) are among those reflecting the experiences of Métis and Aboriginal peoples. In addition to these writers, who have received publication by major houses, the praise of critics, awards from various groups, and the satisfaction of seeing their books included in libraries from coast to coast, there are other ethnic and Aboriginal writers who have not yet achieved critical or popular recognition because they have not produced a large body of work or because they are published by small presses, whose editions are not widely distributed and may sometimes look crude compared to those from larger houses. Among the small presses encouraging minority writers are Sister Vision (books by black women and women of colour), Theytus Books (titles on Native themes by Native authors), and Pemmican Publications (books by and about Métis and Aboriginal peoples). In addition, Native and cultural groups across the country have developed numerous publishing projects to celebrate and to preserve their traditions. For example, Alberta's Kayas Cultural Centre and the Little Red River Board of Education, in co-operation with the Little Red River Band, produced several illustrated booklets retelling Native legends. Most encouraging, however, is the tendency of publishers large and small to issue books in which the racial or ethnic identity of the main characters is a fact, not the main theme. Such books move beyond the multicultural didacticism that made characters from minority groups important only insofar as they could teach lessons in tolerance to readers who belonged to the majority culture. Like books about characters of European ancestry, that is, these books insist that their characters are noteworthy not simply as members of a group but as individuals with significant or interesting experiences.

Our Scots colleague has moved away, but if we could speak to her today, we would respond to her question about what is worth studying by recounting some of the above history of the development of Canadian children's literature. The rest of our answer appears in the entries that follow, entries that together constitute a picture of the main streams of English-Canadian children's publishing: we include artists who have produced various kinds of books, who lived in different periods and regions, who have been published by big and small presses alike, and who have a variety of ethnic or cultural backgrounds. We have included also some French-language authors who are known in English Canada through translations.

Each of the 133 entries is designed to introduce adults—teachers, librarians, parents, grandparents, students of childhood and children's literature, all those interested in Canadian culture or Canadian children's books—to some of the women and men who have created a rich and varied literature. Each of the articles is designed to give adult readers factual and critical information that will help them to engage more fully with specific books. Each entry thus provides an overview of the individual's career; an introduction to major themes, character types, and techniques; and a more detailed look at major works. The focus is on the person as author and/or illustrator, rather than on the author/illustrator as person. Thus, biographical facts are kept to a minimum, most being presented in tabular form before the article itself. Over the years we have been fortunate to interview dozens of Canadian authors, illustrators, and publishers, who freely discussed their work and their creative processes. We have frequently drawn on these interviews in writing our essays.

Preceding each article are bibliographies of the subject's books for children. To the best of our knowledge, they contain all works published prior to January 1999. In some cases, however, we have been able to include information on works published after that date and to include discussions of them. Immediately following the publication data of each title published after 1967 is a list of selected reviews of that book. Lists of related works by each subject and of critical discussions about that person follow the primary bibliographies. At the end of each author essay, we include, where available, a list of selected reference works containing information about the subject. It is our hope that the articles will not only provide useful introductions to the subjects, but that the bibliographical materials will also provide students of Canadian children's literature with starting points for further research. Because of space limitations, we have used an abbreviated form for bibliographical notations, an explanation of which appears after this introduction. To supplement information included in the entries, we have included appendices listing the winners of major Canadian book awards and sources of information for those who wish to undertake further study.

The subjects of the following essays are writers and illustrators of what is often called imaginative literature: fiction, picture books, written versions of traditional tales, and poetry. Because we are concerned with books, we do not discuss dramatists, whose art is concrete and requires performance. We do, however, discuss plays when their author has been included primarily because of works produced in one of our areas of concentration. Similarly, we discuss non-fiction, or 'information books', only to round out discussion of subjects chosen primarily because of their work in other areas.

We have chosen our subjects for a number of reasons: some are historically important, having pioneered various genres and having established patterns that influenced later artists; some have received significant critical acclaim; some have been honoured with major awards; some have attained popularity, indicated by the dedication of their readers, the sales statistics for individual titles, the number of copies of their books in libraries, or the sheer volume of their artistic output; some have produced one or more books that have been influential or unusual; some still at the beginning of their careers have shown the early signs of becoming important in the field.

The essays do not, of course, include all the writers and illustrators who meet these criteria. We have had to settle for a representative sample of the writers and illustrators who have created Canadian children's literature. The process of selection has involved difficult choices and some compromises. For example, even though he is historically important, as we indicate above, we have not included James De Mille because he had little or no influence on other children's authors, and because his children's books, which have long been out of print, are nearly impossible to find outside of large university libraries. We have also had to exclude some promising writers because they have not yet produced a significant body of high-quality work. We hope, however, that such artists will continue to develop so that we can include discussions of their work in any future books we publish.

Because we have had to choose, we will, undoubtedly, have omitted some people our readers believe to be worthy of inclusion. Nevertheless, we hope that we have included studies of at least some writers and illustrators who are not familiar to our readers and that our discussions will stimulate them to explore further or to re-evaluate the works of those writers with whom they are familiar. We also hope that this book will lead adults to discover for themselves some of the rich pleasures offered by Canadian books for children and that it will then encourage them to share these pleasures with children, whether in the library, the classroom, or the home.

ABBREVIATIONS

AAYA	*Authors and Artists for Young Adults* (Detroit: Gale Research)
APBR	*Atlantic Provinces Book Review*
BiC	*Books in Canada*
BYP	*Books for Young People*
CA	*Contemporary Authors* (Detroit: Gale Research)
CAFR	*Contemporary Authors First Revision Series* (Detroit: Gale Research)
CANR	*Contemporary Authors New Revision Series* (Detroit: Gale Research)
CAP	*Contemporary Authors Permanent Series* (Detroit: Gale Research)
CBRA	*Canadian Book Review Annual* (Reviews appearing in the unpaginated 1993 volume are cited by item number, preceded by the symbol #.)
CCB-B	Center for Children's Books—*Bulletin*
CCL	*Canadian Children's Literature*
ChL	*Children's Literature*
ChLQ	*Children's Literature Association Quarterly*
CL	*Canadian Literature*
CLC	*Contemporary Literary Criticism* (Detroit: Gale Research)
CLR	*Children's Literature Review* (Detroit: Gale Research)
CM	*CM: Canadian Materials*
DLB	*Dictionary of Literary Biography* (Detroit: Gale Research)
EL	*Emergency Librarian*
HB	*The Horn Book Magazine*
IR	*In Review*
JR	*Journal of Reading*
Junior 1	*Junior Books of Authors*, 2nd edn, eds Stanley J. Kunitz and Howard Haycraft (New York: H.W. Wilson, 1951)
Junior 2	*More Junior Authors*, ed. Muriel Fuller (New York: H.W. Wilson, 1963)
Junior 3	*Third Book of Junior Authors*, eds Doris De Montreville and Elizabeth D. Crawford (New York: H.W. Wilson, 1972)
Junior 4	*Fourth Book of Junior Authors and Illustrators*, eds Doris De Montreville and Elizabeth D. Crawford (New York: H.W. Wilson, 1978)
Junior 5	*Fifth Book of Junior Authors and Illustrators*, ed. Sally Holmes Holtze (New York: H.W. Wilson, 1983)
Junior 6	*Sixth Book of Junior Authors and Illustrators*, ed. Sally Holmes Holtze (New York: H.W. Wilson, 1989)
Junior 7	*Seventh Book of Junior Authors and Illustrators*, ed. Sally Holmes Holtze (New York: H.W. Wilson, 1996)
MAICYA	*Major Authors and Illustrators for Children and Young Adults* (Detroit: Gale Research, 1993)

MCAI	*Meet Canadian Authors and Illustrators: 50 Creators of Children's Books*, Allison Gertridge (Toronto: Scholastic Canada, 1994)
NYTBR	*New York Times Book Review*
Ocean	*One Ocean Touching: Papers from the First Pacific Rim Conference on Children's Literature*, ed. Sheila Egoff (Metuchen, NJ and London: Scarecrow, 1979)
Profiles	*Profiles*, rev. edn, ed. Irma McDonough (Ottawa: Canadian Library Association, 1975)
Profiles 2	*Profiles*, ed. Irma McDonough (Ottawa: Canadian Library Association, 1982)
QQ	*Quill and Quire*
RT	*Reading Teacher*
SAAS	*Something About the Author Autobiography Series* (Detroit: Gale Research)
SATA	*Something About the Author*
SL	*School Librarian*
SLJ	*School Library Journal*
TCCW	*The St. James Guide to Children's Writers* (Detroit: Gale Research, 1999), the new name for the fifth edition of *Twentieth-Century Children's Writers*. Many of the entries we cite also appear in *Twentieth-Century Children's Writers*, 4th edn (Detroit: St James Press, 1995).
TCYAW	*Twentieth-Century Young Adult Writers* (Detroit: St James Press, 1994)
TES	*Times Education Supplement*
TLS	*Times Literary Supplement*
WSMP	*Writing Stories, Making Pictures: Biographies of 150 Canadian Children's Authors and Illustrators* (Toronto: Canadian Children's Book Centre, 1994)
VOYA	*Voice of Youth Advocates*

Author Entries

Sue Ann Alderson

Born: 11 September 1940, in New York City.

Principal Residences: New York City; Columbus, Ohio; Berkeley, Calif.; Vancouver.

Education: Antioch College (BA 1962); Ohio State University (MA 1964); University of California, Berkeley.

Career: editorial assistant, *Parents' Magazine*; assistant preschool teacher, New Haven, Conn.; professor of creative writing, University of British Columbia; writer.

Works for Children

Bonnie McSmithers You're Driving Me Dithers, illus. Fiona Garrick (Edmonton: Tree Frog, 1974). **Rev:** *IR* 9 (Summer 1975): 18.

Hurry Up, Bonnie!, illus. Fiona Garrick (Edmonton: Tree Frog, 1976). **Rev:** *CCL* 34 (1984), 88; *EL* 18 (Sept. 1990): 60; *IR* 12 (Sept. 1978): 31.

The Adventures of Prince Paul, illus. Jane Wolsack (Vancouver: Fforbez, 1977). **Rev:** *CCL* 15/16 (1980): 94; *IR* 12 (Summer 1978): 40.

The Finding Princess, illus. Jane Wolsack (Vancouver: Fforbez, 1977). **Rev:** *CCL* 15/16 (1980): 94; *IR* 12 (Summer 1978): 41.

Bonnie McSmithers Is At It Again!, illus. Fiona Garrick (Edmonton: Tree Frog, 1979). **Rev:** *CCL* 34 (1984): 88; *EL* 18 (Sept. 1990): 60; *IR* 14 (Oct. 1980): 34; *SLJ* 27 (Jan. 1981): 46.

Comet's Tale, illus. Georgia Pow Graham (Edmonton: Tree Frog, 1983). **Rev:** *EL* 12 (Nov. 1984): 22; *QQ* 49 (Nov, 1983): 24.

The Not Impossible Summer, illus. C. Rother (Toronto: Irwin, 1983). **Rev:** *BiC* 12 (Nov. 1983): 17; *QQ* 49 (Nov. 1983): 24.

The Something in Thurlo Darby's House, illus. Deborah Drew-Brook-Cormack (Toronto: Ginn, 1984).

Ida and the Wool Smugglers, illus. Ann Blades (Toronto: Groundwood, 1988). **Rev:** *BiC* 17 (June 1988): 37; *CCL* 52 (1988): 27; *CL* (Autumn 1989): 246; *CM* 16 (Sept. 1988): 180; *HB* 64 (May 1988): 336; *SLJ* 34 (Aug. 1988): 77.

Maybe You Had to be There, by Duncan (Vancouver: Polestar Press, 1989). **Rev:** *EL* 17 (Mar. 1990): 60.

Chapter One (Toronto: General Publishing, 1990). **Rev:** *CCL* 66 (1992): 76.

Sure As Strawberries, illus. Karen Reczuch (Red Deer, Alta: Red Deer College Press, 1992). **Rev:** *CM* 21 (Jan. 1993): 19; *EL* 21 (Mar. 1994): 16; *QQ* 58 (Dec. 1992): 27.

A Ride for Martha, illus. Ann Blades (Toronto: Groundwood, 1993). **Rev:** *QQ* 59 (Oct. 1993): 38.

Ten Mondays for Lots of Boxes (Vancouver: Ronsdale Press, 1995).

Pond Seasons, illus. Ann Blades (Toronto: Groundwood, 1997). **Rev:** *EL* 25 (Mar. 1998): 27; *QQ* 63 (Apr. 1997): 37.

A love of wordplay, careful observation of the antics of her two children, and an understanding of child and family psychology are major elements that Sue Ann Alderson has used in the creation of her books for children and young adults. When her first book, *Bonnie McSmithers You're Driving Me Dithers*, appeared in 1974, it was enthusiastically reviewed and she wrote two sequels. Since then she has created the texts for picture books, two literary fairy tales, and several novels.

Each Bonnie McSmithers book focuses on the conflicts between the title character and her mother. In *Bonnie McSmithers You're Driving Me Dithers*, the little girl keeps getting into trouble—using a banana peel as a hat, washing the walls with toothpaste, cutting the dog's hair. After each episode the mother begins her despairing refrain, 'Bonnie McSmithers you're driving me dithers' and sends her child either outside or to her room. The resolution occurs when Bonnie asks her mother to join her in an activity, and the mother realizes that she has been as responsible as her child for the conflict. This summary reveals the psychological basis of the story and its careful observation of children and parents. Its popularity arises not only from the humour of the situations, but also from the rhythmic poetic prose in the refrain concluding each episode. Young children can easily learn the words and say them along with an adult reader. In *Hurry Up, Bonnie!* and *Bonnie McSmithers Is at It Again*, mother and child engage in further activities together and work towards resolving their conflicts.

Alderson's novels also deal with relationships between children and adults, but include a larger number of characters. *Comet's Tale* is about Wanda, Willy, and Walter II; their father, Max, a painter whose favourite subjects include 'poached eggs', 'mermaids', and 'long woolen underwear'; their mother, Vanessa, a poet who writes such lines as 'there's a rose in every cabbage'; Aunt Tweedle, who forces cream of rosehip soup on everyone; and Theodore Rexford Fripple, the local poundkeeper, who spends much of his time standing on his head. The plot involves two sinister characters who wish to close the pound and who kidnap the baby, a dreaded visit from Aunt Tweedle, and the appearance of Hartley's comet, supposedly the cause of the unusual events of the novel. Underlying the humorous plot is a serious theme: the need for individuals to feel special and to belong to a loving group. At the end of the story, everyone realizes that, as Max says, 'We have a pretty special family.'

Maybe You Had to Be There, by Duncan, an autobiographical novel written as an English project by a grade six boy who considers himself very average, also presents the humorous adventures of children encountering zany adult characters. With his new friend Magnolia, Duncan thwarts the plans of Hoskins, the school bully, and his uncle to steal an ancient tooth reported to have come from the mouth of Saint Anthony of Padua. Duncan's mother has a hobby of stripping old chairs and has dozens stored in her basement. Magnolia's father likes to create what he calls ancient manuscripts. Duncan's friendship with Magnolia, who declares him a knight near the end of the story, gives him a stronger sense of self-worth. In the concluding chapter, his passive resistance to Hoskins, who has been taking protection money from small children, results in the bully's defeat.

The Not Impossible Summer, intended for older readers, is more serious in tone. Jenny and her mother are spending a summer vacation on one of the Gulf Islands of British Columbia. The mother, busy writing a historical article, has little time for her daughter, who feels somewhat antagonistic but wants to please her parent. During the vacation Jenny achieves a sense of self-worth, gains her mother's admiration and respect, and is able to let go of Debra, an imaginary friend she had turned to in times of loneliness and rejection.

At the beginning of *Chapter One*, another novel for older readers, Beth is annoyed that she must give up her bedroom for her grandmother, who is suffering from Alzheimer's disease, and that she must care for the old lady when she would rather spend time with her grade eight friends, whose approval she seeks. Gradually she realizes how important her mother and grandmother are to her and faces the inadequacy of the two important males in her life. Chris, her boyfriend who 'liked to live on the edge', often scorns her for being a 'goody-goody', begins to date one of her friends, and commits acts of petty vandalism. When she visits her father, who now lives in Toronto, he is more interested in his newest, and very chic, lady friend and his important meetings than he is in her.

In two picture books illustrated by Ann Blades, Alderson depicts events in the life of a girl living on British Columbia's Salt Spring Island at the beginning of the twentieth century. In *Ida and the Wool Smugglers*, the heroine, the middle member of her family, feels left out and wishes that, like her big brother, she could participate in the annual sheep drive. However, she demonstrates great courage during an errand to a neighbour's house when she rescues a ewe and lamb from rustlers. In *A Ride for Martha*, her conflict is with her little sister who is always demanding to be carried and with two friends who have done better at school than she has. After her friends have rescued Martha, who had been sitting in a boat that drifted out into the bay, Ida realizes the depth of her love for her baby sister and the value of her friendship with the other girls.

Alderson's books are noteworthy for their memorable characters, psychologically realistic conflicts, and frequent humorous episodes. During their adventures, Alderson's heroines display an independence of spirit, and they grow in their understanding of the people close to them. This underlying portrayal of character growth gives added dimensions to Alderson's books, making them more than entertaining and sometimes funny stories; the books present significant examinations of the girls' relationships to the worlds in which they live.

See also: *Profiles* 2; *SATA* 48, 59; *TCCW* 5; *WSMP*.

Warabé Aska
(pen name of Takeshi Masuda)

Born: 3 February 1944, in Kagawa, Japan.

Principal Residences: Kagawa; Tokyo; Toronto; Mississauga, Ont.

Education: Takmatsu Technological School; Polytechnic School, Kagawa, Japan.

Career: graphic designer; painter; illustrator; author.

Major Awards: City of Toronto Book Award (1985, for *Who Goes to the Park*); Gold Medal, Studio Magazine Awards (1990, for *Seasons*); First Prize, Tehran International Biennale of Illustration (1993, for *Aska's Birds*).

Works for Children

Written and Illustrated by Warabé Aska

Who Goes to the Park (Montreal: Tundra, 1984). **Rev:** *CCB-B* 38 (Dec. 1984): 14; *CCL* 57 (1990): 114–16; *QQ* 51 (Feb. 1985): 14–16.

Who Hides in the Park (Montreal: Tundra, 1990). **Rev:** *BiC* 15 (Nov. 1986): 35; *CCL* 52 (1988): 25; *CM* 15 (Jan. 1987): 32; *QQ* 52 (Dec. 86): 13.

Illustrated by Warabé Aska

Seasons, ed. Alberto Manguel (Toronto: Doubleday, 1990). **Rev:** *BiC* 19 (Oct. 1990): 29; *CBRA* (1991): 327; *EL* 18 (Mar. 1991): 22; *QQ* 56 (Aug. 1980): 24, and 56 (Sept. 1980): 19; *SLJ* 37 (Jan. 1991): 103.

Aska's Animals, by David Day (Toronto: Doubleday, 1991). **Rev:** *APBR* 19 (Apr. 1992): 13; *BiC* 20 (Dec. 1991): 36; *CCB-B* 45 (Feb. 1992): 152; *CCL* 67 (1992): 66; *CM* 20 (Mar. 1992): 78; *EL* 19 (Mar. 1992): 15; *SLJ* 38 (Mar. 1992): 245.

Aska's Birds, by David Day (Toronto: Doubleday, 1992). **Rev:** *BiC* 22 (Feb. 1993): 37; *CBRA* (1992): 287; *QQ* 58 (Oct. 1992): 32; *SLJ* 40 (Jan. 1994): 105.

Aska's Sea Creatures, by David Day (Toronto: Doubleday, 1994). **Rev:** *CBRA* (1994): 439; *QQ* 61 (Jan. 1995): 40; *SLJ* 41 (May 1995): 112.

Trained in commercial art and employed as a graphic designer, Warabé Aska decided at the age of 30 to devote himself to a career as a painter. Quitting his job, he travelled around Japan for three months, creating the drawings and paintings that formed the basis for his first one-man show in Tokyo. An editor who saw this show encouraged Aska to write and illustrate a children's book about his trip. That book, *Discovering Japan in Eighty Days* (1973), led Aska to focus on book illustration. By the time he moved to Canada in 1979, he had illustrated 14 books, including four he created for children. Since his arrival, he has established an international reputation as a painter and has produced six more children's books.

Aska is not a narrative artist. Instead of telling stories with pictures, he uses them to express emotions and to communicate visions. The source of his work is an intense love of nature. He has said that 'Natural objects such as trees, flowers, birds, animals, the sun and moon, clouds and water, trigger my imagination.' The resulting paintings, usually classified as magic realism or surrealism, are vibrant and luminous. In them, the mundane and the fantastic mingle: children ride geese across the sky or dance on lily pads, baby angels flit around with butterflies, a tree conducts the birds in song, and the breath exhaled by skaters turns into lilies in the cold air.

Two of Aska's books celebrate particular Canadian parks. *Who Goes to the Park* was originally published as a paean to Toronto's High Park, but paperback reprints have made the park into one that could be in any urban centre. Aska's overly sentimental verses trace activities in the park from the spring, when the pond ice melts and the geese return, through to winter, when skaters frolic on the frozen pond and throw into the air snow that magically transforms into snow geese. The progress through the seasons, as well as the verbal and graphic motif of the geese, unifies the book, but its appeal comes from the details in the pictures, which depict people of many ethnic backgrounds and of all ages engaging in activities appropriate to each season. *Who Hides in the Park* celebrates Vancouver's Stanley Park. Text and explanatory notes in English, French, and Japanese describe the legendary past of and the current activities in fourteen locations within the park. Aska's paintings again transform the setting into a magical realm where playing children fly into the sky and Native gods appear within the clouds. Nevertheless, the book does not cohere as well as the earlier one. It lacks a strong organizing principle, such as the passage of the seasons used in the first book, and its text is too bland to complement the paintings. Consequently, it is more compelling in its parts than as a unified work.

Aska has also produced four books about various elements of nature. Like *Who Goes to the Park*, *Seasons* moves from spring scenes to winter scenes, but it lacks visual and verbal continuity. The paintings, most of which were not specifically produced for this book, do not focus on one setting or one group of people. In addition, the text, which consists of poetic excerpts that Alberto Manguel has chosen from a variety of adult sources, too often fails to complement the picture or has an obscure relationship to it. The other three books contain original verses by David Day that purport to make the pictures part of a game. In *Aska's Animals* the 'guessing game' asks the reader to imagine the origin of various beasts. Actually, the text openly posits an origin for each animal: for example, it states that horses were sea foam, deer were trees, the musk ox was a haystack that sprouted legs, and elephants were trumpeting angels whose wings turned into ears. Nevertheless, the text supports the pictures, many of which are appealingly dramatic and colourful. In *Aska's Birds* the text provides rather uninspired answers to the question, 'If birds were people, what jobs would they do?' Although the pretext for a game is even flimsier in *Aska's Sea Creatures*, the book is the most dramatic and coherent of the four concept books. The game asks readers to imagine that they are sea creatures. The text then describes the situations in which the creatures would find themselves, and 15 pictures (a small one at the beginning, 13 page-and-one-half paintings in the middle, and a concluding small one) illustrate them. Changing in hue from yellow-orange, through blue-green, dark blue, yellow-green, and back to yellow-orange, these paintings effectively evoke both the passage of a day from sunrise to sunset and the movement from shallow to deep water and back again.

Aska is an original and distinctive artist, producing works in which depictions of light and colour dramatically add to an atmosphere of magic or mystery. His publications, however, are more collections of art than truly unified books. His own writing, possibly because he composes in Japanese and then translates his words, is either cloying or bland. The text he has had others produce seldom is an effective complement to the paintings. Because his books lack unity and a narrative element and because their illustrations are surreal, many people have questioned whether they actually appeal to children. Many children may pass them by, but those who do pause to enter will find a magical world that will stimulate their imaginations.

See also: *MCAI*; *SATA* 56; *WSMP*.

Margaret Atwood

Born: 18 November 1939, in Ottawa.

Principal Residences: Ottawa; Toronto; Vancouver; Montreal; Edmonton.

Education: University of Toronto (BA 1961); Radcliffe College, Harvard University (AM 1962).

Career: university lecturer; poet; novelist; essayist; critic; anthologist; editor.

Works for Children

Up in the Tree, illus. Atwood (Toronto: McClelland & Stewart, 1977). **Rev:** *CBRA* (1978): 192; *QQ* 44 (July 1978): 36.

Anna's Pet, with Joyce Barkhouse, illus. Anne Blades (Toronto: James Lorimer, 1980). **Rev:** *APBR* 10 (Nov. 1983): 5; *BiC* 9 (Dec. 1980): 18; *CCL* 21 (1981): 65; *CL* 92 (Spring 1982): 95; *CM* 9, 2 (1981): 120; *QQ* 47 (Jan. 1981): 27.

For the Birds, boxes and sidebars written by Shelley Tanaka, illus. John Bianchi (Toronto: Douglas & McIntyre, 1990). **Rev:** *APBR* 18 (Feb. 1991): 13; *CCL* 65 (1992): 83; *CM* 19 (Mar. 1991): 93; *EL* 19 (Sept. 1991): 57; *QQ* 56 (Nov. 1990): 11.

Princess Prunella and The Purple Peanut, illus. Maryann Kovalski (Toronto: Key Porter, 1995). **Rev:** *BiC* 24 (Dec. 1995): 18; *CBRA* (1995): 460; *QQ* 61 (Sept. 1995): 73.

Other

'Production Problems', *CL* 78 (Autumn 1978): 13–15.

Selected Discussions

Beckmann, Susan. 'Margaret Atwood: Can. Lit. to Kid Lit.', *CCL* 12 (1978): 78–81.

Ross, Catherine Sheldrick, and Cory Bieman Davies. 'An interview with Margaret Atwood', *CCL* 42 (1986): 9–16.

An internationally acclaimed poet, novelist, and essayist, Margaret Atwood has produced four children's books. To some degree, each reflects themes prominent in her adult works: three involve relationships between people and nature, and one focuses on a female's development of a satisfactory identity.

Economic constraints forced Atwood to draw the illustrations and to hand-letter the text for her first children's book, *Up in the Tree*. Her drawings are primitive, static, and devoid of an adequate sense of perspective. Furthermore, because she was limited to using two colours, her pictures contain such inappropriate elements as a blue tree and a red sun. The text, a nonsense poem written during a time when Atwood says she was 'feeling quite dippy', shows that nature can both frustrate and satisfy people. The frustration occurs when porcupines chew the ladder that two children need to get down from their home in a tree. The satisfaction comes when a wise owl summons a bird to rescue them (this motif of the bird helper probably developed from the tales of Grimm, which Atwood avidly read as a child). Realizing that they need a more secure way of getting back to the tree, the children show their maturity by wisely nailing stairs to its trunk.

Atwood collaborated with her aunt, Joyce Barkhouse, on *Anna's Pet*, for which Ann Blades provided colourful illustrations. An educational tale with a deliberately controlled vocabulary, it tells of a lonely girl who searches for a pet, catching in turn a toad, a worm, and a snake. Each of Anna's mistaken efforts to make her pets happy produces an overtly didactic speech about that pet's habitat and needs, but the book remains entertaining because Anna's efforts are mildly amusing. Even more overtly didactic is *For the Birds*, a book that reflects Atwood's environmental activism and her interest in birdwatching. When Samantha throws a stone at a bird, her elderly neighbour, Phoebe Merganser, teaches her what a bird's life is really like. After turning Samantha into a scarlet tanager, Phoebe becomes a crow and the two begin a migration to South America. During their journey Phoebe, an archetypal Wise Old Woman, becomes a tutor figure who instructs Samantha about bird habits and the ways in which humans constantly endanger birds. Although Samantha is never certain whether she dreamed the entire adventure, her observations and experiences make her sensitive to the plight of birds; once restored to her own body, she therefore builds a bird feeder. Although the didacticism dominates the fantasy, *For the Birds* is both educational and mildly entertaining.

Atwood's most recent picture book, *Princess Prunella and The Purple Peanut*, is a comical variant of 'Beauty and the Beast' in which a beautiful girl is made ugly so that she can learn the folly of her ways. When the vain and selfish Princess Prunella refuses to give food to a pauper, who is actually a Wise Woman in disguise, the pauper casts a spell that makes a purple peanut sprout on Prunella's nose. Prunella can rid herself of the peanut only by doing three good deeds. Regretting her previous selfishness, Prunella soon becomes concerned about others and unconsciously performs the deeds, the last being the rescue of a potential suitor. Atwood's verbal pyrotechnics give this relatively conventional fairy tale a manic edge: every sentence is filled with alliterations that begin with 'p'. Although these alliterations are clever and prevent the didacticism from becoming heavy-handed, they are so numerous that the device loses the appeal of novelty and distracts somewhat from the plot. Nevertheless, *Princess Prunella* entertainingly develops its theme about a silly girl's maturation into a considerate woman.

See also: *AAYA* 12; *CA* 49–52; *CANR* 3, 24, 33; *CLC* 2, 3, 4, 8, 13, 15, 25, 44, 84; *DLB* 53; *SATA* 50.

Claude Aubry

Born: 23 October 1914, in Morin Heights, Que.

Died: 1984.

Principal Residences: Morin Heights; Montreal; Ottawa.

Education: University of Montreal (BA 1936); McGill University (BLS 1945).

Career: accountant; chief librarian, Ottawa Public Library; writer.

Major Awards: Canadian Library Association (French) Book of the Year for Children (1962).

Writings for Children

King of the Thousand Islands, trans. Alice Kane (Toronto: McClelland & Stewart, 1963).

The Christmas Wolf, trans. Alice Kane (Toronto: McClelland & Stewart, 1965).

The Magic Fiddler and Other Legends of French Canada, trans. Alice Kane (Toronto: Peter Martin, 1968). **Rev:** *CCL* 3 (1975): 90.

Agouhanna, trans. Harvey Swados (Toronto: Doubleday, 1972).

OTHER:

'The Canadian Author for Children Still Lost in the Barren Lands', *Ocean:* 197–201.

'I began writing for children because I wanted to keep the poetical side of myself alive and the freshness of the child I knew was within me. One needs to have a poet within to write well for children.' In this way, the late Claude Aubry described his beginnings as a children's writer; he also discussed the influences of his childhood and teenage years. Born in rural Quebec, he used to exercise his imagination on the two-mile walk to and from school, creating exciting adventures involving savage Indians and wild animals.

Aubry's first story for children, *The King of the Thousand Islands*, a literary folktale set along the St Lawrence River hundreds of years before the coming of the Europeans, is about the Yellow Ant people, a mound-building culture that, at the beginning of the story, is 'prosperous and respected and peaceful'. However, because an evil and ambitious counsellor gives the king bad advice, the happiness is shattered. Enamoured of a mysterious siren, the king follows his counsellor's advice and orders his people to build a beautiful garden of islands. But, in so doing, he loses 'the most precious thing in the world, the affection of my people'. Now, only the islands remain, monuments to human foolishness. Aubry combined extensive research on pre-Columbian cultures, an understanding of the literary folktale, and wry satire of human nature to create one of Canada's few modern *pourquoi* legends.

Aubry wrote *The Christmas Wolf* to recapture the fast-disappearing festivals of rural Quebec and to encompass in a story the celebrations that brightened the hard lives of the people. During the harsh Laurentian winter, Maître Griboux, an aging wolf who was once the terror of the North, is reduced to creeping into the village to find food. It is Christmas Eve, and, slinking into the church during midnight Mass, he is surrounded by angry, yet fearful people. The priest saves him, reminding them that it is a time of love and mercy and that they, too, have been guilty of wolf-like behaviour. The story is a combination of three genres, the animal story, the Christmas miracle, and the satire on human behaviour.

The Magic Fiddler contains 10 French-Canadian legends, many dealing with the intrusion of extraordinary events and beings into the lives of ordinary people. In 'The Magic Fiddler' and 'Rose Latulippe', the Devil wins the souls of the unsuspecting. 'La Courriveau' is about a witch who confronts a lonely traveller. In 'Loup-Garou', a werewolf comes to live with a miller. The narrator often casts doubt on the marvellous adventures he recounts. For example, at the conclusion of 'The Witch Canoe' readers are left wondering whether excessive drinking had anything to do with the supposed adventures. Three of the stories, 'The Caughnawaga Bell', 'The Legend of Percé Rock', and 'Pilotte', are historical legends. In his preface, Aubry draws attention to his 'somewhat ironical tone' and, indeed, one is often aware in the stories of the sardonic tone and satirical view of human nature.

Aubry wrote his final children's book, *Agouhanna*, 'because I wanted to see the Iroquois as they were, not as they'd been shown in movies. I'd done a great deal of background research and wanted to combine it with a story about a young person who embodied the creative, poetic side of life.' The chief's timid son, whose name means 'brave among the braves', is afraid of being alone in the forest during his initiation rites. His closest friend, Little Doe, a girl to whom he is betrothed by the end of the story, is his direct opposite and wishes to become a great warrior. Although the story portrays the cultural details accurately and sensitively, aspects of plot and characterization are somewhat forced, and the blend of historical facts and adventure story conventions is only partially successful.

Discussing the role of the creator of literature for Canadian children, Aubry frequently stressed the necessity of integrating Native, British, and French folklore with the harsh, rugged landscape. His greatest achievement was in writing stories that did this. He was, in a sense, a modern 'myth-maker', drawing on legends, motifs, and character types frequently found in traditional literature. He wrote for two audiences, children and adults. While his younger audience responded to the adventures and the human emotions of a story, older readers enjoyed the witty, ironic satire of human weaknesses.

See also: *CA* 106; *Profiles*; *SATA* 29, 40.

Robert Michael Ballantyne

Born: 24 April 1825, in Edinburgh, Scotland.

Died: 8 February 1894, in Rome, Italy.

Principal Residences: Edinburgh; London; various Canadian outposts; Rome.

Career: clerk for Hudson's Bay Company; employee of printing and publishing company; writer; artist.

Works for Children

Selected Novels Based on Ballantyne's Canadian Experiences

Snowflakes and Sunbeams; or, The Young Fur Traders (London: Thomas Nelson, 1856).

Ungava: A Tale of the Esquimaux Land (London: Thomas Nelson, 1857).

Away in the Wilderness; or, Life Among the Red Indians and Fur Traders of North America (London: J. Nisbet, 1869).

The Wild Man of the West: A Tale of the Rocky Mountains (London: Routledge, 1863).

The Pioneers: A Tale of the Western Wilderness Illustrative of the Adventures and Discoveries of Sir Alexander Mackenzie (London: J. Nisbet, 1872).

The Red Man's Revenge: A Tale of the Red River Flood (London: J. Nisbet, 1880).

The Buffalo Runners: A Tale of the Red River (London: J. Nisbet, 1891).

Selected Novels Set Elsewhere

The Coral Island: A Tale of the Pacific Ocean (London: Thomas Nelson, 1858).

Other

Hudson's Bay; or, Everyday Life in the Wilds of North America (Edinburgh: Blackwood, 1847).

Selected Discussions

Quayle, Eric. *Ballantyne the Brave: A Victorian Writer and His Family* (London: Rupert Hart-Davis, 1967).

Rodd, Lewis Charles. *The Young Fur Trader: The Story of R.M. Ballantyne* (Melbourne: Cheshire, 1966).

'Ballantyne the brave', as Stevenson called him in the introductory poem to *Treasure Island* (1883), is best known for his tropical survival story, *The Coral Island*. Because of R.M. Ballantyne, however, generations of English boys grew up with a romantic view of Canada as an endlessly challenging land of wild animals and wilder Indians, a land in which boys used to Victorian restraint could enjoy endless adventures. Although he romanticized experiences, Ballantyne had first-hand knowledge of the country: at the age of 16, he was enlisted in the Hudson's Bay Company and served at various posts in Canada from 1841 to 1847.

Ballantyne's first book, *Hudson's Bay; or, Everyday Life in the Wilds of North America*, was a non-fictional record of his life in Canada. Its material also provided the basis for *Snowflakes and Sunbeams; or, The Young Fur Traders*, the novel that launched his career as the foremost writer of romances for boys. Assembled episodically rather than by skilful plotting, richly detailed in its descriptions of the exotic Canadian north, and filled with scenes of exciting adventure, it set the pattern for more than a hundred children's books he wrote later. His characterization is somewhat rudimentary and stereotypical. The young white heroes who prove their manhood in the wilderness are Christians who never swear or drink. The Natives include a Noble Savage who converts to Christianity and works with a missionary, as well as a bloodthirsty, cowardly devil who slaughters a woman without thought. Behind all of this romance of wish fulfilment, however, is something else: an authentic picture of the northern landscape and a small glimpse of life in the wilderness forts.

See also: *DLB* 163; *SATA* 24.

Michael Bedard

Born: 26 June 1949, in Toronto.

Principal Residences: Toronto.

Education: University of Toronto (BA 1971).

Career: library clerk; print shop pressman; full-time author.

Major Awards: Governor-General's Literary Award (1990); CLA Book of the Year Award (1991); Violet Downey Book Award (1991); IODE (Toronto) Children's Book Award (1991).

Works for Children

Woodsedge and Other Tales (Toronto: Gardenshore, 1979). **Rev:** *IR* 13 (Oct. 1979): 30, and 14 (Feb. 1980): 34.

Pipe and Pearls: A Gathering of Tales (Toronto: Gardenshore, 1980). **Rev:** *IR* 15 (Aug. 1981): 28.

A Darker Magic (New York: Atheneum, 1987). **Rev:** *BiC* 17 (Apr. 1988): 36; *CCB-B* 41 (Sept. 1987): 2; *CCB-B* 41 (Sept. 1987): 2; *CM* 16 (May 1988): 85; *EL* 19 (Nov. 1991): 66; *SLJ* 34 (Sept. 1987): 177.

The Lightning Bolt, illus. Regolo Ricci (Toronto: Oxford UP, 1989). **Rev:** *EL* 17 (Mar. 1990): 24, and 19 (Nov. 1991): 66; *HB* 66 (May 1990): 366; *QQ* 55 (Nov. 1989): 15.

Redwork (Toronto: Lester & Orpen Denys, 1990). **Rev:** *CCL* 63 (1991): 72; *QQ* 56 (Sept. 1990): 20; *SLJ* 36 (Oct. 1990): 139; *VOYA* 13 (Dec. 1990): 293, and 16 (Apr. 1993): 34.

The Tinder Box, illus. Regolo Ricci (Toronto: Oxford UP, 1990). **Rev:** *APBR* 17 (Nov. 1990): 10; *CCL* 63 (1991): 83; *CM* 18 (Sept. 1990): 216; *QQ* 56 (Aug. 1990): 14; *SLJ* 39 (Aug. 1991): 99.

The Nightingale, illus. Regolo Ricci (Toronto: Oxford UP, 1991). **Rev:** *CCL* 70 (1993): 92; *CM* 19 (Oct. 1991): 306; *EL* 19 (Mar. 1992): 17; *RT* 45 (Apr. 1992): 639; *SL* 40 (Nov. 1992): 138; *SLJ* 38 (May 1992): 85.

Emily, illus. Barbara Cooney (Toronto: Lester, 1992). **Rev:** *BiC* 21 (Dec. 1992): 31; *CCB-B* 46 (Jan. 1993): 140; *CCL* 73 (1994): 90; *CM* 21 (Jan. 1993): 20; *HB* 69 (Jan. 1993): 72; *NYTBR* 98 (28 Mar. 1993): 21; *QQ* 58 (Dec. 1992): 26; *RT* 47 (Feb. 1994): 406; *SLJ* 38 (Nov. 1992): 88; *TES* (1 July 1994): R2.

Painted Devil (Toronto: Lester, 1994). **Rev:** *BiC* 23 (Sept. 1994): 58; *CCB-B* 47 (May 1994): 281; *CM* 22 (Oct. 1994): 188; *QQ* 60 (Apr. 1994): 124; *VOYA* 17 (June 1994): 96.

The Divide, illus. Emily Arnold McCully (Toronto: Tundra, 1997). **Rev:** *CM* 4 (31 Oct. 1997): on-line; *QQ* 63 (Sept. 1997): 72; *SLJ* 43 (Sept. 1997): 199.

Glass Town, illus. Laura Fernandez and Rick Jacobson (Toronto: Stoddart, 1997). **Rev:** *CCB-B* 51 (Jan. 1998): 154; *HB* 73 (Nov. 1997): 707; *QQ* 63 (Oct. 1997): 41.

Selected Discussions

Davis, Marie C. 'An Interview with Michael Bedard', *CCL* 82 (1996): 22–39.

Findon, Joanne. 'Darkness in the Novels of Michael Bedard', *CCL* 82 (1996): 8–21.

Jones, Raymond E. '"Different Moments in the One Cycle": Alchemical and Blakean Symbolism in Michael Bedard's *Redwork*', *ChLQ* 20 (Spring 1995): 3–8.

Michael Bedard is an intellectual and literary writer: he is concerned, that is, with ideas, often presenting them in symbolic form, and he makes meaningful allusions to themes developed by such writers as William Blake and Emily Dickinson. In spite of their challenging intellectual content, however, his works are accessible and entertaining because they avoid the pitfalls of pretentiousness and obscurity.

Bedard decided to become a writer when he discovered poetry at the age of 17. By the time he graduated from the University of Toronto, winning the Gold Medal in Philosophy, he concluded that he could not be both an academic and a writer. Consequently, he gave up the idea of going to graduate school and took jobs in a library and then in a printing shop to support himself while he developed his craft. Bedard eventually moved from poetry to prose. He believes, however, that the fairy tales that constituted his first works in prose were natural outgrowths of his poetry because both forms exhibit 'the same devotion to image and sound'.

Bedard self-published two collections of original fairy tales, *Woodsedge and Other Tales* and *Pipe and Pearls: A Gathering of Tales*, the latter volume markedly inferior to its predecessor. The tales in these collections contain motifs, such as the figure of the controlling wizard or magician, dangerous settings, and powerful dreams, that become important in his novels. They also exhibit Bedard's characteristic concern with serious themes. In the first collection, for example, complementary tales, 'Woodsedge', about a king who refuses to die, and 'The Pool of Paradise', about a boy who wishes to stay young forever, suggest the foolishness of resisting the cycle of life. Bedard's fairy tales are unsatisfying within the genre because the plots are awkwardly designed to convey philosophic ideas rather than to entertain. Bedard did, however, revise one tale from his first collection, turning it into a good picture book. *The Lightning Bolt*, a variation of the Grimms' 'The Fisherman and His Wife', tells of a poor old woman who receives a wish-granting stick as a reward for releasing a funny old man imprisoned within a tree. Seeing the luxuries that the magic stick provides, her greedy, abusive husband decides to murder her. Before he can do so, however, his wife returns the magic stick to the funny old man, who then sends a lightning bolt that imprisons the husband within a tree. (Bedard's original version is more comical in its conclusion: the husband wakes up believing that he has dreamed everything; his wife then makes him do all of the housework.) Because of this book's success, Bedard's publishers asked him to retell two of Hans Christian Andersen's tales, *The Tinder Box* and *The Nightingale*. Both are clean, competent versions.

Bedard also has done significant original work in the picture-book genre, writing three biographical tales of literary figures. *Emily*, a fictional slice of Emily Dickinson's life, is deceptively simple. Narrated by an unnamed little girl, the story begins with Emily's sending a gift of dried flowers and a note asking the girl's mother to revive Emily's spirits by playing the piano for her. When the girl and her mother arrive, they are told that Emily is too ill to come downstairs. While the mother nevertheless plays the piano, the girl discovers that Emily is hiding on the stairs. She gives Emily a gift of lily bulbs, receiving in exchange a poem. As inconsequential as this plot seems, it celebrates creativity and life. It begins with dead flowers, symbols of a flagging spirit, and closes with the planting of lily bulbs, symbols of renewed hope and the continuance of life. In between, the story links music and poetry, arts that bring joy, to the natural mysteries of spring and childhood. Paintings by American illustrator Barbara Cooney subtly expand and reinforce the meaning of the tale. *Glass Town* is also about the mystery of creation. It describes the imaginative games of the Brontë children, who produced over a hundred miniature books and magazines recording adventures in a fantasy world they called Glass Town. Narrated by Charlotte Brontë, the book alternates descriptions of the children's austere lives and 'the web of dreams' they wove about Glass Town. Although lacking the metaphysical profundity of *Emily*, *Glass Town* shows how the imagination, by creating a 'world within', enriches otherwise dull lives. Bedard's third literary biography, *The Divide*, is slighter than both of these. It focuses on a brief but meaningful period in the life of American writer Willa Cather—her 1885 move to a farm on the Divide. After recounting her feelings of devastating loss at leaving her home, it poetically evokes the changing seasons to underscore the young Cather's movement from hatred to love of the land, a love finally symbolized by the song of a lark rising from the prairie grass.

It is as a novelist, however, that Bedard has achieved his greatest critical and popular recognition. His novels mix realistic family and social-problem stories with elements of the fantastic, making the books difficult to classify. In fact, Bedard has said that he is 'uncomfortable with the writing being tame enough to fit comfortably in one particular genre'. Although they defy generic classifications, his novels do share a family resemblance. Bedard himself noted that his first two novels, *A Darker Magic* and *Redwork*, are complementary because each develops the 'idea of an older character and the younger character meeting and in some way completing each other'. Although the older person is middle-aged, not elderly, in his third novel, the same pattern is evident in *Painted Devil*. In addition, all three novels use plots that show that the past continues, for good and evil, to influence the present.

In *A Darker Magic* and *Painted Devil*, its sequel, the young person and older one come together to stop a force of darkness from the past. (Following William Blake's example, Bedard speaks of light and darkness, not good and evil, because he believes that people historically have defined evil in self-serving ways.) The darkness in these novels, Bedard has said, is 'basically a surrendering of one's own self; it's a mass giving over of oneself unto the power of another'. This darkness manifests itself through a children's entertainment: a magic show or a puppet show that periodically takes place when 8 August falls on a Saturday (any further significance to this particular date is never given). In both cases, the seemingly innocent entertainment destroys, physically and spiritually, those who participate in it.

In *A Darker Magic*, the perpetually returning magician, Professor Mephisto, appears in the disguise of a young outcast, Scott Renshaw. The boy's appearance and actions imply his diabolical reality: he is pale, mechanical, weightless, and silent; he appears and disappears suddenly, frequently within a shadow; black birds hover nearby; and both dreams and waking episodes associate him with pits, an obvious reference to hell. So effective is his creation of illusions, however, that those who go to his apartment do not see that it is actually a long-deserted, decrepit tenement. Only in dreams or in the mirror—a symbol of imaginative intuition—does Craig Chandler, a boy Scott tries to lure into his power, get a momentary glimpse of the truth. One additional image goes beyond these commonplaces of Gothic fiction to suggest the magician's perversity: the magician leaves behind rose petals and a cloying smell of roses. Perhaps Bedard is alluding to the sick rose of William Blake's poem; regardless, the roses suggest that by luring children who long for something special in their lives the magician perverts the love that roses conventionally symbolize.

Opposing the force of darkness is Miss Potts, an elderly school teacher who survived the magic show she attended in 1936, and 11-year-old Emily Endicott, her student. Miss Potts enlists Emily's help to establish that the magician repeatedly returns and that he has assumed Scott Renshaw's identity. She heroically resists the magician's efforts to cloud her mind and to make her appear to others a stereotypically addled, old woman. Made whole by her recovered memory, she bravely breaks into Scott's magic show and saves Emily from becoming the victim of a deadly trick. Miss Potts then assumes the role of Crone, guiding Emily into the next stage of development by passing on both her understanding of the magician's changing ways and her role as protector of the community.

In *Painted Devil*, set 28 years later, Emily herself has become the teacher and protector of her niece, Alice Higginson. Emily does not at first realize, however, that the power of darkness is this time working through a set of Punch and Judy puppets. The puppets are part of a collection in the library where Alice works. When the librarian, Mr Dwyer, decides that he and Alice will use them in a performance, the antique devil puppet, Mephistopheles, who resembles Professor Mephisto in both appearance and name, begins to take control of Mr Dwyer, causing him to lose interest in his work and even to paint his face white the same as the puppet. In a daring and dangerous midnight adventure, Emily and Alice enter the library and destroy the puppet through which the force of darkness has operated. They thereby free Mr Dwyer from the spell that possessed him and, thus, prevent the force of darkness from capturing the children who would have watched the Mephistopheles puppet in the show. The puppet show does go on, however: in a triumphant reassertion of the ideas that evil can be defeated and that the past offers help as well as horror, Alice and Mr Dwyer perform an old version of the Punch and Judy play in which Punch, when Mephistopheles comes to take him to the underworld, is able to drive him away. A tense and atmospheric psychological thriller, *Painted Devil* offers the hope that, although darkness may return, the forces of light—intelligence, intuition, and compassion—can defeat it.

Whereas *A Darker Magic* and *Painted Devil* focus primarily on quests to destroy evil, *Redwork*, Bedard's most complex and successful novel, centres upon a quest to create something good. The elderly Arthur Magnus, the loss of whose leg during World War I also caused psychological maiming, was rescued from a gas attack by a man who later died. He has devoted his life to completing his rescuer's quest, the creation of the Philosopher's Stone, an alchemical substance promising health and longevity to humans. Cass, a lonely boy living in the apartment above Magnus, becomes instrumental in restoring the reclusive old man to psychic wholeness. Cass, who has actually had dreams in which he relives the old man's wartime horrors, begins the process of regeneration when he rescues Magnus, who has passed out after accidentally leaving on an unlit gas burner. This rescue, an archetypal act of heroism that recapitulates the wartime rescue from the gas attack, convinces the boy that he and the old man are similar because they are 'but different moments in the one cycle'. They therefore join forces to seek the Philosopher's Stone.

Although *Redwork* emphasizes the quest for good, it also introduces two battles against evil. In the first, Cass performs a heroic deed by rescuing his female friend, Maddy, when she is attacked by a lascivious movie theatre usher. By exposing the usher's depravity and his thievery, Cass also saves the theatre manager, who, like Magnus, has cut himself off from the world to brood about a form of magic, old movies. In the second battle against evil, Cass confronts a juvenile bully, Sid Spector, whose name suggests his role as an evil spirit, an embodiment of the darkness of ignorance. When Spector spies on the experiments that Magnus is conducting, Cass musters the courage to chase him away. Unfortunately, during the chase, the experiment explodes, and Cass must return to rescue Magnus from the burning garage in yet another recapitulation of the World War I rescue. Because Magnus at first seems to be dead, this rescue resembles the deeds of mythic heroes who bring people back from the land of the dead. Afterwards, both the boy and the old man benefit: Cass conceives a purpose for his life when he plans to continue the quest for the Stone, a quest that symbolizes the search for imaginative fulfilment, and Magnus re-enters the social world, going out for the first time to see an old movie, a symbol of the positive social memories that now can replace his wartime nightmares. A tantalizingly erudite novel filled with references to William Blake, alchemy, and old movies, *Redwork* shows that the young and the elderly can, when they see each other properly, find an intensely meaningful connection to each other.

Bedard has flaws, sometimes striving too hard to be poetic, suggestive, or symbolic, but he is a superbly readable author. He creates novels with intricate strands, but these strands never become hopelessly knotted. He also introduces significant themes, notably those involving the interrelationship of the past and the present, but he never resorts to preaching. Finally, he presents material that offers significant intellectual challenges for young readers, but he makes this material interesting by enclosing it in dramatic and compelling plots. Bedard's achievements signal a new maturity and confidence in writing for Canadian children.

See also: *AAYA* 22; *CLR* 35; *Junior* 7; *MCAI*; *SATA* 93; *TCCW*; *WSMP*.

William Bell

Born: 27 October 1945, in Toronto.

Principal Residences: Toronto; Orillia, Ont.; Beijing, China.

Education: University of Toronto (BA 1968, MA 1969); Ontario Institute for Studies in Education (M.Ed. 1984).

Career: editor; high school teacher, Orillia, Ont.; writer.

Major Awards: Ruth Schwartz Award (1991); Mr Christie's Book Award, ages 12 and up (1998).

Works for Children

Crabbe (Toronto: Irwin, 1986). **Rev:** *BiC* 15 (Oct. 1986): 39; *CCB-B* 40 (July 1987): 203; *CM* 14 (Nov. 1986): 267; *QQ* 52 (June 1986): 25; *SLJ* 33 (May 1987): 106.

Metal Head (Don Mills, Ont.: Macmillan, 1987). **Rev:** *CM* 16 (Jan. 1988): 17; *EL* 15 (Mar. 1988): 55.

The Cripples' Club (Toronto: Irwin, 1988); republished as *Absolutely Invincible!* (Toronto: General Publishing, 1991). **Rev:** *CCL* 67 (1992): 87; *EL* 19 (Sept. 1991): 58.

Death Wind (Don Mills, Ont.: Macmillan, 1989).

Five Days of the Ghost (Don Mills, Ont.: Stoddart, 1989). **Rev:** *CCL* 57 (1990): 120; *CM* 17 (Sept. 1989): 213.

Forbidden City (Toronto: Doubleday, 1990). **Rev:** *CCB-B* 44 (Feb. 1991): 137; *BiC* 19 (Oct. 1990): 28; *CCL* 65 (1992): 111; *CL* 113 (1992): 191; *CM* 18 (July 1990): 188; *EL* 18 (Jan. 1991): 64; *QQ* 56 (June 1990): 16; *SLJ* 37 (Mar. 1991): 211.

No Signature (Toronto: Doubleday, 1992). **Rev:** *CCL* 71 (1993): 78; *CM* 20 (Sept. 1992): 211; *EL* 20 (Nov. 1992): 60; *QQ* 58 (June 1992): 35.

Speak to the Earth (Toronto: Doubleday, 1994). **Rev:** *BiC* 23 (Dec. 1994): 58; *CBRA* (1994): 475; *CCL* 22 (Spring 1996): 72; *CM* 22 (Nov. 1994): 209; *QQ* 60 (Oct. 1994): 43.

The Golden Disk, illus. Don Kilby (Toronto: Doubleday, 1995). **Rev:** *BiC* 24 (May 1995): 50; *CBRA* (1995): 461; *QQ* 61 (Oct. 1994): 78.

River My Friend, illus. Ken Campbell (Victoria, BC: Orca, 1996). **Rev:** *CBRA* (1996): 433; *QQ* 62 (Sept. 1996): 73.

Zack (Toronto: Doubleday, 1998). **Rev:** *BiC* 27 (Summer 1998): 38; *CM* 4 (5 June 1998): on-line; *QQ* 64 (Mar. 1998): 74.

Other

Editor, *Contours* (Toronto: Irwin, 1993) [Canadian drama anthology].

Selected Discussions

Jenkinson, Dave. 'Portraits: William Bell: YA Author', *EL* 18 (Nov. 1990): 67–72.

An English major at college and a high school English teacher, William Bell has combined his skill with the techniques of fiction and his sensitive understanding of the complex problems facing today's teenagers to create a series of novels about young people struggling to come to terms with themselves, their immediate peer groups, and the larger world into which they are moving. Although he had not intended to write for publication, his daughter encouraged him to send out the manuscript that became his first book, *Crabbe*.

Crabbe is the journal of a 17-year-old who is in the psychiatric ward of a hospital. He writes to preserve the memories of his traumatic experiences living for a summer and fall in the Ontario wilderness. Rebelling against the hypocrisies of home and school life, the vodka-drinking narrator seeks his freedom in the north woods, not realizing how poorly prepared he is mentally and physically. A friendship with Mary, a woman who has fled to the woods after the mercy killing of her husband, provides the means by which Crabbe achieves the awareness, both of his own and others' limitations and strengths, that enables him to return on a new footing to his parents' home.

Whereas *Crabbe* focused on the solitary individual and his encounters with adults, Bell's later books have the central figures resolve conflicts with the help of peers. *Cripples' Club* (later retitled the more politically correct *Absolutely Invincible!*), which drew on the author's relationship with two handicapped students, is narrated by George Ma, a refugee whose experiences in Southeast Asia have caused memory loss. Joining with wheelchair-bound Hook; Aimie, a blind girl; and Heather, who is deaf, in a group designed to thwart school bullies and to complement each other, George is able to recover his past and absolve himself of the guilt he felt over his sister's death. The importance of understanding the past is also the theme of *Five Days of the Ghost*, in which Karen, her older brother John, and their friend Weird Noah encounter the ghost of a Native chief who assists Karen in letting go of the grief she carries over the accidental death of her twin brother. In *Zack*, the hero, whose father is Jewish and mother is Black, is angry when the family moves from the city to the country. However, when he discovers objects from the early nineteenth century relating to escaped African-American slaves, he begins a process of investigating his personal and cultural past.

The heroes of *Forbidden City*, *No Signature*, and *Speak to the Earth* encounter larger and even global social problems. In *Forbidden City*, 17-year-old Alex, while accompanying his news photographer father to Beijing in 1989, befriends a number of Chinese students who then rescue him when he is wounded and trapped in Tian An Men (Tiananmen) Square during the great uprising. He does not find a happy resolution of his conflicts. Two of his friends are killed by the soldiers; all he can do, through writing a journal, is to help to keep alive the memory of his friends and the brutality of events. The re-creation of the events is powerful and convincing, not only as a result of Bell's knowledge of Beijing, where he spent a year as an exchange teacher, but also, he has explained, because of the surprise, shock, and anger he felt listening in Canada to media reports of the massacre of 1989.

Whereas Alex is caught up in a cultural conflict involving millions of people, Steve Chandler, in *No Signature*, confronts a more specific, but nonetheless major issue: illiteracy. After meeting his father, who had deserted the family when the boy was five, the narrator is angry and resentful until he realizes the shame his father felt because he could neither read nor write. Just as his father had disguised his problem, Steve's best friend, Hawk, has hidden the fact that he is homosexual. While Steve, like Alex, cannot change conditions, he is able to accept and respect the two males who are important in his life. In *Speak to the Earth*, Bryan Troupe is caught between his mother and his uncle, who are on opposite sides of the conflict over clear-cut logging on Vancouver Island. Not only does he come to understand the values of both people, but also the necessity of taking an individual stand on issues. Arrested at the end of the story for blocking a logging road, Bryan, like Alex, is unable to end the larger conflicts, which here involve political parties and multinational corporations, but he gains an appreciation of the goodness and integrity of those closest to him.

Bell has also written two short high-interest low-vocabulary novels, both dealing with troubled teenagers. In *Metal Head*, the hero is torn between loyalty to members of his heavy-metal gang and responsibility to the track club he has joined. *Death Wind* links a violent storm and parent-daughter conflict. He also wrote the texts for the picture books *The Golden Disk* and *River My Friend*, about young children living in Southeast Asia.

With the exception of *Speak to the Earth*, Bell's novels are written in the first person, an appropriate voice for stories of self-discovery. None ends with a clear and final resolution of the conflicts; furthermore, in each, the future is not predictable. For example, Crabbe coexists uneasily with his unhappy parents;

the atrocities of Tian An Men Square remain unpunished although Alex's closest friends are dead; Steve's father continues to suffer in his illiteracy as does Hawk from social attitudes towards his homosexuality; clear-cut logging with its attendant confrontations continues. However, each central character is a wiser, more fulfilled individual for the experiences undergone.

Crucial to the development of several of the main characters is their acquiring an understanding of the past. Both *Crabbe* and *Forbidden City* are journals the characters write in order to preserve and acquire a fuller perspective on their recent pasts. George Ma must recover the memory of his Southeast Asian boyhood before he can create a future: 'I feel like every word of the story is a weight falling off me', he exclaims. His having spoken only in the present tense during the story indicates an inability to consider his past. Steve Chandler, who begins his narrative announcing 'I remember everything', intersperses accounts of present events with what he calls 'replays'. He comes to terms with his present when he is able to interpret the details of these replays. Karen and Zack must learn of the past from ghosts and artifacts. Although the centre of each novel is one individual, none of Bell's heroes operates alone; working with friends and appreciating their strengths and fears is crucial. All of the central characters also profit from the wisdom of older people, who help them to help themselves.

Dealing as they do with contemporary issues—illiteracy, teenage alcoholism, physical disability, environmental destruction, and cataclysmic political struggles—William Bell's books could be termed problem novels or stories of social realism. In many ways they are. However, through his skill in character portrayal and the nuances of the narrative voices, Bell presents the universal drama of coming-of-age. The traumas and disillusionment his characters experience are contemporary manifestations of the complex rites of passage young people must undergo in their progress to adulthood.

See also: *CA* 155; *SATA* 90; *WSMP*.

Brenda Bellingham

Born: 14 August 1931, in Liverpool, England.

Education: University of Liverpool (Certificate in Social Science, Diploma in Industrial Sociology); University of Alberta (Teacher's Diploma 1970).

Principal Residences: Liverpool; Sherwood Park, Alta.

Career: secretary; personnel manager; social worker; teacher; writer.

Works for Children

Joanie's Magic Boots (Edmonton: Tree Frog, 1979). **Rev:** *CCL* 15/16 (1980): 126; *IR* 14 (Apr. 1980): 36.

Storm Child (Toronto: James Lorimer, 1985). **Rev:** *CCL* 46 (1987): 87; *CM* (May 1991): 156.

Two Parents Too Many (Richmond Hill, Ont.: Scholastic, 1985). **Rev:** *BiC* 14 (Dec. 1985): 14; *CCL* 53 (1989): 61; *QQ* 51 (Dec. 1985): 30.

The Curse of the Silver Box (Richmond Hill, Ont.: Scholastic, 1989). **Rev:** *CCL* 62 (1991): 76; *CM* 18 (July 1990): 184; *QQ* 56 (July 1990): 39.

Like a TV Hero (Don Mills, Ont.: General Publishing, 1991). **Rev:** *CM* 20 (Mar. 1992): 64; *QQ* 57 (July 1991): 52.

Princesses Don't Wear Jeans (Richmond Hill, Ont.: Scholastic, 1991). **Rev:** *CCL* 66 (1992): 77; *CM* 19 (Sept. 1991): 218; *QQ* 57 (Apr. 1991): 20.

Dragons Don't Read Books (Richmond Hill, Ont.: Scholastic, 1991). **Rev:** *QQ* 58 (Nov. 1992): 35.

Lilly to the Rescue (Halifax: Formac, 1997). **Rev:** *CBRA* (1997): 502; *CM* 4 (19 Sept. 1997): on-line.

Drowning in Secrets (Richmond Hill, Ont.: Scholastic, 1998).

Lilly's Good Deed (Halifax: Formac, 1998).

Selected Discussions

Jones, Raymond E. 'The Plains Truth: Indians and Metis in Recent Fiction', *ChLQ* 12: (Spring 1987): 36–9.

Brenda Bellingham has written a historical novel, contemporary novels, and chapter books for beginning readers. Much of her work focuses on characters who feel they are outsiders, especially because they live in single-parent families. Her plots are sometimes melodramatic, but they develop themes about realistic acceptance of one's situation and about discovering one's identity.

Bellingham's first novel, *Joanie's Magic Boots*, is a tale of wish-fulfilment within a realistic setting. Joanie, accused of shoplifting some boots, must endure the identity of thief until she dramatically proves her integrity by capturing an actual thief. Joanie then discovers that her boots are 'magic': she gets her deepest wish, to have a father, when the policeman who had handled her shoplifting charge marries her mother.

Two Parents Too Many portrays the feelings of rejection children develop consequent to divorce. In the first part of the novel, two sisters conduct an amusing campaign to prevent their mother from remarrying. A somewhat darker note, however, sounds underneath the light surface tones: Jenny, the older girl, is developing anorexia because she believes that her father has divorced not only her mother but her, too. The novelist is careful to show that both of the divorced parents love their children despite new marriages.

The narrator of *The Curse of the Silver Box* also has divorced parents, but the novel suggests that divorce does not always traumatize children. In this instance, the narrator, 13-year-old Katy Martin, and her sister live with her mother and her new husband, who are friends with Katy's father and new wife. Both couples are loving and attentive to Katy. The relationships are interesting and unusual, but they are not the main focus. The plot actually raises the issue of whether witchcraft and curses are real after Katy's father and his wife, owners of an antique business, purchase an old silver box. An evil-looking boy, Simon, hands them a note saying that they and their kin will be cursed until the rightful owner has the box back. Disasters soon accumulate: Katy's stepmother is hospitalized for serious complications with her pregnancy, Katy breaks her leg, her father has a fire in his kitchen and then suffers a gall-bladder attack. Whether these disasters are coincidences or products of the curse remains an open question, but Katy takes no chances. She believes she can end the possibility of future curses by having Simon, a self-professed witch, put the box in the mausoleum of his grandfather, who originated the curse, thus ensuring that the rightful owner will forever possess the box. The *Curse of the Silver Box* is somewhat overwrought in its suggestions of the supernatural, but its blending of family story and gothic mystery develops an interesting theme about belief controlling people's perceptions of events.

Less successful is *Like a TV Hero*, in which the narrator, Kris Higgins, whose parents are loving but neglectful, imagines the world in terms of television shows. The theme of parental selfishness and neglect is not drawn to a very satisfying outcome: Kris learns that his parents will not change into TV parents, so he must accept them as they are. The related theme of wishing for excitement is similarly vapid in its resolution. Kris's encounter with some much older bullies ends in improbable slapstick when a trash-picker named Garbage Harry helps him humiliate the bullies. The novel preaches acceptance of others obviously by including an older woman who speaks with an accent and seems at first to Kris to be a meddlesome witch but proves to be a loving protector; a Chinese-Canadian girl who constantly changes her name to make life more exciting; and the dirty, bizarre-looking Garbage Harry, who first is threatening but later shows both consideration and ingenuity. The disparate elements do not cohere, however, and the climactic event, a soapbox derby the children have organized, lacks both the excitement and plausibility necessary to allow it to become the basis of a satisfying resolution to Kris's problems.

The resolution is also the weakness of *Drowning in Secrets*, in which 16-year-old Chloe Griffiths, who has grown up remembering and knowing nothing about her deceased mother, embarks on a journey to discover her roots. While visiting her mother's twin sister and her senile grandmother, Chloe learns that her mother was mentally ill and committed suicide by drowning herself. Her body never was recovered. Chloe also begins her first serious romance with a shy neighbourhood boy. Eventually, Chloe recovers a memory of her mother trying to drown her, a memory that explains the nightmares she has had for years. The plot at this point becomes completely implausible, with Chloe's mother, who had faked her suicide to avoid being committed to a mental institution, returning and trying first to kill Chloe and then save her. In the process, Chloe's mother drowns. Having discovered something about her past, Chloe decides that she must go back to her father and try to mend their relationship. The book has several implausible episodes, including its disappointingly melodramatic climax, but *Drowning in Secrets* is a rather gripping psychological novel when it concentrates on Chloe's desire to learn about herself by learning about her mother and on her fears about her own sanity, given her mother's history of mental illness.

Bellingham's best book is *Storm Child*, a soundly researched historical novel. Based on a common historical situation, the white trader's abandonment of his Native wife and her children, it contrasts white and Indian cultures and explores the question of Métis identity. Isobel Macpherson, a Métis, finds all white ways hateful after her Scots father deserts her mother and, therefore, taking on her Indian name, Storm Child, goes to live with her Peigan grandparents. She discovers, however, that she is neither white nor Indian but 'part Isobel, part Storm Child—a country-born girl'. Wishing after all not to choose between her heritages, she decides she must educate herself so that she can make a significant contribution to the West. The novel too readily abandons some challenging questions about a female's place both in Native and in European cultures, but the first parts of the story are engrossing explorations of cultural limitations.

In addition to novels, Bellingham also has written four chapter books for new readers. *Lilly to the Rescue* is a first-person narrative in which Lilly tries to control her bossiness in order to keep friends. When she prevents her friend Kendall from being attacked by a dog that he is teasing, she learns that bossiness is not always a flaw. In the sequel, *Lilly's Good Deed*, Lilly detests nasty Theresa Green, whom she calls Trees Are Green (she realizes that her own name, Lilly Pond, also is comical). After Theresa helps her to save a kitten snuggled under the hood of a car, Lilly learns they can be friends. Bellingham's other chapter books focus on the relationship between Jeff, who wants to be ordinary, and Tilly, who is extremely imaginative. In *Princesses Don't Wear Jeans*, Jeff faces a dilemma because Tilly's unkempt appearance and habit of telling fanciful lies make her an outsider. Tilly has, for example, told the class that she owns pet bears that prove to be only stuffed bears and she has demonstrated that she has a dragon by showing a photograph of an iguana. Jeff doesn't know if he should believe her when she says that she will give him white mice for his birthday, but he shows an admirable loyalty to the likeable Tilly. In the sequel, *Dragons Don't Read Books*, Jeff has trouble going along with Tilly's insistence that the stuffed toy in the school library is not a bookworm but a dragon. The preposterous plot eventually has Jeff playing the role of a knight who wields a vacuum cleaner to slay the dragon and thereby discovering that two mischievous kindergarten students have been 'feeding' it missing library books. The major interest in both of these chapter books is Jeff's struggle to avoid judging Tilly by appearances, as the other students do.

Bellingham's stories frequently wind up with facile, optimistic conclusions, but they raise interesting issues. Her major strength is the creation of psychologically convincing characters, particularly females searching for identity.

John Bianchi

Born: 23 August 1947, in Rochester, NY.

Principal Residences: Rochester; Ottawa; McDonald's Corners, Ont.; Sandhurst, Ont.; Tucson, Ariz.

Education: attended State University of New York, Oswego, leaving in his second year.

Career: odd jobs; artist; animation artist; publisher; illustrator; author.

Works for Children

Written and Illustrated by John Bianchi

The Bungalo Boys: Last of the Tree Ranchers! (Newburgh, Ont.: Bungalo, 1986). **Rev:** *BiC* 16 (Mar. 1987): 39; *BYP* 1 (Feb. 1987): 3; *CCL* 45 (1987): 94; *EL* 14 (May 1987): 49; *EL* 15 (Mar. 1988): 60; *SLJ* 34 (Nov. 1987): 86.

The Bungalo Boys II: Bushmen Brouhaha (Newburgh, Ont.: Bungalo, 1987). **Rev:** *BYP* 2 (Feb. 1988): 5; *CCL* 50 (1988): 94; *CM* 16 (July 1988): 145.

Princess Frownsalot (Newburgh, Ont.: Bungalo, 1987). **Rev:** *BYP* 2 (Feb. 1988): 6; *EL* 15 (Mar. 1988): 61; *CCL* 52 (1988): 86.

The Swine Snafu (Newburgh, Ont.: Bungalo, 1988). **Rev:** *BYP* 2 (Oct. 1988): 16; *CCL* 51 (1988): 99; *CM*: 17 (Jan. 1989): 33; *SLJ* 35 (May 1989): 77.

The Bungalo Boys III: Champions of Hockey (Newburgh, Ont.: Bungalo, 1989). **Rev:** *APBR* 16 (Nov. 1989): 12; *CCL* 59 (1990): 106; *CM* 18 (Jan. 1990): 11; *QQ* 55 (Dec. 1989): 22.

Snowed In at Pokeweed Public School (Newburgh, Ont.: Bungalo, 1991). **Rev:** *CM* 20 (Jan. 1992): 19; *QQ* 57 (Oct. 1991): 38.

Penelope Penguin: The Incredible Good Baby (Newburgh, Ont.: Bungalo, 1992). **Rev:** *CM* 20 (Sept. 1992): 207; *Small Press Book Review* (Spring 1993): 18.

The Bungalo Boys: Flight of the Space Quester (Newburgh, Ont.: Bungalo, 1993). **Rev:** *QQ* 59 (Apr. 1993): 35.

The Artist (Newburgh, Ont.: Bungalo, 1993). **Rev:** *CBRA* (1993): #6011; *QQ* 59 (Sept. 1993): 68.

Spring Break at Pokeweed Public School (Newburgh, Ont.: Bungalo, 1994). **Rev:** *QQ* 60 (Apr. 1994): 38.

The Toad Sleeps Over (Newburgh, Ont.: Bungalo, 1995). **Rev:** *CBRA* (1995): 462.

The First Big Bungalo Boys Book : Three Stories High (Newburgh, Ont.: Bungalo, 1995) [reprints *Last of the Tree Ranchers!*, *Bushmen Brouhaha*, and *Champions of Hockey*]. **Rev:** *CBRA* (1995): 461.

Welcome Back to Pokeweed Public School (Kingston, Ont.: Bungalo, 1996). **Rev:** *CBRA* (1996): 433.

The Lab Rats of Doctor Eclair (Kingston, Ont.: Bungalo, 1997).

Illustrated by John Bianchi

The Dingles, by Helen Levchuck (Toronto: Groundwood, 1985). **Rev:** *QQ* 51 (Dec. 1985): 24.

The Short Tree and the Bird that Could Not Sing, by Dennis Foon (Toronto: Groundwood, 1986). **Rev:** *BiC* 15 (Dec. 1986): 15; *CCL* 46 (1987): 105; *QQ* 52 (Oct. 1986): 16.

Exploring the Night Sky: The Equinox Astronomy Guide for Beginners, by Terence Dickinson (Camden East, Ont.: Camden House, 1987). **Rev:** *BiC* 16 (Dec. 1987): 14; *BYP* 1 (Dec. 1987): 5; *CM* 16 (Mar. 1988): 61, and 16 (May 1988): 76, and 16 (Nov. 1988): 203; *EL* 15 (Mar. 1988): 24; *SLJ* 34 (June 1988): 110.

Exploring the Sky by Day, by Terence Dickinson (Camden East, Ont.: Camden House, 1988). **Rev:** *BiC* 17 (Dec. 1988): 14; *CM* 17 (Jan. 1989): 43; *EL* 16 (Mar. 1989): 24; *SLJ* 35 (Jan. 1989): 97.

Mortimer Mooner Stopped Taking a Bath, by Frank B. Edwards (Newburgh, Ont.: Bungalo, 1990). **Rev:** *CCL* 63 (1991): 89; *CM* 19 (Mar. 1991): 98; *QQ* 57 (May 1991): 23; *SLJ* 37 (May 1991): 77.

For the Birds, by Margaret Atwood, with boxes and sidebars by Shelley Tanaka (Toronto: Douglas & McIntyre, 1990). **Rev:** *APBR* 18 (Feb. 1991): 13; *CCL* 65 (1992): 83; *CM* 19 (Mar. 1991): 93; *EL* 19 (Sept. 1991): 57; *QQ* 56 (Nov. 1990): 11.

Doris Dingle's Crafty Cat Activity Book, by Helen Levchuck (Toronto: Groundwood, 1990).

Melody Mooner Stayed Up All Night, by Frank B. Edwards (Newburgh, Ont.: Bungalo, 1991). **Rev:** *CM* 19 (Sept. 1991): 228; *QQ* 57 (July 1991): 55, and 62 (Oct. 1996): 47.

Grandma Mooner Lost Her Voice!, by Frank B. Edwards (Newburgh, Ont.: Bungalo, 1992). **Rev:** *QQ* 58 (Dec. 1992): 26.

Snow, by Frank B. Edwards (Newburgh, Ont.: Bungalo, 1992).

A Dog Called Dad, by Frank B. Edwards (Newburgh, Ont.: Bungalo, 1994). **Rev:** *BiC* 23 (Dec. 1994): 55; *CBRA* (1994): 448; *QQ* 60 (Dec. 1994): 32; *SLJ* 41 (May 1995): 84.

Mortimer Mooner Makes Lunch, by Frank B. Edwards (Newburgh, Ont.: Bungalo, 1995). **Rev:** *BiC* 24 (Summer 1995): 47; *CBRA* (1995): 468; *CCL* 88 (1997): 83; *QQ* 61 (Apr. 1995): 37.

[illus. with David Egge] *Other Worlds: A Beginner's Guide to Planets and Moons*, by Terence Dickinson (Willowdale, Ont.: Firefly, 1995).

Kids, Computers & You : What Parents Can Do Now to Prepare Their Children for the Future, by Frank B. Edwards and Thomas H. Carpenter (Kingston, Ont.: Bungalo, 1995).

Melody Mooner Takes Lessons, by Frank B. Edwards (Kingston, Ont.: Bungalo, 1996).

Downtown Lost and Found, by Frank B. Edwards (Kingston, Ont.: Bungalo, 1997).

Peek-a-Boo at the Zoo, by Frank B. Edwards (Kingston, Ont.: Bungalo, 1997).

The Zookeeper's Sleepers, by Frank B. Edwards (Kingston, Ont.: Bungalo, 1997).

Is the Spaghetti Ready?, by Frank B. Edwards (Kingston, Ont.: Bungalo, 1998).

Troubles with Bubbles, by Frank B. Edwards (Kingston, Ont.: Bungalo, 1998).

John Bianchi says of children that 'Their path to early literacy should be a happy one.' Hence, when he and Frank B. Edwards founded Bungalo Books as an outlet for their own work, they adopted as their motto, 'Reading for the Fun of It!' In the books he both writes and illustrates, Bianchi creates fun by mixing nonsense, slapstick, puns, a comic discrepancy between words and pictures, and cartoonish illustrations.

Bianchi is author/illustrator of two series. The first, *The Bungalo Boys* books, are nonsense adventures that arise from a literal interpretation of words. In *Last of the Tree Ranchers!*, a spoof of cowboy stories, the four Bungalo Boys, because they are tree ranchers, saddle, ride, lasso, and brand trees. The plot, such as it is, has the Boys capture some tree rustlers, the Beaver Gang. The Gang escapes, however, when the youngest of the Boys, Little Shorty, becomes bored with guarding them and sneaks off for a midnight tree ride. In the ironic conclusion, Little Shorty, unaware that the Gang is free, contentedly imagines his brothers telling Ma how helpful he has been. Much of the fun in their second adventure, *Bushmen Brouhaha*, depends on the discrepancy between words and pictures. For example, the text indicates that the Boys are parachuting into Africa's Serengeti so that they will not disturb the animals, but a two-page illustration shows the animals fleeing in panic as the Boys and their equipment plummet from the sky. Nonsense, like that in the first book, drives the ragged plot in which the Boys save the bushmen, people actually formed from bushes, from the blue-nosed baboons feasting on their berries. The plot is more focused in *Champions of Hockey*, in which the Boys defend their Natural Hockey League trophy, the Bungalo Birdbath, against a team of penguins and enormous bruins. The slapstick finale depends on a pun: 'the heavy action' of the bears converging on the Boys' net shatters the pond's ice. Little Shorty, alone with the puck on an ice floe, drifts towards the opponents' net to score the winning goal. *Flight of the Space Quester*, the most disappointing of the series, has the Boys treating an amusement park ride as if it were a real journey into space. Because the pictures make the reader aware of the true situation from the very beginning, the plot has no surprise twists, making the humour seem exceptionally forced. *The Bungalo Boys* books are appealing because of their zany illustrations, but ultimately their stories are disappointing because the nonsense episodes do not cohere into satisfying plots.

The plotting in Bianchi's other series, the *Pokeweed Public School* books, is also weak, but the focus on school life provides some unity. Most of the complications and much of the fun in this series come from the fact that Principal Slugmeyer, a dog who resembles a bespectacled Snoopy, is incompetent. In *Snowed In at Pokeweed Public School*, for instance, Principal Slugmeyer, announces that he is too busy to be disturbed. Consequently, Ms Mudwortz, the teacher, is unable to call the bus to take the students home early, so they all are trapped in the school by a snowstorm. A picture shows, however, that the principal, having read a book on coping with stress, is not really busy: he is merely taking a nap. In *Spring Break at Pokeweed Public School*, about a camping trip during which the children try to photograph the food-stealing monster Ogopokeweed, pictures make clear to the readers what the children do not understand: the real thief is the hungry principal. Similarly, in *Welcome Back to Pokeweed Public School*, an illustration shows a class of students doing a variety of tasks on their new computers, but Principal Slugmeyer's screen contains a system-error message. The irony and the mocking of adult authority figures in this series provide some amusement, and the pictures have a manic energy, but their lack of strong story lines makes these books flat and disappointing.

In those titles that do not belong to a series, Bianchi's plots are generally tighter, and he includes themes that attempt to make the stories provide more than fun. In *Princess Frownsalot*, for example, the old threat to frowning children that their faces might become stuck is the basis for a lesson about the joy of sharing. When Princess Frownsalot can't undo the frown she uses to get her own way with everybody in the kingdom, Dr Katzinbottin transplants her cat's smile. The Princess sees, however, that her cat is now unhappy, and so she gives the smile back. Ironically, because doing things for others makes the Princess happy, her own smile is restored. A less heavy-handed but more sentimental didacticism controls *The Artist*, the life story of Amelio, a dog who dreams of being a great artist. Duties of supporting a family and raising children repeatedly prevent Amelio from pursuing his dream, but he never complains and finds pleasure in everything he does. When he dies and goes to heaven, God gives him the task of painting sunrises, thus fulfilling Amelio's dream of painting great landscapes. Although it ends as a *pourquoi* tale explaining the glories of sunrise, the main theme is that people do not have to be famous or to do great work to lead happy, loving lives.

In his other overtly didactic tales, Bianchi is especially concerned with acceptance. In *The Swine Snafu*, the urbane Pigs have disdain for their messy, noisy, lower-class neigbours, Wild Bill Boar and his wife, Wild Flora. After both wives give birth on the same day, Mrs Pig fears that the hospital mixed up the babies because her children are wild and seem to be developing tusks. Once the doctor reassures the Pigs that their children merely have teeth that need braces, the Pigs realize that, in spite of their social differences, they can be friends with the Boars and join them for a friendly ball game. This story starts off well with its contrast of social types, but its blatantly contrived conclusion, which has little connection with earlier episodes, overwhelms with earnestness. In contrast, *The Toad Sleeps Over* maintains a tighter focus on thematic issues. When Tony Bufo, a toad, comes to sleep over with Minifield the mouse, his bouncing exuberance and habit of catching insects with his tongue is so different from mouse behaviour that it angers Minifield's father. While the two friends are out walking, Tony uses his tongue, his ability to inflate himself, and his foul-tasting venom to help Minifield and himself escape from a hungry coyote. Minifield's grateful father hence accepts Tony's differences. Although the account of this gratitude drags on too long, the story is otherwise successful. A different kind of acceptance is the theme of *Penelope Penguin: The Incredible Good Baby*, which inverts normal child development to suggest that children and adults need to accept childish limitations in behaviour as normal. When her parents, who had worried about how they would cope with an infant, see the incredible good behaviour of newborn Penelope Penguin, initially they are astonished and delighted. Eventually, however, Penelope's good deeds become troublesome: she makes a mess while preparing breakfast for her parents, loses her father's slippers while vacuuming, shrinks her mother's sweater while washing, and takes the car to get them snacks and a video. After her distressed parents have a good talk with her, Penelope, to their delight, becomes a normal baby who makes noise early in the morning and spills her food at dinner. The idea that parents and children should not have unreasonable expectations is laudable, but the fact that Penelope causes trouble by attempting to do things beyond her competence clouds the issue of what constitutes good behaviour and makes the story more bizarre than meaningful.

Bianchi's most recent solo effort, *The Lab Rats of Doctor Eclair*, is better in its illustrations than in its story, which is not only creaky in plot but also devoid of the nonsense that provided fun in earlier books and of the didacticism that gave them some substance. The science-fiction plot has three lab rats, who gained special powers when lightning struck their laboratory, seeking to save some ratlings from a mechanical rat developed by Professor Eclair. The conclusion, in which the mechanical rat is to be launched into space, leaves room for a sequel, but the characters aren't engaging enough nor are the episodes entertaining enough to warrant one.

Although he was born in the United States and now lives there, John Bianchi qualifies as a Canadian writer and illustrator because he lived in Canada from 1969 to 1993 and because he continues his involvement with the publishing company he co-founded here. In terms of his contribution to children's literature, that publishing company has been both a blessing and a liability. It is a blessing because it originally published books that established firms did not want, books that have entertained many children and gave Bianchi an entrance into the field of children's books. At the same time, however, it has published severely flawed stories. Bianchi is a gifted illustrator: his cartoons are energetic and appealing. As a writer, however, he is severely in need of editorial help. Too often, he is unsure of his audience, aiming remarks over their heads to adults. More seriously, he has been unable to create satisfying plots in which comedy and nonsense make meaningful contributions. Unless independent and gifted editors guide him, he is likely to remain a footnote in Canadian children's literature, a good illustrator of others' books, but a writer whose own creations are, regardless of their commercial success, severely flawed.

See also: *WSMP*.

Geoffrey Bilson

Born: 27 January 1938, in Cardiff, Wales.

Died: 25 July 1987, in Saskatoon.

Principal Residences: Cardiff; Liverpool, England; Stanford, Calif.; Saskatoon.

Education: University of Wales (BA); University of Omaha (MA); Stanford University (Ph.D.).

Career: history professor, University of Saskatchewan; writer.

Works for Children

Goodbye, Sarah (Toronto: Kids Can Press, 1981). **Rev:** *BiC* 11 (June 1982): 31; *CCL* 29 (1983): 45; *EL* 12 (Nov. 1984): 23.

Death Over Montreal (Toronto: Kids Can Press, 1982). **Rev:** *BiC* 11 (Dec. 1982): 10; *QQ* 49 (Jan. 1983): 33; *SLJ* 29 (Mar. 1983): 169.

Hockey Bat Harris (Toronto: Kids Can Press, 1984). **Rev:** *BiC* 13 (Dec. 1984): 12; *CCL* 43 (1986): 60; *EL* 12 (Mar. 1985): 46; *SLJ* 31 (Mar. 1985): 162.

Other

A Darkened House: Cholera in Nineteenth-Century Canada (Toronto: U of Toronto P, 1980).

The Guest Children: The Story of the British Child Evacuees Sent to Canada during World War II (Saskatoon: Fifth House, 1988).

Many authors of historical novels for children often focus on major events of the past and place their heroes in the midst or on the edge of these events; history professor and novelist Geoffrey Bilson did not. He took lesser-known, but nonetheless important, events and showed how they influenced the lives of young teenagers.

Although he had often made up stories for his children, it was not until the late 1970s, while they were away on summer holidays, that he sat down to write them a novel. *Death Over Montreal* made use of Bilson's studies in Canadian medical history to tell the story of Jamie Douglas, who arrived in Montreal early in the nineteenth century in the middle of a cholera epidemic. *Goodbye, Sarah*, set in Winnipeg during the General Strike of 1919, is the account of a young girl's struggles with friendship and family. Saskatoon is the scene of *Hockey Bat Harris*, the story of David Harris, one of the children evacuated from England early in World War II.

The central character in each novel is cut off from a secure past and, essentially alone, must face his or her major crisis. Jamie Douglas has come with his family from Scotland, reluctantly accepting his father's hope that Canada will provide their 'big break'. When, after having given all his money to a swindler, his father dies of cholera Jamie must fend for himself. He proves his heroism working for Dr Ayres, a naturalistic healer, whose faith in him gives the boy courage and self-confidence. Mary Jarrett's security is destroyed by the General Strike, of which her father is an organizer. Not only does the family find itself in severe financial difficulties, but Mary's relationship with her best friend is destroyed by the tensions generated by the conflict. At the conclusion, Mary is able to accept the fact that Sarah is no longer her friend and that she will never be able to say goodbye to her in person. Like Jamie Douglas, David Harris is an unwilling immigrant. Worried about his mother back in bomb-ravaged England and his father on active duty in Egypt, he is hostile to his adoptive Canadian family, especially his new 'brother', Bob. He steals from the family cookie jar, blames Bob for a number of bed-wetting incidents, and refuses to help with family chores. The patience of the adult members of the family and David's growing skill at hockey, using what he calls his 'hockey bat', help him to overcome his unhappiness and belligerence.

Ordinary kids in extraordinary circumstances: this phrase captures the essence of Geoffrey Bilson's novels. Readers will gain knowledge of little-known events of Canadian history; but they will be most interested in the conflicts of the main characters, coming to understand and respect the difficulties of their lives and the strengths they develop in confronting them.

See also: *SATA* 99; *WSMP*.

Ann Blades

Born: 16 November 1947, in Vancouver.

Principal Residences: White Rock, BC; Vancouver; Mile 18, BC; Tache, BC; Surrey, BC.

Education: University of British Columbia (Teaching Certificate 1967); British Columbia Institute of Technology (RN 1974).

Career: teacher at Mile 18 and Tache, BC; nurse in Vancouver; writer/illustrator.

Major Awards: Canadian Library Association Book of the Year for Children (1972); Canada Council Children's Literature Prize for Illustration (1978); Amelia Frances Howard-Gibbon Illustrator's Award (1979); Elizabeth Mrazik-Cleaver Canadian Picture Book Award (1986).

Works for Children

Written and Illustrated by Ann Blades

Mary of Mile 18 (Montreal: Tundra, 1971). **Rev:** *CCB-B* 25 (May 1972): 135; *CCL* 1 (1975): 77; *IR* 6 (Winter 1972): 22; *SLJ* 23 (Feb. 1977): 54.

A Boy of Tache (Montreal: Tundra, 1973). **Rev:** *CCB-B* 30 (June 1977): 154; *CCL* 1 (1975): 77; *HB* 53 (Oct. 1977): 530; *IR* 8 (Spring 1974): 28; *SLJ* 20 (Apr. 1974): 55.

The Cottage at Crescent Beach (Toronto: Magook, 1977). **Rev:** *IR* 12 (Spring 1978): 35; *SLJ* 27 (Sept. 1980), 43.

By the Sea: An Alphabet Book (Toronto: Kids Can Press, 1985). **Rev:** *EL* 13 (Mar. 1986): 15; *QQ* 51 (Aug. 1985): 37.

Seasons Board Books (Toronto: Groundwood, 1989). **Rev:** *CM* 18 (Mar. 1990): 61; *EL* 17 (Mar. 1990): 23; *SLJ* 36 (Mar. 1990): 118.

Back to the Cabin (Victoria, BC: Orca, 1996). **Rev:** *BiC* 26 (Mar. 1997): 34; *QQ* 62 (Sept. 1996): 72.

Illustrated by Ann Blades

Jacques the Woodcutter, by Michael Macklem (Ottawa: Oberon, 1977). **Rev:** *IR* 12 (Spring 1978): 58.

A Salmon for Simon, by Betty Waterton (Vancouver: Douglas & McIntyre, 1978). **Rev:** *CCB-B* 33 (July 1980): 225; *CCL* 21 (1981): 58; *IR* 13 (Apr. 1979): 64; *SLJ* 26 (Aug. 1980): 58.

Six Darn Cows, by Margaret Laurence (Toronto: James Lorimer, 1979). **Rev:** *BiC* 7 (Dec. 1979): 15; *CCL* 21 (1981): 58.

Anna's Pet, by Joyce Barkhouse and Margaret Atwood (Toronto: James Lorimer, 1980). **Rev:** *BiC* 9 (Dec. 1980): 18; *CCL* 21 (1981), 65; *IR* 15 (Feb. 1981): 28; *QQ* 47 (Jan. 1981): 27.

Pettranella, by Betty Waterton (Vancouver: Douglas & McIntyre, 1980). **Rev:** *BiC* 10 (Oct. 1981): 33; *CCL* 35 (1984): 25; *IR* 15 (Apr. 1981): 56; *QQ* 47 (June 1981): 34; *SLJ* 27 (Aug. 1981): 72.

A Candle for Christmas, by Jean Speare (Vancouver: Douglas & McIntyre, 1986).

Rev: *BiC* 15 (Dec. 1986): 16; *CCL* 46 (1987): 109; *EL* 14 (Mar. 1987): 27; *QQ* 52 (Oct. 1986): 16; *SLJ* 34 (Oct. 1987): 33.

Ida and the Wool Smugglers, by Sue Ann Alderson (Vancouver: Douglas & McIntyre, 1987). **Rev:** *BiC* 17 (June 1988): 37; *CCL* 52 (1988): 27; *CL* (Autumn 1989): 246; *CM* 16 (Sept. 1988): 180; *HB* 64 (May 1988): 336; *SLJ* 34 (Aug. 1988): 77.

The Singing Basket, by Kit Pearson (Toronto: Groundwood, 1990). **Rev:** *CCL* 65 (1992): 97.

A Dog Came, Too, by Ainslie Manson (Toronto: Groundwood, 1992). **Rev:** *CCB-B* 46 (Mar. 1993): 219; *CM* 20 (Sept. 1992): 208; *EL* 20 (Mar. 1993): 12; *QQ* 58 (Apr. 1992): 32.

A Ride for Martha, by Sue Ann Alderson (Toronto: Groundwood, 1993). **Rev:** *QQ* 59 (Oct. 1993): 38.

Pond Seasons, by Sue Ann Alderson (Toronto: Groundwood, 1997). **Rev:** *EL* 25 (Mar. 1998): 27; *QQ* 63 (Apr. 1997): 37.

'During Easter vacation when I was teaching at Mile 18, I felt quite isolated and lonely. So I began to think of a story about one of the children in my class and started to paint some watercolours to go with it. None of the books the children had at school related to them at all, and I thought it would be nice for them to have a story about something familiar.' From that week's vacation came one of Canada's most famous picture books, *Mary of Mile 18*. Blades began painting when she was 11; but she never gave any thought to professional art until she began publishing books. It was only after several years' work as a teacher and nurse that she devoted herself full-time to painting and to illustrating books.

Mary of Mile 18 presents a simple story: awakening in the middle of a freezing winter night, Mary Fehr watches the northern lights and sees in them the promise of something special the next day. The promise seems to have come true when, on the way home from school, she discovers a lost half-wolf pup. However, her father tells her that she cannot keep it because 'our animals must work for us or give us food', and she is forced to abandon the pup in the woods. Late that night, the whines of the animal warn the family that a wolf is breaking into the hen house, and now that he has proved his worth, the pup is brought into Mary's bedroom by her father. The simplicity of the plot may lead some to categorize *Mary of Mile 18* as just another dog story. The book, however, is really a tribute to the Fehr family, who moved North in response to the government's promise of title to the land they clear. They live a hard life without plumbing, electricity, or telephones; they obtain water by melting snow; and their nearest neighbours are two miles away. But the family works and plays together, older children helping younger ones, and all helping their mother who expects a new baby. Mr Fehr suffers emotional hardships, for he must often refuse to give the children what they want, concealing his sorrow in anger.

The artistry of the illustrations makes up a large part of the strength of this book. Blades's watercolours capture the bleak quality of the northern wilderness in which the family lives. In contrast to the pale blues, drab greys, and dull browns of the landscape are the rich colours of human tools: the warm yellows of the lanterns, the vivid scarlet of the tractor. Particularly effective are the illustrations that reveal Mary's changing emotions. When she first discovers the pup, she kneels before it, extending her bright yellow mittens, a faint smile on her lips. The horizon appears distant, the slender trunks of the bare trees less overwhelming than in other pictures. However, as she walks into the woods to abandon the pup, the grey and brown tree trunks dominate. There is no brightness on the page, just as there is no happiness in Mary's heart. When Mary is finally given the pup, warmth radiates from the illustration. Sitting up in her bed, she cradles the dog in her arms. Her rich, golden hair is down, a full smile plays on her face, and her eyes twinkle. On her bed is a gaily coloured quilt; the browns of the bedstead and walls are rich and warm.

Like *Mary of Mile 18*, *A Boy of Tache* draws on people Blades knew while she was teaching in northern British Columbia. She has said that, although the story was based on an actual event in which a teenage boy brought help for his sick grandfather, 'I made the boy much younger, so that he'd be about the age of the children who'd be reading it. The events, however, are very true to the experiences of Native children. Their lives are much less protected than those of children growing up in the city; they see violence and death at an early age.' *A Boy of Tache* is more than a rescue story; it is the account of a boy's growth to maturity, his development of an understanding of aging and death in a rugged and demanding environment. In the illustrations, Blades contrasts the harsh elements with the courageous, but vulnerable, human beings. There are no people in the opening picture; bare, black tree trunks are silhouetted against a cold, blue-grey, early spring sky. Several illustrations, however, do emphasize human warmth: Charlie looks admiringly at Za as the old man talks to him about trapping; both crouch before a campfire roasting a grouse; and, in the concluding picture, the old man, recovered from his illness, puts his arm on Charlie's shoulder as the two look at the bright red hues of the setting sun. The two face not only the horizon, but also the future that awaits the boy who has proved his courage and love.

Blades also has written and illustrated three picture books based on her own childhood experiences and those of her children. *The Cottage at Crescent Beach* and *By the Sea* are simple accounts of children's everyday experiences on the beaches near White Rock, British Columbia. In addition to illustrating various seashore activities, she gives a strong sense of the colours and the details of the beach and the sea. Green is the dominant colour of *The Cottage at Crescent Beach*: the rich foliage of the trees and the bottle-green underwater areas the girls explore. Blue dominates *By the Sea*; it is as if one were looking at a hazy west coast summer day. In both, one senses the security of the children as they play in a familiar environment. *Back to the Cabin* recounts in words and pictures the summer activities of two boys and their mother at a northern lake and cabin. The simple text and pictures emphasize the happiness the people feel together in the woods, on the lake and, during rainy days, in the snug, warm cabin.

Not surprisingly, all but one of the books Blades has illustrated for other writers portray children engaged in realistic activities and aware of the support of loving families. In fact, the success of Blades's art lies in its communication of both adventure and security. At the beginning of Betty Waterton's *A Salmon for Simon*, the title hero fishes alone, a pensive expression on his face. At the end, he is fishing again, but now he is grinning. His rescue of a trapped salmon has given him a sense of accomplishment and has made him feel like the others in the village, all of whom are successful fishermen. His unhappiness early in the story, when he cannot catch a fish, is emphasized in an illustration of him hunched over a tidal pool, gazing at the small sea creatures. The page is designed around a series of downward curves—his hairline, eyebrows, mouth, shoulders, and the hill on which he slouches all reinforce the downturned line of his mouth. Later, when he has freed the fish, he leans contentedly on his shovel, a small smile on his face. In the distance, a bright sun casts a cheery glow.

From the time she leaves her Old World home to the time when she discovers the blooms in the Manitoba wilderness from the seeds her grandmother gave her, the heroine of Betty Waterton's *Pettranella* feels many emotions, all of which are communicated clearly by the illustrations. At first, the prospect of a voyage to the New World thrills the child, and she smiles radiantly; but her enthusiasm fades as she sits slouched on her family's trunk in a dingy waiting room. When she loses her grandmother's gift, she slumps dejectedly, looking down sadly at the empty seed bag. She is surrounded by leafless yellow birch trees. In contrast, when she discovers the flowers, she smiles and holds them in her hands, surrounded by pale green spring grass, delicately coloured blossoms, a powder-blue sky, and new foliage on the birch trees. And she wears a bright yellow bonnet that symbolizes her inner happiness and new hope.

Turn-of-the-century Salt Spring Island, BC, provides the settings for Sue Ann Alderson's *Ida and the Wool Smugglers* and *A Ride for Martha*. In the former, the title heroine, a middle child, feels insignificant until she courageously saves a ewe and her lamb from rustlers. In *A Ride for Martha*, Ida is unhappy with her two friends and her tag-along little sister Martha. However, when the friends rescue the little girl, who has been trapped by a rising tide, Ida appreciates both them and her sibling. In each book, Blades accurately depicts period costumes and dwellings, as well as the rural landscapes of the West Coast. She also illustrates the tensions and conflicts of her central character. Double-spread aerials depict the moments of greatest danger. From above, viewers see Ida walking through a forest clearing, the sheep nearby, and menacing men crouching in the woods on either side of the clearing. An overhead view of the bay into which the canoe containing baby Martha drifts reveals how distant she is from other children. Early in both stories, Blades depicts Ida's sense of isolation by positioning her apart from other people; at the conclusions, she centres her in the illustrations, an indication of her new happiness and self-confidence.

A recurrent subject among Blades's illustrations is the home, the place of security for children. Snug in her bed, Mary cuddles her new-found pet; Charlie and his grandparents travel to a distant but warm trapper's cabin; having rescued the salmon, Simon strides confidently towards his house; Pettranella's family builds a log cabin in the lonely Manitoba countryside; Ida has a loving home and family to return to after her adventures. Blades emphasizes the importance of the home in several ways. First, she contrasts it to the wilderness around: through the window of the Fehr home appear the bleak expanses of the winter landscape; Pettranella's small, but strongly built, cabin is the only building on the vast prairie. In Jean Speare's *A Candle for Christmas*, a boy waiting for his family on a stormy night lights a candle, a beacon to set in the window of his home. Second, Blades uses warm colours for homes. Often, as in *A Salmon for Simon*, these are seen from the outside, with a yellow light shining from the windows; inside, the dwellings may be plain, but they are homey, and the families within generally are grouped together.

Blades's illustrations are less successful for Michael Macklem's adaptation of a French-Canadian folktale, *Jacques the Woodcutter* (republished as *The Singing Basket*, with a new text by Kit Pearson). Here Blades is approaching a different, unfamiliar culture; she had experienced neither the customs nor the landscape. Moreover, her subjects are adults rather than children. While the illustrations are accurate, they lack spontaneity and warmth. The adults appear awkward and even grotesque, and the visualizing of ironic situations seems forced and unnatural.

The watercolour art of Ann Blades has been called primitive, and in a sense it is. She captures emotions and situations as simply as possible. This very simplicity, however, enhances the texts of the stories. She understands the changing emotions of her characters and the beauty and powers inherent in the landscapes that shape them; she conveys these elements with a purity that has made her one of Canada's foremost illustrators of children's books.

See also: *CA* 77-80; *CANR* 13, 48; *CLR* 15; *Profiles*; *SATA* 16, 69; *TCCW*; *WSMP*.

Mary Blakeslee

Born: 12 December 1938, in Calgary.

Principal Residences: Calgary; Vancouver; Kamloops, BC; Fort Worth, Texas; Winnipeg.

Education: University of British Columbia (BSW, MSW).

Career: social worker; educational consultant; writer.

Works for Children

It's Tough To Be a Kid (Richmond Hill, Ont.: Scholastic-TAB, 1983). **Rev:** *CCL* 42 (1986): 52; *EL* 16 (Jan. 1989): 51, and 19 (Nov. 1991): 61.

Halfbacks Don't Wear Pearls (Richmond Hill, Ont.: Scholastic-TAB, 1986). **Rev:** *QQ* 52 (Dec. 1986): 17.

Carnival (Toronto: Overlea House, 1987). **Rev:** *BYP* 1 (Dec. 1987): 10; *CM* 16 (Jan. 1988): 114.

Edythe with a Y (Richmond Hill, Ont.: Scholastic-TAB, 1987). **Rev:** *BYP* 1 (Apr. 1987): 8; *CM* 16 (Jan. 1988): 14.

Outta Sight (Richmond Hill, Ont.: Scholastic-TAB, 1987). **Rev:** *CM* 16 (Jan. 1988): 14.

Chocolate Pie for Breakfast (New York: Avon, 1988).

It's Still Tough To Be a Kid (Richmond Hill, Ont.: Scholastic-TAB, 1988). **Rev:** *BYP* 2 (Dec. 1988): 8; *EL* 16 (Jan. 1989): 51, and 19 (Nov. 1991): 61.

Museum Mayhem (Markham, Ont.: Overlea House, 1988). **Rev:** *BYP* 3 (Feb. 1989): 8; *CM* 17 (Mar. 1989): 67.

Rodeo Rescue (Markham, Ont.: Overlea House, 1988). **Rev:** *CM* 17 (Mar. 1989): 67; *EL* 19 (Sept. 1991): 60.

Will to Win (Toronto: Overlea House, 1988). **Rev:** *BYP* 2 (Aug. 1988): 6; *CM* 16 (Nov. 1988): 211; *EL* 16 (Mar. 1989): 51.

Say Cheese (Richmond Hill, Ont.: Scholastic-TAB, 1989). **Rev:** *APBR* 17 (Feb. 1990): 7; *CCL* 59 (1990): 95; *QQ* 56 (Mar. 1990): 22.

Stampede (Toronto: Overlea House, 1989). **Rev:** *BYP* 3 (June 1989): 10; *CCL* 65 (1992): 114; *CM* 17 (May 1989): 114; *SLJ* 35 (Aug. 1989): 138.

Holy Joe (Toronto: Stoddart, 1990). **Rev:** *QQ* 56 (Sept. 1990): 20.

Death Drop! (Don Mills, Ont.: General Publishing, 1991). **Rev:** *BiC* 21 (Summer 1992): 38; *CM* 20 (May 1992): 150; *QQ* 58 (Mar. 1992): 67.

Four Eyes and French Fries (Toronto: General Paperbacks, 1991). **Rev:** *CBRA* (1995): 492; *CCL* 81 (1996): 65; *CM* 19 (Sept. 1991): 218.

Hal (Toronto: Stoddart, 1991). **Rev:** *CBRA* (1995): 493; *CCL* 67 (1992): 86; *CM* 19 (Sept. 1991): 237; *QQ* 57 (June 1991): 25.

Ida Mae Evans Eats Ants (Toronto: McClelland & Stewart, 1990). **Rev:** *BiC* 19 (Dec. 1990): 33; *CM* 18 (Nov. 1990): 264; *QQ* 56 (Dec. 1990): 18.

The Ghost in the Old Roxy (Goderich, Ont.: Moonstone, 1993). **Rev:** *BiC* 23 (Feb. 1994): 50; *CM* 22 (Jan. 1994): 19; *EL* 22 (Sept. 1994): 55; *QQ* 59 (Dec. 1993): 36.

Stop the Presses, Ida Mae! (Toronto: McClelland & Stewart, 1994). **Rev:** *BiC* 23 (Sept. 1994): 57; *CBRA* (1994): 475; *CM* 22 (Sept. 1994): 124; *QQ* 60 (May 1994): 37.

Other

'Bubblegum and Birthdays: Writing Poetry for Children', *School Libraries in Canada* 11 (Spring 1991): 38–43.

The Wheelchair Gourmet: A Cookbook for the Disabled (Don Mills, Ont.: General Publishers, 1981). **Rev:** *QQ* 48 (Feb. 1982): 16.

Selected Discussions

Jenkinson, Dave. 'Mary Blakeslee: Poetry, Mysteries and Realistic Fiction', *EL* 16 (Mar.-Apr. 1989): 60–4.

Mary Blakeslee has established herself as a popular writer of crime adventures, family and school novels, and young adult problem fiction. Her output is varied, but Blakeslee tends to focus on the falsity of appearances, the foolishness or danger of judging by appearances alone, and, as a corollary, the need for young people to accept and be themselves.

Although she is known as a novelist, Blakeslee began her career as a children's poet. *It's Tough To Be a Kid* and its companion, *It's Still Tough To Be a Kid*, are collections of light humorous verse. Some poems, such as 'Telephone', in which the child narrator unwittingly runs up a large telephone bill and then orders presents using her mother's credit card, or 'The Sandwich', in which the child combines a sickening array of ingredients in a sandwich for his father but does not understand why his dog later throws up, rely on the reader's having an understanding of circumstances superior to that of the narrator. Many critics believe such ironic poems are condescending in mocking naïve youngsters, but children who have achieved some degree of domestic competence and who understand relationships enjoy the silliness they have outgrown. Other poems depend on nonsense. In 'Fade Out', for instance, a child puts on vanishing cream to get rid of freckles, but the freckles remain while the rest of his or her face disappears. Still other poems look at common problems: the title poem of the first volume amusingly catalogues difficulties in dealing with adults, who are always right, and one of the few serious poems in the collections, 'Hurting', recounts the pain of having a best friend move away. Filled with musical alliteration and euphony, Blakeslee's amusing verse is pleasing to read aloud.

Blakeslee's crime adventures, written for competent middle-school readers, focus on the exploits of two or more members of the Lemon Street Gang, a group of boys who repeatedly stumble upon serious crimes. The stories involve some detection, but they are primarily thrillers that focus on the attempts of at least one captured child to escape in order to prevent a criminal from fleeing or committing sabotage. A common motif in the books is the reluctance of adults to believe what children say, inadvertently encouraging the children to engage in perilous actions. The first of the series, *Carnival*, focuses on two gang members, Jason Ogilvie, a 'superjock' who is the group's natural leader, and Matthew

Wilson, a stereotypical 'brain'. Because he overhears some men plotting a crime at a carnival, Jason is captured and nearly killed. Eventually, Matthew deduces his whereabouts and the location of stolen loot. Chapters alternately focus on Matthew and Jason, keeping Jason, even though he is tied up for most of the novel, an active force. In *Museum Mayhem*, four gang members, Jason, Matthew, Kyle, and David, go on a class trip to a museum. When their teacher is accused of stealing a newly discovered dinosaur skull, the boys set out to prove his innocence. Trailing the thief (a research assistant hired to steal because of his history of cheating), Kyle and Matthew are captured. At this point, the action rapidly shifts between their efforts to escape from possible death and the efforts of their friends to locate and rescue them. Part wilderness survival story and part crime adventure, *Museum Mayhem* also uses the dinosaur theft to criticize the one who engineered the theft, an unscrupulous professor who placed career advancement ahead of both genuine achievement and others' welfare. *Stampede* also deals with deceptions and adult dishonesty. When Jason, Matthew, and Kyle go to Calgary for the Stampede, they become suspicious about all the bad luck besetting the chuckwagon Jason's uncle has sponsored. Poking around, the boys discover a plot to sabotage the wagon, but they have trouble convincing adults. Only after Kyle is kidnapped, escapes, and stands in the middle of the course to prevent a sabotaged wagon from racing are the gang members able to show that gamblers have been trying to prevent the top wagon from winning.

The problem of believing children, especially those who report abuse, forms a serious theme in *Death Drop*. When Jason and David visit Gerry, a gang member who has moved away, they become caught up both in issues of child abuse and in commercial sabotage. While exploring a giant mall in Gerry's new hometown, Edmonton, the boys meet Penny, who has run away to live in the mall because her mother refuses to believe that her stepfather abuses her. Penny and the boys soon discover that her stepfather is planning to sabotage the mall's giant rollercoaster so that a rival mall can gain customers. The predictable kidnapping occurs when the stepfather finds Penny spying on him and locks her into the Death Drop, a ride he has rigged to crash. Because of the ingenuity, persistence, and bravery of the gang, Penny is saved, the criminals are arrested, and the rides are repaired before anyone is hurt. *The Ghost in the Old Roxy*, one of the weakest in the series because the true criminal is obvious and the plot employs gothic clichés, has Gerry and Penny visiting Jason and David in Pinterville. When Ronnie Albright, a reformed thief, disappears on the same night a lottery prize is stolen, the four children begin an investigation that nearly costs them their lives. Having seen a ghost in the reputedly haunted Roxy Theatre, the gang discovers Ronnie hiding there. They then deduce that Colonel Bluff has stolen the money and framed Ronnie. As usual, the gang is captured and has to escape. This time, however, they are responsible for saving themselves, the falsely accused Ronnie, and the actual thief, who becomes trapped after setting fire to the theatre.

In addition to the Lemon Street Gang crime adventures, Blakeslee has produced the similar but more elaborately plotted *Rodeo Rescue*. This story also concentrates on four children out to solve a crime, the kidnapping of the Queen of the Calgary Stampede. Because the resolution depends on the actions of the four children and several adults, especially the queen's fiancé, the story lacks the tight focus that would make it a gripping adventure. Furthermore the early portion of the story contains too much awkwardly presented local colour. Nevertheless, tension develops when the queen's young rescuers are themselves captured, and when it becomes apparent that the criminal is the queen's demented mother, who is intent on killing her.

Several of Blakeslee's novels of home and school life develop comedy through the mistakes and disasters that flow from misrepresentation and the concern for appearances. When 14-year-old Edith Cowan, the narrator of *Edythe with a Y*, moves to a new school, she is so ashamed that her father is a magician that she declares on a form that he is a government agent. Furthermore, in an effort to make herself more exotic, she changes the spelling of her name. Edith does become a focus of attention, but her deceptions become increasingly more difficult to maintain. Furthermore, believing that others are snobs who judge by appearances, Edith succumbs to the same fault by assuming that her friends won't like her if they know her mother delivers milk. Eventually, Edith learns that only honest acceptance of herself and her family can ensure happiness by freeing her from the web of troubles woven by her lies.

A similar pattern appears in *Ida Mae Evans Eats Ants*, an accomplished comic novel about a girl who must learn how to fit into a new school and yet be true to her own identity. Having attended a permissive private school, Ida Mae finds difficulty in adjusting to the restrictions of a public school. Her troubles begin when a teacher refuses to allow her to go to the washroom and she wets her pants. Subsequently, her math teacher accuses her of cheating because she uses a calculator during a test and her art teacher lashes out because she draws an abstract picture. Feeling like an oddball, Ida Mae adopts a flamboyant personality, causing the snobs to reject her and the other children to imitate her. Befriended by Erika, a bright girl branded as a dummy because of her dyslexia, Ida Mae grows in confidence and shows her true character by not exacting a petty revenge on an arrogant, rich girl who has tried to cheat during an essay contest. Although the characters are eccentrics or stereotypes, the novel is fast-paced, amusing, and reassuringly insistent on honesty and integrity. The sequel, *Stop the Presses, Ida Mae!*, tends more to farce than the pointed exaggeration of the first volume. Writing a plagiarized astrology column for the school newspaper, Ida Mae becomes celebrated for the accuracy of her predictions. Soon, however, her advice leads some students into trouble, and Ida has to rely on her eccentric Great Aunt Glory Paradise for help in extricating herself. Because of the weak premise, the episodes in this predictable novel lack the humour and significance of those of its predecessor.

The theme of false appearances developed in *Ida Mae Evans Eats Ants* is central also to two earlier novels, *Outta Sight* and *Say Cheese*. These novels have similar plot patterns. In each, the narrator is a teenaged girl who likes a handsome, popular, and shallow boy. In turn, a boy of sound character likes her. When the girl changes her appearance to look more conventionally beautiful, she manages to attract the handsome boy. When this boy becomes sexually aggressive, she finally realizes that the boy who never judged her by appearances is a much better person and a more desirable boyfriend. The issue of judging by appearances is also multiplied through subplots in both novels. In *Outta Sight*, a novel set in 1944, Hope Elise Mather, a fat girl who loses weight to attract the dashing Troy Farnham, initially feels repelled by the fact that Raymond Round, a boy who liked her even when she was fat, has lost a finger. Troy's bigoted and superficial character also is apparent because he mocks Suzie Suzuki, a Japanese Canadian. For her part, Hope insults her tutor, M. Lasseur, by exclaiming that his beautiful wife, who has endured hardships in Nazi-occupied Germany, looks like an old woman. *Outta Sight* suffers from awkwardly integrated historical references, overemphatic irony in the narrator's constant lack of belief that devices such as television will be invented, and set speeches condemning the government's relocation of Japanese Canadians. Apart from unnecessary historical overlay, it is a fine novel about a girl's becoming aware that looks alone can never form the basis of a meaningful relationship. *Say Cheese*, in which Granada (Granny) Tyler begins using makeup to attract the handsome editor of the school newspaper, parallels the main plot with one in which Granny's stepmother, eager to give her twins a modelling career, plasters them with so much makeup that they no longer resemble the real children advertising agencies desire. The fact that Granny repeatedly comments on the artificiality of the twins but cannot see her own emphasizes the plot parallels at the expense of credibility. Otherwise, *Say Cheese* succeeds as an entertaining exploration of the lengths to which girls will go to make themselves conventionally attractive.

Halfbacks Don't Wear Pearls also touches on issues of appearance, but its primary focus is the complex question of female roles in a changing society. When the boys in one of her classes attack the idea of female equality, the narrator, Jane Fellows, and her friends challenge them to a touch football game, which the girls subsequently win. Later, when Jane further defeats her boyfriend in a game of pool, he storms out angrily. Their relationship becomes even more strained when she decides to take up auto mechanics and begins to practice secretively so that she can make one play in a boy's football game. When she does enter the game in disguise, she scores a touchdown, but suffers a broken leg and concussion. She is reconciled to her boyfriend, however, when he reveals that he was not angry because she beat him at pool but because she previously had deceived him by deliberately losing. Complicating the main issue of female liberation are the decisions of Jane's sisters-in-law: Marion, a nurse, decides to return to medical school, which she quit when she married, to become a doctor;

Gwen, a lawyer, decides to quit, at least temporarily, her promising political career to raise a family. Although it is dated in its strident defences of the women's liberation movement and somewhat implausible in presenting the climactic football game, *Halfbacks Don't Wear Pearls* is an intelligent problem novel in refusing to offer simplistic solutions.

Four-Eyes and French Fries also touches on stereotyping while dramatizing a boy's need to accept change. Eddie Chandler becomes worried that his close relationship with his widower father will end when Mr Chandler begins dating Pauline Fordyce, Eddie's teacher. Eddie, who has nicknamed Pauline 'Four Eyes', resents her criticism of his family's diet heavy with French fries and her participation in events he formerly shared with his dad alone. After Eddie is injured while helping a friend who has run away from his alcoholic and abusive mother, Eddie learns that Pauline is not a domineering and intolerant woman, and that she would never come between Eddie and his father. He therefore accepts her. The ending, in which Pauline shows that she would, for Eddie's sake, sacrifice her own relationship with Mr Cochrane and reveals that since childhood she has been an expert at making French fries, is sentimental and compromises some of the issues raised earlier by making Pauline a stereotypically nurturing female. The earlier parts, however, entertainingly develop a boy's need to adapt to change and to avoid pigeon-holing people.

Confined to a wheelchair since contracting polio at the age of 22, Blakeslee has employed her understanding of the psychological effects of physical disabilities in two novels. *Will to Win* and *Hal* are first-person narratives told by a boy who has become handicapped. In both, the bitter narrator fears that others will treat him as different. Self-conscious, he thinks that his handicap makes him the centre of mocking or pitying attention. Both narrators thus repeatedly misinterpret situations and nearly alienate those who care the most for them. Both books also provide the narrator with a knowledgeable, compassionate, and pushy female friend, who has a relative with a handicap like the narrator's. In both cases, the narrator benefits from his friendship with this girl, a redhead who does not have conventional good looks, but he feels attracted to the popular, relatively shallow, school beauty whom all the other boys desire. Both novels also use a contest, a debating competition in *Will to Win* and a chess tournament in *Hal*, as climactic public trials in which the narrator proves to himself and others that his physical difference is not an overridingly important one and therefore becomes more accepting of himself and others. In *Will to Win*, Phil Marsden, a 12-year-old self-professed 'superjock', eventually realizes both that he can still do many things and that people who get to know him will appreciate him for who he is. One of the novel's strengths is its presentation of the debates between his parents, who argue about whether to force him into the outside world or to let him hide himself away. The narrator is even angrier in *Hal*. Blinded by firecrackers when he was 10, 17-year-old Hal Drucker becomes a recluse who uses his exceptional intelligence as a weapon, thereby causing many people to regard him as an arrogant jerk. His success in a chess tournament, his friendship with red-headed Nancy Adams, whose grandfather is blind, the overt support of a shy and nerdish friend, and the unflagging dedication of his family finally enable him to get rid of the chip on his shoulder. Rounding out Hal's story is a subplot in which his brother, who mistakenly blames himself for the accident that blinded Hal, has allowed his parents to turn him into Hal's nursemaid. Both novels succeed in making the reader understand and care for protagonists who are unlikeable at various points. Both also fill the background with idiosyncratic or troubled characters to emphasize that the protagonists are not alone in experiencing feelings of difference. Finally, both stories end with the triumph of substance over appearance, with the protagonist coming to like the red-headed girl who has been his strongest support.

Holy Joe, a story of transformations, also focuses on a handicap, this time one brought on a boy's reputation. Joe Larriby, a minister's son known as Holy Joe because he seems devoted to church activities, tells of how he, his family, and his best friend changed attitudes during a turbulent school year. Wanting to shed the Goody Two-Shoes image that he thinks has branded him a loser at school, Joe feels himself forced into an escalating series of lies when he becomes a member of a rock group, acquires a girlfriend who seems to care about social prestige, and joins an illegal fraternity. Joe believes that his father is overly strict and is a town laughing-stock for holding decidedly old-fashioned views. Joe therefore lies about his activities and sneaks out of the house although he is 'grounded'. Only when his younger sister has been seriously injured in an automobile accident after she herself sneaks out of the house does Joe reassess his values and come to see what a positive force and likeable person his father is. At the same time, his father realizes that he, too, must adapt. In a subplot, Joe's nerdish friend, Woody, blossoms into a talented mime and loses his own social insecurities. The characterization of the adults is weak. Dr Larriby's speeches, designed to reveal his hostility to things modern, are wooden at best, and his wife's understanding tolerance of her son's deceits makes her a problematical model of motherhood. The characterization of the adolescents is better, but it contains weaknesses. First, the dramatic and life-changing success of Woody, who becomes enormously popular as a mime, stretches credibility. Second, the shifting attitudes of Amy, Joe's girlfriend, who seems to be using him but later appears as compassionate and unconcerned about social prestige, are never adequately explained. *Holy Joe* is a well-intentioned but entirely conventional problem novel.

Blakeslee's fiction may concentrate on the theme of appearances, and it may repeatedly employ such character types as the snob and the handsome but dangerous boy, but it is varied in plot and tone. Sometimes serious and sometimes comical, her fiction touches on issues of concern to children and adolescents trying to come to terms with their own identities and social relationships. Blakeslee's novels don't offer profound analysis of the issues, but they are good reads because they posit them in entertaining ways.

See also: *WSMP*.

Jo Ellen Bogart

Born: 20 October 1945, in Houston, Texas.

Principal Residences: Houston; Austin, Texas; Ruston, La; Guelph, Ont.

Education: University of Texas, Austin (BS 1967, BA 1969).

Career: supply teacher; teacher of mentally retarded teens; reporter; writer.

Major Awards: Ruth Schwartz Award (1998).

Works for Children

Dylan's Lullaby, illus. Cheryl Lowrey (Willowdale, Ont.: Annick, 1988). **Rev:** *BYP* 2 (Apr. 1988): 227; *CCL* 51 (1988): 99; *CM* 16 (Nov. 1988): 227, and 17 (Sept. 1989): 216.

Malcolm's Runaway Soap, illus. Linda Hendry (Richmond Hill, Ont.: North Winds, 1988). **Rev:** *BiC* 17 (Dec. 1988): 13; *BYP* 3 (Feb. 1989): 8; *CCL* 63 (1991): 97; *EL* 18 (Mar. 1991): 59.

10 for Dinner, illus. Carlos Freire (Richmond Hill, Ont.: North Winds, 1989). **Rev:** *BiC* 18 (Oct. 1989): 36; *BYP* 3 (Apr. 1989): 12; *CCL* 61 (1991): 96; *EL* 18 (Mar. 1991): 59.

Daniel's Dog, illus. Janet Wilson (Richmond Hill, Ont.: North Winds, 1990). **Rev:** *CCB-B* 43 (June 1990): 233; *CCL* 59 (1990): 81; *CM* 18 (May 1990): 117; *EL* 18 (Sept. 1990): 52, and 19 (Mar. 1992): 58; *QQ* 56 (Mar. 1990): 20; *SLJ* 36 (Mar. 1990): 188.

Sarah Saw a Blue Macaw, illus. Sylvie Daigneault (Richmond Hill, Ont.: North Winds, 1991). **Rev:** *CCL* 66 (1992): 82; *CM* 19 (May 1991): 170; *QQ* 57 (Mar. 1991): 20, and 58 (Dec. 1992): 28.

Mama's Bed, illus. Sylvie Daigneault (Richmond Hill, Ont.: North Winds, 1993). **Rev:** *CM* 22 (Oct. 1994): 45; *QQ* 59 (Oct. 1993): 38.

Two Too Many, illus. Yvonne Cathcart (Richmond Hill, Ont.: North Winds, 1994). **Rev:** *CCL* 78 (1995): 69; *CM* 22 (Oct. 1994): 183; *QQ* 60 (Apr. 1994): 36.

Gifts, illus. Barbara Reid (Richmond Hill, Ont.: North Winds, 1994). **Rev:** *CBRA* (1994): 443; *CCL* 78 (1995): 77; *CM* 22 (Nov. 1994): 208; *EL* 22 (Nov. 1994): 45, and 22 (Mar. 1995): 18, and 25 (Jan. 1998): 45; *QQ* 60 (Sept. 1994) 70; *SLJ* 42 (Mar. 1996), 166.

Jeremiah Learns to Read, illus. Laura Fernandez and Rick Jacobson (Richmond Hill, Ont.: North Winds, 1997). **Rev:** *CM* 4 (16 Jan. 1998): on-line; *QQ* 64 (Jan. 1998): 37.

The texts that Jo Ellen Bogart writes for picture books are notable for their repetition of words and events, their manipulation of sound, and their choice of words that are refreshingly different among books aimed at the very young. Many of her texts are also spare and suggestive, requiring of her illustrators that they play a complementary role. Her books are of various kinds and do not follow a pattern or formula, but certain thematic concerns are prominent in them, most notably the mutually fulfilling relationship between the generations.

Bogart began her career with a story exaggerating a frustration many children feel: their inability to hold on to slippery soap at bath time. *Malcolm's Runaway Soap* sends a young boy in mad pursuit of the bar of strawberry soap that, 'POP!', slips out of his hands and flies down the stairs and out the door. Various persons, including a letter carrier, policeman, and paperboy, try to grab the slippery soap, but it pops out of their hands also and shoots off towards someone else. Eventually Malcolm grabs the soap in a public fountain, where he bathes until the troublesome soap dissolves into bubbles. The story lacks the inventiveness of similar stories by Robert Munsch: each new effort to capture the soap merely repeats the last failure. Furthermore, none of the efforts has anything of the slapstick absurdity that makes Munsch's texts hilarious to youngsters. In spite of needless repetition of episodes and lack of humorous invention, *Malcolm's Runaway Soap* is a mildly amusing tale that, like Munsch's books, shows the ingenuity of a child in solving problems that frustrate even adults.

Bogart has also written three concept books that depend heavily upon illustrations to achieve their ends. Two of these are variations on the common counting book. *10 for Dinner* is about Margo's birthday party, to which she invites 10 friends. The text describing what the various children wear, what they eat, and what they do divides them into groups that require the reader to add them to arrive at the total of 10. The description of what the guests wore, for example, indicates that three wore shorts, one wore a dress, two wore jeans, three wore jogging suits, but one wore a Halloween costume. In each case, this last guest is different and stands apart from the group, a point amusingly developed in the illustrations, which keep him or her separated from the other children. At the end, the boy who is different is the only one who helps to clean the dishes, underlining the idea that people who are different can both frustrate us because of their lack of conformity and please us by demonstrating unusual consideration or kindness. *10 for Dinner* is thus successful in blending an entertaining tale, a mathematical challenge, and didacticism that works because it is not blatant. Bogart's other counting book variant, *Two Too Many*, uses rhyming couplets that often contain alliteration to make the point about another kind of difference, excess quantities. One part of a typical couplet shows the freshness and effectiveness of Bogart's lines: 'Walter's balsa biplane had two too many wings.' The accompanying illustration shows a plane with four wings. One joke depends entirely on the pictures. The line indicating that Marvin has two too many Brussels sprouts shows a plate containing only two of the vegetables, subtly telling the reader about Marvin's attitude to this vegetable. The ending, in which those with two too many of anything are invited to share their excess, may be a trifle heavy-handed and predictable, but the rhymes and pictures preceding the conclusion invite frequent rereadings. Pictures are even more important in *Sarah Saw a Blue Macaw*, a book inspired by Bogart's trips to South America with her husband, a university zoologist. The book employs an unusual device to describe a day in the jungle. Through a series of questions and answers, it focuses on the observations of Sarah, a spider monkey examining her surroundings. Sarah can be found hidden in each of the accompanying illustrations, inviting children to explore the illustrations to learn about the various animals pictured in them. The text consists of alliterative poetic quatrains, in which the first line rhymes with the fourth, and the second and third lines form a rhyming couplet based on a different rhyme. A 'Cast of Characters' at the end of the book identifies all of the animals pictured in the illustrations. *Sarah Saw a Blue Macaw* is a beautiful introduction to exotic wildlife that rewards both eyes and ears.

The majority of Bogart's books explore elements of family life. *Dylan's Lullaby* celebrates the imaginative life of a child who sings his own bedtime lullaby, thus taking himself on a journey to the sky that his mother, because she is an adult, can no longer take. The prose has a poetic quality, treating the song that Dylan sings as a ribbon that carries him into the sky. There he encounters birds, a horse, and the gigantic Face in the Sky. To share his imaginative experiences, Dylan brings back fruit from a marvellous tree, even though he knows it will be invisible to his mother. The text is too long and the various adventures are not particularly meaningful or entertaining. The theme is also hackneyed and overly sentimental, awkwardly suggesting that adults will recover something of their lost imaginative power by listening to the tales their children tell. In contrast to this lengthy, elaborate book, *Mama's Bed* is stark and simple. Nevertheless, it is one that very young readers will find emotionally reassuring. Consisting of a series of very simple statements about the various reasons that a girl likes her mother's bed, this book creates vignettes portraying the security and love of a happy family. Its conclusion, which reveals that Mama liked her own mother's bed, indicates the importance of sharing experiences by suggesting that happy, loving families develop a tradition of love and security.

A similar generational connection is in the background of *Daniel's Dog*, whose foreground issue treats a child's feelings of abandonment when a new sibling arrives. In the first part of the story, Daniel copes with the loneliness and alienation he feels because his mother pays so much attention to his new sister. Remembering his deceased grandfather's stories of a 'ghost dog' that once kept him company, Daniel imagines that the very same invisible dog is keeping him company. Daniel's observant and understanding mother then makes him feel important by including him in the care and entertaining of the baby. The second part of the story shows that experience has given Daniel the maturity and sensitivity to understand how others feel. When he realizes that his friend Norman is sad because his father is going away, he promises to send Norman an invisible dog to keep him company. The story not only shows that parents must make children feel important when a baby arrives, but that the memories passed on by grandparents can be effective years later in helping children to cope with problems and in forming their characters.

The elderly, who are only mentioned in the previous stories, are a visible presence in Bogart's two finest books. *Jeremiah Learns to Read*, winner of the Ruth Schwartz Children's Book Award, is the story of an elderly man who decides that he wants to learn to read. The story begins with meaningful repetition, recitations of elderly Jeremiah's many skills and accomplishments. Each expression of accomplishments concludes with the statement that, in spite of these skills, Jeremiah could not read. This repetitive structure emphasizes both that illiteracy does not signal worthlessness and that reading is a valuable, desirable skill. The story then recounts how Jeremiah goes to school, where he not only learns to read but also teaches the children some entertaining skills. At the end, when he finally reads to his wife, an act that brings them lovingly closer to each other, Jeremiah inspires her to learn to read also. Without preaching, Bogart shows children two things that can enhance life: reading and a respectful relationship with someone of another generation.

Partly because of Barbara Reid's award-winning illustrations, *Gifts* is Bogart's most satisfying book. Told in lively rhymes that avoid the pitfalls of sing-song rhythm and mechanical rhyme, this book tells of the lengthy and rich relationship between a girl and her globe-trotting grandmother. The tale depends on a repetitive structure of various journeys and repetitive wording introducing them. Thus, before each trip, the grandmother asks the girl, 'What would you have me bring?' The girl's responses reveal that she doesn't want material things, only the joy of shared experiences, of hearing her grandmother's stories. For example, when the grandmother leaves for Hawaii, the girl requests 'Just the secret wish / of a flying fish, / and a rainbow to wear as a ring.' The progress of time is recorded by Reid's plasticine illustrations, which show the grandmother gaining more travel patches on her backpack and becoming so old that she eventually requires a wheelchair. An illustration is also central to the conclusion because it clarifies that the narrator is actually a grown woman who has been telling her own daughter about the travelling grandmother. Aided by the pictures, Bogart movingly, yet without sentimentality, shows that the love between generations carries on, affecting the lives of even those who never met a loving elderly person.

Vocabulary choices, assonance, rhythms, rhyme, and alliteration make Bogart's books a pleasure to read aloud. Nevertheless, these are picture books, and Bogart has shown herself adept at writing texts that invite artists to expand them meaningfully. Especially in *Jeremiah Learns to Read* and *Gifts*, she has shown restraint in developing her themes, writing about relationships between the young and the elderly without succumbing to sentimentality.

See also: *MCAI*; *SATA* 92; *WSMP*.

Paulette Bourgeois

Born: 20 July 1951, in Winnipeg.

Education: University of Western Ontario (Honours B.Sc. in Occupational Therapy 1974); studied journalism at Carleton University, but did not complete degree.

Principal Residences: Winnipeg; Calgary; Ottawa; Beaconsfield, Que.; London, Ont.; Washington; Toronto.

Career: psychiatric occupational therapist; radio reporter; freelance magazine writer; writer.

Works for Children

Franklin in the Dark, illus. Brenda Clark (Toronto: Kids Can Press, 1986). **Rev:** *BiC* 15 (Dec. 1986): 15; *CCL* 50 (1988): 94; *Maclean's* 99 (15 Dec. 1986): 44; *QQ* 52 (Aug. 1986): 38.

The Amazing Apple Book, illus. Linda Hendry (Toronto: Kids Can Press, 1987). **Rev:** *CM* 16 (Jan. 1988): 22, and 16 (May 1988): 76, and 16 (Nov. 1988): 203; *EL* 15 (Mar. 1988): 24.

Big Sarah's Little Boots, illus. Brenda Clark (Toronto: Kids Can Press, 1987). **Rev:** *BiC* 16 (Dec. 1987): 13; *CCL* 52 (1988): 28; *CM* 16 (Mar. 1988): 56; *EL* 15 (Mar. 1988): 23; *SLJ* 35 (Nov. 1989): 74.

On Your Mark, Get Set . . . All About the Olympics, Then and Now, illus. Pat Cupples (Toronto: Kids Can Press, 1987). **Rev:** *CM* 16 (May 1988): 107; *EL* 15 (Mar. 1988): 26; *Maclean's* 100 (7 Dec. 1987): 56.

The Amazing Paper Book, illus. Linda Hendry (Toronto: Kids Can Press, 1989). **Rev:** *CM* 18 (Jan. 1990): 10; *EL* 17 (Nov. 1989): 61, and 17 (Mar. 90): 24; *SLJ* 37 (Mar. 1991): 198.

Grandma's Secret, illus. Maryann Kovalski (Toronto: Kids Can Press, 1989). **Rev:** *CM* 18 (Mar. 1990): 62; *HB* 66 (May 1990): 318; *QQ* 55 (Dec. 1989): 22; *SLJ* 36 (July 1990): 56.

Hurry Up, Franklin, illus. Brenda Clark (Toronto: Kids Can Press, 1989). **Rev:** *BYP* 3 (Apr. 1989): 12; *CM* 17 (Sept. 1989): 216; *EL* 17 (Mar. 1990): 23; *SLJ* 36 (Dec. 1990): 70; *TES* (29 Mar. 1991): 23.

The Amazing Dirt Book, illus. Craig Terlson (Toronto: Kids Can Press, 1990). **Rev:** *CM* 18 (Nov. 1990): 273; *EL* 18 (Jan. 1991): 62; *QQ* 56 (Oct. 1990): 16; *SLJ* 37 (Mar. 1991): 198.

Too Many Chickens, illus. Bill Slavin (Toronto: Kids Can Press, 1990). **Rev:** *CCL* 70 (1993): 84; *CM* 18 (Nov. 1990): 264; *QQ* 56 (Oct. 1990): 15; *Language Arts* 69 (Sept. 1992): 372; *SLJ* 37 (June 1991): 72; *RT* 45 (Apr. 1992): 635.

The Amazing Milk Book, illus. Linda Hendry (Toronto: Kids Can Press, 1991).

The Amazing Potato Book, illus. Linda Hendry (Toronto: Kids Can Press, 1991). **Rev:** *BiC* 20 (Nov. 1991): 36; *CM* 19 (Oct. 1991): 307; *EL* 19 (Mar. 1992): 16; *QQ* 57 (May 1991): 21, and 57 (July 1991): 52; *SLJ* 38 (Feb. 1992): 92.

Franklin Fibs, illus. Brenda Clark (Toronto: Kids Can Press, 1991). **Rev:** *BiC* 20 (June 1991): 58; *CCL* 67 (1992): 81; *CM* 19 (May 1991): 170; *EL* 19 (Mar. 1992): 17; *QQ* 57 (Feb. 1991): 22, and 57 (May 1991): 21; *RT* 45 (Apr. 1992): 635.

Canadian Fire Fighters, illus. Kim LaFave (Toronto: Kids Can Press, 1991). **Rev:** *BiC* 20 (Nov. 1991): 36; *CM* 19 (Sept. 1991): 226; *EL* 19 (Mar. 1992): 16; *QQ* 57 (May 1991): 21, and 57 (June 1991): 24.

Canadian Garbage Collectors, illus. Kim LaFave (Toronto: Kids Can Press, 1991). **Rev:** *BiC* 20 (Nov. 1991): 36; *CM* 19 (Sept. 1991): 227; *EL* 19 (Mar. 1992): 16; *QQ* 57 (May 1991): 21, and 57 (June 1991): 24.

Canadian Police Officers, illus. Kim LaFave (Toronto: Kids Can Press, 1991). **Rev:** *BiC* 21 (Oct. 1992): 50; *CM* 20 (Nov. 1992): 308.

Canadian Postal Workers, illus. Kim LaFave (Toronto: Kids Can Press, 1991). **Rev:** *BiC* 21 (Oct. 1992): 50; *CM* 21 (Jan. 1993): 20; *EL* 20 (Mar. 1993): 12; *QQ* 58 (Aug. 1992): 28.

Franklin Is Lost, illus. Brenda Clark (Toronto: Kids Can Press, 1992). **Rev:** *CM* 20 (Sept. 1992): 207; *QQ* 58 (Feb. 1992): 32.

Franklin Is Bossy, illus. Brenda Clark (Toronto: Kids Can Press, 1993). **Rev:** *CM* 22 (Mar. 1994): 46; *EL* 21 (Mar. 1994): 16; *QQ* 59 (July 1993): 56.

Changes in You and Me: A Book About Puberty, Mostly for Boys, with Martin Wolfish, illus. Louise Phillips and Kam Yu (Toronto: Somerville House. 1994). **Rev:** *CBRA* (1994): 543; *CCL* 21 (1995): 74; *EL* 23 (Sept. 1995): 46; *QQ* 60 (Dec. 1994): 34; *SLJ* 41 (Mar. 1995): 141, 208.

Changes in You and Me: A Book About Puberty, Mostly for Girls, with Martin Wolfish, illus. Louise Phillips and Kam Yu (Toronto: Somerville House. 1994). **Rev:** *CBRA* (1994): 543; *CCL* 21 (1995): 74; *EL* 23 (Sept. 1995): 46; *NYTBR* 100 (12 Mar. 1995): 20; *QQ* 60 (Dec. 1994): 34; *SLJ* 41 (Mar. 1995): 141, 208.

Franklin Is Messy, illus. Brenda Clark (Toronto: Kids Can Press, 1994). **Rev:** *QQ* 60 (Nov. 1994): 34.

Franklin Wants a Pet, illus. Brenda Clark (Toronto: Kids Can Press, 1994). **Rev:** *QQ* 60 (Nov. 1994): 34; *RT* 49 (Feb. 1996): 397.

The Many Hats of Mr. Minches, illus. Kathryn Naylor (Toronto: Stoddart Kids, 1994). **Rev:** *CBRA* (1995): 444; *QQ* 60 (Nov. 1994): 34.

Franklin's Blanket, illus. Brenda Clark (Toronto: Kids Can Press. 1995). **Rev:** *CBRA* (1995): 463.

Franklin Goes to School, illus. Brenda Clark (Toronto: Kids Can Press, 1995). **Rev:** *CBRA* (1995): 462; *EL* 23 (Mar. 1996): 24.

Franklin and Me: A Book about Me, Written and Drawn by Me (with a Little Help from Franklin), illus. Brenda Clark (Toronto: Scholastic, 1995). **Rev:** *CBRA* (1995): 462.

Franklin Plays the Game, illus. Brenda Clark (Toronto: Kids Can Press, 1995). **Rev:** *CBRA* (1995): 463.

Franklin and the Tooth Fairy, illus. Brenda Clark (Toronto: Kids Can Press, 1995). **Rev:** *CBRA* (1995): 462.

The Moon, illus. Bill Slavin (Toronto: Kids Can Press, 1995). **Rev:** *CBRA* (1995): 565; *QQ* 61 (Sept. 1995): 74.

The Sun, illus. Bill Slavin (Toronto: Kids Can Press, 1995). **Rev:** *CBRA* (1995): 565; *QQ* 61 (Sept. 1995): 74.

Franklin Has a Sleep-Over, illus. Brenda Clark (Toronto: Kids Can Press, 1996). **Rev:** *CBRA* (1996): 434.

Franklin's Bad Day, illus. Brenda Clark (Toronto: Kids Can Press, 1996). **Rev:** *CBRA* (1996): 435; *QQ* 62 (Dec. 1996): 38; *SLJ* 43 (May 1997): 93.

Franklin's Halloween, illus. Brenda Clark (Toronto: Kids Can Press, 1996). **Rev:** *CBRA* (1996): 435; *QQ* 62 (Sept. 1996): 32.

Franklin's School Play, illus. Brenda Clark (Toronto: Kids Can Press, 1996). **Rev:** *CBRA* (1996): 435; *EL* 24 (Mar. 1997): 26.

Finders Keepers for Franklin, illus. Brenda Clark (Toronto: Kids Can Press, 1997).

Franklin Rides a Bike, illus. Brenda Clark (Toronto: Kids Can Press, 1997). **Rev:** *SLJ* 43 (Dec. 1997): 87.

Franklin's New Friend, illus. Brenda Clark (Toronto: Kids Can Press, 1997). **Rev:** *SLJ* 43 (Dec. 1997): 87.

Franklin's Secret Club, illus. Brenda Clark (Toronto: Kids Can Press, 1998).

Franklin's Christmas Gift, illus. Brenda Clark (Toronto: Kids Can Press, 1998).

Franklin's Valentine, illus. Brenda Clark (Toronto: Kids Can Press, 1998).

Franklin and the Thunderstorm, illus. Brenda Clark (Toronto: Kids Can Press, 1998).

Franklin's Class Trip, illus. Brenda Clark (Toronto: Kids Can Press, 1999).

Selected Discussions

Jenkinson, Dave. 'Paulette Bourgeois: The "Amazing" Creator of Franklin', *EL* 18 (Mar.-Apr. 1991): 66–71.

Wilde, Leanne. 'Franklin: Ideal Children's Literary Idol or Flavourless Turtle of Privilege?', *CCL* 90 (1998): 38–44.

Paulette Bourgeois is most notable as the author of the *Franklin* books, which are as ubiquitous in both Canada and the United States as those about the Berenstain Bears or Arnold the Aardvark. In fact, the *Franklin* books are now the centre of a lucrative commercial enterprise, having spawned educational activity books, computer programs, an animated television show, and toys. Some critics deplore the bland plotting of the series, but parents and children alike find appealing the way in which a shy turtle illustrates and finds solutions for common problems of childhood.

Franklin was inspired by an episode of the television show *M*A*S*H** in which Benjamin Franklin Pierce exclaimed that he was so claustrophobic he would be afraid of his shell if he were a turtle. The result was *Franklin in the Dark* (French versions name the character Benjamin), the story of a turtle who is so afraid of the dark that he drags his shell behind him. The slim plot depends on the archetypal pattern of the quest journey, and as in folktales, each of its episodes basically repeats the previous one. Thus Franklin asks a series of characters for help, but instead of offering a solution to his dilemma, each reveals his own fears: Duck is afraid of deep water; Lion fears loud noises; Bird is scared of flying too high, and Polar Bear worries about icy, cold nights. Franklin is, of course, afraid of none of these. When he returns and his own mother says that she was afraid he was lost, Franklin finally realizes that everyone has fears. As a result, he decides to overcome his fear of the dark by sleeping in his shell. In a gently humorous conclusion, however, Franklin turns on his night light.

As it does in the first story, fear plays a major role in the subsequent instalments of the series. Many of the fears originate in Franklin's innocence, his status as a child experiencing things for the first time and thus being unaware of how to handle them. In *Franklin Goes to School*, for example, he worries so much about his first day at school that he upsets his stomach. One source of Franklin's worry is his sense of inferiority, his belief that other students already know much more than he does. Once the teacher, Mr Owl, reassures him that he has his own accomplishments and that both he and the other students will learn many other things, Franklin becomes so busy and happy that he forgets all about his stomach. School life nevertheless continues to be a source of fears. During *Franklin's Class Trip*, he worries about seeing dinosaurs at the museum, until he discovers that the dinosaurs are not alive. In *Franklin's School Play*, Franklin must overcome both his doubt that he can memorize his lines and his stage fright. By overcoming both fears on the night of the play, Franklin learns that mastery of his emotions brings rewards because his success in the play, a very public accomplishment, makes him happy. Franklin overcomes another common school fear, that of meeting new people, in *Franklin's New Friend.* When Moose moves into the neighbourhood, Franklin is initially frightened because Moose is so big. Once Mr Owl points out that big persons also have fears, however, Franklin plays with the lonely Moose and discovers that they have much in common.

As this last story suggests, Franklin is not the only character in the series touched by fears. *Franklin Is Lost* focuses on an event that frightens many parents: the search for a lost child. Absorbed in a game of hide-and-seek, Franklin forgets that he is not supposed to go into the woods alone and becomes lost. As night descends, Franklin is frightened, but so are his parents, who conduct a frantic search for him. All ends happily, of course, and Franklin promises never again to forget the warning about going into the woods. Although adult figures normally provide the assurance that helps Franklin to handle his fears, peer support is of central importance in *Franklin and the Thunderstorm.* Franklin is so terrified of storms that he hides in his shell when thunder cracks. When his sympathetic friends begin telling him amusing stories about giants causing thunder, however, Franklin becomes so interested that he accepts without fear an explanation of the real nature of lightning. Thus, Franklin not only gets an object lesson in friendship, but he learns that imagination, which often causes fears, can also dispel them.

Fears and worries are the dominant topics in the series, but problems associated with the socialization of children also appear. *Franklin Fibs* treats the issue of childhood lying. When Franklin responds to the boasting of several characters by claiming that he can eat 76 flies in the blink of an eye, his friends challenge him to prove his assertion. Fortunately, his father finds a solution by telling him to admit his fib and then to show what he *can* do. Franklin therefore not only restores his friends' respect for him by eating a pie containing 76 flies, but he also displays a degree of maturity by resisting the urge to fib when it next arises. *Franklin Is Bossy* focuses on another social skill, the need to respect and co-operate with others. After his friends refuse to play with him because he insists on telling everyone what to do, Franklin accepts that he must give others a chance to be the pitcher in their ball games. He learns another form of co-operation in *Franklin Plays the Game*, in which his soccer team practises teamwork, playing better and having fun as a result, even when they don't win.

Another facet of socialization, coping with the natural desire to be like others, is central to two stories. In *Franklin and the Tooth Fairy*, the toothless turtle wants teeth, like those of his friends, so that he can receive a gift from the tooth fairy. After Franklin puts a stone out to fool the tooth fairy, his parents give him a present to show that, even if he is not like his friends in some ways, he is just like them in growing up. The desire to be as accomplished as others appears in *Franklin Rides a Bike*, in which Franklin, worried that he is the only one riding a bike with training wheels, eventually learns that people have difficulties with different things. The issues are a bit confused in *Hurry Up, Franklin*. Franklin is slow because he becomes easily distracted. When he pauses to play with various friends while on his way to Bear's birthday party, he encounters Snail, whose small size makes him even slower. He carries Snail to the party so that both arrive just in time to give Bear a gift of berries. Because the plot resolves itself with a sentimental scene of sharing, it does not satisfactorily treat the issue of concentration on goals that it first promises.

The series also explores the emotional dimensions of socialization, showing how Franklin learns to be sensitive to the feelings of others and to act as a true friend. *Franklin's Bad Day* has him being ill-tempered with everyone because Otter has moved away. Once his father informs him that he can still be friends and can share thoughts by calling or writing Otter, however, Franklin regains control of his emotions. In *Franklin's Secret Club*, he first excludes Beaver from a club that he starts but then realizes, after she forms her own club, that they can have more fun by joining forces and by making sure than no one feels excluded. Franklin also shows awareness of how others feel in *Franklin Has a Sleep-Over*, in which he helps the visiting Bear to overcome a bout of homesickness. Franklin gains new insight into friendship in *Franklin's Valentine*. After he runs away from a party in tears because he has lost the valentines he made for his friends, Franklin learns that his friends still want him at the party and still want to give cards to him. The following day, he gives his classmates cards celebrating Friendship Day, which he assures them can be any day at all. Franklin shows similar mature consideration in *Franklin's Halloween*, getting his friends to share their treats with Bear, who was sick and could not attend a Halloween party. In *Franklin's Christmas Gift*, a sentimental holiday tale about true giving, Franklin learns that consideration for both the less fortunate and for his relatives gives him a warm feeling inside.

Other Franklin stories treat familiar elements of home life. *Franklin's Blanket*, for instance, has Franklin losing the blue blanket that comforts him each night. Although he receives other things to take to bed, Franklin isn't truly comfortable until he finds his own blanket, which he had hidden with some Brussels sprouts he didn't want to eat. Another search for a missing object is the basis for *Franklin Is Messy*. Because he never cleans his room, Franklin steps on and breaks his toy sword. His parents find a solution to Franklin's messiness when they decide to make him special boxes that can hold all of his possessions. *Franklin Wants a Pet* offers a minor twist on one of the most common situations in childhood. When Franklin finally proves to his parents that he is mature enough to own a pet, he surprises them by insisting that he doesn't want a puppy, or any of the pets his friends have suggested. Instead, he asks for a goldfish, which he says will make him feel calm and quiet. As he promised he would, Franklin shows his love for the fish by taking care of it.

Although they cover many problems of childhood, from fear, through bullying, to selfishness, the Franklin stories follow a pattern. Each begins positively, reassuring the reader of Franklin's accomplishments by listing some of his skills, such as his ability to tie his shoes and to count by twos. Each story then introduces Franklin's current worry or problem. In every case, the story ends positively with Franklin acquiring a new skill or coming to a new understanding of some facet of life. In most cases, Franklin achieves his understanding through the aid of a wise and understanding adult, most often his father or his teacher, Mr Owl. The stories thus gently insist that understanding is the key to solving difficulties and that adults will always help children. For the most part, the narration is direct and unchallenging. Few of the stories contain any wit or overt humour, but both *Franklin Is Bossy* and *Franklin's Class Trip* conclude with puns. In the former, although Franklin does not catch any balls during a ball game, he contents himself by catching many flies, and in the latter, he decides that a museum mummy isn't frightening because he has one at home. Because such wit is so infrequent in the series, many critics dismiss the Franklin books as bland celebrations of a comfortable middle-class life that few children ever experience. Such critics may be correct, but many parents find these books reassuring because they exclude the threats of violence and poverty while quietly reinforcing traditional ideals within the context of middle-class life.

In addition to the Franklin books, Bourgeois has written four picture books and numerous non-fiction titles. Two of her picture books focus on issues of growth and the relationship between people of different ages. In *Big Sarah's Little Boots*, a girl comes to accept that inevitable change brings its own rewards. Sarah refuses to admit that she has outgrown her favourite yellow boots and is unhappy that she has to give them to her brother. However, once she discovers that her new boots make a big-girl sound when she jumps in them, she is happy. *Grandma's Secret* presents a boy's discovery that his eccentric grandmother's scary stories about a bear in the basement have been designed to protect him from falling down the rotting, dangerous stairs. Like the Franklin stories, these are gently didactic tales that urge understanding as the key to happy relationships. In her other picture books, Bourgeois clearly demonstrates that she has little ability to create madcap humour. The better of the two, *Two Many Chickens*, tells of a class project that gets out of hand. Given, in turn, chicken eggs, bunnies, and a goat, Mrs Kerr's class soon finds itself engaged in selling eggs, Angora sweaters, and goat's milk. The events aren't truly comical, and the resolution is a disappointing contrivance. In *The Many Hats of Mr. Minches*, serious Dotty Rupert realizes her wish to become brave and wild when the eccentric Mr Minches arrives in her conservative seaside village, shocking the staid citizens with his behaviour. Dotty finally gets a chance to be brave when she rescues Mr Minches and his wife during a storm. Unfortunately, Mr Minches is eccentric without being funny, and the plot never successfully blends the themes of individualism and bravery.

Bourgeois occasionally injects narrative elements into her non-fiction. Her 'In My Neighbourhood' books about community workers, for instance, provide slight plots to underscore how postal workers, police officers, and garbage collectors perform their tasks. These plots may be mechanical and may remind adults of the documentaries once common in movie theatres, but they do adequately and clearly illustrate their topics.

Bourgeois is primarily a didactic writer. Critics who look for children's books that enlarge children's imaginations, challenge their complacency, and enrich their vocabularies may deplore the commercial success of the Franklin books. Those looking for books that reassure children that their problems are common and that they can cope with them will continue nevertheless to support a series that has become one of the most important commercial, if not literary, publishing enterprises in Canada.

See also: *CA* 137; *MCAI*; *WSMP*.

Karleen Bradford

Born: 16 December 1936, in Toronto.

Principal Residences: Toronto; Buenos Aires, Argentina; Colombia; Philippines; United States; London, England; Bonn, Germany; Ottawa.

Education: University of Toronto (BA 1959).

Major Awards: Canadian Library Association Young Adult Book Award (1993).

Works for Children

A Year for Growing (Richmond Hill, Ont.: Scholastic-TAB, 1977); republished as *Wrong Again, Robbie* (Richmond Hill, Ont.: Scholastic, 1983). **Rev:** *CCL* 14 (1979): 55.

The Other Elizabeth (Agincourt, Ont.: Gage, 1982). **Rev:** *BiC* 12 (Feb. 1983): 33; *CBRA* (1982): 243; *CCL* 34 (1984): 91.

I Wish There Were Unicorns (Agincourt, Ont.: Gage, 1983). **Rev:** *CBRA* (1983): 283; *CCL* 34 (1984): 91; *EL* 11 (Nov. 1983): 37; *QQ* 49 (July 1983): 60.

The Stone in the Meadow (Agincourt, Ont.: Gage, 1984). **Rev:** *CBRA* (1984): 325; *QQ* 50 (Aug. 1984): 35.

The Haunting at Cliff House (Richmond Hill, Ont.: Scholastic-TAB, 1985). **Rev:** *BiC* 14 (Dec. 1985): 14; *CBRA* (1985): 259; *QQ* 52 (Feb. 1986): 14.

The Nine Days Queen (Richmond Hill, Ont.: Scholastic-TAB, 1986). **Rev:** *CCL* 48 (1987): 85; *CM* 16 (Jan. 1988): 5; *QQ* 52 (Dec. 1986): 14.

Write Now!: The Right Way to Write a Story (Richmond Hill, Ont.: Scholastic-TAB, 1988); revised as *Write Now!: How to Turn Your Ideas into Great Stories* (Richmond Hill, Ont.: Scholastic, 1996). **Rev:** *BYP* 3 (June 1989): 11; *CBRA* (1989): 10, and (1996): 514; *CCL* 57/58 (1990): 122; *CM* 17 (July 1989): 170; *EL* 18 (Nov. 1990): 61.

Windward Island (Toronto: Kids Can Press, 1989). **Rev:** *CCL* 62 (1991): 110; *CBRA* (1989): 315; *CM* 18 (Mar. 1990): 70; *QQ* 55 (Oct. 1989): 14.

There Will Be Wolves (Toronto: HarperCollins, 1992). **Rev:** *BiC* 21 (Nov. 1992): 38; *CBRA* (1992): 314; *CCL* 73 (1994): 71; *CM* 20 (Nov. 1992): 304; *QQ* 58 (Dec. 1992): 27.

Thirteenth Child (Toronto: HarperCollins, 1994). **Rev:** *CBRA* (1994): 476; *CCL* 77 (1995): 88; *QQ* 60 (Sept. 1994): 73.

Animal Heroes (Richmond Hill, Ont.: Scholastic, 1995): **Rev:** *BiC* 24 (Summer 1995): 47; *CBRA* (1995): 554; *QQ* 61 (Apr. 1995): 42.

More Animal Heroes (Richmond Hill, Ont.: Scholastic, 1996). **Rev:** *CBRA* (1996): 528; *QQ* 62 (Nov. 1996): 44.

Shadows on a Sword: The Second Book of the Crusades (Toronto: HarperCollins, 1996). **Rev:** *CBRA* (1996): 466; *CCL* 89 (1998): 49.

Dragonfire (Toronto: HarperCollins, 1997). **Rev:** *CBRA* (1997): 504 ; *QQ* 63 (Dec. 1997): 37.

A Different Kind of Champion (Richmond Hill, Ont.: Scholastic, 1998).

Other

'Karleen Bradford, Winner of the 1992 Canadian Library Association Young Adult Book Award for *There Will Be Wolves*, Published by HarperCollins' [acceptance speech], *CM* 21 (Sept. 1993): 141–2.

'The Roads of Research', *CCL* 83 (1996): 75–7.

Karleen Bradford is a writer difficult to fix precisely because her publications for young people include fantasies, contemporary problem novels, historical fictions, an animal novel, and non-fiction. Furthermore, Bradford has developed her craft gradually. Whereas her earlier fiction suffered from obvious limitations in plotting and characterization, her later books are far more accomplished, telling interesting stories, presenting characters with psychological depth, and developing significant themes.

Bradford's fantasies explore issues of identity. Three of these fantasies are time-shift novels in which a modern child who resembles someone in a former time goes back to that time and affects the course of history. In *The Other Elizabeth*, Elizabeth goes back to 1813, during the war with the United States, and saves the life of one of her ancestors, thus ensuring her own existence in the future. In the more complicated *The Stone in the Meadow*, Jenifer goes back to

Druid England, where her experiences cause the Victorian relative who accompanies her to become a historian. In *The Haunting at Cliff House*, events recorded in a diary by Bronwen, a nineteenth-century Welsh girl, parallel those experienced by Alison, who opposes her widower father's relationship with an attractive woman. By becoming sensitive to the pain of others, she undoes the tragedy of the past and willingly mends her strained relationships in the present. Although each of these novels contains interesting historical scenes, the predictable plots and the shallow optimism they support mark them as apprentice works.

Dragonfire, a sword-and-sorcery adventure, makes a significant advance from these early works. It contains a suspenseful plot, complex characters, and moral depth. The elaborate plot involves the quest of young Dahl, rightful heir to the throne of Taun, to wrest control of his kingdom from the evil Usurper. Hidden in another world since infancy, Dahl suffers doubts about his own ability to succeed. Complicating matters for him is Catryn, a girl with whom he was raised. She follows him when the Protector, a mentor with the ability to change shapes, brings Dahl through a portal into Taun. A feisty and stubborn girl plagued by guilt about her ancestry (her mother was burned at the stake as an evil witch), Catryn is clever and brave. In fact, although the others first view her as an unwelcome encumbrance, she eventually plays a crucial role in the success of the quest. The twist in the plot that adds thematic depth is Dahl's realization that the Usurper is not a separate individual but his own evil side. To be whole and confident, therefore, Dahl must not destroy his other self but embrace it as part of his own identity. This theme and its dramatic resolution obviously owe much to Ursula K. LeGuin's *A Wizard of Earthsea*, which also dramatizes a Jungian quest in which the hero becomes whole by embracing his shadow. Nevertheless, *Dragonfire* is not crassly derivative. The world it portrays is original, and its characters are novel and interesting. The ending suggests that a sequel focusing on Catryn is in the offing. If so, it will be interesting to see if its analysis of female psychology echoes those symbolized in the second volume of LeGuin's 'Earthsea' series.

Bradford has more directly approached issues of adolescent identity and relationships in her contemporary problem novels. In *Wrong Again, Robbie* (originally published as *A Year for Growing*) the title character, a conservationist, and his grandfather, an avid hunter and fisher, gradually come to understand each other's views and, thus, to accept each other. In *I Wish There Were Unicorns*, Rachel Larrimer, wounded by her parents' recent divorce, gradually develops sympathy for her mother and an acceptance of the new life the family must lead. Both novels resort to dramatic contrivances to resolve problems, but in their earlier sections, both successfully portray children at odds with their families and the world.

Although they also depend on contrived conclusions, two other problem novels benefit from more complex characterizations. *Windward Island*, winner of the 1990 Max and Greta Ebel Memorial Award for Children's Writing, explores the adolescent anxieties about relationships and change. Best friends Loren and Caleb are the last children on Windward Island, off the Nova Scotia coast. Consequently, their school is closing, and they will have to attend a school on the mainland next year. Loren, however, loves his island home so much that he wants to remain and take correspondence courses instead. Hoping to have the best summer of his life before telling his father, Loren soon finds all his plans being spoiled. For one thing, the arrival of April Lohnes and her widower father sets Loren and Caleb against each other. The novel contains exciting episodes, such as Loren's rescue of April when she becomes lost in a fog, and Loren's rescue of Caleb and April after their fishing boat catches fire and fog then engulfs it. The real interest in the novel, however, resides in its depiction of Loren's mood shifts as he tries to maintain his life-long companionship with Caleb but repeatedly falls into sullen resentment at each of Caleb's overtures to April. Although the conclusion depends on the cliché of a dramatic rescue, Loren's reconciliation with Caleb, his appreciation of April, and his acceptance of the fact that he must move from the island are together elements that form a satisfying resolution. Only the leaden presentation of April, who believes that her father is so grief-stricken by the death of his wife that he no longer cares for his daughter, rings hollow in this otherwise gripping presentation of a way of life seldom portrayed in children's literature.

Thirteenth Child mixes vignettes of three young people from dysfunctional families with a mystery story. The central character is Kate Halston, who writes stories to escape from her tawdry life: her father is a violent alcoholic, her abused mother spends all her time in front of a blaring television set, and she works long hours in the family diner and at the adjacent gas pumps. The second major character is Mike Bridges, whose home life was so bad that he ran away. Starving, he tries to rob Kate, but sensing that he is not a criminal, she feeds him and tells him where to get a job. Shortly thereafter reports of stores being robbed make Kate suspect Mike, who is reluctant to talk about his past, but his friendliness and his helpfulness around the diner belie her suspicions. When Melanie Davis, the school's most popular girl, is murdered and Mike disappears that same night, however, the entire community suspects him. The third child from a troubled home is the school 'nerd', Barney, whose demanding father forces him to study all the time. Barney dreams of owning a motorcycle and of dating Melanie. When Mike is taken into police custody, Barney finally confesses that he committed the robberies to buy a motorcycle and became so enraged when Melanie still rejected him that he killed her; Barney then commits suicide. This mystery story may have a rather pat ending, but it maintains suspense until the conclusion through effective red herrings, and it succeeds in developing Kate's character as she alternates between surly suspicion of and friendship with Mike. Because Barney is a victim of psychological abuse, his story supplements the focus on Kate's dysfunctional family. Kate's story, however, offers the hope missing in Barney's. When Kate's mother discovers that her husband has hit Kate, she comes out of the stupor that has allowed her to excuse him, presses charges, and testifies against him so that he can be forced to receive the treatment he needs to control his alcoholism and rage. *Thirteenth Child* falls short because it attempts too much, but the portraits of Kate, her mother, and Mike make it an intriguing portrayal of reactions to abuse.

In 'The Roads of Research', Bradford has indicated that when she first got the idea for *The Other Elizabeth*, she discovered that it could not become good fiction unless she understood the past. Consequently, she began researching the stories' backgrounds and discovered that historical research fascinated her. Her intensive research not only enables her to bring history alive, but her commitment to truth compels her to offer a far less sanitized portrait of the past than is usual in romances for the young. Bradford thus refuses to ignore the dubious morality of many historical actions, and she makes her characters fallible humans, not conventional larger-than-life heroes. In *The Nine Days Queen*, for example, she focuses on the way Lady Jane Grey becomes victim of her own family's thirst for power. Filled with accounts of intrigue and manipulation, *The Nine Days Queen* is a tense portrayal of a girl whose age, gender, and social station prevent her from having an effective voice in her own tragic destiny.

A similar examination of power and manipulation underlies *There Will Be Wolves*, which traces the organization and progress of the ill-fated People's Crusade, an eleventh-century pilgrimage that was supposed to free Jerusalem from Turkish rule. As Bradford makes clear, religious fervour competed with and often was obscured by bloodlust, greed, and blind ambition. Through a series of dramatic episodes—Christian Crusaders kill most of the Jews before departing; during their trek Crusaders kill Christians and Muslims alike; and vengeful Turks exact appalling retribution by slaughtering nearly everyone—Bradford undermines all traces of the romance and heroism conventionally associated with the Crusades. To give this mass movement a human dimension, she focuses on the moral development of a young couple caught up in events. The central female is Ursula, daughter of an ailing apothecary who demonstrates his morality by hiding a Jew when the Crusaders riot. Sharp-tongued and proud of her skill as a healer, Ursula angers her ignorant neighbours, who conspire to have her condemned to be burned as a witch. After Ursula is allowed to redeem herself by embarking on the Crusade with her father, Bruno, a young stonecutter, joins them. During the journey, Ursula's father dies, Ursula and Bruno suffer immensely, and both change dramatically. Bruno, who opposes the idea of a holy war because he does not believe in killing, is forced to fight and kill; Ursula, who previously lacked sympathy for a thief who was punished by amputation of his hand, must steal food to survive. Eventually, Ursula, Bruno, and a girl they have saved give up the quest and return to Germany. In another of the novel's many pointed ironies, Ursula, who repeatedly demanded money from the cruel, miserly, drug-addicted count her father served, discovers that the count had not lied when he insisted that he owed her nothing: in a secret cellar of her home, Ursula discovers a bag of coins. Although she had long sought the money, Ursula gives it to the Church, believing that life with Bruno, now her husband, is all that she really needs. Her decision to donate money to the very institution that falsely condemned her defies credibility, but the falsity of the conclusion does not seriously weaken a novel that dramatically and intelligently explores the behaviour of people during character-testing crises.

Shadows on a Sword, Bradford's second novel about the Crusades, also involves a love that develops between a couple during the course of an arduous journey to Jerusalem. Theo, made a knight just before setting out on the First Crusade, is a brave but sensitive young man who cannot celebrate bloodshed the way his carefree friend Amalric does. Theo meets Emma, a girl whose noble family has fallen on such hard times that she is employed as a nursemaid to the children of a lascivious relative making the journey to Jerusalem. When her relative's wife and children die, Emma, knowing that she is not safe with him, seeks protection by disguising herself as Theo's groom. Having thus adopted a male's identity, she goes one step further by participating in a battle, during which she is wounded. Like Theo, she thus discovers that killing is not glorious. The climax involves both in further horrors. As the Crusaders overwhelm Jerusalem, Emma sees that one who has long hated Theo is about to kill him; she therefore kills Theo's enemy. Shortly afterwards, Emma and Theo realize that the Crusaders have turned the Holy City into a hell by wantonly slaughtering all of its men, women, and children. Although the life of a male knight and his numerous battles receive considerable attention in *Shadows on a Sword*, it is really about the competing claims of public duty and personal feelings. As in the previous volume, the love story itself becomes a central thematic device. When he marries Emma, Theo sets aside his sword, thus showing that the measure of the man is not his ability to kill but his ability to love and to live in peace. A third novel about the Crusades, *Lionheart's Scribe*, has been announced.

In addition to her fantasies, problem novels, and historical fictions, Bradford has written a guide to story writing and three books about animals. *Write Now!* offers children practical advice about getting ideas, outlining, creating conflicts and characters, and revising short stories. Interestingly, she provides examples of plotting by showing the development of a story called 'Not Ever Again'. A revised version of this story has been published as *A Different Kind of Champion*, about a boy who learns that his three-legged dog may not be able to enter sanctioned obedience trials but still can be both a good companion and a champion in its own right. *Animal Heroes* and *More Animal Heroes* present brief true-life accounts of animals who were, to various degrees, heroic. Crisp and breezy, these stories appeal to children fascinated by animals, especially cats and dogs.

In accepting the CLA Award for *There Will Be Wolves*, Bradford said that 'Cynicism has no place in literature for the young.' This laudable moral stance has, unfortunately, sometimes caused her to create endings that are thematically positive but dramatically false. Nevertheless, such missteps do not seriously damage her best books. Bradford is a versatile writer whose fiction contains interesting characters and intelligent, uncompromising examinations of their problems.

See also: *CA* 112; *SATA* 96; *WSMP*.

Bryan Buchan

Born: 15 August 1945, in Aberdeen, Scotland.

Principal Residences: Aberdeen; Toronto; Richmond Hill, Ont.

Education: University of Toronto (BA 1967); Toronto Teachers' College (Teaching Certificate 1968).

Career: teacher in Richmond Hill, Ont.; writer.

Works for Children

The Forgotten World of Uloc (Richmond Hill, Ont.: Scholastic-TAB, 1970). **Rev:** *IR* 5 (Spring 1971): 17.

Copper Sunrise (Richmond Hill, Ont.: Scholastic-TAB, 1972). **Rev:** *BiC* 20 (Dec. 1991): 39; *CCL* 5 (1976): 10; *EL* 19 (May 1992): 58; *IR* 7 (Spring 1973): 30.

The Dragon Children (Richmond Hill, Ont.: Scholastic-TAB, 1975). **Rev:** *IR* 10 (Summer 1976): 45.

A school teacher who has become involved in sponsoring refugee children, Bryan Buchan has written three novels for children. 'All my writing has been done with a specific audience in mind,' he has said, 'and the children with whom I have worked are often reflected in the composite characters in my novels.'

Buchan's first novel, *The Forgotten World of Uloc*, recounts the relationship between Doug and Uloc, the small creature who is guardian of the polluted pond by which the boy is playing. On a camping trip in northern Ontario, Doug courageously helps Uloc defeat the evil spirit Satika. *Copper Sunrise* is set on the east coast of Canada during early colonial times. Jamie, a young immigrant, hears terrifying rumours about the 'savages'; but he befriends a Native boy who, he discovers, is 'so unlike the savages of the village stories'. In *The Dragon Children*, a contemporary mystery, John, while wandering in the woods, meets Steve, a strange boy who urges him to stop a confidence man from fleecing elderly people. Along with his cousin Cathy and little brother Scott, John spends much of the novel chasing the wrong suspect. Finally they capture the criminal and befriend Mrs Winch, an elderly neighbour thought by many children to be a witch. Steve turns out to be the long-dead son of Mrs Winch; he has returned from the spirit world to find people who will assist his mother.

Buchan's three novels deal with ordinary children who are called on to face extraordinary experiences, whether they be forces of supernatural evil, dangers in colonial times, or modern-day criminals. Although the major characters do not undergo extensive development in the course of their adventures, they do learn the importance of trust and responsibility. *Copper Sunrise* is the most successful of the books, presenting no easy answers, but honestly facing some of the unpleasant truths of our country's past.

See also: *CA* 107; *SATA* 36.

MARGARET BUFFIE

BORN: 29 March 1945, in Winnipeg.

PRINCIPAL RESIDENCES: Winnipeg.

EDUCATION: University of Manitoba (BA 1967, Certificate of Education 1976).

CAREER: art gallery instructor; teacher; artist; author.

MAJOR AWARDS: Canadian Library Association Young Adult Book Award (1989).

WRITINGS FOR CHILDREN

Who Is Frances Rain? (Toronto: Kids Can Press, 1987). **Rev:** *BiC* 16 (Dec. 1987): 11; *CM* 16 (Mar. 1988): 203; *CCL* 53 (1989): 59; *EL* 18 (Mar. 1991): 52; *HB* 64 (May 1988): 390.

The Guardian Circle (Toronto: Kids Can Press, 1989); published in the US as *The Warnings* (New York: Scholastic, 1991). **Rev:** *CCB-B* 44 (Mar. 1991): 160; *CM* 18 (Mar. 1990): 71; *SLJ* 37 (Apr. 1991): 141.

My Mother's Ghost (Toronto: Kids Can Press, 1992); published in the US as *Someone Else's Ghost* (New York: Scholastic, 1994). **Rev:** *CCL* 75 (1994): 73; *CM* 20 (Nov. 1992): 311; *EL* 20 (Mar.–Apr. 1993): 61; *QQ* 58 (Aug. 1992): 25.

The Dark Garden (Toronto: Kids Can Press, 1995). **Rev:** *CCB-B* 51 (Oct. 1997): 44; *EL* 25 (Mar. 1998): 47; *HB* 73 (Sept. 1997): 568.

Angels Turn Their Backs (Toronto: Kids Can Press, 1998). **Rev:** *BiC* 27 (Nov. 1998): 344.

OTHER

'Back on this Side of the Door', *School Libraries in Canada* 11 (Spring 1991): 29–34.

'Reflections on a Personal Case of Censorship', *CCL* 68 (1992): 43–9.

In Margaret Buffie's five young adult novels, ghosts with business that had not been completed during their lives interact with contemporary teenage girls, not only bringing closure to their own conflicts, but profoundly influencing the lives of these young women as they move to adulthood. The author draws on her long-standing interest in and thorough research on the paranormal and combines this with her keen sense of setting and deep understanding of the difficulties of growing up in the modern world to create works of fiction that not only reflect problems of late twentieth-century life, but also reveal how much the well-being of individuals is dependent on their understanding of the connections between themselves and the past.

Before she began to write her first novel, *Who Is Frances Rain?*, Buffie had become an accomplished sketch and watercolour artist and had been a high school teacher. Both of these aspects of her life contribute to her writing: the ability to visualize completely the settings that have such strong influences on her heroines and the sympathetic treatment of the tensions they feel. Memories of her grandmother and of the summer cabin she has vacationed at since her birth find their way into *Who Is Frances Rain?*, as do her childhood sensations of that cabin having a past life of its own and her adult discovery there of a pair of old glasses wrapped in a mug.

The novel takes place during the summer vacation of 15-year-old Lizzie. Hostile towards her family, especially her recently remarried mother and her stepfather, she decides to spend as much time as she can on mysterious Rain Island, near her grandmother's cabin. Here she discovers a pair of glasses that, when worn, enable her to see the island as it was decades ago. She watches Frances Rain and her daughter and witnesses the daughter being taken away by a man who turns out to be the girl's father. On her last visit to the past, Lizzie promises Frances Rain to take a message to the girl who, she now realizes, is her own grandmother. Witnessing the pain of family love and separation in the past, Lizzie becomes progressively more appreciative of her own family. At the novel's conclusion, she and her grandmother exchange objects. She receives Frances Rain's signet ring; her grandmother receives the spectacles that Lizzie had found and that had been her own as a young woman.

The book belongs to many children's literary genres. A problem novel in which Lizzie and her siblings must work out the conflicts that arise from their mother's divorce and remarriage, it is also a female coming-of-age story. A girl on the edge of adulthood is helped by the wise old woman, her grandmother, to understand her mother and, by extension, the woman she is to become herself. Equally important, it is both a time-shift fantasy and a ghost story. The heroine is able to perceive her grandmother's past, but, in addition, Frances Rain, a ghost, travels to the future (Lizzie's present) to establish a relationship with the daughter she had never said goodbye to. As an intermediary, Lizzie herself grows and discovers that she cannot isolate herself from her past or present or from her family. The clearly realized settings; the skilful characterization of Lizzie, her strong-willed mother, and her gritty, sensible, and feisty grandmother; and the convincing wonder Lizzie feels about the time shifts and ghostly intrusions make this, Buffie's first novel, her strongest.

Like *Who Is Frances Rain?*, *The Guardian Circle* deals with the visit of a teenaged daughter of recently divorced parents to the home of an older female relative and her encounter with ghosts from her family's past. However, there are significant differences. Rachel, who travels from the country to Winnipeg and has lived with her father rather than her mother, is not an ordinary person, for she possesses psychic powers that enable her to see future events. Her gift deeply distresses her, and she wishes she could escape from it. However, when she arrives at the large, somewhat rundown Victorian house occupied by Aunt Irene and several other eccentric old people, she senses other beings around her and encounters both good and evil spirits from the past. She is the youngest of a long line of sensitive 'protectors of the Stone', a Scottish family that used magic to help maintain order and balance in the world, and, with her father, must join the old people, members of the 'Guardian Circle', in an ultimately successful struggle to prevent the ghost of an ancestor from controlling the power for selfish, evil reasons.

Although the conflict between strong forces of good and evil gives *The Guardian Circle* a power not generated by the more limited family problems of *Who Is Frances Rain?*, the novel is less successful. Rachel, who, like Lizzie, develops a sense of responsibility as she understands her relationship to past and present family members, is less convincingly portrayed. Her sense of her uniqueness and loneliness, created by her awareness and fear of her powers, is rendered somewhat unconvincing because it is interspersed with sarcastic, flip, typical teenaged remarks about the difficult old people with whom she lives and because of her relatively conventional romance with her neighbour, Will. In addition, the plot is relatively slow moving and, at times, overly complex. The first supernatural event does not occur until nearly a third of the way through the book and the exposition is extremely detailed. Writing both a mystery and a Gothic horror story, the author tends to diminish the force of the latter by extending her explanations of events of the former.

Buffie's next two works both involve further explorations of the intrusion of spirits from the past into the lives of contemporary teenage girls. However, these supernatural beings are not ancestors of the heroines, even though there are many similarities and parallels between the ghosts and the girls. Following the death of her younger brother in a canoeing accident, Jess, in *My Mother's Ghost*, moves with her family from Winnipeg to a ranch in Alberta. The novel is developed in two strands: the first-person narrator's accounts of her relationship with her still grieving, dysfunctional mother and her strong-willed, self-centred, seemingly insensitive father; and excerpts from a journal of the crippled son of the ranch's first owner. As events progress in both times, Jenny and her mother and Ian and his mother become aware of the ghostly presence of the others in their own times. The strong grief of both mothers for their sons (Ian is to die in a riding accident), as well as the pressure the children experience as a result of family conflicts, creates energy fields that make the two aware of each other. Jess matures as she gains understanding of the conflicts in the life of the family from the past and the relationship of these to her own situation. Fairly straightforward in both plot and characterization, *My Mother's Ghost* is a skilfully organized presentation of the parallel lives of the two families.

In *The Dark Garden*, Buffie combines a Gothic romance/ghost story with the psychological-medical problem of amnesia. Like Lizzie and Jess, Thea had been a normal teenager struggling with relatively straightforward family difficulties; her self-absorbed mother and father had delegated increasing responsibilities for the care of her two younger sisters and the household maintenance to her, and she had contemplated running away. However, after a bicycle accident, she lost her memory. The novel begins with her return home from the hospital and her being upset that the house is not the way it used to be. She is, in fact, seeing it as it was 75 years earlier, when it was the home of Susannah and her domineering father. The ghosts of an earlier era have unfinished business and use Thea's present state and her hostilities towards her own family to complete it. As Thea comes to understand and, with the aid of her psychic friend Lucas, to help these people from the past, the ghost Susannah is reunited with her lover, and Thea begins to recover a sense of who she is. She is able to confront her parents and assert her individuality within the shared responsibilities of the family. *The Dark Garden* communicates the brooding intensity of the house very convincingly and employs Thea's traumatic amnesia skilfully as a symbol of a teenager's struggle to define her own identity. As in earlier works, the setting is fully detailed, providing a concrete backdrop against which the intense drama is enacted. However, the explanations of the mysteries of the past are delayed until very late in the novel and are so complex as to be somewhat confusing.

Like Thea, Addy, the heroine of *Angels Turn Their Backs*, suffers a major psychological-medical problem. When her mother leaves her domineering husband and moves to Winnipeg with her daughter, Addy's agoraphobia intensifies, and she refuses to leave their apartment, which is located in an old Victorian home that once belonged to Lotta Engel, a world-famous creator of tapestries. Addy discovers that Engel was also an agoraphobic whose works, which pictured angels, reflected the sadness and guilt of her life and her feeling of having been deserted by these guardian spirits and betrayed by a domineering man. Making contact with the artist's ghost, the girl sets about to complete the woman's last, unfinished tapestry, thus enabling Engel's ghost to rest. However, she refuses to let the woman's spirit dictate a gloomy tapestry pattern to her and finishes the piece in a way that, as well as freeing the uneasy spirit, enables her to make the first steps towards overcoming her own problems. In addition to this main plot, the novel shows two other women, Addy's mother and a young university student, escaping from the men who had controlled, repressed, and, in the student's case, physically abused them. While *Angels Turn Their Backs* bears similarities to Buffie's earlier books, it examines in much fuller detail the importance for the female characters to control their own destinies, not to be repressed and directed by males who, it turns out, use power to compensate for their own weaknesses and problems.

Her young adult novels have established Margaret Buffie as one of Canada's foremost writers of psychological ghost stories. Careful research provides convincing background that does not overwhelm the narratives, although the explanations of this material are sometimes overly complex. Her portrayals of the teenaged heroines are, however, well-delineated accounts of relatively ordinary girls in extraordinary situations. The lives of characters from earlier ages and the girls' encounters with them provide well-developed symbols of the problems of coming of age. The skilled presentation of the houses and landscapes in which the events take place make these events and the central characters' responses convincing.

See also: *AAYA* 23; *CA* 160; *CLR* 39; *SATA* 71; *TCCW* 5; *WSMP*.

Sheila Burnford

Born: 11 May 1918, in Scotland.

Died: 20 April 1984, in Bucklers Hard, Hampshire, England.

Principal Residences: Edinburgh; Port Arthur, Ont.

Education: Harrowgate College, Yorkshire; study in Germany.

Career: ambulance driver in WW II; author.

Major Awards: Canadian Library Association Book of the Year for Children (1963); American Library Association's Aurianne Award (1963); Lewis Carroll Shelf Award (1971) for *The Incredible Journey*.

The Incredible Journey (Boston: Little, Brown, 1961). **Rev:** *APBR* 10 (Nov. 1983): 2; *Booklist* 86 (1 Sept. 1989): 83; *Books and Bookmen* 14 (Aug. 1969): 38; *Five Owls* 3 (May 1989): 70; *HB* 67 (Mar. 1991): 224; *Top of the News* 34 (Winter 1978): 189.

Mr. Noah and the Second Flood, illus. Michael Foreman (Toronto: McClelland & Stewart, 1973). **Rev:** *CCB-B* 27 (Dec. 1973): 59; *NYTBR* (16 Dec. 1973): 8; *Teacher* 91 (Mar. 1974): 110, and 92 (Dec. 1974): 79; *TLS* 91 (Mar. 1974): 386.

Always fascinated by the ways animals communicated with each other, Sheila Burnford used her observations of the relationships between three family pets to create her first and most famous book, *The Incredible Journey*. This novel traces the progress of two dogs and a cat who undertake a dangerous journey across the rugged northern Ontario wilderness to the home of their masters. Along the way, they endure every conceivable test of their friendship and determination. The animals have unique, well-defined personalities. Luath, the young Labrador retriever who leads them, is wise and benevolent; Bodger, the dim-eyed old bull terrier, is fun-loving and eager for a fight in spite of his infirmities; Tao, the Siamese cat, appears aloofly self-centred at the beginning but proves as altruistic as the others. Most critics have complained of the obvious anthropomorphism and sentimentality in the novel, but its simplicity and fast pace made it an immediate commercial success. Winner of several awards, it has been translated into at least 25 languages and made into a full-length Walt Disney film.

Burnford's other children's book, *Mr. Noah and the Second Flood*, is a cautionary tale in which a descendant of the original Noah prepares for a flood brought on by man's interference with the planet's ecology. Occasionally humorous in its portraits of James Noah and his wife as pastoral innocents, the book grows progressively more caustic: in the end, Noah decides that man is so much at fault that he refuses passage on the ark to his own sons and their wives.

Burnford made an important contribution to Canadian letters by becoming internationally successful at a time when Canadian books did not enjoy wide popularity. In spite of its sentimentality, *The Incredible Journey* remains a popular and notable contribution to the fiction about animals.

See also: *CA* 112; *CA* 1–4R; *CANR* 1; *CLR* 2; *MAICYA*; *Profiles*; *SATA* 3, 38; *TCCW*.

Maria Campbell

Born: 6 April 1940, in Park Valley, Sask.

Principal Residences: Park Valley; Vancouver; Edmonton; Batouche, Sask.; Regina.

Career: waitress; writer; women's shelter administrator; editor.

Work for Children

People of the Buffalo, illus. Douglas Tait and Shannon Twofeathers (Vancouver: Douglas & McIntyre, 1976). **Rev:** *CCL* 31 (1983): 98; *IR* 11 (Spring 1977): 34.

Little Badger and the Fire Spirit, illus. David Maclagan (Toronto: McClelland & Stewart, 1977). **Rev:** *CCL* 31 (1983): 105; *IR* (Autumn 1977): 34: *SLJ* 25 (Nov. 1978): 41.

Riel's People, illus. David Maclagan (Vancouver: Douglas & McIntyre, 1978). **Rev.** *CCL* 31 (1983): 93; *IR* 13 (Apr. 1979): 36.

Other

Editor, *Achimoona* [writings by Native children] (Saskatoon: Fifth House, 1985).

Selected Discussions

Stott, Jon C. 'A Conversation with Maria Campbell', *CCL* 31/32 (1983): 15–22.

'I have brothers and sisters all over the country. I no longer need my blanket to survive.' In the closing lines of *Halfbreed*, her autobiography, Métis author Maria Campbell states that she has achieved self-knowledge, and awareness of who she is and where she belongs. This awareness summarizes not only her own life, but also the theme of her books for children.

For Campbell, part of the goal of writing has been to inform her readers, Native and non-Native, of the proud cultural heritage of her people. Perhaps the most important part of that heritage was the Métis' and Plains Indians' strong sense of personal and cultural identity. As she notes at the conclusion of *People of the Buffalo*, writing of the renaissance of old beliefs and customs, 'The most important weapon of all [is] to know who you are and where you come from.' In *People of the Buffalo*, this involves not only appreciating the physical world of the Canadian Plains people—all aspects of whose culture are carefully detailed in the book—but also understanding and sympathizing with their spirituality. The circle, the symbol of the unity of and harmony among all created things, dominated their lives, from tipi design and placement to weapons. The coming of the white people led to violence, drunkenness, and a loss of harmony and unity. The conclusion of her companion volume on the Métis, *Riel's People*, also emphasizes a people's self-awareness: 'History calls them a defeated people, but the Métis do not feel defeated, and that is what is important. . . . They know who they are: "*Ka tip aim soot chic*"—the people who own themselves.' Although the advance of farming and urbanization into the Prairies destroyed their traditional lifestyles, they still adhere to the family as the source of strength.

Campbell's major work for children, *Little Badger and the Fire Spirit*, is a literary folktale describing the acquisition of fire by the Native people of the Prairies. Although the people had good lives, they suffered in the winter because of lack of fire. Badger, who is blind, journeys to the cavern of the Fire Spirit, receives fire for his people, and is rewarded with the gift of sight. The tale is set within a contemporary framework. Visiting her grandparents on the shores of Alberta's Lac LaBiche, Ahsinee asks her grandmother to tell her a story from the old days. Although Maria Campbell created the story, she drew consciously on the traditional wisdom and tales she had learned from both her *cheechum*, her great-grandmother, and from other old people. Underlying the narrative is the belief that all living things have a purpose: 'That purpose was to serve and help each other.' Badger has not acted alone in his journey; moreover he has made new friends: Mountain Goat, Mountain Lion, Grizzly Bear, and Rattlesnake, not to mention the Fire Spirit. He has helped to restore harmony and friendship among all beings. Badger's journey has been one of self-discovery and fulfilment. His new eyesight symbolizes his understanding of friendship and the necessity of co-operation between all beings.

The story's framework reinforces the narrative's meaning. Just as Little Badger must journey into unknown realms to achieve wisdom and fulfilment, Ahsinee must leave the familiar town of Lac LaBiche to visit her grandparents, people who live close to the old ways and remember the old traditions. She is aware of her need to learn the old ways as she asks her grandfather a question about the origin of fire, hoping that he will tell a traditional tale. When she returns to the town at the end of the summer, not only will she remember this and other stories told to her by her grandparents, but also she will possess some of the old wisdom and will, therefore, be surer of who she is and where she belongs. She will have a sense of her Native heritage.

See also: *CA* 106; *CANR* 54; *Profiles* 2.

Brenda Clark

Born: 10 February 1955, in Toronto.

Principal Residences: Toronto; Nestleton, Ont.

Education: Three-year program in illustration at Sheridan College, Oakville, Ont.

Career: freelance illustrator.

Major Awards: IODE (Toronto) Book Award (1989).

Works for Children

The Yellow Flag, by Suzanne McSweeney (Toronto: PMA Books, 1980). **Rev:** *BiC* 10 (Apr. 1981); 28; *IR* 15 (Apr. 1981): 44; *QQ* 47 (Feb. 1981): 46; *SLJ* 27 (May 1981): 54.

Ski for Your Mountain, by Sharon Siamon (Toronto: Gage, 1983). **Rev:** *CCL* 34 (1984): 92; *EL* 11 (Nov. 1983): 37; *QQ* 49 (Aug. 1983): 39.

Christopher and the Dream Dragon, by Allen Morgan (Toronto: Kids Can Press, 1984). **Rev:** CC 43 (1986): 70; *EL* 13 (Mar. 1986): 15, 44; *SLJ* 31 (May 1985): 80.

Sadie and the Snowman, by Allen Morgan (Toronto: Kids Can Press, 1985). **Rev:** *EL* 21 (May 1994): 55; *QQ* 51 (Aug. 1985): 37.

Night and Day, by Catherine Ripley (Toronto: Greey de Pencier, 1985). **Rev:** *EL* 13 (Nov. 1985): 43, and 13 (Mar. 1986): 16; *QQ* 51 (Aug. 1985): 36.

We Celebrate Winter, by Bobbie Kalman and Susan Hughes, black-and-white illus. Elaine Macpherson, colour illus. Brenda Clark (Toronto: Crabtree, 1986).

How Does Your Garden Grow, by Pat Patterson (Toronto: Greey de Pencier, 1986).

Franklin in the Dark, by Paulette Bourgeois (Toronto: Kids Can Press, 1986). **Rev:** *BiC* 15 (Dec. 1986): 15; *CCL* 50 (1988): 94; *Maclean's* 99 (15 Dec. 1986): 44; *QQ* 52 (Aug. 1986): 38.

Big Sarah's Little Boots, by Paulette Bourgeois (Toronto: Kids Can Press, 1987). **Rev:** *BiC* 16 (Dec. 1987): 13; *CCL* 52 (1988): 28; *CM* 16 (Mar. 1988): 56; *EL* 15 (Mar. 1988): 23; *SLJ* 35 (Nov. 1989): 74.

Little Fingerling: A Japanese Folktale, by Monica Hughes (Toronto: Kids Can Press, 1989). **Rev:** *BiC* 18 (Dec. 1989): 23; *EL* 17 (Mar. 1990): 25, and 18 (Sept. 1990): 53, and 18 (Nov. 1990): 54, and 21 (Sept. 1993): 61; *QQ* 55 (Sept. 1989): 22; *RT* 45 (Apr. 1992): 637; *SLJ* (Apr. 1993): 111.

Puddleman, by Ted Staunton (Toronto: Scholastic: 1988). **Rev:** *CM* 17 (Mar. 1989): 88.

Hurry Up, Franklin, by Paulette Bourgeois (Toronto: Kids Can Press, 1989). **Rev:** *BYP* 3 (Apr. 1989): 12; *CM* 17 (Sept. 1989): 216; *EL* 17 (Mar. 1990): 23; *SLJ* 36 (Dec. 1990): 70; *TES* (29 Mar. 1991): 23.

Franklin Fibs, by Paulette Bourgeois (Toronto: Kids Can Press, 1991). **Rev:** *BiC* 20 (June 1991): 58; *CCL* 67 (1992): 81; *CM* 19 (May 1991): 170; *EL* 19 (Mar. 1992): 17; *QQ* 57 (Feb. 1991): 22, and 57 (May 1991): 21; *RT* 45 (Apr. 1992): 635.

Franklin Is Lost, by Paulette Bourgeois (Toronto: Kids Can Press, 1992). **Rev:** *CM* 20 (Sept. 1992): 207; *QQ* 58 (Feb. 1992): 32.

Franklin Is Bossy, by Paulette Bourgeois (Toronto: Kids Can Press, 1993). **Rev:** *CM* 22 (Mar. 1994): 46; *EL* 21 (Mar. 1994): 16; *QQ* 59 (July 1993): 56.

My Cat, by Marilyn Baillie (Toronto: Kids Can Press, 1993). **Rev:** *CM* 22 (May 1994): 77; *QQ* 60 (Jan. 1994): 38.

My Dog, by Marilyn Baillie (Toronto: Kids Can Press, 1993). **Rev:** *QQ* 60 (Jan. 1994): 38.

Franklin Is Messy, by Paulette Bourgeois (Toronto: Kids Can Press, 1994). **Rev:** *QQ* 60 (Nov. 1994): 34.

Franklin Wants a Pet, by Paulette Bourgeois (Toronto: Kids Can Press, 1994). **Rev:** *QQ* 60 (Nov. 1994): 34; *RT* 49 (Feb. 1996): 397.

Franklin's Blanket, by Paulette Bourgeois (Toronto: Kids Can Press. 1995). **Rev:** *CBRA* (1995): 463.

Franklin Goes to School, by Paulette Bourgeois (Toronto: Kids Can Press, 1995). **Rev:** *CBRA* (1995): 462; *EL* 23 (Mar. 1996): 24.

Franklin and Me: A Book about Me, Written and Drawn by Me (with a Little Help from Franklin), by Paulette Bourgeois (Toronto: Scholastic, 1995). **Rev:** *CBRA* (1995): 462.

Franklin Plays the Game, by Paulette Bourgeois (Toronto: Kids Can Press, 1995). **Rev:** *CBRA* (1995): 463.

Franklin and the Tooth Fairy, by Paulette Bourgeois (Toronto: Kids Can Press, 1995). **Rev:** *CBRA* (1995): 462.

Franklin Has a Sleep-Over, by Paulette Bourgeois (Toronto: Kids Can Press, 1996). **Rev:** *CBRA* (1996): 434.

Franklin's Bad Day, by Paulette Bourgeois (Toronto: Kids Can Press, 1996). **Rev:** *CBRA* (1996): 435; *QQ* 62 (Dec. 1996): 38; *SLJ* 43 (May 1997): 93.

Franklin's Halloween, by Paulette Bourgeois (Toronto: Kids Can Press, 1996). **Rev:** *CBRA* (1996): 435; *QQ* 62 (Sept. 1996): 32.

Franklin's School Play, by Paulette Bourgeois (Toronto: Kids Can Press, 1996). **Rev:** *CBRA* (1996): 435; *EL* 24 (Mar. 1997): 26.

Finders Keepers for Franklin, by Paulette Bourgeois (Toronto: Kids Can Press, 1997).

Franklin Rides a Bike, by Paulette Bourgeois (Toronto: Kids Can Press, 1997). **Rev:** *SLJ* 43 (Dec. 1997): 87.

Franklin's New Friend, by Paulette Bourgeois (Toronto: Kids Can Press, 1997). **Rev:** *SLJ* 43 (Dec. 1997): 87.

Franklin's Secret Club, by Paulette Bourgeois (Toronto: Kids Can Press, 1998).

Franklin's Christmas Gift, by Paulette Bourgeois (Toronto: Kids Can Press, 1998).

Franklin's Valentine, by Paulette Bourgeois (Toronto: Kids Can Press, 1998).

Franklin and the Thunderstorm, by Paulette Bourgeois (Toronto: Kids Can Press, 1998).

Franklin's Class Trip, by Paulette Bourgeois (Toronto: Kids Can Press, 1999).

Selected Discussions

Wilde, Leanne. 'Franklin: Ideal Children's Literary Idol or Flavourless Turtle of Privilege?', *CCL* 90 (1998): 38–44.

As a child, Brenda Clark has said, she was fascinated by the illustrations in her school readers, and she longed to be the person who drew them. After graduating from a three-year course in illustration at Sheridan College, she realized her ambition. Working as a freelance illustrator, she soon had commissions for anthologies and other school texts. She also provided pictures for *Chickadee*, a nature magazine for children. In 1980, however, she began a new phase in her career by illustrating a trade book, Susanne McSweeney's *The Yellow Flag*. Increasingly, publishers turned to her with commissions to illustrate children's books. She thus came to illustrate books by Allen Morgan, Ted Staunton, and, most notably, Paulette Bourgeois, creating the image of Franklin the turtle, one of the most recognized fictional creations in Canadian publishing history.

Clark's first book, *The Yellow Flag*, showed her indebtedness to the textbook tradition of illustration. Her somewhat stiff and dull-coloured figures are not entirely realistic, but their clothing and their settings contain enough detail to establish a sense of believability. It is clear that Clark researched the background of the story and took particular pains to ensure accuracy in her drawings, especially those of sailing ships. As Clark began to do commercial books, her style became more fluid, but she continued to do research in order to give her work an aura of authenticity. She also developed a method for ensuring that the printed versions of her pictures were colourful. Her use of thick layers of watercolours, or glazes, gives a vibrancy to her pictures. Clark's early compositions were relatively straight-forward and not notably distinctive. From the beginning, she filled them with details, but she has occasionally employed variation effectively. In Paulette Bourgeois's *Big Sarah's Little Boots*, for example, she eliminates backgrounds in some pictures in order to focus attention on Sarah's feelings. In her most complex work, *Little Fingerling*, a book for which she conducted extensive research into Japanese art and history, she effectively varies the format, inserting some double-page illustrations to underline dramatic turns in the course of the story.

Clark's reputation depends principally on her creation of Franklin. Indeed, it is Clark who has given Franklin whatever personality he possesses. By portraying him as walking upright on his hind legs and by giving him large, somewhat sad eyes, Clark has appealingly, if somewhat sentimentally, humanized this turtle. She has also made him stand apart by drawing the other animals with comparative realism. Because Franklin seems so much more human than they are, readers probably find it easy to identify with him. In any case, Clark further underscores Franklin's underlying identity with that of the child by giving him a richly detailed environment, one that she has said she hopes children will pore over. Details, such as pull toys and dolls shaped like turtles instead of humans, add a humorous touch, but they make Franklin's world recognizably middle-class. Furthermore, Clark makes this middle-class world emotionally supportive by portraying parents as gazing fondly on both each other and their child, who is always the centre of their concerns. The world she thus portrays is warm, comfortable, and secure. Occasionally, however, as is the case with the fly pie that Franklin makes in *Franklin Fibs*, Clark adds details to remind readers that he is an animal, and a fictional one at that. On other occasions, Clark uses the details to support political correctness. Thus, in *Franklin's School Play*, she suggests the need for inclusiveness and acceptance, even though the text says nothing about it, by portraying Badger as requiring crutches. At other times, Clark omits details to ensure that the books will be acceptable to international publishers. To forestall objections by American censors, for example, she made sure that none of the characters attending the party in *Franklin's Halloween* was wearing a witch's costume.

Although the authentic Japanese atmosphere of the pictures in *Little Fingerling* clearly indicates that she can illustrate with noteworthy artistry, Brenda Clark has concentrated on work that is not especially distinctive or ground-breaking. She has, however, given life to Franklin the turtle, making him a recognizable fixture of children's lives in Canada and abroad. Even those who find the mild didacticism and sentimentality of the Franklin books distasteful must acknowledge that such an achievement is worthy of respect.

See also: *MCAI*; *WSMP*.

Catherine Anthony Clark

Born: 5 May 1892, in London, England.

Died: 24 February 1977, in Victoria, BC.

Principal Residences: London, England; Nelson, BC; Victoria, BC.

Education: Convent of Jesus and Mary, Ipswich, Suffolk.

Career: rancher; newspaper columnist; author.

Major Awards: Canadian Library Association Book of the Year Medal (1952).

Works for Children

The Golden Pine Cone (Toronto: Macmillan, 1950).

The Sun Horse (Toronto: Macmillan, 1951).

The One-Winged Dragon (Toronto: Macmillan, 1955).

The Silver Man (Toronto: Macmillan, 1958).

The Diamond Feather; or, The Door in the Mountain: A Magic Tale for Children (Toronto: Macmillan, 1962).

The Man with the Yellow Eyes (Toronto: Macmillan, 1963).

The Hunter and the Medicine Man (Toronto: Macmillan, 1966).

Selected Discussions

Kealy, J. Kieran. 'The Flame-Lighter Woman: Catherine Anthony Clark's Fantasies', *CL* 78 (1978): 32–42.

Murray, Heather. 'The Geography of the Imagination: The Fantastic Frontier of Catherine Anthony Clark', *ChLQ* 8 (Winter 1983): 23–5.

Razzell, Mary. 'Canadian Fantasy: Thoughts on *The Golden Pine Cone*', *CCL* 89 (1998): 22–6.

Selby, Joan. 'The Creation of Fantasy: The Fiction of Catherine Anthony Clark', *CL* 11 (Winter 1962): 39–45.

Catherine Anthony Clark is generally recognized as the first fantasy writer to make substantial use of Canadian materials. After coming to Canada in 1914 and marrying, Clark spent a number of years on a ranch in the West Kootenay region of British Columbia, where she gained a particularly sharp understanding of the rugged mountain landscape that is the setting for her six fantasies and one historical novel.

Individual novels vary the details, but Clark's fantasies are essentially similar in pattern: they present the circular journey of a pair of children who, except in *The Golden Pine Cone*, feel alienated. These children, a boy of either 10 or 11 and a slightly younger girl, set out from home and soon find that they have crossed over from the Outer World of mundane life into a special, magical world. Here they discover that they are important: people in the magic realm depend on them to undertake a quest that will lead to a restoration of moral order. Unable to return to the Outer World before completing this quest, the children display courage, compassion, and generosity. Success in the quest also makes them certain of their own worth and capable of appreciating others.

Although the pattern of each novel is clear, Clark tends to complicate matters by putting her characters through an almost bewildering variety of incidents. Even the quests tend to multiply as a novel progresses. In *The Golden Pine Cone*, Bren and Lucy begin with the idea of returning a golden pine cone necessary for Tekontha, the good ruler of the magic realm, to hold power. Along the way they become involved in a quest to free an Indian princess by finding her heart, which has been replaced by a crystal, and another to earn the freedom of their dog. All of the quests are thematically united because they display the power of love, but they seem more the product of extemporizing than of careful plotting. *The Sun Horse* similarly begins with a pair of clear quests when a boy and girl search for both the girl's lost father and a magical golden stallion. During their search, however, they learn that they must seek the Love Magnet, a metal plate that will destroy the Thunderbird. Unfortunately, this new quest seems more of a story-stretching contrivance than an integral part of the main story. *The One-Winged Dragon* is particularly shaky in its multiplication of quests because Clark unsuccessfully tries to combine Chinese and Pacific Coast Indian strands. Thus, the two children set out in search of an old Chinese farmer's luck stone, which, in turn, leads them to a quest for his missing daughter, which, along the way, involves them in a quest for a whale that is destroying the Indians' fishery. Similar plotting complexities are evident in *The Silver Man*, *The Diamond Feather*, and *The Hunter and the Medicine Man*.

In addition to their numerous episodes, Clark's fantasies are characterized by a unique, sometimes jarring mixture of mythic and folkloric elements. Through mythic devices, Clark creates grandeur. Thus, she populates her novels with Indian princesses, warriors, and medicine men who embody basic moral attributes. The children who enter the magic realm also take on new heroic identities, a point stressed in *The Sun Horse*, *The One-Winged Dragon*, and *The Silver Man* by the fact that they earn new Indian names. Furthermore, familiar characters of the pioneer past—miners and settlers—take on added dignity and significance as helper figures. Sometimes, these characters become effectively symbolic. In *The Sun Horse*, for example, Old Beard, a miner who refuses to move from his mine, symbolizes the futility of the life dedicated to materialistic pursuit. All of these elements give the adventures within the Canadian landscape a universality and a timeless dignity.

Clark's use of folkloric elements works in the opposite way, leavening the tone of moral grandeur, often through comedy. Thus, she begins her first two books with variations on the 'once upon a time' opener. She also introduces a variety of talking animals, many of whom have significant roles as helper figures. Some of these, such as the Head Canada Goose in *The Golden Pine Cone* and the Rock Puck in *The Diamond Feather*, are memorable and original. Folkloric creatures like the comical Rock Puck, the bats in *The Sun Horse*, Foxy and Mammoth in *The Silver Man*, and the beavers in *The Hunter and the Medicine Man* do not, however, always make a positive contribution to the novels: in fact, by distracting from the seriousness of the mythic elements, such characters frequently make the novels somewhat cartoonish.

Clark also wrote an historical adventure novel that employs the quest pattern to show a boy's achievement of manhood. In *The Man with the Yellow Eyes*, young Steve races over the mountain to file a silver claim before a corrupt prospector can cheat his father out of it. This novel fails because of its melodramatic plotting and the stereotypical presentation of the yellow-eyed prospector as a vicious animal.

Clark's books have obvious limitations, but she deserves respect for pointing out to a later generation that Canadian settings and materials can be the basis for compelling fantasy.

See also: *CA* 11–12; *CAP* 1; *DLB* 68; *TCCW*.

Joan Clark

Born: 12 October 1934, in Liverpool, NS.

Principal Residences: Liverpool, NS; Sussex, NB; Edmonton; Calgary; Dartmouth, NS; St John's, Nfld.

Education: Acadia University (BA 1957).

Career: teacher in New Brunswick, Alberta, and Nova Scotia; freelance writer.

Major Awards: Geoffrey Bilson Award for Historical Fiction (1995); Mr Christie's Book Awards, ages 12 and up (1995).

Works for Children

Girl of the Rockies (Toronto: Ryerson Press, 1968).

Thomasina and the Trout Tree, illus. Ingeborg Hiscox (Montreal: Tundra, 1971). **Rev:** *CCB-B* 25 (Mar. 1972): 103; *Publishers Weekly* 204 (24 Sept. 1973): 187.

The Hand of Robin Squires (Toronto: Clarke, Irwin, 1977). **Rev:** *APBR* 10 (Nov. 1983): 17, and 13 (Nov. 1986): 1; *CCL* 14 (1979): 73; *EL* 14 (Mar. 1987): 49; *QQ* 52 (Dec. 1986): 12; *TES* (4 Apr. 1980): 29

The Leopard and the Lily, illus. Velma Foster (Lantzville, BC: Oolichan, 1984). **Rev:** *CCL* 39 (1985): 158; *QQ* 52 (Dec. 1986): 12

Wild Man of the Woods (Markham, Ont.: Viking Kestrel, 1985). **Rev:** *BiC* 14 (Dec. 1985): 14; *Booklist* 83 (1 Sept. 1986): 59; *QQ* 51 (Dec. 1985): 30, and 52 (Dec. 1986): 12; *SLJ* 33 (Sept. 1986): 132.

The Moons of Madeleine (Markham, Ont.: Viking Kestrel, 1987). **Rev:** *BiC* 16 (Mar. 1987): 37; *CCL* 50 (1988): 86; *QQ* 52 (Dec. 1986): 12.

The Dream Carvers (Toronto: Viking, 1995). **Rev:** *CCL* 80 (1995): 79.

Other

'What Is History?', *CCL* 83 (1996): 79–81.

Selected Discussions

Luthy, Jean. 'Profile: Joan Clark', *IR* 12 (Winter 1978): 18–20.

At the end of her entry in *Canada Writes!*, Joan Clark lists as one of her favourite quotations E.B. White's comment that 'Anyone who writes down to children is simply wasting time. You have to write up, not down.' In her effort to follow White's dictum, Clark has shown herself unafraid of writing children's books that tackle serious and complex ideas in sophisticated ways. Unfortunately, her execution does not always match her conception, and her books frequently falter both aesthetically and intellectually.

In much of her writing for children, Clark has shown a preoccupation with symbolism, parallel stories, and the theme of identity. Her first book, *Girl of the Rockies*, symbolically parallels the amusing story of a bear cub's growth into an unpredictable yearling and an account of the development of the girl who has kept it as a pet. The connection of Heather's development and the bear's growth to maturity is at best, however, tenuous. Attempts at symbolic meaning are also evident in two picture books for which Clark provided the text. In *Thomasina and the Trout Tree*, illustrated by Ingeborg Hiscox, Clark tries with only partial success to make a girl's search for the mysterious Trout Tree suggest that art is everywhere. In *The Leopard and the Lily*, illustrated by Velma Foster, she parallels the story of a caged black leopard who dreams of a lily and that of a girl with gossamer wings who eventually presents him with the lily. Here the symbols are too vague and enigmatic to make the tale anything other than an unsolvable puzzle.

The Hand of Robin Squires, a first-person fictional explanation for the mysterious 'Money Pit' on Oak Island, Nova Scotia, suggests that the young hero is telling the tale in order to begin a new life. Most of the identity theme, though, occurs in the story of Auctadin, a Micmac whose powers of observation and intelligence have caused him to rebel against tribal traditions and taboos. His tale of rebellion and conformity is not an effective parallel to Robin's tale of victimization by his cruel piratical uncle. Furthermore, it forces Clark to violate point of view, shifting to the third person in three chapters. Although this novel contains several sharply drawn, exciting scenes, stereotyped minor characters and a strained conclusion further weaken it.

Wild Man of the Woods and *The Moons of Madeleine*, which are far more ambitious in narrative design than her earlier novels, are related by plot and theme. Both explore themes of identity by trying to fuse the adolescent problem novel and a symbolic fantasy. *Wild Man of the Woods* is the less successful because it does not convincingly integrate its literal and symbolic levels. The story of Stephen Gibson, a boy terrified of bullies and fascinated by Native masks, it seeks to show the interrelationship of mythic and mundane worlds. Stephen dons a Native mask to confront his tormentors and becomes an evil creature who lusts for power over them. He is saved from his darker self only when the mask is knocked off and he falls into the lake to be symbolically reborn.

Stephen's symbolic transformations are intriguing, but his too-rapid acceptance of himself when he views a postcard showing a white Grecian temple with columns 'like gods and goddesses holding back the dark' not only violates the Native symbolism used throughout, but it also strains credibility. Indeed, the literal level is so contrived that it undermines the symbolic one. Thus, Clark fails to explain why a Kwakiutl carver lives in a Plains tipi in eastern British Columbia and hangs his masks on trees. Most significantly, she fails to convince us that bullies would be frightened of boys wearing Native masks, no matter how much those boys feel internally transformed. The ending, in which the bullies unite in friendship with their former victims may express noble anti-war sentiments, but the bullies' change of heart is improbable, and this thematic extension is too forced to be an effective message.

The Moons of Madeleine also employs mythic patterns and symbols, most notably Greek ones, to explore female identity. 'Mad' (short for 'Madeleine') is a loner spending time in Calgary with her cousin Selena, a rebellious teenager whose very appearance upsets the staid visitor. Mad enters a parallel moon world, where she discovers that she has a quest to prevent the return to Chaos by entering a cave to prove that First Woman still lives. Mad's successful quest, which takes her to 'the womb of the universe', offers hints about the continuity of the female principle, immortality through memory of others, and acceptance of differences.

The Moons of Madeleine is far more successful than *Wild Man of the Woods* in blending the mundane and the fantastic. It is not, however, completely free from puzzling inconsistencies and excesses characteristic of Clark's work. For instance, the novel does not satisfactorily explain why donning an Indian moon mask, which has been carved by a man, should enable Mad to see a world of Greek moon goddesses and priestesses. Perhaps the mixing of mythic elements reflects Mad's own knowledge of and interests in Greek mythology, for Clark suggests that the quest may be a dream. The parallel actions of Selena and the rebellious moon goddess Aneles (Selena backwards), for instance, clearly suggest that Mad may be working out her mundane problems by dreaming of a mythic world. In any case, although the characterization in the fantasy or dream sections is wooden, the dialogue and actions of characters in the realistic sections are believable and consistent enough to make the novel an interesting study of female maturation.

Fantastic or mystical elements also weaken *The Dream Carvers*. A captivity novel set in AD 1015, it uses two narrators to compare Native and European cultures. The dominant narrator is 14-year-old Thrand, a Greenlander captured by natives while he is on a wood-gathering expedition in the New World. At first he regards his captors, members of the Osweet tribe and fictional forerunners of the Beothuk of Newfoundland, as wretches and savages. During his long captivity, however, during which he is renamed Wobee and made part of the tribe, he realizes that they are a gentle people who are in many respects superior to his own bloodthirsty nation. The secondary narrator is a young girl, Abidith, who initially resents Thrand because he was instrumental in killing her brother. The juxtaposition of their narratives creates an intriguing comparison of cultures, allowing readers to appreciate the differences in what each considers normal. Unfortunately, Clark also gives Abidith the ability to enter Wobee's dreams. This ability may have a foundation in Native beliefs, but it strains the novel's realism. Furthermore, it has little substantive influence on plot or theme. Even if Abidith did not know about them, for example, Thrand's dreams would be just as effective in providing background information. Furthermore, the fact that he himself dreams of the fate of his father and his other companions, only to realize that he has no idea about what happened to them, suggests that dreams are not accurate guides in life or that Europeans are not as gifted psychically as Natives. The former trivializes a major narrative element in the novel, and the latter suggests an implicitly racist notion of culture.

The Dream Carvers has other problems. Its detailed accounts of Native customs seem anthropologically plausible for the most part, but it is unlikely that a young girl such as Abidith would claim that one does not have to believe in the literal truth of her people's mythology because each person finds a personal truth in stories. Furthermore, the descriptions of Native activities sometimes overwhelm the dramatic tension created by Thrand's conflicting desires to return to Greenland and to join the Osweet. When Thrand runs away and is wounded in precisely the same way that he wounded Abidith's brother, thematic architecture triumphs over realism. Regardless, as in Clark's other novels, issues of identity become central. After undergoing a ceremony in which he is dyed red with ochre, Thrand realizes that he can know who and what he is by living among the red men, and he ultimately accepts that he can be happy as Wobee. In tracing this change of attitude, however, the novel is ideologically heavy-handed, idealizing the Natives and demonizing the Norse. Thus, it repeatedly celebrates the tribe's reverence for nature, its pacifism, and its communal sharing of property, pointedly contrasting these qualities with the suspicion, selfishness, rapacity, and violence that Thrand himself sees as characteristic of Norse life.

Clark deserves credit for trying 'to write up, not down' to children. Even though her plotting deficiencies, symbolic ambiguities, and thematic confusions prevent her books from being entirely successful, at least two of her novels, *The Moons of Madeleine* and *The Dream Carvers*, will both entertain and reward many young readers.

See also: *CA* 93–6; K.A. Hamilton, ed., *Canada Writes!* (1977); *Profiles* 2; *SATA* 59; *WSMP*.

Elizabeth Cleaver

Born: 19 November 1939, in Montreal.

Died: 27 July 1985, in Montreal.

Principal Residences: Montreal; Toronto.

Education: The Gymnazium, Sàrospatak, Hungary; Sir George Williams University, Montreal; School of Art and Design of the Montreal Museum of Fine Arts; l'École des Beaux Arts, Montreal; Concordia University, Montreal (MFA 1980).

Career: artist in Toronto advertising agency; freelance writer, designer, and illustrator of children's books (1968-85).

Major Awards: Award of Merit, New York Illustrators Society (1968, for *The Wind Has Wings*); Amelia Frances Howard-Gibbon Illustrator's Award (1971, 1978); Canadian Association of Children's Librarians Bronze Medal (1974); Canada Council Children's Literature Prize for English-Language Illustration (1980).

Posthumous Honours: The Elizabeth Mrázik-Cleaver Canadian Picture Book Award was established in her honour; the Elizabeth Cleaver Memorial Lecture series is held every second year at Vanier College, Montreal.

Works for Children

Written and Illustrated by Elizabeth Cleaver

The Miraculous Hind: A Hungarian Legend (Toronto: Holt, Rinehart and Winston, 1973). **Rev:** *CCB-B* 27 (June 1974): 155; *RT* 35 (Apr. 1982): 38.

Petrouchka (Toronto: Macmillan, 1980). **Rev:** *BiC* 9 (Dec. 1980): 19; *CCL* 25 (1982): 55; *HB* 56 (Dec. 1980): 631; *IR* 15 (Apr. 1981): 27; *Maclean's* 93 (15 Dec. 1980): 52; *QQ* 46 (Nov. 1980): 44; *SLJ* 27 (Nov. 1980): 72.

ABC (Toronto: Oxford UP, 1984). **Rev:** *CCB-B* 38 (May 1985): 162; *CCL* 39 (1985): 122; *EL* 13 (Sept. 1985): 44; *QQ* 51 (Feb. 1985): 14, and 51 (Mar. 1985): 74; *SLJ* 32 (Sept. 1985): 228; *TES* (3 May 1985): 30.

The Enchanted Caribou (Toronto: Oxford UP, 1985). **Rev:** *BiC* 14 (Dec. 1985): 12;

CM 19 (May 1991): 156; *EL* 13 (Mar. 1986): 15; *HB* 62 (Mar. 1986): 190; *Maclean's* 98 (9 Dec. 1985): 45; *QQ* 52 (Feb. 1986): 15; *Scientific American* 255 (Dec. 1986): 34; *SLJ* 32 (Mar. 1986): 158.

Illustrated by Elizabeth Cleaver

The Wind Has Wings: Poems from Canada, eds Mary Alice Downie and Barbara Robertson (Toronto: Oxford UP, 1968). **Rev:** *CCB-B* 22 (July 1969): 173; *CCL* 18–19 (1980): 135, and 42 (1986): 53; *HB* 45 (Apr. 1969): 181; *LJ* (15 Mar. 1969): 1325; *TLS* (3 Apr. 1969): 353.

How Summer Came to Canada, by William Toye (Toronto: Oxford UP, 1969). **Rev:** *APBR* 10 (Nov. 1983): 2; *Five Owls* 3 (May 1989): 68; *Teacher* 96 (May 1979): 117.

The Mountain Goats of Temlaham, by William Toye (Toronto: Oxford UP, 1969). **Rev:** *LJ* (15 Apr. 1970): 1626.

Canadian Wonder Tales, by Cyrus MacMillan (Toronto: Clark, Irwin, 1974). **Rev:** *Books and Bookmen* 20 (May 1975): 74; *Growing Point* 13 (Apr. 1975): 2610; *Junior Bookshelf* 39 (Feb. 1975): 12; *TLS* (4 Apr. 1975): 370.

The Witch of the North, by Mary Alice Downie (Ottawa: Oberon, 1975).

The Loon's Necklace, by William Toye (Toronto: Oxford UP, 1977). **Rev:** *CCL* 15/16 (1980): 134, and 60 (1990): 31; *HB* 54 (Apr. 1978): 157; *TLS* (7 Apr. 1978): 385.

The Fire Stealer, by William Toye (Toronto: Oxford UP, 1979). **Rev:** *BiC* 9 (Feb. 1980): 21; *CCB-B* 33 (June 1982): 203; *CCL* 15–16 (1980): 134; *HB* 56 (June 1980): 288; *IR* 14 (Apr. 1980): 283; *RT* 35 (May 1982): 916; *SLJ* 27 (Oct. 1980): 140; *TLS* (19 Sept. 1980): 1029.

The New Wind Has Wings: Poems from Canada, eds Mary Alice Downie and Barbara Robertson (Toronto: Oxford UP, 1984). **Rev:** *CCL* 41 (1986): 5, and 42 (1986): 53; *Five Owls* 3 (May 1989): 70.

Other

Love and Kisses Heart Book, by Luko Paljetak (Montreal: Melville Press, 1975; mini-accordion fold version, 1979) [illustrator of adult book].

'The Visual Artist and the Creative Process in Picture Books', *CCL* 4 (1976): 71–9.

'Picture Books as an Art Form', *Ocean*: 195–6.

'Fantasy and Transformation in Shadow Puppetry', *CCL* 15/16 (1980): 67–79.

'Idea to Image: the Journey of a Picture Book', *The Lion and the Unicorn* 7/8 (1983–4): 156–70.

Selected Discussions

Nodelman, Perry. 'Non-Native Primitive Art: Elizabeth Cleaver's Indian Legends', *CCL* 31/32 (1983): 69–79.

Thompson, Hilary. 'Transformation and Puppetry in the Illustrations of Elizabeth Cleaver', *CCL* 70 (1993): 72–83.

Toye, William. 'Elizabeth Cleaver (1939-1985)', *CCL* 39–40 (1985): 33–4 [reprinted from *QQ* 51 (Oct. 1985): 21].

Turbide, Deane. 'Elizabeth Cleaver Enchants with Colour and Collage', *QQ* 51 (June 85): 26.

Although she produced only a dozen books over the course of a 17-year career, Elizabeth Cleaver established herself as Canada's leading illustrator of children's books. A formally trained artist, Cleaver devoted her Master of Fine Arts thesis to the children's picture book, but the subject was of more than academic interest to her. She was deeply committed to the picture book as 'a precious art form'. She believed in its importance in the lives of children, declaring that 'artistically valuable books will educate the child's taste and visual sense. They will stimulate imagination.' To produce such 'artistically valuable' works herself, she set limits on what she would illustrate: 'For me to do my work it is necessary to be inspired by the piece of literature I am working with, and to believe in it, to have a great feeling and love for it.' What is notable about Cleaver's career is that she found a significant number of texts that inspired her to undertake the time-consuming meditation and research she found necessary before she could even begin to create one of her unique pictures.

Cleaver began her career as a freelance illustrator after undergoing surgery for cancer near the end of 1967. As she later told her editor, William Toye, she had promised in prayer that she would, if she survived the operation, devote herself to the production of beautiful books for children. Therefore, in January 1968, having accepted a commission from Toye, she quit her job at a Toronto advertising agency. That same year her coloured and black-and-white pictures for *The Wind Has Wings*, her first published work, won her an Award of Merit from the New York Illustrators Society and, in 1971, the very first Amelia Frances Howard-Gibbon Illustrator's Award. She produced a revised version, *The New Wind Has Wings*, in 1984.

After completing her initial commission, Cleaver pursued her own interests in later work: 'I love fairy tales, myths and legends; they are my "inner world", the world I love and want to re-create.' Her re-creations fall into several well-defined categories. First were the legends of North American Indians. She was, in fact, a pioneer in the development of the picture-book presentation of Canadian Native tales. Such tales had fascinated her since childhood, when she would go on family outings to a reserve near Montreal. Working with William Toye, who produced the text, Cleaver illustrated four Native legends: *How Summer Came to Canada*, a Micmac myth about Glooskap and the origin of the seasons; *The Mountain Goats of Temlaham*, a Tsimshian legend about mountain goats who avenge the wanton cruelty committed against one of their number; *The Loon's Necklace*, a Tsimshian story in which a blind man, whose vision is restored by Loon, rewards the bird with a shell necklace, thus creating the loon's distinctive markings; and *The Fire Stealer*, an Ojibway tale about the trickster Nanabozho, who brought fire to his people. Cleaver also produced black-and-white linocuts for *Canadian Wonder Tales*, a one-volume collection of Cyrus MacMillan's retellings of Native tales and other Canadian stories. Finally, she both wrote and illustrated with shadow puppets *The Enchanted Caribou*, an Inuit transformation tale about a woman changed into a white caribou.

A second interest, the folklore of French Canada, where she was educated and spent most of her life, found expression in illustrations for Mary Alice Downie's *The Witch of the North*. Her third interest was the tales and legends of Hungary, the country of her family's origin. She developed this interest in the 1950s, when she accompanied her parents to Hungary. For three years she studied at Sàrospatak, where, she would fondly recall, Amos Comenius produced *Orbis Pictus*, the first picture book for use in schools. This interest found expression in *The Miraculous Hind*, a meticulously researched and documented retelling of the legend of two brothers, Hunor and Magyar, whose pursuit of a hind leads them far from their home to found the country that became Hungary. Developed first as a National Film Board filmstrip (1971), the book version won the Canadian Association of Childrens' Librarians Bronze Medal.

Cleaver also had a deep love for two other art forms, both of which are associated with tales of wonder. Her love of ballet and stage design led to *Petrouchka*, a retelling of Stravinsky's ballet about a puppet with a soul who vainly tries to win the love of a ballerina. Cleaver was at work on *The Wooden Prince*, based on a Bartok ballet, at the time of her death. Part of her joy in doing such work was in translating an experience that depended upon a complex interaction of music and movement: 'A ballet has many ways to express character and plot. . . . With a book you have only a two-dimensional world, but there is a lot happening in that tiny universe.'

The other art form that attracted her was puppetry, especially shadow puppetry. When she was a child, her father had entertained her by casting hand-shadows of animals on the walls. With the assistance of Canada Council grants, Cleaver travelled in 1971 to Europe, Iran, and Turkey to study shadow puppetry and in 1972 to Baker Lake, NWT, to work with Inuit children in adapting their tales to presentation with shadow puppets. Because 'Shadows are mysteries', Cleaver felt that shadow puppetry was especially suited to the kind of fairy tale and mythic material that most attracted her: 'It can be the most poetic form of puppetry since it is ideal for presenting dreams, visions and transformation scenes.' Cleaver herself designed shadow puppets based on Inuit tales for a Christmas performance at Montreal's Centaur Theatre in 1971 and for her last published book, *The Enchanted Caribou*.

Cleaver's childhood heavily influenced the techniques characteristic of her work. Her happiest childhood hours were those in which she was left alone with cut-out books, to be 'transposed to another world': 'Cut-out books are associated in my mind with play and happiness.' As an adult, she found that she still enjoyed cutting paper, hence the collages she assembled to 'create feelings and moods in a contemporary way'.

Typically, Cleaver began an illustration only after long contemplation of a text and, often, considerable research into its meaning and the visual elements necessary to picture it accurately. For example, before beginning *The Mountain Goats of Temlaham*, she obtained a Canada Council travel grant to visit British Columbia, where she was able to see the mountain setting and view Tsimshian artifacts in museums. She continued the research in museums and libraries in Toronto, Montreal, and Ottawa. The actual preparation of a picture began with pencil drawings, which she transferred onto linoleum blocks. She would also prepare textured paper (monoprints) upon which she printed the blocks and which she used for her backgrounds. She would then cut and tear the elements of her collage, manipulating them to find pleasing arrangements: 'It is not planned completely, but is in part discovered and revealed.' Cleaver's materials and methods encouraged creativity: 'I can exploit the accidental.' Thus, for example, she used the white edges of torn monoprints to form snowcaps in *How Summer Came to Canada*, *The Mountain Goats of Temlaham*, and *The Loon's Necklace*.

Cleaver was always experimenting. She used such things as leaves, grass, pine needles, bark, and lace to give her two-dimensional pictures a three-dimensional quality and to form a contrast between the sharply delineated natural object and her own stylized linocuts. In *The Miraculous Hind*, she even cut out letters for the text because 'children should feel and see that there is beauty in the sound and look of words.' Cleaver readily admitted that some would see her process as creative play, but she added that 'one has to use the mind, the hands, the eyes and the heart to create a picture.'

The most striking feature of Cleaver's collages is their use of colour. In *How Summer Came to Canada* and *The Mountain Goats of Temlaham*, she uses brightly coloured strips of paper arranged in layers to establish stylized settings and, thus, to suggest a mythic world. In the former, she also uses blues and purples to convey the chill of winter and shocking reds, oranges, and greens to suggest the fertility, vibrancy, and joy of summer. In the latter, colour conveys mood. The book begins with bright, light colours to represent the world before man violated the sanctity of life by abusing the mountain goats. The central illustrations contain darker colours. These are appropriate to both the smoky lodge and the violent retribution the goats exact. When peace is restored, the bright colours return.

Less obvious, but just as powerful, is Cleaver's use of symbolism. For Cleaver, who termed herself 'an amateur Jungian', a major attraction of a story was 'the verbal or visual images, the symbols, in it'. In particular, she was concerned with the motif of transformation, using pictures to intensify or extend the meaning of the text.

Such symbolism is apparent in *How Summer Came to Canada*, where the coming of vegetation and the cycle of the seasons indicate the theme: 'life and death and change'. Cleaver intensifies this symbolic pattern with pictorial symbolism. Thus, when Glooskap dreams and defeats the power of the giant Winter, Cleaver portrays him with a tree sprouting by the side of his head, an illustration she has interpreted as 'a use of the tree as a symbol of imaginative thought'. *The Mountain Goats of Temlaham*, in which goats transform themselves into humans in order to exact retribution from people who do not respect the sacred bond of life, shows totem poles placed and coloured symbolically. In the beginning, the totem pole separating the villagers from the goats is orange, the initial colour of the sky and the villagers. To attack the goats, the villagers move to the right past this totem, symbolically moving beyond human law and restrictions. Later, on their way to the lodge of the strangers, they again move beyond their totem, but it is now green, the colour of the natural world of the goats, thereby suggesting that they have entered a territory where the goats and their laws reign. After the boy is saved, he appears between two totems. Behind him, an orange and green totem, suggestive of the blending of village life and natural life, separates him from the world of goats. The totem he approaches, tree-coloured like the one that saved him, suggests that the village will now have a protective ceremonial spirit.

Cleaver develops symbols in other ways. In *The Loon's Necklace*, she composes her design in two facing pictures. The circular form of the pictures illustrating the loon's healing of the blind man suggests a cyclic healing process. As Cleaver pointed out, in fact, the tale has profound meaning: 'Symbolically, he attains inner vision and becomes whole as he is cleansed by the deep water, symbol of purification, regeneration and birth.' In *The Fire Stealer*, she employs a device reminiscent of the transformation sequence in Gerald McDermott's *Arrow to the Sun* (1974). Like McDermott, she works within four panels resembling the frames of a film strip. Her sequence shows Nanabozho transforming himself into a birch tree and represents his psychic wholeness by having his roots cling strongly to the earth. Finally, the very technique of shadow puppetry used in *The Enchanted Caribou* was richly symbolic to Cleaver, who consciously related it to Jung's theory of the shadow, claiming that both 'attempt to lead man to self-realization and transformation'. Indeed, she interpreted the book in psychological or spiritual terms, suggesting that this tale of a girl who is transformed into a white caribou when she violates an injunction and then back into a woman when her lover seeks her out, is a symbolic presentation of the notion that girls must accept their animal natures before attaining womanhood.

Whenever Elizabeth Cleaver addressed audiences, particularly those of young artists, she conveyed her message strongly: 'I tell them how important I think children's books are, particularly how important images and story-telling can be in transforming children into adults. Actually, I think life is one big process of transformation for all of us.' Picture books played an important role in Cleaver's own development.: 'I love picture-books and one of the greatest pleasures in creating them is the way I change and grow and travel on to many new levels of existence.' Her brightly coloured *ABC* was her way of giving future generations the same loving start with books as her own. Like all of her books, it is an expression of her theory that 'The picture acts like a living person with whom I can converse. If the picture can talk back to me, it will also be capable of talking to others.' Cleaver's pictures will be talking to Canadians for many years to come.

See also: *CA* 97–100; *Junior* 4; *Profiles*; *SATA* 23.

Lindee Climo

Born: 1948, in Massachusetts.

Principal Residences: Massachusetts; Los Angeles; Prince Edward Island; Halifax.

Career: artist; illustrator; farmer.

Major Awards: Amelia Frances Howard-Gibbon Illustrator's Award (1983).

Works for Children

Chester's Barn (Montreal: Tundra, 1982). **Rev:** *BiC* 11 (Dec. 1982): 9; *CCL* 30 (1983): 69; *EL* 10 (Nov. 1982): 35; *HB* 59 (Feb. 1983): 35; *QQ* 48 (Nov. 1982): 25.

Clyde (Montreal: Tundra, 1986). **Rev:** *BiC* 15 (Nov. 1986): 35; *CCL* 52 (1988): 15; *CM* 16 (Jan. 1988): 6; *QQ* 52 (Dec. 1986): 16.

When Lindee Climo arrived on Prince Edward Island, she expressed her enthusiasm for the landscape by creating the paintings for *Chester's Barn*. Animals and art had long been very important to the artist. When she lived in Los Angeles, she spent much of her free time in the country, breeding sheep, many of which won prizes, and after moving to Canada, she divided her time between farming and painting.

Chester's Barn is a tribute to a past way of life and farming. However, the author notes, 'Here on the Island, more often than in many other places, even a specialized farmer might keep an old barn fixed up and full of all sorts of animals, simply out of appreciation and love for the old ways. Chester has that kind of barn.' The text and the 24 full-colour illustrations describe a day in the life of the barn. The central figure, Chester, works busily caring for, feeding, and loving his animals.

While the text explains in detail the habits of the animals and the nature of Chester's work, the illustrations communicate the feelings of harmony and love that permeate the farm. Nearly every picture is filled with activity: animals frolic in the barnyard, a Clydesdale prances proudly into the barn, goats leap across bags of feed, lambs clamber over Chester as he bottle-feeds them, and a newborn calf suckles. Although Chester is depicted in only five of the illustrations, his presence is evident everywhere: in the special structures he has built in the barn, in the bags and bales of food he has distributed, and in the loving look the animals give him as he closes up the barn for the night. Throughout, the brown colours create an impression of warmth and security.

If *Chester's Barn* is a tribute to an old way of life, *Clyde* is a story about how that life is threatened by modern technology. The hero, a Clydesdale, is very upset when, looking out the barn window, he sees a new tractor and fears that he will become useless and unloved. In a dream, he assumes a number of fantastic shapes that he hopes will restore his self-esteem and make him valuable to his master. If he had wheels instead of back legs, for example, he could supplant the tractor; if he had cheetah legs on the front, he could work faster than the machine. However, each of his transformations is unsatisfactory, and he wakes up to discover that the farmer still loves him and that he has a new role, taking the local children for rides. The 10 full-colour illustrations not only depict Clyde's transformations, but also reveal his foolishness. The wheels, wings, and variety of legs he sprouts make him look ridiculous. In the last illustration, he has resumed his horse form, an indication of his rejection of his fantasies; but more important, he is not alone. For the first time in the illustrations, *Clyde* is surrounded by people, five loving children who take him for a walk.

Climo's books deal with themes common to children's books: a nostalgia for a simpler, happier way of life in the country, and the use of fantasy as an escape from inner fears. In *Chester's Barn*, she has realistically presented a place where the old ways still exist; in Clyde, she has humorously depicted the resolution of inner fears—fears that most younger readers will recognize.

George Clutesi

Born: 1905, in Port Alberni, BC.

Died: 1988.

Principal Residences: Port Alberni, BC.

Career: fisherman; piledriver operator; writer; artist; lecturer.

Works for Children

Son of Raven, Son of Deer (Sidney, BC: Gray's Publishing, 1967). **Rev:** *CCL* 5 (1976): 71; *IR* 1 (Autumn 1967) 13.

Potlatch (Sidney, BC: Gray's Publishing, 1969). **Rev:** *CCL* 5 (1976): 71; *IR* 4 (Summer 1970): 19.

Like many of his people, George Clutesi, one of the best-known Native retellers of Indian legends, grew up at a time when white society was attempting to suppress awareness of and belief in traditional customs. Born in Port Alberni, British Columbia, Clutesi had heard the old stories from his father, but it was not until the 1940s, when a back injury forced him to give up his job as a piledriver operator, that he had time to reconsider his heritage. After that, he became active as an artist, folklorist, writer, and lecturer, helping his own people and sympathetic whites to discover a proud heritage that had almost been destroyed.

Clutesi's 'Introduction' to *Son of Raven, Son of Deer*, a collection of the tales of his people, the Tse-shaht, is an important statement about the nature and significance of traditional tales. Clutesi emphasized that 'tales were used widely to teach the young the many wonders of nature; the importance of all living things, no matter how small and insignificant; and particularly to acquaint [them] with the closeness of man to all animal [and] bird life and the creatures of the sea'. The tales gave the young a feeling of deep respect for creation. Moreover, they were parables illustrating good and bad behaviour. An awareness of these stories is vital for Native children, he emphasized, for the European tales they generally read in school present an alien system of values. 'This could be part of the reason so many of the Indian population of Canada are in a state of bewilderment today.'

The central figures of the 12 stories in the collection are Ah-tush-mit, Son of Deer, and Ko-ishin-mit, Son of Raven. In the opening and, perhaps, best tale, Ah-tush-mit steals fire from the dreaded Wolf People. He is a classic unlikely hero, succeeding only after the bravest, strongest, fastest, and wisest males of the village have failed. In later stories, however, he is not so heroic, and his naïvety and weakness for flattery lead him into dangerous situations. The Ko-ishin-mit stories present the well-known Raven character in his most foolish moments. Three of the tales are built around the 'bungling host' motif found in folktales around the world. Always the glutton, Raven inveigles free meals from a variety of animals and then, bound by the laws of hospitality, is forced to invite them to his home. But when he uses their methods of procuring food, he fails miserably, often injuring himself in the process.

As a consequence of their actions, both Son of Raven and Son of Deer acquire physical characteristics now common to their species. For example, deer have black smudge marks at the backs of their knees because Ah-tush-mit carried fire to the people in bands attached to his knees; ravens are black today because Ko-ishin-mit burned himself using someone else's way of cooking food. Listening to the stories, young audiences learn such lessons as 'Children should not always believe other people' and 'It is not good to copy other people.' These short stories are told in a lively, entertaining style suitable for children in the early elementary grades.

Potlatch is a longer, more complex, and detailed work. Clutesi gives a full account of the preparations, songs, dances, and other ceremonies of the 28 days of a great winter festival. What emerges is a sense of the physical and psychological quality of the event and an awareness of the communal bonds it strengthens. The book is most appropriate for junior high and high school readers.

See also: *Profiles*.

Mary-Ellen Lang Collura

Born: 1 August 1949, in Vancouver.

Principal Residences: Vancouver; Campbell River, BC.

Education: University of British Columbia (B.Ed. 1972).

Career: high school teacher; writer.

Major Awards: Canadian Library Association Young Adult Book Award (1985); IODE Violet Downey Children's Book Award (1985).

Works for Children

Winners (Saskatoon: Western Producer Prairie Books, 1984). **Rev:** *EL* 13 (Sept. 1985): 46; *HB* 62 (Sept. 1986): 627; *SLJ* 33 (Jan. 1987): 81.

Sunny (Toronto: Irwin, 1988). **Rev:** *Booklist* 86 (15 June 1990): 2000; *CM* 20 (Jan. 1992): 13.

Dreamers (Vancouver: Douglas & McIntyre, 1995). **Rev:** *CBRA* 96: 470; *CCL* 24 (Spring 1998): 43.

Drawing on her experiences as a high school teacher and on her love of horses, Mary-Ellen Lang Collura has written three young adult novels that present the personal, familial, and social pressures teenagers confront as they move towards adulthood. Her convincing delineations of the conflicts of the central characters are placed against the realistically and knowledgeably depicted backgrounds of the activities of training horses in *Winners* and *Sunny*, and of the relationships between members of a high school rock band in *Dreamers*.

In *Winners*, Jordy Threebears, a 15-year-old orphan who has lived in 11 foster homes in eight years, develops a sense of self-worth as he discovers his southern Alberta Blackfoot heritage. Living with his grandfather, a former rodeo rider who had served time in prison for killing his daughter's killer, and befriended by tribal elders, Jordy experiences the true freedom and fulfilment of riding a half-wild horse and, in doing so, learns about his deceased parents, his grandfather, and the values of his Native community. The title character of *Sunny* is an injured race horse who is befriended by Sophie and her brother Mike, who is handicapped by Down's Syndrome. Not only must the girl face the routine difficulties of adolescence, but she must deal with the hostility between and eventual breakup of her parents, caused, in part, by her father's inability to cope with his son's disability. In both stories, the central character must deal with prejudice: Jordy with vicious racism; Sophie with outsiders' attitudes to her brother. Although the heroes of these novels face their main conflicts without the help of parents, each is befriended by wise older people who draw on their own pasts to provide guidance to the teenagers. The climactic event in each novel, the horse's victory in a major competition, symbolizes the achievement of the central characters, who, in working with the horses, have developed self-confidence and better relationships with other people.

In *Dreamers*, Sam's narrative of his grade 12 year traces his painful transition from adolescence to adulthood. A member of a rock band led by Jack, his best friend since elementary school, Sam must deal with the breakup of the band, a serious injury to Jack and the ending of their friendship, and a sense of partial responsibility for the suicide of a disliked classmate. At the end of the story he accepts, for the first time, the possibility of achieving his secret ambition of becoming a writer and acknowledges the end of his youth. More complex than Collura's first two novels, *Dreamers* is less successful. In dealing with the struggles of three other teenagers, as well as Sam, along with all of their relationships with their parents, the author is unable to develop any of the characters in sufficient depth. Furthermore, the use of the band as a symbol for the tenuous bond among teenage boys is not adequately realized. Collura's considerable strengths as an author of novels for young adults are most successful when she focuses directly on one main character and presents the physical activities of horse training and riding in a concrete and detailed manner that is at once factually accurate and symbolically evocative.

See also: *CA* 165.

John Craig

Born: 1 July 1921, in Peterborough, Ont.

Died: 23 January 1982.

Principal Residences: Peterborough; Toronto.

Education: University of Manitoba (BA 1951); University of Toronto (MA 1952).

Career: market researcher; writer.

Major Awards: Vicky Metcalf Award (1980).

Works for Children

Wagons West (Toronto: Dent, 1955).

The Long Return (Toronto: McClelland & Stewart, 1959). **Rev:** *IR* 10 (Winter 1976): 18.

No Word for Good-bye (Toronto: Peter Martin, 1969). **Rev:** *CCL* 3 (1975): 88; *EL* 12 (1984): 14; *IR* 3 (Summer 1969): 9; *SLJ* 25 (May 1979): 84.

Zach (New York: Coward McCann, 1972); published as *Who Wants to be Alone?* (Richmond Hill, Ont.: Scholastic, 1974). **Rev:** *CCL* 3 (1975): 88; *IR* 7 (Summer 1973): 27; *SLJ* 27 (Sept. 1980): 43.

The Clearing (Toronto: Longman, 1975). **Rev:** *IR* 9 (Summer 1975): 25.

The Wormburners (Richmond Hill, Ont.: Scholastic, 1975).

Chappie and Me (New York: Dodd, Mead, 1979); published as *Ain't Lookin'* (Richmond Hill, Ont.: Scholastic, 1979).

The Last Canoe (Toronto: Peter Martin, 1979).

Selected Discussions

Ferns, John. 'John Craig: An Under-Estimated Writer?', *CCL* 33 (1984): 32–9.

John Craig spent his childhood and teenage years enjoying two activities that appear frequently in his books for children and young adults: playing team sports in winter and spring and, in the summer, vacationing on a lake in central Ontario. His understanding of athletics and love of the outdoors inform his novels, which could be categorized under several headings: adventure stories, historical novels, sports novels, captivity narratives, mysteries, modern problem fiction, and summer vacation stories.

However, one category encompasses them all: the *bildungsroman*—the development of a young person, usually male, who grows in understanding of himself, other people, and his role in the world. As his character Zach remarks, 'How can a man know what to believe in unless he first knows what he is?' For Zach, last member of the Agawa tribe, this involves a long journey across the Canadian and American Prairies searching for clues about his ancestors. In *The Long Return*, Thad Cameron, captured by Ojibway warriors, learns to understand and respect his captors before he returns home a mature and confident young man. Joe Giffen, narrator of *Chappie and Me*, barnstorming during the Depression with an African-American baseball team, initially thinks 'the world I found myself part of was completely foreign to me.' By the end of the summer, he is accepted by the group and understands his teammates as individuals.

The most important lessons Craig's young heroes learn are the need to understand others and to work with a group. The runners in *The Wormburners*, a group of poor and racially mixed inner-city children, earn their way to the national cross-country championships by co-operating. Zach leaves his home alone, but returns with four other people—a disillusioned African-American athlete, a runaway teenage boy, a rich hippie girl, and a middle-aged man who has left a successful business life—all determined that, as a group, they will beat the odds against them. Playing with the All Stars, a diverse group united by their love of baseball and bitterness about the prejudice they face, Joe Giffen learns to understand true teamwork.

Craig's best two books dealing with the theme of maturation portray the relationship between a white teenager and Native people. In *The Long Return*, Thad realizes that if he is going to escape he must learn the skills of his captors; in learning these he develops love and loyalty for his Ojibway 'mother and father'. *No Word for Good-bye*, Craig's most acclaimed novel, focuses on Ken Warren, a 15-year-old spending the summer with his parents at their lake cabin. Early in July he meets Paul Onaman, an Ojibway teenager with whom he develops a close friendship, learning the Ojibway ways of fishing from him. More importantly, he learns about the dignity and hardships of the Ojibways' lives. Ken hopes to overcome the injustices suffered by Paul and his family. On one level he is successful, solving the mystery of a series of break-ins that prejudiced summer residents have blamed on the Native people. On another, Ken fails: a large land-development corporation claims the Indians' camp, and, when he returns to the lake at Thanksgiving for a visit with Paul, he discovers that the Indians have left for the North. He cannot help them, and he learns the painful truth that there is no word for 'good-bye'.

At times, Craig falls into the clichés typical of the genres he uses. In *The Wormburners*, the underdog team wins against seemingly impossible odds. Both *The Long Return* and *No Word for Good-bye* make use of the staples of boys' adventure stories: cliff-hanger chapter endings, overdeveloped mysteries, and stereotypical 'bad guys'. However, he writes sympathetically and knowledgeably about the traditions and present hardships of Native people. They are courageous when dealing with an insensitive and exploitative white bureaucracy, and, although no easy solutions to their plight are possible, they combat despair and injustice with dignity and fortitude. Craig is at his best when presenting his young heroes as they grow to maturity in a natural setting. Thad Cameron must respond not only to his captors but to the harsh, magnificent landscape. Ken Warren comes to understand that Lake Kinnewabi is more than an idyllic setting for two summer months each year; it is a place where the Ojibway have lived for centuries with dignity and in harmony with nature. He realizes that life is not simple, that the individual must develop inner integrity and strength in order to live successfully with himself and those around him.

See also: *CA* 101; *Profiles*; *SATA* 23; *TCCW*; *WSMP*.

Beatrice Culleton

(now Beatrice Mosionier)

Born: 27 August 1949, in St Boniface, Manitoba.

Principal Residences: Toronto; Winnipeg.

EDUCATION: George Brown College, Toronto; Banff School of Fine Arts.

CAREER: accounting clerk; bookkeeper; publisher; writer.

WORKS FOR CHILDREN

In Search of April Raintree (Winnipeg: Pemmican, 1983); revised as *April Raintree* (Winnipeg: Pemmican, 1984). **Rev:** *BiC* 13 (Feb. 1984): 30; *QQ* 49 (Nov. 1983): 20; *EL* 13 (Nov. 1985): 45; *Queen's Quarterly* 94 (Spring 1987): 191.

Spirit of the White Bison (Winnipeg: Pemmican, 1985).

Christopher's Folly, as Beatrice Mosionier, illus. Terry Gallagher (Winnipeg: Pemmican, 1996).

OTHER

'Native Peoples', *Writers on Writing: Guide to Writing and Illustrating Children's Books*, ed. David Booth (Markham, Ont.: Overlea House, 1989), 120–3.

SELECTED DISCUSSIONS

Fee, Margery. 'Upsetting Fake Ideals: Jeannette Armstrong's "Slash" and Beatrice Culleton's "April Raintree"', *Native Writers and Canadian Writing*, ed. W.H. New (Vancouver: U British Columbia P, 1990).

Rowan, Norma. 'The Outsider Within: The Portrayal of the Native Child in Some Recent Canadian Children's Stories', *CCL* 61 (1991): 6–18.

Stott, Jon C. *Native Americans in Children's Literature* (Phoenix: Oryx Press, 1995), 171–6.

'It's not meant to be accusatory; it's something for the reader to read and think about.' So spoke Beatrice Culleton about her novel *In Search of April Raintree*, one of the few novels about contemporary Canadian Native life written by a Native author. Culleton grew up in a number of foster homes, as did the title heroine of her novel, experiencing the prejudices directed against her people: 'White-skinned people cannot possibly understand what it feels like to be another colour. That fact causes separation.' After she lost two sisters to suicide, she decided to create the novel, in part as an outlet for her grief.

The novel is the first-person account of a young Métis woman's long quest for her personal and cultural identity. Alcoholism and illness cause the breakup of the Raintree family, and April spends her childhood in a series of foster homes. Although some of the foster parents are loving, most are not. In an attempt to find happiness, she denies her Native heritage, which upsets her activist sister, Cheryl. Marriage to a Toronto socialite ends disastrously, and when April returns to Winnipeg, she discovers that her sister has fallen victim to prostitution and drugs. Brutally raped by three white men, April is filled with hatred. Only after her sister's suicide and the discovery of her sister's child does April find the focus for her life and a hope for her nephew and her people. Whereas some reviewers were upset by the anger and the harshness in the novel, it has generally been praised for the vivid realism and the fairness with which it presents social conditions. In 1984, a revised edition, *April Raintree*, was published. Strong language and graphic scenes were modified to make the novel suitable for use in high school literature programs.

Spirit of the White Bison, Culleton's second book, is intended for younger readers. The first-person narrative of a buffalo, it recounts the decimation of the herds during the last half of the nineteenth century. 'It was not a quiet, accidental extermination', Culleton notes in her 'Introduction'. 'The horror was that the killings were deliberate, planned, military actions. Destroy the livelihood of the Indians and win a war.' During its long life, the White Bison sees the arrival of more and more hunters, the building of the railroad, and the disastrous effects of European civilization and disease on the Native people. At the story's conclusion, the bison and its Native friend, Lone Wolf, are buried side by side. Their deaths symbolize the end of a way of life that has been needlessly and atrociously destroyed.

Using a series of dream visions, *Christopher's Folly* also recounts the ways in which people have destroyed the ideal harmony between humans and animals. When Christopher receives a toy ship for his birthday, he becomes so absorbed in playing with it that he completely neglects Princess, his dog. In a dream, Christopher then sails his ship to a land where all creatures live in harmony. The animals generously provide for Christopher, but he becomes greedy, demanding so much from Buffalo that Buffalo disappears. He then demands so much fur of Wolf that it, too, disappears. Eventually, Christopher realizes that all of the remaining animals avoid him. Finally, the lonely Christopher loses the arrogance that made him abuse the kindness of the animals. He realizes that he cannot undo the harm that he did to Buffalo and Wolf, but he decides that he can show love and respect for the remaining animals. Waking from one of his dreams, Christopher shows this change in attitude by paying attention to his neglected pet.

Although Culleton's works do contain anger and sadness because of the wrong committed against her people and the waste of so many lives and so many natural resources, the tone of her books is optimistic. As April holds her nephew, Henry Liberty, she thinks, 'Cheryl had once said, "All life dies to give new life." Cheryl had died. But for Henry Lee and me, there would be a tomorrow. And it would be better. I would strive for it.' At the conclusion of *Spirit of the White Bison* are the words, 'My spirit would return again in the future to walk with those who were gentle but strong.' At the end of *Christopher's Folly*, the reformed Christopher enjoys some of the ideal harmony he saw in his dream visions because Princess 'nuzzled him, as if she understood exactly what he was promising'. Culleton's works thus embody the sense of hope, the belief in a renaissance of Native culture that characterizes much contemporary Native writing.

See also: *CA* 120.

Kady MacDonald Denton

Born: 22 July 1942, in Winnipeg.

Principal Residences: Winnipeg; Toronto; Brandon, Man.

Education: University of Toronto; Banff Centre for Fine Arts; Niagara College; Chelsea School of Art, London, England.

Career: stage designer; art instructor; author; illustrator.

Major Awards: Amelia Frances Howard-Gibbon Illustrator's Award (1990, 1999); Mr Christie's Book Award (1990); Governor-General's Award for Illustration (1998).

Works for Children

Written and Illustrated by Kady MacDonald Denton

The Picnic (New York: Dutton, 1988). **Rev:** *CCB-B* 41 (June 1988): 202; *NYTBR* (11 Mar. 1988): 103.

Granny Is a Darling (Toronto: Collier Macmillan, 1988). **Rev:** *CM* 17 (Jan. 1989): 34; *CM* 17 (Jan. 1989): 34; *HB* 67 (Jan. 1991): 109; *SLJ* 35 (Feb. 1989): 69.

Dorothy's Dream (Toronto: Kids Can Press, 1988). **Rev:** *CM* 17 (Jan. 1989): 34; *RT* 43 (Oct. 1989): 57; *SLJ* 35 (Feb. 1989): 69.

The Christmas Boot (Toronto: Little, Brown, 1990). **Rev:** *SLJ* 36 (Oct. 1990): 35.

Janet's Horses (London: Walker, 1990).

Would They Love a Lion? (New York: Kingfisher, 1995). **Rev:** *CCB-B* 48 (July 1995): 381; *EL* 23 (Mar. 1996): 24; *QQ* 61 (Sept. 1995): 76; *SLJ* 41 (July 1995): 55.

Watch Out William (New York: Kingfisher, 1997).

Illustrated by Kady MacDonald Denton

Let's Go Shopping, Ned, by Pam Hope-Zinnemann (London: Walker, 1986). **Rev:** *SLJ* 33 (May 1987): 120.

Time for Bed, Ned, by Pam Hope-Zinnemann (London: Walker, 1986). **Rev:** *SLJ* 33 (May 1987): 120.

Find Your Coat, Ned, by Pam Hope-Zinnemann (London: Walker, 1987). **Rev:** *SLJ* 35 (Sept. 1988): 175.

Let's Play Ball, Ned, by Pam Hope-Zinnemann (London: Walker, 1987). **Rev:** *SLJ* 35 (Sept. 1988): 175.

Til All the Stars Have Fallen: Canadian Poems for Children, selected by David Booth (Toronto: Kids Can Press, 1989). **Rev:** *BiC* 18 (Dec. 1989): 19; *CM* 18 (Mar. 1990): 69; *EL* 17 (Mar. 1990): 25; *QQ* 55 (Nov. 1989): 14; *SLJ* 36 (Dec. 1990): 114.

The Story of Little Quack, by Betty Gibson (Toronto: Kids Can Press, 1990). **Rev:** *CM* 18 (Nov. 1990): 267; *QQ* 56 (Sept. 1990): 19; *SLJ* 37 (May 1991): 78.

Before I Go to Sleep: Bible Stories, Poems, and Prayers for Children, edited by Ann Pilling (New York: Crown, 1990). **Rev:** *CCL* 61 (1991): 90; *CM* 18 (Nov. 1990): 271; *QQ* 56 (Oct. 1990): 17; *SLJ* 37 (Mar. 1991): 117.

The Traveling Musicians of Bremen, retold by P.K. Page (Toronto: Kids Can Press, 1991). **Rev:** *CCL* 70 (1993): 84; *QQ* 57 (Aug. 1991): 24; *SLJ* 38 (May 1992): 105.

Jenny and Bob, by David Wynn Millward (New York: Delacorte Press, 1991). **Rev:** *CM* 19 (Oct. 1991): 306; *EL* 19 (Mar. 1992): 17; *SLJ* 38 (Jan. 1992): 94.

The Kingfisher Children's Bible, retold by Ann Pilling (New York: Kingfisher, 1993). **Rev:** *EL* 21 (Mar. 1994): 46; *TES* (10 Dec. 1993): 30.

Realms of Gold: Myths and Legends from Around the World, retold by Ann Pilling (New York: Kingfisher, 1993). **Rev:** *CCB-B* 46 (July 1993): 356; *EL* 22 (Sept. 1994): 48; *SLJ* 39 (May 1993): 120.

Toes Are to Tickle, by Shen Roddie (Toronto: Reed Books Canada, 1997). **Rev:** *CCB-B* 51 (Sept. 1997): 24; *QQ* 63 (May 1997): 44; *SLJ* (Sept. 1997): 192.

A Child's Treasury of Nursery Rhymes, compiled by Kady MacDonald Denton (Toronto: Kids Can Press, 1998).

The Umbrella Party, by Janet Lunn (Toronto: Groundwood, 1998). **Rev:** *QQ* 64 (Mar. 1998): 71.

The Arctic Fox, by Mary Ellis (Toronto: HarperCollins, 1998).

Selected Discussions

Jenkinson, Dave. 'Kady MacDonald Denton: Watercolorist Extraordinaire', *EM* 21 (May 1994): 61–4.

During a year she spent with her husband in England, Kady MacDonald Denton put to good use her lifelong love of reading stories and drawing. While she was taking a course at the Chelsea School of Art, she met author Pam Hope-Zinnemann and began discussing ideas for a series of books for young readers. The two collaborated on *Let's Go, Ned*, published in 1986, and three sequels. Since then Denton has illustrated poetry collections, traditional tales, realistic and fantasy stories, and non-fiction, adapting her pen-and-ink and watercolour pictures to reflect and expand on the meanings of the words.

Denton has written and illustrated four books about the fantasy worlds created by young children. *Granny Is a Darling* deals with a familiar subject: a small child's night-time fear of monsters. When Billy hears the snores of his visiting grandmother, he imitates the noises, which he thinks are made by monsters, to drive them away. The early and later single-page pictures of the child's daytime world are surrounded by borders, while the night-time events are presented in borderless double-spreads. As his imagination expands, transforming ordinary night noises into the fearful sounds of monsters, Billy is without the secure frameworks of his normal world. White and pale blue backgrounds are replaced by shadowy brown walls and dark blue closets. When he scares the creatures away, light blue washes are again used for backgrounds. Unlike Billy, who can't sleep, the heroine of *Dorothy's Dream* fears that she will miss something if she does go to sleep. Her older brother and sister are seen in single-spreads enclosed by borders; she dances around in borderless double-spreads. When she does fall asleep, the rocking horse in her room becomes part of a marvellous carousel she dreams about, and her dolls, now life-sized, dance with her.

Denton's illustrations provide readers with a surprise ending in *Janet's Horses*, the story of a girl who likes to pretend she has horses while her mother is out shopping. The meadow and hill around which the horses gallop are the green carpeted hallway and stairs. However, when the mother returns, the pictures show that the make-believe horses are the little girl's real brother and sister, who have become tired of being objects in Janet's imaginative games. Anna, in *Would They Love a Lion?*, also concerns a younger sibling. Feeling inadequate after the arrival of a new baby, she imagines herself as various animals and decides to become a lion that, although it can scare people with its roar, can take naps with the family and be loved. Crayon-and-watercolour-wash illustrations communicate the humour of the girl's using her reversible coat to assume the shapes of various animals. The baby is not mentioned in the written text; however, her presence in five of the illustrations reveals the focus of Anna's unhappiness.

Denton has created award-winning illustrations for two collections of poetry. *Til All the Stars Have Fallen* presented her with the challenge of developing visual continuity for a collection of short poems that were about a variety of subjects and had been selected by someone else. She did this, in part, by using as her dominant medium pen-and-ink sketches usually highlighted with one or more washes. When more than one poem is printed on a page, Denton arranges her illustrations so that one leads to another as if each were linked by an invisible, flowing, curved line. Frequently, continuity from one double-spread to the next is achieved through the first picture on the new page standing in the same location as the last one on the previous page. Generally, there are no sharp contrasts between illustrations on successive pages, the main exception being between the double-spreads illustrating 'The North Wind' and 'Poems can give you'. In the first, black washes and streaks of red surround a horse leaping through the sky with a child clinging to its neck. In the next, a girl stands playing a flute in a room coloured soft pinks and blues. The power of the first illustration is so intense that the gentler, more relaxed one provides a rest for the viewer. Individual illustrations satisfyingly depict the content and enhance the tones of the various poems. Small pen-and-ink sketches present the humour of a child sitting in a mud puddle and a boy hiding behind a hedge preparing to throw an apple at his unsuspecting brother.

In illustrating the 12-dozen poems she selected for *A Child's Treasury of Nursery Rhymes*, Denton wanted, she wrote, 'to catch those images I saw springing from the rhymes; to please those who read pictures and not words by telling my own visual stories'. The pictures depict clothing styles and objects from the Renaissance to the late nineteenth century, as do those from many other collections. Often there are several small pictures on a page, each one depicting a character or incident from a short poem or from a verse of a longer poem. Occasionally a longer poem will be complemented with a double-spread. While many of the water-colour paintings merely depict what is stated in the words, others add new meanings and interpretations. For example, the title character for 'Jack Be Nimble' is presented as a mouse that leaps into the air after a cat has surprised it nibbling at a large wedge of cheese.

Denton's skill at portraying humorous relationships between animals and people is seen in her illustrations for P.K. Page's adaptation of the Grimms' *The Traveling Musicians* and Betty Gibson's *Little Quack*. In the former, about a group of displaced animals who achieve happiness by co-operating, the cover, endpapers, and half-title page all depict a procession, from left to right, of the donkey, dog, rooster, and cat moving away from unhappy pasts. During the first half of the story, the illustrations present, in cumulative fashion, the formation of the group. When first encountered, each animal looks despondent, but after it joins the procession, it walks, dances, or flies happily. The cowardly robbers are modern miscreants dressed in 'punk' clothing, spiked hair, and earrings and surrounded by the TV sets, stereo equipment, and microwave ovens they have stolen. Their cockiness quickly changes to fear when the animals attack.

The opening and concluding double-spreads for *Little Quack* reveal the change in the emotional situation of a small boy. Both are set in a barnyard and, in both, Jackie is the dominant figure. In the first, he leans unhappily on a rail, lonely because none of the animals pay attention to him; all are facing away from him. In the distance his father walks away, the family dog following. At the end, Jackie is happy; Little Quack, a duck he'd befriended, but who had gone missing for a month, is back. The boy hugs his pet, who, with its ducklings, paddles happily in an old bathtub. Jackie's mother and father look smilingly on, while surrounding him are all of the barnyard animals who earlier had ignored him. The intervening illustrations reveal the boy's changing emotions: the joy and then deep satisfaction when he acquires his pet; the anxiety, loneliness, and sadness when it disappears; and, finally, the surprise and recovered happiness when Little Quack and the ducklings are found.

Denton also has illustrated Ann Pilling's three collections of traditional stories. On the title page of *Before I Go to Sleep*, a collection of Bible stories and related poems, a small girl holding a candle is followed by a small boy and an older boy and girl. All wear pajamas and she leads them into the book and the bedtime pieces that follow. The illustrations for the Old and New Testament stories depict traditional costumes and architecture and communicate the emotional tones of the narratives through the use of one or two dominant colours. *The Kingfisher Children's Bible* includes all of the major stories, including such darker ones as 'God Destroys the City of Sodom' and 'The Ten Plagues of Egypt'. Denton does not include the small pajama-clothed figures, focusing directly on the stories, including two or three small illustrations for each piece. The illustrations accompanying *Realms of Gold*, a collection of myths and legends from many lands, use the appropriate architecture and costumes for each story and also include coloured sketches of artifacts that are important in the individual stories.

Kady MacDonald Denton's illustrations for both her own and others' stories reveal her versatility with the combined media of pen-and-ink and watercolour. Whether she is dealing with the fantasies of small children, poems reflecting many moods, traditional stories from many lands, or humorous adventures of animals, she carefully designs her pictures, using line patterns, colours, and details that precisely reflect and often enhance both the subject matter and mood she is depicting.

Jacques de Roussan

Born: 12 February 1929 in Paris, France.

Principal Residences: Paris; Montreal.

Education: University of Paris (BA 1948); Sorbonne (MA).

Career: accountant; publisher; writer/illustrator; translator.

Major Awards: Amelia Frances Howard-Gibbon Illustrator's Award (1973).

Works for Children

Au-delà du soleil/Beyond the Sun (Montreal: Tundra, 1972). **Rev:** *IR* 7 (Winter 1973): 18; *HB* 53 (Dec. 1977): 652.

If I Came From Mars/Si j'étais martien (Montreal: Tundra, 1977). **Rev:** *IR* 12 (Winter 1978): 47; *HB* 53 (Dec. 1977): 652.

Montreal picture-book author Jacques de Roussan is a person of many talents. Born in Paris, he was twice captured while working with the French Resistance during World War II. Since coming to Canada, he has worked as a printer, journalist, art critic, biographer, and poet. His interest in scientific concepts and abstract painting resulted in the creation of his two picture books.

A bilingual work, *Beyond the Sun* is at once factual, imaginative, and creative. The story is simple. Peter dreams one night that he is an astronaut and explores the solar system and outer reaches of the universe before returning home. De Roussan presents astronomical information about the heavens through words and illustrations, but focuses more strongly on the imagination. Peter is a young boy just beginning to understand his potential for growth and discovery. The silk-screened illustrations are composed mainly of geometrical shapes and have bold primary and secondary colours. They accurately depict objects of outer space while at the same time giving an impression of Peter's sense of wonder and discovery.

Peter also is the central character of *If I Came from Mars*. This time he dreams he is the first human being to have been born in a Martian colony. Flying his spaceship towards Earth, he sees the beauty of the planet from a distance and then views the grandeur of mountains and oceans and, more importantly, the wonder of animals and people. Reluctantly, he heads back to Mars. The simple, abstract drawings depict the sights Peter sees and suggest the beauty of the planet he has never known. If the implicit message of *Beyond the Sun* is that we grow by exploring the unknown, that of *If I Came From Mars* is that we must never forget the joy of life on our own planet; we must refamiliarize ourselves with a beauty to which an outward focus may make us insensitive.

Although he is the hero of both books, Peter is not depicted in the illustrations. Consequently, young readers can identify with Peter, imagining themselves as space explorers and entering into Peter's emotions. Having read the two books, young readers not only will have acquired knowledge about space, but also will have become more sensitive to their own potential and to the world in which they live.

See also: *CA* 123; *Profiles*; *SATA* 31.

Mary Alice Downie

Born: 12 February 1934, in Alton, Ill.

Principal Residences: Alton; Toronto; Kingston, Ont.

Education: University of Toronto (BA 1955).

Career: secretary; editor; librarian; writer.

Works for Children

The Wind Has Wings: Poems from Canada, edited with Barbara Robertson, illus. Elizabeth Cleaver (Toronto: Oxford UP, 1968). **Rev:** *CCB-B* 22 (July 1969): 173; *CCL* 42 (1986): 53; *HB* 45 (Apr. 1969): 181; *IR* 3 (Winter 1969): 23.

Honor Bound (Toronto: Oxford UP, 1971; rev. edn, Kingston: Quarry Press, 1991). **Rev:** *CCL* 21 (Fall 1995): 96; *IR* 6 (Winter 1972): 26.

Dragon on Parade (Toronto: Peter Martin, 1974). **Rev:** *IR* 9 (Spring 1975): 36.

The Magical Adventures of Pierre (Toronto: Nelson, 1974).

Scared Sarah, illus. Laszlo Gal (Toronto: Nelson, 1974).

The Witch of the North: Folk Tales of French Canada, illus. Elizabeth Cleaver (Ottawa: Oberon, 1975). **Rev:** *CCL* 11 (1978): 93; *IR* 10 (Winter 1976): 30.

The King's Loon, illus. Ron Berg (Toronto: Kids Can Press, 1979). **Rev:** *CCL* 29 (1983): 77; *SLJ* 27 (Oct. 1980): 144.

The Last Ship (Toronto: Peter Martin, 1980). **Rev:** *CCL* 29 (1983): 77; *IR* 15 (Feb. 1981): 35; *QQ* 48 (June 1982): 3.

A Proper Acadian, with George Rawlyk, illus. Ron Berg (Toronto: Kids Can Press, 1981). **Rev:** *BiC* 10 (Apr. 1981): 29; *CCL* 26 (1982): 60; *IR* 15 (Apr. 1981): 35; *QQ* 47 (May 1981): 14.

Seeds and Weeds: A Book of Country Crafts, illus. Jillian Hulme Gilliland (Toronto: North Winds, 1981).

The Wicked Fairy-Wife: A French-Canadian Folktale (Toronto: Kids Can Press, 1983). **Rev:** *BiC* 13 (June 1984): 26; *SLJ* 30 (May 1984): 78.

Alison's Ghosts, with John Downie (Toronto: Nelson, 1984). **Rev:** *QQ* 50: (June 1984): 35.

Jenny Greenteeth, illus. Barbara Reid (Toronto: Kids Can Press, 1984). **Rev:** *CCL* 41 (1986): 56; *QQ* 50 (Nov. 1984): 13; *SLJ* 31 (May 1985): 72.

The New Wind Has Wings, edited with Barbara Robertson, illus. Elizabeth Cleaver (Toronto: Oxford UP, 1984). **Rev:** *BiC* 13 (Dec. 1984): 12; *CCB-B* 38 (Apr. 1985): 145; *CCL* 39 (1985): 95; *QQ* 50 (Nov. 1984): 11; *SLJ* 32 (Nov. 1985): 83.

Stones and Cones: Country Crafts for Kids, illus. Jillian Hulme Gilliland (Toronto: Scholastic, 1984).

The Window of Dreams: New Canadian Writing for Children, edited with Elizabeth Greene and M.A. Thompson (Kingston: Quarry Press, 1986). **Rev:** *BiC* 15 (Oct. 1986): 38; *CCL* 57 (1990): 142; *QQ* 52 (July 1986): 10.

How the Devil Got His Cat, illus. Jillian Hulme Gilliland (Kingston: Quarry Press, 1988). **Rev:** *CCL* 57 (1990): 116; *EL* 17 (Sept. 1989): 57.

Doctor Dwarf and Other Poems for Children by A.M. Klein, edited with Barbara Robertson (Kingston: Quarry Press, 1990).

The Buffalo Boy and the Weaver Girl, with Mann Hwa Huang-Hsu, illus. Jillian Hulme Gilliland (Kingston: Quarry Press, 1989). **Rev:** *EL* 17 (May 1990): 59; *QQ* 55 (Sept. 1989): 22.

Cathal the Giant Killer and the Dun Shaggy Filly, illus. Jillian Hulme Gilliland (Kingston: Quarry Press, 1991). **Rev:** *CCL* 73 (1994): 86; *CM* 19 (Oct. 1991): 304; *EL* 19 (Mar. 1992): 58; *QQ* 57 (June 1991): 25.

The Cat Park, illus. Kathryn Naylor (Kingston: Quarry Press, 1993).

Snow Paws, illus. Kathryn Naylor (Toronto: Stoddart, 1996). **Rev:** *CBRA* (1996): 439; *CCL* 86 (1997): 59; *QQ* 62 (Aug. 1996): 43.

Other

'But What About Canadian History?', *CCL* 83 (1996): 86–9.

Mary Alice Downie has described herself as an author of 'false starts': '[*The Wind Has Wings*] sprang from the ashes of an anthology for four to six-year olds . . . ; *Honor Bound* from an eighteenth-century diary owned by a landlady. *The Witch of the North* resulted from reading done for an ill-fated sequel to *Honor Bound*.' However, from these false starts have come books that have made Downie a significant creator of historical novels, editor of anthologies, and reteller of legends and folktales.

When Downie's children began school, she discovered that there were no suitable books of Canadian poetry for children their age. She and co-compiler Barbara Robertson set about collecting poems for what became *The Wind Has Wings*, which has become a Canadian classic. Because it includes a number of poets published before 1945, the anthology presents a considerable challenge to younger readers or listeners. Nonetheless, it is a significant landmark for Canadian children's literature — the first publication of a major anthology for children consisting entirely of Canadian poetry. The second edition, *The New Wind Has Wings*, contains more contemporary poems. Downie and Robertson also have edited *Doctor Dwarf and Other Poems for Children*, a selection of the works of A.M. Klein, while Downie worked with M.A. Thompson and Elizabeth Greene in editing *The Window of Dreams: New Canadian Writing for Children*.

When told that her proposed edition of an eighteenth-century diary was unsuitable for publication, Downie used it as the basis for her first historical novel, *Honor Bound*, written in collaboration with her husband, John. It is the story of the Averys, an eighteenth-century Loyalist family that flees from Philadelphia to the eastern end of Lake Ontario to create a new life on a wilderness homestead. As she prepares to leave her lovely home, the mother laments, 'Canada! . . . that's a wilderness. There's nothing up there but Indians and wild beasts!' However, the courage of the family, their loyalty to each other, and the new and generous friends they meet give them a fulfilling life. The main character is Miles, a hot-headed boy who dreams of the glorious life of a soldier. In his new environment, he acquires maturity and a sense of honour, even if it means warning a notorious thief of impending capture. Although the novel does not delve deeply into character and has a relatively slight plot, it gives a strong sense of the life of the immigrant family in its new environment.

Downie's other historical stories, *Scared Sarah*, *The King's Loon*, *The Last Ship*, and *A Proper Acadian* are, like *Honor Bound*, carefully researched works that provide an impression of the daily lives of early Canadians. Of these, *The King's Loon*, in which the young hero, Andre, comes to appreciate the foster home from which he ran away, and *A Proper Acadian*, in which a Bostonian staying with relatives in Nova Scotia bravely casts his lot with the persecuted Acadians, are the strongest, with the main characters facing and resolving conflicts central to their lives.

Downie has adapted two types of French-Canadian legends: the involved story of a questing young man who, after many tests, earns the hand of a beautiful princess, and the tale of people who match their wits against the devil. *The Magical Adventures of Pierre* and *The Wicked Fairy-Wife* are of the former type, and *How the Devil Got His Cat* and most of the stories in the collection *The Witch of the North* are of the latter. In *The Witch*, Downie uses the device of a grandmother telling a group of wondering children stories that supposedly happened to her deceased husband or to other people whom she knew. The devil, always anxious for souls, is the major actor, enticing unwitting but often overly confident people away from the security of home and church. There is a balanced mixture of humour and terror in the stories. In *How the Devil Got His Cat*, the title character is fooled by a clever Mother Superior, who is able to give up the convent cat rather than a human soul, in order to honour her part of a bargain.

Downie has retold traditional stories from other lands, including *Cathal the Giant Killer and the Dun Shaggy Filly*, a Scottish tale about a man who receives help from animals in his quest to recover his stolen wife, and *The Buffalo Boy and the Weaver Girl*, in which a young Chinese man driven from his home achieves success with the aid of a magic buffalo. *Snow Paws* is a picture-book fantasy for young children, while *Seeds and Weeds* and *Stones and Cones* are craft books for younger readers.

See also: *CANR* 10, 26, 52; *CAR* 25–8; *Profiles* 2; *SATA* 13, 87; *TCCW* 4; *WSMP*.

Brian Doyle

Born: 12 August 1935, in Ottawa.

Principal Residences: Ottawa.

Education: Carleton University (BJ 1957, BA 1958).

Career: journalist; high school English teacher; children's writer.

Major Awards: Canadian Library Association Book of the Year Award (1983, 1989, 1997); Mr Christie's Book Award (1990, 1996); Vicky Metcalf Award (1991).

Works for Children

Hey Dad! (Vancouver: Groundwood, 1978). **Rev:** *CCL* 22 (1981): 47–9; *IR* 12 (Autumn 1978): 57; *SLJ* 27 (Sept. 1980): 43.

You Can Pick Me Up at Peggy's Cove (Vancouver: Groundwood, 1979). **Rev:** *BiC* 9

(Aug. 1980): 32; *CCL* 22 (1981): 49; *CM* 8 (Autumn 1980): 227; *IR* 14 (Aug. 1980): 45; *QQ* 46 (Aug. 1980), 30; *SLJ* 27 (Sept. 1980): 43.

Up to Low (Vancouver: Groundwood, 1981); **Rev:** *APBR* 10 (Nov. 1983): 2; *BiC* 12 (Feb. 1983): 32; *CCL* 37 (1985): 67, and 50 (1988): 71; *HB* 60 (Feb. 1984): 101–3; *Maclean's* 95 (13 Dec. 1982): 56; *QQ* 48 (Nov. 1982): 26, and 48 (Dec. 1982): 27.

Angel Square (Toronto: Groundwood, 1984). **Rev:** *BYP* 1 (Apr. 1987): 1; *CCL* 44 (1986): 69; *Quarry* 34 (Winter 1985), 90; *QQ* 50 (Nov. 1984): 18; *SLJ* 33 (May 1987): 97.

Easy Avenue (Toronto: Groundwood, 1988). **Rev:** *BiC* 17 (Dec. 1988): 11; *BYP* 2 (Oct. 1988): 12: *CCL* 54 (1989): 71; *Maclean's* 101 (26 Dec. 1988): 60; *QQ* 54 (Oct. 1988): 12.

Covered Bridge (Toronto: Groundwood, 1990). **Rev:** *CCL* 64 (1991): 90; *CM* 19 (Mar. 1991): 88; *EL* 18 (Mar. 1991): 22, 50; *QQ* 56 (Oct. 1990): 16.

Spud Sweetgrass (Toronto: Groundwood, 1992). **Rev:** *QQ* 58 (Sept. 1992): 72.

Spud in Winter (Toronto: Groundwood, 1995). **Rev:** *CCL* 80 (1995): 80; *QQ* 61 (Mar. 1995): 75.

Uncle Ronald (Toronto: Groundwood, 1996); **Rev:** *CBRA* (1996): 471; *CCB-B* 50 (Feb. 1997): 203; *EL* 24 (Mar. 1997): 28; *HB* 73 (May 1997): 318; *QQ* 62 (Oct. 1996): 49, and 63 (Feb. 1997): 51.

Selected Discussions

Dunnion, Kristyn. 'Making Magic: An Interview with Brian Doyle', *CCL* 76 (1994): 39–47.

Garvie, Maureen. 'Up Doyle Way', *QQ* 61 (Mar. 1995): 74–5.

Harker, Mary J. 'Textual Capers: Carnival in the Novels of Brian Doyle', *CCL* 63 (1991): 41–52.

——. 'Crafting a Story: Brian Doyle on the Act of Writing', *CCL* 76 (1994): 31–8.

Katz, Wendy R. '"Dying and Loving Somebody"', *CCL* 22 (1981): 47–50.

Vanderhoof, Ann. 'Prankster, Teacher, Writer: Brian Doyle is Up to Good', *QQ* 48 (Dec. 1982): 27.

Although he writes about the problems of adolescence, Brian Doyle is not a topical novelist. Instead of treating the issue of the moment, he examines what he calls 'the classic concerns, the ones with the capital letters'. As dauntingly serious as this statement sounds, Doyle's novels are actually comic, reflecting his vision of life: 'Laughter and tears are very close together. I can't do one without the other. When I work on a serious question, a mirror of humour always presents itself.'

Doyle's serio-comic novels fall into distinct groups. *Hey, Dad!* and its sequel, *You Can Pick Me Up at Peggy's Cove*, were inspired by his relationship with his children, Megan and Ryan, whose names he used for the central characters. Five novels, some inspired by Doyle's memories of his own childhood or by the stories his father told, are set in the past in Ottawa or nearby Low, Quebec: *Up to Low*, *Angel Square*, *Easy Avenue*, *Covered Bridge*, and *Uncle Ronald*. Two more ephemeral books, mysteries focusing on the adventures of a Métis teenager, are set in present-day Ottawa.

Although Doyle has mined family life and stories for his novels, his work is not strictly autobiographical. The first-person viewpoint used in all of his novels compels Doyle to respect the independence of his characters: 'My stories may begin as autobiography, but I become so absorbed in the character that it takes over and the story develops a life of its own.' First-person narration also has thematic and aesthetic functions. Thematically, it allows a fresh, colloquial exploration of the traditional 'capital letter' themes of death, love, and reconciliation. Aesthetically, it enables him to mix comic and serious moods. The innocence of the youthful narrators, for example, generates comic irony, whereas their acute sensitivity elicits sympathy, forcing readers to take seriously their pain and distress.

In many ways, *Hey, Dad!* set the pattern for Doyle's novels. It uses a basically realistic description of a family's troubled vacation trip from Ottawa to the west coast to convey a symbolic journey to maturation. For 13-year-old Megan, who does not want to go, the trip ironically becomes educational. She begins by irrationally hating her father, even attempting to run away from him, but she gradually learns to love him deeply.

Running throughout the novel is a powerful motif stressing the inevitability of death and the transience of human life and relationships. Episodes develop these ideas in various ways. An early episode is painfully funny: a terminally ill boy at a picnic site assures Megan that she too must be dying because families undertake such trips only because a child is dying. A later episode is dramatic: Megan thinks that a dying man at the hot springs is her father. Another is seriously philosophic: thinking about the Athabaska River and trying to understand human time and geologic time, Megan realizes that the life span of her parents is brief.

Although somewhat contrived, *Hey, Dad!* is engaging because its episodes effectively and humorously develop character. The scene in which Megan watches her wise-cracking father playfully mock a group of adolescents at a swimming pool is a master stroke. It is amusing and moving: the father wins the friendship of all the young people except his daughter, who longs for a father like all other fathers. It is also painful: the embarrassment of a sensitive teenager whose father is ignorant of her feelings is made palpable.

You Can Pick Me Up at Peggy's Cove, which has been made into a film, is more conventionally plotted and less humorous, although it has some fine passages satirizing tourists. Reversing the situation of the first book, it shows the consequences of a father leaving his family. Deeply hurt by the situation, Ryan,

Megan's brother, is sent to Peggy's Cove. The majority of the characters he encounters and many of the episodes show in some way either the pain of loss or the power of love. Ryan shows his immaturity by befriending a petty thief and by writing a letter to his father telling of his part in some thefts. At the same time, Ryan experiences unselfish companionship when he takes up fishing with Eddie, even going so far as to pretend to be his son when tourists come around. Unfortunately, the novel has a highly contrived ending, one in which Ryan proves his maturity through physical action. When Eddie is attacked by a shark, Ryan has enough presence of mind to radio for help, something his companion, the mentally deficient Wingding, cannot do. This competence is not meaningfully connected to his reconciliation with his father. His father comes for him shortly after the rescue, but he has not yet received Ryan's letter, indicating that he comes purely from love.

Doyle's most successful fusion of comedy and serious themes comes in the five books set in the past. The ideas about love and reconciliation developed in his first two novels receive their finest expression in *Up to Low*. The children's version of a cross between works by Mark Twain and William Faulkner, this tall tale employs an episodic and unrealistic plot, contains an abundance of memorable eccentrics, and concludes in a highly symbolic manner. Structurally, it depends on two journeys. In the first, Frank, an alcoholic, drives Tommy and his father to their summer cabin in his new 1950 Buick, which he gradually turns into a wreck. Stopping at every hotel along the way, the men become progressively more inebriated and hear rumours of the impending death of Mean Hughie, an event most of the men won't accept because 'He's too mean to die.'

The second journey begins at the cabin after Tommy has re-established his childhood friendship with Mean Hughie's daughter, Baby Bridget, who lost part of her arm in an accident caused by her father's carelessness. Tommy takes her by boat to Mean Hughie, who, lying in a coffin, confesses sorrow for his treatment of Bridget, thus healing her heart. No longer too mean, he then dies. Tommy places the coffin across the boat to form a cross, an act that symbolizes the redemption of Hughie, his daughter, and, because of his own mature compassion, Tommy. This new maturity expresses itself in the novel's final section. Now able to see Bridget as a woman instead of the mutilated victim of her father's carelessness, Tommy asks to kiss her. The novel that begins with talk of the death of his mother and includes the death of Bridget's father thus concludes with the comic affirmation of the power of love and the joy of life.

Angel Square, which Doyle jokingly calls a 'prequel', is set four years before the events of *Up to Low*. Tommy lives in a comic world of Catholics, Jews, and Protestants, all of whom fight each other every day in the inappropriately named Angel Square. Able to be friends with members of all groups 'Because I'm not anything', Tommy joins in the daily battles, constantly changing sides. These battles form the comic motif of racial and religious prejudice, the darker side of which is the beating of the father of a Jewish boy by a hooded man.

Alongside the theme of tolerance, Doyle presents a comic theme about the development of identity. Tommy, unable to fit into the distinct religious groups, tries to be something and takes on the role of Lamont Cranston, the Shadow. After a number of false starts, he exposes the identity of the hooded man. The novel ends triumphantly on a note of wish fulfilment: for at least a while, the rival groups co-operate, and the boy who thought he was nothing gains the romantic identity of a hero and the love of the hero's girl.

Doyle's next two novels set in the past feature a new narrator, Hubbo (Hulbert) O'Driscoll, a poor orphan. *Easy Avenue* and *Covered Bridge* are more heavy-handed in their repeated jokes and use of comic eccentrics than the two novels about Tommy, but they entertainingly explore serious issues. *Easy Avenue*, a novel of manners, concerns itself with various definitions of the term 'success'. After he suddenly comes into some money, Hubbo changes for the worse. Trying to be accepted by the rich kids at school, he becomes ashamed of Mrs O'Driscoll, the cleaning lady who raised him. He also becomes estranged from Fleurette Featherstone Fitchell, a neighbouring girl trying to live down her bad reputation. Eventually, Hubbo learns that financial success is not the same as success as a human being. Rejecting the arrogant materialism of the rich kids, he affirms the redemptive power of love by publicly expressing his love for Mrs O'Driscoll and by reconciling with Fleurette.

In *Covered Bridge* slapstick and tall tale elements dominate, but the novel presents a serious conflict, the clash between past and present values. In doing so, it returns to one of Doyle's dominant themes, the need for tolerance. Hubbo, who has moved to Low, Quebec, is tending an old covered bridge slated for demolition. His efforts to preserve the bridge lead to conflict with Father Foley. Intolerant and unforgiving, Father Foley (his name suggests 'folly') has refused to allow the body of Ophelia Brown, who committed suicide years ago by jumping from the bridge, to be buried in the church graveyard. He also insists that the bridge should be torn down. Matters are resolved in an unexpected and comical way: Hubbo helps Ophelia's lover move the fence so that Ophelia's grave is inside the cemetery; that night Father Foley sees a goat, which has become entangled in a sheet, thinks that it is a ghost crossing the bridge, and dies of fright; Mrs O'Driscoll saves the bridge by having it declared a monument to Father Foley.

Uncle Ronald is more truly historical than the other novels set in the past. Narrated by 112-year-old Mickey McGuire, it is an extended anecdote that touches on familiar themes about love and change. The main action occurs in 1895, when Mickey and his mother flee from her abusive husband and seek sanctuary with Uncle Ronald O'Rourke. Paralleling the bullying of Mickey's father is the bullying of the government, which sends police to collect the taxes or seize the goods of the residents of Low. The twin O'Malley sisters cleverly sabotage the tax collectors, and the gigantic Uncle Ronald chases away Mickey's father, who is killed trying to beat a train to a crossing. Young Mickey, whose bed-wetting stopped when he reached the security of Uncle Ronald's house, learns to feel and to accept love. He comes also to appreciate the beauty of change.

Spud Sweetgrass and *Spud in Winter* are contemporary mysteries. Like Doyle's other novels, these contain slapstick episodes and eccentric characters; they differ in having pronounced multicultural elements and in being thematically thin. In the first, John (Spud) Sweetgrass, whose deceased father was Native and whose mother is part Irish, solves an ecological crime. Working on a chip wagon after being expelled from school, Spud learns that Angelo (Dumper) Stubbs has been pouring used cooking oil into the sewer system. With the help of his friend Dink the Thinker, he exposes Dumper and earns the affection of Connie Pan, who is part Vietnamese and part Chinese. In *Spud in Winter*, Spud witnesses a murder. After the killer is arrested, Spud and Connie are instrumental in capturing the getaway driver, the extravagantly named B. Faroni ('Beefaroni'), following a slapstick chase on skates down the frozen Rideau Canal.

Doyle's novels are sometimes patently contrived, straining for comic or thematic effects, and they are sometimes too anecdotal. Furthermore, an excessive reliance on eccentric characters with improbable names blunts the comic force of some of his creations. Nevertheless, Doyle's novels, especially those inspired by his own childhood, have the merits of deft characterization, engaging humour, and the presentation of important themes all in language that is effective without being artificially poetic or literary. Alternately amusing and moving, his novels both demand and reward rereadings.

See also: *CA* 35; *CLR* 22; *MAICYA*; *SAAS* 16; *SATA* 67; *TCYAW*; *WSMP*.

Sandy Frances Duncan

Born: 24 January 1942, in Vancouver.

Principal Residences: Vancouver; Toronto; Regina; Gabriola, BC.

Education: University of British Columbia (BA 1962, MA 1963).

Career: psychologist; writer.

Works for Children

Cariboo Runaway (Don Mills, Ont.: Burns & MacEachern, 1976).

Kap-Sung Ferris (Toronto: Burns & MacEachern, 1977). **Rev:** *CM* 20 (Jan. 1992): 13; *SLJ* 27 (Sept. 1980): 43.

The Toothpaste Genie (Richmond Hill, Ont.: Scholastic, 1981). **Rev:** *APBR* 10 (Nov. 1983): 2, 13; *CCL* 21 (Spring 1995): 69; *IR* 16 (Apr. 1982): 44; *QQ* 48 (Feb. 1982): 16.

Finding Home (New York: Avon, 1982). **Rev:** *SLJ* 29 (Nov. 1982): 98

Listen to Me, Grace Kelly (Toronto: Kids Can Press, 1990). **Rev:** *CCL* 75 (1994): 79; *CM* 18 (Nov. 1990): 275; *EL* 18 (Mar. 1991): 60; *QQ* 56 (Sept. 1990): 20.

Other

'The Young Adult Novel: One Writer's Perspective', *HB* 57 (Apr. 1981): 221–8.

Dragonhunt (Toronto: Women's Educational Press, 1981) [adult novel].

Pattern Makers (Toronto: Women's Educational Press, 1989) [adult novel].

'I am primarily interested in individuals and how they cope with situations, external crises, and crises of their own making', Frances Sandy Duncan has said. Because of her background, education, and professional work, Duncan has an especially keen understanding of the ways young people cope with pressure and pain. She experienced the pain of parental loss when her father died while she was just entering adolescence and the loss of familiar places and friends when her mother subsequently moved her from Vancouver to Toronto and then Regina. After university, where she gained a theoretical understanding of human psychology, she worked for nine years as a child psychologist, a job that gave her firsthand knowledge of the ways children think about issues and the ways they respond to personal problems. This understanding is most evident in her adolescent problem novels, *Kap-Sung Ferris*, *Finding Home*, and *Listen to Me, Grace Kelly*, but it also adds tension to her historical novel, *Cariboo Runaway*, and depth to her whimsical fantasy, *The Toothpaste Genie*.

Set during the Cariboo gold rush of the 1860s, Duncan's children's book, *Cariboo Runaway*, is about a girl and her brother who set off from Victoria in search of their missing prospector father. In addition to testing their physical and emotional resources, the children's perilous adventures provide vivid, well-researched portraits of gold rush society. The adventure ends on a positive psychological note: by finding their father at Barkerville, the children re-establish their identity as members of a family that can win out over the dangers of a 'hard country'.

Duncan has said that she has a special interest in 'Canadian identity, but within the framework of individual identity'. This interest unifies *Kap-Sung Ferris*, an exploration of the anxieties of three adolescent girls who feel themselves to be different but eventually find their identities both as individuals and Canadians. Barbara Kim Ferris, an adopted Korean, learns to accept herself and Canada after coming to terms with racial prejudice and the facts of her adoption. Bhindu, a Ugandan Asian driven from her country for looking unusual, learns to love Canada as a land of possibilities. Mish, the narrator, who had once felt inordinately ungainly, accepts herself, establishes a new relationship with her mother, from whom she had grown distant, and feels the stirrings of patriotism when watching her friends develop love for Canada. Although it contains some gripping and meaningful events, *Kap-Sung Ferris* is primarily a novel of character in which plausible adolescents seek to know themselves and their parents.

An even more complex and intense investigation of internal and external pressure is *Finding Home*, a novel for young adults. Presented in chapters that alternate the point of view of 15-year old Rondo, whose parents have been killed in an auto accident, and 35-year old Margery Grey, the best friend of Rondo's mother, it explores how grief, impotent rage, and alienation affect relationships. Only when Margery engages in a frank exchange of ideas and feelings with Rondo, who has run away from the Grey household to commit suicide, do the two achieve an understanding that allows them both to cope with their losses and to find where they belong.

Although it is not as tense, *Listen to Me, Grace Kelly* successfully explores the meanings a young girl finds in a variety of relationships. In the summer of 1955, the narrator, 12-year-old Jessica Crawford struggles to come to terms with changes brought on by her elderly father's death, her subsequent move from Vancouver to Toronto, and the confusing changes of adolescence. While her mother spends the weekdays working in Toronto, Jess stays at a cottage with elderly Agatha Adams. Lonely and troubled by memories of her father, Jess conducts imaginary conversations with Grace Kelly, who always provides a sympathetic ear. Eventually, Jess learns that her father suffered from what is now known as Alzheimer's disease and that during his illness he may have come close to sexually abusing her. Realizing the truth about her father both in better times and in his illness, Jess matures to the point that she no longer requires Grace Kelly to help her explore her feelings. The scenes in which Jess converses with Grace Kelly, with elderly Agatha, and with her mother are effective in revealing Jess's character. Unlike the plausible and thematically rich episodes involving adults, those in which Jess copes with an adolescent boy's unwelcome advances and in which she and a girlfriend discuss menstruation and practise kissing are poorly integrated and artificial. In spite of plotting deficiencies, *Listen to Me, Grace Kelly* is nevertheless an interesting study of a female balanced between fantasy and reality, childhood and adolescence.

Duncan's most popular book, *The Toothpaste Genie*, appeals to younger audiences. This highly amusing tale is about Amanda, who finds a wish-giving, apprentice genie in a tube of toothpaste. Because the genie is a practical joker who constantly makes her wishes go awry, Amanda learns that magic is not always the best way of handling life's problems. Many of the wishes, such as her desire to be always neat, humorously explore Amanda's search for a satisfying identity. Gradually, Amanda becomes less self-centred; she helps the genie earn his identity as a Master Genie and accepts the fact that her own wishes for a horse and a baby sister will have to come through the ordinary 'magic' of life.

Duncan is an intelligent, often witty writer. Occasionally, in trying to clarify themes or to illustrate the clash of ideas, she resorts to episodes that are too schematic or too contrived. Plots are not, however, the most important elements in her novels because, as she has said, 'Characters control the story, the action, and the plot.' The characters who control her stories are vivid and plausible, and their stories thus become interesting and informative psychological portrayals of youth.

See also: *CA* 97–100; *CANR* 17, 37; *SATA* 48; *Profiles* 2; *WSMP*.

Sarah Ellis

Born: 19 May 1952, in Vancouver.

Principal Residences: Vancouver; Toronto.

Education: University of British Columbia (BA 1973, MLS 1975); Simmons College, Boston (MA 1980).

Career: librarian; lecturer; critic; writer.

Major Awards: Governor-General's Award for Children's Literature (1991); IODE Violet Downey Children's Book Award (1995); Mr Christie's Book Award, ages 12 and up (1994); Vicky Metcalf Award (1995).

Works for Children

The Baby Project (Toronto: Groundwood, 1986); published in the US as *A Family Project* (New York: Atheneum, 1988). **Rev:** *BiC* 15 (Dec. 1986): 17; *CCL* 47 (1987): 90; *CL* 116 (Spring 1988): 236; *CM* 15 (Mar. 1987): 90; *HB* 64 (May 1988): 350; *QQ* 52 (Oct. 1986): 19; *SLJ* 34 (Mar. 1988): 188.

Next-Door Neighbours (Toronto: Groundwood, 1989). **Rev:** *CCB-B* 43 (Mar. 1990): 137; *CCL* 57–58 (1990): 149; *HB* 66 (May 1990): 334; *QQ* 55 (Sept. 1989): 23; *SLJ* 36 (Dec. 1990): 21.

Putting Up with Mitchell: My Vancouver Scrapbook (Vancouver: Brighouse Press, 1990). **Rev:** *CCL* 61 (1991): 107; *EL* 18 (Nov. 1990): 61.

Pick-Up Sticks (Toronto: Groundwood, 1991). **Rev:** *CCB-B* 45 (Feb. 1992): 154; *CCL* 67 (1992): 87; *CM* 20 (Mar. 1992): 90; *EL* 19 (Mar. 1992): 18; *HB* 68 (Mar. 1992): 208; *QQ* 57 (Nov. 1991): 25; *SLJ* 38 (Dec. 1992): 20

Out of the Blue (Toronto: Groundwood, 1994). **Rev:** *CCB-B* 48 (Apr. 1995): 271; *CBRA* (1994): 481; *CM* 22 (Nov. 1994): 209; *EL* 22 (Mar. 1995): 13; *HB* 71 (July 1995): 456; *QQ* 60 (Nov. 1994): 36; *SLJ* 41 (May 1995): 156.

Back of Beyond: Stories (Toronto: Groundwood, 1996). **Rev:** *CCB-B* 50 (Nov. 1997): 83; *BiC* 26 (June 1997): 33; *CBRA* (1996): 472; *CCL* 24 (Spring 1998): 39; *EL* 25 (May 1998): 40; *HB* 73 (Nov. 1997): 680; *QQ* 62 (Oct. 1996): 51; *SLJ* 43 (Dec. 1997): 24.

Other

'Books and Bibliotherapy', *CCL* 55 (1989): 83–6.

'News from the North', *The Horn Book* (a series of short critical articles on Canadian children's literature appearing on a regular basis since 1984).

Selected Discussions

Saltman, Judith. 'An Appreciation of Sarah Ellis', *CCL* 67 (1992): 6–18.

'I am endlessly fascinated with the subject of family', Sarah Ellis remarked to an interviewer about her novels. She went on to explain that 'my child self, a girl about twelve, is still alive in me', but that, because her own childhood had been happily ordinary, she enjoyed making up interesting events and imagining the emotional impacts these might have had on a girl like her. In each of her four novels, girls on the edge of adolescence must come to terms with major changes in their lives, changes that come as great surprises and that shatter the security of their family lives to this point. To use the title of one of her novels, these changes come 'Out of the Blue', and, like the players in the game pick-up sticks, which provided the title of another of her books, they must learn how to deal with the delicately balanced new arrangements of aspects of their lives.

None of Ellis's heroines is extraordinary; each occupies a secure position within her home and family and enjoys times with a best friend. However, the adjustments the girls must make require that they develop emotional strength and courage and insights into their own natures and those of the people with whom they interact: siblings, parents, best friends and other peers, and adults outside the home. In *The Baby Project*, Jessica and her older brothers learn that their 41-year-old mother is pregnant. A girl who had complained, 'Why do things have to *change* all the time' and who 'was used to her family the way it was' adapts well to her new baby sister. However, she faces a far greater adjustment when the baby suddenly dies. Peggy, the shy, self-conscious main character of *Next-Door Neighbours*, moves from the country to the city, where her minister father has taken a new parish. Hoping to fit in during the waning weeks of the school year, she lies to her classmates, telling them that she owns a horse. When the lie is discovered, she is ostracized. However, during the summer, she befriends George, an immigrant boy who also is a school outcast, and Sing Lee, a Chinese gardener who is badly treated by his racist employer. With the man's help, she and George produce a prize-winning puppet show, and she learns the values of co-operation and friendship. When Sing Lee is fired, the girl courageously overcomes her shyness to confront his employer; however, she is unable to reverse the old woman's decision.

The families in *The Baby Project* and *Next-Door Neighbours* are fairly conventional two-parent units espousing traditional values. However, in her next two novels, Ellis presents more unusual and, in a limited way, more contemporary family situations. In *Pick-Up Sticks*, the heroine lives with her single mother, while in *Out of the Blue* the mother of a 'typical' family reveals that she had had a child before her marriage and gave it up through adoption. Yet each of the central characters must face major changes in her life. Thirteen-year-old Polly and her stained-glass designing mother must leave the apartment that has been the girl's home all her life. Angry at her mother, who she thinks would be able to find a new apartment that they could afford if only the woman had a regular job, Polly goes to live in the home of her affluent uncle before healing the split with her mother. When her 24-year-old long-lost half-sister enters her family circle, Megan reacts angrily to this person who has arrived 'Out of the Blue'. Feeling shut off from her mother, who has enthusiastically entered into her rediscovered child's wedding preparations, Meg struggles with hurt feelings and a sense of rejection, before accepting the half-sister into a family that she briefly felt had become 'too crowded'.

After a long period of wrestling with the conflicts occasioned by such dramatic changes, Ellis's central characters are able to experience a revelation, an epiphany in which they understand and accept the new circumstances of their lives. Interestingly, it is in literal darkness that they figuratively 'see the light'. In *The Baby Project*, Jessica and her 14-year-old brother, who had displayed hostility to other members of the family before and after the birth and death of the baby, ride their bikes through the city in the predawn hours. The two rediscover a bond of affection that will keep the family united as it overcomes its grief. Creeping into the darkness of her next-door neighbour's basement, Peggy discovers the dreadful conditions in which the old lady had forced her Chinese employee to live and also understands George's experience as a refugee escaping from eastern Europe. When she is pushed from a car by Stephanie because she refuses to join her rich cousin in a spree of petty vandalism, Polly, of *Pick-Up Sticks*, wanders at night lost and terrified in a rundown section of the city. Hiding in a crate, she recalls a happy childhood incident and re-emerges with a sense of purpose and an understanding of the value of her life with her mother: 'she knew exactly which way was home'. Invited to look through the university telescope by her half-sister, Megan, in *Out of the Blue*, begins to understand Natalie's need for family and begins to accept the changes in the pattern of her family.

Although, as she told critic Judith Saltman, 'I have only one major idea and I have it to death—a preadolescent girl discovers that life is more complicated than she thought', Ellis deals with her basic theme in different ways. In the first two books, a stable traditional family provides the backdrop for the heroine's understanding of death and prejudice. In the second two novels, the heroine must confront her changing attitudes towards and relationship with her mother. Both Peg and Megan progress through and resolve what may be considered an archetypal conflict: the daughter's separation from and reunion with the mother. The resolutions may be rather swiftly accomplished at the conclusions of *Pick-Up Sticks* and *Out of the Blue*; however, the painful struggles and tensions along the way are carefully delineated and fully realized.

Ellis's third-person narrators focus almost exclusively on the central characters. Secondary figures, whose own conflicts are occasionally presented, are frequently sketched in and often seem two-dimensional and static. Jessica's best friend, Margaret, who 'was very good at talking about plans and projects', or Polly's companion Vanessa, who leaned 'toward the dramatic and . . . also managed to turn most conversations to herself', tend towards being caricatures, as does Polly's rich, land-developer uncle. However, the old, lonely, and prejudiced Mrs Manning, Peggy's next-door neighbour, and Ernie, the retarded adult who is Polly's neighbour, are presented in ways that permit readers to share the main characters' growing understanding of these people's inner needs and struggles.

Ellis clearly and vividly presents the concrete realities of the worlds in which her characters live. In addition, she employs many of the objects in the novels as symbols. The baby project that Jessica and Margaret undertake as a school research report signifies the discoveries Jessica's family makes as a result of the birth, brief life, and death of the new member of their home. *Next-Door Neighbours*, the title of a grade-one reading text that new-Canadian George used to learn English, becomes the symbol for Peggy's process of understanding people she meets in her new home. As she murmurs lines from the old counting rhyme 'Pick-up sticks', Polly sees parallels between her interactions with people and the traditional rhyme: each involves a precarious balance re-created in a new way after each action. The blue Japanese fishing float that Megan discovers on the seashore is not only a surprise, something from the past like her half-sister, it becomes a link in a new family relationship, a wedding gift that will help to keep the changed family network afloat.

The four novels also include a series of set pieces, short scenes, in most of which the central figure is either an actor or observer. At the mall, Jessica and Megan try unsuccessfully to interview adults about the shopping centre's apparent lack of concern for the needs of babies and small children or the mothers who must bring them along while they shop. Apart from the girls' research for their baby project report, their actions provide a humorous picture of the gulf between adults' and children's views of situations and of the types of individuals found at malls. Polly's observations, during her stay at her uncle's home, of that family's daily habits and interactions, form a satiric picture of the inner poverty of an affluent, middle-class family. In these two examples, the set pieces are related to plot, conflict, and character development. Other set pieces, such as the description of the church rummage sale in *Next-Door Neighbours*, seem more like interesting interludes related to, but not essential for the development of the novels' conflicts.

Ellis has also written a travel story and a collection of short stories. In *Putting Up with Mitchell: My Vancouver Scrapbook*, Elizabeth's account of a visit to Vancouver mixes lively accounts of the city's famous tourist attractions with expressions of exasperation over her little brother's antics. The 12 stories in *Back of Beyond* are, in many ways, in marked contrast to the novels. Each is told by a first-person narrator, who is the central character, a teenager who has passed beyond the threshold stage of Ellis's heroines in the novels. Three of the narrators are male, and each of the stories deals with magic and the supernatural rather than with realistic events. The supernatural events frequently involve connections with past and future times. One character visits a mysterious garden that her grandfather had entered decades earlier; another encounters in human form a seal he had observed during a summer vacation several years earlier; a third accompanies her midwife mother to a home that has yet to be built. These time shifts and the characters' responses to them emphasize the need for individuals to perceive the interconnectedness of past and present events in their lives and the impact these may have on their futures. Underlying the different points of view and events of the stories is Ellis's concern with the family and the conflicts that must be confronted and resolved if a family is to be a viable unit. In *Back of Beyond*, these conflicts are more intense and painful than in the novels: hatred towards an absent father, confusion engendered by a runaway sibling, anxiety over a mentally unstable mother. Yet because of their encounters with different time periods, the narrators are able to put their present family relationships in order and to see their own lives in new and healthier perspectives.

In her four novels and her short-story collection, Ellis has combined elements of the traditional family story, with its focus on unity and understanding, with the complex issues of the more contemporary social-problem novel to create narratives that honestly, if perhaps sometimes a little optimistically, examine the tensions that individuals on the edge of and in early adolescence experienced in the later part of the twentieth century.

See also: *CA* 123; *CANR* 50; *CLR* 42; *Junior* 7; *SATA* 68; *WSMP*.

Peter Eyvindson

Born: 20 January 1946, at Carberry, Man.

Principal Residences: Carberry; Winnipeg; Melita, Man.; Snow Lake, Man.; Clavet, Sask.

Education: University of Manitoba (BA 1967, B.Ed. 1971).

Career: teacher; school librarian; professional storyteller.

Works for Children

Kyle's Bath, illus. Wendy Wolsak (Winnipeg: Pemmican, 1984).

Old Enough, illus. Wendy Wolsak (Winnipeg: Pemmican, 1986).

The Wish Wind, illus. Wendy Wolsak (Winnipeg: Pemmican, 1987).

Chester Bear, Where are You?, illus. Wendy Wolsak-Frith (Winnipeg: Pemmican, 1988).

Circus Berserkus, illus. Doug Keith (Winnipeg: Pemmican, 1989).

A Crow Named Joe, illus. Doug Keith (Winnipeg: Pemmican, 1990).

Jen and the Great One, illus. Rhian Brynjolson (Winnipeg: Pemmican, 1990).

The Backward Brothers See the Light: A Tale from Iceland, illus. Craig Terlson (Red Deer, Alta: Red Deer College Press, 1991). **Rev:** *CM* 20 (May 1992): 158; *QQ* 58 (Jan. 1992): 32.

The Yesterday Stone, illus. Rhian Brynjolson (Winnipeg: Pemmican, 1992). **Rev:** *QQ* 59 (Jan. 1993): 33.

The Missing Sun, illus. Rhian Brynjolson (Winnipeg: Pemmican, 1993). **Rev:** *BiC* 23 (Apr. 1994): 49; *CM* 22 (May 1994): 79; *QQ* 60 (Mar. 1994): 82.

The Night Rebecca Stayed Too Late, illus. Rhian Brynjolson (Winnipeg: Pemmican, 1994). **Rev:** *BiC* 24 (Apr. 1995): 57; *CBRA* (1994): 449.

Red Parka Mary, illus. Rhian Brynjolson (Winnipeg: Pemmican, 1996).

Peter Eyvindson's stories are variously ironic, silly, sentimental, and didactic. Equally varied are his themes, which concern time, growth, imagination, changing perceptions, or the environment.

Eyvindson first book, *Kyle's Bath*, uses children's logic as the basis of comedy. Inspired by Eyvindson's son's attitudes, the story focuses on Kyle, who enjoys messy activities but doesn't like his nightly baths because his mother makes the water too hot, scrubs him roughly, and always gets shampoo in his eyes; furthermore, she refuses to let him play in the tub and always sends him to bed right after his bath. Kyle decides that the only way he can avoid baths is to give up all his messy amusements. His radical change of habits has ironic results, however: believing that the neat and quiet Kyle must be ill, his mother gives him a bath and sends him to bed early. Realizing that he is always going to have baths, Kyle decides to make them worth his while, so he returns to his messy amusements. (The Afternote indicates that, after reading the book, Kyle's mother also changed, allowing Kyle to play in the bath.) Without being overtly didactic, *Kyle's Bath* amusingly illustrates that adults who respect their children's growth and feelings can eliminate some of the conflicts of family life.

The comforts and terrors of imagination are central in three tales. *Chester Bear, Where are You?*, another story inspired by Eyvindson's son, recounts Kyle's attachment to his teddy, Chester, whom he relies on to protect him at night from the 'booglely men' in the closet. When Kyle is unable to find Chester at bedtime, his brothers laugh and his father is too busy to help him search. Mom helps, but they fail to find the bear. Once in bed, however, Kyle finds Chester beneath his pillow and, after hearing the bear whisper peek-a-boo, happily falls asleep. Although it shows that children imaginatively animate toys to provide themselves with security, the quest's conclusion is anticlimactic and reduces the tale to little more than a bland anecdote about a common event. *The Night Rebecca Stayed Too Late*, which also treats night fears, has a far stronger and more consequential plot. Rebecca, having stayed late at her friend's house, becomes too scared to walk home alone, so Suzie, after insisting it will be the last time, agrees to accompany her. Rebecca's talk about ghosts so frightens her escort, however, that Suzie races ahead into Rebecca's house. In a comical reversal, Rebecca, insisting that she will do it for the very last time, agrees to walk the frightened Suzie home. The girls' parallel statements and situations generate comic irony, and not only show that different things frighten people but, more importantly, they effectively suggest that people who need help in one situation may be able to give help in another. Eyvindson's third exploration of the power of imagination, *Circus Berserkus*, is a rhymed story. To amuse himself when he is alone, a daydreaming boy lets his imagination run riot as he imagines an absurdly comical circus coming to town. Pleased with his own powers of imagination, the boy reasserts self-control by banishing the circus. The illustrations are manic, although a bit grotesque, but neither the basic plot nor the rhymes that describe the circus are of sufficient innovation to make this book compelling nonsense.

Time figures prominently in a number of Eyvindson's books. The least accomplished, the sentimental *Old Enough*, is about a father who is so busy that he fails to establish a meaningful relationship with his growing son. When the son has his own child, the man receives a second chance because, now that he is a grandfather, he is 'old enough' to do with his grandson all the things he failed to do with his son. A companion tale, *The Wish Wind*, is a dream fantasy that uses the folkloric motif of the foolish wish to explore youth's impatience. Boy is continually displeased with the present moment. In winter, he refuses to play in the snow with Wish Wind, instead wishing it were spring. When he gets his wish, he becomes bored and wishes it were summer. In summer, he becomes so resentful of Wish Wind's warnings of danger that he angrily wishes he were old so that no one could tell him what to do. He thus finds himself an old man regretting that time passed so swiftly. Wishing that Boy had had the patience to appreciate the present moment, the old man is whirled back to his own time, where he awakens as Boy, who eagerly runs out to play in the snow with Wish Wind. A semi-poetic allegorical tale that avoids extreme sentimentality and didacticism, *The Wish Wind* is one of Eyvindson's best stories.

The Yesterday Stone is also about time and the relationship between the generations. This story awkwardly combines a girl's fears about sharing secrets with a friend and an examination of the deep bonds between the young and the elderly. Anna loves to look into a stone that grandmother has polished over the years because grandmother's stories seem to become visible in it. When grandmother helps Anna to find her own yesterday stone, Anna finds that she has something that will help her remember her life and something that she can share with her best friend. Unfortunately, Eyvindson does not limit the stone to showing scenes of one's own past, so its symbolism is too diffuse. Additionally, Anna's concern about sharing the secret of the stone with a friend is a contrivance that distracts from the focus on the relationship between members of different generations.

Far more effective and touching is *Red Parka Mary*, which uses the growing friendship of a boy and an elderly woman to develop themes about overcoming fear of strangeness and difference, and about appreciating character instead of appearances. Told as a flashback about the time when the narrator was seven, it recounts how he was initially frightened of old Mary because of her withered appearance and strange clothes. Because his mother sends him on errands to Mary's house, the boy comes to know and like Mary, who teaches him many of the traditional skills, such as trapping and preparing furs. The boy grows so fond of Mary that he buys her a red parka for Christmas. In return, she promises to give him the biggest gift in the world. When the boy opens Mary's parcel, he finds in it only a small heart-shaped bead. Told that it represents Mary's love, the boy realizes that he likes everything about Mary and cannot imagine why people made him fear her. In showing that experience of another's character can enable a person to overcome the prejudices that strange appearances may foster, the story teaches an important lesson. Because the pictures represent the boy and Mary as members of a First Nations group, people who have suffered from similarly hasty judgements about their differences, the lesson becomes even more powerful.

The Missing Sun is notable for the way in which it balances science with a retelling of an Inuit *pourquoi* myth to show the continuing vitality of myth. When she and her meteorologist mother move from Regina to Inuvik, Emily makes friends with Josie Tucktoo. Although Emily's mother provides a scientific explanation for the long winter darkness, Josie gives one that Emily can understand when she says that Raven stole the sun. The humour in this tale resides in the fact that the reader knows that Josie's belief that the new spring sun is too big for Raven to steal is naïve: whether or not one accepts the Raven myth, winter inevitably comes. Eyvindson has retold another traditional tale, this time one from Iceland, in a more direct way. *The Backward Brothers See the Light* is a conventional numbskull tale about three brothers who are so foolish they believe that they can use coffee cups to empty the darkness from their unlighted house. When evening comes and the sun sets, the foolish brothers believe that they emptied so much darkness from their house that they turned the world dark.

Neither of Eyvindson's other books is especially notable. *Jen and the Great One* employs the convention of the child as romantic innocent to issue a heavy-handed call for ecological responsibility. Jen, listening to the wind in the branches of Great One, an old tree, learns that Big Businessman, Politician, and Road Builder were so greedy and short-sighted that they destroyed the forests that once covered the land. Great One is dying in the polluted atmosphere, but adults don't hear his cries of distress, so Jen and her friends take Great One's seeds and begin planting them. Although earnest in trying to show that children alone seem to care for the environment they will inherit, this tale is so insistently didactic and contrived that it is more sermon than story. *A Crow Named Joe*, on the other hand, makes insufficient use of a common childhood event, children adopting wounded animals as pets. In this case, the children adopt a crow, whom they name Joe. Joe proves to be mischievous, stealing household items, destroying the garden, and attacking a neighbour's cat. In the anticlimactic ending, Joe suddenly leaves and the children agree to find another crow if he doesn't return in the spring. What saves this tale from complete banality are the illustrations, which portray the oversized Joe Crow wearing a sweater and appearing very much anthropomorphic. The illustrations thus suggest something the text does not imply: that Joe is an imaginary friend who makes lonely children happy.

Eyvindson has yet to produce an outstanding book, but those stories in which he restrains his overt didacticism are both entertaining and thematically rewarding.

See also: *CA* 124; *SATA* 52; *WSMP*.

Eugenie Fernandes

Born: 25 Sept. 1943, in Huntington, NY.

Principal Residences: Huntington; New York City; Peterborough, Ont.; Buckhorn Lake, Ont.

Education: attended School of Visual Arts, New York City (1963–5).

Career: freelance illustrator and author; writer, designer, and producer of animated television segments for *Sesame Street* television series.

Works for Children

Written and Illustrated by Eugenie Fernandes

Wickedishrag (Norwalk, Conn.: C.R. Gibson, 1968).

Jenny's Surprise Summer (Racine, Wis.: Western Publishing, 1981).

The Little Boy Who Cried Himself to Sea (Toronto: Kids Can Press, 1982). **Rev:** *BiC* 11 (Dec. 1982): 8; *CCL* 34 (1984): 73; *EL* 10 (May 1983): 29.

A Difficult Day (Toronto: Kids Can Press, 1983); rev. edn with colour pictures (Toronto: Kids Can Press, 1987). **Rev:** *BYP* 1 (Oct. 1987): 24; *CCL* 74 (1994): 90; *CM* 16 (Sept. 1988): 181; *EL* 11 (Jan. 1984): 40; *QQ* 50 (Mar. 1984): 72; *SLJ* 30 (May 1984): 64.

Ordinary Amos and the Amazing Fish, written and illustrated with Henry Fernandes (Racine, Wis.: Western Publishing, 1986).

My Bath Time Book; My Bedtime Book; My Going Out Book; and My Playtime Book (Auburn, England: Ladybird Books, 1987).

My Birthday Book; My Busy Day Book; and My Rainy Day Book (Auburn, England: Ladybird Books, 1988).

The Very Best Picnic (Racine, Wis.: Western Publishing, 1988).

Jolly Book Box: Early Learning for Toddlers [contains *ABC and You*; *Alone-Together*; *Picnic Colours*; *Dreaming Numbers*; and *Busy Week*] (Auburn, England: Ladybird Books, 1990).

Just You and Me, illus. Eugenie Fernandes and Kim Fernandes (Toronto: Annick, 1993). **Rev:** *CM* 21 (Nov. 1993): 217; *QQ* 59 (Aug. 1993): 36.

Waves in the Bathtub (Richmond Hill, Ont.: North Winds, 1993). **Rev:** *BiC* 22 (Summer 1993): 28; *CCL* 76 (1994): 80; *CM* 21 (Sept. 1993): 146; *QQ* 59 (Feb. 1993): 34.

The Tree That Grew to the Moon (Richmond Hill, Ont.: North Winds, 1994). **Rev:** *CBRA* (1994): 449; *QQ* 60 (Sept. 1994): 73.

Written by Eugenie Fernandes

Little Toby and the Big Hair, illus. Kim Fernandes (Toronto: Doubleday, 1997).

Illustrated by Eugenie Fernandes

Dog Goes to Nursery School, by Lucille Hammond (Racine, Wis.: Western Publishing, 1982).

My Book of the Seasons, by Stephanie Calmenson (Racine, Wis.: Western Publishing, 1982).

Ned's Number Book, by Ronne Peltzman (Racine, Wis.: Western Publishing, 1982).

When Dog Was Little, by Lucille Hammond (Racine, Wis.: Western Publishing, 1983).

The Adventures of Goat, by Lucille Hammond (Racine, Wis.: Western Publishing, 1984).

I Had a Bad Dream: A Book About Nightmares, by Linda Hayward (Racine, Wis.: Western Publishing, 1985). **Rev:** *CCB-B* 39 (Sept. 1985): 10.

Once Upon a Time, by Barbara Rennick, illustrated by Eugenie Fernandes and others (Toronto: McGraw-Hill Ryerson, 1985).

Little Sister, by Kathleen N. Daly (Racine, Wis.: Western Publishing, 1986).

Belly Buttons, by Anne Baird (New York: Simon & Schuster, 1987.)

Look At Me!: A Book of Occupations, by Dorothy Marcic Hai (Racine, Wis.: Western Publishing, 1986).

Who's The Boss Here? A Book About Parental Authority, by Barbara Seuling (Racine, Wis.: Western Publishing, 1986).

Ride Away!, by Anne Baird (New York: Simon & Schuster, 1987).

Sky Full of Babies, by Richard Thompson (Toronto: Annick, 1987). **Rev:** *BYP* 2 (Feb. 1988): 4; *CCL* 49 (1988): 58; *CM* 16 (May 1988): 100.

When Dog Grows Up, by Lucille Hammond (Racine, Wis.: Western Publishing, 1987).

Foo, by Richard Thompson (Toronto: Annick, 1988). **Rev:** *BiC* 17 (June 1988): 36; *BYP* 2 (June 1988): 6; *CCL* 57 (1990): 108; *CM* 16 (Sept. 1988): 184; *SLJ* 35 (Sept. 1988): 173.

I Have To See This!, by Richard Thompson (Toronto: Annick, 1988). **Rev:** *CCL* 51 (1988): 98; *CM* 17 (Jan. 1989): 36.

One Light, One Sun, by Raffi (New York: Crown Publishers, 1988). **Rev:** *SLJ* 34 (June 1988): 98.

Effie's Bath, by Richard Thompson (Toronto: Annick, 1989). **Rev:** *CCL* 62 (1991): 98; *CM* 17 (Dec. 1989): 269.

Daddies at Work, by Eve Merriam (New York: Simon & Schuster, 1989).

Gurgle, Bubble, Splash, by Richard Thompson (Toronto: Annick, 1989). **Rev:** *CCL* 57 (1990): 135; *CM* 17 (July 1989): 192; *SLJ* 35 (Aug. 1989): 133.

Mommies at Work, by Eve Merriam (New York: Simon & Schuster, 1989).

Jesse on the Night Train, by Richard Thompson (Toronto: Annick, 1990). **Rev:** *BiC* 19 (Dec. 1990): 32; *CCL* 64 (1991): 74; *CM* 19 (Jan. 1991): 31; *QQ* 57 (May 1991): 23.

Going to the Dentist: A Pop-Up Book, by Marianne Borgardt (New York: Simon & Schuster, 1991).

Going to the Doctor, by Stacie Strong (New York: Simon & Schuster, 1991).

Glow in the Dark—Under the Sea, by Jean Lewis (Racine, Wis.: Western Publishing, 1991).

Maggee and the Lake Minder, by Richard Thompson (Toronto: Annick, 1991). **Rev:** *BiC* 20 (Sept. 1991): 53; *CCL* 74 (1994): 90; *CM* 19 (Jan. 1991): 31; *QQ* 57 (May 1991): 22.

Grandpa Dan's Toboggan Ride, by Suzan Reid (Richmond Hill, Ont.: Scholastic, 1992). **Rev:** *CM* 21 (Jan. 1993): 23; *QQ* 58 (Nov. 1992): 35.

Lace Them Up, by Lilly Barnes (Toronto: Somerville House, 1992). **Rev:** *CM* 21 (Jan. 1993): 17; *QQ* 58 (Sept. 1992): 70.

Brush Them Bright, by Patricia Quinlan (Toronto: Somerville House, 1992).

Little Kitten Dress-Up, by Lucille Hammond (Auburn, England: Ladybird Books, 1992).

Tell Me One Good Thing: Bedtime Stories, by Richard Thompson (Toronto: Annick, 1992). **Rev:** *CCL* 77 (1995): 73; *CM* 20 (Oct. 1992): 266; *QQ* 58 (Apr. 1992): 32.

My Mommy Comes Back, by Ginny Clapper (Racine, Wis.: Western Publishing, 1992).

Don't Be Scared, Eleven, by Richard Thompson (Toronto: Annick, 1993). **Rev:** *BiC* 22 (May 1993): 31; *CCL* 76 (1994): 80; *QQ* 59 (Feb. 1993): 34.

Good Morning, by Jan Colbert (Toronto: HarperCollins, 1993). **Rev:** *CM* 21 (Nov. 1993): 216; *QQ* 60 (Jan. 1994): 39.

Good Night, by Jan Colbert (Toronto: HarperCollins, 1993). **Rev:** *CM* 21 (Nov. 1993): 216; *QQ* 60 (Jan. 1994): 39.

Nature in the Home, by David Suzuki (Toronto: Stoddart, 1993). **Rev:** *BiC* 22 (Nov. 1993): 58; *EL* 21 (Nov. 1993): 47, and 21 (Mar. 1994): 16.

Today I Took My Diapers Off, by Judy Rothman (Racine, Wis.: Western Publishing, 1993).

Elliot Fry's Good-bye, by Larry Dane Brimner (Honesdale, Penn.: Boyds Mills Press, 1994). **Rev:** *QQ* 60 (Mar. 1994): 80; *SLJ* 40 (May 1994): 89.

If We Could See the Air, by David Suzuki (Toronto: Stoddart, 1994). **Rev:** *CBRA* (1994): 550; QQ 61 (Jan. 1995): 42.

Katie's Hand-Me-Downs, by Laurie Wark (Toronto: Kids Can Press, 1994).

The Backyard Time Detectives, by David Suzuki (Toronto: Stoddart, 1995). **Rev:** *CBRA* (1995): 563.

Kapoc, the Killer Croc, by Marcia Vaughan (Morristown, NJ: Silver Burdett Press, 1995). **Rev:** *SLJ* 40 (Nov. 1994): 92.

Aaron's Awful Allergies, by Troon Harrison (Toronto: Kids Can Press, 1996).

Make It Better, by Lilly Barnes (Toronto: Somerville House, 1996).

On the Phone, by Patricia Quinlan (Toronto: Somerville House, 1996).

Rise and Shine, by Raffi (Toronto: Random House, 1996). **Rev:** *CCL* 90 (1998): 84.

Lavender Moon, by Troon Harrison (Toronto: Annick, 1997). **Rev:** *CCL* 91/92 (1998): 166.

The Long Wait, by Budge Wilson (Toronto: Stoddart, 1997). **Rev:** *CBRA* (1997): 496.

A Cat in a Kayak, by Maria Coffey (Willowdale, Ont.: Annick, 1998).

Tom and Francine: A Love Story, by Sylvia Fraser (Toronto: Key Porter, 1998).

Ribbon Rescue, by Robert Munsch (Toronto: Scholastic, 1999).

The prolific Eugenie Fernandes has produced illustrations for her own texts as well as those by a number of writers. She has also produced a varied body of work, publishing board books, pop-up books, Little Golden Books, science books, and conventional picture books. Such productivity is probably not surprising because art has always been an integral part of her daily family life. When she was growing up, her father, Creig Flessel, worked in a home studio as an illustrator for D.C. Comics. He set up a desk next to his own so that his daughter could spend many happy hours next to him drawing her own pictures. After attending art school she married Henry Fernandes, also an artist. They moved to Canada in 1974, and she began working in a home studio that was actually only a part of a bedroom marked off from the rest with tape. As she herself did with her father, her children spent hours beside her while she worked; both children grew up to be artists. As part of the union of family life and professional life, Fernandes has produced a book with her husband and two with her daughter, Kim.

One of the most notable features of the books that Fernandes has herself written and illustrated is the seamless blending of mundane reality and fantasy. Fernandes established the pattern for such blends in her first Canadian-published book, *The Little Boy Who Cried Himself to Sea*. The story begins with a scene familiar to most parents: when a mother puts her tired little boy into bed for a nap, he begins crying because he doesn't want a nap. Once his mother leaves, reality shades into fantasy. The boy cries so much that he creates an ocean and his bed becomes a boat in which he escapes from the confinement of his room. The pictures illustrating what is obviously a dream adventure are black-and-white line drawings, with a blue wash used mostly to indicate tears and the ocean. In spite of the crudeness of the pictures, which are designed to seem as if a child drew them, the graphic design is sophisticated. In a manner slightly similar to that employed by Maurice Sendak in his classic dream-journey picture book, *Where the Wild Things Are*, Fernandes uses the layout to suggest meaning. Thus, as the boy enters the fantasy world, she eliminates the border that surrounds the pictures of events in the waking world, thereby symbolizing the boy's escape from confinement. Like Sendak, she also makes the pictures into double-page spreads when the boy is fully in the fantasy world, thus graphically suggesting the breadth and freedom of his imagination. Unlike Sendak, however, Fernandes has the mother appear, not only in the waking section but also in the dream sequence. The point of having her set out herself to bring back the boy, who has fallen asleep at sea, is to reassure children that, even if the child has thrown a tantrum, a mother's protective love continues while the child sleeps.

A somewhat similar use of the double-page layout signals entry into fantasy in *A Difficult Day*, a book originally published with black-and-white pictures but reissued with coloured pictures that are far more effective in highlighting details and in suggesting mood. The story again begins with a common household conflict. Melinda, having one of those days in which many things go wrong, enters her room, slams the door, and, asking why her mother doesn't love her better, crawls under her bed. Melinda then enters a fantasy or dream in which she imagines running to the other side of the world, where people will hug her. Unlike the pictures of her real life, these pictures are double-page spreads and they show Melinda so big that the Earth is like a big ball beneath her. The pictures again become confined to a single page when Melinda's mother enters the room and begins searching for her. In the resolution, Melinda, reassured that her mother loves her, comforts her mother, and the two lovingly share milk and cookies, an act that physically symbolizes the emotional sharing and nurture that has taken place.

Both format and pictorial details combine to show the power of a little girl's imagination in *Waves in the Bathtub*. The scenes of mundane life, in which Kady makes waves in the bath water while her mother asks her to stop, are presented in framed, single-page pictures. The format changes when Kady sings a song about seeing the ocean and such sea creatures as fish and dolphins. The double-page pictures, which contain at most a framing line at the bottom, represent Kady's expansive imagination. They are effective because, instead of offering an objective view of a girl in a tub, they dramatize her subjective vision, being filled with colourful fish, dolphins, and even a huge whale. This gentle bedtime book, which even includes the words and music to Kady's song, does not contain a serious conflict because the loving mother does not get angry at Kady, whom she soon puts to bed. Its conclusion, which children will see as validating their imaginations and which adults may perceive as a testimonial to how children keep their parents' imaginations vigorously alive, has the mother enter the tub, sing the song, and see the same animals her daughter saw.

Although she does not hold to the format quite as rigidly, Fernandes also makes the scenes of fantasy larger than those of reality in *The Tree that Grew to the Moon*. Bright colours and the welter of details communicate the excitement of a girl who imagines growing in her bedroom a tree that will become the centre of the entire neighbourhood's life. As in her other books, Fernandes has the mother nearby as a witness who lovingly validates her daughter's flights of fantasy.

Fernandes has also written the text to two books illustrated by her daughter, Kim. *Just You and Me* is a nonsense fantasy. Heather and her mother want some time together, but Auntie Pearl refuses to watch the baby unless it is asleep. When Heather and her mother try to calm it by taking it out in the stroller, they receive advice from a variety of sources, including a river and the moon. Nothing that the various representatives of nature advise helps: baby just falls asleep by itself as they return home. The story is slight, but the collaboration is effective because Eugenie Fernandes draws the scenes of reality in gouache, which makes them flat and ordinary, whereas Kim Fernandes renders the fantasy scenes in three-dimensional fimo, which makes the fantasy seem more rounded and interesting than reality. Kim Fernandes provided all the illustrations for her mother's *Little Toby and the Big Hair*. When Toby lets her hair grow to her knees, it becomes unruly. It frightens some adults and causes Toby a number of problems, but she refuses to cut it. Eventually, by showing that she can keep it neat and pretty in braids, her parents come to accept her unruly hair. Although more visually stunning than satisfying as a narrative, this story comically suggests that appearance is not the most vital part of a person's identity, while also stressing that individualism can eventually earn acceptance.

The sheer number of books Fernandes has illustrated makes it impossible to discuss this side of her career in detail. Her collaboration with Richard Thompson, however, has been fairly successful. The Jesse adventure series, all of which involve at least a degree of fantasy, has not allowed significant experimentation with format, but it has permitted her to illustrate subjective reality and to add details not mentioned in the text. In *Jesse on the Night Train*, for instance, she indicates Jesse's fear of a tunnel by portraying it as a wolf with an open mouth. In *I Have To See This!*, she adds to the comedy by making the Man in the Moon, whom Jesse's father vainly tries to see, look exactly like her father. The beginning of Thompson's *Effie's Bath* resembles *Waves in the Tub* in that Fernandes pictures two young girls submerging themselves in their bathtub and then swimming with angel fish and a porpoise. In the later stages of this fantasy, Fernandes reinforces Thompson's allusions to Edward Lear through her superb renditions of Lear's famous 'Owl and Pussycat'. In Larry Dan Brimner's *Elliot Fry's Goodbye*, Fernandes uses colour, notably in the garish monsters in the subjective double-page spread illustrating the scary stories that Elliot tells. Throughout her books, Fernandes also adds comical details. Nearly all the pictures for Suzan Reid's *Grandpa Dan's Toboggan Ride*, for example, include a dog, who is not mentioned in the text. As Nicki and her grandfather hurtle down the mountain, adding unwilling passengers as their toboggan passes through the village, the little dog grabs a doughnut knocked out of the baker's bag, Nicki's teddy bear, and then someone's mitten. Even more comical are the details Fernandes incorporates in Robert Munsch's *Ribbon Rescue*. In the final wedding scene, for example, in which the disheveled Jillian acts as a flower girl, Fernandes shows the girl holding a frog, as well as a bouquet.

Over the years, Fernandes has improved in her draughtsmanship. She has left behind the flat cartoonishness characteristic of the Little Golden Books that were a prominent source of income in the early stages of her career. Her more recent work shows her skill in creating textures and in filling pictures with interesting detail. She has not developed a style that instantly sets her apart from other professional illustrators, and she has yet to produce a book that is fully satisfying textually and graphically, but she has produced some very entertaining books that offer satisfying read-aloud moments for parents.

See also: *MCAI*; *SATA* 77; *WSMP*.

Sheree Fitch

Born: 3 December 1956, in Moncton, NB.

Principal Residences: Moncton; Fredericton; Wolfville, NS.

Education: St Thomas University (BA 1987); Acadia University (MA 1994).

Career: author.

Major Awards: Mr Christie's Book Award (1992); Ann Connor Brimer Award (1995).

Works for Children

Toes in My Nose and Other Poems, illus. Mary Lamb Bobak (Toronto: Doubleday, 1987). **Rev:** *CCL* 50 (1988): 76; *EL* 16 (Jan. 1989): 57.

Sleeping Dragons All Around, illus. Michele Nidenoff (Toronto: Doubleday, 1989). **Rev:** *BiC* 19 (June 1990): 14; *CCL* 61 (1991): 77; *CM* 18 (Mar. 1990): 63; *QQ* 55 (Dec. 1989): 22

Merry-Go-Day, illus. Molly Lamb Bobak (Toronto: Doubleday, 1991). **Rev:** *BiC* 20 (Oct. 1991): 53; *CM* 20 (May 1992): 162; *QQ* 57 (July 1991): 52.

There Were Monkeys in My Kitchen!, illus. Marc Mongeau (Toronto: Doubleday, 1992). **Rev:** *BiC* 21 (Dec. 1992): 32; *CCL* 81 (1996): 43; *QQ* 58 (Oct. 1992): 34.

I Am Small, illus. Kim LaFave (Toronto: Doubleday, 1994). **Rev:** *CBRA* (1994): 450; *CCL* 78 (1995): 69; *CM* 22 (Oct. 1994): 187; *QQ* 60 (June 1994): 47.

Mabel Murple, illus. Maryann Kovalski (Toronto: Doubleday, 1995). **Rev:** *CBRA* (1995): 468; *CCL* 81 (1996): 43; *QQ* 61 (June 1995): 56.

The Hullabaloo Bugaboo Day (Eastern Lawrencetown, NS: Pottersfield Press, 1997).

If You Could Wear My Sneakers: A Book About Children's Rights, illus. Darcia Labrosse (Toronto: Doubleday, 1997). **Rev:** *BiC* 26 (Sept. 1997): 33; *QQ* 63 (Apr. 1997): 37.

There's a Mouse in My House!, illus. Leslie Elizabeth Watts (Toronto: Doubleday, 1997). **Rev:** *CM* 30 (Jan. 1998): on-line; *QQ* 63 (Dec. 1997): 36.

If I Were the Moon, illus. Leslie Elizabeth Watts (Toronto: Doubleday, 1999).

The Other Author Arthur (Eastern Lawrencetown, NS: Pottersfield Press, 1999).

Selected Discussions

Jenkinson, David. 'Sheree Fitch: Prize Winning Writer of "Utterature"', *EL* 20 (Sept. 1993): 66–70.

Sheree Fitch has been called the poet of 'utterature', a term she uses to describe poetry, which she believes should be presented orally to a community of young listeners. In her many books of poems, she has experimented with a variety of voices and different line lengths and has presented a wide array of real and imaginary experiences as perceived by young children. A Master of Arts in English whose thesis was on 'The Oral Tradition in Children's Poetry', she seeks the rhymes, rhythms, and images that capture the worlds of childhood.

Although Fitch's first book, *Toes in My Nose*, did not appear until she was 31, poetry had been an important part of her life since her early childhood. Her father frequently read aloud from the classic English poets, inviting her to enjoy the 'big words' they used; her mother used to share tongue-twisters with her. An avid reader and writer who enjoyed class recitation, she later wrote poems for her own children, many of them based on their experiences or shared conversations. However, she faced 12 years of rejection slips before Doubleday accepted her first collection. As a university student, she became interested in the English poet William Blake's study of the imagination as a way of perceiving reality and in Dennis Lee's use of the forms and techniques of oral poetry in work that related to the lives of contemporary Canadian children.

Toes in My Nose presents a young child's responses to character and situations both real and imaginary. Putting rocks in a brother's socks and visiting a favorite grandmother are reality-based contrasts to watching a boy who overindulged in popcorn and exploded or another who floated away after blowing an enormous bubble. Observing window washers creates a sense of wonder; hearing thunder raises a number of questions. The speaker has such imaginary pets as a worm, an orangutan, and a porcupine and describes such imaginary people as Zelba Zinnamon and Mabel Murple. The three dozen poems are short, from eight to 39 lines, as are the lines themselves, which usually contain four to six syllables. Strong rhythms and pronounced rhymes, along with frequent onomatopoeia and alliteration, emphasize the comic tone of most of the pieces. However, a quieter more reflective tone captures the voice of a sensitive, reflective child in the poems 'I Wonder About Thunder' and 'I Can Fly'.

Sleeping Dragons All Around, Fitch's second book, is the first containing one long poem detailing a child's specific experience. The rhythm of a line from English poet John Keats's 'The Eve of St Agnes' appealed to the author, who used it as the title and starting point for the account of a child's nighttime trip to the refrigerator for 'Mocha Maple Chocolate Cake'. Gentle rhythms describe the progress past the dragons Priscilla, who sleeps 'in pink Pantaloons', and Beelzebub, who 'blows purple bubbles'. The eccentric character of each creature is described. After the girl has accidentally awakened the dragons, the rhythm accelerates. In the poem, Fitch reveals her love of challenging words such as 'temperamental', 'bizarre', 'precision', and 'ancestral', inviting her readers to enjoy their sounds and to discover the meanings.

Three other single-poem volumes illustrate the author's ability to employ rhythm and sound to reflect a child's varying responses to a day's experiences. *Merry-Go-Day* presents a trip to the Exhibition, entering contests, taking rides, and eating midway food. Waiting in line, licking a rapidly melting cone, the thrill of a roller-coaster ride, and the disappointment of not winning a stuffed parrot are precisely communicated. In *There Are Monkeys in My Kitchen!*, the heroine tries unsuccessfully to summon aid to get rid of the hordes of primates that have invaded her home. The frenetic pace of the event is emphasized by the short lines, frequent rhymes, and lists of details. Her frustration is revealed in the regularly repeated refrain in which she calls the police, but to no avail. This refrain is altered near the conclusion when, instead of dialing for help, she confronts the animals herself, driving them away. *There's a Mouse in My House!* is a fantasy about the night-time encounter between a boy and Scheherezade, a stray mouse whom the boy is supposed to kill. Written in ballad form, it recounts how the tall-tale-telling rodent is able to arouse the boy's pity and guilt feelings and to enchant him with her dubious accounts of her family's adventures.

I Am Small and *Mabel Murple* each contain several poems that, considered as a group, define the creation of a personality, one real, one imaginary. The former begins, 'This is Small talking', and concludes, 'I am small. But I think big.' In between, the untitled poems present the voice of a little child thoughtfully responding to the various elements of her life. Troubled by her size and the fact that she cannot perform the activities that her parents can, she wonders, 'if I were not inside my body, who would be me?' She enjoys sharing with parents and grandparents and with two friends, one real, the other imaginary, and delights in rolling down a hill, visualizing the days of the week as colours and squares, and making up nonsense words for the texts of books she is unable to read. In bed, her thoughts expand as she wonders about the reality and nature of God. Unlike the earlier books, *I Am Small* does not rely on rhyme, onomatopoeia or strong rhythms. The longer, more gently flowing unrhymed free-verse lines, accompanied by the visual imagery, communicate the child's growing sense of herself. By contrast, in *Mabel Murple*, the portrait of an imaginary girl from a purple planet, alliteration and rhyme contribute to a comic effect. The make-believe creation of an ordinary child, the title heroine is a wild skier, skate boarder, and motorcycle driver, who careens through her monochromatic world. A kind of alter-ego for her creator, she embodies the power of the imagination to provide a brief, exhilarating escape from everyday reality.

The majority of the 14 poems in *If You Could Wear My Sneakers* are longer than most of those in Fitch's other collections, an expansion appropriate to the older audience for whom they were created. Written to illustrate the United Nations Rights of the Child Declaration, they describe the relationships between individuals in families and with those beyond the family circle. The focus is on the importance to both the self and others of unique and universally shared characteristics and needs. The characters, a collection of animals from around the world, explore such concerns as accepting differences, recognizing individuality, co-operating, acquiring an education, and fighting war. In the opening poem, the speaker remarks: 'The you I see / You try to be / Never ever speaks to me.' A raccoon whose 60-letter alliterative name includes all the letters of the alphabet, states that 'every name is a story.' An unusual assortment of animals gladly welcomes newcomers to its 'All Are Welcome Crew', special friends assist a giraffe who cannot laugh, and a sloth agrees to accept others' lifestyles if they will accept his unusual one. The personalities of the unusual animals and situations, coupled with the alliteration and tongue-twisting lines, give a humorous tone to the book's underlying serious themes.

Sheree Fitch's books of poetry speak to children from preschool to middle elementary ages, embodying their emotions, thoughts, and experiences. Her 'utterature', which embodies what she has called the 'lipslipperyness' of language, is addressed to a community of readers and listeners, allowing them to recognize the unique and shared aspects of their lives. A skilled poetic technician who is sensitive to the varied characteristics of words, she communicates the many voices of children as they experiment with language to engage their expanding inner and outer worlds.

See also: *TCCW*; *WSMP*.

Joanne Fitzgerald

Born: 17 February 1956, in Montreal.

Principal Residences: Montreal; Toronto; Georgetown, Ont.

Education: Mount Allison University (BFA).

Career: artist, Royal Ontario Museum; freelance artist; illustrator.

Major Awards: Governor-General's Award for Illustration (1991).

Works for Children

Illustrated by Joanne Fitzgerald

Plain Noodles, by Betty Waterton (Toronto: Groundwood, 1989). **Rev:** *BiC* (Dec. 1989): 23; *CCL* 59 (1990): 83; *CM* (Mar. 1990): 69; *QQ* 55 (Dec. 1989): 22.

Emily's House, by Niko Scharer (Toronto: Groundwood, 1990).

Doctor Kiss Says Yes, by Teddy Jam (Toronto: Groundwood, 1991). **Rev:** *CM* 20 (May 1992): 159; *EL* 19 (Mar. 1992): 17; *QQ* 57 (July 1991): 51.

Ten Small Tales, by Celia Barker Lottridge (Toronto: Groundwood, 1993). **Rev:** *CBRA* (1994): 518; *CCB-B* 47 (May 1994): 293; *HB* 70 (1994): 112; *QQ* 59 (Oct. 1993): 37; *SLJ* 40 (June 1994): 122.

Jacob's Best Sisters, by Teddy Jam (Toronto: Groundwood, 1996). **Rev:** *CBRA* (1996): 445; *CCL* 86 (1997): 59; *QQ* 62 (Nov. 1996): 47; *SLJ* 43 (Apr. 1997): 106.

As a child, Joanne Fitzgerald used to imagine better pictures than those accompanying the stories she read. This activity was the first step in her becoming a children's book illustrator. Art training at Mount Allison University was followed by work as an artist for the Royal Ontario Museum. An art director at Groundwood Books, impressed with her illustrations in the children's magazine *Chickadee*, invited her to illustrate Betty Waterton's *Plain Noodles*, the story of a lonely lighthouse keeper's wife who discovers a drifting rowboat full of babies. Fitzgerald's illustrations capture the humour as the woman tries to feed and change all of them, as well as the chaos they create trying to wash dishes and operate the lighthouse equipment. The final picture of the woman walking quietly along the beach presents a contrast to the activity and clutter of the earlier pictures.

Fitzgerald is best-known for her illustrations for two books by Teddy Jam. The heroine of *Doctor Kiss Says Yes* climbs out of her bedroom window during the night so that she can ride into the forest to tend to a knight who has been injured in battle. After giving him the apple, a box of pineapple juice, and the hugs and kisses she had received from her parents when they tucked her in bed, she returns to her modern home. Fitzgerald's watercolours emphasize the contrast between the girl's daytime and night-time worlds. The former is dominated by pale brown washes; her room is relatively bare, with no decorations or pictures on the wall. By contrast, the tent of the injured knight contains a golden goblet and bowl, a crimson rug, and tasseled pillows. Although the little girl, dressed in a white sweat shirt, blue jeans, and sneakers seems out of place, she efficiently goes about her business, bandaging his wounds and gently kissing his forehead. One of the details of Fitzgerald's illustrations suggests that the girl has not dreamed, but made an actual journey into some other realm. As she prepares to leave the tent, the knight gives Doctor Kiss a pendant he is wearing; the next day at the breakfast table, she has it on a chain around her neck.

Jacob's Best Sisters also deals with the nighttime adventures of a child. A school-aged boy discovers that the tiny dolls in a toy log cabin he has received are alive. During the night, he pours a bath for them in the basin, makes them new nightclothes, plays hide and seek with them, and tells them a story. Fitzgerald renders the fantasy convincing through her depiction of the boy's reactions, first to the doll's coming to life and later to their ongoing, selfish demands. She also highlights the size differential. The tiny figures are contrasted to the head and shoulders of the boy who looms, unthreateningly, above them. As in *Doctor Kiss*, she contrasts the dominant background colours of the ordinary and fantasy worlds. Whites are prominent in the former; deep blues, in the latter. The book's four double-spreads all depict his interactions with the little people; these are the times when he is most fully engaged with the world of the dolls.

Fitzgerald's illustrations for Celia Lottridge's *Ten Small Tales* emphasize the humour of the situations in the folktales. A realistically drawn mouse sits at a dinner table; another paddles a walnut-shell boat down a river. A boy, dog, cat, goat, and horse huddle frightened on a bed, alarmed at a noise that turns out to be the squeaking of hinges. Members of a family line up from largest to smallest, the father pulling on an enormous turnip, the others pulling on him.

Although her output is small, Joanne Fitzgerald has achieved recognition as a creator of illustrations that convincingly depict fantastic experiences and that capture the humour of the often foolish actions of human beings and animals. Her works invite young readers to go beyond the words, using the pictures to interpret events and characters.

See also: *WSMP*.

Bill Freeman

Born: 21 October 1938, in London, Ont.

Principal Residences: London; Hamilton; Montreal; Toronto.

Education: Acadia University (BA 1964); McMaster University (MA 1970, Ph.D. 1979).

Career: probation officer; lecturer; financial consultant; writer.

Major Awards: Canada Council Children's Literature Prize (1976).

Works for Children

Shantymen of Cache Lake (Toronto: James Lorimer, 1975). **Rev:** *CCL* 5 (1976): 94; *IR* 10 (Winter 1976): 32; *QQ* 48 (June 1982): 4.

The Last Voyage of the Scotian (Toronto: James Lorimer, 1976): **Rev:** *CCL* 11 (1978): 83; *IR* 11 (Winter 1977): 27; *QQ* 48 (June 1982): 4.

Cedric and the North End Kids (Toronto: James Lorimer, 1978): **Rev:** *CCL* 18 (1980): 130; *IR* 12 (Autumn 1978): 59.

First Spring on the Grand Banks (Toronto: James Lorimer, 1978). **Rev:** *CCL* 26 (1982): 80; *IR* 13 (Apr. 1979): 48.

Trouble at Lachine Mill (Toronto: James Lorimer, 1983). **Rev:** *CCL* 41 (1986): 92.

Harbour Thieves (Toronto: James Lorimer, 1984). **Rev:** *CCL* 43 (1986): 64; *EL*12 (Mar. 1985): 46; *QQ* 51 (Apr. 1985): 75.

Trouble on the Tracks (Toronto: James Lorimer, 1987). **Rev:** *BiC* 16 (June 1987): 35; *CCL* 51 (1988): 74.

Prairie Fire! (Toronto: James Lorimer, 1998). **Rev:** *QQ* 64 (Aug. 1998): 38.

'I wanted Canadian children to explore their historical roots, to come to know Canada of the 1870s. This was largely still the traditional time—before modern uniformity. It was a diverse country, but economic factors shaped ordinary people's lives, although in different ways in different places.' Bill Freeman was discussing the novels that make up his 'Adventures in Canadian History' series and was describing his basic focus: an economic perspective and a concern for the common, often marginalized people. In *Cedric and the North End Kids*, he also dealt with social problems, as an immigrant from Jamaica confronts prejudice in his new country.

Although *Shantymen of Cache Lake*, the first novel of the series, was not published until 1975, Bill Freeman's life to that time could be called a preparation for his writing. He acquired a love of history from his mother, a teacher, and an interest in left-wing politics from his father. He was an avid reader, devouring countless adventure novels. During the 1960s, Freeman vagabonded around Canada and England, working at a variety of jobs, as do his young protagonists, the Bains children. At university, he studied Canadian economic history and the history of the workers of Canada.

The first six novels of the 'Adventures in Canadian History' series—*Shantymen of Cache Lake*, *The Last Voyage of the Scotian*, *First Spring on the Grand Banks*, *Trouble at Lachine Mill*, *Harbour Thieves*, and *Danger on the Tracks*—follow similar patterns. Meg Bains is a young teenager who must leave home to find work to help her widowed mother. She is accompanied at first by her older brother, John, and later by her younger brother, Jamie. At a lumber camp, on a square-rigged ship, on a fishing boat, in a Montreal clothing factory, on the streets of Toronto, and on the western Ontario 'frontier', they encounter the dangers that provide the plot for each book and meet the characters whose motivations illuminate the social-economic themes. Working for very low wages, the two children learn that a few rich and relatively uncaring wealthy men control the destinies of thousands of poor people. Meg and her brothers develop close bonds with the workers. In fact, they become leaders, inspiring the men to unite in an effort to ameliorate intolerable conditions and to achieve a sense of self-respect. Often, the rich owners of the various operations are ignorant of the miseries of their workers, and they frequently fail to see the evil of their selfish foremen and managers. Only through the agency of the children are they enlightened and the conflicts resolved.

In *Prairie Fire!*, Meg and her younger siblings are joined in Manitoba by their strong-willed and hard-working mother and establish a homestead on lands that used to belong to the Métis. When they befriend the Dauphin family, they incur the anger of the other English farmers, who fear and hate the people they have displaced. In the end, the racial conflicts are settled, Meg marries Louis Dauphin, and the Bains, by dint of their courage, determination, integrity, and hard work, have established the home they have been longing for.

Shantymen of Cache Lake follows the basic format of the stories and displays Freeman's art at its best. After the suspicious death of their father in a logging accident, Meg and John 'already . . . knew the hardships working people had to undergo.' Feisty, independent, and determined not to be ignored because of her gender, Meg decides to join her brother, John, in looking for work at her father's old camp. John is timorous and frightened when he perceives the ambiguities of the issues they confront. The two children become capable workers and earn the trust of the men. Although the foreman, Hardy, is a stereotypical villain, a bully who finally turns coward, the other characters are convincingly portrayed. Freeman is particularly adept at describing in lively fashion the technical details of logging and at giving a sense of the grandeur and desolation of the wilderness around the logging camp.

Although John develops as a character during the next two works, becoming surer of himself and discovering his true vocation as an Atlantic fisherman, Meg remains relatively unchanged. In *Trouble at Lachine Mill* and *Harbour Thieves*, she is somewhat of a mother figure, taking care of her younger brother, and in the latter book her role diminishes. Freeman pictures vividly the various locales and clearly explains details of sailing, fishing, and factory operation. Characterization and plot, however, become progressively more formulaic. After the second novel, readers expect the young characters to be working in miserable conditions for near starvation wages and to play central roles in management-labour confrontations. The noble adult leader of the workers, the rich owner, and the nasty foreman are almost interchangeable stereotypes between the novels.

Freeman's 'Adventures in Canadian History' novels depart from the approach of much historical fiction. In each novel, he provides valuable insights into the lives of ordinary people, the unsung heroes and heroines of the country, and he gives young readers insight into ways of life long past. In *Shantymen of Cache Lake* he has created a minor Canadian classic, a well-written novel containing memorable characters, exciting action, and significant themes.

See also: *Profiles* 2; *SATA* 48, 58; *TCCW*; *WSMP*.

Laszlo Gal

Born: 18 February 1933, in Budapest, Hungary.

Principal Residences: Budapest; Toronto; Verona, Italy.

Education: Academy of Dramatic Arts, Budapest; Superior School of Pedagogy, Budapest (Diploma, 1955).

Career: freelance artist; teacher; graphic designer; illustrator; author.

Major Awards: IODE (Toronto) Children's Book Award (1978); Canada Council Children's Literature Prize for Illustration (1979, 1983); Amelia Frances Howard-Gibbon Illustrator's Medal (1980); Canadian Library Association Book of the Year for Children Award (1971).

Works for Children

Written and Illustrated by Laszlo Gal

Prince Ivan and the Firebird (Toronto: McClelland & Stewart, 1991). **Rev:** *BiC* 21 (Apr. 1992): 45; *CCL* 67 (1992): 71; *CM* 20 (May 1992): 158; *EL* 19 (Mar. 1992): 17; *QQ* 57 (Nov. 1991): 26; *SLJ* 38 (July 1992): 68.

East of the Sun and West of the Moon (Toronto: McClelland & Stewart, 1993). **Rev:** *BiC* 23 (Feb. 1994): 49; *CCL* 77 (1995): 55; *CM* 22 (May 1994): 80; *QQ* 59 (Oct. 1993): 37.

Merlin's Castle (Toronto: Stoddart, 1995). **Rev:** *CBRA* (1996): 442; *CCL* 87 (1977): 85.

The Parrot, with Raffaella Gal (Toronto: Groundwood, 1997): **Rev:** *CM* 4 (14 Nov. 1997): on-line; *QQ* 63 (Aug. 1997): 37.

Illustrated by Laszlo Gal

El Cid: Soldier and Hero, by Maria Luisa Gefaell de Vivanco (London: Paul Hamlin, 1968).

Siegfried: The Mighty Warrior, by Maria Luisa Gefaell de Vivanco (London: Paul Hamlin, 1968).

Cartier Discovers the St. Lawrence, by William Toye (Toronto: Oxford UP, 1970). **Rev:** *CCB-B* 25 (Dec. 1971): 66; *IR* (Winter 1971): 21; *TON* 34 (Winter 1978): 191.

Raven, Creator of the World, by Ronald Melzack (Toronto: McClelland & Stewart, 1970). **Rev:** *CCB-B* 24 (May 1971): 141; *HB* 47 (Apr. 1971): 166; *IR* 5 (Spring 1971): 28.

The Moon Painters and Other Estonian Folk Tales, by Selve Maas (New York: Viking, 1971). **Rev:** *CCB-B* 25 (Nov. 1971): 47; *HB* 47 (Oct. 1971): 483.

How the Chipmunk Got Its Stripes, by Nancy Cleaver (Toronto: Clarke, Irwin, 1973). **Rev:** *CCL* 5 (1976): 111; *IR* 8 (Winter 1974): 31.

Scared Sarah, by Mary Alice Downie (Toronto: Nelson, 1974).

My Name is Not Odessa Yarker, by Marian Engel (Toronto: Kids Can Press, 1977). **Rev:** *CCL* 21 (1981): 80; *IR* 12 (Summer 1978): 61.

The Shirt of the Happy Man, by Mariella Bertelli (Toronto: Kids Can Press, 1977). **Rev:** *CCL* 20 (1980): 57; *IR* 12 (Summer 1978): 44.

Sword of Egypt, by Bert Williams (Richmond Hill, Ont.: Scholastic, 1977). **Rev:** *IR* 12 (Summer 1978): 82.

Why the Man in the Moon is Happy, by Ronald Melzack (Toronto: McClelland & Stewart, 1977). **Rev:** *IR* 12 (Spring 1978): 62.

The Twelve Dancing Princesses, by Janet Lunn (Toronto: Methuen, 1979). **Rev:** *BiC* 8 (Dec. 1979): 13; *CCB-B* 34 (Jan. 1981): 94; *CCL* 15/16 (1980): 140; *IR* 14 (Apr. 1980): 51; *QQ* 48 (June 1982): 3; *SLJ* 26 (Mar. 1980): 131.

Christobel: A Story for Young People, by Catherine Ahearn (Ottawa: Golden Dog, 1982).

Hans Christian Andersen's 'The Little Mermaid', by Margaret Crawford Maloney (Toronto: Methuen, 1983). **Rev:** *BiC* 12 (Dec. 1983): 14; *CCL* 39 (1985): 145; *EL* 12 (Nov. 1984): 20; *TLS* 39 (Mar. 1984): 339.

Canadian Fairy Tales, by Eva Martin (Toronto: Groundwood, 1984). **Rev:** *BiC* 13 (Dec. 1984): 13; *CCB-B* 38 (May 1985): 171; *CCL* 38 (1985): 95; *HB* 61 (Jan. 1985): 89; *QQ* 50 (Nov. 1984): 10.

The Willow Maiden, by Meghan Collins (Toronto: Groundwood, 1985). **Rev:** *CCL* 45 (1987): 68; *EL* 13 (Mar. 1986): 15; *QQ* 51 (Dec. 1985): 24; *SLJ* 32 (Jan. 1986): 55.

The Enchanted Tapestry, by Robert D. San Souci (Toronto: Groundwood, 1987). **Rev:** *BiC* 16 (Nov. 1987): 38; *CCL* 53 (1989): 48; *EL* 15 (Mar. 1988): 26; *SLJ* 33 (June 1987): 89.

The Goodman of Ballengiech, by Margaret Crawford Malony (Toronto: Methuen, 1987). **Rev:** *BiC* 16 (Dec. 1987): 14; *CCL* 53 (1989): 52; *EL* 15 (Mar. 1988): 24.

Iduna and the Magic Apples, by Marianna Mayer (New York: Macmillan, 1988). **Rev:** *SLJ* 35 (Apr. 1989): 114.

A Flask of Sea Water, by P.K. Page (Toronto: Oxford UP, 1989). **Rev:** *CCL* 59 (1990): 104; *CM* 17 (Dec. 1989): 263; *EL* 17 (Mar. 1990): 25; *HB* 66 (Jan. 1990): 60; *QQ* 55 (Sept. 1989): 22.

Pome and Peel, by Amy Erhlich (New York: Penguin, 1990). **Rev:** *CCB-B* 44 (Sept. 1990): 6; *SLJ* 36 (July 1990): 76.

The Spirit of the Blue Light, by Marianna Mayer (New York: Macmillan, 1990). **Rev:** *SLJ* 37 (Feb. 1991): 79.

Sea Witches, by Joanne Robertson (Toronto: Oxford UP, 1991). **Rev:** *CM* 20 (Jan. 1992): 24; *EL* 19 (Mar. 1992): 17; *QQ* 52 (Aug. 1991): 24; *SLJ* 37 (Nov. 1991): 112.

The Moon and the Oyster, by Donia Blumenfeld Clenman (Victoria, BC: Orca, 1992). **Rev:** *BiC* 21 (Dec. 1992): 31; *CCL* 73 (1994): 261; *CM* 20 (Oct. 1992): 261; *QQ* 58 (Oct. 1992): 32.

Islands, by Anne Smythe (Toronto: Groundwood, 1995).

Tiktala, Margaret Shaw-MacKinnon (Toronto: Stoddart, 1996). **Rev:** *CBRA* (1996): 457.

Dracula, by Bram Stoker, adapted by Tim Wynne-Jones (Toronto: Key Porter, 1997): **Rev:** *CM* 4 (16 Jan. 1998): on-line; *QQ* 63 (Dec. 1997): 38.

Beowulf, by Welwyn Wilton Katz (Toronto: Groundwood, 1999).

Other

'Illustrating the Text', in *Writers on Writing: Guide to Writing and Illustrating Children's Books*, ed. David Booth (Markham, Ont.: Overlea House, 1989), 12–15.

Selected Discussions

Jenkinson, Dave. 'Laszlo Gal: Award Winning Illustrator', *EL* 19 (Mar. 1992): 65–9.

Theatre's loss was children's literature's gain in the case of Hungarian-born illustrator Laszlo Gal. After he had finished high school, he entered drama school. However, after a year, he was told he did not have acting talent and became an art teacher. His career as a children's book illustrator began in 1962, when, on a vacation to Italy, he showed his portfolio to publisher Arnoldo Montadori. His art was well received and he worked for the firm for several years before returning to Canada.

In 1970, he published his first Canadian book, William Toye's *Cartier Discovers the St. Lawrence*. A condensation of one part of Toye's earlier *The St. Lawrence*, it draws heavily on the explorer's journals to re-create their feelings as they entered a strange new world. Gal's full-colour illustrations, which contrast the size of small human figures against a rugged landscape, the plain dress of the Native people with the elaborate costumes of the French, and portray the winter sufferings of the Europeans, are a perfect complement to the text.

During much of the 1970s Gal was restricted, because of the high cost of publishing full-colour picture books, to using one or occasionally two colours for his illustrations. Within these constraints, however, he achieved a variety of effects. For example, using only blue and black for *Raven, Creator of the World* and *Why The Man in the Moon is Happy*, he created illustrations that resemble Inuit soapstone carvings. The blue suggests the cold of the Arctic, and the design of the drawings communicates the spirit power infusing many of the stories. For the Algonkian legend *How the Chipmunk Got Its Stripes*, he used brown inks and brown paper appropriate to the woodland setting of the story.

In 1979, Gal returned to full-colour illustrations, providing the paintings for a number of traditional tales, beginning with Janet Lunn's adaptation of *The Twelve Dancing Princesses*. The seven watercolour-and-tempera-wash double-spreads accompanying the text create a formal elegance in the style of the Italian High Renaissance. Set completely apart from the text, they are visual islands to contemplate before continuing with the written narrative. By contrast, in *The Little Mermaid*, Margaret Maloney's retelling of the Hans Christian Andersen classic, Gal varies size and shape, incorporating the illustrations into the text and making them part of the rhythm of the story.

Gal next created full-colour illustrations for retellings of myths, legends, and folktales from several different cultures. For each he carefully researched backgrounds, re-creating settings, buildings, and costumes that would have been familiar to original audiences of the stories, and he varied colours, lights, and shadows appropriately to evoke the moods of the narratives. While the costumes for *The Willow Maiden*, Meghan Collins's adaptation of a Celtic tale, are late medieval, Gal's illustrations emphasize the timeless, supernatural realm a young man enters on his way home one midsummer night. Illumination from a full moon backlights many of the scenes, creating mysterious lights and shadows. The young farmer's brown homespun garments relate to his normal world, while the pale green, gossamer-thin gowns of the willow maiden represent the realm of magic with which he must come to terms.

The *Goodman of Ballengiech*, a legend retold by Margaret Maloney, is set firmly in sixteenth-century Scotland. To emphasize the contrasts in the friendship between farmer and king, Gal depicts two styles of clothing and architecture: those of royalty and of the peasantry. Three scenes of subjects kneeling to the king reveal the movement between the worlds of court and barnyard. Early in the story, King James in full regalia sits on his throne, surrounded by courtiers. However, when the King, in disguise, is rescued from thieves by the farmer, he sits on a bench in yeoman's clothing while his unsuspecting benefactor kneels to dress his wounds. Back in the palace, the farmer kneels before the now-revealed king, who still wears simple clothing. The bonds between the two worlds have been demonstrated.

The Enchanted Tapestry, Robert D. San Souci's retelling of a Chinese folktale, and *Iduna and the Magic Apples*, a Norse myth adapted by Marianna Mayer, are narratives from cultures unfamiliar to most North American readers. In the former, in which a woman weaves a work of art so realistic that she and her son are able to enter into its scenery, Gal adapts the oriental style of landscape painting and tapestry art. The harsh world in which the widow and her family lives and the ideal one in which she finds lasting happiness are contrasted in the landscapes. Gnarled trees and rocky hillsides in the real world are replaced by a tranquil garden to be entered by crossing a delicate, arched bridge. In the Norse tale, the evil created by the Norse giant Loki, who abducts Iduna, whose magic apples keep the gods young, is emphasized by shifts in landscape and in dominant colours. Early in the story, the goddess sits in her garden under a tree that bears both blossoms and fruit. When a monster bird abducts her, dark clouds settle over the land and snow covers the ground. After her rescue she returns to her garden and bright hues return to the land.

Gal has illustrated original stories by other writers and by himself. The 11 full-page paintings for P.K. Page's literary fairy tale, *A Flask of Sea Water*, highlight the hero's long, dangerous quest. Star-bedecked arches about each illustration, along with the turban and robes of the characters, are Arabian touches that complement the style of the text. *For The Moon and the Oyster*, by Donia Blumenfeld Clenman, Gal's washes produce the undersea world of shell fish, the pale light of the moon, and the reflections of its rays on the water. *Tiktala*, Margaret Shaw-McKinnon's story about a contemporary Inuit girl who undertakes a spirit journey to discover her vocation as a traditional carver, is developed around a series of contrasts: land and sea, animals and human beings, spirit and natural worlds, traditional and modern ways. The central part of the book, in which the girl transforms into a seal, is dominated by a variety of green and blue hues that evoke not only winter seas and ice, but also the spirit powers she encounters. Dark, isolated castles and black, grey, and crimson hues dominate the illustrations for *Dracula*, Tim Wynne-Jones's abridgement of the nineteenth-century horror story.

In adapting *East of the Sun and West of the Moon*, a traditional Norwegian tale, Gal modified elements of the original narrative. He shortens the journey of the heroine in search of her lover by having one wind, rather than four help her reach her destination; he removes specific religious references by having the North Wind, rather than captive Christians, play a role in her success; and he emphasizes family unity by having the girl's parents and siblings join her and her new husband at the Prince's palace. The illustrations, which accurately depict Scandinavian architecture and landscape, reinforce the theme of a quest for a secure, happy home. In addition to the family's small cottage and the humble dwellings of the helpers along the way, Gal implicitly contrasts three grand dwellings: the Winds' home atop a bare, cloud-covered hill; the troll princess's castle built on a great rock 'supported in the dark emptiness by four giants'; and the prince's palace, a gold-walled, luxuriously furnished building. The first is merely a resting place on an arduous journey; the second, a place of deception and evil; the third, a secure, beautiful place that she has proved herself worthy of inhabiting.

Merlin's Castle celebrates both the courage of a brother and sister and the validity of creations of the literary imagination. Raphaella and Marco, with their tiny pet lizard, step into the pages of a book created by their illustrator father. Through the aid of the magician Merlin, who tells them, 'If you use the power of your imagination, everything you read will become alive', they enter the pages of J.R.R. Tolkien's *Farmer Giles of Ham* (a work Gal is contemplating illustrating) and play a role in the destruction of a dragon. Donatello, the lizard, who has grown large during the adventure, decides to return home with the children, stating that 'the power of friendship is the strongest of all.' The story, which bears resemblance to Chris Van Allsburg's *Jumanji* and *The Polar Express*, is illustrated with double-spreads showing the main events and, with their luminescent shades and hues, suggesting the heroes' imaginative powers.

The Parrot, co-written and co-illustrated by his daughter Raffaella, is an adaptation of an Italian folktale that also celebrates the power of the literary imagination. In order to save a beautiful maiden, a prince from a neighbouring kingdom is transformed into a storytelling parrot. As long as he continues telling a narrative about a princess who rescues a prince, the beautiful maiden will be safe. Castles, furnishings, and costumes of sixteenth-century Italy give the illustrations the look of its setting. Pictures of the maiden listening to the tale are drawn with black crayon, effecting detachment and passivity, as though she has escaped, through story, from the males who control her life.

Gal's works are not the type of picture book in which narrative and characterization are incomplete without the visual elements. Rather, they are illustrated books; the texts could stand, and, in some cases, have stood alone. Gal illustrates place, time, and mood, so that throughout the pictures the readers' responses to written text are guided and reinforced. Carefully researched, meticulously designed, and rigorously executed are the tableaus in which individuals and groups of characters are placed in interior or exterior settings. The separation of many of the illustrations onto pages facing the text and the frequent surrounding of these pictures with culturally and thematically appropriate border designs enhance the formal, sometimes static quality of the designs and link Gal with classical children's artists whose illustrations parallel, rather than involve, the printed text.

See also: *CA* 161; *Profiles* 2; *SATA* 32, 52, 96; *TCCW*; *WSMP*.

Marie-Louise Gay

Born: 17 June 1952, in Quebec City.

Principal Residences: Quebec City; Montreal.

Education: Institute of Graphic Arts (Montreal); Montreal Museum of Fine Arts School; Academy of Art College (San Francisco).

Career: designer of children's clothing; art director; set designer; editorial illustrator; lecturer; writer; illustrator.

Major Awards: Canada Council Children's Literature Prize for Illustration, English (1984); Canada Council Children's Literature Prize for Illustration, French (1984); Amelia Frances Howard-Gibbon Illustrator's Award (1987, 1988); Governor-General's Award for Illustration, English (1987); Mr Christie's Book Award, ages 7 and under (1996).

Works for Children

Works Written and Illustrated by Marie-Louise Gay

The Garden (Toronto: James Lorimer, 1985). **Rev:** *EL* 14 (Sept. 1986): 49.

Moonbeam on a Cat's Ear (Toronto: Stoddart, 1986). **Rev:** *BiC* 21 (Summer 1992): 37; *CCL* 52 (1988): 25; *CM* 16 (Jan. 1988): 8; *EL* 15 (Nov. 1987): 65; *QQ* 52 (June 1986): 28; *SLJ* 33 (Dec. 1986): 85.

Rainy Day Magic (Toronto: Stoddart, 1987). **Rev:** *BiC* 16 (Dec. 1987): 12; *CCL* 46 (1987): 107; *CM* 15 (Sept. 1987): 205; *EL* 16 (Sept. 1988): 68; *SLJ* 36 (May 1990): 85.

Angel and the Polar Bear (Toronto: Stoddart, 1989). **Rev:** *BiC* 18 (Apr. 1989): 36; *CCL* 54 (1989): 66; *CL* 29 (Summer 1991): 175.

Fat Charlie's Circus (Toronto: Stoddart, 1989). **Rev:** *BiC* 18 (Dec. 1989): 23; *CCL* 59 (1989): 75; *CM* 18 (Mar. 1990): 64; *EL* 17 (Mar. 1990): 23; *QQ* 55 (Dec. 1989): 22.

Willy Nilly (Toronto: Stoddart, 1990). **Rev:** *CCL* 63 (1991): 87; *EL* 18 (Mar. 1991): 24; *HB* 67 (Sept. 1991): 631; *QQ* 57 (Jan. 1991): 22; *SLJ* 37 (Mar. 1991): 171.

Mademoiselle Moon (Toronto: Stoddart, 1992). **Rev:** *BiC* 22 (Apr. 1993): 36; *QQ* 58 (Nov. 1992): 33.

Rabbit Blue (Toronto: Stoddart, 1993). **Rev:** *QQ* 59 (Dec. 1993): 33.

Midnight Mimi (Toronto: Stoddart, 1994). **Rev:** *CBRA* (1994): 451; *QQ* 60 (Dec. 1994): 32.

The Three Little Pigs (Toronto: Groundwood, 1994). **Rev:** *CBRA* (1994): 520; *QQ* 60 (Oct. 1994): 41

Rumpelstiltskin (Toronto: Groundwood, 1997). **Rev:** *CM* 4 (28 Nov. 1997): on-line; *QQ* 63 (Aug. 1997): 38; *SLJ* 43 (Nov. 1997): 107.

Stella: Star of the Sea (Toronto: Groundwood, 1999).

Works illustrated by Marie-Louise Gay

Lizzy's Lion, by Dennis Lee (Toronto: Stoddart, 1984). **Rev:** *BiC* 13 (Dec. 1984): 12; *CCL* 41 (1986): 74; *QQ* 50 (Nov. 1984): 11.

That's Enough Maddie, by Louise Leblanc, trans. Sarah Cummins (Halifax: Formac, 1991). **Rev:** *CCL* 74 (1994): 92; *CM* 20 (Mar. 1992): 70; *QQ* 58 (Mar. 1992): 68.

Maddie in Goal, by Louise Leblanc, trans. Sarah Cummins (Halifax: Formac, 1992). **Rev:** *CCL* 74 (1994): 92.

The Last Piece of Sky, by Tim Wynne-Jones (Toronto: Groundwood, 1993). **Rev:** *BiC* 22 (Dec. 1993): 56; *QQ* 59 (Oct. 1993): 38.

Maddie Goes to Paris, by Louise Leblanc, trans. Sarah Cummins (Halifax: Formac, 1994). **Rev:** *CBRA* (1994): 489.

When Vegetables Go Bad!, by Don Gillmor (Toronto: Doubleday, 1994). **Rev:** *BiC* 23 (Sept. 1994): 56; *CBRA* (1994): 452; *QQ* 60 (Aug. 1992): 33.

Maddie in Danger, by Louise Leblanc, trans. Sarah Cummins (Halifax: Formac, 1995). **Rev:** *CBRA* (1994): 509.

The Fabulous Song, by Don Gillmor (Toronto: Stoddart, 1996). **Rev:** *CBRA* (1996): 443; *CCL* 86 (1997): 57; *QQ* 62 (Mar. 1996): 75.

The Christmas Orange, by Don Gillmor (Toronto: Stoddart, 1998). **Rev:** *QQ* 64 (Dec. 1998): 35.

Dreams Are More Beautiful Than Bathtubs, by Susan Musgrave (Victoria, BC: Orca, 1998).

How to Take Your Mother to the Museum, by Lois Wyse and Molly Rose Gold (New York: Workman Publishing, 1998).

Related Works

Bonne Fête Willy, children's puppet play written by Gay, who also designed sets, puppets, and costumes. Produced, National Arts Centre Atelier, Montreal, 26 Nov. 1989.

Selected Discussions

Davis, Marie. 'Un penchant pour la diagonale: An Interview with Marie-Louise Gay', *CCL* 60 (1990): 52–74.

Jenkinson, Dave. 'Marie-Louise Gay: Award-Winning Picture Book Author and Illustrator', *EL* 19 (May 1992): 65–8.

Marie-Louise Gay, the only person to have won two major French-Canadian and two major English-Canadian awards for illustration, did not originally intend to become an artist. She had planned to work as a teacher, but after high school and study at the Academy of Art College, she worked as a freelance artist and wrote and illustrated children's books for Quebec publishers. Her *La soeur de Robert* won the Alvine-Belisle Prize for the best French-Canadian children's book of the Year. *Drôle d'école* received the French-Canadian Canada Council Illustration Award. Her illustrations for Dennis Lee's *Lizzy's Lion*, her first book for an English-speaking audience, also won the Canada Council Prize for Illustration.

Speaking of her work, Gay has stated, 'I feel that I'm principally an illustrator who can add words to round out the illustration.' She notes that for *Moonbeam on a Cat's Ear*, the illustrations are more important than the words: 'If you just looked at the pictures, you would understand the whole story.' In her illustrations, Gay reinforces the rhythms of the poem, develops characterization, and gives fuller expression to actions.

Lizzy's Lion takes place in Lizzy's bedroom, where a burglar is confronted by the girl's pet. Gay uses a double-spread for each four-line verse. The opening pen-and-watercolour illustration shows the friendly clutter of her room, the tousle-haired heroine, and only the lion's tail. On the following page, the lion is revealed; he is huge, but completely controlled by the heroine, who casually wraps his tail around her neck. These two illustrations foreshadow scenes to come. The lion is not seen when the robber enters the room; when he encounters it later, his face reveals shock and fear. Soon the clutter of the room is replaced by torn pieces of the robber's clothing, and Lizzy controls the lion as she did at the beginning. Although Lee's verse carries the story along, Gay's exaggerated, cartoon-like illustrations emphasize the humour.

Gay's 14-line poem for *Moonbeam on a Cat's Ear* provides the barest plot outline. Toby arrives at his sister's bedroom one moonlit night and invites her to come outside. He climbs the apple tree to pull down the moon, which they ride over the sea and through the sky. At the conclusion, the poet asks the reader, 'Was it a dream or did they really try to steal the moon right out of the sky?' By looking at the last two illustrations, readers find the answer. At the beginning of the story, the cat and mouse have been sleeping on Rosie's bed; at the end, they are dozing on the curve of the crescent moon.

Realizing that events have really happened, the reader/viewer can go back and look carefully at the illustrations as a record of an exciting adventure. The double-spread showing the children standing at the front door, silhouetted against the moonlit sky, indicates that no ordinary nocturnal stroll awaits them. Bolts of lightning zigzag across the wallpaper, and the landscape outside contains no familiar objects, as if the two were stepping into an alternate world. Four double-spreads depict the children's changing emotions as they ride the moon. They smile quietly as it bobs across the waves, break into excited smiles as it becomes airborne, and cry out in fear as lightning strikes their craft, forcing them to jump overboard.

The heroine of *Midnight Mimi* does not like sleeping at night and enjoys the magical effects created by the moon shining into her room. Dancing with her toys, she protects them from invading toys. Purple and white hues distinguish the imaginative world the child creates, while the wild rhythms and cartoon-like drawings suggest her exuberance and release as she plays.

Rainy Day Magic is the fantasy adventure of two small children caught in the basement when the lights go out. On a rainy day, they have been wildly playing upstairs, racing tricycles around and over the wonderful clutter they have made. Banished to the basement by their exasperated father, they create a pyramid of old chairs, on which they stand while playing musical instruments and dancing. The opening illustrations are not only humorous exaggerations of normal children's play, but also symbols of the emotional state of the children. They are filled with energy they cannot release because they are confined indoors and repressed by adults. In addition, the illustrations contain several details that will be seen again in the children's adventures after they follow a mysterious blue light shining in a corner of the darkened basement. Gay ends *Rainy Day Magic* ambiguously. The father asks, 'What's that in your hair?' The illustration shows Joey wearing a small purple starfish like the one the children had met on their adventure. As in the conclusion of *Moonbeam on a Cat's Ear*, the reality of magic is made a distinct possibility.

In *Angel and the Polar Bear* and *Willy Nilly* fantastic events occur in the ordinary world. Angel, who tries unsuccessfully to get the attention of her sleeping parents, must act resourcefully when her apartment fills with water and a polar bear emerges from the refrigerator. Willy Nilly, sent outside while his mother prepares for his birthday party, finds a box containing magical equipment and instructions and uses the magic words to transform other children and his aunt into animals. In the two books, however, the children's responses to these fantastic events is very different. Angel, who cannot swim, makes a tightrope to reach the bureau that contains her flippers and rubber giraffe and, donning these, makes her way to the kitchen where she opens the refrigerator to freeze the water. Willy, hastily casting spells, misuses his new-found power, with the result that people become monsters—half-human and half-animal. He needs the help of an adult, Vladimir the Magician, to set things right.

Although the written texts are longer than in her earlier works, the illustrations of these books expand on the narratives and communicate the emotions of the characters. In *Angel and the Polar Bear*, a white border embraces the upper half of one side of each double-spread, indicating the world of the real apartment. However, the illustrations of the magical world extend beyond the borders, across the bottoms of both sides of the double-spreads. The opening and closing single-page illustrations are dominated by purple and light blue washes. In the first, Angel, lying on her pillow, calls out to her parents. In the final one, she sprawls on the kitchen floor, facing the crouching polar bear with whom she is playing dominoes. The similarity in colours implies she is on equal terms with reality, and with the wonderful world that has invaded her house. Small details in the pictures reinforce the girl's character. For example, a tiny kitten dons a snorkel mask and later skates and then joyfully slides down the bear's back. It, like the girl, is enthusiastically engaged in her events. In *Willy Nilly*, when he is proud of his accomplishments, the boy is the largest figure in the illustrations. However, he is very small when he needs help from the magician. In many pictures, a rabbit and turtle who came with the magic kit laugh at the ridiculous situations the boy creates and, by implication, at his foolish pride.

The hero of *Fat Charlie's Circus* does not encounter magical worlds or powers; rather, he comes to understand the difference between his fantasies and reality. Planning to become a circus performer, he practices lion-taming with the family cat and juggling with the dinner plates. However, when he climbs a tree to perform a daredevil dive into a glass of water, he becomes frightened and must be helped to the ground by his grandmother. Gay's illustrations underscore differences between make-believe and reality. The borders surrounding Charlie practicing give the pictures the appearance of circus posters. They also contain his world and imply security. However, when he climbs the tree, the borders disappear. The frightening reality destroys the safe framework of harmless make-believe.

Gay's art for Don Gillmor's *The Fabulous Song* and her retelling of the Brothers Grimm's *Rumpelstiltskin* are representative of her approach to illustrating others' stories. The former deals with a familiar Gay theme: a child's learning his own strengths; the latter is about a woman who is under the control of others and saved only by luck. Frederic, whose parents want him to become a musician, fails miserably at piano, clarinet, and other lessons. However, after watching the conductor at his sister's concert, he proves his talents, conducting his family at a birthday party. Early in the story, he is the smallest figure in the illustrations; however, as he assembles and conducts his family, he becomes larger on the pages. Pictured earlier as a baby slopping food and waving his spoon, he now sits proudly eating his ice cream with the spoon he used as a baton. Zigzag pieces of torn musical scores are now replaced by waving, rainbow-coloured ribbons of music.

Rumpelstiltskin is about the power the father, the king, and a magical little man have over the heroine. Only after she announces her benefactor's true name does she achieve a measure of freedom. Although Gay is limited by the fact that the text is well-known to many and can stand on its own and by the fact that the tone is far more sombre than the tones of her earlier books, she successfully uses the borders of her pictures and the size and position of the heroine within them to reflect the woman's struggles with the males in her life. Early in the narrative, the girl, who is shorter than her father, is dominated by the king. His horse towers over her; later, his shadow, pointing to the room of straw, looms on the wall. Rumpelstiltskin strides confidently into her presence. However, when she is in danger of losing the child, she assumes a more dominant position in the pictures, and, as she prepares to defeat the little man, she stands tall above him, an indication of her new power. Whereas earlier she had been confined within the borders of most of the illustrations, and her head extends above the border, and her long flowing hair and full skirt extend into the side margins. The book's final illustration, in which the queen joyously dandles her child, is not framed: she is completely free.

Whether she is presenting strong, courageous, and clever heroines confronting dangerous situations or children exploring imaginary or magical realms, Gay draws her characters with bold, cartoon-like lines that convey their physical exuberance and imaginative vitality, qualities that propel them beyond the limits of mundane experiences, just as the figures in many of the illustrations burst from the constraints of borders. The worlds they inhabit or visit are splashed with a variety of colours, each in varying degrees of brilliance. As her characters' moods change, so do the hues of the pictures. Her apparently simple texts and plots and her seemingly child-like illustrations are quite fully celebrations of the complex emotional and imaginative exuberance of children as they explore the many and varied worlds of their lives.

See also: *CA* 135; *CLR* 27; *SAAS* 21; *SATA* 68; *TCCW*; *WSMP*.

Tony German

Born: 28 September 1924, in Ottawa.

Principal Residences: Ottawa.

Education: Royal Canadian Naval College (Victoria).

Career: naval officer; businessman; school administrator; personnel consultant; writer.

Works for Children

Tom Penny (Toronto: Peter Martin, 1977). **Rev:** *CCL* 23 (1981): 96; *EL* 14 (Jan. 1987): 53; *IR* 12 (Spring 1978): 46.

River Race (Toronto: Peter Martin, 1977): **Rev:** *BiC* 9 (Feb. 1980): 22; *CCL* 29 (1983): 63; *EL* 14 (Jan. 1987): 53; *IR* 14 (Aug. 1980): 48.

Tom Penny and the Grand Canal (Toronto: McClelland & Stewart, 1982). **Rev:** *BiC* 12 (Feb. 1983) 33; *CCL* 23 (1981): 96; *EL* 10 (May 1983): 30; *QQ* 49 (Feb. 1983): 39.

A Breed Apart (Toronto: McClelland & Stewart, 1985). **Rev:** *CCL* 41 (1986): 82.

OTHER

'Time and Place', *CCL* 83 (Fall 1996): 89–91.

'We're all immigrants, as are my characters. Their stories are fictional, but I try to conjure up some of the adventures, problems, and difficulties a young person of the earlier nineteenth century might experience.' Tony German's young immigrant heroes live in pre-Confederation Canada; they respond to the dangers and excitement of the new country and mature as they confront their environment and their own inner doubts and hopes. German says that he discovered the romance of Canadian history by reading the journals of Alexander Mackenzie.

For German, the writing of the novels is preceded by a great deal of research: 'I must know the times and the settings of a story thoroughly before I can begin developing character and plotting events.' German's first three novels, 'The Tom Penny Trilogy', are set in the Ottawa Valley during the early nineteenth century. He has called Penny 'an unusual boy, a hero. Young people then had to be tough, resourceful, and determined. It was an active time and sparks flew. We need to look back at our forebears, people like Tom, with pride.' At the beginning of *Tom Penny*, the boy's father is murdered just as the family prepares to sail for Canada. As events follow thick and fast in the tradition of the adventure story, Tom requires all the toughness, resourcefulness, and determination he can muster. The ship carrying him and his mother to the New World is wrecked, he is picked up by rum-runners, and when he finally joins his Uncle Matthew on the family land, he must contend with the winter weather and the villainous Dirk Black. In *River Race*, Tom and his uncle are on a lumber raft, determined to reach Montreal in time to get the best prices for their timber. Along the way Tom is accused of a murder committed by Oliver Sharpe, who seeks to become rich through others' misfortunes. In *Tom Penny and the Grand Canal*, Matthew and Tom's new father-in-law hope to become rich by building a canal to Georgian Bay.

Donald Cameron, the teenage hero of *A Breed Apart*, is half Cree and half Scots. Returning after several years at school in Montreal to the trading fort run by his father, he becomes embroiled in the struggles between the Hudson's Bay and North West companies and is forced to face and to resolve his conflicting thoughts about his dual heritage. Along the way, he is able also to expose Harry Whistler in his attempt to manipulate both companies for his own illegitimate gain.

German's stereotypical minor characters will be familiar to readers of mystery and adventure stories and his major characters are not overly complex. They emerge as symbols: Tom Penny and Donald Cameron represent the youthful, masculine spirit possessed by thousands of unknown pioneers. One of the strongest elements of these historical adventures is the presentation of setting. German knows the rugged landscapes of his stories well and portrays these concretely and convincingly.

See also: *CA* 97–100; *WSMP*.

Phoebe Gilman

Born: 4 April 1940, in New York.

Principal Residences: New York; Jerusalem; Toronto.

Education: Art Students' League (New York); Hunter College (New York); Bezalel Academy (Jerusalem).

Career: college instructor; artist; author; illustrator.

Major Awards: Ruth Schwartz Children's Book Award (1993); Vicky Metcalf Award (1993).

Works for Children

Written and Illustrated by Phoebe Gilman

The Balloon Tree (Richmond Hill, Ont.: Scholastic, 1984). **Rev:** *CCL* 39 (1985): 145; *QQ* 51 (Feb. 1985): 10.

Jillian Jiggs (Richmond Hill, Ont.: Scholastic, 1985). **Rev:** *QQ* 51 (Feb. 1985): 22.

Little Blue Ben (Richmond Hill, Ont.: Scholastic, 1986). **Rev:** *CCL* 45 (1987): 94; *QQ* 52 (Dec. 1986): 14.

The Wonderful Pigs of Jillian Jiggs (Richmond Hill, Ont.: Scholastic, 1988). **Rev:** *BiC* 17 (Dec. 1988): 11; *CCL* 57 (1990): 111; *EL* 18 (Nov. 1990): 61.

Grandma and the Pirates (Richmond Hill, Ont.: Scholastic, 1990). **Rev:** *CCL* 63 (1991): 114; *CL* 135 (Winter 1992): 189; *CM* 18 (Nov. 1990): 267; *QQ* 56 (June 1990): 16; *SLJ* 37 (Jan. 1991): 72.

Something from Nothing (Richmond Hill, Ont.: Scholastic, 1992). **Rev:** *BiC* 21 (Nov. 1992): 36; *CCB-B* 47 (Feb. 1994): 186; *CCL* 72 (1993): 52; *CM* 20 (Sept. 1992): 207; *EL* 20 (Mar. 1993): 13; *HB* 69 (Nov. 1993): 770; *QQ* 58 (July 1992): 44; *SLJ* 40 (Jan. 1994): 107.

Jillian Jiggs to the Rescue (Richmond Hill, Ont.: Scholastic, 1994). *CBRA* (1994): 452; *CL* 147 (Winter 1995): 205; *CM* 22 (Sept. 1994): 132; *QQ* 60 (Mar. 1994): 80.

The Gypsy Princess (Richmond Hill, Ont.: North Winds, 1995). **Rev:** *BiC* 25 (Feb. 1996): 20; *CCB-B* 50 (Mar. 1997): 247; *CBRA* (1995): 469; *EL* 23 (Mar. 1996): 24; *QQ* 61 (Dec. 1995): 37; *SLJ* 43 (Mar. 1997): 152.

Pirate Pearl (Markham, Ont.: North Winds, 1998).

Illustrated by Phoebe Gilman

Once Upon a Golden Apple, by Jean Little and Maggie Devries (Toronto: Penguin, 1991).

Although Phoebe Gilman did not publish her first children's story until she was 44, the experiences of her life to that point provided the foundation for *The Balloon Tree* and the books that followed. Her childhood dreams of becoming a princess, love of fairy tales, ability to make messes, and tendency to criticize illustrations that did not complement the texts she read find their way into her own works, as do her extensive training in art and design and portrait painting and her study of classical art.

Gilman began *The Balloon Tree* after noticing her daughter's unhappiness over a burst balloon. It is a literary fairy tale in which a princess's courage, resourcefulness, and love of balloons lead to her escape from her evil, power-hungry uncle. With the exception of a magic tree that blossoms with millions of balloons, the plot is relatively conventional. However, the character strengths of the princess and the somewhat chaotic play as the balloons proliferate in the pictures anticipate Gilman's later works. Traditional borders introduce visual elements similar to others of Gilman's books, as do the inclusion of visual details not mentioned in the text. Unfortunately, because human figures are made small, facial expressions that could reveal character and emotions are difficult to perceive.

Little Blue Ben relates to her own children's occasional fussiness about the food she served them. A tiny man and his brother, Blue Cat, tired of a constant diet of eggs served by their mother, Blue Hen, engage in a game of hide-and-seek, with the loser required to eat the winner's eggs. Gilman's double-spreads communicate the sense of freedom the brothers experience after leaving the house. In her rhyming text, she invites readers to look carefully for the tiny man hidden in the pictures, a use of detail she expands in later works.

Jillian Jiggs embodies Gilman's own, her children's, and by extension, most children's love of creative, if somewhat messy and chaotic play. The repeated refrain, 'It looks like your room has been lived in by pigs', indicates the mother's growing annoyance as the girl and her friends continue to make costumes and toys from boxes, paper, old clothing, and other objects. As Jillian's creative enthusiasm expands, the number of small objects in the pictures increases and details spill beyond the borders of the illustrations. Six double-spreads present the height of activities, as the girl is joined by her little sister and two friends. Although the heroine obeys her mother at the conclusion and sets about tidying things, the reader is left with suspicions that her creativity and clutter are only temporarily contained. These suspicions are confirmed in the sequels, *The Wonderful Pigs of Jillian Jiggs* and *Jillian Jiggs to the Rescue*.

Grandma and the Pirates presents two strong, resourceful female characters and parodies the conventions of the nineteenth-century pirate story. When a hungry crew of buccaneers invade an old woman's house, devour all her food, and then shanghai her and her parrot, young Melissa comes to the rescue, only to become a prisoner herself. The two must devise a clever plan to get rid of their captors and sail the ship home. Much of the humour of the story is communicated through contrasting facial expressions: the pirates, in spite of attempts to appear fierce, look foolish; the two women, who at first looked fearful and alarmed, become increasingly more resolute and devious. The borders around the illustrations are varied to reflect the different situations. For example, when Grandma is captured, there are several knots in the ropes, and borders of fish traps accompany the illustration of the trapped girl and woman. A brave princess and a parody of pirates are found also in *Pirate Pearl*, in which an abandoned princess adopted by pirates becomes a swashbuckling adventurer who overcomes the evil count who usurped her throne. After her victory, Pearl declines a prince's marriage proposal, preferring the life of a buccaneer.

Something from Nothing and *The Gypsy Princess* reveal the author's finest use of illustrations to expand the textual meanings of stories built from traditional motifs. The former, based on an eastern European Jewish folktale, portrays the relationship between a tailor and his grandson. The old man makes baby Joseph a blue blanket. When, over the years, the cloth becomes smaller and more tattered, the grandfather makes it into new, but smaller articles of clothing. When the boy loses the button made from the last piece of cloth and is told that a person 'can't make something from nothing', he disagrees and uses his memories of his grandfather's work as the basis of a story he shares with school friends and family. The story, like *Jillian Jiggs*, celebrates creativity—both grandfather's with cloth and Joseph's with memories and words. Futhermore, it is a tribute to family and community, a theme presented through the details and overall designs of the pages. In addition to depicting the family's activities in their tiny apartment, Gilman presents people interacting in the street outside, at market, town pump, and school. Activities extend beneath grandfather's work area, where a growing family of mice salvages scraps of material that have fallen between the floor boards. Cutaway views of the house help to integrate all three areas. For example, in the second-floor apartment, Joseph's father works as a cobbler; below, grandfather works on the blue cloth while the boy and a customer look on; behind a curtain, the grandmother tends Joseph's little sister; under the floorboards, the mouse family engages in chores, including school lessons. Outside, Joseph's mother hangs laundry from the upper porch, a girl knocks at the tailor's door, two boys watch an organ grinder, and the neighbours stand in their doorway watching passersby.

The Gypsy Princess adopts a theme familiar in children's stories; a young person yearning for a different life leaves home and, discovering that the new life is not so fulfilling as expected, returns to her own community a wiser person. Cinnamon, who laments, 'If only I could live in a palace,' ignores her old aunt's caution that 'there are things more precious than a crown of gold' and accepts a passing princess's invitation to become her companion. However, the gypsy girl begins to lose her identity, becomes dispirited, and finds herself ignored. When the old woman and a dancing bear, the girl's companion and pet, communicate to her through magical dreams, Cinnamon escapes from the palace and, after washing away all traces of her aristocratic life in a forest pond, joyously rejoins her community. Underlying the narrative are the themes of true and false identity, freedom and imprisonment, dream and reality.

Gilman uses page design, portrait-style pictures, and small, but very significant details to reveal character, theme, and conflict. Each double-spread contains three closely related illustrations: on the left are a small framed picture above the text and, surrounding the text, another illustration. Opposite, a full-page picture is surrounded by a border resembling the gilt frames of formal paintings. These three illustrative forms display conflicting aspects of the heroine's life. Early in the story, a tiny picture reveals her dream of dancing with a prince; the surrounding one contains many images from the imaginative tales the old woman tells her; on the opposite page, the girl, her aunt, and the tame bear are grouped happily together. When she has left home, the bear sits lonely in the forest, and she stands awkwardly in a confining dress while maids create a fashionable hairdo. On the opposite page, Cinnamon stands unhappily alone in the formal enclosed palace garden, dipping her fingers in an ornamental pool.

Gilman contrasts several pairs of visual details in order to imply the change in the girl's life after she has withdrawn from her community. Unlike the gypsy caravan with a windowbox of herbs at its side, the ornate carriage has only a stylized floral decoration painted on its side panels. Her dancing bear is replaced by a wind-up toy bear; her head scarf, by a coronet; and her bare feet, by tight, pinching shoes. Whereas she had ridden her aunt's horse bareback and danced as a member of the gypsy group, in the palace she sits side-saddle on a wooden hobby horse and stands apart from the other people at the ball. When Cinnamon escapes the castle, she leaves the artificial objects behind, discards her shoes and coronet and, her gown in tatters, tears a strip from it to make a new kerchief for her head. In the castle, she had stared in the mirror and not recognized herself; in the forest, she looks in a pond and declares, 'I know who I am.' The style of portraiture showing her at the ball is formal, in the manner of the eighteenth century. That of her emerging from the pond uses the same ornate framework; however, lines of vitality swirl in the picture, and water splashes out beyond the frame. She is no longer confined.

In a publicity flyer for *The Gypsy Princess*, Gilman wrote that, as a child, 'When the pictures didn't match the images that the words [of the books she was reading] had painted in my head, I would cover them up with my hands.' Gilman's own illustrations are not designed just to match the words; they are designed to expand on them. She asks her readers to approach creatively her own illustrations, freely liberating meanings she has suggested and making their own meanings. Thus, readers, like the characters in the stories who respond imaginatively and creatively to their worlds, will find their own freedom and fulfilment.

See also: *SATA* 58; *TCCW*; *WSMP*.

Martyn Godfrey

Born: 17 April 1949, in Birmingham, England.

Principal Residences: Birmingham; Toronto; St Albert.

Career: elementary and junior high school teacher in Ontario and Alberta; children's writer.

Education: University of Toronto (BA Honours 1973, B.Ed. 1974).

Awards: Vicky Metcalf Short Story Award (1985); University of Lethbridge award for best children's book (1987); Geoffrey Bilson Award for Historical Fiction for Young People (1989).

Works for Children

The Vandarian Incident (Richmond Hill, Ont.: Scholastic-TAB, 1981); republished as *The Day the Sky Exploded* (Richmond Hill, Ont.: Scholastic Canada, 1991). **Rev:** *IR* 15 (Aug. 1981): 40; *QQ* 47 (June 1981): 33.

Alien Wargames (Richmond Hill, Ont.: Scholastic, 1984). **Rev:** *EL* 12 (Mar. 1985): 48.

The Beast (Don Mills, Ont.: Collier Macmillan, 1984).

Spin Out (Don Mills, Ont.: Collier Macmillan, 1984).

Here She Is, Ms Teeny-Wonderful (Richmond Hill, Ont.: Scholastic, 1984).

Ice Hawk (Don Mills, Ont.: Collier Macmillan, 1985).

Fire! Fire! (Don Mills, Ont.: Collier Macmillan, 1985).

The Last War (Don Mills, Ont.: Collier Macmillan, 1986).

Plan B Is Total Panic (Toronto: James Lorimer, 1986). **Rev:** *BiC* 15 (Dec. 1986): 16; *CCL* 45 (1987): 72; *QQ* 52 (Dec. 1986): 17; *SL* 39 (Feb. 1991): 29.

It Isn't Easy Being Ms Teeny-Wonderful (Richmond Hill, Ont.: Scholastic, 1987). **Rev:** *BYP* 1 (Apr. 1987): 8; *CM* 16 (Jan. 1988): 15; *CCL* 56 (1989): 78.

Wild Night (Don Mills, Ont.: Collier Macmillan, 1987).

More Than Weird (Don Mills, Ont.: Collier Macmillan, 1987) **Rev:** *CM* 16 (July 1988): 127.

Rebel Yell (Don Mills, Ont.: Collier Macmillan, 1987).

Baseball Crazy (Toronto: James Lorimer, 1987). **Rev:** *BYP* 2 (Feb. 1988): 5; *CCL* 56 (1989): 78; *CM* 16 (July 1988): 127; *CM* 20 (Jan. 1992): 12.

It Seemed Like a Good Idea at the Time (Edmonton: Tree Frog, 1987). **Rev:** *CM* 16 (Sept. 1988): 169.

Send in Ms Teeny-Wonderful (Richmond Hill, Ont.: Scholastic, 1988).

Mystery in the Frozen Lands (Toronto: James Lorimer, 1988). **Rev:** *BYP* 3 (Apr. 1989): 12; *CCL* 56 (1989): 91; *CL* (Winter 1990): 124; *CM* 17 (May 1989): 123; *EL* 16 (May 1989): 53; *EL* 17 (Mar. 1990): 24; *Maclean's* 101 (26 Dec. 1988): N6; *SL* 39 (Feb. 1991): 23.

Break Out (Toronto: Collier Macmillan, 1988).

In the Time of the Monsters (Don Mills, Ont.: Collier Macmillan, 1989).

Why Just Me? (Toronto: McClelland & Stewart, 1989).

Can You Teach Me to Pick My Nose? (New York: Avon, 1990). **Rev:** *BiC* 19 (Oct. 1990): 29; *VOYA* 13 (Oct. 1990): 217.

I Spent My Summer Vacation Kidnapped Into Space (New York: Scholastic, 1990). **Rev:** *BiC* 19 (Dec. 1990): 33; *CCL* 64 (1991): 85; *CM* 18 (Nov. 1990): 275; *QQ* 56 (Oct. 1990): 16.

Monsters in the School (Richmond Hill, Ont.: Scholastic, 1991) **Rev:** *BiC* 20 (Dec. 1991): 37; *CCL* 77 (1995): 69; *CM* 19 (Nov. 1991): 350.

There's a Cow in My Swimming Pool, with Frank O'Keeffe (Richmond Hill, Ont.: Scholastic, 1991). **Rev:** *CCL* 77 (1995): 77; *CM* 19 (Nov. 1991): 340; *CM* 20 (Jan. 1992): 17; *QQ* 57 (Nov. 1991): 28.

Wally Stutzgummer, Super Bad Dude (Richmond Hill, Ont.: Scholastic, 1992). **Rev:** *CCL* 80 (1995): 82; *CL* (Spring 1993): 170.

Don't Worry About Me, I'm Just Crazy (Toronto: Stoddart, 1992). **Rev:** *QQ* 58 (May 1992): 32.

The Great Science Fair Disaster (Richmond Hill, Ont.: Scholastic, 1992). **Rev:** *CM* 20 (Nov. 1992): 305; *QQ* 58 (Aug. 1992): 26.

Is It Okay If This Monster Stays for Lunch?, illus. Susan Wilkinson (Toronto: Oxford UP, 1992). **Rev:** *BiC* 21 (May 1992): 58; *CM* 20 (May 1992): 159; *QQ* 58 (Mar. 1992): 65.

Meet You in the Sewer (Richmond Hill, Ont.: Scholastic, 1993). **Rev:** *CM* 22 (May 1994): 75; *EL* 21 (Jan. 1994): 57; *QQ* 59 (Oct. 1993): 41.

Please Remove Your Elbow From My Ear (New York: Avon, 1993). **Rev:** *QQ* 59 (Aug. 1993): 38.

Just Call Me Boom Boom (Richmond Hill, Ont.: Scholastic, 1994). **Rev:** *BiC* 23 (Summer 1994): 58; *CBRA* (1994): 482; *CCL* 80 (1995): 82–4; *CL* (Spring 1996): 198; *CM* 22 (Oct. 1994): 179; *QQ* 60 (Mar. 1994): 82.

Mall Rats (Edmonton: oz New Media/Duval, 1994). **Rev:** *CBRA* (1994): 482; *QQ* 60 (July 1994): 58.

The Things (Edmonton: oz New Media/Duval, 1994). **Rev:** *CBRA* (1994): 482; *QQ* 60 (July 1994): 58.

Do You Want Fries With That? (Toronto: Scholastic Canada, 1996). **Rev:** *BiC* 25 (Oct. 1996): 31.

Adventures in Pirate Cove #1: The Mystery of Hole's Castle (New York: Avon, 1996). **Rev:** *SLJ* 42 (July 1996): 84.

Adventures in Pirate Cove #2: The Hunt for Buried Treasure (New York: Avon, 1996).

Adventures in Pirate Cove #3: The Desperate Escape (New York: Avon, 1997).

'There are two kinds of books', Martyn Godfrey says. 'First, there are the stories that kids devour. Then there are the ones that get the gold crests—you and I enjoy them; librarians love them; they're super books. But their covers don't fall off because kids don't take them home.' As the torn and tattered covers of his books in libraries across Canada indicate, Godfrey has definitely succeeded in his goal of becoming 'a popular author in the sense that kids ask for a Martyn Godfrey book because they enjoy it'. Although Godfrey is admittedly a commercial writer, he believes that he plays an important role: 'I am a first step. By giving children enjoyable reading, I may be encouraging some of them to take the next step and to read the books with the gold crests.'

Godfrey has become popular as the author of tales about pre-teen life, but he began his career writing science fiction, a genre to which he occasionally returns. Written in response to a challenge from a student, his first novel, *The Vandarian Incident* (reissued as *The Day the Sky Exploded*), is a conventional space adventure complete with evil, reptilian aliens. His second, *Alien War Games*, contains considerable violence, but it is more substantial. It effectively criticizes racism and imperialism by winning sympathy for an indigenous hunting people whom colonists from Earth deceive and mistreat. Godfrey also chose a science fiction theme for his first foray into picture books, *Is It Okay If This Monster Stays for Lunch?*, in which a boy repeatedly asks his family to invite his alien and monster playmates for lunch. Pictures and text clearly establish that only the boy notices the monsters, which comically keeps open the question of whether they are real or imaginary. Godfrey's later science fiction novels are, however, decidedly inferior to *Alien War Games*. For example, *I Spent My Summer Vacation Kidnapped into Space*, a work written for younger readers, combines disparate elements unsuccessfully. The story of two adolescents who are kidnapped by aliens, sold as slaves to fight slime worms in a circus, and then sent to rescue a princess, its adventures are too predictable and stereotypical to be gripping, and its presentation of bizarre aliens, ludicrous heroics, and juvenile repartee is not witty enough for an entertaining spoof of space operas. Other science fiction books, such as *The Last War*, a grim picture of the aftermath of an atomic war, *The Things*, about teens fighting monsters from an experimental laboratory, and *More Than Weird*, about a female robot from the future trying to kidnap an average human for display in a zoo, concentrate on action at the expense of character development. The limitations of these last three titles are deliberate, however, because Godfrey wrote them for reluctant readers. Narrated in the first person to establish what Godfrey calls 'the instant hook of character identification', these books employ a limited, unchallenging vocabulary. The short chapters, which typically conclude with cliff-hangers, are packed with fast-paced action. In *Wild Night*, for example, a boy working at a convenience store must cope with a robbery, an attempted suicide, a birth, and a nearly fatal accident. In addition to relying on action, these novels compel interest by focusing on situations that concern many teens. *Ice Hawk*, for example, explores the moral conflict of a hockey 'goon' ordered to injure an opposing superstar, *Rebel Yell* presents the experiences of an inner-city teen contending with a prejudiced vice-principal and a gun-carrying gang member, and *Mall Rats* recounts the frustrations and violence facing troubled teens who hang around a large urban mall.

Like his books for reluctant readers, Godfrey's mainstream fiction is formulaic. First-person narration invites identification with the central character, a relatively dramatic opening engages the reader, extensive dialogue creates a quick pace and sense of immediacy, and the slapstick episodes and numerous jokes hold interest. Although many of the characters exhibit comic eccentricities, the central characters display anxieties and insecurities typical of youth. In spite of their absurd events, these novels treat relatively serious problems involving friendship with members of the opposite sex and relationships with parents, particularly divorced parents, and their themes clearly stress the need to understand and accept others.

The most light-hearted and popular of these books are undoubtedly those in the *Ms Teeny-Wonderful* series. In *Here She Is, Ms Teeny-Wonderful*, Carol Weatherspoon, whose talent is jumping garbage cans on her bicycle, enters a pre-teen beauty contest. The obnoxious Campbell twins repeatedly try to sabotage Carol's chances, initiating a series of ludicrous retaliations. Reminiscent of Gordon Korman's *Bruno and Boots* books, this farce has a unified plot, lively pace, comic reversals, and eccentric characters. As is often the case, however, the sequels are disappointing. Lacking the focus that the beauty contest provides in the first story, *It Isn't Easy Being Ms Teeny-Wonderful* awkwardly combines episodes about Carol's maturing sense of identity and implausible physical heroism. The third instalment, *Send in Ms Teeny-Wonderful*, in which Carol saves a teenage Middle Eastern prince from kidnappers, has manic energy, but its chase scenes, during which Carol and her companion, Wally, outwit and humiliate the kidnappers, are too hackneyed and too long to be funny. Although the final title in the series, *Wally Stutzgummer, Super Bad Dude*, concludes farcically with Wally, dressed in a superhero's costume, capturing a thief who stole a valuable comic, it lacks the zaniness that makes the earlier volumes entertaining.

Similar deficiencies weaken other titles. The humour is forced in *It Seemed Like a Good Idea at the Time*, more an extended anecdote than a novel, in which disasters descend upon a boy who disguises himself in order to attend an all-girl party. Although written for children relatively new to chapter books, *Monsters in the School* has little to commend it. Ignoring the issues raised by the lies eight-year-old Selby tells in order to gain attention, this novel falls back on the creaky plot device of having her accidentally become responsible for catching a robber. The resolution of the conflict between the narrator and her parents in *The Great Science Fair Disaster* depends on predictable slapstick, and the novel leaves unresolved an important subplot about an underachieving student. In *Baseball Crazy*, about 14-year-old Brent Hutchins, who wins a contest to become bat boy for the Blue Jays during spring training in Florida, the compelling baseball atmosphere is not sufficient compensation for the decidedly pedestrian mystery. Godfrey's two attempts at starting series are marginally better. *The J.A.W.S. Mob* books, *Meet You in the Sewer* and *Just Call Me Boom Boom*, first-person narratives about the adventures of students in a writing class at a Toronto school, contain action and lively adolescent dialogue. *The Adventures in Pirate Cove* series combines elements of the Hardy Boys books and English vacation novels. The central joke in them is that the aspiring youthful detective constantly jumps to false conclusions. Each series has some entertaining moments, but neither is noteworthy.

Although they differ in plot, many of Godfrey's other books are similar in their focus on changes. In *Plan B Is Total Panic*, a somewhat heavy-handed multicultural adventure, a teen discovers his inner resources and realizes that he is not a 'wimp'. *There's a Cow in My Swimming Pool*, which Godfrey co-authored with Frank O'Keeffe, shows Nicole Peters, whose father was killed in an accident, overcoming resentment when her mother decides to remarry. In *Please Remove Your Elbow From My Ear*, the issue is social perception. Stormy Sprague, who views himself and is viewed by others as a social misfit, ends his social isolation by stopping a gang from extracting protection money from students and then by helping other social outcasts to win both a floor hockey tournament and acceptance. In *Why Just Me?*, Shannon MacKenzie learns to accept the changes of puberty and then displays maturity by refusing to let a quarrel ruin a friendship, by forming a closer relationship with her divorced mother, and by trying to share her new boyfriend's interest in hockey. Roob Fowler, the narrator of *Don't Worry About Me, I'm Just Crazy*, must reorient his attitudes. In the beginning, he foolishly fantasizes about being stranded with Rachel Parsons, and he entertains the misguided dream of solving his problems at school by moving in with his divorced father. Roob learns that he cannot run away from trouble, a point highlighted by a subplot in which he saves the life of a friend despondent because his father refuses to let him be himself. Hence, Roob gains a more mature vision of both Rachel and his drunken father. The need for parents to change is central in two books. In *Do You Want Fries with That?* the presentation trivializes the theme of parents needing to adapt as their children mature. Brittany Prentice's smotheringly over-protective divorced father is a gross caricature whose change of heart depends on a melodramatic plot contrivance, her rescues of a drowning boy. *Can You Teach Me to Pick My Nose?* (the title refers to a skateboard manoeuvre) is more effective because Jordy Shepherd's overprotective mother, who refuses to let him try skateboarding, is not a caricature and is not dominant. Furthermore, the novel amplifies the theme, showing not only that Jordy's mother must give him freedom but also that Jordy must have faith in himself and that his strange friend, Pamela, must stop hiding herself behind bizarre costumes and alienating manners.

Godfrey has also written a historical novel, *Mystery in the Frozen Lands*, about an expedition to discover what happened to Sir John Franklin's ill-fated Arctic expedition. Narrated by young Peter Griffin, this novel conveys the dangers faced by explorers and shows how through these adventures the protagonist comes of age. Although the characterization of Peter's Inuit companion is a bit stilted, the book contains sharply delineated scenes of the life of nineteenth-century sailors. It shows that Godfrey may be capable of writing serious literature for young adults.

Like much commercial fiction, Godfrey's books frequently have contrived plots, one-dimensional characters, and weak themes. On the positive side, the jokes, slapstick episodes, and engaging characters are often genuinely amusing, and his themes interest young people. Such novels don't win gold crests, but they may achieve Godfrey's aim of convincing children that reading is pleasurable.

See also: *CA* 126; *MCAI*; *WSMP*.

Grey Owl

also Wa-Sha-Quon-Asin, or He-Who-Flies-By-Night (pseudonym of Archibald Stansfeld Belaney)

Born: 18 September 1888, in Hastings, Kent, England.

Died: 13 April 1938, in Prince Albert, Sask.

Principal Residences: Hastings, England; Toronto; vicinities of Temiskaming, Biscotasing, and Doucet, Ont.; vicinity of Touladi, Que.; Riding Mountain National Park, Man.; Prince Albert National Park, Sask.

Education: Hastings Grammar School.

Career: clerk; guide; trapper; mail carrier; fire ranger; lecturer; writer; naturalist; filmmaker.

Works for Children

The Adventures of Sajo and Her Beaver People (London: Lovat Dickson, 1935); reprinted as *Sajo and the Beaver People* (New York: Scribner, 1936).

Other

The Men of the Last Frontier (London: Country Life, 1931).

Pilgrims of the Wild (London: Lovat Dickson, 1932).

Grey Owl and the Beaver, with Harper Cory (London: Nelson, 1935).

Tales of an Empty Cabin (London: Lovat Dickson, 1936).

A Book of Grey Owl: Pages from the Writings of Wa-Sha-Quonasin, ed. E.E. Reynolds (London: Davies, 1938).

Grey Owl's Farewell to the Children of the British Isles (London: Lovat Dickson, 1938).

Selected Discussions

Anahareo [Gertrude Bernard]. *Devil in Deerskins: My Life with Grey Owl* (Toronto: New Press, 1972); published in England as *Grey Owl and I: A New Autobiography*, London: Davies, 1972).

Brower, Kenneth. 'Grey Owl', *Atlantic Monthly* 265 (Jan. 1990): 74–84.

Dickson, Lovat. *Wilderness Man: The Strange Story of Grey Owl* (London: Macmillan, 1973).

Kirk, Heather. 'Grey Owl as Necessary Myth: A Reading of *Pilgrims of the Wild*', *CCL* (1991): 44–56.

Few Canadians have achieved the international popularity of Grey Owl; probably none have been so soundly denounced. Following the publication of his second book, *Pilgrims of the Wild*, the British acclaimed him as the incarnation of the Noble Savage, standing against mechanization and greed to defend the wilderness. After his death, the very newspapers that had celebrated this romantic figure denounced him as a fraud, a white who passed himself off as a Native to achieve fame and fortune. The scandal delayed for years acknowledgement and fair assessment of his achievements as both conservationist and author.

Throughout his unhappy childhood in Hastings, England, Archibald Stansfeld Belaney dreamed about becoming an Indian. When he came to Canada in 1906, he thus began to pass himself as the son of a Scots father and an Apache mother. Moving to northern Ontario, he lived among the Ojibway and became a guide and trapper. After serving with the Canadian army in France during World War I, Belaney again took up his life as a trapper. His Iroquois common-law wife, Anahareo (Gertrude Bernard), profoundly changed him, however, by convincing him of the need for conservation. Grey Owl, as Belaney now became universally known, thus made respect for and preservation of the wilderness the theme of a number of articles and four popular books, *The Men of the Last Frontier*, *Pilgrims of the Wild*, *The Adventures of Sajo and Her Beaver People*, and *Tales of an Empty Cabin*. He also actively promoted conservation through his work as a filmmaker, acting in and directing two National Film

Board productions, *The Little People* (1930) and *The Beaver Family* (1931), and producing a third, *The Trail: Winter Men Against the Snow* (1936). The Canadian government officially offered support in 1931 by appointing him warden of a beaver conservation program, first in Riding Mountain National Park, Manitoba, and then in Prince Albert National Park, Saskatchewan.

Grey Owl based his only book for children, *The Adventures of Sajo and Her Beaver People*, on his own experiences with the beavers McGinnis and McGinty, who had previously become famous as subjects of some of his writings for adults. The story of a Native girl, Sajo, whose father presents her with two beaver kittens, this novel is both a realistic animal story and an urbane maturation tale. The Canadian animal story tradition is evident in the first part, an exposition of beaver habits. The narrator discusses the beaver's living arrangements and defensive strategies, before showing the development of the two kittens, Chikanee (Little Small) and Chillawee (Big Small). Throughout, he stresses their charm and their harmlessness, evoking sympathy for them by strongly indicating their personalities, intelligence, and feelings: 'don't let anyone ever tell you that animals cannot feel despair!'

The opening episode, an attack of an otter upon a beaver dam, shows that nature can be cruel, but the novelist's major concern is the contrast between the cruelty of men, who callously exploit animals in zoos, and the ideal harmony of Sajo and the beavers. This theme develops after the father is forced to sell one of his children's pets to pay a debt owed to the trading post. At this point, the novel becomes a maturation tale, following English conventions typical of the period: it depends on an obtrusive narrator, uses a physical journey and the resulting changes in setting to develop character, and keeps to a restricted yet significant time scheme.

The journey is a spiritually inspired, perilous quest that tests and displays their love and dedication. Sajo, hearing a message from her deceased mother, convinces her brother to help her to save her pet. Narrowly avoiding destruction in a forest fire, the brave siblings travel to the city, where they locate their pet and, after displaying their concern for its well-being, obtain its release from the park's owner. In addition to revealing the character of the children, this journey also illustrates through the financial contributions that the American tourists and the trader make that people, if given a proper understanding of situations, will display kindness for both humans and animals.

In addition to employing the conventional journey motif, the novel effectively advances its maturation theme through a compressed time scheme. It opens with the discovery of the stranded beavers in the spring, the symbolic time of new beginnings. It then follows the development of both the beavers and Sajo through a long summer and into the fall, the symbolic time of ripeness and maturity. *The Adventures of Sajo and Her Beaver People* is dated in its technique, but it is important as both a significant development of the animal story and as a novel in its own right. Alive with humour and the passionate concern for animals, it is not the work of Archie Belaney, expatriate Englishman: it is the legacy of the symbol he became, the man who spoke for inarticulate nature, Grey Owl.

See also: *CA* 114; *CLR* 32; *DLB* 22; *SATA* 24; *TCCW*.

Roderick Haig-Brown

Born: 21 February 1908, in Lancing, England.

Died: 9 October 1976.

Principal Residences: Lancing, England; London, England; Campbell River, BC.

Career: logger; trapper; fisherman; civil magistrate; writer.

Major Awards: Canadian Library Association Children's Book of the Year Award (1947, 1964); Vicky Metcalf Award (1965).

Works for Children

Silver: The Life of an Atlantic Salmon (London: A. and C. Black, 1931).

Panther (London: Cape, 1934).

Starbuck Valley Winter (London: Collins, 1944).

Saltwater Summer (Toronto: Collins, 1948).

Captain of the Discovery: The Story of Captain George Vancouver (Toronto: Macmillan, 1956).

The Farthest Shores (Toronto: Longman, 1960).

Fur and Gold (Toronto: Longman, 1962).

The Whale People (London: Collins, 1962).

Selected Discussions

Birks, John. 'The Work of Roderick Haig-Brown', *Junior Bookshelf* 17 (July 1953): 95–102.

Ellis, Sarah. 'News From the North', *HB* 60 (Sept. 1990): 640–2.

Keith, W.J. 'Roderick Haig-Brown', *CL* 71 (1976): 7–20.

Kirk, Heather. 'Unity with Natural Things: Roderick Haig-Brown as a Writer for Children', *CCL* 51 (1988): 25–42.

Lucas, Alex. 'Haig-Brown's Animal Biographies', *CCL* 1 (1978): 21–38.

Osler, Ruth. 'Haig-Brown: Fisherman, Nature Lover, Author', *IR* 1 (Winter 1967): 16–19.

Stow, Glenys. 'A Conversation with Roderick Haig-Brown', *CCL* 2 (1975): 9–22.

Perhaps no Canadian writer for children has achieved such high excellence in so wide a range of literary genres as did Roderick Haig-Brown. *Starbuck Valley Winter* and *Saltwater Summer* describe a boy's coming of age on Vancouver Island. *The Whale People* is a historical novel about the Nootka nation. In addition, he wrote two animal biographies, *Silver: The Story of an Atlantic Salmon* and *Panther*; a historical biography, *Captain of the Discovery: The Story of Captain George Vancouver*; and *The Farthest Shores* and *Fur and Gold*, historical documentaries about British Columbia. He also wrote 18 books for adults, most on outdoors subjects.

When he was a child, Haig-Brown knew he wanted to become a writer. His father, a naturalist and author, introduced him to the English novelist Thomas Hardy. The works of Ernest Thompson Seton and Sir Charles G.D. Roberts were regular gifts from an aunt living in Canada. When he began his writing career, his deep knowledge of and love for the west coast landscape, its people, and other living beings were the sources of his inspiration.

In *Panther*, the animal hero must engage in frequent combat against other animals and man. Its main conflict is with David Milton, a professional hunter. Haig-Brown presents this as a heroic confrontation between the most noble animal of the area and the most dedicated hunter, a man who respects and understands the adversary he will eventually kill and who has a deep sense of the responsibility attached to his profession. The book's naturalistic portrayal of the panther makes it a significant work in the tradition of the realistic animal story.

In *Starbuck Valley Winter*, Don Morgan, the teenage hero, spends a winter trapping in order to earn money to buy a fishing boat. The book records his struggle and, more importantly, his growth to maturity. He proves his worth in the wilderness and comes to understand Jetson, a renegade old trapper he had at first viewed with suspicion and hostility. Haig-Brown is very successful in depicting the hero's outdoor activities and inner thoughts. *The Whale People*, about the pre-contact Nootka people of the west coast, again centres on the growth to maturity of a young man. There is no doubt that Atlin, son of the great whale-chief Nit-gas, will become chief himself. The question that arises is, 'Will he prove worthy of the title he will eventually inherit?' Like his father, Atlin is ambitious and impatient; he wants to rush into the whale hunt without sufficient preparation. He learns that his training must be according to a ritual that involves spiritual readiness and practical instruction. There is little inner conflict in *The Whale People*. Instead, Haig-Brown presents the logical and ritual steps in the creation of a whale chief. It is, in fact, his ability to convey the dignity of this ritual, along with his sensitive and accurate treatment of the west coast landscape, that gives the book its great beauty.

In his historical writings, especially in *Captain of the Discovery*, Haig-Brown combines factual accuracy with interesting characters and sensitive awareness of the land. The author calls Vancouver a 'quiet hero', whose greatness lay not in one or two spectacular deeds but in the day-to-day strength he revealed over many years. Friendship was important to Vancouver, as is evident in the descriptions of his relationship with the Spanish explorer Quadra and the Hawaiian king Tamaahmaah. Vancouver also showed respect for the rights of Native peoples, whose ruthless exploitation by other Europeans he strongly opposed.

Some critics have suggested that Haig-Brown's writing is dated, that it is an outgrowth of literary tastes no longer shared by young adult readers. He was influenced by two popular literary forms of the early twentieth century: the realistic animal story and the boy's adventure tale. Within the frameworks of these genres, however, his novels achieved considerable depth. Most evident is his response to the land. 'The only real ownership of the land is knowing and feeling it', he once stated. In addition, he displayed remarkable ability to project himself into characters different from himself and to understand their lives as they might have seen them. Although Haig-Brown's novels are not so widely read as they were four decades ago, they justly deserve their status as Canadian classics.

See also: *CANR* 38; *CLR* 31; *DLB* 88; *SATA* 12; *TCCW*.

Pam Hall

Born: 10 July 1951, in Kingston, Ont.

Principal Residences: Kingston; Montreal; St John's.

Education: Sir George Williams University (BFA 1972); University of Alberta (M.Ed. 1978).

Career: art teacher; educational consultant; illustrator; writer.

Major Awards: Amelia Francis Howard-Gibbon Illustrator's Award (1977).

Works for Children

Written and Illustrated by Pam Hall

On the Edge of the Eastern Ocean (Toronto: GLC Publishers, 1982). **Rev:** *BiC* 11 (Dec. 1982): 9; *QQ* 48 (Oct. 1982): 32; *SLJ* 80 (Sept. 1983): 106.

Illustrated by Pam Hall

Down by Jim Long's Stage, by Al Pittman (Portugal Cove, Nfld: Breakwater Books, 1976). **Rev:** *CCL* 12 (1978): 45; *IR* 11 (Winter 1977): 42.

When Pam Hall, an art consultant for the Newfoundland Department of Education, was asked by a friend to illustrate a collection of his children's poems, she had no idea her first book would win the Howard-Gibbon Award for illustration. *Down by Jim Long's Stage*, written by Al Pittman, was about

Newfoundland fishes, but the words and pictures quickly became popular with children across Canada. Creating the illustrations for the book was, she said, a real challenge: 'I started with research, mainly because I wasn't visually familiar with the fish. The publisher allowed me to design the entire book, so I did the graphic layout and decided where the type would be set amidst the illustrations.' The result was a mixture of zoological accuracy and humorous personification. Characters like Lucy Lumpfish and Rodney Cod preserve their anatomical peculiarities but also have distinct personalities. This results, in part, from the expressions of the eyes: Rodney looks supercilious, Rosie Rosefish is flirtatious, and Lucy is bewildered.

On the Edge of the Eastern Ocean, which Hall wrote and illustrated, is a long free-verse poem combining elements of the archetypal solitary journey of initiation with an ecological warning. A fledgling puffin finds himself alone on the ocean after he has fled from Goth, a black-backed gull. At the Sacred Island of Funk, home of the spirits of the extinct auks, he is given wisdom by the leader/teacher and learns of the dangers living birds face from oil spills. He returns to his own kind and teaches them about threats to their well-being. Thirteen full-colour illustrations enhance the story, suggesting the emotions and status of the puffin as he moves from vulnerable infant to lost seeker, dedicated student, and finally respected leader of his flock.

Although Hall's literary output is limited at present to two books, she has established herself as a significant Canadian author-illustrator. The illustrations for *Down by Jim Long's Stage* demonstrate her talents as a creative illustrator and book designer. *On the Edge of the Eastern Ocean* is noteworthy for her ability to use both words and pictures to present a story that is both timely and universal in its implications.

See also: *Profiles* 2.

MARILYN HALVORSON

BORN: 17 January 1948, in Olds, Alta.

PRINCIPAL RESIDENCES: Calgary; Sundre, Alta.

EDUCATION: University of Calgary (B.Ed.).

CAREER: teacher; rancher; writer.

WORKS FOR CHILDREN

Cowboys Don't Cry (Toronto: Clarke, Irwin, 1984). **Rev:** *CBRA* (1984): 331; *CM* 12 (Nov. 1984): 242.

Let It Go (Toronto: Irwin, 1985). **Rev:** *CBRA* (1985): 145; *CM* 14 (May 1986): 114.

Nobody Said It Would Be Easy (Toronto: Irwin, 1986); published in the US as *Hold*

On, Geronimo (New York: Delacorte, 1988). **Rev:** *CCL* 53 (1989): 75; *CM* 15 (July 1987): 150.

Dare (Toronto: Stoddart, 1988). **Rev:** *CBRA* (1988): 288; *CCL* 61 (1991): 87.

Bull Rider (Toronto: Collier Macmillan, 1989).

Brothers and Strangers (Toronto: Stoddart, 1991). **Rev:** *CCL* 67 (1992): 106; *CM* 19 (Sept. 1991): 238; *QQ* 56 (Oct. 1990): 16.

Stranger on the Run (Toronto: Stoddart, 1992). **Rev:** *CBRA* (1992): 319; *CCL* 76 (1994): 72.

But Cows Can't Fly and Other Stories (Toronto: Stoddart, 1993). **Rev:** *BiC* 23 (Mar. 1994): 49; *CBRA* (1993): #6141; *QQ* 59 (Nov. 1993): 38.

Blue Moon (Don Mills, Ont.: Maxwell Macmillan, 1994).

Cowboys Don't Quit (Toronto: Stoddart, 1994). **Rev:** *CBRA* (1994): 485 *CM* 22 (Nov. 1994): 209; *QQ* 60 (Dec. 1994): 33.

Stranger on the Line (Toronto: Stoddart, 1997). **Rev:** *CBRA* (1997): 509; *CCL* 91/92 (1998): 149.

Other

To Everything a Season: A Year in Alberta Ranch Country (Toronto: Stoddart, 1991). **Rev:** *CBRA* (1992): 53.

Marilyn Halvorson combines local colour—life on the ranches, at the rodeos, and in the small-town schools of southern Alberta—with the universal problems of adolescents, especially their stormy love-hate relationships with parents. Both elements are authentically rendered because they spring from her experience. Halvorson, a confirmed country dweller, grew up on a ranch near Sundre, Alberta, and was, she says, 'a rodeo freak'. After graduating from university, she moved back to the family ranch and took up a teaching position at the nearby Sundre school, where she had once attended. Teaching shaped her writing, enabling her to develop plausible teenage characters and situations: 'the emotions, the problems, and even the vocabulary of the kids', she has said, 'come straight from the classroom.'

Halvorson tends to present characters who do not belong to the comfortable middle class, whose lives are in upheaval because of alcohol or drug abuse, school violence, or the estrangement of family members. Although she sticks to first-person narration, a conventional approach in adolescent novels, her narrators come plausibly alive because they speak a genuine adolescent jargon and show a mixture of wise-cracking cynicism and vulnerability.

The narrator of Halvorson's first novel, *Cowboys Don't Cry* (winner of the Clarke Irwin/Alberta Culture Writing for Youth Competition), is Shane Morgan, a hot-tempered redhead, who blames his alcoholic, rodeo cowboy father for the highway accident that killed his mother. Ranch and rodeo life provide the two most important events in the novel. In one overtly symbolic scene, Shane realizes that his desperate lashing out against circumstances makes him just like his mother's horse, which seriously wounds itself when it tries to fight free after becoming tangled in barbed wire. In the climactic scene, Shane's father saves him from a charging bull at a rodeo. His father, no longer running away from his responsibilities, and Shane, no longer letting the past fill him with hatred, lovingly accept each other.

The sequel, *Cowboys Don't Quit*, again tests Shane and his feelings for his father. When his father, Josh Morgan, is overdue from a trip to Montana to sell rodeo bulls, Shane begins to think the worst, believing that Josh is on an alcoholic bender. Although neither he nor Casey Sutherland, a girl who lives nearby, has a driver's licence, the two take his father's camper and head to the US to find Josh. The trip tests their ingenuity, their faith, and their courage. Eventually, they discover that bear poachers, whom he accidentally discovered, have imprisoned Josh in a refrigerator truck, where they are freezing him to death. Naturally, Shane and Casey are instrumental in rescuing him and in breaking up the illegal trade in bear parts. The plot depends on far too many coincidences and implausible situations, but the novel is mildly entertaining in advancing the theme of maintaining faith in others.

Acceptance and understanding of others is also the primary message of *Let It Go*, which balances two stories showing the tension between parents and children. The primary story is not that of the narrator, Jared (Red) Cantrell, but that of his Métis friend, Lance Ducharme, who was deserted in childhood by his mother, a country and western singer. Rebellious and despondent, Lance takes up with a drug pusher when his mother returns to fight a custody case. In the end, a symbolic exchange of gifts indicates that, although they will not live together, Lance and his mother do love each other. The less dramatic plot involving Red Cantrell also shows that understanding begins only when fighting stops. Red feels that his policeman father has been so attached to Red's older, more gifted brother that he has been unable to appreciate Red. The brother has, however, suffered irreparable brain damage from drug experimentation, something the father refuses to acknowledge. More devoted to the comatose son than the one living with him, the dictatorial father alienates Red. Only after Red shows courage and devotion in helping Lance does the father appreciate Red's qualities and feel proud of him. Although this story has a quieter, less complete resolution than Lance's, it illustrates a primary message in Halvorson's novels: true love requires the strength to let another be himself.

The sequel, *Nobody Said It Would Be Easy* (US title, *Hold On, Geronimo*), combines a problem novel with a wilderness survival tale. Lance, the narrator, discovers that he may never regain full use of his injured hand and, thus, may never realize his dream of becoming an artist. At the same time, he is involved in an emotionally charged battle with his cousin, Kat, a beautiful and wilful girl who accuses him of posturing to make himself look important. When Lance,

Red, and Kat escape an airplane crash that kills Kat's father, and then must survive in the wilderness, Lance makes important discoveries. He learns that he can establish meaningful relations with his friends and relatives only by sharing his feelings with them. He also discovers that he will regain use of his hand when he uses it to save Kat from drowning. *Nobody Said It Would Be Easy* successfully portrays Lance's painful maturation as he learns 'to accept what life gives you, instead of holding out for everything—and ending up with nothing'.

A secret from his past haunts 15-year-old Darren Jamieson, a tough kid whose recklessness has earned him the nickname of Dare. Orphaned after the death of their mother, Dare and his younger brother, Ty, have been living with their grandmother. When she, too, dies, an English teacher, Laura McConnell takes them in to save them from a foster home. Dare, however, repeatedly betrays Laura's trust, sneaking out at night to go to a concert and unwittingly ending up with two robbers. Another careless act of disobedience leads to the destruction of one of Laura's prized horses. Eventually, Dare faces the ghosts that haunt him when a horse is trapped in a burning barn. Accepting that he accidentally started the fire that killed his mother, he overcomes his fears and leads a horse from the burning barn, an act of heroism that allows him to face both his own past and those who have tried to befriend him. *Dare* may be contrived in its use of the climactic fire, and it may contain an impossibly idealized adult, Laura McConnell, who is more patient than Job, but it is still a gripping novel. Its power resides in the portrait of Dare: although he is tough and somewhat selfish at times, it is apparent that he can consider the feelings of others and that many of his bad acts are results of errors of judgment or a hardness resulting from his own feelings of guilt. *Dare* plausibly recounts the feelings of an ostensible delinquent who needs only to gaze into his own heart to mature and become a responsible young adult.

The past also haunts Steve Garrett in Halvorson's 'Stranger' series. Having run away years before and become a drug dealer in Vancouver, Steve has served time in jail. Paroled, he helped the police arrest Carlos Romero, a drug dealer whom Steve holds responsible for the death of the girl who saved him from the streets and became his lover. Knowing that Romero was intent on killing him, Steve violated his parole and is thus a fugitive from the law and from Romero. In each instalment of the series, Steve shows that he has reformed, that he has come to terms with the bitterness towards his father that caused him to run away, and that he can form meaningful relationships. Each time he does so, however, Romero finds him, and Steve must again become a fugitive.

The first novel in the series, *Brothers and Strangers*, is narrated by Steve's younger brother, Beau, who lives with their father. Steve, who is adept at handling horses, soon lands a job on a ranch owned by the father of Beau's girlfriend. The novel contains descriptions of ranch life that are interesting because they develop the character of the two brothers, who become rivals in various ways. Interspersed are dramatic and violent moments. At a rodeo, a bully named

Russ Donovan, who once had Steve's job and blames him for its loss, viciously attacks Steve with a whip. Although Steve eventually beats him, Donovan decides to exact revenge by later teaming up with Romero. In the climactic final scenes, Romero confronts Steve at a horse sale, but Steve, although shot in the arm, escapes. Mixing portraits of troubled family members trying to understand and accept each other, a love triangle (Steve and Beau temporarily become rivals), scenes of ranch and rodeo life, and a criminal revenge story, *Brothers and Strangers* is fast-paced entertainment focusing on characters with whom young readers can empathize.

Stranger on the Run continues the story with Steve as narrator. The major portion of the tale recounts Steve's growing relationship with two people after he takes a job on a ranch in the foothills. The first is Jesse Firelight, a Native with his own troubled past and an avid conservationist trying to save a valley from destruction. The second is Lynne Tremayne, whom Steve meets when he returns to school under an assumed name. Lynne becomes Steve's girlfriend, but she leaves because Romero again tracks him down. Both help Steve to develop emotionally. Steve's continuing adventures in *Stranger on the Line* fall into three parts. The first is a wilderness survival story in which the ill-equipped Steve barely manages to hike over the mountains from Alberta to Montana. The second part recounts his experiences on a North Dakota ranch, where he helps Reece Kelly, a former jockey, train horses for chuckwagon racing. In the final section, Steve drives the chuckwagon to victory at the Calgary Stampede, reunites with Lynne, but must send her away when the still-vengeful Donovan brings Romero to the Stampede. Once again, Steve must leave Lynne and set out alone on the road, an ending that promises at least one more book in the series.

Halvorson has also written three books that are somewhat different from the novels described above. *But Cows Can't Fly* stands apart because it is a series of connected tales, not a novel; is Halvorson's only book without first-person narration; focuses on a female protagonist; tells of a loving, well-adjusted family; and is aimed at a slightly younger audience. The eight stories describe the discoveries of 10-year-old Jodie McCrimmon, a girl raised in Vancouver, as she spends a year with her grandparents on an Alberta ranch. These gentle stories lack the violence and complications of Halvorson's young adult novels, but they convey a genuine love for nature. Halvorson has also written two novels for a series designed for reluctant readers. Both are first-person narratives about ranch life. *Blue Moon* focuses on horse-crazy Bobbie Jo Brooks who learns to judge a tough-looking boy by his character, not his reputation, and who later faces an ethical decision when she discovers that she innocently bought a stolen horse at auction. *Bull Rider* recounts how Layne McQueen, whose father was killed riding a rodeo bull, finally gets his mother to accept his dream of riding bulls.

Halvorson's plots are sometimes mechanical, and they too frequently rely on implausible crime elements to give them dramatic tension, but her books have the compensating strength of convincing characterization and a colourful background. She reveals the vulnerability and fears beneath the wise-cracking, confident surface her characters present to the world. She shows their painful attempts to understand life and to come to grips with their emotions. Although she acknowledges the power of sentiment, Halvorson does not herself descend into sentimentality. She may not have produced any enduring classics, but she has succeeded in one of her stated aims, the writing of books that 'show what life is like from the kids' point of view'.

See also: *CA* 132.

Christie Harris

Born: 21 November 1907, in Newark, NJ.

Principal Residences: Abbotsford, BC; Prince Rupert, BC; Vancouver.

Education: Provincial Normal School, Vancouver, BC.

Career: teacher; radio scriptwriter; broadcaster; journalist; children's author.

Major Awards: Canadian Association of Children's Librarians Book of the Year Award for Children (1967, 1977); Vicky Metcalf Award (1973); Canada Council Children's Literature Prize (1980).

Works for Children

Cariboo Trail (Toronto: Longman, 1957).

Once Upon a Totem Pole (Toronto: McClelland & Stewart, 1963). **Rev:** *APBR* 10 (Nov. 1983): 2; *HB* 39 (Apr. 1963): 173, and 61 (July 1985): 468; *LJ* 88 (15 May 1963): 2144; *NYTBR* (12 May 1963): pt 2, 28; *SLJ* 26 (Nov. 1979): 43.

You Have to Draw the Line Somewhere (Toronto: McClelland & Stewart, 1964). **Rev:** *HB* 40 (June 1964): 290; *NYTBR* (16 Aug. 1964): 18

West with the White Chiefs (Toronto: McClelland & Stewart, 1965).

Raven's Cry (Toronto: McClelland & Stewart, 1966). **Rev:** *HB* 42 (Oct. 1966): 574; *LJ* 91 (15 Oct. 1966): 5251; *NYTBR* (20 Nov. 1966): 55.

Confessions of a Toe-Hanger (Toronto: McClelland & Stewart, 1967).

Forbidden Frontier (Toronto: McClelland & Stewart, 1968).

Let X Be Excitement (Toronto: McClelland & Stewart 1969). **Rev:** *CCB-B* 22 (July 1969): 176; *LJ* 94 (15 Sept. 1969): 3218.

Secret in the Stlalakum Wild (Toronto: McClelland & Stewart, 1972). **Rev:** *CCB-B* 25 (July 1972): 169; *CCL* 15 (1980): 29; *LJ* 97 (15 May 1975): 1913; *QQ* 48 (June 1982): 7.

Once More Upon A Totem Pole (Toronto: McClelland & Stewart, 1973). **Rev:** *CCB-B* 27 (Nov. 1973): 43; *HB* 49 (June 1973): 266; *LJ* 98 (15 May 1973): 1681; *SLJ* 26 (Nov. 1979): 43.

Sky Man on the Totem Pole? (Toronto: McClelland & Stewart, 1975). **Rev:** *CCB-B* 29 (Dec. 1975): 63; *CCL* 15 (1980): 29; *HB* 51 (Aug. 1975): 380; *JR* 19 (Mar. 1976): 509; *SLJ* 21 (May 1975): 55.

Mouse Woman and the Vanished Princesses (Toronto: McClelland & Stewart, 1976). **Rev:** *CCB-B* 30 (Nov. 1976): 43; *HB* 52 (June 1976): 286; *SLJ* 22 (Apr. 1976): 86, and 22 (May 1976): 34.

Mouse Woman and the Mischief-Makers (Toronto: McClelland & Stewart, 1977). **Rev:** *CCB-B* 31 (Jan. 1978): 78; *CCL* 15/16 (1980): 98; *HB* 53 (Aug. 1977): 436; *Language Arts* 55 (Feb. 1978): 216; *SL* 27 (Mar. 1979): 36; *SLJ* 23 (Apr. 1977): 67.

The Mystery at the Edge of Two Worlds (Toronto: McClelland & Stewart, 1978). **Rev:** *CCB-B* 32 (Dec. 1978), 62; *CCL* 15/16 (1980): 29, 100; *SLJ* 25 (Dec. 1978): 68.

Mouse Woman and the Muddleheads (Toronto: McClelland & Stewart, 1979). **Rev:** *BiC* 8 (Oct. 1979): 28; *CCL* 15/16 (1980): 103; *HB* 55 (Oct. 1979): 542; *RT* 33 (June 1980): 482; *SL* 29 (Mar. 1981): 30; *SLJ* 26 (Sept. 1979): 139; *TES* (20 Feb. 1981): 27.

The Trouble with Princesses (Toronto: McClelland & Stewart, 1980). **Rev:** *CCB-B* 33 (July 1980): 213; *CCL* 20 (1980): 42; *CL* 84 (Spring 1980): 151; *HB* 56 (Aug. 1980): 419; *IR* 14 (Aug. 1980): 50; *QQ* 46 (May 1980): 31; *RT* 34 (Jan. 1981): 485.

The Trouble with Adventurers (Toronto: McClelland & Stewart, 1982). **Rev:** *CCL* 31/32 (1983): 100; *HB* 58 (Aug. 1982): 420; *Maclean's* 95 (28 June 1982): 57; *QQ* 48 (June 1982), 36; *SLJ* 28 (Aug. 1982): 116.

Something Weird Is Going On (Victoria, BC: Orca, 1994). Rev: *QQ* 60 (Dec. 1994): 33.

Other

Figleafing Through History: The Dynamics of Dress, with Moira Johnston (Toronto: McClelland & Stewart, 1971).

Mule Lib, with Tom Harris (Toronto: McClelland & Stewart, 1972).

'In Tune with Tomorrow', *CL* 78 (Autumn 1978): 26–30.

'The Shift from the Feasthouse to Book', *CCL* 31/32 (1983): 9–11.

'On Fantasy', *IR* 15 (Oct. 1981): 5–8.

'Caught in the Current', *CCL* 74 (1994): 5–15.

Selected Discussions

Davies, Cory. 'Bridges between Two Realities: An Interview with Christie Harris', *CCL* 51 (1988): 6–24.

Ellison, Shirley, and Mary Mishra. 'The Award-Winning Canadian Author Christie Harris', *Bookbird* 4 (1981): 19–22.

Evans, Gwyneth. 'Mouse Woman and Mrs. Harris', *CCL* 31/32 (1983): 53–62.

Wood, Susan. 'Stories and Stlalakums: Christie Harris and the Supernatural World', *CCL* 15/16 (1980): 47–56.

Christie Harris did not publish her first book until she was 50 years old. She began writing in high school, however, reporting news for a rural weekly. As a teacher, she discovered that she could entertain her students with her own stories, and she sold some of these to the *Vancouver Province*. Forced by provincial regulations to quit teaching after she married, she devoted herself to writing, mostly for radio, often creating stories based on family incidents. Over the years, she wrote dramas for both adults and children, women's talks, and hundreds of school broadcasts. After receiving a commission to turn one of her school broadcasts into *Cariboo Trail*, she began the career that made her one of the most honoured of Canadian children's writers.

Harris has strong beliefs about the significance of her craft. She says that story, by removing the 'hodge podge' from life, satisfies a basic human need: 'Story puts pattern and order to the world.' She is equally concise and emphatic about children's literature, declaring that it requires 'a good story' and 'graceful language'. Harris has tried to meet these requirements in a variety of types of children's books—historical fiction, fictionalized biography, contemporary fiction, fantasy, and retellings of Northwest Coast myths and tales. In spite of their differences in form, all reflect her background and intellectual interests.

Harris's interest in the early days of the Canadian West and her own experiences on a homestead led to three novels, *Cariboo Trail*, *West with the White Chiefs*, and *Forbidden Frontier*. The first two emphasize the hardships and heroism of the ordinary people who crossed the mountains. *West with the White Chiefs* and *Forbidden Frontier* enhance the adventure elements with significant themes about racism and concern for reputation. All three bring historical conditions and hardships to life, but their characters are wooden.

Harris jokingly said that she turned to a more personal form of history, fictionalized biographies of three of her children, 'because they won't sue or charge Mother'. All three are episodic first-person narratives. *You Have To Draw the Line Somewhere* is a series of nine 'sketches' tracing the career of Linsey Ross-Allen from childhood in rural British Columbia to life in New York as a freelance *Vogue* fashion artist. *Confessions of a Toe-Hanger* is the story of Linsey's sister, Feeny, who feels inconsequential and ordinary because the rest of her family is more talented. *Let X Be Excitement* traces the development of Ralph Ross-Allen, who finds excitement and meaning in a dual career as an aeronautical engineer and test pilot. *You Have to Draw the Line Somewhere* dispels the glamorous image of the fashion world, but it is dated. The other two have interesting moments, but they depend on too many sketchy episodes to be gripping or convincing.

In 1958, Harris and her husband moved to Prince Rupert, where she became fascinated with the remnants of Northwest Coast Native culture. Researching a series of school broadcasts, she became convinced that this culture had produced 'one of the world's great art styles and . . . one of its great oral literatures'. Her research provided the basis for *Once Upon a Totem*, her first retelling of this oral literature.

As a reteller of Native stories, Harris is a mediator: she tries to reflect the character of the oral original while meeting the needs of the modern reader. Harris understands that the Northwest tales are 'complex and sophisticated' expressions of a particular outlook and that modern white readers are unlikely to find the versions recorded by anthropologists comprehensible. Therefore, she builds into her work a sense of the Native value system, and to make motives clear, she devotes more effort to character portrayal and emotions than the sources do. She also shapes the story by choosing from various versions episodes that are true to Native culture yet likely to be comprehensible to modern readers. Her tales are, therefore, more structured and less anecdotal or episodic than the originals. Furthermore, she uses devices of European folklore, such as repetition of key speeches and descriptions, to suggest both the oral nature of the tale and the 'fairy tale' world it portrays. Her changes reflect a belief that 'Always, it's the *story* that's important. The pattern must be satisfying to modern readers while still remaining true to its origins.'

Harris's favourite device of mediation is an introduction drawing comparisons between European and Native culture. In *Once Upon a Totem*, for example, she compares the figures on a totem pole to a European knight's coat-of-arms and explains that Prince Hayis, the hero of a 'historical adventure, based firmly on actual happenings, . . . was as wrongfully deprived of his rights as was Robin Hood living in Sherwood Forest, or as was Richard the Lion Hearted.' In *The Trouble with Princesses*, Harris insists that the princesses of the New World's 'fairy tales', although they dressed differently and lived in different kinds of houses, were 'just as important' as those in the Old World's tales. Her prefaces to individual tales cite similarities between her characters and the more familiar European ones. Likewise, in *The Trouble with Adventurers* she pointedly connects Native adventurers to such familiar Old World heroes as 'Ulysses, Marco Polo, Sinbad the Sailor'.

Harris herself has deepened her understanding of the tales and the culture that produced them. In *Once Upon a Totem*, she spoke of the dangers Coastal Natives saw in the forest: 'ignorance and imagination added even more terrors.' She also clearly revealed a patronizing outsider's view: 'Lacking science, the aborigines found fanciful reasons for the mysteries of nature.' Later collections avoid such condescending references.

Her change in attitude came, according to Harris, when she was doing research for *Raven's Cry*, a fictionalized history of the decline of the mighty Haida nation: 'I became so engrossed in that world that I began to think I was tuning in on an old Haida spirit.' Her sympathy led to a new valuation of her material: 'the old Indian notions are very much in tune with today, maybe even more in tune with tomorrow.' She believes, in fact, 'that science is tending to validate this spirituality'. Thus, although she tries to make her retellings accessible by showing their similarities to European tales, she also, at least in her public statements, shows how different they are: 'While Old World folklore tends to feature the struggle of Good vs. Evil, Light vs. Dark, this is not so in the Northwest Coast legends. In them, there are mighty forces out there in the world, but all have potential for Good OR Evil, depending on what the character does.' According to Harris, 'that's an ethic today's children can identify with.'

Although she has changed her attitudes towards her material, Harris has been fairly consistent in the themes she develops in her retellings. Her primary theme is an ecological-spiritual one stressing the necessity of respect for all nature and the need for maintaining balance in nature. She announced this theme and stressed its authenticity by describing the purpose of Native tales in the introduction to *Once More Upon a Totem* and again in *The Trouble with Princesses*: 'Many were also a warning. An emotional reminder of what happened to a proud, wealthy people when it forgot to be worthy of its wealth and importance. When it failed to keep the sacred laws of life.' This theme finds its earliest expression, however, in the first tale of *Once Upon a Totem*, 'The One-Horned Mountain Goat', in which hunters are destroyed for wantonly violating the old law.

Perhaps the most authentic and artistic presentation of this theme, though, comes in the Mouse Woman trilogy, *Mouse Woman and the Vanished Princesses*, *Mouse Woman and the Mischief Makers*, and *Mouse Woman and the Muddleheads*. Harris treats Mouse Woman, a *narnauk*, or spirit, who can appear as either a mouse or the 'tiniest of grandmothers', as 'Good Fairy of the Northwest Coast', the helper and protector of erring young people. The major concept Mouse Woman supports is evident in 'The Princess and the Bears', in the first book of the series. Because a princess's people do not show respect for the bears they kill, Prince-of-Bears, who can be either human or bear, kidnaps and marries the princess. Consequently, he forces her people to learn the necessity of showing reverence for all life, of giving gifts when they take the gift of life.

In addition to expressing themes about the balance of nature, Harris's tales are alike in their portrayal of violence. Harris sees this characteristic violence as a natural product of the rugged setting that produced the tales: 'If you're going to cope with a ruthless land, you're going to have to have a certain ruthlessness in your culture.' She also says that the blood code, which demanded revenge when anyone was killed, represents 'Violence cloaked in a sort of beauty of concept.' This concept is, of course, the maintenance of equality or balance. Harris insists that we should not deny the reality of death in stories for children, but she is equally insistent that formulaic distancing in the tales protects children. Thus, she opens many Mouse Woman tales with, 'It was in the time of very long ago, when things were different.'

Although she has achieved her greatest success as a reteller of tales, Harris has also used Native material in other books. In *Raven's Cry*, she combined history and fiction to portray the decline of the Haida nation. Covering more than 200 years by focusing on several generations of chiefs, all named Edinsa, Harris shows how the once-mighty Haida became victims of white ignorance and prejudice and of their own feuding and inability to meet the challenges of white society. The vast span of the book forces Harris to resort to textbook chronicle and does not permit full development of the characters. The dramatized scenes are, however, effective and emotional. Combined with the choric repetition of key statements, these scenes give the book some qualities of tragedy.

A complex work, *Raven's Cry* has two major themes. The first is the humiliation of a people whose pride was the basis of their culture. The second stresses the art that was the most demonstrable sign of pride. The Haida society succumbs, but Tahayghen, the last Edinsa (named Charlie Edenshaw by whites), keeps the art alive. He is the artist-hero who replaces the earlier warrior-hero.

Harris's other attempts to incorporate Native material into her work have had limited success. The best of these, *Secret in the Stlalakum Wild*, is also the earliest. Combining problem novel, Native mythology, and fantasy, it shows the moral development of Morann, an unhappy girl whose encounter with *stlalakums*, or spirits, tests her. She passes her most significant test when she decides to remain quiet about a nugget of gold she has found because the undisturbed natural beauty of the wilderness is a treasure far more valuable. Her moral decision thus supports Harris's recurring ecological concerns.

Sky Man on the Totem Pole? and *Mystery at the Edge of Two Worlds* use Native materials far less significantly. The former combines science fiction with a retelling of Native myths in order to suggest that stories about Sky Man had a logical origin: Earth was visited by men from a dying planet. Unfortunately, the novel makes the Natives appear the gullible victims of space tricksters, not humans finely attuned to a spiritual world. The attempt to combine adolescent identity problems, mystery-adventure, and Native mysticism also fails in *Mystery at the Edge of Two Worlds*. Lark Doberly's adventures do not command credence, and her psychological and spiritual awakening is too indefinite.

In her most recent work, *Something Weird Is Going On*, Harris tries to combine a conventional problem novel, the domestic tales of her early career, and a ghost story. After weird events repeatedly interfere with the attempts lonely Xandra (Alexandra) Warwick makes to find a friend, she realizes that the imaginary companion of her early childhood is actually a ghost who is continuing to haunt her. Heavy-handed repetitions, an insipid ghost story, a contrived, unexciting climax, and stilted characterization make this one of Harris's weakest books, a novel not even redeemed by its portrait of Xandra's grandmother, a writer who resembles Harris herself.

Harris's reputation depends on her work as a mediator of Northwest Coast Native legends. Because she changed tales to meet the perceived needs of readers accustomed to European narrative structures, her work is open to the charge of cultural misappropriation and may come to be less valued than it once was.

Nevertheless, her best collections, *Mouse Woman and the Vanished Princesses* and *The Trouble with Princesses*, are historically important. Unified by a focus on a character type and by thematic concerns, they are witty and artistic attempts at giving regional materials universal significance. If we no longer consider such an enterprise desirable, we can still admire Harris for making children and adults aware of the rich resources of Native legend.

See also: *CA* 5–8R; *CANR* 6; *CLC* 12; *DLB* 88; *MAICYA*; *Profiles*; *SAAS* 10; *SATA* 6, 74; *TCCW*; *WSMP*.

Ted Harrison

Born: 28 August 1926, in Wingate, England.

Principal Residences: Wingate, England; Hartlepool, England; Malaysia; Carcross, Yukon; Whitehorse, Yukon; Victoria, BC.

Education: Hartlepool College of Art; University of Durham (Art Teacher's Diploma 1951); University of Alberta (B.Ed. 1977).

Career: teacher; artist; writer; illustrator.

Works for Children

Written and Illustrated by Ted Harrison

Children of the Yukon (Montreal: Tundra, 1977). **Rev:** *CCB-B* 31 (Apr. 1978): 127; *CCL* 13 (1978): 77; *RT* (Apr. 1992): 635.

A Northern Alphabet (Montreal: Tundra, 1982). **Rev:** *BiC* 11 (Dec. 1982): 8; *CCL* 35 (1984): 134; *EL* 10 (Nov. 1982): 35; *QQ* 48 (Dec. 1982): 25; *RT* 36 (May 1983): 944; *SLJ* 29 (Aug. 1983): 51.

The Blue Raven (Toronto: Macmillan, 1989). **Rev:** *CCL* 60 (1990): 116; *CM* 17 (July 989): 173; *EL* 7 (Mar. 1990): 23; *RT* 45 (Apr. 1992): 635.

Illustrated by Ted Harrison

The Cremation of Sam McGee, by Robert Service (Toronto: Kids Can Press, 1986). **Rev:** *BiC* 15 (Nov. 1986): 35; *CCB-B* 40 (June 1987): 27; *HB* 63 (May 1987): 353; *SLJ* 33 (Mar. 1987): 165.

The Shooting of Dan McGrew, by Robert Service (Toronto: Kids Can Press, 1986). **Rev:** *CM* 17 (Jan. 1989): 38; *EL* 16 (Nov. 1989): 23; *HB* 65 (Mar. 1989): 222; *SLJ* 35 (Dec. 1988): 129.

O Canada (Toronto: Kids Can Press, 1992). **Rev:** *CCB-B* 47 (Sept. 1993): 11; *CM* 20 (Oct. 1992): 258; *EL* 20 (May 1993): 50; *HB* 70 (May 1994): 218; *QQ* 58 (July 1992): 45; *SLJ* 39 (Apr. 1993): 174.

Other

'Images of the North', *Writers on Writing: Guide to Writing and Illustrating Children's Books*, ed. David Booth (Markham, Ont.: Overlea House, 1989), 16–19.

Selected Discussions

Paul, Lissa. 'The Lay of the Land: Turbulent Flow and Ted Harrison', *CCL* 70 (1993): 63–71.

'My first impression of the Yukon was one of absolute joy. I had seen the movie *Lost Horizon* with Ronald Coleman when he finally reached Shangri-La. The music breaks out as he gazes out on the scene of this earthly paradise. I felt similar to that. I suddenly had a light—this is the place, this is the place I've been looking for all my life and never knew existed.' This joyful response to the Yukon has remained with Ted Harrison since he first looked down on Crag Lake in 1968 and has provided the inspiration that has made him Canada's best-known painter of the contemporary North.

An exhibition of his paintings drew the attention of Montreal publisher May Culter and resulted in the publication of his first book *Children of the Yukon*. As the preface notes, 'Children in the towns of the Yukon do many things other North American children do. . . . But they do other things children further south never do, and this is what I have presented.' Each of the 21 paintings is filled with busy activity. Children build snowmen, tease ravens, create skating 'trains' pulled by dogs, and fish through the ice. Of particular interest is Harrison's non-naturalistic use of colours, as, for example, in his depiction of a blue moose. Such colours help to create the fantasy atmosphere that he feels is an important aspect of his vision of the Yukon: 'Fantasy is a marvelous escape. And the blue moose and the pink dogs and the coloured suns are the world of fantasy. In *Lord of the Rings*, we disappear into a medieval world, and in my painting I like to think we disappear into a wonderful world of colour and line.'

Harrison notes that his second picture book, *A Northern Alphabet*, 'is also a puzzle book, a story book, and a games book.' Children are invited to look at the illustrations for examples of the objects that begin with the illustrated letter and are encouraged to use the accompanying short text as the opening sentence for their own stories. For example, the letter 'B' includes the caption 'Brenda and Betty are being chased by a bear.' The illustration includes, among other things, a beaver, berries, and boots. The reader can ask why the children found themselves in the predicament and how they escaped.

Harrison has illustrated Yukon poet Robert Service's two best-known poems: *The Cremation of Sam McGee* and *The Shooting of Dan McGrew*. In the former, his illustrations depict the narrator's journey to fulfil Sam's dying wish, a magnificent cremation. The dominant blues and whites early in the book emphasize the frigid climate that Sam complains about. Warmer colours gradually increase until the climactic illustration in which Sam, resplendent in red long-johns and with a smile on his face, reclines in the red-hot furnace that is his crematorium.

The Shooting of Dan McGrew is, as Harrison notes in his introduction, filled with mystery about motive and character, but it reflects the power that the Klondike, with its bitter cold and the lust for gold, has over people's hearts. The dominant colours of the illustrations are blue, reflecting the cold, and bright oranges, embodying the violent passions of the mysterious stranger. Two illustrations suggest the world outside of the Yukon. The joys of a happy home in the south are evoked by the stranger's piano playing. In the final picture, Lou, dressed in her best outfit stands aboard a departing steamer, Dan's poke of gold in her hand. The intensity of the blues is muted, while oranges and pinks in the sky suggest a happier future for her after she has left the Klondike.

In his 'Foreword' to *O Canada*, an illustrated version of the national anthem, Harrison writes that during World War II, 'the magic name CANADA [was] a symbol of all that was good in the world.' The 12 illustrations, one for each of the provinces and territories, depict the varied landscapes and homes of Canada and are a tribute to the land and the people. Although Harrison portrays the diversity of the country, all of the paintings are in his Yukon style, which may limit the diversity he is trying to present.

The Blue Raven, an original story, combines the artist's sensitive appreciation of the North and its Native peoples with the conventions of the male coming-of-age story. At a time of great hardship for his people, Nik, a young hunter, makes a long and dangerous journey to seek aid from the Shaman of the West. In his quest he has to prove his worth and receives guidance from the great Blue Raven and assistance from the Shaman, who provides him with gifts and the advice 'the magic will always be with yourself.' Nik uses the boon to help his people, and his story becomes one of their legends. As Harrison's illustrations of modern clothing and dwellings indicate, the story may well be an allegory of Native peoples' recovering their ancient traditions. The circular journey to and from a supernatural realm is represented stylistically. Early in the story, landscape and people are rendered realistically, whereas the encounters with the Blue Raven and Shaman emanate waving lines suggestive of the presence of spiritual power. The two realms are joined in the concluding illustration as the celebrating villagers wear a mixture of contemporary and traditional costume while dancing around a fire, the blue smoke from which recalls the Raven and the Shaman's home.

The vivid acrylic illustrations for Harrison's books depict three main elements. The towering mountains, flaming suns, and icy moons in the background embody the enduring power of nature. The adults and children at work and play in the foregrounds emphasize the vitality of the people who live in this rugged environment. Between these are two kinds of buildings: abandoned hotels, churches, and outbuildings are reminders of the days of the gold rush; homes and modern buildings are symbols of the abiding human spirit.

See also: *CA* 116; *CANR* 39; SATA 56; *WSMP*.

Kathleen Hill

Born: 7 April 1917, in Halifax.

Principal Residences: Halifax; Ketch Harbour, NS.

Career: secretary; court reporter; radio dramatist; writer.

Major Awards: Canadian Library Association Book of the Year for Children (1969); Vicky Metcalf Award (1971).

Works for Children

Glooscap and His Magic: Legends of the Wabanaki Indians (Toronto: McClelland & Stewart, 1963). **Rev:** *HB* 40 (Apr. 1964): 175.

Badger, the Mischief Maker (Toronto: McClelland & Stewart, 1965). **Rev:** *HB* 42 (Sept. 1966): 53.

And Tomorrow the Stars: The Story of John Cabot (Toronto: McClelland & Stewart, 1968). **Rev:** *CCB-B* 23 (Nov. 1969): 46; *IR* 3 (Spring 1969): 32.

More Glooscap Stories (Toronto: McClelland & Stewart, 1970). **Rev:** *HB* 46 (Aug. 1970): 383; *IR* 5 (Winter 1971): 12.

Joe Howe: The Man Who Was Nova Scotia (Toronto: McClelland & Stewart, 1980). **Rev:** *CCL* 23 (1981): 93; *IR* 15 (Feb. 1981): 38.

Kay Hill became a children's writer almost by accident. She had been writing radio and television scripts for several years when, as she remembers, 'One day, a producer gave me a collection of Indian legends and asked me to create a pilot for a projected series. I did, it was accepted, and I was commissioned to do a thirteen-week-series. The next twelve were a lot harder than the first one!' The legends, focusing on the Wabanaki trickster-hero Glooscap, formed the basis of her first book, *Glooscap and His Magic*, and two sequels, *Badger, the Mischief Maker* and *More Glooscap Stories*.

The adaptation of traditional Native stories presented Kay Hill with many challenges. She had to select those that were accessible to and appropriate for younger readers, and then make them both entertaining to her audience and faithful to the original culture. She achieved her goals by including dialogue not found in the originals and by highlighting those elements of Native life that would appeal to children: courage and concern for others. The central character, Glooscap, creator of people and animals, wants all his creatures to respect each other. Although his presence is felt in all of the stories, he plays a minor role in many of them, being content most of the time to allow people and animals to act as much as possible for themselves. The characters are placed in situations that test their inner strengths and weaknesses. Only when they have exhausted their inner resources does Glooscap step in to help. However, he is not above having fun with his people while he is working on their behalf, for he is a benevolent trickster.

The title character of *Badger, the Mischief Maker* is both fearless and impudent. Perpetually causing trouble, he would have found himself in even more trouble except for the indulgence of Glooscap, who admires his indomitable spirit. Badger has a saving grace—his devotion to his little brother, whom Glooscap has hidden. This devotion sends him on a long search for the missing boy, and the hero becomes an almost picaresque figure as he moves from village to village in his quest. He must learn, as Glooscap says, 'how much better it is to give pleasure than pain'. *More Glooscap Stories* introduces a new theme, the quest of the individual for a sense of identity. This is humorously presented in the opening story, 'The Rabbit Makes a Match', in which Ableegumooch discovers that he is engaged to an otter and must remain true to his rabbit identity. The theme is more seriously presented in several stories about orphans who, not always through wise means, try to find out who they are.

In writing *And Tomorrow the Stars*, Kay Hill was faced with another difficult problem: the name of John Cabot is famous, but very little is known about him. As a result, she wrote what might be called fictional biography, a blending of a few biographical facts with general historical and geographical knowledge, understanding of human nature, and imagination. 'This', she notes in her introduction, 'is how it might have been.' *Joe Howe*, the biography of the Nova Scotia statesman, presented more challenges. How did one create an interesting story where there was little physical action and a lot of politics? 'It wasn't like writing a biography about an almost legendary American hero where there are plenty of tales of derring-do. So I fell back on the writer's primary tool, imagination, trying to make my readers understand the inner courage of the man and how he felt about the things which were happening in his time, a time far distant from my readers.'

Although Hill frequently refers to her use of imagination, that does not mean her works are not true. She does invent certain details for the sake of the story, but she captures the essence of her subject, whether it be the mythical history of the Wabanaki, the boyhood and adulthood of a sixteenth-century explorer, or the determination of a nineteenth-century statesman.

See also: *CAFR* 9–12; *CANR* 3; *Profiles*; *SATA* 4; *WSMP*.

James Houston

Born: 12 June 1921, in Toronto.

Principal Residences: Toronto; Northwest Territories; New York City; Stonington, Conn.; Tlell, BC.

Education: Ontario College of Art; École Grand Chaumière (Paris); Unichi-Hiratsuka School (Tokyo).

Career: territorial administrator, Northwest Territories; arts administrator; writer; illustrator; designer of blown-glass art.

Major Awards: Canadian Library Association Book of the Year Award (1966, 1968, 1980); Vicky Metcalf Award (1977).

Works for Children

Written and illustrated by James Houston

Tikta'liktak (Toronto: Longman, 1965). **Rev:** *CCC-B* 20 (Dec. 1966): 59; *HB* 41 (Dec. 1965): 633; *SLJ* 27 (Sept. 1980): 423.

Eagle Mask (Toronto: Longman, 1966). **Rev:** *CCB-B* 20 (Jan. 1967): 74; *HB* 42 (Dec. 1966): 716; *IR* 1 (Winter 1967): 32.

The White Archer (Toronto: Longman, 1967). **Rev:** *HB* 43 (Oct. 1967): 588; *IR* 2 (Winter 1968): 16; *SLJ* 27 (Sept. 1980): 43.

Akavak (Toronto: Longman, 1968). **Rev:** *CCB-B* 22 (Apr. 1969): 127; *HB* 45 (Feb. 1969): 54; *IR* 3 (Winter 1969): 26.

Wolf Run (Toronto: Longman, 1971). **Rev:** *CCB-B* 25 (Sept. 1971): 701; *HB* 47 (June 1971): 287; *IR* 5 (Summer 1971): 28

Ghost Paddle (Toronto: Longman, 1972). **Rev:** *CCB-B* 26 (Nov. 1972): 43; *HB* 49 (Feb. 1973): 48; *IR* 7 (Winter 1973): 22; *SLJ* 27 (Sept. 1980): 43

Kiviok's Magic Journey (Toronto: Longman, 1973). **Rev:** *CCB-B* 27 (Apr. 1974): 130; *HB* 50 (Apr. 1974): 146; *IR* 8 (Sept. 1974): 40.

Frozen Fire (Toronto: McClelland & Stewart, 1977). **Rev:** *CCB-B* 31 (Mar. 1978): 113; *HB* 54 (Feb. 1978): 47; *IR* 12 (Spring 1978): 52; *RT* 32 (Oct. 1978): 43; *SLJ* 24 (Nov. 1977): 57.

River Runners (Toronto: McClelland & Stewart, 1979). **Rev:** *CCB-B* 33 (Apr. 1980): 153; *CCL* 20 (1980): 84; *HB* 56 (Apr. 1980): 176; *IR* 14 (Fall 1980): 44; *SLJ* 26 (Feb. 1980): 67

Long Claws (Toronto: McClelland & Stewart, 1981). **Rev:** *BiC* 10 (Oct. 1981): 33; *CCB-B* 35 (Mar. 1982): 130; *IR* 15 (Oct. 1981): 38; *QQ* 47 (Nov. 1981): 25; *SLJ* 28 (Feb. 1982): 76.

Black Diamonds (Toronto: McClelland & Stewart, 1982). **Rev:** *EL* 11 (Nov. 1983): 37; *RT* 36 (Dec. 1982): 338; *SLJ* 29 (Dec. 1982): 72.

Ice Swords (Toronto: McClelland & Stewart, 1985). **Rev:** *BiC* 14 (Dec. 1985): 14; *CCL* 45 (1987): 58; *EL* 13 (Mar. 1986): 15

The Falcon Bow (Toronto: McClelland & Stewart, 1986). **Rev:** *BiC* 16 (Mar. 1987): 37; *CCB-B* 40 (Jan. 1987): 89; *CCL* 45 (1987): 74; *CM* 16 (Jan. 1988): 4; *QQ* 52 (Aug. 1986): 40; *SLJ* 33 (Jan. 1987): 75; *VOYA* 9 (Feb. 1987): 285.

Whiteout (Toronto: Greey de Pencier, 1988). **Rev:** *BiC* 18 (Apr. 1989): 32; *CM* 17 (Mar. 1989): 71.

Drifting Snow (Toronto: Maxwell Macmillan, 1992). **Rev:** *BiC* 22 (Sept. 1993): 30; *CCB-B* 46 (Jan. 1993): 148; *CM* 21 (May 1993): 97; *EL* 20 (Mar. 1993): 14; *QQ* 58 (Dec. 1992): 25; *VOYA* 15 (Dec. 1992): 279.

Illustrated by James Houston

Songs of the Dream People, ed. James Houston (Toronto: Longman, 1972).

First Came the Indians, by M.J. Wheeler (New York: Atheneum, 1983).

Other

Confessions of an Igloo Dweller (Toronto: McClelland & Stewart, 1995).

'The Vision of that Mask', *CCL* 31 (1983): 12–14.

Selected Discussions

Harker, Mary. 'An Interview with James Houston', *CCL* 61 (1991): 19–28.

Jobe, Ron. 'Profile: James Houston', *Language Arts* 60 (Oct. 1983): 907–13.

Jones, Raymond E. 'Heroes in the Perilous Land: Pattern and Meaning in Arctic Fiction for Children', *CCL* 31 (1983): 30–40.

Stott, Jon C. 'An Interview with James Houston', *CCL* 20 (1980): 3–16.

———. 'Form, Content, and Cultural Values in Three Inuit (Eskimo) Survival Stories', *American Indian Quarterly* 10 (Summer 1986): 213–26.

In 1948, while on a trip with a bush pilot to a remote Inuit village in the Northwest Territories, James Houston made a quick decision that changed the course of his life. When the plane prepared to return south, he stayed, with only his sketch books and a sleeping bag. 'I guess the doctor [who had accompanied them] thought I was crazy—winter was coming and I didn't know any of the language. It took me over four years to learn it.' Faced with a new situation, he used the skills he possessed, drawing pictures to communicate, and he learned new skills from the patient and kindly people he met. Houston stayed in the Arctic for 14 years, becoming territorial administrator and teaching the Inuit the art of printmaking. After he left the Arctic, he used his artistic ability and his experiences and observations of the animals, landscape, and people there as the basis of his children's books and adult novels, six screenplays, and innumerable glass sculptures.

Although most of his heroes are Inuit and three are Native, the central characters of Houston's books are much like the author, reacting quickly to rapidly changing circumstances. Stranded on broken sea ice, the title character of *Tikta'liktak* must act quickly and decisively and must improvise, using found objects and ages-old techniques to survive. Kungo, in *The White Archer*, alone after his family has been murdered, matures when he, as Houston often did, accepts the wisdom of an old man who befriends him. Matthew, the white boy of *Black Diamonds*, finds himself first in an isolated contemporary Inuit community and then lost, with an Inuit friend, in the wilderness. By pooling their resources and learning from each other, the boys are able to make their way back to the settlement—not, however, before having experiences similar to those in the adventure novels Houston read as a child.

Houston's children's books can be divided into three categories: adapted retellings of traditional Inuit legends and myths (*Tikta'liktak, The White Archer, Akavak, Wolf Run, Kiviok's Magic Journey, Long Claws*, and *The Falcon Bow*); Northwest Coast Native legends (*Eagle Mask* and *Ghost Paddle*); and six adventure novels set in the contemporary North (*River Runners*; *Frozen Fire, Black Diamonds*, and *Ice Swords*—a trilogy; *Whiteout*; and *Drifting Snow*).

Houston's Inuit legends, which evolved from stories his friends told him about places and customs he observed in the North, are considerably longer than their sources. Writing for younger readers who would not be familiar with the environments and lifestyles he depicts, he includes considerable background material. In addition, he portrays character conflicts and inner growth in detail, making the legends resemble the shorter novels and chapter books with which his audience would be familiar. The legends involve long perilous journeys in which the hero (or, in *Long Claws*, the hero and heroine) must leave the security of home and family and confront the dangers of weather and wild animals. Tikta'liktak, caught on broken ice while hunting for his starving family, survives on a barren island before devising the means to return to the mainland. When Kungo has learned the skills of survival and archery, he travels by himself to the Land of Little Sticks to avenge his family's murder. Akavak travels through blizzards and other dangers to take his dying grandfather to the home of the old man's brother. Punik, the hero of *Wolf Run*, wanders into the barren lands in search of food for his starving family. The children in *Long Claws* fight off a grizzly bear so that they can bring food from a distant cache back to the village.

At the beginning of his adventure, Tikta'liktak 'wished most of all to be a good hunter' like his father. Marooned, he must remember the survival skills of his people and draw on inner courage if he is to be reunited with them. The exciting adventures give him the opportunity to mature as an individual. In *The White Archer*, Kungo must learn to overcome hatred. After the massacre of his family, 'a terrible anger started to grow within [Kungo]'. Journeying to a distant island, he lives for several years with a wise old teacher and his wife, assimilating their practical knowledge and spiritual wisdom. As a result he is able to forgive the killers of his family.

Although most of the heroes' adventures in these stories take place in solitude, the importance of family is a dominant theme in Houston's retelling of the old legends. Alone on his island, Tikta'aliktak is sustained by his hope of rejoining his people. Punik and the brother and sister of *Long Claws* face danger in order to help their families. Kiviok undertakes his magic journey so that he can rescue his wife and children, who have been abducted by the evil Raven. During their adventures, the heroes make use of the lessons taught by wise old people. Ittok and his wife instruct Kungo. As he prepares to take his grandfather on the long journey, Akavak is told by his father: 'Listen to his words and learn from him, for that is the way in which all knowledge has come to this family.' In *Wolf Run*, an old grandmother is the teacher: 'She carried ancient knowledge deep inside herself, wisdom that women have always possessed, wisdom that they have carefully handed down to their children and grandchildren since the beginning of mankind.'

Houston's stories about the Northwest Coast deal with an entirely different social structure. Rather than small, loosely organized groups of nomadic hunters, the villages of the British Columbia coastline embodied complex social structures and intricate clan genealogies. Whereas the Inuit heroes have only to find their places within their families, his Native heroes must learn their roles in a highly political, rigorously defined social system. They must develop a full awareness of their family, village, and cultural histories and value systems and must carefully and ritualistically prepare themselves for their assigned roles. This preparation provides the basis for the plot of *Eagle Mask*. Early in the story, Skemshan, whose name means Mountain Eagle, hears a mysterious voice in the night. He is told, 'If it were a spirit, he must wait until it revealed itself secretly to him alone.' He learns those things he must know in order to understand his eagle spirit and assume his role as a nobleman in his clan. *Ghost Paddle* examines a young son's political role in ending hostilities between neighbouring peoples. Hooits, when told by his father that he will join a group of unarmed people on a peace mission to an enemy village, is unsure of himself: 'He loved the idea of peace, but he did not know whether he had the courage.' Not only does he prove instrumental in bringing peace, but he falls in love with the rival chief's daughter, cementing the political union with personal love.

Personal admiration and cultural respect are the dominant themes of Houston's contemporary adventure novels. Their point of view is that of a white teenager, Matthew Morgan, in *Frozen Fire*, *Black Diamonds*, and *Ice Swords*; Andrew Stewart, in *River Runners*; and Jon Aird, in *Whiteout*. Placed in a completely new environment, Matthew comes to understand his new home and to develop a deep friendship with Kayak, an Inuit teenager. At the conclusion of the third book, Matthew remarks, 'this is hard country, . . . but somehow I feel that I belong here. It has come to seem like a home to me.' Andrew Stewart, the son of an international banker, has been sent to northern Quebec to serve as an apprentice to a fur-trading company. At first, he is lonely and bewildered, but, with the help of his Naskapi friend, he acquires a knowledge of and love for the land and its people. At the novel's end, he 'felt as though he . . . had become a part of everything upon this earth'.

Whiteout and *Drifting Snow*, Houston's most recent novels for children, present a different approach to the meeting between cultures. In the former, 19-year-old Jon Aird must spend a year in Nanuvic with his crusty uncle in order to prove himself worthy of his inheritance. Although he befriends one Inuk teenager and falls in love with another, he returns to the south after a year. The gap that separates the two cultures is too great to bridge. Elizapee, the main character of *Drifting Snow*, returns to her homeland after having lived most of her life in a major Canadian city. The main events of the novel depict the gradual loss of her white ways and acceptance of the more traditional lives of her new friends. Again, the ways of the two cultures are seen as incompatible.

Houston brings to his stories his intimate knowledge of the Arctic and its people and his love of telling a fast-paced and exciting story. He is at his best in the Inuit survival legends, depicting the heroes' physical and psychological adventures in simple, concrete, clear language. The Northwest Coast legends, while very interesting, do not achieve the clarity or intensity of the Inuit stories, perhaps because the necessary descriptions of such a complex society blur the focus on the main character. The novels are at their best when dealing with the relationships between the young heroes and the land and its animals; they are less convincing when they deal with the intricate relationships between cultures, and they become somewhat forced when they fall into the standard patterns of the adventure story.

When James Houston's children's books first appeared, they broke new ground in the creation of children's literature about Canada's indigenous peoples. They are accurate, based on his own experiences and backed up by thorough anthropological and historical research. They also are sympathetic portrayals of Native cultures that, at the same time, emphasize universal qualities of character.

See also: *CA* 65–8; *CANR* 38, 60; *CLR* 3; *Junior* 4; *Ocean*; *SAAS* 17; *SATA* 13, 74; *TCCW*; *WSMP*.

Jan Hudson

Born: 27 April 1954, in Calgary.

Died: 22 April 1990, in Edmonton.

Principal Residences: Edmonton; Calgary; Vancouver.

Education: University of Calgary (BA 1978); University of Alberta (LL.B. 1984).

Career: legal editor and writer; legal researcher, administrative assistant, and editor for Attorney-General of BC.

Major Awards: Canada Council Children's Literature Prize (1984); Canadian Library Association Book of the Year for Children (1984); Writers Guild of Alberta R. Ross Annett Award (1991).

Works for Children

Sweetgrass (Edmonton: Tree Frog, 1984). **Rev:** *CCB-B* 42 (Apr. 1989): 196; *CM* 19 (May 1991): 156; *EL* 17 (Sept. 1989): 51; *JR* 35 (Nov. 1991): 237; *RT* 43 (Apr. 1990): 588; *SL* 34 (Dec. 1986): 362; *SLJ* 35 (Apr. 1989): 102.

Dawn Rider (Toronto: HarperCollins, 1990). **Rev:** *CCB-B* 44 (Feb. 1991): 143; *BiC* 19 (Oct. 1990): 28; *EL* 18 (Mar. 1991): 23; *HB* 67 (Mar.-Apr. 1991): 198–9; *QQ* 56 (Oct. 1990): 16; *SLJ* 36 (Dec. 1990): 103.

Other

'Author Gives Thank You's' [sic], *Canadian Library Journal* 41 (Oct. 1984): 287.

Selected Discussions

Jenkinson, Dave. 'Portraits: Jan Hudson', *EL* 12 (Sept.-Oct. 1984): 46–7.

Jones, Raymond E. 'The Plains Truth: Indians and Metis in Recent Fiction', *ChLQ* 12 (Spring 1987): 36–9.

Stander, Bella. 'Jan Hudson', *Publishers Weekly* (22 Dec. 1989): 32.

Jan Hudson's tragically short career—she died before the publication of her second novel—began with exceptional critical acclaim: her first novel, *Sweetgrass,* won two major awards. Hudson was not, however, an overnight success. She took more than five years, and at least 17 drafts, to write *Sweetgrass.* As she often told young people, 'I'm a rewriter, not a writer.' Hudson also had false starts. Believing that only boys' adventures were publishable, she initially wrote about a young boy. After listening to an inner voice, Hudson decided to make the central character a girl, Sweetgrass, thereby transforming the story into more than a formulaic adventure.

Although the focus throughout *Sweetgrass* is the maturation of the title heroine, a Blackfoot growing up in Alberta in 1837, the novel divides into two parts, each with a separate emphasis. In the first part, a historical study of manners, Sweetgrass must accept the limitations her culture imposes on women. She endures life in a time of cultural change brought on by contact with white traders. Blackfoot men, eager for horses, guns, and white trade goods, have abandoned many old customs, including monogamy, because additional wives can tan more hides for trading. Drunkenness and smallpox are even more visible signs of the destructive changes brought on by contact with the whites.

Dramatic tension comes from the conflict between female desire and the rigid restraint imposed on girls. In love with a young warrior, Sweetgrass knows that her people believe that 'Wanting is not right for a young woman.' She repeatedly fails to convince her father that she is mature enough for marriage and that she should be allowed to choose her own husband. As a test of her maturity, she endures the drudgery of pemmican-making and of preparing hides, all the while silently envying the freedom granted to her brother and other males.

The second part of the novel is a survival story that reveals the power and heroism within Sweetgrass. Heroically resisting the urge to give into her own desires, Sweetgrass does her duty and saves her family when smallpox strikes them during the winter. She even overcomes a taboo against eating fish when eating it becomes the only way to save her family. Sweetgrass thus shows that women, although not warriors, can be heroic. Her father then recognizes that she is ready for marriage and worthy of the man she loves.

Sweetgrass is a remarkable work of anthropological accuracy and feminist realism. As a study of Native manners, it provides a clear, accurate picture of Blackfoot life. To ensure this accuracy, Hudson thoroughly researched the book, as her bibliography suggests, and she also sent the manuscript to several Blackfoot for comment. As a sensitive exploration of female identity, the novel dramatizes the pressures on females to follow strict codes of conduct, but it also shows the heroic grandeur of females who selflessly devote themselves to saving others. Brilliantly, Hudson combines Native expressions and colloquial diction in the first-person narration. Consequently, Sweetgrass seems neither a Hollywood Indian nor the kid next door. Making Sweetgrass the only person with a face unmarked by the smallpox is her only concession to popular romantic formulae.

Although it, too, is thoroughly researched and is just as concerned with portraying Native manners and the limitations imposed on females as *Sweetgrass*, *Dawn Rider*, Hudson's second novel, is less successful because it is too diffuse. Set in the early eighteenth century, when the introduction of both horses and rifles was about to change Blackfoot culture, *Dawn Rider* includes scenes of a buffalo hunt, a celebratory dance during which petty jealousies become evident, a war party, a young man's first ritual display of bravery in capturing an eagle with his hands, and a marriage ceremony. Interspersed are domestic scenes showing the behaviour of three generations of the central family. Insofar as it focuses on the central character, 16-year-old Kit Fox, the novel is a female coming-of-age story. Kit Fox, who believes that she is 'nothing special to anyone', dreams of riding a horse, an activity that her tribe believes should be left to males. She is also struggling to understand relationships, especially her sister's choice of a suitor. Eventually, Kit Fox becomes special, a hero who saves the tribe by riding a horse for help when her camp comes under a surprise attack. She also matures, gaining self-understanding by recognizing that the young man she considers a friend is actually the one she loves and will marry.

Writers who dramatize the lives of primal cultures often face charges of cultural misappropriation. Jan Hudson, however, was a sensitive and knowledgeable student of Native life. She once declared that her primary interest was 'social anthropology—the little things that make up most people's lives'. In *Sweetgrass* she turned this interest into gripping fiction that compels readers to think about both the limitations of white society and their views of indigenous peoples. By doing so, she secured a small but permanent place in Canadian children's literature.

See also: *CA* 136; *CLR* 40; *SATA* 77.

Monica Hughes

Born: 3 November 1925, in Liverpool, England.

Principal Residences: Liverpool; Edinburgh; London, England; Cairo, Egypt; Bulawayo, Rhodesia (now Zimbabwe); Umtali, Rhodesia; Ottawa; Edmonton.

Education: attended Edinburgh University (1942–3).

Career: dress designer; Women's Royal Naval Service; bank clerk; laboratory technician; writer.

Major Awards: Canada Council Prize for Children's Literature (1981, 1982); Vicky Metcalf Award (1981); Canadian Library Association Young Adult Book Award (1983); Children's Literature Association Phoenix Award (2000, for *The Keeper of the Isis Light*).

Works for Children

Gold-Fever Trail: A Klondike Adventure (Edmonton: John LeBel, 1974). **Rev:** *EL* 18 (May 1991): 57.

Crisis on Conshelf Ten (Toronto: Copp Clark, 1975). **Rev:** *APBR* 10 (Nov. 1983): 2; *CBRA* (1975): 182, and (1995): 504; *CCL* 73 (1994): 66; *CCB-B* 30 (June 1977): 160; *HB* 60 (Sept. 1984): 663; *SLJ* 27 (May 1977): 62; *TLS* (19 Sept. 1975): 1052.

Earthdark (London: Hamish Hamilton, 1977). **Rev:** *CBRA* (1995): 504; *CCL* 73 (1994): 66.

The Ghost Dance Caper (London: Hamish Hamilton, 1978). **Rev:** *RT* 35 (Nov. 1981): 237.

The Tomorrow City (London: Hamish Hamilton, 1978). **Rev:** *CBRA* (1995): 504; *TES* (18 Aug. 1978): 17; *TLS* (29 Sept. 1978): 1089.

Beyond the Dark River (London: Hamish Hamilton, 1979). **Rev:** *CBRA* (1992): 321; *CCB-B* 34 (June 1981): 195; *CCL* 17 (1980): 25; *EL* 20 (Mar. 1993): 14, 48; *HB* 57 (June 1981): 308; *RT* 35 (Nov. 1981): 237; *SLJ* 27 (Mar. 1981): 146, and 39 (June 1993): 106; *VOYA* 4 (Aug. 1981): 31.

The Keeper of the Isis Light (London: Hamish Hamilton, 1980). **Rev:** *CCL* 73 (1994): 63; *RT* 45 (Apr. 1992): 636.

The Guardian of Isis (London: Hamish Hamilton, 1981). **Rev:** *CBRA* (1995): 505; *CCL* 73 (1994): 63.

Beckoning Lights (Edmonton: J.M. LeBel, 1982). **Rev:** *BiC* 11 (Dec. 1982): 11; *CCL* 65 (1992): 107; *HB* 60 (Sept. 1984): 663; *QQ* 49 (Feb. 1983): 39.

Hunter in the Dark (Toronto: Clarke, Irwin, 1982). **Rev:** *BYP* 1 (Apr. 1987): 1; *CBRA* (1982): 247; *EL* 14 (Sept. 1986): 22; *RT* 45 (Apr. 1992): 637.

The Isis Pedlar (London: Hamish Hamilton, 1982). **Rev:** *CBRA* (1995): 505; *CCL* 73 (1994): 63.

Ring-Rise, Ring-Set (London: J. MacRae, 1982). **Rev:** *CBRA* (1995): 505.

The Treasure of the Long Sault (Edmonton: LeBel, 1982). **Rev:** *CCL* 63 (1991): 76; *EL* 18 (May 1991): 57.

Space Trap (Toronto: Groundwood/London: J. MacRae, 1983).

My Name is Paula Popowich! (Toronto: James Lorimer, 1983). **Rev:** *BiC* 13 (Mar. 1984): 28; *CBRA* (1983): 288; *CM* 19 (May 1991): 156; *QQ* 49 (Nov. 1983): 22.

Devil on My Back (London: J. MacRae, 1984). **Rev:** *CBRA* (1995): 504; *EL* 13 (Mar. 1986): 15, 16, 46; *TES* (1 Nov. 1985): 26.

Sandwriter (London: J. MacRae, 1984). **Rev:** *CCB-B* 41 (Mar. 1988): 138; *SLJ* 34 (Mar. 1988): 214; *TES* (30 Jan. 1987): 31; *VOYA* 11 (Aug. 1988): 138.

The Dream Catcher (London: J. MacRae, 1986). **Rev:** *BYP* 1 (June 1987): 4; *CCB-B* 40 (1987): 211; *QQ* 52 (June 1986): 24; *SLJ* 33 (Jan. 1987): 31; *VOYA* 10 (June 1987): 90.

Blaine's Way (Toronto: Irwin, 1986). **Rev:** *BiC* 15 (Dec. 1986): 18; *CBRA* (1986): 149; *CCL* 46 (1987): 66; *CM* 16 (Jan. 1988): 4; *EL* 15 (Mar. 1988): 24; *Maclean's* 99 (15 Dec. 1986): 45.

Log Jam (Toronto: Irwin, 1987); published in England as *Spirit River* (London: Methuen, 1988).

Little Fingerling: A Japanese Folktale, illus. Brenda Clark (Toronto: Kids Can Press, 1989). **Rev:** *BiC* 18 (Dec. 1989): 23; *CBRA* (1989): 251; *EL* 17 (Mar. 1990): 25, and 18 (Sept. 1990): 53, and 18 (Nov. 1990): 54, and 21 (Sept. 1993): 61; *QQ* 55 (Sept. 1989): 22; *SLJ* 39 (Apr. 1993): 111.

The Promise (Toronto: Methuen, 1990). **Rev:** *CM* 18 (May 1990): 128; *QQ* 56 (Jan. 1990): 16; *SLJ* 38 (June 1992): 115; *TES* (16 Feb. 1990): 68.

Invitation to the Game (Toronto: HarperCollins, 1990). **Rev:** *CCB-B* 45 (Oct. 1991): 40; *CCL* 73 (1994): 65; *EL* 18 (Jan. 1991): 51; *QQ* 56 (Nov. 1990): 14; *SLJ* 37 (Sept. 1991): 281, and 38 (Mar. 1992): 176; *VOYA* 14 (Dec. 1991): 323.

The Refuge (Toronto: Doubleday Canada, 1990). **Rev:** *CBRA* (1989): 320; *CCL* 59 (1990): 77.

The Crystal Drop (London: Methuen, 1992). **Rev:** *CM* 20 (Mar. 1991): 91; *QQ* 58 (Mar. 1992): 66; *RT* 47 (Apr. 1994): 564; *VOYA* 16 (Dec. 1993): 310.

The Refuge (Don Mills, Ont.: Stoddart, 1992). **Rev:** *CBRA* (1992): 322.

A Handful of Seeds, illus. Luis Garay (Toronto: Lester, 1993). **Rev:** *BiC* 22 (Sept. 1993): 57; *CBRA* (1993): #6041; *CCB-B* 49 (June 1996): 339; *CCL* 83 (1996): 132; *CM* 21 (Oct. 1993): 187; *QQ* 59 (Apr. 1993): 35; *SLJ* 42 (Mar. 1996): 176.

The Golden Aquarians (Toronto: HarperCollins, 1994). **Rev:** *CBRA* (1994): 486; *CCB-B* 49 (Oct. 1995): 57; *CM* 22 (Sept. 1994): 138; *HB* 71 (Sept. 1995): 600; *SLJ* 41 (Aug. 1995): 154, and 42 (Mar. 1996): 176; *VOYA* 18 (Aug. 1995): 172.

Where Have You Been, Billy Boy? (Toronto: HarperCollins, 1995). **Rev:** *CBRA* (1995): 505; *EL* 23 (Mar. 1996): 25; *QQ* 61 (Nov. 1995): 44.

Castle Tourmandyne (Toronto: HarperCollins, 1995). **Rev:** *BiC* 25 (May 1996): 20; *CBRA* (1995): 503.

The Seven Magpies (Toronto: HarperCollins, 1996). **Rev:** *CBRA* (1996): 480.

The Faces of Fear (Toronto: HarperCollins, 1997). **Rev:** *CBRA* (1997): 511.

Jan's Big Bang (Halifax: Formac, 1997). **Rev:** *CBRA* (1997): 512.

The Story Box (Toronto: HarperCollins, 1998). **Rev:** *CCL* 94 (1999): 108.

Jan and Patch (Halifax: Formac, 1998).

Other

'The Writer's Quest', *CCL* 26 (1982): 6–25.

'The Writer as Mask-Maker and Mask-Wearer', *HB* 68 (Mar. 1992): 178–85.

What If . . . ?: Amazing Stories, editor (Toronto: Tundra, 1998).

Selected Discussions

Evans, Gwyneth. 'The Girl in the Garden: Variations on a Feminine Pastoral', *ChLQ* 19 (Spring 1994): 20–4.

Jones, Raymond E. 'Re-Visioning *Frankenstein*: *The Keeper of the Isis Light* as Theodicy', *CCL* 93 (1999): 6–19.

——. 'The Technological Pastoralist: A Conversation with Monica Hughes', *CCL* 44 (1986): 6–18.

——. '"True Myth": Female Archetypes in *The Keeper of the Isis Light*', *Science Fiction and the Young Reader*, ed. C.W. Sullivan III (Westport, Conn.: Greenwood, 1993), 169–78.

Kertzer, Adrienne E. 'Setting, Self, and the Feminine Other in Monica Hughes's Adolescent Fiction', *CCL* 37 (1985): 18–28.

Rubio, Gerald. 'Monica Hughes: An Overview', *CCL* 17 (1980): 20–6.

Wytenbroek, J.R. 'The Debate Continues: Technology or Nature—A Study of Monica Hughes's Science Fiction Novels', *Science Fiction and the Young Reader*, ed. C.W. Sullivan III (Westport, Conn.: Greenwood, 1993), 145–55.

Monica Hughes has emerged as one of the most prolific and internationally respected writers for Canadian children. An award-winning writer of both science fiction and novels of contemporary adolescent life, Hughes has also written historical, adventure, and fantasy novels, a couple of chapter books for beginning readers, and two picture books. Throughout her career Hughes has shown an interest in tackling significant issues, especially the question of evil and the need to respect the natural environment.

Hughes has frequently noted that her own childhood reading influenced her writing. From the fantasies of E. Nesbit she acquired a love of magic and the idea of alternative worlds. She was also influenced by James Jean's *The Mysterious Universe*. In conjunction with Nesbit's fiction, this book gave her what she calls 'the magical universe', a 'sense of the marvellous magic of space'. From Charles Dickens, Hughes acquired a sense of the power of language, a delight in idiosyncratic characters, and possibly, her concern for treating social matters in fiction. From Jules Verne and nineteenth-century adventure novelists like Anthony Hope, R.M. Ballantyne, Richard Blackmore, and Robert Louis Stevenson, she gained a sense of 'the adventure and the making real'. The influence of these writers of swashbuckling adventures is particularly evident in such early books as *Crisis on Conshelf Ten*, in which she resorts to mechanical plot devices to create excitement. In later works she shows less concern for swashbuckling adventure and more for meaningful action, significant settings, and convincing motivations.

Hughes has generally insisted that she is foremost a writer of science fiction, which she sometimes calls speculative fiction because of its tendency to be based on the question 'What if?' Many of her stories do, in fact, depend on such speculation. Thus, *Crisis on Conshelf Ten* and *Earthdark*, respectively, treat the possibility of colonies undersea and on the moon being exploited by Earth corporations, just as multinational corporations exploit underdeveloped countries. *The Golden Aquarians* considers the possibility that humans interested only in their ability to create habitations for themselves or to exploit resources would inflict permanent damage on other planets. *The Tomorrow City* and *Devil on My Back* explore societies in which the computer dominates, thereby reducing human freedom and choice. *Beyond the Dark River* speculates about the survivors of a nuclear war, and *The Crystal Drop* about those attempting to survive the desertification that would follow ozone depletion. Hughes insists on the logic of these projections, asserting that her science fiction worlds follow the principles of Newtonian physics. In her most revealing comment, though, she claims for science fiction both the moral concerns and the external wonders of traditional stories: 'Speculative fiction is the mythology of today. . . . It is good versus evil.'

One major evil in Hughes' modern myths is limited knowledge, especially scientific knowledge that fails to value human feelings, individual freedom, and even life itself. In *The Tomorrow City*, the visible villain is a giant computer that establishes totalitarian rule of the city. The hidden villain is the deification of science and logic. The heroine, Carol Henderson, matures when she recognizes that compassion and freedom are essential to humanity and therefore tries to destroy the computer. *Devil on My Back* takes a similar stand. In a rigidly caste-structured futuristic society dedicated to preserving knowledge, the leaders stoop under the weight of computer packs that feed information directly through sockets in their necks. Lord Tomi Bentt (his name symbolizes the idea that unalloyed logic distorts, or bends, humans) discovers that no possible future benefit justifies enslaving people and that true humanity demands both compassion and freedom for all citizens.

The computer is not, however, her only villain. In *The Dream Catcher*, the sequel to *Devil on My Back*, Hughes reverses the situation to show that even benevolent conformity can be evil. Ruth, the psychokinetic heroine, initially humiliated when she is unable to fit into a telepathic society that values group identification above individuality, is able to free Lord Tomi's city only because of her individuality. Even more limiting than conformity is ethnocentrism, the group's refusal to respect ideas and values outside of its own. In *Beyond the Dark River*, a brilliant novel set in the period after a nuclear war, the surviving Hutterites again face destruction because they cling to the belief that their traditional ways are the only valid ones. Refusing to have contact with the world, they become susceptible to disease and remain ignorant of its cures.

Another major source of evil in Hughes's myths is a lack of respect for the environment. In *The Golden Aquarians*, Colonel Angus Elliot, a 'hardbitten terraformer', takes pride in his ability to transform planets into places suitable for human habitation or for the exploitation of raw materials. Elliot, who assumes an almost god-like power in changing the worlds that he visits, does not respect life forms unlike his own, even superior life forms. Therefore, even after Walter, his son, discovers an intelligent, telepathic amphibian species inhabiting the planet Aqua, he ignores an injunction against disturbing planets containing intelligent life. Walter, whose youthful sensitivity symbolizes hope for the future, becomes an environmental hero by forcing the evacuation of the planet, an evacuation that actually saves his father from being killed by tidal waves. *The Crystal Drop* also offers hope that people will learn to respect nature. Megan and Ian Dougal live on a once-thriving poultry farm that is now in the middle of the desert that has developed in southern Alberta. When their mother dies, the two children know that the farm can no longer sustain them, so they set out to find a new home. Their subsequent adventures teach them that the ecological devastation surrounding them is the product of poor agricultural practices. Thus, when they finally arrive at Gaia, a new community of environmentalists in the

Rockies, they are prepared to change their ways in order to help the land heal and humans to survive.

Hughes's contention that speculative fiction is a contemporary form of mythology receives its most complex and extensive support in the Isis trilogy. The first volume, *The Keeper of the Isis Light*, her most original and her finest novel, can be read as a myth about female development, as a variation of Shelley's *Frankenstein* myth that explores both morality and the concept of the Other, and as a colonization myth. All of these myths, however, focus on the individual's knowledge of self and others. When Earth-settler Mark London lands on the planet Isis, he meets Olwen Pendennis, a girl surgically altered by her robot Guardian into a lizard-like being able to withstand the radiation and thin atmosphere of her planet. Because Guardian makes Olwen conceal her appearance with a mask, Mark does not realize that Olwen differs from him in appearance and he falls in love with her. When he climbs a mesa and sees Olwen for the first time without the mask, a symbol of the social facade all people erect, Mark falls both literally and morally, refusing to accept Olwen's humanity, declaring her to be a monster. For her part, Olwen embarks on a journey into the wilderness. Seeking shelter in a cave during a cosmic storm, she is symbolically reborn and comes to understand her own powers. She subsequently displays morality and heroism by rescuing a child stuck in a sink hole during a cosmic storm (an act symbolic of motherhood). After refusing to consider an operation that would make her again appear like the settlers, she displays her maturity: knowing the pain of loneliness, the emotion that makes her human and distinguishes her from the robot Guardian, she nevertheless decides that she must remain apart from the settlers, but that she will aid them by sending warnings of storms. In its concern for the connection between female identity and nature, its exploration of both childish selfishness and adolescent desire, and its commitment to a morality of loving service to others, *The Keeper of the Isis Light* ranks as one of the most intellectually and dramatically satisfying science fiction novels ever written for young people in any country.

The Guardian of Isis, the next in the trilogy, develops a social myth by dramatizing the dangers of blind faith. Mark London, now the colony's ruler, turns violently against science, which he blames for altering Olwen and humiliating him. Mark governs by superstition, teaching that Olwen is 'the Ugly One': death. He also becomes socially regressive, refusing to admit new ideas and constraining women to a subservient position. Only Jody, an iconoclastic African boy who violates the colony's purposeless taboos and enlists the aid of Olwen and Guardian, is able to save it from certain destruction. The final volume, *The Isis Pedlar*, is a contact myth that duplicates the basic outlines of European imperialism. A confidence man from a more sophisticated society arrives on Isis to victimize the settlers by playing on their naïvety and greed. He thus gets them to abandon their harvesting to search for gemstones. Abandoning both productive activity and sound values, the gullible settlers nearly destroy their community.

Only because the pedlar's daughter is moral do the settlers gain the liberating knowledge that they have been duped and return to productive labour.

In addition to their focus on questions of knowledge and evil, the majority of Hughes's speculative fiction novels display another characteristic of traditional literature, the use of the journey as an organizing device. In all cases, the journeyer is young, and the journey both tests identity and leads to maturity. Hughes reveals her status as a modern mythologist, however, by providing a large number of female heroes who discover an identity separate from that imposed by society. She does not, however, try to blur gender distinctions. Although she knows that she risks charges of chauvinism in defining separate male and female qualities, Hughes says that 'feminine qualities are the nurturing qualities as opposed to making, wisdom as opposed to intelligence, caring and intuiting as opposed perhaps to finding out and thinking'. She often identifies the feminine with the indigenous peoples, who have a deep commitment to the land, and the masculine to technocrats, who see the universe as man-centred and the land as something challenging them, something to change and dominate.

Both of these ideas are apparent in *Ring-Rise, Ring-Set*. Liza Monroe, living in a rigidly structured society that emphasizes women's inferiority, seeks adventure in the polar world outside her domed city. She must be rescued by the indigenous people, the Ekoes, who show her familial love, individual worth, and a connection to nature that she had never before experienced. Symbolically reborn, she becomes a nurturer and a healer of the dying tundra.

Symbolic rebirth journeys also take prominence in other novels. In *Devil on My Back*, Lord Tomi leaves his domed city when he falls through a garbage chute that plunges him into a river. When he returns, significantly enough, nine months later, hoping to work within the city for the well-being of those outside, the dominating technocrat has been reborn as a nurturer. In *Beckoning Lights*, Julia Christie undergoes a rebirth when she climbs up a mountain and, in spite of her fear of the dark, enters a narrow cave in order to save aliens who require a fungus that grows there. Although more subtly, the Isis books also present symbolic rebirths through journeys beyond the settlers' valley and a visit to a cave.

Not all of Hughes's mythic journeys develop rebirth imagery; sometimes they define the growth of personal or cultural awareness. In *The Tomorrow City*, Caroline Henderson journeys when she climbs within a building (climbing up is always a significant and positive action in Hughes's novels) and destroys the computer that has taken complete control of people's lives. In *Beyond the Dark River*, a Native girl and a Hutterite boy, who understand neither themselves nor the culture of the other, journey to the destroyed city (obviously Edmonton) to search at the University for books that will explain a mysterious illness killing the Hutterite children. The Hutterite learns that his people, who have shut out the world, thus have not developed immunities to protect them from diseases.

His companion learns that she cannot selfishly avoid her destiny as the one who is to serve the needs of others: she must fulfil her place in a pattern. The children in *The Crystal Drop* similarly experience an educational journey, learning about the selfishness of survivalists who hoard resources and about the respect for the land that was traditional with Native peoples, before they finally arrive at a colony that offers hope for a new beginning because it is based on respect for nature.

That hope for a fresh start is central also to *Invitation to the Game*, in which a group of young people make a journey, unaware that they are doing so. The narrator, Lisse, lives at a time when robots do most of the work and overcrowding has given few people a chance for meaningful employment. Consigned after graduation to live with other unemployed persons in a Designated Area where they must fend for themselves, Lisse learns to co-operate with her companions. Lisse's group is soon invited to play The Game, a hypnotically induced test of survival skills. Only after one of their members becomes ill do they realize that previous episodes of The Game were training sessions and that they have actually been transported to another world to build a new civilization. This myth of renewal offers the hope that humans who co-operate and have a knowledge of the mistakes of the past can build a pastoral utopia.

Although earlier in her career she was adamant that she wrote science fiction, Hughes has written several fantasy novels. Her first, *Sandwriter*, uses the death and rebirth symbolism present in her science fiction to explore values and questions of identity. Princess Antia, who has long desired freedom, journeys from her wealthy home to the caves at the heart of the desert kingdom of Roshan, where she symbolically undergoes a rebirth. Antia is taught by an archetypal wise old woman, the mysterious Sandwriter, who says that she is charged with the well-being of the desert kingdom. From Sandwriter, Antia learns that her feeling of being nothing is the first step to a valid spiritual identity. A subplot pits the spiritual values of the desert and the simple subsistence-level way of life it fosters against the commercial claims of Antia's wealthy homeland. Antia's courtly tutor, Eskoril, seeks the valuable secret at the heart of the desert. He thinks he has discovered it in a pool of methli (a combustible oil-like substance); as Antia realizes, however, the true secret, is found in water, the source of all life. Fittingly, Eskoril, who is about to exploit the methli commercially, dies in a storm, his mouth full of sand. In the sequel, *The Promise*, Antia is now queen and mother of a girl, Rania. On Rania's tenth birthday, Sandwriter summons the girl to begin training as her successor. Four years later, Rania experiences a spiritual crisis, being torn between her duty to Sandwriter and her desire for a young man named Atbin. In a reversal of the journey pattern of the first novel, Rania is sent away from the caves to a social setting so that she can discover what she wants and thus who she is. Rania eventually realizes that her power to foresee makes people want to exploit her as a fortune teller. Finally accepting her true identity, Rania returns to Sandwriter to be a spiritual nurturer, not the wife and mother she would have become in the secular world. With its focus on spiritual values instead of secular or carnal fulfilment, *The Promise* is an unusual and provocative story of a female's coming of age.

The Story Box has notable weaknesses, but it also develops significant intellectual and psychological conflicts. Its premise, that a community would ban not only storytelling but dreaming as well, is preposterous. Otherwise, this fantasy, which recalls the Salem witch trials in many of its particulars, erects a case against intolerance and utilitarianism. The elders of the isolated island of Ariban, fearful that stories of other countries will lead the young to abandon their austere home, not only forbid stories and dreams, but they also ban strangers. When young Colin discovers Jennifer, a storyteller, washed ashore, he is thus involved in a conflict between his culture's traditions and his own observations of the healing power of stories. Predictably, Colin decides that he must save Jennifer after the community condemns her to death. Although it makes a gripping romantic adventure, *The Story Box* founders thematically because the stories that are supposed to celebrate the power and beauty of narrative are hackneyed. As a consequence, Hughes must advance her case by making those who ban stories into cold, cruel, stereotypical villains, even giving one elder hands reminiscent of a snake's skin and a voice that hisses.

Hughes has set two fantasies in the modern world. *Where Have You Been, Billy Boy?* is a time-slip fantasy in which a boy is transported from 1908 to 1993. Billy, an orphan given shelter and a job by Johannes, caretaker of a carousel, discovers that the carousel is a time machine when it transports him into the future. Susan Paterson, who finds the confused Billy in the barn housing the now dilapidated carousel, vows to fix the carousel so that Billy can return to his own time. The plot illustrates themes about friendship and trust in both the past and the future. Billy, feeling lost in the future, learns that he cares about Johannes; when Billy returns to 1908, Johannes realizes that he can trust Billy and symbolically adopts him by calling him 'son'. Susan, whose family has had a long-standing feud with a neighbouring family, enlists the aid of one of her neighbours and thereby makes the restoration of the carousel a way of healing the rupture between the families. The healing of torn relationships is also vital in *Castle Tourmandyne*, a psychological fantasy. When her grandmother gives her an antique paper dollhouse for her twelfth birthday, Marg Pargeter is sure that she will obey the printed warning that she must make it with love. Her visiting cousin Peggy, a mean girl who is upset that her parents don't seem to value her, insists that Marg is too little to assemble the intricate house. Filled with anger and spite, Peggy builds it herself. Peggy then becomes subject to a series of terrifying nightmares in which she is an abused Victorian child held prisoner in the house. Only when Marg realizes that the dollhouse designer, who committed suicide, is an evil force using their negative feelings against them is she able to free both Peggy and herself from his spell. Using conventional associations between a house and the psyche and between weather and emotions, *Castle*

Tourmandyne is a tense, brooding novel in which love and respect prove themselves to be the most powerful and liberating forces in the world.

Hughes has combined fantasy and contemporary problem fiction in *The Faces of Fear*, using the world of virtual-reality games to develop an allegory of life. Confined to a wheelchair after an automobile accident that killed her mother, 15-year-old Joan Sandow is a bitter recluse who feels whole only on the Internet, where she calls herself Joanna, 'a warrior kind of name'. She and Steve Andersen, an on-line acquaintance who calls himself Whizkid, begin to play a virtual-reality game, unaware that its programmer, Jason Bedard, whom Joan once insulted, has maliciously designed it to terrify them. As an allegory of life, the game casts Jason as the devil who frustrates humans, and Adrienne Harris, who modifies Jason's evil program, as a guardian angel who offers the hope of success. By forcing Joan and Steve to be both heroic and co-operative, the game enables them to face their problems and to accept themselves. Joan thus goes out of the house for the first time and introduces herself to Steve; Steve, realizing that he is a poor fielder in baseball only because of a childhood trauma, gains the confidence not only to play well but to let his father know that he wants to live his own life, not his father's. *The Faces of Fear* has an interesting premise, but the virtual adventure is bland, and the characterization of the competing programmers is awkward.

Several other novels combine realistic description and symbolic resolution of significant problems. As its title suggests, *My Name is Paula Popowich!* concerns a search for identity. Paula Herman, raised without any real knowledge of her father or her Ukranian ancestry, eventually discovers her own identity, symbolized by a half-German and half-Ukranian Easter egg she paints at the end of the novel. In *The Ghost Dance Caper*, Tom Lightfoot, confused because he is part Native and part white, steals a medicine bundle from the Provincial Museum in order to partake in the ghost dance ceremony and thus to discover his spirit or identity.

A Native's ceremonial search for his spirit also forms the symbolic core of *Log Jam*, in which the separate journeys of two adolescents converge, providing them with an understanding of themselves and their choices in life. Isaac Moneyfeathers, a Native escaping from prison, rescues from a canoeing accident Lenora Ridz, a troubled white girl. Both are transformed. Lenora, symbolically reborn after nearly drowning, accepts her foster father and her new life. Isaac, who heroically finds his spirit by slaying a bear attacking Lenora, comes to terms with his past and finds new hope for his future.

Symbolic allusions are at the core of *The Refuge*, which varies the story of Frances Hodgson Burnett's classic *The Secret Garden*. Like Burnett's Mary Lennox, Hughes's Barb Coutts suffers the breakdown of her family and a physical dislocation that eventually leads to psychological renewal. Barb's dislocation begins when her father leaves and her mother must move with her from their fancy house to an apartment in a poorer section of town. Like Mary Lennox,

Barb is sour and bitter. Whereas a robin leads Mary to an abandoned garden at wealthy Mistlethwaite Manor, a jackrabbit is instrumental in guiding Barb to a wild patch between some factories that becomes her 'secret garden'. Barb, like Mary, changes even more dramatically after she shares her secret with a boy, who also benefits from contact with nature. In Barb's case, she invites into her refuge Stan, a clumsy stammerer dismissed as a sissy by his family because he loves art. Hughes varies from the pattern of Burnett's novel when she has an escaped murderer, who had made the garden his place of refuge years ago, enter it and make Barb his prisoner. She also differs by noting that industrial progress will destroy the garden, which is on the site where a new factory will be built. Although the plot becomes melodramatic, *The Refuge* successfully explores a girl's growing understanding of friendships, her mother's sacrifices, her father's callous betrayals, and the need for a natural refuge in which one can find spiritual renewal.

Hunter in the Dark, the most celebrated of Hughes's problem novels, is a story of maturation and identity. Mike Rankin, a teenager who discovers that he has leukemia, is desperate for a trophy head, his symbol of manhood. Mike sneaks off alone to the woods, but as he is about to kill a prize buck, Hughes makes her symbolism overt. Mike recognizes that both the game tag he is about to clip to the buck's ear and the hospital tag that he wears around his wrist are symbols of victimization. His refusal to kill the deer affirms life. Knowing that he cannot run from death, he comes to terms with the dark—the death that had terrified him—and with his own situation and identity. Although a victim of disease, Mike is a hero because he takes conscious charge of his feelings and of his life.

Hughes has written four works of historical fiction. *The Treasure of the Long Sault*, an early adventure published only after she established her reputation, is set during the building of the St Lawrence Seaway. Young Neil Anderson discovers that he wants to be an archaeologist after he finds lost artifacts proving that a man accused of being on the side of the Americans during the Battle of Crysler's Farm in 1813 was innocent. *Gold-Fever Trail: A Klondike Adventure* uses the adventures of two children heading to the Klondike to find their father as the basis for a description of that historical event. *Blaine's Way*, based on her husband's life, is a social history of the Depression and early war years that uses two trains as symbols. The first is the New York Central train that passes by the Ontario farm where Blaine Williams lives. His mother repeatedly suggests that it promises a better life elsewhere. The second is the one he encounters near his grandparents' home after his parents lose their own farm. This train, the Toonerville Trolley, also known as the Grim Reaper because it has killed several unwary people crossing its tracks, symbolizes the hardships and disasters of life. Blaine, who grows up dreaming of the time when he can move away, eventually lies about his age to join the army. After he loses both of his hands in the war, he realizes that he has boarded the Grim Reaper, not the New York Central. Cured of his illusion that other places are better, he returns to the girl who loves him, happy to make his home in the place he once thought was a trap. *The Seven Magpies* is also set during the war. The plot follows a prophetic rhyme, and it includes episodes involving offerings to carvings representing Celtic forces of good and evil, but this novel is essentially a conventional boarding-school story about social cliques and the acceptance of differences. With her father called up to active service and her mother joining the Wrens, Maureen Frazer is sent to a new school in Scotland because it is supposed to be safe from German invasion. Although initially excluded from a group known as the Seven Magpies by the group's domineering leader, Kathleen Buchanan, Maureen eventually gains admission to the group. She earns full acceptance, however, only after being kidnapped by the father of an army deserter who fears that she may spoil his escape. The novel is most notable for its presentation of class biases as Maureen discovers that the other girls put on false airs of superiority and are condescending to a local farm woman, the archetypal Celtic wise woman.

The two chapter books that Hughes has written for beginning readers are about a third grader named Jan MacLeod (unaccountably renamed MacDonald in the second book). In *Jan's Big Bang*, Jan and her friend Sarah Smith convince their teacher to let them enter the science fair. After a couple of disasters, the girls enter an exhibit on methane, but a pompous school official causes it to explode, resulting in comic disaster. In *Jan and Patch*, Jan wants a dog but her grandmother refuses to allow her to have one. After Jan shows her responsible nature by rescuing an escaped budgie, a store owner rewards the ingenious Jan by allowing her to walk one of the store's dogs. One of the two picture books that Hughes has written is a didactic tale and the other is a version of a traditional story. In *A Handful of Seeds*, published in collaboration with UNICEF Canada, Concepcion, an orphan, brings hope to the starving children of the barrio by teaching them to grow food. *Little Fingerling* retells a Japanese folktale about a tiny boy who shows such courage that eventually he is magically transformed so that his outward appearance finally reflects the magnificent character he developed in spite of his diminutive stature.

As might be expected of such a prolific author, Hughes has produced work of uneven quality. Her early novels, for instance, rely too much on the mechanical plot devices common in nineteenth-century adventure fiction. Their dialogue also is somewhat artificial. She has, however, produced some superb novels: *The Keeper of the Isis Light* is a landmark in children's science fiction; *Sandwriter* and *The Promise* are compelling works of mythic fantasy; *Hunter in the Dark* and, in spite of some lapses, *The Refuge* are provocative problem novels. In these and most of her other novels, Hughes develops gripping plots that explore the psychological and social implications of a variety of serious themes. By doing so, she demonstrates conclusively that intelligent children's books can also be exciting ones.

See also: *CA* 77–80; *CANR* 23, 46; *CLR* 9; *Junior* 6; *MCAI*; *Profiles* 2; *SATA* 15, 70; *TCYAW*; *WSMP*.

Bernie Thurman Hunter

Born: 3 November 1922, in Toronto.

Principal Residences: Toronto.

Career: bookkeeper; writer.

Major Awards: Vicky Metcalf Award (1990).

Works for Children

That Scatterbrain Booky (Richmond Hill, Ont.: Scholastic, 1981). **Rev:** *BiC* 10 (Dec. 1981): 6; *CCL* 29 (1983): 63; *EL* 9 (May 1982): 28; *IR* 16 (Feb. 1982): 46; *QQ* 48 (Jan. 1982): 35.

With Love from Booky (Richmond Hill, Ont.: Scholastic, 1983). **Rev:** *BiC* 12 (Dec. 1983): 16; *CCL* 44 (1986): 73; *QQ* 49 (Nov. 1983): 24.

A Place for Margaret (Richmond Hill, Ont.: Scholastic, 1984). **Rev:** *EL* 12 (May 1985): 46; *QQ* 51 (Oct. 1985): 21.

As Ever, Booky (Richmond Hill, Ont.: Scholastic, 1985). **Rev:** *CCL* 44 (1986): 73.

Margaret in the Middle (Richmond Hill, Ont.: Scholastic, 1986). Rev: *QQ* 52 (Dec. 1986): 13.

Lamplighter (Richmond Hill, Ont.: Scholastic, 1987). **Rev:** *EL* 15 (Mar. 1988): 24.

Margaret on Her Way (Richmond Hill, Ont.: Scholastic, 1988). **Rev:** *CM* 17 (May 1989): 124; *EL* 16 (Jan. 1989): 51.

The Railroader (Richmond Hill, Ont.: Scholastic, 1990). **Rev:** *CCL* 62 (1991): 62; *CM* 18 (July 1990): 180; *EL* 18 (Sept. 1990): 60.

The Firefighter (Richmond Hill, Ont.: Scholastic, 1991). **Rev:** *CM* 20 (Mar. 1992): 68; *CCL* 81 (1996): 65; *EL* 19 (Mar. 1992): 58; *QQ* 57 (Nov. 1991): 24.

Hawk and Stretch (Richmond Hill, Ont.: Scholastic, 1993). **Rev:** *CM* 22 (May 1994): 76; *QQ* 59 (Nov. 1993): 38.

Amy's Promise (Richmond Hill, Ont.: Scholastic, 1995). **Rev:** *CBRA* (1995): 506; *CCL* 84 (1996): 108; *EL* 25 (Jan. 1998): 45; *QQ* 61 (Nov. 1995): 46.

Janey's Choice (Richmond Hill, Ont.: Scholastic, 1998).

Other

'Inspirations', *CCL* 84 (1996): 87–9.

Selected Discussions

Conway, Eileen. 'Public Images, Private Images: Photographic Illustrations in the *Booky* Trilogy', *CCL* 60 (1990): 45–51.

Like thousands of Canadian girls, Toronto-born author Bernice Hunter read the novels of L.M. Montgomery. Unlike nearly all of them, she had the opportunity to have tea with the creator of Anne Shirley, and she received encouragement from Montgomery to continue her own writing. However, although she had written stories for her siblings and for her own children, it was not until she became a grandparent that her first novel was published. *That Scatterbrain Booky* was based on her experiences growing up in Toronto during the Depression.

For Booky, as her mother affectionately calls her, life in 1932 is not easy. Her father is often out of work, her mother is expecting another baby, and the family moves frequently because it is unable to pay the rent. Christmas is bleak: they have no tree, they rely on charity for presents and food, and Mother and Father are fighting. However, even though *That Scatterbrain Booky* unflinchingly portrays the unhappy aspects of the heroine's life, the tone is generally joyous. Through Booky's eyes, readers experience more of the happy than the unhappy times. Hunter successfully evokes the sights and sounds of a large 1930s city as it would have been perceived by a 10-year-old girl.

With Love from Booky focuses more directly on the heroine's growing pains. Mr Jackson, her teacher, encourages her writing. She feels shame when her father rummages for coal at the dump, suffers the indignities of babysitting for a rich couple, and is kissed for the first time at a mixed party. At the end of the novel, her grandfather dies and the girl feels guilty that she has not visited him more often. At the beginning of *As Ever, Booky*, she is in high school and is encouraged by L.M. Montgomery to continue her own writing. Although she receives several rejection slips for her stories, she does win a newspaper prize for her essay, 'The Bravest Man I Know Is a Woman'. The novel closes with an epilogue describing her adult life.

While the Booky stories are not developed around any major conflicts and do not contain significant character growth, they are very successful in their evocation of a girl's response to the world around her. The vignettes that comprise them not only give readers an idea of what it was like to live in the 1930s, but also capture the reactions of a character who, though she experienced events of 70 years ago, is not unlike modern girls in her emotional responses.

A Place for Margaret, *Margaret in the Middle*, and *Margaret on Her Way* are set in the 1920s. The title heroine, sent to her aunt and uncle's farm to recover from tuberculosis, comes to love her relatives as a second family and reveals her love of animals, especially the horse Starr. She realizes that she wants to become a veterinarian, helps to discover a treasure of 100 dollars, breaks her leg rescuing a kitten from a tree, and acquires the self-confidence necessary to pursue her chosen career. Though not so lively as the Booky series, the 'Margaret Trilogy' believably re-creates rural life of 70 years ago.

Toronto in the 1920s is the setting for *Amy's Promise*, in which a girl must take over the running of her family, including dealing with an alcoholic father, after the death of her mother. Like Booky, she finds joy in her own talents, in her case playing the piano. *Janey's Choice*, a sequel, deals with the changes the family makes when, after many years of widowhood, the father remarries. Amy fights against relinquishing her role as the woman of the family, while her younger sister, Janey, who like Booky wishes to be a writer, welcomes her stepmother. Hunter's interest in her family's pioneer roots underlies *Lamplighter*, *The Railroader*, and *The Firefighter*, a group of stories dealing with occupations in the later nineteenth century.

Although Bernice Thurman Hunter's books do not deal with sensational adventures, they are very successful presentations of times now past and of the timeless emotions of growing up. Drawing on her own childhood and on family memories and historical research, she has created a strong sense of how life was for children in a time that is seldom portrayed in Canadian children's books.

See also: *CA* 119; *CANR* 52; *SATA* 45, 85; *TCCW*; *WSMP*.

Hazel Hutchins

Born: 9 August 1952, in Calgary.

Principal Residences: Calgary; Canmore, Alta.

Education: University of Calgary.

Career: store clerk; waitress; writer.

Works for Children

The Three and Many Wishes of Jason Reid (Willowdale, Ont.: Annick, 1983). **Rev:** *BiC* 12 (Dec. 1983): 16; *CCB-B* 41 (June 1988): 208; *QQ* 50 (Feb. 1984): 39; *SL* 34 (May 1988): 97; *TES* (26 June 1987): 23.

Anastasia Morningstar and the Crystal Butterfly (Willowdale, Ont.: Annick, 1983). **Rev:** *SLJ* 36 (Aug. 1990): 148.

Leanna Builds a Genie Trap, illus. Catharine O'Neill (Willowdale, Ont.: Annick, 1984). **Rev:** *CCL* 44 (1986): 93 *CM* 14 (July 1986): 184; *EL* 14 (Mar. 1987): 47; *QQ* 52 (Apr. 1986): 26; *SLJ* 33 (Jan. 1987): 65.

Ben's Snow Song: A Winter Picnic, illus. Lisa Smith (Willowdale, Ont.: Annick, 1987). **Rev:** *BiC* 16 (Dec. 1987): 13; *CM* 16 (May 1988): 99; *EL* 15 (Mar. 1988): 23.

Casey Webber, The Great (Willowdale, Ont.: Annick, 1988). **Rev:** *CCB-B* 42 (Jan. 1989) 124; *CCL* 56 (1989): 82; *CM* 17 (Jan. 1989): 17; *EL* 16 (Jan. 1989): 51.

Norman's Snowball, illus. Ruth Ohi (Willowdale, Ont.: Annick, 1989). **Rev:** *CM* 18 (Jan. 1990): 12.

Nicholas at the Library, illus. Ruth Ohi (Willowdale, Ont.: Annick, 1990). **Rev:** *CCL* 64 (1991): 73; *CM* 19 (Jan. 1991): 27; *QQ* 56 (Nov. 1990): 12.

Katie's Babbling Brother, illus. Ruth Ohi (Willowdale, Ont.: Annick, 1991). **Rev:** *BiC* 20 (June 1991): 58; *CCL* 66 (1992): 93; *CM* 19 (Sept. 1991): 229; *QQ* 57 (Apr. 1991): 18.

A Cat of Artimus Pride (Willowdale, Ont.: Annick, 1991). **Rev:** *CCL* 75 (1994): 76; *CM* 20 (Mar. 1992): 69; *QQ* 57 (Dec. 1991): 24.

And You Can Be the Cat, illus. Ruth Ohi (Willowdale, Ont.: Annick, 1992). **Rev:** *BiC* 22 (Sept. 1993): 58; *CCL* 74 (1994): 90; *CM* 20 (May 1992): 159; *EL* 20 (Nov. 1992): 58; *QQ* 58 (Mar. 1992): 66.

The Catfish Palace, illus. Ruth Ohi (Willowdale, Ont.: Annick, 1992). **Rev:** *CCL* 76 (1994): 80; *CM* 21 (Oct. 1993): 188; *QQ* 59 (July 1993): 56.

The Best of Arlie Zack (Willowdale, Ont.: Annick, 1993). **Rev:** *BiC* 22 (Sept. 1993): 58; *CCL* 81 (1996): 65; *CM* 21 (Sept. 1993): 137; *NeWest Review* 20 (June 1995): 26; *QQ* 59 (May 1993): 34.

Within a Painted Past (Willowdale, Ont.: Annick, 1994). **Rev:** *CBRA* (1994): 487; *CCL* 82 (1996): 89; *CCB-B* 48 (Apr. 1995): 278; *QQ* 60 (Dec. 1994): 31; *SLJ* 41 (Mar. 1995): 204.

Believing Sophie (Martin Grove, Ill: A. Whitman, 1995). **Rev:** *SLJ* 42 (Jan. 1996): 85.

Tess, illus. Ruth Ohi (Toronto: Annick, 1996). **Rev:** *BiC* 24 (Nov. 1995): 40; *CBRA* (1995): 472; *NeWest Review* 21 (Feb. 1996): 28; *QQ* (Aug. 1995): 34.

Yancy and Bear, illus. Ruth Ohi (Toronto: Annick, 1996). **Rev:** *BiC* 25 (Oct. 1996): 32; *CBRA* (1996): 445; *QQ* 62 (Oct. 1996): 46.

The Prince of Tarn (Toronto: Annick, 1997). **Rev:** *BiC* 26 (Oct. 1997): 34; *QQ* 63 (June 1997): 64; *SLJ* 44 (Feb. 1998): 109.

Shoot for the Moon, Robyn (Halifax: Formac, 1997). **Rev:** *CM* 4 (31 Oct. 1997): online; *QQ* 63 (July 1997): 50.

It's Raining, Yancy and Bear, illus. Ruth Ohi (Toronto: Annick, 1998).

Robyn's Want Ad (Halifax: Formac, 1998).

'I like good opening lines', a character in *The Prince of Tarn* announces. Hazel Hutchins's opening lines are good—abrupt, surprising statements of the basic premise of her novels: the sudden introduction of magic into the lives of ordinary boys and girls. For example, this is the beginning of *Anastasia Morningstar and the Crystal Butterfly*: 'On a bright morning in May, the lady at the corner grocery store turned Derek Henshaw into a frog. It happened very quietly.' The author has stated that she starts with the idea of something magical and then considers how it changes the people who come in contact with it. A boy granted a seemingly endless supply of wishes, another who finds a jacket of invisibility, a girl who is given a crystal butterfly that comes to life, and a girl who can step into the paintings in her aunt's guest room all discover their own strengths and weaknesses as they deal with magic.

On his way home from school, the title hero of *The Three and Many Wishes of Jason Reid* encounters a being from another universe who must grant the boy three wishes before he can complete his journey back to his own world. An inept baseball player, Jason first wishes for a magic glove and then devises a scheme to extend the wishes indefinitely. However, with the aid of his friend Penny, he is able to perceive the disastrous effect of his continued wishing on the giver of the magic gift and the importance of wishing both wisely and worthily. Sarah, worried about creating a successful science project, befriends the magician Anastasia Morningstar, whose ability to transform people and whose crystal butterfly are symbols of the changes the girl must undergo herself. From the woman, she learns, 'I know perfectly well who I am and I like it.'

In *Casey Webber, The Great*, a boy's desire to appear on a popular talent show seems possible when he discovers a jacket that makes him invisible. Old Mrs Anderson has provided him with it in the hope of sparking his imagination. When he finally returns it willingly to its rightful owner, Casey learns the importance of believing in himself, not in magical powers. *A Cat of Artimus Pride* recounts how a very old cat provides Claire with the opportunity of creating a winning float for the Heritage Days' Parade. The cat, who can talk, helps her to discover the selflessness of its original owner and the unhappiness of the neighbourhood 'bad boy'.

Living with his single-parent mother, the title hero of *The Best of Arlie Zack* plays hooky and hangs around with bad kids. However, when old Mrs Spinx, who claims to have lived for 210 years, gives him a magic rock, conch shell, and toque, and his classmate Jan befriends him, he becomes aware of his inner strengths and weaknesses and is able to establish a new and healthier attitude to his absent father.

Within a Painted Past tells of the summer vacation of Allison, who fancies herself independent, but feels insecure around her peers. She discovers that she can step into the paintings depicting the Alberta foothills region as it was a century ago. There she befriends Lily, a girl her age, and her little brother Jo-Jo. In the past, she discovers that 'she liked knowing the things she did well made an immediate difference to the lives of other people.' However, she is happy to return to the present, where, as often happens in time-shift fantasies, she learns that she is descended from Lily and that, in the past, her actions have influenced her own life. In *The Prince of Tarn*, Fred, the central character, is able to help a character who has come to life from a story written by his deceased mother. The boy helps the visitor, a prince, return to and save his kingdom and, at the novel's conclusion, gives the prince his mother's pen, explaining, 'You've got to write your own story.'

Hutchins has also created the written text for several picture books. *Leanna Builds a Genie Trap*, *Ben's Snow Song*, *Norman's Snowball*, *The Catfish Palace*, and the Yancy stories are realistic narratives often based on incidents in the lives of the author's children. *Katie's Babbling Brother* and *Nicholas at the Library* resemble the novels in their study of the influence of magic on ordinary children. Wearied of his constant wordless chatter, an older sister sprinkles shrinking powder on her little brother. She is able to accept his noise when, after he returns to normal size, she learns that her mother also finds him occasionally annoying. Nicholas, who has reluctantly accompanied his mother to the library, finds the place more interesting when he discovers a tiny monkey and, with the aid of the librarian, locates the storybook from which it has escaped. *Shoot for the Moon, Robyn* and *Robyn's Want Ad* are short chapter books about a girl who must deal with the consequences of her sometimes rash actions.

Hazel Hutchins's characters are engaging, the magic intriguing, and the plots exciting. However, there is much more to her books than their entertainment value. As one of her characters is told, 'like most stories, it's about a lot of other things too. But it takes time to figure it out.' Like readers of her books, the main characters in the novels must work to understand the significance of the people they encounter, the events they experience, and the magic they briefly possess. Although magic is a plot device, each type of magic is an appropriate catalyst for the specific character's development. Jason learns that action and wise choices are as significant as wishes. Mrs Spinx explains to Arlie Zack that the magic gifts she gives him are only 'the simple strength everyone has inside'. As the heroes grow in self-knowledge and self-confidence, they achieve fuller appreciation of their friends, their parents, and the other adults in their lives. At the end of each novel, the magic is gone; the characters no longer need it. They can now accept responsibility for their own actions and the courses of their own lives.

See also: *CA* 123; *CANR* 50; *SAAS* 24; *SATA* 51, 81; *TCCW*; *WSMP*.

Julie Johnston

Born: 21 January 1941, in Smiths Falls, Ont.

Principal Residences: Smiths Falls; Kingston; Peterborough, Ont.

Education: University of Toronto (Diploma in Occupational Therapy 1964); Trent University (BA 1984).

Career: occupational therapist; creative writing instructor; writer.

Major Awards: Governor-General's Prize for Children's Literature (1992, 1994); Canadian Library Association Young Adult Book of the Year Award (1995); IODE Violet Downey Book Award (1993); Ruth Schwartz Children's Book Award (1995).

Works for Children

Hero of Lesser Causes (Toronto: Lester Publishing, 1992). **Rev:** *CCB-B* 46 (Apr. 1993): 254; *CM* 20 (Oct. 1992): 272; *EL* 20 (Mar. 1993): 14; *HB* 69 (July 1993): 457; *QQ* 58 (Apr. 1992): 31; *SLJ* 39 (June 1993): 107; *VOYA* 16 (Aug. 1993): 152.

Adam and Eve and Pinch-Me (Toronto: Lester Publishing, 1994). **Rev:** *BiC* 23 (Dec. 1994): 18; *CCB-B* 47 (May 1994): 290; *CM* 22 (Sept. 1994): 138; *EL* 22 (Mar. 1995): 67; *HB* 70 (Sept. 1994): 599; *QQ* 60 (May 1994): 37; *SLJ* 40 (July 1994): 119; *VOYA* 17 (Aug. 1994): 146.

The Only Outcast (Toronto: Tundra, 1998).

Love Ya Like a Sister: A Story of Friendship (Toronto: Tundra, 1999).

Selected Discussions

Little, Jean. 'Julie Johnston: An Exciting New Voice', *CCL* 77 (1995): 33–8.

In 1964, Julie Johnston received a diploma in occupational therapy and began work in her field; two decades later, she earned a BA in English and Creative Writing and started to teach creative writing and submit her own work to periodicals. In the 1990s, she drew on her relationships with disabled children and her study of literature to create young adult novels that sensitively portray the experiences of traumatized teenagers as they approach birthdays that mark thresholds to new phases of their lives.

Hero of Lesser Causes is the first-person narrative of 12-year-old Keely who, in the first chapter, confesses, 'I've always had this vision of myself charging through a sort of mist on a silver-white stallion . . . fixing things, making everything all better.' However, when her brother, 14-year-old Patrick, is crippled in the polio epidemic that swept Ontario in 1946, her visions and courage are shaken. She is unable to make contact with Patrick, a person she'd felt connected to like 'Siamese twins joined at the mind'. Wishing to escape childhood, to be taken seriously by her family, Keely enlists her brother's help in search for the missing fiancé of his live-in nurse and attempts to set up a friendship between Patrick and a neighbourhood boy. By the time she reaches her thirteenth birthday, which is described in the final chapter, she has grown out of her fantasies of heroism and horsemanship. Ironically, in fact, Patrick has twice rescued her from horse-riding mishaps, once before his polio attack, and once just before her birthday. He has also told her to 'see me the way I am'. She must accept him as a separate person with a life he must learn to control on his own. Similarly, she must acknowledge her own uniqueness and understand the heroism involved in facing the realities of both of their lives. Then she can take pride in being a 'hero of lesser causes'.

Critics have praised the novel for its refusal to accept simplistic solutions to the complex problems it examines. Keely must abandon her romantic quest to reunite nurse Peggy with her lost lover, and, like the nurse, she must deal with situations as they are. Although he is regaining limited mobility, the real possibility remains that Patrick may be an almost total paraplegic for the rest of his life. Johnston's complexity of vision is achieved in large part through the depth of her characterization of the brother and sister. While Keely's is a 'coming-of-age story', her movement from childhood to adolescence is complicated by Patrick's devastating illness. In dealing with her altered relationship with him, she is forced to understand change in an extreme manner. Johnston's focus is on the young narrator; however, her presentation of the changes taking place for

Patrick as he moves from anger, self-pity, and despair towards hope is movingly and convincingly portrayed.

The novel has also been praised for the skill with which the author creates a network of secondary characters to surround Keely and Patrick. Mrs Whinney, a domineering nurse who bullies Patrick to the brink of suicide, is contrasted with Peggy Doyle, the nurse who not only cares for the boy's physical needs but ministers to his psychological requirements as well, encouraging, sympathizing, and gently scolding as needed. Her ability to cope with the loss of her fiancé provides an example of dealing with change against which the two siblings' conflicts can be compared. Two neighbouring children dealing with change also are presented. Alex, who works with horses at a nearby farm, has lost his father during World War II, but refuses to accept pity for himself or self-pity in others. Although his gruff, outspoken manner rankles both Keely and Patrick, he is instrumental in getting the invalid to leave the self-imposed prison of his room. Charlotte, a newcomer to the area, deals with changes in her life by attempting to manipulate Patrick and Keely, playing favourites with one or the other.

Whereas Keely, approaching her thirteenth birthday, must deal with major change for the first time in her life, Sara Moone, the narrator of *Adam and Eve and Pinch-Me*, looks forward to her sixteenth birthday as a time when she can control the changes that have occurred so often in her life. A foster child since the death of her adoptive parents many years earlier, she has lost count of the times she has moved. By the time she reaches her present home she has withdrawn into herself, speaking seldom to others and refusing to react to the people she encounters. However, by the time of her birthday, she has undergone changes she could not have imagined, becoming emotionally involved with her foster family and the rural Ottawa Valley community in which she lives. Significantly, her new attitudes have been brought on, in part, by changes over which she has no control: the appearance at a nearby bed-and-breakfast of her birth mother, who wishes to have the girl live with her, and the sudden death of her foster father, whose quiet affection has helped her to relate to others.

'I want to get into the future, but I keep getting distracted by the past and bogged down in the present', Sara complains to herself after she has been with the new foster family for a few months. For her the future is after her rapidly approaching birthday, and she plans to live it in a hermit-like existence in northern Ontario. The past she must confront is not only hers, but that of other people she encounters. Understanding it, she better understands herself and the others. In the present, she reluctantly finds herself becoming interested in and responsive to other people and is upset, as it breaks down her defences and increases her vulnerability. However, as she learns to love her four-year-old foster brother Josh and her foster parents Ma and Hud, she develops confidence in herself.

As in *Hero of Lesser Causes*, Johnston skilfully portrays the relationships among Sara and the people around her. Unlike another foster child, Nick, who had seen his mother work at destroying relationships and die of a drug overdose, the heroine learns to create relationships, becoming a big sister to Josh, a friend to teenaged Matt, and a daughter to Hud. Nick's anger, Hud's affection, Josh's timidity, her birth mother's rigidity—all convincingly depicted by Johnston—influence Sara's change from an introverted rejecter of people to a caring young woman.

Johnston also introduces and very effectively develops several symbols through the novel. The child question-and-answer joke that provides the title is one in which the giver of the answer is a victim. Only by learning to respond to the question, 'Who do you think was saved?' in a different way does a person escape victimization. When Sara tells Josh that they could be brother and sister, both with the name 'Pinch-Me-Not', she is defining a bond between them in which they both know how to protect themselves from those who would harm them. The new foster home also is symbolic, for the Huddlestons' own a sheep farm, carefully tending newborn lambs, especially those that are orphaned, mending fences to keep the flock safe within boundaries, and bringing strays back home. As they do with the animals, so, too, do Ma and Hud with their foster children, lost lambs who need the security of the fold. A lost lamb herself, Sara becomes a shepherd, helping little Josh find the love and security he needs. However, neither she nor Ma and Hud can save the malicious, destructive black sheep, Nick.

The computer on which Sara records her story is the novel's major symbol, representing her movement from a silent, withdrawn foster child to a participating member of her new family and the larger community. At first, she enjoys the control she has over the machine: she can save or delete the words that describe her past and present with the tap of a key. Moreover, because she does not have a printer, what she writes is totally private. However, the very act of recording is a step towards accepting the past she has attempted to reject: 'The danger of keeping your thoughts to yourself is that they tend to disappear, like everything in my life.' However, when she acquires a printer, the possibility exists of her words being communicated to others. And, when her text accidentally falls into other hands, her barriers are broken down; she is vulnerable. The computer has helped her to discover a voice and how to share that voice with other people.

Set in eastern Ontario, *The Only Outcast* is 16-year-old Fred Dickinson's account of his 1904 summer vacation. The first-person narrative presents two accounts: the first, in a journal given him by his grandmother, briefly reports activities and events; the second, a record of his thoughts, presents, in great detail, emotions and experiences of which his father, siblings, and relatives are unaware. Suffering from a severe speech impediment, Fred cannot and does not reveal to those around him his deepest thoughts and feelings. He must, on his own, come to terms with his harsh and domineering father, with his sense of himself as an insignificant fool, and with the disappointment of falling in love with a teenage girl much older than he.

During much of the narrative, Fred reports on the daily life at the summer cabin: performing chores with his brothers and cousins, swimming and riding in boats, and attending ice-cream socials and a dance at the local resort hotel. Swimming naked in the early morning, he is noticed by Nora, the older girl; talking to her at the social, he becomes infatuated; and seeing her kiss her beau at the dance, he feels foolish. By the end of the summer, however, he realizes that he does not really love her and accepts his changed emotions. The most dramatic events take place when, with his father, who is looking for vacation property, he inspects the John Oliver shack, the location, according to legend, of a long-ago murder. Fred discovers that the legend is true when he breaks through rotting floorboards and lands on a skeleton. He also discovers that his father, who had always stressed that he become more manly, is a coward, fainting when he sees the grizzly contents of the shack. Fred confronts his father when the man wants to report the findings to the police, explaining that the disclosure would serve no purpose other than to shame the murderer's son, now a frail old man. As the summer holidays end, Fred leaves the lake a changed person, surer of himself and stronger in his relationship with his father.

In *The Only Outcast*, Johnston effectively combines several genres: the summer vacation story, the problem novel, the mystery-adventure, the historical novel, and the coming-of-age story. She skilfully presents period details of early twentieth-century cottage life and piques the reader's interest with the horror and mystery plot. Most important, she presents a strong and convincing portrait of Fred as he works to articulate who he is, particularly in relation to his father. When, at the end of the story, he talks back to his father for the first time, stressing the need for compassion rather than for legal correctness, he has found his own voice and his own sense of identity.

Julie Johnston's novels can be placed into three categories of contemporary children's and young adult fiction: the historical novel, the problem novel, and the coming-of-age story. In *Hero of Lesser Causes*, Keely's movement out of childhood is achieved as she deals with the physical handicap of her brother. In *Adam and Eve and Pinch-Me*, Sara Moone's passage to an age when she will no longer be a ward of the court is marked by coming to terms with the positive as well as negative elements of her life as a foster child. Fred, in *The Only Outcast*, ends his summer vacation having discovered how to define himself. Johnston also links her stories to two early twentieth-century classics dealing with similar themes. Like Mary Lennox and Dickon helping the apparently crippled Colin in Frances Hodgson Burnett's *The Secret Garden*, Keely and Alex work with Patrick. Fred's father covers his grief over the death of his wife through acting severely to his son, as did Archibald Craven in *The Secret Garden*. Sara is not unlike the heroine of L.M. Montgomery's *Anne of Green Gables*, only discovering where she truly belongs after the death of a beloved foster parent. While Johnston's works reflect contemporary genres and echo established classics, they

Other

'My Own Story: Plain and Coloured', *CCL* 54 (1989): 31–6.

Selected Discussions

Jenkinson, Dave. 'Portrait: Welwyn Wilton Katz', *EL* 21 (Nov. 1993): 61–5.

Micros, Marianne. 'When Is a Book Not a Book?', *CCL* 47 (1987): 23–8.

Kertzer, Adrienne. 'Mad Voices: The Mothers of Welwyn Wilton Katz', *CCL* 77 (1995): 6–18.

A great distance separates the cold, precise rationality of mathematics from the intense, emotional power of mythology and legends. However, London, Ontario, mathematics teacher Welwyn Katz travelled the distance in the early 1980s when she began a career as a writer of fantasy. An avid reader of fiction as a child and, as an adult, a student of mythology, particularly that of Celtic Britain, she published her first children's book in 1982. *The Prophesy of Tau Ridoo* is the story of five brothers and sisters who, during their summer vacation on a farm, search a dark cupboard for lost toys and enter into a strange universe. The story, which shows the influence of the fantasies of Edith Nesbit and C.S. Lewis and bears some resemblance to Pierre Berton's *The Secret World of Og*, anticipates many of the themes of Katz's later work. In it, ordinary children are confronted by conflicting forces of light and dark and, although often unsure of themselves, are instrumental in the defeat of evil powers.

Katz's next two books, *Witchery Hill* and *Sun God, Moon Witch*, focus on a North American child spending a summer vacation in Britain. In the former, Mike Lewis, an insecure 14-year-old, travels with his author father to Guernsey. There, with his new friend Lisa, he uncovers a witches' coven. Mike learns to stand on his own, while Lisa must face the truth about her stepmother's wicked nature. Although the two children are safe at the story's conclusion, the ending is not happy. Mike realizes that he will never have a close relationship with his father; and Lisa's father and stepmother are dead, killed as a result of the forces unleashed partly because of the stepmother's evil. In *Sun God, Moon Witch*, Hawthorn McCall is sent to western England to stay with her aunt while her domineering father and his new bride honeymoon in Europe. When a local industrialist threatens to destroy Awen-Un, a prehistoric stone circle, Hawthorn is drawn into a power struggle between ancient forces of good and evil. Told by a mysterious White Lady that she must work to save the powers embodied in the stones, Hawthorn protests, 'I'm just a kid!' However, she conquers her inner uncertainties and, with the assistance of her cousin Patrick, courageously prevents the disaster that threatens the area.

The setting of *False Face* is Katz's hometown of London, Ontario. Living unhappily with her selfish mother and her sister, young teenager Laney McIntyre discovers an Iroquois False Face mask in the marsh near her home.

However, when her mother takes it from her, its evil powers are released. With her Native friend, Tom Walsh, Laney struggles against her transformed mother, seeking to contain the dangerous forces of the mask. The two also fight against developers who want to destroy the marshlands. In the end, not only is Laney successful, but she has gained a sense of her own self-worth and an unhappy recognition of her mother's inherent inadequacies. Solidly based on Katz's careful research into Native spiritual beliefs, the novel is more disciplined than the author's earlier works and is a powerful portrait of intense family conflicts.

Morgan Lefevre, 15-year-old heroine of *The Third Magic*, on a trip to England with her film-maker father, is drawn into Britain's mythic past, where she becomes involved in the struggles between the Circle, which is feminine power, and the Line, which is masculine power. With Arddu, from the ancient kingdom of Nwm, she recovers the power of the Third Magic that restores a balance between the opposing forces and, through its power, is transported to Arthurian England, where she discovers that the legendary king is not the noble character he is usually portrayed to be. One of her prized possessions, what she considers a lucky charm, proves to be a jade talisman empowered to bring peace in the past. In engaging in battles of cosmic significance, the girl learns the importance of using mystic forces wisely and responsibly. Compelling in its presentations of character, especially in its revisionist interpretation of Arthur, the novel is slightly weakened by the sometimes confusing complexity of its plot.

Whalesinger also involves time-shifting, a movement from the present-day coast of California, where the hero Nick is a member of a whale study project, to the sixteenth century, where sailed the explorer Sir Francis Drake, who, like Arthur, is portrayed in unheroic terms. Filled with anger over the death of his brother, a conservation activist, Nick learns that his sibling had been murdered by Ray Pembroke, who is using the project as a cover for illegal treasure hunting. With his friend Marty, who has learned from a mother whale about accepting her own limitations, the boy discovers Pembroke's scheme and finds out that Drake, like the director, had murdered a boy who came too close to his evil secrets. As in her other works, Katz links a young person's coming of age to historical forces. Evil is a continuing presence that must be constantly confronted.

The Stratford, Ontario, and Edinburgh, Scotland, Shakespeare Festivals are the settings of *Come Like Shadows*, in which Kinny O'Neil discovers truths about herself and the historical Macbeth, who has been much maligned as a result of his presentation in Shakespeare's play. Sent by her parents to Stratford to get her interest in theatre out of her system, the girl becomes increasingly involved in the production of the tragedy and with a mysterious old woman from ancient times who takes over the body of a young girl in order to continue to exercise her powers. *Macbeth*, described as 'a play about power . . . Who has it, who wants it, who takes it, who abuses it. And who is defeated by it', provides the backdrop for struggles between the director and actors, as well as among beings from the past. Kinny becomes enmeshed in the struggles when she buys an antique mirror that was made in the time of the historical Macbeth and through which the ancient females exercise their quests for power. As she perceives the power of the mirror, the girl realizes that she must assume the responsibility for its use.

Sara, the 12-year-old heroine of *Time Ghost*, encounters, not major historical figures, but her own grandmother as a girl. In 2044, she travels to the Arctic, one of the few places where the natural world has not been destroyed, with her grandmother and her best friend, Dani. There, through the agency of her birthday present, a pendant that had belonged to her grandmother since she was young, she visits 1993. In this past, she lives in her grandmother's body and, in coming to understand why the now-feisty old woman behaves as she does, learns about herself as well. In a subplot, Adam Duguay, an offshore oil driller, also is sent to the past where he learns about the importance of preserving the natural world that he has treated so casually.

Although he does not time-shift, 13-year-old Ben, in *Out of the Dark*, uses his understanding of characters from the past to come to terms with the demons of his present. Like his mother, who had been killed during a convenience-store robbery, Ben loves the Norse myths and sagas, and, when he accompanies his family to his father's hometown, a Newfoundland outport, he becomes interested in the Viking settlements of the eleventh century. As Ben's father notes: 'Nobody's ever really gone from a place if they've once lived there', and Ben finds himself identifying with Tor, like him a woodcarver, who had lived in the area centuries earlier and had become involved in the bitter struggles between the Vikings and the Native peoples. Although his interest is in part to escape from his grief over his mother's death and the hostility between himself and the local children, it becomes a way for Ben to resolve his conflicts and to discover the truth of his mother's words that after Ragnorak, the great battle between the Norse Gods and the Frost Giants, 'There will be life, and new life. . . . That was the end, and this is the beginning.' At the story's conclusion, he flings a Norse ax, a symbol of violence, into the bog where he had found it.

An eighth-century Scandinavian warrior is the subject of Katz's first picture book, a retelling of *Beowulf*, the oldest extant English epic. Her descriptions of Beowulf's battles against the monster Grendel, Grendel's vengeful mother, and the dragon that delivers his death blow are faithful to scenes in the original epic. Katz does, however, add a frame story in which an old bard tells his grandson, Wiglaf, about the adventures Beowulf had as a young man. In the second part of the story, Wiglaf becomes the only warrior who goes to the aid of the elderly Beowulf during the battle against the dragon. Katz also gives Beowulf and his line troublesome magic gifts, Beowulf's being an enormous strength that he cannot always control. The bard's ability to enter people's thoughts and Wiglaf's ability to see the future enable Katz to explain how people are able to describe events that occurred when Beowulf was alone. In spite of such possibly controversial departures from the original, Katz's *Beowulf* adheres to the spirit of the epic in its descriptions of both the proud Beowulf and his ferocious battles against monsters.

Although they are in the tradition of such high fantasy novels as those of J.R.R. Tolkien, C.S. Lewis, and Susan Cooper, Katz's works are strongly original creations. In addition to presenting, as those novelists do, the cosmic clashes of good and evil, she uses her mythological materials as symbols to delineate the intense struggles of young people on the verge of adulthood. In her novels Katz deals with both male and female children and teenagers; however, her focus is profoundly feminine, particularly in her analysis of supernatural female beings, whose positive and negative influences the characters must come to terms with. As they contact the mythical and historical pasts, the characters learn that their lives are not lived alone, that forces of earlier ages continue into the present, influencing them. In some of the earlier novels, the characters have gained self-respect and self-confidence, but also the unhappy knowledge of the inadequacies of their parents and the impossibility of ever achieving happy, fulfilling relationships with them. The later novels emphasize reconciliation and new beginnings, as the young people, wiser because of their experiences, willingly accept the worlds in which they live.

See also: AAYA 19; *CA* 154; *CLR* 45; *SAAS* 25; *SATA* 62, 96; *TCCW*; *WSMP*.

Dayal Kaur Khalsa

Born: 17 April 1943, in New York City.

Died: 17 July 1989, in Vancouver.

Principal Residences: New York; Toronto; Montreal; Vancouver.

Education: City College of New York (BA 1963).

Career: artist; yoga instructor; writer.

Works for Children

BAABEE Books 'Series I', 4 vols (Montreal: Tundra, 1983). **Rev:** *BiC* 12 (Dec. 1983): 14; *CCL* 37 (1985): 75.

BAABEE Books 'Series II', 4 vols (Montreal: Tundra, 1983). Rev: *QQ* 49 (1983): 12.

BAABEE Books 'Series III', 4 vols (Montreal: Tundra, 1984). **Rev:** *BiC* 13 (Dec. 1984): 11; *QQ* 51 (Mar. 1985): 74; *SLJ* 31 (Apr. 1985): 80.

Tales of a Gambling Grandma (Montreal: Tundra, 1986). **Rev:** *BiC* 15 (Nov. 1986): 35; *CCB-B* 40 (Nov. 1986): 52; *CCL* 47 (1987): 91; *CM* 15 (Jan. 1987): 32; *EL* 14 (Mar. 1987): 28; *HB* 65 (May 1989): 394; *NYTBR* (18 Sept. 1986): 36; *QQ* 52 (June 1986): 28.

I Want a Dog (Montreal: Tundra, 1987). **Rev:** *BiC* 16 (Dec. 1987): 13; *CCB-B* 41 (Mar. 1988): 140; *CCL* 52 (1988): 27; *EL* 15 (Mar. 1988): 23; *HB* 64 (May 1988): 342; *RT* 41 (May 1988): 950; *SLJ* 34 (Feb. 1988): 62.

My Family Vacation (Montreal: Tundra, 1988). **Rev:** *BiC* 17 (Dec. 1988): 11; *CCL* 57 (1990): 105; *CM* 17 (Mar. 1989): 86; *EL* 16 (Mar. 1989): 21; *HB* 65 (May 1989): 394; *SLJ* 35 (Nov. 1988): 89.

Sleepers (Montreal: Tundra, 1988). **Rev:** *CCL* 53 (1989): 86; *CM* 16 (Nov. 1988): 228; *HB* 64 (Sept. 1988): 616; *NYTBR* (8 May 1988): 35; *SLJ* 35 (June 1988): 91.

How Pizza Came to Our Town (Montreal: Tundra, 1989); published in the United States as *How Pizza Came to Queens*. **Rev:** *BiC* 18 (June 1989): 33; *CCL* 56 (1989): 116; *CM* 17 (July 1989): 189; *NYTBR* (17 Sept. 1989): 39; *SLJ* 35 (May 1989): 86.

Julian (Montreal: Tundra, 1989). **Rev:** *BiC* 18 (Dec. 1989): 23; *CCL* 56 (1989): 109; *CM* 18 (Jan. 1990): 13; *EL* 17 (Mar. 1990): 23; *HB* 65 (Nov. 1989): 761; *QQ* 55 (Oct. 1989): 13; *SLJ* 35 (Sept. 1989): 228.

Cowboy Dreams (Montreal: Tundra, 1989). **Rev:** *BiC* 19 (June 1990): 15; *CCB-B* 43 (July 1990): 269; *CCL* 59 (1990): 74; *CL* 130 (Autumn 1990): 151; *CM* 18 (July 1990): 181; *EL* 18 (Mar. 1991): 24; *HB* 66 (Sept. 1990): 592; *QQ* 56 (Mar. 1990): 20; *SLJ* 36 (Aug. 1990): 131.

The Snow Cat (Montreal: Tundra, 1992). **Rev:** *BiC* 21 (Nov. 1992): 36; *CCL* 81 (1996): 80; *CM* 21 (Jan. 1993): 21; *EL* 20 (Mar. 1993): 13; *HB* 69 (Mar. 1993): 197; *QQ* 58 (Sept. 1992): 72; *SLJ* 39 (Aug. 1993): 146.

Selected Discussions

Edwards, Gail. 'Dayal Kaur Khalsa: The Art of Remembering', *CCL* 70 (1993): 48–62.

Ellis, Sarah. 'News From the North', *HB* 65 (May 1989): 393–5.

When Dayal Kaur Khalsa was a girl with dreams of becoming an author, her mother told her that she would find the best stories in her own backyard. Nearly 40 years later, these words came true, as Khalsa created several picture books based on memories of her childhood in New York City. Motivated in part by the author's awareness that she was dying of cancer and wanted to tell her own story, these books present the life of a girl growing up in the 1950s. The vivid, folk-like illustrations and the often deceptively simple written texts deal with her relationships with family and friends, her imaginary life, and her hopes and dreams. The pictures vividly recall the styles of the 1950s, while at the same time offering a child's view of her own life.

At the opening of Khalsa's first book, *Tales of a Gambling Grandma*, the now-adult narrator states: 'This is the story of her life as she told it to me and as I remember it.' Escaping from Cossacks in Russia, the heroine had arrived in Brooklyn, married, and, to help with expenses, become a poker player. When she moved into her daughter's house, she formed a close bond with her granddaughter, who recounts the woman's stories and the times they shared. The engaging character of the resourceful and lively old lady, along with the child's response to her stories, gives the book its humour and charm. The chalk, pastel, tempera, and acrylic paintings present the child's point of view and interpretation of what she both sees and hears. Events and settings at which she was present are realistically depicted; those based on what she only heard are more exaggerated. For example, a picture of the old lady and the girl sitting outside their home is contrasted to one immediately following in which the girl imagines her grandmother's advice. The woman had said, 'Never, ever go into the woods alone because the gypsies will get you.' In the illustration, the granddaughter, dressed in a cowgirl outfit, hiding behind a tree, watches colourfully attired gypsies preparing traps. On the next page, scarlet- and blue-uniformed Cossacks invade a modern kitchen. The final illustration, picturing the girl's reaction to her grandmother's death, reveals the woman's room, the bed empty and neatly made. Just inside the half-open closet, the girl is seen embracing the old lady's dresses. The simplicity of the action and the depth of the quiet grief it reveals are communicated in the clear design and subdued colours of the illustration.

My Family Vacation and *How Pizza Came to Our Town* also celebrate memories of childhood. In the former, the heroine, her brother, and her parents make a winter automobile trip to Florida. Khalsa presents her reactions to roadside motels, amusement parks, and 1950s Florida hotels. From the postcards that decorate the endpapers, to a used car lot, fake-Indian souvenir stand, and coral-coloured seaside swimming pool, the book is a pop-art guide to mid-twentieth-century east coast resorts. Its charm comes from the portrayal of May, the heroine, who hates to leave the snow but loves hotel soaps, postcards, feathers from Parrot Jungle, and a drink served in a coconut. She is the smallest figure in each of the illustrations, but her bright red hair and delighted smiles contrast her vitality to the tacky settings around her.

How Pizza Came to Our Town, also set in the 1950s, tells of the relationships among May, her friends, and an old lady who visits from Italy. In spite of their attempts to make the new arrival happy, the visitor mopes about muttering 'No pizza'. Only when the children discover the meaning of the strange word, find a recipe at the library, and purchase the necessary ingredients, does she become animated. The most tightly plotted of Khalsa's stories, it is a kind of modern-day *pourquoi* tale. Contemporary readers will laugh both at the parody of a traditional genre and at the possibility of there once having been people who didn't know what pizza was. They also will respond to the warmth of the emotional relationships developed between the children and the old lady. The visitor's changing emotions are reflected in the illustrations. When she first arrives, she stands in the background, a small, frowning figure. Often she sits apart from other people, usually the children who are trying to befriend her. But when she is teaching the children how to stretch the dough, joyously flinging a circle of it into the air, she is in the center of the picture, smiling and surrounded by her young helpers. Soon after, she joins them outside at the backyard picnic table.

I Want a Dog reveals Khalsa's great skill at creating humorous effects and capturing a child's point of view through her brilliantly coloured, folk-art styled illustrations. A child's unfulfilled yearning for a pet is seen in the details of her room, where dog pictures cover the walls, and in the classroom, where she daydreams so much about pets that the rest of the students are depicted with the heads of dogs. Noticing that her roller skate looks like a small white dog, she makes a leash for it, hoping that walking it will be good training for when she gets the real thing. A series of illustrations show May taking the skate to the playground, on her Halloween rounds, and downtown. The almost tall-tale humour of the narrative is emphasized by the brightness of the paintings, in which the 1950s objects in each of the pictures assume surrealistic intensity.

A real dog provides the humour and conflict in *Julian*. In the endpapers, several breeds of dogs stand quietly facing in one direction, while a yellow dog races the opposite way. He is Julian, who loves to chase everything. With the exception of the first full-page illustration, in which the human narrator sits quietly on the grass watching her two cats, and the last, when the conflicts are resolved and the owner, cats, and the dog rest quietly together indoors, each picture is filled with motion as the hyperactive dog causes chaos. Only after he rescues a lost kitten does he become a member of the family group.

Cowboy Dreams is another presentation of a child's yearnings, this time for a horse. The narrator, who wanted to be a cowboy when she was a child, remembers riding on her father's back, a rocking horse, and a merry-go-round stallion. Realizing that her parents will not get her a real horse, she builds one on the basement banister and sings cowboy songs 'that would carry me away, into the world of my dreams, into the land of the cowboys.' At this point, single-page illustrations depicting the girl's real world are replaced by double-spreads; the basement room dissolves into a southwestern landscape; the clothesline becomes a cowboy's lariat. The girl rides through scenes from the songs she sings, watching wagon trains and herds of buffalo and antelope.

While the illustrations and text of *Cowboy Dreams* reflect the child's view of her real imaginary worlds, they also reflect the adult author's present attitudes towards her own past. In fact, much of the wit and humour of this and other books by Khalsa can be more fully appreciated by adults, who can both reimagine these pasts and observe them. Khalsa specifically celebrates the past of her 1950s childhood and fills her pictures with crisply, vividly, and accurately painted physical details from them. However, her artistic style, which has been termed naïve or folk, with its bright colours and sharp designs and outlines, creates the sense of wonder with which children of all eras have perceived their worlds.

See also: *CA* 137; *CLR* 30; *Junior* 7; *SATA* 62; *TCCW*; *WSMP*.

Murray Kimber

Born: 1964, in Lethbridge, Alta.

Principal Residences: Lethbridge; Calgary.

Education: University of Calgary; Alberta College of Art, Calgary (1984).

Career: Commercial artist; art instructor; illustrator.

Major Awards: Governor-General's Award for Illustration (1994); Elizabeth Mrazik Cleaver Award (1995).

Works for Children

Illustrated by Murray Kimber

Josepha: A Prairie Boy's Story, by Jim McGugan (Red Deer, Alta.: Red Deer College Press, 1994). **Rev:** *BiC* 23 (Nov. 1994): 58; *CBRA* (1994): 487; *CCB-B* 48 (Nov. 1994): 94; *CCL* 81 (1996): 48; *CM* 22 (Nov. 1994): 209; *EL* 22 (Mar. 1995): 18; *QQ* 60 (July 1994): 60; *SLJ* 40 (Nov. 1994): 84.

Fern Hill, by Dylan Thomas (Red Deer, Alta: Red Deer College Press, 1997). **Rev:** *CM* (8 May 1999): on-line.

When Murray Kimber was a boy, he wanted to become a comic-book artist. However, his skill as a narrative artist did not reach its fulfilment until the early 1990s, when, having become a successful artist whose oil paintings had appeared on magazine covers, in advertising campaigns, and in gallery showings, he accepted an invitation to illustrate Jim McGugan's children's story about rural Alberta life at the beginning of the twentieth century.

Set in 1900, *Josepha* presents the narrator's recollections of an immigrant boy who had briefly attended his one-room school. Unable to speak English and bullied by older boys, Josepha befriended the younger children, including the narrator. The immediate present of the story takes only a few minutes as Josepha and the narrator stand in the schoolyard at the end of term. Before he leaves with his brothers the 14-year-old immigrant presents the teacher with an exquisitely carved miniature violin and the narrator with his prized possession, an old pen knife.

Kimber's 15 oil paintings depict the narrative's few events and effectively capture the emotional intensity of the main characters. Josepha's loneliness is emphasized by the fact that, although he is the largest figure in most of the pictures, he seldom looks directly at other people. Barefooted, clothed only in overalls held up by rope suspenders, he appears out of place in the school room, sitting at a tiny desk, slouching unhappily as younger boys smirk at him. Elsewhere, his tenderness is captured as he dances happily around his younger sisters and then kneels to dust off the narrator's new boots. His sadness is revealed in a double-spread in which he stands in the foreground, the only person in the picture, his head bent forward pensively. To his right, bathed in sunlight on a hill behind him, is the schoolhouse in which he was a misfit; to the left, in the distance, is a sod house, its windows dark, the home to which he must return. Caught between the two worlds symbolized by these buildings, he will find happiness in neither.

The oil paintings that Kimber created for an edition of Dylan Thomas's *Fern Hill* not only complement the Welsh poet's lyric account of the spirit of youth, they also emphasize a theme implicit in the words: the unstoppable passage of time that brings childhood to an end. The opening illustration depicts a white-faced old man, his eyes closed as he remembers his youth. In subsequent pages, a red-headed boy races horses, runs along tree-lined roads, and stands in a stream blowing a horn. Significantly, in the pictures of him holding hands with the girl he will marry, the old man looks on, a reminder of the aging process. He reappears three illustrations later, calling and then leading the red-headed boy's son across the fields. In the book's final picture, the old man, his shoes in hand, wades in a pond, as if remembering the childhood he once enjoyed.

Kimber, in his children's books, has extended the emotional meanings of the texts. He has transformed relatively simple reminiscences into often intense portrayals of childhoods now past.

Gordon Korman

Born: 23 October 1963 in Montreal.

Principal Residences: Montreal; Thornhill, Ont.; New York; Pompano Beach, Fla; Toronto.

Education: New York University (BFA 1985).

Career: writer.

Works for Children

This Can't Be Happening at Macdonald Hall! (Richmond Hill, Ont.: Scholastic-TAB, 1978). **Rev:** *CBRA* (1978): 190; *CCL* 14 (1979): 55.

Go Jump in the Pool! (Richmond Hill, Ont.: Scholastic-TAB, 1979). **Rev:** *CBRA* (1979): 209; *CCL* 20 (1980): 39; *IR* 14 (June 1980): 46.

Beware the Fish! (Richmond Hill, Ont.: Scholastic-TAB, 1980). **Rev:** *CBRA* (1980): 168; *CCL* 20 (1980): 39.

Who Is Bugs Potter? (Richmond Hill, Ont.: Scholastic-TAB, 1980). **Rev:** *CBRA* (1980): 170.

I Want to Go Home! (Richmond Hill, Ont.: Scholastic-TAB, 1981). **Rev:** *APBR* 10

(Nov. 1983): 2, 13; *CBRA* (1981): 226; *EL* 9 (Sept. 1981): 29; *IR* 15 (Aug. 1981): 46, and 16 (Feb. 1982): 41; *QQ* 47 (June 1981): 33.

Our Man Weston (Richmond Hill, Ont.: Scholastic-TAB, 1982). **Rev:** *CBRA* (1982): 249.

The War With Mr. Wizzle (Richmond Hill, Ont.: Scholastic-TAB, 1982). **Rev:** *BiC* 11 (Dec. 1982): 10; *CBRA* (1982): 249; *CCL* 77 (1995): 70; *QQ* 49 (Jan. 1983): 34, and 59 (Oct. 1993): 19; *SLJ* 30 (Sept. 1983): 136.

Bugs Potter LIVE at Nickaninny (Richmond Hill, Ont.: Scholastic-TAB, 1983). **Rev:** *BiC* 12 (1983): 16; *CBRA* (1983): 290; *Maclean's* 96 (4 July 1983): 52; *QQ* 49 (Nov. 1983): 24.

No Coins, Please (Richmond Hill, Ont.: Scholastic-TAB, 1984). **Rev:** *CBRA* (1985): 264; *CCB-B* 39 (Nov. 1985): 50; *CCL* 43 (1986): 55; *EL* 13 (Sept. 1985): 44.

Don't Care High (New York: Scholastic, 1985). **Rev:** *CCB-B* 39 (Dec. 1985): 71; *CCL* 46 (1987): 83; *EL* 14 (Jan. 1987): 49; *HB* 62 (Mar. 1986): 208; *QQ* 51 (Dec. 1985): 27; *SLJ* 32 (Dec. 1985): 102; *VOYA* 8 (Dec. 1985): 320, and 10 (June 1987): 49.

Son of Interflux (New York: Scholastic, 1986). **Rev:** *CCB-B* 40 (Nov. 1986): 53; *SLJ* 33 (Nov. 1986): 104; *VOYA* (Dec. 1986): 219.

A Semester in the Life of a Garbage Bag (New York: Scholastic, 1987). **Rev:** *CCL* 52 (1988): 63; *EL* 15 (Mar. 1988): 19; *HB* 63 (Nov. 1987): 744.

The Zucchini Warriors (New York: Scholastic, 1988): **Rev:** *BYP* 2 (Dec. 1988): 10; *CCL* 77 (1995): 70; *CM* 20 (Jan. 1992): 12; *EL* 16 (Mar. 1989): 22; *SLJ* 35 (Sept. 1988): 184; *VOYA* 11 (Oct. 1988): 182.

Radio Fifth Grade (New York: Scholastic, 1989). **Rev:** *CCL* 67 (1992): 89; *EL* 17 (Mar. 1990): 24; *QQ* 55 (Oct. 1989): 14; *SLJ* 35 (Sept. 1989): 252.

Losing Joe's Place (New York: Scholastic, 1990). **Rev:** *BiC* 19 (Oct. 1990): 29; *CCL* 80 (1995): 82; *CL* (Summer 1992): 191; *CM* 18 (July 1990): 184; *EL* 18 (Mar. 1991): 21; *QQ* 56 (Apr. 1990): 15; *SLJ* 36 (May 1990): 124; *VOYA* 13 (June 1990): 106, and 14 (Feb. 1992): 408.

Macdonald Hall Goes Hollywood (New York: Scholastic, 1991): **Rev:** *BiC* 20 (Sept. 1991): 48; *CCL* 67 (1992): 89; *CL* (Spring 1993): 170; *CM* 19 (May 1991): 168; *EL* 19 (Mar. 1992): 18, and 20 (Sept. 1992): 36; *QQ* 57 (Apr. 1991): 19; *VOYA* 14 (June 1991): 98.

The D- Poems of Jeremy Bloom: A Collection of Poems about School, Homework, and Life (Sort of), with Bernice Korman (New York: Scholastic 1992). **Rev:** *SLJ* 39 (Feb. 1993): 100.

The Twinkie Squad (New York: Scholastic, 1992). **Rev:** *CBRA* (1992): 323; *CCB-B* 46 (Nov. 1992): 77; *CCL* 80 (1995): 82; *CM* 20 (Nov. 1992): 311; *QQ* 58 (Aug. 1992): 26; *SLJ* 38 (Sept. 1992): 254; *VOYA* 15 (Dec. 1992): 281.

The Toilet Paper Tigers (New York: Scholastic, 1993). **Rev:** *CBRA* (1993): #6153; *CM* 22 (Jan. 1994): 19: *QQ* 59 (Sept. 1993): 68; *SLJ* 39 (Sept. 1993): 233.

Why Did the Underwear Cross the Road? (New York: Scholastic, 1994). **Rev:** *CBRA* (1994): 488; *CCL* 88 (1997): 76; *CM* 2 (26 Apr. 1996): on-line; *QQ* 60 (Oct. 1994): 44; *SLJ* 41 (Jan. 1995): 108.

Something Fishy at Macdonald Hall (New York: Scholastic, 1995). **Rev:** *CBRA* (1995): 508; *CCL* 89 (1998): 51; *EL* 23 (Mar. 1996): 25; *QQ* 61 (Aug. 1995): 34; *SLJ* 41 (Sept. 1995): 202.

The Chicken Doesn't Skate (New York: Scholastic, 1996). **Rev:** *BiC* 25 (Dec. 1996): 36; *CBRA* (1996): 480; *QQ* 62 (Nov. 1996): 44; *SLJ* 42 (Nov. 1996): 107.

The Last-Place Sports Poems of Jeremy Bloom: A Collection of Poems about Winning, Losing, and Being a Good Sport (Sometimes), with Bernice Korman (New York: Scholastic, 1996). **Rev:** *CBRA* (1996): 480; *QQ* 62 (Dec. 1996): 39; *SLJ* 43 (Apr. 1997): 112.

Liar, Liar, Pants on Fire (Markham, Ont.: Scholastic, 1997). **Rev:** *CBRA* (1997): 513; *CM* 4 (24 Apr. 1998): on-line; *QQ* 63 (Nov. 1997): 44; *SLJ* 43 (Sept. 1997): 185.

The 6th Grade Nickname Game (Markham, Ont.: Scholastic, 1998). **Rev:** *CM* 16 (9 Apr. 1999): on-line.

Selected Discussions

Ferns, Chris. 'An Interview with Gordon Korman', *CCL* 38 (1985): 54–65.

Jenkinson, Dave. 'Gordon Korman: ALA Best Book Author and Fan Favorite', *EL* 20 (Jan.-Feb. 1993): 66–70.

In the seventh grade, Gordon Korman became carried away with an English assignment. That project turned into *This Can't Be Happening at Macdonald Hall!*, a novel published when he was only 14. To prove to himself and to others that the publication of this book was not a 'fluke', Korman completed another by the time his first was in print. He thus established a pattern, writing a new book every summer during school vacation and getting five published by the time he graduated from high school in 1981. In the more than 20 years since his first book, Korman has continued to publish at a steady rate, becoming one of Canada's most famous and popular children's writers.

The bulk of Korman's work consists of farces aimed at middle-school readers, an audience he understands because he tours extensively to speak at schools. These farces generally follow a formula. Set primarily in a school or camp, they focus on a pair of boys who use their ingenuity to overcome restrictions that adults impose. Although one of the central characters may appear to lack any talents beyond the ordinary, at least one major character tends to be intellectually superior to others or to have extraordinary powers of manipulation. The protagonists also consistently ignore adult rules and strictures because they find them unreasonable. Secondary characters tend to be either eccentrics passionately devoted to one subject or people identifiable by a single dominant trait. As in most traditional farces, the action consists of a series of slapstick episodes in which disasters, often physically destructive, accumulate until order is restored in a happy ending, one that comes as the result of the protagonists' plans, but not always in the form they hoped. Repetition of the absurd situations and statements is also a basic comic device. In spite of all the violations of rules, the novels uphold basic moral principles, because, as Korman has noted in an interview with Dave Jenkinson, they 'set a pretty good example, I think, of friendship, loyalty, honesty, and indomitable courage.' Nevertheless, the characters exist to entertain, not to provide moral instruction, and Korman avoids deep themes or messages.

Korman's formula governs the seven Bruno and Boots books, which are set in a fictitious boys' boarding school outside of Toronto. The practical-joking protagonists, Bruno Walton and Melvin 'Boots' O'Neal, are roommates who constantly break the school's rules, although often for a good reason. The initial conflict in the first volume, *This Can't Be Happening at Macdonald Hall!*, arises because the school's headmaster, William Sturgeon, nicknamed the Fish, decides that the way to curtail the boys' pranks is to separate them. Bruno, who is forced to move in with Elmer Drimsdale, a scientific genius, and Boots, who must room with George Wexford-Smyth III, a wealthy hypochondriac, launch a campaign to be reunited. Unfortunately, each of their efforts backfires, confirming the Fish in his belief that they should remain separate. It is not until they become heroes by rescuing the Malbonian ambassador's son from a drifting balloon that they win back the right to room together. In *Go Jump in the Pool!*, the two devise elaborate schemes to raise money for a pool so that parents won't be tempted to enrol their sons in a school with better facilities. The comedy depends on the absurdity of the fund-raising efforts, the repeated arguments between the Headmaster and Miss Scrimmage, the Head Mistress of an adjacent girls' school who constantly waves around a shotgun that she cannot aim properly, and the accidents that befall Miss Scrimmage. Similarly, in *Beware the Fish!*, Bruno and Boots also have the best interests of the school at heart. Knowing that the school is in financial trouble, they contrive a series of publicity stunts to get the media coverage they believe will attract new students. As with all of their previous plans, these stunts cause trouble and nearly ruin the school; only the accidental use of one of Elmer Drimsdale's inventions saves the day. In the fourth volume, *The War with Mr. Wizzle*, self-interest and school spirit coincide. When Melvin C. Wizzle, a new teacher, determines to modernize Macdonald Hall and introduces an oppressive demerit system to coerce compliance, Bruno and Boots spring into action to preserve the school as they like it. Fortunately, their friends at Miss Scrimmage's Finishing School have a similar problem, being burdened with a former Marine drill sergeant as new assistant headmistress. After numerous failed and messy attempts to rid themselves of their oppressors, the boys and girls succeed in getting the teachers to fall in love with each other, to marry, and to leave to start a new life.

Because his publishers were not initially interested in more Bruno and Boots books, Korman put the series aside for six years. When he returned to it with *The Zucchini Warriors*, he maintained his basic formula, but he gave the girls at Miss Scrimmage's Finishing School greater roles, lengthened the stories slightly, reduced some of the repetitious joking, and made the farcical events more elaborate. When millionaire zucchini king Hank the Tank Carson donates a football stadium to Macdonald Hall, which doesn't even have a football team, Bruno and Boots once again kick into action by getting him to promise to build a recreation centre if the school fields a winning team. They therefore help Cathy Burton, a brilliant quarterback, disguise herself as Elmer Drimsdale. Cathy then leads the team to a championship. The farcical complications arise from three events. First, because the students don't want to insult Hank Carson, they pretend to love his fried zucchini sticks and must take elaborate measures to dispose of the vast quantities he donates. Second, Kevin Klapper, an agent from the Ministry of Education who is determined to write a devastating report on the school, catches football fever and stays on to be a coach, leading his boss to believe that he has been murdered. Third, Elmer Drimsdale's Manchurian bush hamsters escape and take up residence under the stadium stands, propagating wildly when they eat the zucchini sticks thrown there. A police raid, a field overrun with hamsters, and a near riot follow before peace returns to the school.

Macdonald Hall Goes Hollywood adds a further wrinkle to the formula: Korman attempts to add a theme. When a Hollywood movie company arrives to shoot on the Macdonald Hall campus, Bruno repeatedly tries to get into the movie, generating comedy by ruining every scene. Although Bruno is initially jealous of the movie's young star, Jordie Jones, he soon realizes that Jordie is lonely and really wants to be like other kids. Bruno and Boots thus smuggle him into their activities, such as a midnight poker game, a dance at Miss Scrimmage's, and a hockey game, in which the masked Jordie plays goal. Most of these events end in chaos: for instance, when the girls at the dance discover that Jordie is present in disguise they nearly riot. Although it has its moments, this novel has three major problems. First, Jordie, the normal kid, is so bland next to the colourful caricatures surrounding him that he never comes alive. Second, the overly long plot is too involved. The sequence in which Jordie stows away on the bus taking the boys on the school's compulsory wilderness survival trip does offer an opportunity for an wilderness accident and the confusing arrival of Miss Scrimmage and her girls, the Fish, and numerous reporters, but the attempts at typically chaotic comedy are rather vapid when compared to the movie set themes. Third, the theme of understanding Jordie's humanity and his needs is belaboured at most points and negligible at the end.

A little shorter but far more polished is *Something Fishy at Macdonald Hall*. When someone begins to play clever pranks at Macdonald Hall, everyone naturally suspects Bruno and Boots. This time, however, they are innocent. Their attempts to discover the real culprit repeatedly land them in more trouble.

Although filled with such conventional set pieces as Miss Scrimmage's schemes to keep intruders out of her school and Elmer Drimsdale's ridiculously inept attempt to court a girl by sending her samples of bird droppings, the plot skilfully creates suspense by setting up red herrings: Bruno and Boots thus wrongly assume that Edward, Boots's younger brother, is the prankster. Most young readers will be surprised to learn that the culprit is Mrs Sturgeon, who is merely seeking to rekindle her husband's sense of purpose so that he will not retire from Macdonald Hall. *Something Fishy at Macdonald Hall* is vintage Korman, but the plotting, dialogue, and pace are far smoother than in the first volume of the series.

Korman has also applied the pattern and techniques of his Bruno and Boots books to stories touching on settings or subjects of interest at various times to growing children. *Who Is Bugs Potter?* and its sequel, *Bugs Potter LIVE at Nickaninny*, thus farcically present the youthful obsession with rock and roll and the adult distaste of it. *Our Man Weston* shows the desire of every adolescent to have his summer job become something exciting. A kind of Hardy Boys farce, the novel is the story of twins, one of whom tries to be a detective. He causes numerous disasters, but he eventually stops a plot to steal a secret airplane. None of these books has the light-hearted zest of the Bruno and Boots books.

Although most of the violations of adult regulations in Korman's books are for good purposes, those in two novels are more ambiguous. Both concern summer camps, which Korman himself disliked. In *I Want To Go Home!*, Rudy Miller, a genius and a gifted athlete, is determined to escape from camp, where fun is regulated by the 'clones', the counsellors. Insofar as it has a theme, the book suggests that children find their meaning, their identities, and considerable joy in opposing the conformity that adults demand. A similar idea seems to be behind *No Coins, Please*, the first of Korman's books with an American setting. Here, however, the focus is on the teenage counsellors who must somehow keep in check Artie Geller, a precocious financial wizard who is part of a group making a camping tour across the United States. The point seems to be that Artie simply wants to show that he can outsmart adult society. What is disconcerting here, however, is that he, even more than Rudy Miller and Bugs Potter, is so self-absorbed that he can spare no thought for others or their feelings.

Korman's other middle-school books focus on students in American public schools. *The Twinkie Squad*, like *Macdonald Hall Goes Hollywood*, which was published the previous year, tries to make the typical Korman chaos illustrate a theme about the injustice of judging by appearances. Douglas Fairchild, son of an ambassador, is enrolled in a Washington public school because private schools will no longer accept him. His unco-operative attitude lands him with other misfits in the Special Discussion Group, derisively known as the Twinkie Squad. He soon becomes friends with another Twinkie, Armando Rivera, known as Commando. Douglas is behind a number of things that go wrong at school, but the principal, judging only by economic class, repeatedly blames Commando. The most satisfying part of the novel comes when Douglas fools the entire school, which believes that a secret club has been pulling elaborate pranks, into joining the Twinkie Squad. The novel also tries to show that Douglas is an under-achiever because he fears that he cannot compete with his father and successful older siblings. As a defence mechanism, he makes up stories about the frolicking ways of Pefkakia, where he was born. His sense of isolation is emphasized by the contrast between his parents, who remain aloof because of their busy lives, and Commando's father, who has a daily game of booby-trapping their apartment. After Douglas botches a school play, his father finally realizes that his son needs parental attention and 'frolics' with him. Too heavy-handed in its development of its themes and too belaboured in its farcical episodes, *The Twinkie Squad* is a weak entry into the field of fiction about lonely rich kids.

The 6th Grade Nickname Game does not have as many wildly farcical moments as most Korman novels, and may be only mildly amusing instead of hilarious, but it makes better use of its hints at theme than does *The Twinkie Squad*. *The 6th Grade Nickname Game* presents two best friends, Wiley and Jeff, who pride themselves on giving people appropriate nicknames. For example, they call a boy who constantly spies on people Snoopy, and they give their substitute teacher, a gigantic football coach named Mr Hughes, the obvious nickname of Mr Huge. When Cassandra Levy moves into town, however, she proves to have so many facets to her character that the boys are stumped. The entire nickname game introduces a two-sided theme. On one side, the failure of the boys to find an appropriate nickname for Cassandra shows that labels do not always explain people or reality. On the other side, however, a boy formerly ignored by everyone becomes popular and significant when Wiley and Jeff jokingly call him the Iceman. In this case, the name creates the reality. Korman works these themes into two subplots. In the first, Mr Hughes's class, who have believed in their nickname, The Dim Bulbs, learn that he is about to be fired because their reading-test scores are low. To save his job, everyone in the class becomes an avid reader. Predictably, the class scores highest in the state on their examination, thereby showing that they are shining beacons whose belief in an inaccurate label held them back. Unfortunately, the praise of reading as fun and the efforts to make Mr Hughes a comical eccentric who treats every class as if it were a football game are overdone. The second plot line, in which Wiley and Jeff become rivals for Cassandra's affection, is much stronger. It shows them nearly losing their lifelong friendship when they begin to sabotage each other's chances with Cassandra. Its ironic ending, in which Cassandra chooses to go to a Sadie Hawkins dance with the Iceman, may be predictable, but it again supports the theme that labels can govern perceptions.

Two books about school projects generate the entertaining mayhem more typical of Korman's middle-school books. In *Radio Fifth Grade*, three students are in charge of a radio program that becomes the centre of numerous disasters. In part the problems arise because the students have a new teacher, who imposes what they consider to be unrealistic demands. Benjamin Driver, a boy who wants to become 'an immortal radio broadcaster', thus comes up with the idea of creating a radio quiz that will have listeners phone in with homework answers. The students' elaborate schemes to keep the teacher from hearing the program, their ongoing efforts to keep a sponsor happy by trying to sell a parrot, and their fear of a bully who insists on reading inane stories about a pair of fighting kittens, combined with a cast of eccentrics, make this fast-paced, vintage Korman. In *Why Did the Underwear Cross the Road?*, a contest to see which group can earn the most points by doing good deeds generates the disasters. Justin Zeckendorf, a member of the Three Zs, a group consisting of two girls whose names also begin with the letter Z, prides himself on being an idea man. His plans repeatedly go awry, of course, costing the group demerit points. Ironically, as soon as Justin gives up his elaborate ideas and devotes himself to an honest effort at performing good deeds, the Three Zs achieve one of Justin's goals, catching a car-theft ring, a good deed that wins the contest. The plot is a bit hackneyed, but its fast pace and the unity that the contest imposes on them make this a book that Korman fans will breeze through.

Much like *The Zucchini Warriors*, two further middle-school books use sports as a major source of comedy. In *The Chicken Doesn't Skate*, Milo Neal, son of a famous scientist, decides that his science fair project will be 'The Complete Life Cycle of a Link in the Food Chain'. He brings to school a chick, which he intends to raise, slaughter, and serve as food at the fair. His classmates, however, don't understand his intentions. In fact, they fall in love with the chick, which grows into a hen they name Henrietta and make the mascot of the hockey team. The team gains inspiration from the chicken, winning the championship. Although the jokes and slapstick events are similar to those in Korman's other books, *The Chicken Doesn't Skate* stands apart because it employs a number of first-person narrators, including two adults. The multiple points of view effectively show how the three main eccentrics have such different attitudes towards things that comical misunderstandings are inevitable. The other sports book, *The Toilet Paper Tigers*, also tries for a bit of narrative novelty. Although the book has a single narrator, baseball-mad Corey Johnson, each chapter dwells on a different member of his team, telling how that member changed from an inept performer to a valuable member of a championship team. Of course, nothing is ever straightforward in a Korman novel, and the wrinkle here is that the team, sponsored by a toilet paper company, has a coach who doesn't understand anything about baseball. Consequently, his granddaughter, a hip-talking 12-year-old from New York, runs the team, coercing obedience by threatening to show everyone in town a photograph she took when the team was changing into their uniforms. The individual chapters are filled with slapstick as the team members are tricked into gaining confidence. The final joke, however, is that the New York girl is not really from New York City and that she had placed her finger over the lens when she took the blackmail picture. Although sports are prominent in both books, the bulk of the humour occurs off the playing field, making these titles accessible even to those who don't like sports stories.

Korman's novels for young adult readers suggest but do not fully develop themes common in problem novels. In *Don't Care High*, two boys attending the notoriously apathetic Don Carey High in New York get the students to exhibit exceptional school spirit when they promote a strange, inarticulate eccentric as student leader. Somehow, this helps one of the two, Paul Abrams, adjust to his move from Saskatoon to New York. Even weaker in connecting the problem story and comedy is *Son of Interflux*, an attempt to treat a variety of adolescent concerns, including parent-child and boy-girl relationships, and pollution by powerful corporations. Simon Irving, whose father wants him to become a businessman with Interflux, a notorious polluter, insists on becoming an artist. He leads the opposition to Interflux's plans to destroy a green belt separating the school from the factory. Korman initially raises issues of pollution and corporate manipulation of the law, but he does not develop them sufficiently. In *A Semester in the Life of a Garbage Bag*, Raymond Jardine, a boy who believes that winning a trip to a Greek island will bring luck into his disaster-filled life upsets the staid existence of Sean Delancey, his partner in an English poetry project, when he convinces Delancey's grandfather to play the role of a deceased and insignificant Canadian poet. The novel combines a decidedly light approach to such problems as low self-esteem, conformity, the generation gap, and attitudes towards the elderly—none of which receive a satisfying resolution—with slapstick satire mocking technology and the bureaucratic deceptions that permit expensive technological failures to continue receiving government funding.

The only one of these young adult novels with a Canadian setting, *Losing Joe's Place*, succeeds because it does not vitiate the comedy with social concerns. Instead, it describes how three 16-year-olds from Owen Sound spend what they anticipate as a magical summer of fun and romance in the Toronto apartment leased by Joe Cardone, brother of Jason, the narrator. Jason, Don Champion (who considers himself to be 'Mr Wonderful'), and Ferguson Peach, a genius variously called 'the Peach' and 'Peachfuzz', have only one restriction: they must not imperil Joe's lease. Predictably, everything the boys do causes their unscrupulous and miserly landlord, Mr Plotnik, to threaten cancellation of the lease. The novel contains the predictable mixture of repeated disasters, jokes, situations, and eccentric characters, including the gigantic Rootbeer Racinette, who changes hobbies daily and who performs incredible physical acts, such as allowing himself to be hit in the stomach with a two-by-four, to earn money for the boys' food and rent. The repetition is excessive and the episodes become increasingly more farcical, but the retrospective narration—Jason is explaining to Joe precisely how he lost the lease—appropriately gives the entire novel the air of a tall-tale excuse. Furthermore, the story contains a bit of character development normally absent in Korman's novels. Jason Cardone thus discovers that he has talents in home economics, but he also belatedly realizes that the girl who has been chased by his friends has actually been chasing him. As one might expect in a Korman novel, the seemingly disastrous loss of the apartment ultimately becomes a blessing: Joe no longer needs it because he is going to tour as manager of Rootbeer, whom everybody thinks is a new-wave comedian. This amusing novel thus includes both climactic disasters and a happy ending.

In addition to the middle-school and young-adult novels, Korman has also written a chapter book and two volumes of poetry. *Liar, Liar, Pants on Fire*, a disappointing book for younger readers, is heavily didactic and not particularly funny. Zoe Bent constantly lies because she is insecure, believing that she is a nobody. Ironically, after she lies about having an eagle's nest in her backyard, a real eagle lands in the wok that she has decorated to look like a nest, but her pictures don't turn out and everyone again laughs at her. Only after Michael tells her that she has the best imagination in the third grade does Zoe realize that she does not need to lie to be important. The two volumes of poetry that Korman has written with his mother are uneven. The best parts of *The D-Poems of Jeremy Bloom* and *The Last-Place Sports Poems of Jeremy Bloom* are the prose introductions to the various sections of each book. In typical Korman fashion, these introductions tell stories of comic disasters and misunderstandings. The first volume tells how Jeremy gets on the bad side of his poetry teacher, Ms Terranove, by doing such things as blurting out her nickname, Ms Pteradactyl, and inadvertently sending her a gift of plastic barf. The repeated joke is that the reader must decide if the poems in each section deserved the D- that the teacher subsequently gave them. In the second volume, the situation is reversed. Jeremy plays a variety of sports, but every time his teacher shows up for a game, she causes a disaster that results in the team losing such confidence that it does not win again for the rest of the season. The poems in these volumes are not distinguished or hilarious, but occasionally they are amusing examples of light verse.

Korman's books are unrealistic and highly predictable. They rely on the repetitious and exaggerated slapstick of the type found in *Archie* comic books. The characters are essentially one-dimensional caricatures. They contain lots of conflict, but in most cases their plots are remarkably devoid of significant themes. Nevertheless, Korman's stories of children successfully opposing adult authority are undeniably popular. Although not specifically designed for them, these stories appeal to reluctant readers. Perhaps Korman's greatest contribution, then, is that his fast-paced farces have convinced many children that reading can indeed be fun.

See also: *AAYA* 10; *CA* 112; *CANR* 34; *CLR* 25; *MCAI*; *SATA* 41, 49, 81; *Profiles* 2; *TCCW*; *WSMP*.

Maryann Kovalski

Born: 4 June 1951, in New York City.

Principal Residences: New York City; Montreal; Toronto.

Education: New York School of Visual Arts.

Career: commercial artist; writer; illustrator.

Works for Children

Written and Illustrated by Maryann Kovalski

Brenda and Edward (Toronto: Kids Can Press, 1984). **Rev:** *BiC* 13(Dec. 1984): 11; *CCL* 60 (1990): 135; *QQ* 50 (Nov. 1984): 12; *SLJ* 31 (Apr. 1985): 80.

The Wheels on the Bus (Toronto: Kids Can Press, 1987). **Rev:** *BiC* 16 (Dec. 1987): 13; *CCL* 60 (1990): 135; *CM* 16 (Mar. 1988): 57; *EL* 15 (Mar. 1988): 23; *NYTBR* (20 Mar. 1988): 35; *TES* (10 June 1988): 28.

Jingle Bells (Toronto: Kids Can Press, 1988). **Rev:** *BiC* 17 (Dec. 1988): 16; *CM* 17 (Mar. 1989): 87; *EL* 16 (Mar. 1989): 21; *SLJ* 35 (Oct. 1988): 35; *TES* (1 Dec. 1989): 31.

Frank and Zelda (Toronto: Kids Can Press, 1990); published in the United States as *Pizza for Breakfast*. **Rev:** *BiC* 20 (Apr. 1991): 37; *CCB-B* 44 (Mar. 1991): 168; *CM* 19 (Jan. 1991): 27; *HB* 67 (May 1991): 316; *QQ* 56 (Sept. 1990): 19.

Take Me Out to the Ball Game (Richmond Hill, Ont.: Scholastic, 1992). **Rev:** *BiC* 21 (Mar. 1992): 50; *CCL* 70 (1993): 94; *CM* 20 (May 1992): 160; *EL* 22 (Jan. 1995): 56; *QQ* 58 (Mar. 1992): 65; *SLJ* 39 (Apr. 1993): 112.

Queen Nadine (Victoria: Orca Books, 1998). **Rev:** *QQ* 64 (June 1998): 58.

Illustrated by Maryann Kovalski

Molly and Mr. Maloney, by Allen Morgan (Toronto: Kids Can Press, 1981). **Rev:** *BiC* 11 (Aug. 1982): 39; *QQ* 48 (Dec. 1982): 25; *SLJ* 29 (Jan. 1983): 63.

Puddleman, by Ted Staunton (Toronto: Kids Can Press, 1983). Rev: *EL* 11 (Jan. 1984): 40; *QQ* 50 (Jan. 1984): 28.

Mother Goose: Songs, Finger Rhymes, Tickling Verses, Games and More, selected by Sharon, Lois, and Bram (Vancouver: Groundwood, 1985). **Rev:** *CCL* 42 (1986): 96; *QQ* 51 (Dec. 1985): 22; *SLJ* 32 (Aug. 1986): 87.

I'll Make You Small, by Tim Wynne-Jones (Toronto: Groundwood, 1986). **Rev:** *BiC* 15 (Dec. 1986): 15; *CCL* 54 (1989): 66; *QQ* 52 (Oct. 1986): 16.

My King Has Donkey Ears, by Frances Harber (Richmond Hill, Ont.: North Winds Press, 1986). **Rev:** *BYP* 1 (Feb. 1987): 10.

The Cake That Mack Ate, by Rose Robart (Toronto: Kids Can Press, 1986). **Rev:** *BiC* 15 (Dec. 1986): 15: *CCL* 46 (1987): 106; *EL* 14 (Mar. 1987): 27; *HB* 63 (Sept. 1987): 649; *QQ* 52 (Aug. 1986): 38.

Grandma's Secret, by Paulette Bourgeois (Toronto: Kids Can Press, 1989). **Rev:** *CM* 18 (Mar. 1990): 62; *HB* 66 (May 1990): 318; *QQ* 55 (Dec. 1989): 22.

Alice and the Birthday Giant, by John Green (Richmond Hill, Ont.: Scholastic, 1989). **Rev:** *BiC* 29 (June 1991): 58; *CCB-B* 43 (July 1990) 264; *CCL* 61 (1991): 98; *CM* 17 (Dec. 1989): 266; *QQ* 56 (Jan. 1990): 17; *RT* 45 (Oct. 1991): 132; *SLJ* 36 (July 1990): 60.

Junkpile Jennifer, by John Green (Richmond Hill, Ont.: Scholastic, 1991). **Rev:** *CM* 19 (Nov. 1991): 532; *QQ* 57 (July 1991): 51.

The Big Storm, by Rhea Tregebov (Toronto: Kids Can Press, 1992). **Rev:** *QQ* 58 (July 1992): 45.

I Went to the Zoo, by Rita Golden Gelman (Richmond Hill, Ont.: Scholastic, 1993). **Rev:** *CM* 21 (Nov. 1993): 217; *QQ* 59 (Aug. 1993): 35; *SLJ* 39 (Nov. 1993): 79.

Doctor Knickerbocker and Other Rhymes, ed. David Booth (Toronto: Kids Can Press, 1993). **Rev:** *BiC* 22 (Oct. 1993): 56; *CCB-B* 47 (Sept. 1993): 5; *CCL* 21 (1995): 62; *CM* 21 (Oct. 1993): 189; *QQ* 59 (June 1993): 36.

Mabel Murple, by Sheree Fitch (Toronto: Doubleday Canada, 1995). **Rev:** *CBRA* (1995): 468; *CCL* 81 (1996): 43; *QQ* 61 (June 1995): 56.

Princess Prunella and the Purple Peanut, by Margaret Atwood (Toronto: Key Porter, 1996). **Rev:** *BiC* 24 (Dec. 1995): 18; *CBRA* 1995: 460; *QQ* 61 (Sept. 1995): 73; *TES* (8 Dec. 1995): 12.

The Marvelous Market on Mermaid, by Laura Krauss Melmed (New York: Lothrop, Lee and Shepherd, 1996). **Rev:** *RT* 51 (Oct. 1997): 134; *SLJ* 42 (May 1996): 94.

The Seven Chairs, by Helen Lanteigne (Toronto: Key Porter, 1998).

Other

'Patterns and Structures for Writing', *Writers on Writing: Guide to Writing and Illustrating Children's Books*, ed. David Booth (Markham, Ont.: Overlea House, 1989), 36–9.

'Beginning, Middle, End', *School Libraries in Canada* 11 (Spring 1991): 39–40.

Selected Discussions

Jenkinson, Dave. 'Maryann Kovalski—an Illustrator and Author', *EL* 18 (May 1991): 64–9.

In discussing the creative process, Maryann Kovalski has emphasized the importance of the 'writer's own life experiences and interests'. For her, these included her childhood in New York's Bronx, her adult life in Toronto, and her careful study of the work of significant picture book artists, including William Steig and Ken Nutt. These influences are seen in the many books she has illustrated for such writers as Tim Wynne-Jones, Sheree Fitch, and Margaret Atwood, and the six works she has written and illustrated herself. Her illustrations feature settings and activities from Toronto and New York. Like the pictures of Maurice Sendak's books, hers extend the meanings communicated by the words; her accurately depicted building exteriors and interiors, like those in the illustrations of Ken Nutt, reveal the personalities of the occupants; and her representations of the stories' main characters portray a gently satiric attitude towards human nature, as do the illustrations of William Steig.

Brenda and Edward and *Frank and Zelda*, which use Toronto and New York settings respectively, present what Kovalski considers a basic story conflict: 'a change of circumstance or place . . . that challenges the character's mettle'. In the former, the happy life of two dogs is disrupted when Brenda becomes lost on the subway. Although the two are separated for many years, the love of each for the other remains unshaken. In the latter, Frank and Zelda's once prosperous pizza business falls off drastically when the neighbourhood factory closes, and it is only saved when one of their rare customers pays them in wishes rather than cash. The resulting explosion in business all but destroys the husband and wife's happiness, until they plan sensibly rather than impulsively for the future.

The happiness of the canine couple is evident in the portrayal of them together in their neighbourhood and in their cosy home. However, each dog, when alone, seems dwarfed by the city through which it wanders. While the illustrations communicate the varying emotions the dogs experience, they do not expand on the story's narration or themes. By contrast, the illustrations make a considerable contribution to the meaning and tone of *Frank and Zelda*. Double-spreads of the pizza parlor and neighbouring buildings reveal the changes of fortune in the couple's business. Early in the story, summer activities in the nearby park and a happy group of people on the sidewalk in front of the restaurant indicate not only the prosperity of the business but also the couple's happiness. However, when the magic wishes bring them more business than they imagined, the double-spread suggests that their happiness will not last. The large, brightly lit, art deco pizza palace seems out of place in the old neighbourhood, and Frank and Zelda seem bewildered as they stand in the street gaping at the new building. The depictions of the interior indicate the changing volume of business, the increasing chaos and stress that result, and finally the peace that arrives when they wish their success away. Frank and Zelda's changing body language and facial expressions reveal their changing emotional reactions to failure and then success.

Queen Nadine is also about change and separation. In its farm setting, the cows speak to each other, often expressing human emotions, but act as normal barnyard animals around people. The heroine, who is scorned by the rest of the herd because of her attachment to Farmer Pete and her hobby of collecting stones, is disconsolate when the old man sells his cows and has them moved to a distant farm. When the lonely farmer brings Nadine back home, she discovers that one of her favourite rocks, which is really an egg, has hatched, and she and the chick become fast friends. Kovalski treats the theme of change and separation more lightly than she has in her other stories, achieving humour through the depictions of Nadine, who looks at times contented, bewildered, panic-stricken, and filled with joy.

The illustrations and brief texts that Kovalski adds to the well-known lyrics in *The Wheels on the Bus*, *Jingle Bells*, and *Take Me Out to the Ball Game* give new meanings to the popular songs. In each book, an energetic grandmother and her two grandchildren sing the words to accompany their activities. In the first, they wait for a bus after an afternoon's shopping; in the second, the trio takes a sleigh ride through New York's Central Park; while in the third, they attend a major league baseball game. But in each, the actions are in contrast to the relatively peaceful activities described in the songs. As she sings the words to 'The Wheels on the Bus', Grandma begins to remember a childhood experience on a London double-decker. For example, the words 'the people on the bus go up and down' are accompanied by an illustration in which an organ grinder stretches his arms upward in a vain attempt to catch his escaped monkey, a startled woman nearly drops her baby, and a dignified man drops the bouquet of roses he is carrying. As the grandmother and children sing 'Jingle Bells', the startled horse bolts and the driver falls off the sleigh as it careens through the park. Grandma saves the day by controlling the runaway team. When she takes her granddaughters, who are fanatical fans, to the baseball game, the pictures depict the trio performing the actions indicated in the song, but with a zany interpretation of the final lines: Grandma climbs onto the field in quest of a lost souvenir balloon and inadvertently makes the final out at 'The Old Ball Game'. In the books, Kovalski's crayon, ink, or pencil drawings, each vividly coloured with watercolour or gouache, are filled with swirling lines of motion. Her cartoon-like style embodies both the vitality and humour of the events, which present such comically unexpected additions to the content of the familiar songs.

Kovalski's techniques for illustrating others' works are best seen in John Green's *Alice and the Birthday Giant*, Tim Wynne-Jones's *I'll Make You Small*, and Sheree Fitch's *Mabel Murple*. Green's and Wynne-Jones's stories contrast with each other in tone and plot, and offer the challenge of creating a sense of excessive largeness and excessive smallness in illustrations that are of uniform size. In Green's narrative, humorous problems are caused when a giant is accidentally wished into a girl's house on her birthday. In the latter, a boy who wishes to befriend the neighbourhood recluse is shrunk by the old man. The incongruity of having so large a person in a normal world is achieved by presenting the giant in relation to normal objects. While he sleeps on top of Alice's bed, the giant's arms and legs spill over the edges. He is cramped in this setting as he sits on the bed, chin between his knees, listening to the girl proposing a solution to the problem. Having scared away children from her birthday party, he sits among the party favours crying. Although the giant is the physically dominant figure in these scenes, his body language and facial expressions make him seem like a frightened, disoriented baby. By contrast, when Roland is trapped in Mr Swanskin's dark and run-down Victorian house and then transformed into a tiny person, normal-sized toys appear large and the old man's little dog becomes huge and ferocious. The terror of the situation is increased by the fact that Mr Swanskin's hands dominate several illustrations: reaching for the boy, lifting him into the air, and holding him over the trash can.

Kovalski's illustrations for Fitch's *Mabel Murple*, a collection of poems about a girl who lives in a purple world, extend the meanings of the written text, as do those for the old songs she adapted and illustrated. On the opening page, a full-colour illustration accompanies the two words 'what if'. The next two pages show a purple planet and a girl springing out of the bathtub; she is the title character and comes from a parallel or alternate universe. Until the final double-spread, in which full-colour is used in a picture of the girl lying in bed, purple is the dominant and often the only colour. Kovalski's colour shifts indicate what the words of the poems do not, that Mabel is an imaginary alter ego; that the girl in the first picture creates; she is a being whose wild, carefree activities provide a vicarious escape from the ordinary world. The majority of the pictures present a kind of exuberant, barely controlled chaos as Mabel rides a motorcycle and crashes it into a garbage can, careens through a grocery store on a skateboard, and stands on tiptoe tasting soup she's made, while behind her teeters a tower of precariously balanced pots. In the second-to-last drawing, in which Mabel sits in her bed reading, more yellow is introduced into the picture, perhaps an indication that the imaginings of the ordinary girl are winding down and that she, now tired, is returning to her normal world.

As a narrative illustrator, Maryann Kovalski povides art that adds dimensions and new implications for the written texts, whether it is making the title hero of Rose Robart's *The Cake That Mack Ate* a dog, something not mentioned in the words, or the narrator of *Mabel Murple* an ordinary girl creating an alter ego, or evoking the emotional lives of two city dogs or partners in a pizza parlour. She is most successful when the colours and sweeping lines of her cartoon-style art convey the vitality and good-natured humour with which her central characters engage in the often preposterous events in their lives.

See also: *CA* 153; *CLR* 34; *SAAS* 21; *SATA* 58, 97; *WSMP*.

PAUL KROPP

BORN: 22 February 1948, in Buffalo, NY.

PRINCIPAL RESIDENCES: Buffalo; New York City; London, Ont.; Hamilton; Toronto.

EDUCATION: Columbia College, New York City (BA 1970); University of Western Ontario (MA 1972).

Career: teacher; editor; author.

Works for Children

Burn Out (Don Mills, Ont.: Collier Macmillan, 1979).

Dope Deal (Don Mills, Ont.: Collier Macmillan, 1979).

Hot Cars (Don Mills, Ont.: Collier Macmillan, 1979).

Runaway (Don Mills, Ont.: Collier Macmillan, 1979).

Dead On (Don Mills, Ont.: Collier Macmillan, 1980).

Dirt Bike (Don Mills, Ont.: Collier Macmillan, 1980).

Fair Play (Don Mills, Ont.: Collier Macmillan, 1980).

No Way (Don Mills, Ont.: Collier Macmillan, 1980).

Wilted (New York: Coward, McCann and Geohagen, 1980); revised as *You've Seen Enough* (Don Mills, Ont.: Maxwell Macmillan, 1991). **Rev:** *BiC* 21 (Summer 1992): 38; *CBRA* (1992): 324; *CCL* 37 (1985): 59; *CM* 20 (May 1992): 168.

Baby, Baby (Don Mills, Ont.: Collier Macmillan, 1982). **Rev:** *CCL* 37 (1985): 59.

Gang War (Don Mills, Ont.: Collier Macmillan, 1982). **Rev:** *CCL* 37 (1985): 59.

Snow Ghost (Don Mills, Ont.: Collier Macmillan, 1982). **Rev:** *CCL* 37 (1985): 59.

Wild One (Don Mills, Ont.: Collier Macmillan, 1982). **Rev:** *CCL* 37 (1985): 59.

Amy's Wish (Don Mills, Ont.: Collier Macmillan, 1984). **Rev:** *CBRA* (1984): 330.

Micro Man (Don Mills, Ont.: Collier Macmillan, 1984): **Rev:** *CBRA* (1984): 330.

Take Off (Don Mills, Ont.: Collier Macmillan, 1985). **Rev:** *CBRA* (1985): 265.

Death Ride (Don Mills, Ont.: Collier Macmillan, 1986).

Getting Even: A Novel for Young Adults (Toronto: McClelland & Stewart-Bantam, 1986). **Rev:** *CCL* 53 (1989): 61.

Jo's Search (Don Mills, Ont.: Collier Macmillan, 1986). **Rev:** *CCB-B* 42 (May 1989): 213; *SLJ* 35 (June 1989): 122.

Justin, Jay-Jay, and the Juvenile Dinket (Richmond Hill, Ont.: Scholastic-TAB, 1986); republished as *Fast Times with Fred* (Richmond Hill, Ont.: Scholastic, 1990). **Rev:** *CL* 135 (Winter 1992): 191; *EL* 15 (Nov. 1987): 53; *QQ* 52 (Dec. 1986): 17.

Get Lost (Don Mills, Ont.: Collier Macmillan, 1987). **Rev:** *CBRA* (1987): 232; *CM* 16 (Jan. 1988): 17; *EL* 15 (Mar. 1988): 55.

Not Only Me (Don Mills, Ont.: Collier Macmillan, 1987). **Rev:** *CM* 16 (Sept. 1988): 171.

Under Cover (Don Mills, Ont.: Collier Macmillan, 1987). **Rev:** *CM* 16 (Sept. 1988): 171.

Cottage Crazy (Richmond Hill, Ont.: Scholastic-TAB, 1988).

Head Lock (Don Mills, Ont.: Collier Macmillan, 1988).

Moonkid and Liberty (Toronto: Stoddart, 1988). **Rev:** *CBRA* (1988): 290; *RT* 45 (1991): 138.

Tough Stuff (Don Mills, Ont.: Collier Macmillan, 1988).

Baby Blues (Don Mills, Ont.: Collier Macmillan, 1989). **Rev:** *CBRA* (1989): 321.

The Rock (Toronto: Stoddart, 1989). **Rev:** *CBRA* (1990): 319; *CCL* 62 (1991): 86

Split Up (Don Mills, Ont.: Collier Macmillan, 1989). **Rev:** *CBRA* (1989): 321.

We Both Have Scars (Don Mills, Ont.: Collier Macmillan, 1990): **Rev:** *CCL* 66 (1992): 90.

The Victim Was Me (Don Mills, Ont.: Collier Macmillan, 1991).

Ellen/Eléna/Luna (Don Mills, Ont.: Collier Macmillan, 1992). **Rev:** *CBRA* (1992): 323; *CCL* 78 (1995): 74.

Ski Stooges (Richmond Hill, Ont.: Scholastic, 1992). **Rev:** *CBRA* (1992): 324; *CCL* 80 (1995): 82; *CM* 20 (May 1992): 152; *QQ* 58 (July 1992): 49.

Riot on the Street (Don Mills, Ont.: Collier Macmillan, 1993). **Rev:** *CBRA* (1993): #6154.

Moonkid and Prometheus (Toronto: Stoddart, 1997). **Rev:** *CBRA* (1997): 514.

Other

The Reading Solution: Making Your Child a Reader for Life (Toronto: Random House, 1993); revised for the US as *Raising a Reader: Make Your Child a Reader for Life* (New York: Doubleday, 1996).

The School Solution: Getting Canada's Schools to Work for Your Children, with Lynda Hodson (Toronto: Random House, 1995).

Selected Discussions

McGillis, Roderick. 'Master Teague, What Is Your Story? Male Negotiation in Fiction for Children', *CCL* 76 (1994): 6–21.

Vanderhoof, Ann. 'Hot Topics for Cool Readers', *QQ* 46 (Jan. 1980): 6–8.

Paul Kropp began writing because reluctant readers in the Hamilton vocational school at which he was teaching had no books that appealed to them: available materials were unsuitable because they were designed for much younger audiences. Wanting something that would lure students into beginning a book and keep them turning pages, Kropp wrote a story especially for them. Eventually published as *Burn Out*, this story about two boys who try to capture arsonists set the pattern for Kropp's later high-interest, low-vocabulary books for reluctant readers. Each title employs a restricted vocabulary and relatively short, straightforward sentences. Description is kept to a necessary minimum, and the proportion of dialogue to narration is high. Chapters are short and typically end with some kind of cliff-hanger to make the reader begin the next chapter.

Physically, the books have appealing covers, snappy titles (such as *Dope Deal*, *Runaway*, *Gang War*, and *Hot Cars*), large print, and extra spacing between lines to make them easier to read and to give readers the sense of progress by lessening the time required before it is necessary to turn the page. To make them more relevant to readers, they use Canadian settings and refer to Canadian social and cultural institutions. Most importantly, however, the books focus on topics of interest to teens, including teenage pregnancy, sexual abuse, running away from home, shoplifting, drug use, gang violence, and suicide. In spite of their somewhat lurid subject matter and fast-paced action, however, the stories contain little in the way of graphic violence. Furthermore, they conclude on a positive, reassuring note, affirming traditional moral values. The success of Kropp's titles is evident from the number published and from the fact that Kropp was later hired as general editor of a new series of books for this audience. His dedication to reading is also evident in his guide to children's books, *The Reading Solution: Making Your Child a Reader for Life* (revised for the US market as *Raising a Reader*).

Kropp has also written mainstream fiction, novels that don't limit vocabulary, sentence structure, or chapter length. Like those for reluctant readers, these novels benefit from Kropp's experience as a teacher and his obvious understanding of what young people are like and what appeals to them. His experience is especially evident in the convincing dialogue, which, because these novels employ first-person narration, creates plausible and interesting protagonists. Certain elements repeatedly appear in these books—the awkward but brilliant nerd, the bully, the balding and befuddled father, and the dysfunctional family—but Kropp employs them in sufficiently diverse ways to make a number of his books both entertaining and thematically satisfying.

Most of the elements evident in later books are present in Kropp's first mainstream novel, *Wilted* (updated and relocated to a Canadian setting as *You've Seen Enough*). Fourteen-year-old Danny Morrison lives in the midst of chaos: his heavy-drinking father beats his mother; his sister, who goes out with a boy nicknamed Mangy Bob, constantly smokes dope; his seven-year-old brother is frightened that their parents are going to separate. To make matters worse, as far as he is concerned, Danny not only needs glasses, but the affordable pair his mother chooses make him look like a Wilt, or nerd. Danny's life becomes even more complicated after he forms a relationship with attractive Samantha Morgan. Ron Marsten, a bully, threatens Danny, declaring that Sam is his girl. Naturally, Danny ends up with Sam, the first of Kropp's attractive, spirited girls who do not judge boys entirely by appearance. *You've Seen Enough* is not entirely successful; perhaps because he was too used to the brevity of his reluctant-reader books, Kropp crammed too much material into a short book. As a result, the complex characterization is hinted at but never developed. In particular, Danny is unconvincing as a boy who is sensitive, yet can fly into such a rage that he nearly kills the bully in a fight.

Although it includes more material and covers a greater time span, from graduation from elementary school to entrance into university, *The Rock* is more successful because the narrator is predominantly an observer and commentator, rather than the centre of the action. Brian Robinson, another in Kropp's long line of peculiar-looking boy geniuses, is called Beak because of his big nose. The summer after his first year of university, he looks back on his life and his friendships with three neighbours: Antony LaRoche, known as the Rock; Nikki, the Rock's sister; and Simon Van Geet, a fat kid and perennial follower. The four were inseparable, but the Rock was the magnet that pulled and held them together. He was loyal and feisty, saving the two boys from a humiliating hazing when they entered high school and preventing Simon's father from beating him. Beak fondly recalls the good times swimming and their trip to a cabin, where they accidentally crashed a car they were driving in a field. As the years pass, however, the group begins to split: Beak's parents move to a wealthier neighbourhood, Simon begins spending time at a girlfriend's house to avoid abuse at home, and the Rock, who is failing at school, begins to drink and do dope, becoming a follower of his wild fellow-workers at a car wash. The Rock, having given up on his childhood dream of business success, hurtles out of control, dying in a car crash. *The Rock* is an elegy mourning both the loss of a life and of the promises of youth. Major themes include the idea that maturation brings inevitable changes, including the end of idyllic friendships, and that the qualities that make some children leaders are not necessarily the ones that enable them to become adequate as adults. Although it never fully develops either Simon or Nikki, *The Rock* is an interesting coming-of-age story in which the senseless destruction of a friend and the loss of a relationship teach Beak that growing up is never simple.

The issue of growing into one's identity implicit in *The Rock* is overt in *Ellen/Eléna/Luna*. Ellen Bertrand, tired of being bland and boring, is convinced by her friend Janey, the school newspaper editor, to adopt a new identity so that she can have some blind dates and write an article about them. On her first date, with Tooner, an aspiring cartoonist and sponge, she adopts the identity of Luna, a punk rocker, and discovers the phony world of alternative art. For the second, with Garrett, a rich boy attending Upper Canada College, she becomes wealthy Eléna Hilton. Naturally, she and Garrett fall for each other, and she must decide whether the truth will destroy a relationship based on deception. Eventually the realization that Garrett likes her for who she is convinces her that she is more complex than she previously imagined, that her various roles are parts of her character. Although the novel plays off Ellen's story of deception with one involving feisty Granny Bo, who herself adopts roles, it is too predictable to be entirely satisfying.

Getting Even is a far more skilful story of teen relationships. It employs two narrators to recount the romance developing between an unlikely couple whose personal histories contain ironic parallels. Shy and awkward Keith Hartman is ignorant about girls and lives in the shadow of his brilliant brother, who now attends university. Jane Flemming, a bright and athletic girl, who constantly lies in order to cover her pain, has refused to talk to her mother ever since she separated from Jane's father four years earlier. Working together on a yearbook project, Keith and Jane learn to respect each other. After he visits his brother, Keith realizes that his brother is not infallible and that he himself has notable talents. When Jane's father is felled by a stroke, Jane begins to talk to and accept her estranged mother. Now able to feel and care for another, she can express her feelings for Keith. Convincingly recounting the rivalries, misunderstandings, and experiments that characterize teen life, *Getting Even* succeeds, in spite of the contrived drama of the stroke, as both a love story and a novel of maturation.

Dual narration is also a feature of Kropp's most successful books, the two novels about Ian Callisto McNaughton, called Moonkid because his middle name is the name of the fourth moon of Jupiter. *Moonkid and Liberty* balances Ian's account of home and school life with that of his older sister, Liberty, or Libby. Physically short, brilliant, and quick with witty retort, Ian is an outsider who fantasizes that he is an alien from another planet so that he can take a dispassionate and cynical look at others. Picked on by a bully he nicknames the Missing Link, Ian exacts revenge, but his own cruelty in doing so teaches him that he is wrong to consider himself morally superior to other humans. Whereas Ian protects himself by cultivating his status as an outsider, Libby is sick of appearing weird to others. While toying with the idea of going to live with her mother in California, she tries to fit in with a rich, fast crowd. When her ex-hippie father, a bookstore owner, is accused of distributing pornography, however, her new friends desert her. Eventually, she realizes that being different is not necessarily bad if the alternative is conforming to the mindless and cruel bigotry practised by her snobbish former friends. Both Ian and Liberty then show their maturity by refusing to run away from their problems: Ian refuses a transfer to a school for gifted students, and Libby decides that she won't go to California. Witty in its dialogue and narration, *Moonkid and Liberty* develops two authentic voices, includes a variety of compelling and interesting scenes, and works towards a conclusion that is full of sentiment without being sentimental.

Set two years later, the sequel, *Moonkid and Prometheus*, intersperses Ian's witty and literate narrative with excerpts from the journals of Prometheus John Gibbs, a six-foot tall, seventh-grade black boy whom Ian has been assigned to tutor. Ian initially tutors Pro out of self-interest: although he does not fit in at his current school, he does not want to be transferred forcibly to a much worse one. Ian soon takes the assignment seriously, tutoring even after Pro's teacher, a conservative who dislikes Ian's methods, refuses to allow him into the school. Ian thus becomes friends with Pro, helping his mother with a legal problem, introducing him to the wonders of astronomy, and, of course, motivating him to read and write. For his part, Pro gives Ian advice on getting along with others and teaches him to play basketball, enabling Ian to gain confidence and to fit in better at school. The descriptions of basketball practice and games are too extensive, but the novel effectively portrays kids from different worlds developing a meaningful and rewarding friendship. The narration is especially effective. Ian's narrative sparkles with wit and sarcasm. It conveys the changes in Libby, who has become a conservative college student determined to move to California with her mother. It also makes adults, such as Ian's father and his teachers, convincingly alive. Pro's journal entries, which alternate with Ian's account, brilliantly convey both his developing literacy and his appreciation of his new friend, becoming longer, better written, and more insightful as the novel progresses. *Moonkid and Prometheus* is Kropp's best book, a testament to his ability to make intelligent and amusing stories for young adults.

Kropp has also made one of his characteristic misfits the centre of three novels for younger readers. *Fast Times with Fred* (originally titled *Justin, Jay-Jay, and the Juvenile Dinket*), *Cottage Crazy*, and *Ski Stooges* focus on Fred, a clumsy, bizarre-looking teen oblivious to the chaos he creates. In all three books, Fred is the unlikely babysitter of six-year-old Justin, who cries to get his way, and Jason, a 10-year-old intellectual. In the first book, Fred, who has the reputation of being a delinquent ('dinkent' in Justin's pronunciation) has numerous run-ins with Beefy, a bully who hates him. In the end, Fred becomes a hero by saving Beefy's life. The problem with this book is not that the plot is improbable—farcical comedy is always improbable—but that its piled-on disasters are neither fresh nor particularly funny. The same is true of the sequels. *Cottage Crazy*, in which Fred takes the boys to a beat-up shack that he has claimed is almost a mansion and out onto a leaky boat that he has claimed is almost a cabin cruiser, is full of unfunny disasters. Even naïve Justin's unalloyed faith in Fred's abilities and his repeated request for Fred to perform a disastrous activity again do not make these events amusing. As with the previous book, its climax tries to make the inept Fred into something approaching a hero. Fred thus engages in a swimming contest with a rich, arrogant bully for the right to ask a girl to a dance. The rich bully cheats, and Fred loses, but in the only unpredictable element of this stale novel, the girl, insisting that she is not an object, refuses to go with either boy. At the dance, however, she willingly dances with Fred, whom she likes for his character, not his appearance. The final volume of the series, *Ski Stooges*, in which Fred goes skiing with the boys, similarly mixes romantic attraction (the attraction this time is Chantal, a French-Canadian ski instructor), slapstick (a wild slalom race, an attempt to change diapers that culminates with Fred gluing his hand to his face), and improbable heroics (Fred goes out into a blizzard to the rescue of Chantal, who has been injured in an automobile accident). The various episodes are weaker than similar ones in the previous novels, especially the requisite display of Fred's heroism because it is told in an excessively abbreviated flashback, losing any chance of dramatic intensity.

Kropp's junior novels suggest that he lacks the gift for creating the comic mayhem that has made Gordon Korman's books so popular. His forte is really fiction for teens, both those who are reluctant readers and those who devour books. His Moonkid books are particularly notable achievements: they are amusing because wit is integral to the narration; honest because they convey a genuine sense of the joys and frustrations of teen life; and inspiring because they touch on important attitudes and values without condescension or preachiness.

See also: *CA* 112; *MCAI*; *SATA* 34, 38; *WSMP*.

William Kurelek

Born: 3 March 1927, in Whitford, Alta.

Died: 3 November 1977, in Toronto.

Principal Residences: Winnipeg; London, England; Toronto.

Education: University of Manitoba (BA 1949); Ontario College of Art; Instituto Allende (Mexico).

Career: picture framer; artist; writer.

Major Awards: Amelia Frances Howard-Gibbon Illustrator's Award (1974, 1976); IODE (Toronto) Children's Book Award (1975).

Works for Children

Written and Illustrated by William Kurelek

A Prairie Boy's Winter (Montreal: Tundra, 1973): **Rev:** *CCB-B* 27 (Mar. 1974): 112; *EL* 12 (Mar. 1985): 46; *HB* 49 (Oct. 1973): 456; *IR* 8 (Winter 1974): 37; *NYTBR* (4 Nov. 1973): 57; *SLJ* 27 (Sept. 1980): 43.

Lumberjack (Montreal: Tundra, 1974): **Rev:** *CCB-B* 28 (Apr. 1975): 132; *HB* 50 (Dec. 1974): 684; *IR* 9 (Winter 1975): 33; *TLS* (21 Oct. 1977): 1245.

A Prairie Boy's Summer (Montreal: Tundra, 1975): **Rev:** *CCB-B* 28 (July 1975): 179; *EL* 12 (Mar. 1985): 46; *HB* 51 (Aug. 1975): 381; *IR* 9 (Summer 1975): 35; *SLJ* 22 (Sept. 1975): 106.

A Northern Nativity (Montreal: Tundra, 1976): **Rev:** *CCB-B* 30 (Feb. 1977): 93; *CCL* 14 (1979): 46; *HB* 53 (Apr. 1977): 151; *IR* 11 (Spring 1977): 57.

They Sought a New World: The Story of European Immigration to North America, ed. Margaret S. Engelhart (Montreal: Tundra, 1985). **Rev:** *BiC* 14 (Nov. 1985): 36; *CCB-B* 39 (Jan. 1986): 89; *HB* 62 (Mar. 1986): 221; *QQ* 51 (Dec. 1985): 24.

Illustrated by William Kurelek

Fox Mykyta, by Ivan Franko, trans. by Bohdan Melnyk (Montreal: Tundra, 1978). **Rev:** *CCL* 17 (1980): 81.

Selected Discussions

Morley, Patricia. 'The Good Life, Prairie Style: The Art and Artistry of William Kurelek', *ChL* 6 (1977): 141–9.

——. 'William Kurelek's Persona', *The Voice of the Narrator in Children's Literature*, ed. Charlotte Otten and Gary Schmidt (New York: Greenwood, 1989), 43–53.

Sybesma-Ironside, Jetske. 'Through a Glass Darkly: William Kurelek's Picture Books', *CCL* 39 (1985): 8–21.

'I have found that Canadian artists are far in advance of Canadian writers. . . . And this being so, I found it easier in Canada to produce quality children's books starting with the artists rather than with writers. I asked William Kurelek to do his prairie childhood. . . . He did the pictures and then he added the text.' This is how publisher May Cutler described the genesis of the children's books of one of Canada's best-known painters, William Kurelek.

The dedications of his first two books, *A Prairie Boy's Winter* and *A Prairie Boy's Summer*, present the dual aspects of Kurelek's painting as he described it: 'nostalgic-pastoral' or 'religious commentary'. The former bears the inscription: 'For everyone who ever spent a winter on the prairies—and for all the others who wonder what it was like.' The dedication to the latter is more complex: 'With love for my sister, Nancy, who more than anyone else shared with me the surprise and wonder of the prairie seasons as a child—who has added to that surprise and wonder a sense of awe and love for the Creator of those wonders. Many call it the living whole—ultimate cause—nature. We two call it: God.'

Unlike many picture books in which the illustrations are merely the gloss on the text, the paintings for these two volumes are the reasons for the books; the text is an addition. Both contain 20 chapters, each with a full-page painting of a prairie activity accompanied by three or four paragraphs discussing it. The theme of *A Prairie Boy's Winter* is the relationship between people and the land. From October to May, the horizon, snow, and cold dominate. As the accounts of the blizzard indicate, winter can be a dangerous, life-threatening time. Yet, working and playing together, living with rather than in opposition to the land, the people thrive. The book opens with the autumn departure of the crows and concludes with their spring return. In between are such events and activities as the first snowfall, the making of a rink, skiing behind the hayrack, and skating on the bog ditch. The hero is the artist as a young boy existing on the fringes of his society. He has been made the goaltender in hockey because of his poor skating, and often he is on the edge of the action, at best a reluctant participant. One of his greatest joys is skating for miles along the bog ditch, 'because it appealed to his exploring instinct'.

A Prairie Boy's Summer follows the life of young William from his school activities in early June, through the summer, to his September return to school. He is still inept at school sports: children laugh at his awkward attempts at high jumping, and, during softball games, he is relegated to the distant outfield. Much of his summer involves doing chores, but even these allow him plenty of time to daydream. The book ends with the arrival of threshing time, signalling the beginning of autumn. As he admires straw stacks rising in the distance, William engages in the one activity at which he really excels—archery. 'It seemed to the boys that they were conquering the awesomeness of the prairie expanses at last. The arrow went clear out of the school yard into the pasture on the other side of the highway.' Obviously, they have not conquered the Prairie, for the illustration reveals the always-present but distant horizon and, between it and the boys, the golden, rich, enduring land.

Comparing the contents of these two books with Kurelek's record of his childhood in his autobiography, *Someone With Me*, one is immediately struck by the fact that the picture books emphasize the happier times; the autobiography stresses the many unhappy ones. Perhaps Kurelek felt that, writing for children, he must tone down the extreme unhappiness, making the central character, William, merely a typical outsider, not unlike those loners often found in children's books.

Lumberjack deals with the time Kurelek went to work in northern Ontario so that he could earn money to pay for art school. He also, as he reports, had a deeper motive: 'I did it to prove to my father (and myself) that I could make it on my own. . . . What I felt I was really working for all that summer was my independence, my manhood.' In the book, Kurelek again captures a way of life now past. His 'Epilogue' specifically captures the pastoral note. After talking about the machines that revolutionized the lumbering industry, he muses, 'Was our old way, for all its hardships, more romantic, more humane, more socially satisfying? . . . I only know I am glad to have been a part of that good life before it passed into history.' The pictures capture the beauty of the old life of lumber camps: times in the cookhouse and bunkhouse, the joys of swimming in icy lakes after a sauna, and the demanding but satisfying work in the bush. The book also traces the further growth of William's character. Still a loner, he is determined to stick out his time in the bush and gains a great deal of self-confidence. Interestingly, more of the pictures in this volume deal with people interacting: working in the woods, chatting together in the evenings.

A Northern Nativity, considered by many critics to be Kurelek's finest children's book, presents a hypothesis: what would have happened had Christ been born in twentieth-century Canada? Kurelek's sense of the Canadian landscape is evident in the depictions of 20 Canadian locations that are the settings for this hypothetical birth. In each, the bleakness of the scene mirrors the loneliness of the Holy Family and provides a contrast to the warmth of their love for each other. The illustrations are of two types. When the Holy Family is rejected, mother, father, and child are isolated and usually ignored by people who busily pursue their materialistic concerns. But when they are given charity, they are with others, generally inside poor, but warm and cosy homes. Young William is present in many of the paintings. He looks yearningly at the family, with love and devotion and with a feeling of sorrow for their predicament. He also has intimations that he, too, will reject them during his period of atheism. His sorrow is well founded, for the theme of the book is that the Nativity would not be well received by large numbers of twentieth-century Canadians. This is dramatically depicted in the final illustration, where young William dreams that he is chasing a Mennonite carriage that contains the fleeing Holy Family who tell him: 'We will return one day—when *you* are ready to receive Us with undivided love.'

Some critics have maintained that Kurelek's books should not be considered children's literature, that their nostalgic look at a vanished childhood represents an adult point of view and that their social-religious themes are beyond children's interests and understanding. The majority of critics, however, consider them Canadian classics. Kurelek's detailed presentations of work and play in a harsh and demanding landscape introduce children to a way of life now past. In pictures and words, Kurelek depicts the joy, loneliness, and humour experienced by the central character. And the religious and social themes are certainly not too sophisticated for children in the upper elementary and junior high grades. Each of Kurelek's children's books is a unique and moving work; and each is also very Canadian in its presentation of a harsh and difficult life lived in the presence of a dominating and demanding landscape.

See also: *CA* 49–52; *CANR* 3; *CLR* 2; *Junior* 5; *SATA* 8, 27; *TCCW*; *WSMP*.

Donn Kushner

Born: 29 March 1927, at Lake Charles, La.

Principal Residences: Lake Charles; Sault Ste Marie, Ont.; Ottawa; Toronto.

Education: Harvard University (B.Sc. 1948); McGill University (M.Sc. 1950, Ph.D. 1952).

Career: research scientist; professor; writer.

Major Awards: Canadian Library Association Book of the Year for Children (1981); IODE Violet Downey Children's Book Award (1988).

Works for Children

The Violin-Maker's Gift (Toronto: Macmillan, 1980). **Rev:** *BiC* 9 (Dec. 1980): 19; *EL* 17 (Nov. 1989): 68; *IR* 15 (Apr. 1981): 43; *QQ* 47 (May 1981): 14.

Uncle Jacob's Ghost Story (Toronto: Macmillan, 1984). **Rev:** *CCB-B* 39 (May 1986): 170; *CCL* 43 (1986): 69; *EL* 17 (Nov. 1989): 69; *SLJ* 32 (May 1986): 94.

A Book Dragon (Toronto: Macmillan, 1987). **Rev:** *CCL* 49 (1988): 68; *CM* 16 (May 1988): 88; *EL* 16 (Mar. 1989): 22; *HB* 64 (Sept. 1988): 627; *SLJ* 34 (June 1988): 118.

The House of Good Spirits (Toronto: Lester & Orpen Dennys, 1990). **Rev:** *CM* 19 (Mar. 1991): 105; *QQ* 57 (Feb. 1991): 23.

The Dinosaur Duster (Toronto: Lester, 1992). **Rev:** *BiC* 22 (Feb. 1993): 36; *CCL* 71 (1993): 82; *CM* 21 (Jan. 1993): 22; *QQ* 58 (Nov. 1992): 33.

A Thief Among Statues (Toronto: Annick, 1993). **Rev:** *CCL* 21 (1995): 55; *CM* 22 (Mar. 1994): 44; *QQ* 59 (Mar. 1993): 69.

The Night Voyagers (Toronto: Lester, 1995). **Rev:** *BiC* 25 (May 1996): 20; *CBRA* (1995): 508; *CCB-B* 51 (Nov. 1996): 89; *CCL* 22 (1996): 60; *QQ* 61 (Dec. 1995): 37.

Life on Mars (Toronto: Childe Thursday, 1998). **Rev:** *CCL* 94 (1999): 107.

Donn Kushner is a person of many talents. A microbiologist who has authored over 100 articles on his subject, he is also a musician who enjoys playing the violin and viola with friends in Canada and abroad. And he is an accomplished storyteller who has used his considerable talents to produce several moving novels for children and young adults.

Kushner's first children's book, *The Violin-Maker's Gift*, set in the French Pyrenees in the early nineteenth century, is the story of Gaspard l'Innocent, a hardworking but ungifted violin-maker, and Matthias, a stolid tollman. Both of their lives are changed after Gaspard gives the tollman a small bird he has rescued. When the bird proves to be magical—it can talk and foretell the future—and Matthias sets out to make his fortune, Gaspard realizes that he must provide the bird with a gift: freedom. Stealing the creature from the tollman, he allows it to join its own kind, and the bird, in gratitude, gives him the secret of making violins that can sing with a human voice. In the manner of traditional folktales, *The Violin-Maker's Gift* mixes the ordinary and the fabulous. Marvellous events occur in the lives of undistinguished individuals, who are tested. Gaspard's violins have been a mirror of his character: they are 'as carefully made as ever—and as undistinguished'. Modest, peaceful, and respected, he rescues the bird as a simple act of kindness. But when he realizes how its exploitation by Matthias is killing it, he liberates the bird and proves worthy of the gift he receives. Although Matthias later becomes a prosperous innkeeper, he has changed little as a result of his contact with the bird. He has been as selfish as the people who pay to hear it predict their own futures; the recipient of a wondrous gift, he has given nothing in return.

Uncle Jacob's Ghost Story combines Kushner's interests in science, music, and storytelling: the title hero is a rationalist, looking for natural causes for all occurrences; two of the ghosts in the story are street musicians; and a young boy to whom Jacob's story is told realizes that he has a responsibility to keep it alive. After his closest friends, Simon and Esther, are killed in a typhoid epidemic, Jacob leaves his Polish village to seek a new life in the United States. His demand for natural proof for everything is tested when he meets the street players, who closely resemble his dead friends. Only gradually does he accept the fact that they are the ghosts of these friends. Jacob's story is enclosed in a framework. Paul, a young boy of the 1980s, learns about his great uncle as he sits in his grandfather's nursing home, listening to the old man and his crony, Mr Eisbein, recall events of Jacob's life and discuss rumours they have heard about him. During his listening, Paul's attitude fluctuates between scepticism and belief. However, he realizes that in hearing the story he has assumed an obligation: 'Someday, only I will know it, and it must be told.' When Paul becomes a scientist (a microbiologist, like the author), the story fades from his mind. Only after the ghosts of Jacob, Simon, and Esther appear before him does he remember his unfulfilled duty. Kushner is here dealing with a sophisticated theme: the importance of story as a record of human perceptions of realities of the past. More than mere entertainment, story is a vital element of human life and must be given continued existence.

The importance of works of art and of maintaining a continuity between the past and present are the main themes of *A Book Dragon*. Told by his grandmother that 'a dragon without a treasure is nothing', Nonesuch, the title hero, develops a love of illuminated manuscripts and, later, printed books. Because, over the centuries, he has been shrinking in size, he is able to live in libraries and bookstores, unseen by all but the most observant of book lovers. At the novel's climax, the dragon, now the size of a tiny bird, is able to thwart plans of greedy land developers to expropriate a bookstore and other small shops in an Atlantic seacoast village. As in *The Violin-Maker's Gift*, insensitive, materialistic people are satirized; those, like Nonesuch, who defend the beauty of books and who believe that they preserve the wisdom of the past are the truly heroic. Underlying the whimsical humour of the book, with its plot premise that dragons can shrink, are serious moral themes.

Like Nonesuch and Uncle Jacob, the central characters of Kushner's next three books are exiles seeking better lives in the New World. *A Thief Among Statues* is a fantasy depicting a Christmas miracle and explaining the origins of famous Nativity carvings at a church in the town of Merchantville. An English orphan who has been sent to Canada in the late nineteenth century, Brian Newgate takes refuge in a church where he hears voices telling him, 'You're the one who's going to get us out.' The voices belong to statues of two of the Christmas Wise Men who, when liberated, explain how the boy, with the aid of the ghost of an old carver, will recover the other figures, all of whom have been sold to townspeople by insensitive church leaders. Brian finds his own fulfilment through freeing and reuniting the members of the Nativity scene. The ennobling power of art for those who appreciate it is contrasted with the attitudes of the townspeople, whose response to the miracle of the return to the church of the Nativity statues seems to be motivated mainly by their sense of the fame it will bring the town.

Both *The House of Good Spirits* and *The Night Voyagers* present a specifically political focus to a familiar Kushner theme. Each deals with a boy who has come to Canada from a land controlled by repressive tyrants, and each discovers his own destiny through his interaction with ghosts and spirit beings. By relating his present conflicts to the past, each is able to look forward to a fulfilling future.

Amos, the young hero of *The House of Good Spirits*, has joined his mother and father, who are on a medical exchange trip from Nigeria to Kingston, Ontario. He soon learns that the small town in which the family lives was a destination for American slaves, and after befriending four old men of the town he comes to realize that two of them—Mr Stern, who escaped the Nazis, and Mr Hick, a descendant of escaped slaves—are in a sense exiles. Amos's great adventure comes when he enters the old house that gives the book its title and encounters the ghosts of escaping slaves who tell him that he is needed to complete their story. Travelling magically into the past and to present-day Nigeria, he discovers the great evil oppressing many people and courageously fights for their freedom. In this novel, Kushner moves from gentle satire of human weakness to strong, although implicit, condemnation of people who destroy others' freedom: slave catchers, Nazis, Nigerian soldiers, and even the racists who still live in eastern Ontario. Like Paul from *Uncle Jacob's Ghost Story*, Amos learns that he has an important role in completing and conserving the stories of people from the past. Although at times the plot is cluttered and slightly confusing, the novel is notable for the intensity of its presentation, which often resembles the magic realism of contemporary Latin American novelists.

The Night Voyagers continues Kushner's examination of diaspora, the exile of peoples from their homelands. After his father has been killed by the authorities, Manuel and his family flee their Central American country to the United States and then to eastern Ontario. The boy, who has refused to speak since his father's disappearance, is aided by the spirits of a young boy and girl and of his dead father, as well as by helpful Americans who, distressed at their country's neglect of political refugees, have formed what Kushner calls a new 'Underground Railroad', one like that used over a century earlier to help fugitive slaves. Manuel, who recovers his voice when he must call for help for his drowning brother, confronts powerful evil throughout his journey: the Lords of Death of Mayan mythology, their human emissaries, military forces from the repressive regime, and greedy Americans who capture escapees for bounty. Manuel's silence is a symbol for the voicelessness of the victims both in their homeland and during their escape. The courage he displays and his speaking out bring safety for his family. However, he realizes that the evil his enemies represent cannot be utterly defeated: 'They would surely change their faces and reappear in other forms when they chose.'

Life on Mars is something of a scientific game, an amusing explanation of how intelligent life could exist on Mars even though the Viking Landers failed to detect any, but also looks at myths to create both a social satire and a symbolic social history. The heart of the joke is Kushner's thesis that Mars is inhabited by tiny mushroom-shaped beings who carefully stayed out of camera range when the Viking Landers touched down. In describing the culture of these Martians, Kushner satirizes human racism and violence. He shows, that is, that the Martians, who once received some television broadcasts from Earth, imperfectly understood the stories they told and therefore transformed their violent content into a ritualistic series of peaceful mathematical contests. By then concentrating on a Martian who rejects the blind faith of the others in order to investigate the ancient artifacts, Kushner symbolically investigates belief systems, myths, and culture. The inquisitive Martian discovers that the god-like voice that has directed Martian activities for years does not belong to a divine being but to a computer. He also learns the Martian myth of a Catastrophe (an obvious parallel to Earth's numerous flood myths) has a historical basis, that Mars was once a green planet inhabited by giants, and that the computer is the last remnant of a once-great race. In spite of some narrative awkwardness, *Life on Mars* is amusing and provocative, closing with the idea that stories from old times and from new will eventually comfort, if not guide, the Martians.

Donn Kushner's novels present a world in which the ordinary and the fabulous, the physical reality of daily life and magical, spiritual realms and powers interrelate. Through the power of myths, stories, music, and art, his characters come in contact with the fabulous world, and by responding positively to it, they are able to achieve more fulfilled lives. A mediocre maker of musical instruments, boys far from their homelands, lovers of books, and a logical Martian interact with talking birds, tiny dragons, ghosts, gods, and a computer, acquiring the wisdom and courage necessary to make decisive actions to better themselves and those around them. Neither the ordinary nor the fabulous worlds are perfect: greedy dragons and land developers, malignant deities and repressive political forces are formidable adversaries who must be faced and defeated. Each character must live and complete his own story and help others to complete their stories.

See also: *CA* 113; *CANR* 35; *SATA* 52; *TCCW*.

Michael Arvaarluk Kusugak

Born: 27 April 1948, in Repulse Bay, NWT.

Principal Residences: Repulse Bay; Yellowknife, NWT; Churchill, Man.; Saskatoon; Rankin Inlet, NWT.

Education: University of Saskatchewan.

Career: community programs director; government clerk; writer.

Major Awards: Ruth Schwartz Children's Book Award, with Vladyana Krykorka (1994).

Works for Children

A Promise Is a Promise, with Robert Munsch, illus. Vladyana Langer Krykorka (Willowdale, Ont.: Annick, 1988.). **Rev:** *BiC* 17 (Aug. 1988): 36; *CCL* 53 (1989): 55; *CM* 16 (Nov. 1988): 228; *EL* 16 (Mar. 1989): 22; *SLJ* 35 (Feb. 1989): 74.

Baseball Bats for Christmas, illus. Vladyana Langer Krykorka (Willowdale, Ont: Annick, 1990). **Rev:** *BiC* 20 (May 1991): 52; *CCL* 61 (1991): 61; *CM* 19 (Mar. 1991): 99; *EL* 18 (Mar. 1991): 23; *HB* 67 (May 1991): 45; *QQ* 56 (Oct. 1990): 14.

Hide and Sneak, illus. Vladyana Langer Krykorka (Willowdale, Ont: Annick, 1992). **Rev:** *BiC* 21 (Sept. 1992): 36; *CCL* 72 (1993): 84; *CM* 20 (Sept. 1992): 208; *QQ* 58 (Mar. 1992): 65.

Northern Lights: The Soccer Trails, illus. Vladyana Langer Krykorka (Willowdale, Ont.: Annick, 1993). **Rev:** *CCL* 77 (1995): 55; *CM* 22 (Jan. 1994): 21; *QQ* 59 (Sept. 1993): 67; *RT* 49 (Feb. 1996): 398.

My Arctic 1, 2, 3, illus. Vladyana Langer Krykorka (Toronto: Annick, 1996). **Rev:** *BiC* 25 (Oct. 1996): 28; *CBRA* (1996): 446; *EL* 24 (Mar. 1997): 27; *QQ* 62 (Oct. 1996): 46; *SLJ* 43 (May 1997): 120; *TES* (13 June 1997): R7.

Arctic Stories, illus. Vladyana Langer Krykorka (Toronto: Annick, 1998). **Rev:** *QQ* 64 (Dec. 1998): 35.

Selected Discussions

Ellis, Sarah. 'News from the North', *HB* 67 (May 1991): 366–8.

Michael Kusugak's stories celebrate a period of transition for the Inuit people: the 1950s, when the traditional way of life in which the author spent his childhood was rapidly disappearing. Drawing on his own experiences and on tales told by his grandmother, he creates realistic and fantasy narratives that capture the rapidly passing old customs, including the belief in spirit beings and the sense of surprise and wonder that children and adults alike felt as they witnessed the advances of the modern world. Each of Kusugak's stories is about a modern Inuk child. Two are based on his own experiences in the mid-1950s; others are about fictional characters. Three include traditional spiritual beliefs or encounters with supernatural beings.

In *Baseball Bats for Christmas* a seven-year-old asthmatic boy, as the author was, recounts how, at Christmas 1955, a bush pilot left six evergreen trees at the village, much to everyone's bewilderment. Only after the boy receives a rubber ball for Christmas do the children decide that the trees have been given to them so that they will have wood to make baseball bats. This short episode is more than an autobiographical reminiscence; it is a humorous account of the differences between two cultures that only then were beginning to interrelate in the Far North. *Arctic Stories*, also based on personal memories and experiences, describes episodes in the life of Agatha, a feisty little girl who responds emotionally to the world around her. She, along with the rest of the villagers, is terrified when a helium-filled airship flies overhead; but when she angrily calls out 'go away' and it changes direction, she becomes a hero. Her love of the birds of the Arctic is rewarded when a raven befriends her. And she becomes heroic a second time when, sent to a southern residential school, she rescues a pompous priest who falls through thin ice. By presenting the events as experienced by the young girl, Kusugak is able to capture both the amazement and excitement these events brought to the people. *Northern Lights: The Soccer Trails* is a testimony to the continuing vitality of the belief that the shifting patterns of the northern lights mark the movements of the spirits of dead loved ones playing soccer in the sky. After her mother dies, Kataujaq feels very lonely. However, one winter night, while the villagers play ball on the ice, her grandmother points to the northern lights above and explains that the spirit of Kataujaq's mother is playing there. The girl no longer feels lonely. Her people's old beliefs, communicated by her grandmother, sustain her.

On the surface, *My Arctic 1, 2, 3* is a simple counting book, using northern animals as the subject matter. Beneath is a sensitive, subtle presentation of the relationships among the animals and between them and the traditional and modern Inuit. A polar bear hunts two seals on the sea ice; five Arctic foxes watch their mother hunt six ground squirrels, and so forth. With the exception of seven men repairing a stone fishing weir and a group of people picking millions of berries, human beings are not present in the scenes. The introduction discusses traditional people hunting for food, clothing, and fuel. Now, the author states, 'We do not hunt animals all the time. Mostly we watch them.' The conclusion, 'The Arctic World of Michael Kusugak', explains, 'There are no farms. And there are no zoos. But there are many animals', and discusses how the author, his wife, and his children have observed the habits of the creatures using telescopes, snowmobiles, four-wheelers, and boats with outboard motors. Although their physical lives have become modernized and they no longer depend on the animals, their respect for the creatures remains strong.

Kusugak's two best-known books narrate the adventures of Allashua, a little girl who is captured by, but then escapes from two supernatural beings that had always been threats to little children. In *A Promise is a Promise*, the girl breaks her promise not to go near the dangerous spring sea ice where, her parents warn her, the Qallupilluit trap solitary children. Because she has seen Santa Claus, fairy godmothers, and the Tooth Fairy on the television, she believes in them. But she does not believe in the existence of Qallupilluit and sings mocking songs. However, they are real and she is captured. Selfishly, she gains her freedom by promising to bring her brothers and sister to them. The conflict is resolved only through her mother's cleverness. On one level, the story is a modern example of a traditional Inuit story designed to teach appropriate behaviour. On a deeper level, it is the story of a girl who learns that television programs from a non-Inuit culture do not tell the whole story, that the old beliefs also are true.

In *Hide and Sneak*, a much older Allashua is able to escape from another supernatural being, this time on her own. The Ijiraq is a creature who lures children away by pretending to play hide and seek. Because the heroine is not very good at the game, she is an easy victim. Once again she uses non-Inuit folklore to justify ignoring her mother's warnings: 'Elves don't hide you forever; dwarves don't hide you forever; leprechauns don't hide you forever.' Trapped, she relies on one of her people's old customs to engineer an escape: she ridicules the creature and stares at him, using mockery as a means of shaming him into proper behaviour. When he disappears in the tundra, she uses an inuksugaq, an old stone statue, to guide her home, just as her people have always done. Because she has relied on traditional practices, she has escaped from one of the Inuit's more dangerous supernatural beings.

Kusugak stands as a pioneer in Canadian children's literature, the first Inuk writer to create books exclusively for children. Using his knowledge of traditional beliefs and Inuit life in the middle of the twentieth century, along with his ability to create engaging characters and believable events, Kusugak has both perpetuated his people's heritage and shared it with children from other parts of Canada and the world.

See also: *TCCW*; *WSMP*.

Kim LaFave

Born: 12 January 1955, in Vancouver.

Principal Residences: Vancouver; Calgary; Toronto; Sechelt, BC; Roberts Creek, BC.

Education: Capilano College, North Vancouver; Alberta College of Art, Calgary (Diploma 1976).

Career: commercial artist; illustrator.

Major Awards: Governor-General's Award for Illustration (1988); Amelia Frances Howard-Gibbon Illustrator's Award (1989).

Works for Children

Illustrated by Kim LaFave

The Mare's Egg, by Carole Spray (Camden East, Ont.: Camden House, 1981). **Rev:** *BiC* 11 (Mar. 1982): 26; *CCL* 30 (1983): 69; *IR* 15 (Oct. 1981): 54; *QQ* 48 (Feb. 1982): 36; *SLJ* 29 (Oct. 1982): 156.

A New World Bestiary, by Mary Hamilton (Vancouver: Douglas & McIntyre, 1985). **Rev:** *CCL* 47 (1987): 58; *QQ* 52 (Apr. 1986): 27.

Goldie and the Sea, by Judith Saltman (Toronto: Groundwood, 1987.). **Rev:** *BiC*

17 (June 1988): 37; *CCL* 53 (1989): 52; *CL* (Aug. 1989): 246; *HB* 66 (May 1990): 367.

Amos's Sweater, by Janet Lunn (Toronto: Groundwood, 1988). Rev: *EL* 16 (Mar. 1989): 21; *CCL* 57 (1990): 115.

Duck Cakes for Sale, by Janet Lunn (Toronto: Groundwood, 1989). **Rev:** *CCL* 59 (1990): 83; *CM* 18 (Mar. 1990): 66; *QQ* 55 (Nov. 1989): 14.

Pumpkin Time, by Jan Andrews (Toronto: Groundwood, 1990). Rev: *CM* 19 (Jan. 1991): 25; *QQ* 56 (Nov. 1990): 12.

Canadian Fire Fighters (In My Neighbourhood Series), by Paulette Bourgeois (Toronto: Kids Can Press, 1991). **Rev:** *BiC* 20 (Nov. 1991): 36; *CM* 19 (Sept. 1991): 226.

Canadian Garbage Collectors (In My Neighbourhood Series), by Paulette Bourgeois (Toronto: Kids Can Press, 1991). **Rev:** *EL* 19 (Mar. 1992): 16; *QQ* 57 (May 1991): 21.

Canadian Police Officers (In My Neighbourhood Series), by Paulette Bourgeois (Toronto: Kids Can Press, 1991). **Rev:** *BiC* 21 (Oct. 1992): 50; *CM* 20 (Nov. 1992): 308.

Canadian Postal Workers (In My Neighbourhood Series), by Paulette Bourgeois (Toronto: Kids Can Press, 1991). **Rev:** *BiC* 21 (Oct. 1992): 50; *QQ* 58 (Aug. 1992): 28.

The Bones Book and Skeleton, by Stephen Cumbaa (Toronto: Somerville House, 1991). **Rev:** *CM* 20 (May 1992): 164.

Sharon, Lois & Bram Sing A-Z, by Sharon, Lois, and Bram (Toronto: Groundwood, 1991). **Rev:** *CM* 20 (May 1992): 115; *EL* 19 (Mar. 1992): 18.

Cyril the Seagull, by Patricia Lines (Gibsons, BC: Nightwood Editions, 1991). **Rev:** *BiC* 21 (Apr. 1992): 44; *CCL* 72 (1993): 66; *QQ* 58 (Feb. 1992): 32.

Oliver's Chickens, by Lois Simmie (Toronto: Groundwood, 1991). **Rev:** *QQ* 58 (Sept. 1996): 80.

Puccini and the Prowlers, by Adele Wiseman (Gibsons, BC: Nightwood Editions, 1992). **Rev:** *BIC* 22 (Apr. 1993): 30; *CCL* 81 (1996): 80; *CM* 21 (May 1993): 90; *QQ* 59 (Mar. 1993): 58.

The Bones Book and Skeleton Gamebook, by Stephen Cumbaa and Karen C. Cumbaa (Toronto: Somerville House, 1993). Illus. Bill Kimber and Steve MacEachern. **Rev:** *CM* 22 (May 1994): 83; *QQ* 60 (Jan. 1994): 39.

Follow That Star, by Kenneth Oppel (Toronto: Kids Can Press, 1994). **Rev:** *CBRA* (1994): 461; *QQ* 60 (Aug. 1994): 33.

I Am Small, by Sheree Fitch (Toronto: Doubleday, 1994). **Rev:** *CBRA* (1994): 450; *CCL* 78 (1995): 69; *CM* 22 (Oct. 1994): 187; *QQ* 60 (June 1994): 47.

Bear Stories, by Hubert Evans (Gibsons, BC: Nightwood Editions, 1991). **Rev:** *CM* 20 (Sept. 1992): 203; *QQ* 58 (Apr. 1992): 34.

Silversides: The Life of a Sockeye, by Hubert Evans (Gibsons, BC: Nightwood

Editions, 1991). **Rev:** *CM* 20 (Sept. 1992): 203; *EL* 19 (May 1992): 58.

Bats About Baseball, by Jean Little and Claire Mackay (Toronto: Penguin, 1995). **Rev:** *BiC* 24 (Sept. 1995): 50; *CBRA* (1995): 76; *CCL* 87 (1997): 66; *EL* 23 (Mar. 1996): 24; *QQ* 61 (Mar. 1995): 78.

Paul Bunyan on the West Coast, by Tom Henry (Madeira Park, BC: Harbour Publishing, 1995). **Rev:** *CBRA* (1995): 531; *CCL* 83 (1996): 107; *QQ* 61 (Nov. 1995): 46.

Doggerel, by Sheila Dalton (Toronto: Doubleday, 1996). **Rev:** *CBRA* (1996): 496; *CM* 4 (5 June 1998): on-line; *QQ* 62 (Apr. 1996): 38.

Catalogue, by Sheila Dalton (Toronto: Doubleday, 1998).

The Neanderthal Book and Skeleton, by Stephen Cumbaa and Kathlyn Stewart (Toronto: Somerville House, 1997). **Rev:** *QQ* 64 (Feb. 1998): 45.

Andrew's Magnificent Mountain of Mittens, by Deanne Lee Bingham (Toronto: Fitzhenry & Whiteside, 1998). **Rev:** *QQ* 64 (Nov. 1998): 45.

Kim LaFave's career as a children's book illustrator began when an invitation to do the pictures for *The Mare's Egg*, Carole Spray's adaptation of a maritime folktale, offered a break from his work as a commercial artist and a chance to return to his childhood love of illustrated books. Since 1981, he has illustrated over two dozen books, the majority of them in his characteristic cartoon style. With few exceptions, the most notable being *The Mare's Egg* and *Follow That Star*, LaFave has used ink outlines and watercolour washes that capture the sense of movement bordering on chaos, which is characteristic of most of his pictures. In all his works, he embodies, enhances, and expands on the humour of the written characterization and narrative; however, he is at his best when depicting the interrelationships and often laughable conflicts between animals and human beings.

Although *The Mare's Egg*, his first book, was executed in oils, it shows many of the characteristics of the works to follow. The narrative delineates the foolishness of a naïve settler who purchases and cares for a giant pumpkin, believing it is an egg that will hatch a horse. In a series of paintings in which neighbours instruct the man about judging horses, he looks intent, then confused, and finally bewildered. When he takes the huge pumpkin home, he looks ridiculous sitting on it like a hen. When the pumpkin, now rotten, is smashed, scaring a nearby rabbit, the hero, believing that it is a newly hatched horse, kneels on the ground, befuddled as he looks for the long-awaited but now escaped animal. While the illustrations capture the absurdity of the situations, they lack the sense of movement of LaFave's subsequent books. They seem to be more illustrations of, rather than extensions of, the meanings of the words.

The sense of movement is found in the later works, as the lack of borders, the pen-sketched outlines of figures, and the watercolour washes create a sense of incompleteness, of art in process that parallels the actions, which are segments of ongoing conflicts not resolved until the conclusions. This quality is most fully embodied in Janet Lunn's *Amos's Sweater*. The conflict is between a disgruntled sheep, the woman who has shorn him, and the man who wears the sweater knitted from his wool. The opening illustration presents a side view of Amos, standing in the field resplendent in his wool; however, in the next side view several pages later, he stands in the barn, completely shorn, with bandaids on his blue skin and a sullen, resentful expression on his face. In the final illustration, he is again in the field, proudly wearing the purple and yellow sweater. Between these are several double-spreads depicting the struggles between the human beings and the animal. The wife, her glasses askew, has fallen backward, and the back end of Amos is seen as he bolts off the page. Then husband and wife, on one side of a page, pull a rope, while a scowling Amos pulls against them on the other side. Later, Amos tugs at the sweater when the farmer is wearing it. After the people and the sheep reach an 'understanding' and Amos is given the sweater, all are pictured closer to the middle of a double-spread, facing each other with smiles on their faces.

In *Duck Cakes*, another Janet Lunn story, a woman who has left the city to find a quiet simple life discovers the opposite when two ducks she bought reproduce dozens of offspring, LaFave captures the humorousness of the increasing chaos. The excitement is sandwiched between opening and closing double-spreads in which the heroine sits quietly in her living room. But more and more ducks appear in the yard, and, when she gathers the eggs to use in baking, the kitchen is cluttered with dirty dishes, stacks of uneaten food, and ducklings; the woman leans exhausted against a counter. When she seeks to get rid of her excess baking by selling it, the chaos spreads to her living room. Over a dozen adult customers bump into each other, spilling tea and biscuits onto the floor across which more ducks waddle.

Cyril the Seagull, set near a west coast village like that in which the author lives, reveals LaFave's ability to combine the story of an anthropomorphized bird, in this case a gull who is afraid of the water because he becomes seasick, with realistic settings. In the opening picture, a wharf, a boathouse, the sea, and a small inlet form the backdrop for the young seagull and his mother, who stands on a rock above him, looking down with motherly concern. Later, he perches on the railing of a ferry boat listening to his friend, the ship's cook, play his guitar. However, when his illness first manifests himself, Cyril is again next to his mother, looking queasy while she gazes anxiously at him. The storm during which Cyril courageously overcomes his fear of the rough water to rescue the ferry boat from running aground, is realistically pictured. The lighthouse, with grey waves pounding against it, and the cliffs on which the birds huddle during the storm, provide an appropriate background that lends credibility to the fears and courage the hero reveals.

In Kenneth Oppel's *Follow That Star*, LaFave uses acrylics rather than watercolours to capture the sense of wonder when a shepherd boy makes a Christmas Eve journey in search of the angels announcing the birth of Jesus. The publishers, in their publicity material, explain that LaFave carefully studied the lighting effects of the night sky and then chose cobalt blue and burnt orange as the colours best suited for creating the visual and emotional effects he desired. Cobalt blue dominates the pictures as the colour of the night skies and the boy's annoying sheep. He wears a rust-coloured robe and is frequently sitting within a circle of orange light. The solidity and intensity of the acrylics suggests the spiritual powers that he comes into contact with. The humour arises because of the problems the sheep create. One is caught in a tree, several have to be propelled up a hillside with a giant slingshot, and all wear foolish expressions on their faces. Yet they all face him, helpless themselves, totally dependent on his leadership. Because of his dependability, the boy is rewarded with seeing the angels he seeks.

Kim LaFave's pictures are essential ingredients of the books to which he has contributed. They go beyond merely depicting characters, settings, and events. They furnish details and create tones that expand on characterization and conflict, and produce humorous tones that are not present in the written texts. The exaggerated realism that he has created through his cartoon-like art has helped to make the stories he has co-created into minor classics of humorous Canadian children's literature.

See also: *WSMP.*

Margaret Laurence

Born: 18 July 1926, in Neepawa, Man.

Died: 5 January 1987, in Lakefield, Ont.

Education: United College, Winnipeg (BA 1947).

Principal Residences: Neepawa; Winnipeg; London, England; Somaliland; Ghana; Vancouver; Penn, Buckinghamshire, England; Lakefield.

Career: reporter; writer.

Works for Children

Jason's Quest (Toronto: McClelland & Stewart, 1970). **Rev:** *BiC* 10 (Apr. 1981): 28; *CBRA* (1981): 226; *CCB-B* 24 (Oct. 1970): 29; *CCL* 15 (1980): 29; *IR* 15 (Aug. 1970): 48.

The Olden Days Coat, illus. Muriel Wood (Toronto: McClelland & Stewart, 1979). **Rev:** *BiC* 8 (Dec. 1979): 15; *CCL* 15/16 (1980): 138; *IR* 14 (Aug. 1980): 55; *Maclean's* 92 (17 Dec. 1979): 49; *SLJ* 27 (Sept. 1980).

Six Darn Cows, illus. Ann Blades (Toronto: James Lorimer, 1979). **Rev:** *BiC* 7 (Dec. 1979): 15; *CCL* 21 (1981): 58.

The Christmas Birthday Story, illus. Helen Lucas (Toronto: McClelland & Stewart, 1980). **Rev:** *BiC* 9 (Dec. 1980): 18; *CBRA* (1980): 159; *CCB-B* 24 (Oct. 1980): 35;

CCL 39/40 (1985): 104; *IR* 15 (Feb. 1981): 40; *QQ* 46 (Nov. 1980): 44; *SLJ* 27 (Oct. 1980): 161.

Selected Discussions

Besner, Neil. 'Canadian Children's Regional Literature: Fictions First', *CCL* 86 (1997): 17–26.

Letson, D.R. 'Mother of Manawaka: Margaret Laurence as Author of Children's Stories', *CCL* 21 (1981): 17–24.

Morley, Patricia. *Margaret Laurence* (Boston: Twayne, 1981).

The winner of Governor-General's Awards for two of her adult novels, *A Jest of God* (1966) and *The Diviners* (1974), Margaret Laurence gained international recognition for her Manawaka books, which were based on life in a small prairie town much like Neepawa, Manitoba, where she was born and raised. Laurence's four children's books are distinctly different from each other and from her adult work, although her first, *Jason's Quest*, is thematically connected to the Manawaka books. As in *The Stone Angel* (1964) and *The Diviners*, the past exerts an oppressive hold on the characters in this animal fantasy. Jason, a mole, lives in Molanium, a city governed by the contradictory motto 'Hasten Slowly'. Accompanied by an owl and two cats with their own quests, he sets out to find a cure for the invisible sickness destroying Molanium. After a number of adventures, including a battle with rats running a protection racket, all of the animals succeed, Jason becoming the new leader of the moles for discovering that the illness is boredom. Although Laurence makes it clear that resistance to change is destructive, the new life of the moles, patterned after nightclub life in modern London, seems every bit as shallow as the old way. Obviously inspired by Kenneth Grahame's *The Wind in the Willows* (1908), another story of a mole who leaves his home to seek a better life, *Jason's Quest* lacks both its engaging characters and thematic depth.

Laurence's other children's works are far more successful. *Six Darn Cows*, illustrated by Ann Blades, is remarkably rich for a book written with a limited vocabulary for beginning readers. Jen and Tod Bean, two farm children tired of having to tend the family's 'darn cows', wish the cows would get lost. They subsequently must accept responsibility when the cows wander away through a gate they left open. This simple tale deftly develops themes about the irony of wishes, the power of duty, the need for co-operation on a farm, and the love of family.

The Olden Days Coat is Laurence's best work for children. Like Philippa Pearce's *Tom's Midnight Garden* (1958), it is a time-shift fantasy in which a child discovers the child within an older person. Sal, bored and miserable with having to spend Christmas at Grandma's house, puts on an old-fashioned coat and is transported back in time. Aided by a blue jay, she helps a girl recover a beautiful box lost in the snow. When Sal returns to her own time, her Grandma gives her a present: the very box she had helped the girl recover. Sal thus realizes that the girl she helped was really her own Grandma. With its subtle use of the symbolic blue jay and its simple plot, *The Olden Days Coat* is an elegant statement of continuity in time.

Laurence's last children's book, *The Christmas Birthday Story*, is a revision of a story that she wrote when her own children were young. A simple retelling of the birth of Christ, it stresses the parental love of Mary and Joseph.

Although Laurence's continuing reputation depends on her achievement as an adult writer, *The Olden Days Coat*, which was released in a film version in 1980, is still popular. In Canada, it probably will last as a minor seasonal classic.

See also: *CA* 121; *CA* 5–8R; *CANR* 33; *CLC* 3, 6, 13, 50, 62; *DLB* 53; *SATA* 50.

Julie Lawson

Born: 9 November 1947, in Victoria, BC.

Principal Residences: Victoria; Sooke, BC.

Education: University of Victoria (BA 1979).

Career: teacher; writer.

Works for Children

The Sand Sifter (Victoria, BC: Beach Holme, 1990).

A Morning to Polish and Keep, illus. Sheena Lott (Red Deer, Alta: Red Deer College Press, 1992). **Rev:** *CCL* 69 (1993): 80; *CM* 20 (Oct. 1992): 264; *QQ* 58 (May 1992): 32.

Kate's Castle, illus. Frances Tyrell (Toronto: Oxford UP, 1992). **Rev:** *CCL* 69 (1983): 80; *CM* 26 (Nov. 1992): 309; *QQ* 58 (Aug. 1992): 21.

My Grandfather Loved the Stars, illus. Judy McLaren (Victoria, BC: Beach Holme, 1992). **Rev:** *CM* 29 (Oct. 1992): 264.

The Dragon's Pearl, illus. Paul Morin (Toronto: Oxford UP, 1992). **Rev:** *BiC* 21 (Nov. 1992): 37; *CCB-B* 46 (May 1993): 287; *CCL* 75 (1994): 58; *CM* 20 (Oct. 1992): 264; *EL* 21 (Sept. 1993): 49; *QQ* 58 (Aug. 1992): 24; *SLJ* 39 (July 1993): 62.

White Jade Tiger (Victoria, BC: Beach Holme, 1993). **Rev:** *QQ* 59 (Aug. 1993): 38.

Blown Away, illus. Kathryn Naylor (Red Deer, Alta: Red Deer College Press, 1995). **Rev:** *CBRA* (1995): 474; *CL* (Summer 1996): 200; *QQ* 62 (Jan. 1996): 42.

Fires Burning (Toronto: Stoddart, 1995). **Rev:** *QQ* 61 (Mar. 1995): 76.

Cougar Cove (Victoria, BC: Orca, 1996). **Rev:** *CBRA* (1996): 480; *QQ* 62 (May 1996): 34; *SLJ* 42 (Sept. 1996): 204.

Too Many Suns, illus. Martin Springett (Toronto: Stoddart, 1996). **Rev:** *BiC* 25 (Nov. 1996): 34; *CBRA* 1996: 446; *QQ* 62 (Mar. 1996): 73.

Whatever You Do, Don't Go Near That Canoe! illus. Werner Zimmerman (Richmond Hill, Ont.: Scholastic, 1996). **Rev:** *BiC* 25 (Oct. 1996): 28; *CBRA* (1996): 447; *QQ* 62 (Oct. 1996): 46.

Emma and the Silk Train, illus. Paul Mombourquette (Toronto: Kids Can Press, 1997). **Rev:** *CM* 4 (3 Oct. 1997): on-line; *QQ* 63 (July 1997): 50.

Goldstone (Toronto: Stoddart, 1997). **Rev:** *QQ* 63 (July 1997): 48.

In Like a Lion, illus. Yolaine (Richmond Hill, Ont.: Scholastic, 1998). **Rev:** *QQ* 65 (Jan. 1999): 43.

Midnight in the Mountains, illus. Sheena Lott (Victoria, BC: Orca, 1998). **Rev:** *QQ* 64 (Dec. 1998): 35.

Turns on a Dime (Toronto: Stoddart, 1998).

'When I was teaching', Julie Lawson remembers, 'I loved reading Farley Mowat's *The Dog Who Wouldn't Be* and *Owls in the Family*. And I realized that you could make your own memories, your own experiences interesting to readers. That helped me to realize my lifelong ambition of being a writer; I could tell stories about things I'd known.' For her, these included the summers spent at the family cabin at Sooke, southwest of Victoria. During the early 1950s, she took the family boat out on the lagoon, often imagining the mist-enshrouded area to be the scene of marvellous adventures in which she was the main character, and, on rainy days, she, her younger brother, mother, and father would read. The Andrew Lang coloured 'Fairy Books', Marguerite Henry's horse stories, Nancy Drew mysteries, and, later, historical novels were her favourites. From them she acquired a sense of traditional stories, fast-paced plots, and the romance of the past that characterize her picture books and novels; from the Sooke land and seascapes came the fully realized settings for her stories.

The Sand Sifter, Lawson's first book, introduced themes, character types, and settings found in her later works. Spending a summer in Sooke, Jessica and her older brother Andrew meet an old man who claims to make the sand and who tells them remarkable legends from Pacific Rim countries. As the summer comes to an end, the old man disappears, and the children return to the routines of school life. Ordinary children on a summer vacation encounter elements of the marvellous in a familiar landscape. Although character and plot are relatively slight, Lawson reveals her skill in creating a fully realized setting, developing symbolism—the grains of sand that represent the stories of the world—and relating the ordinary and fabulous dimensions of children's lives.

Lower Vancouver Island is the setting for five short stories published as picture books. *Kate's Castle*, a simple cumulative rhyme that originated as a language arts activity for the author's students, recounts a child's activities with sand, seashells, and seaweed. In *A Morning to Polish and Keep*, a young girl, her brother, and her parents go on an early-morning fishing trip. One of the last family activities of the summer, the events of the morning seem magical to the girl, who will keep them alive in her memory. *My Grandfather Loved the Stars* memorializes a girl's grandfather and his accounts of star myths drawn from various cultures. The passage of the seasons reflects the aging process of the old man and, after his death, the girl accepts the wisdom of his words about dying: 'cause that's the way it is'. In *Whatever You Do, Don't Go Near That Canoe* is a humorous ballad in which two disobedient children are captured by pirates whose boat mysteriously appears on the lagoon near their home. *In Like a Lion* is based on a true event: the discovery of a wild cougar hiding in the parking lot of a downtown Victoria hotel.

The Dragon's Pearl and *Too Many Suns*, retellings of traditional tales, reflect Lawson's interest in the customs and legends of China. The former embodies the Oriental beliefs in dragons as powerful creatures who reward deserving people with life-giving rain. Xiaou Sheng, a poor, hard-working, good-natured grass cutter discovers a magic pearl, which he generously shares with his village. When evil neighbours attempt to steal it, the youth swallows the pearl and is transformed into a dragon who ends the drought that has plagued the area. Unlike many adaptors of traditional stories from other cultures, Lawson does not attempt to dismiss the traditional elements of the story as make-believe or foolish superstition. Instead, she emphasizes the important relationships between supernatural powers and beings and ordinary people, a relationship symbolized by the hero's transformation. In *Too Many Suns*, the youngest of 10 brothers, a hard-working boy who dreams of becoming an artist and painting pictures of the setting sun, plays a significant role in ending a drought and in preventing a spirit being from destroying the last of 10 suns.

Ancient Chinese traditions and British Columbia history combine in Lawson's first novel, *White Jade Tiger*. During her research, she discovered a picture of an amulet supposed to contain a supernatural, powerful animal. This event, combined with interest in the use of Chinese labour in the building of the railroad through British Columbia, a school field trip to Victoria's Chinatown, and her long-time interest in individuals' memories of their own pasts or searches for roots led to the creation of a novel that is not only a time-shift fantasy, but also a problem novel and a historical narrative. After her mother's death in an automobile crash, Jasmine goes on a school field trip to Chinatown and is transported into the 1880s, where she befriends a newly arrived immigrant searching for his father, a railroad labourer. Jasmine learns not only about British Columbia's history, but also about her own past, a Chinese ancestry that her mother had rejected.

Lawson's use of time-shifts, seen in such other Canadian novels as Janet Lunn's *The Root Cellar* and Margaret Buffie's *Who is Frances Rain?*, is more than a technical device for moving a fairly average contemporary girl into a past era where historical events can be portrayed. Although the description of the condition of Chinese railroad workers and the white prejudices against them are accurately and convincingly presented through the eyes of the amazed girl, the shifts also relate to character development and theme. Bereft of a mother and, therefore, of part of her immediate past, the girl can only move into a future if she discovers her roots as they extend back to Victoria's earlier years and beyond. Because she is instrumental in the survival of the immigrant boy, she makes possible her own life, for she is one of his descendants. Just as she is able to travel to the past, the spirit of Bright Jade, the original possessor of the amulet that gives the book its title, is able to travel into the future—both into the nineteenth century and into the dreams of the present-day Jasmine. Lawson has thus incorporated into the novel an Oriental sense of time, which is conceived not as linear but circular, allowing individuals to encounter and influence other individuals from their pasts and/or futures.

Emma and the Silk Train, a picture book set in the 1920s, deals with another element in the history of British Columbia's railroads, in this case the high-speed trains that carried silk from China across Canada and to New York. When a train wreck scatters bales of cloth into the Fraser River, five-year-old Emma decides to fish for silk. Unsuccessful at first, 'Emma didn't give up easily.' However, she falls into the river, is cast up on an island, and resourcefully engineers her rescue by making silk banners that are spotted by a passing train. Like the characters of folktales, Emma is a gritty and clever person, an unlikely hero who courageously succeeds against great odds.

Eastern British Columbia at the beginning of the twentieth century is the setting of *Goldstone*, a historical novel in which a girl must come to terms with her mother's death. Although Karin had been embarrassed by her mother's clinging to old Swedish ways, she realizes after the death how deep her mother's love was. The goldstone, like the white jade tiger, provides not only the title, but also the story's central symbol. A semi-precious stone that was her mother's favourite piece of jewellery, it is reputed to give a person who sleeps with it the ability to dream of the future. However, grieving over the past, Karin will not test its powers, as she cannot imagine happiness ahead of her. Only when she has accepted the death does she sleep with it on the pillow. In addition to portraying the girl's character development, the novel presents a vivid account of life in a small railway town a century ago. In *Turns on a Dime*, a sequel set in Victoria in the 1950s, 11-year-old Jo learns that she is not a descendent of Karin, but an adopted child. However, from her grandmother, Karin's stepmother, she learns the importance of ties of love rather than blood. For her birthday, she receives the goldstone, a gift that re-establishes her in the heritage she thought she had lost and that will help her to envision a happier future.

Lawson sets two of her novels in present-day Sooke, where troubled outsiders have come to spend time with relatives. In *Fires Burning*, Chelsea, after the death of her father and remarriage of her mother, spends the summer with her cousins. Resented as an interloper, she both envies and rejects the family's long-established traditions before a crisis makes her accept her problems and establish better relationships with her mother and other family members. In *Cougar*

Cove, Samantha Ross feels insecure away from the big city of Toronto and resentful of her cousins who are so comfortable in their rural surroundings. However, in a series of encounters with cougars that live in the area, she develops a surer sense of herself and acquires memories that will sustain her when she returns home at the end of the summer.

Whether they are written for very young readers, older children, or young adults, whether they are adapted folktales, humorous ballads, or historical, fantasy, or problem novels, Julie Lawson's books share many elements in common. Often they focus on sensitive, different children, lonely or solitary individuals. The narrators are distinguished by their sensitive responses to the natural environments and the people who surround them. However, Lawson does not merely repeat familiar story patterns with the slight novelty of superficially different material. She blends form with content, making the former a natural, appropriate vehicle for the latter. The content emerges out of her own personal experiences and memories and her loves of the lower Vancouver Island landscape. The adventures, however, are moved beyond the local and personal. The books sensitively reflect the complexities of the ways children respond to their natural and human environments. A language arts teacher who loves words and understands childhood, Lawson has painstakingly revised and polished her words until they are the most appropriate vehicles for the thoughts and emotions she conveys.

See also: *SATA* 79; *WSMP*.

Dennis Lee

Born: 15 August 1939, in Toronto.

Principal Residences: Toronto.

Education: University of Toronto (BA 1962, MA 1964).

Career: professor; editor; writer.

Major Awards: IODE (Toronto) Book Award (1974); Canadian Library Association Book of the Year (1975, 1978); Vicky Metcalf Award (1986); Mr Christie's Book Award (1991).

Works for Children

Wiggle to the Laundromat, illus. Charlie Pachter (Toronto: New Press, 1970). **Rev:** *IR* 5 (Spring 1971): 25.

Alligator Pie, illus. Frank Newfeld (Toronto: Macmillan, 1974). **Rev:** *CCB-B* 29 (Mar. 1976): 113; *CCL* 1 (1975): 68; *HB* 51 (Dec. 1975): 608; *IR* 9 (Winter 1975): 35; *SLJ* 22 (Dec. 1975): 47.

Nicholas Knock and Other People, illus. Frank Newfeld (Toronto: Macmillan, 1974).

Rev: *CCL* 1 (1975): 68; *HB* 53 (Dec. 1977): 675; *IR* 9 (Winter 1975): 35; *NYTBR* (13 Nov. 1977): 47; *SLJ* 24 (Feb. 1978): 59.

Garbage Delight, illus. Frank Newfeld (Toronto: Macmillan, 1977). **Rev:** *CCB-B* 32 (Apr. 1979): 140; *CCL* 12 (1978); 72; *IR* 12 (Winter 1978): 55; *RT* 33 (Oct. 1979): 92; *SLJ* 25 (Jan. 1979): 55.

The Ordinary Bath, illus. Jon McKee (Toronto: McClelland & Stewart, 1979). **Rev:** *BiC* 9 (Feb. 1980): 21; *CCL* 15 (1980): 91; *IR* 14 (Apr. 1980): 48.

Jelly Belly, illus. Juan Wijngaard (Toronto: Macmillan, 1983). **Rev:** *BiC* 12 (Dec. 1983): 15; *CCL* 33 (1984): 15; *EL* 12 (Nov. 1984): 20; *QQ* 49 (Nov. 1983): 25; *TES* (16 Mar. 1984): 31.

Lizzy's Lion, illus. Marie-Louise Gay (Toronto: Stoddart, 1984). **Rev:** *BiC* 13 (Dec. 1984): 12; *CCL* 41 (1986): 74; *QQ* 50 (Nov. 1984): 11.

The Dennis Lee Big Book, illus. Barbara Klunder (Toronto: Macmillan, 1985).

The Ice Cream Store, illus. David McPhail (New York: HarperCollins, 1991). **Rev:** *CCB-B* 46 (Dec. 1992): 116; *CCL* 67 (1992): 102; *CM* 20 (Mar. 1992): 86; *EL* 19 (Jan. 1992): 50; *QQ* 57 (Oct. 1991): 35; *SLJ* 38 (Sept. 1992): 221.

Ping and Pong (Toronto: HarperCollins, 1993). **Rev:** *BiC* 23 (Mar. 1994): 47; *CM* 22 (Mar. 1994): 46.

Other

'Roots and Play: Writing as a 35-Year-Old Children [*sic*]', *CCL* 4 (1976): 28–58.

Selected Discussions

Davies, Cory Bieman, and Catherine Ross. 'Re-realizing Mother Goose: An Interview with Dennis Lee on *Jelly Belly*', *CCL* 33 (1984): 6–14.

Nodelman, Perry. 'The Silverhonkabeest: Children and the Meaning of Childhood', *CCL* 12 (1978): 26–34.

——. 'Who's Speaking? The Voices of Dennis Lee's Poems for Children', *CCL* 25 (1982): 4–17.

——. 'Cadence and Nonsense: Dennis Lee's Poems for Children and for Adults', *CCL* 33 (1984): 22–31.

Parsons, Marnie. '"Like a Muscle that Sings in the Dark": Semiotics and Nonsense in Dennis Lee's Poetry for Children', *CCL* 63 (1991): 61–71.

Thompson, M.A. 'Jelly Belly in the Perilous Forest', *CCL* 33 (1984): 15–22.

Dennis Lee's career as a poet for children began when, in the 1960s, he was reading Mother Goose rhymes to his young daughters. 'It was completely unpremeditated', he later recalled. 'I just started making rhymes for my kids. Rhythms would knock around in my head, and I'd start finding words for them.' Many of these found their way into the companion volumes *Alligator Pie* and *Nicholas Knock*, which were published in 1974 and quickly became two of the best-selling Canadian children's books of all time. The two works are complementary: *Alligator Pie* embodies the poet's belief that nursery rhymes linguistically contain the elements of play that are also found in the physical games and body language of young children; *Nicholas Knock* involves the older child's awareness of the conflicts between the inner liberating impulses and the social constraints he feels.

Lee contends that nursery rhymes 'reflect a sense of community, a sense of a stable world, of an at-homeness. In their play with words, sound, rhythm, and imagery, they parallel the child's sense of play.' Although he admired and enjoyed the traditional nursery rhymes, as did his children, he realized that the poems 'were no longer on home ground. . . . Shouldn't the child also discover the imagination playing on things he lived with every day?' The 32 poems of *Alligator Pie* celebrate the play of the young child, the joys of his or her liberated imagination, and, at the same time, the securities of the familiar world. The title poem, which opens the collection, is, in a sense, the child's request or demand to be allowed the freedom of the imagination. She is willing to give away familiar, everyday things, but not her alligator pie, stew, or soup, for without them she worries that she may die, may droop, and may be unable to cope. There follow a number of short, chanting poems that mix the familiar with the unusual: ice cream, rattlesnakes, and an elephant who sits on the speaker. The volume closes with a sense of security in 'Windshield Wipers', the musings of a sleepy child being driven home late at night.

Nicholas Knock and Other People creates a much different tone. Lee has noted that underlying the collection is the question: 'Can we sustain play, joy, or any of the deeper and more vibrant modes of being which tantalize us?' The answer is, at best, a very qualified 'yes'. More often than not, repression and restriction impede movement towards fulfilment. The vibrant aspects of life are symbolized by the owl Ookpik, who, in the opening poem, 'Ookpik and the Animals', acts as a liberator, releasing a number of animals from the zoo. In the penultimate poem, the speaker addresses a plea to Ookpik, asking for grace to 'Help us / Live in / Our own / Space'. Although friendship is the theme of many of the poems, including 'With My Foot in My Mouth', 'The Cat and the Wizard', and 'The Question', the strongest poems in the collection deal with the failure of individuals to achieve full relationships with unusual creatures that represent what Lee has called the 'emissaries of larger life'. Mister Hoobody, who helps children release their repressions, disappears when a young child deliberately searches for him. In 'The Thing', three boys lead a tormented Ancient Mariner-like existence after they refuse to acknowledge the strange creature who, they later realize, wants friendship and the right 'to be'.

Nicholas Knock, the hero of the title poem, had a mind with 'funny edges', a quality that enabled him to make contact with the Silver Honkabeest, a creature symbolizing imaginative power and integrity. However, the adults in the poem deny that such a being can exist and send Nicholas to psychologists and finally to the Supreme Court, where he is sentenced to death by beheading for his firm insistence on the reality of the creature. Nicholas escapes. Although he remains faithful to his vision, he no longer sees the honkabeest and wanders the town searching for it. He is at once an admirable and pathetic person in his perseverance. Not surprisingly, here and in other poems in the collection, adults are the repressive figures. They seem, like the adults who fear sunshine in Mordecai Richler's *Jacob Two-Two Meets the Hooded Fang*, frightened of children's visionary powers and intent on making sure that these powers do not survive.

Lee's third collection, *Garbage Delight*, contains many echoes of his earlier poems. There are short chants, tongue-twisters, and poems containing Canadian place names. However, the focus and tone are different from those of the earlier collections. Lee remarked: 'After finishing the first two books, I didn't know if I'd write any more children's poems. But two years ago, things started again as I began making poems for my five-year-old son. I wanted wild and woolly hijinks; but I also wanted to capture the inward, musing voice of the younger child. When I gathered the poems together, I found I could move back and forth between the two types.'

'Between' would be an appropriate word to describe the tone of the book, a tone embodied in the opening piece, 'Being Five', in which the speaker concludes that what he likes best about his age is that 'it's In Between.' On the one side are solitary, quiet moments. In 'Half Way Dressed', the child complains of the difficulty of getting a sweater on; in 'The Moon', he gazes out of his window and wonders about other children who may be looking at the moon at the same time. 'The Coming of Teddy Bears' is a record of his jumbled thoughts as he falls asleep. On the other side are his active moments, when he remembers a visit to Stanley Park in Vancouver, where he enjoyed a strawberry soda, or to the Summerhill Fair, where he met a special girl. 'The Last Cry of the Damp Fly' details his observations of a fly in his soup; 'The Worm' is a portrait of an unusual pet; in 'Smelly Fred', he contemplates the heroic climbing of a little bug only to discover that the creature has fallen off his shoe.

Garbage Delight also contains a gallery of memorable characters, the most important of which are the narrator's three stuffed animals: McGonigle, Bigfoot, and Hannah V. Varoom. They are introduced in 'The Animals', in which the speaker indicates his position as an authority figure: 'All of them are friends of mine / So none of them are scared.' In 'McGonigle's Tail', the narrator tries a variety of methods to attach the character's tail, which, he notes, was lost because of its foolishness. The animals provide him with a sense of security. 'Bigfoot' celebrates the heroism of the title character—when the boy plays scary games, his friend is always ready to protect him from dangers. The narrator is not always kind to his friends, and, in 'The Operation', his solicitude for Hannah, who has lost stuffing from a rip in her head, is a result of his guilt—he has mishandled her.

As in earlier volumes, Lee includes several silly and exaggerated characters. 'Suzy Grew a Mustache' recounts the foolish ways in which two girls try to rid themselves of facial hair. In 'Inspector Dogbone Gets His Man', a famous detective commits himself to jail because he allowed a fugitive to escape by devouring himself. 'I Eat Kids, Yum, Yum!' describes a girl who is not frightened by the approach of a cannibalistic monster. 'Bloody Bill' avoids being pressured into a fight with a bully by recounting his spectacular victory over a ferocious pirate.

Lee's other two collections, *Jelly Belly* and *The Ice Cream Store*, are less successful than the first three books. Only 17 of the 75 poems in *Jelly Belly* are over 10 lines. Most are short chants. While length is not the only quality of a good poem, many of Lee's best pieces have been considerably longer, tracing mood and developing character and theme. In this book, the short poems emphasize rhyme and rhythm without capturing as successfully as in the earlier works the element of play and the child's view of the world. In addition, the grouping of several poems together, often up to six on a double-spread, tends to overwhelm the reader rather than create a cumulative effect. *The Ice Cream Store*, written nearly a decade after *Jelly Belly*, is, like *Alligator Pie*, designed for younger listeners. A large majority of the 58 poems are very short, often only four lines, and strong rhymes and rhythms predominate. While a few deal with relationships, most focus on single children, those too young to deal with friendships. Lee once again plays with place names, expanding beyond Canada to include such places as Costa Rica and Patagonia, and emphasizes such basic childhood activities as eating and sleeping, making music and dancing. There are poems warning against bad table manners and lying, along with several night poems and lullabies. These suggest the presence of an older person, perhaps even a grandparent reading at bedtime to a small child.

Lizzy's Lion, a longer poem illustrated by Marie-Louise Gay, is set in a girl's bedroom and tells of the fate of a night-time robber who is devoured by the girl's pet. The initial situation, as is the case in many of Lee's poems, is exaggerated and ridiculous: a pet lion is under the complete domination of a girl, who controls it by calling out its very ordinary name: Lion. When the burglar confidently enters through the window, he brings candy with him to tame the beast, but, because he does not know its name, he is devoured. The sources of the poem's popularity are easy to spot: its humorous situation; the control exhibited by the girl; the exaggerated justice dealt to the robber; and, most important, the skill of Lee's verse. The quatrains move rapidly, carrying the reader quickly from event to event, and there is plenty of alliteration, as well as exaggerated sounds to parallel the exaggerated events.

Dennis Lee's poems for children have achieved the status of classics. As successive groups of Canadian children move through the various age levels, they respond to the different poems. The reasons for the success of the works are many. As he set out to, Lee has created contemporary *and* Canadian nursery rhymes: short poems capturing the strong rhymes and rhythms that children love to repeat and using these to depict familiar characters, situations, and settings. In his longer poems, Lee exhibits his mastery of a number of complex rhythm patterns and stanza forms, which he skilfully employs to commentate a variety of tones. He has also created a gallery of characters that reflects the growing sensibilities of children, and he treats these sensibilities with understanding and respect.

See also: *CAFR* 25–8; *CANR* 11, 31, 57, 61; *CLR* 3; *DLB* 53; *Junior* 7; *Profiles*; *SATA* 14; *TCCW*; *WSMP*.

Mireille Levert

Born: 20 December 1956, in St Jean-sur-Richelieu, Que.

Principal Residences: St Jean-sur-Richelieu; Quebec City; Montreal.

Education: Université de Québec, Montréal (BA).

Career: batiking teacher; bookseller; window dresser; artist; author; illustrator.

Major Awards: Governor-General's Award for Illustration (1993).

Works for Children

Written and Illustrated by Mireille Levert

Little Red Riding Hood (Toronto: Groundwood, 1995). **Rev:** *CBRA* (1995): 532; *CCL* 89 (1998): 69; *QQ* 61 (Aug. 1995): 34; *SLJ* 42 (Sept. 1996): 198.

Molly's Bath, Molly's Breakfast, Molly's Clothes, Molly's Toys (Molly Bear Series) (Willowdale, Ont.: Annick, 1997). **Rev:** *CCL* 86 (1997): 95; *QQ* 63 (Apr. 1997): 38.

Rose by Night (Toronto: Groundwood, 1998). **Rev:** *QQ* 64 (Aug. 1998): 37.

Illustrated by Mireille Levert

Jeremiah and Mrs. Ming, by Sharon Jennings (Willowdale, Ont: Annick, 1990). **Rev:** *CCL* 62 (1991): 98; *CM* 18 (July 1990): 180; *HB* 67 (Jan. 1991): 110; *QQ* 56 (June 1990): 16.

When Jeremiah Found Mrs. Ming, by Sharon Jennings (Willowdale, Ont.: Annick, 1991). **Rev:** *BiC* 21 (Nov. 1992): 36; *CCL* 72 (1993): 64; *CM* 20 (Oct. 1992): 263; *QQ* 58 (Sept. 1992): 71.

Sleep Tight, Mrs. Ming, by Sharon Jennings (Willowdale, Ont.: Annick, 1993). **Rev:** *CCL* 78 (1995): 79; *CM* 21 (Nov. 1993): 218; *QQ* 59 (Sept. 1993): 66.

Tiny Toes, by Donna Jakob (New York: Hyperion, 1995). **Rev:** *SLJ* 41 (June 1995): 87.

When Mireille Levert was asked to name the picture-book illustrators who most influenced her, she listed Maurice Sendak, Chris Van Allsburg, Tony Ross, and Marie-Louise Gay. Like many of Sendak's, her illustrations deal with the relationships between a child's waking and sleeping worlds; like Van Allsburg, she suggests the presence of strange forces in everyday life; and, like Ross and Gay, she humorously presents wild, chaotic scenes. Known best for her pictures in Susan Jennings's three books about Jeremiah and his friend Mrs Ming, Levert has also adapted the Grimm Brothers' *Little Red Riding Hood* and has written or illustrated other stories about the real and imaginary lives of children.

Levert's watercolour illustrations for *Jeremiah and Mrs. Ming, When Jeremiah Found Mrs. Ming*, and *Sleep Tight, Mrs. Ming* expand on the meanings of the simple repetitive texts, adding dimensions of characterization and amplifying the humour of situations. In the first book, the child comes into the living room to explain that he is unable to sleep because, among other reasons, his books are reading their stories aloud and his shoes are dancing. Levert depicts large books floating above his bed, pictures mounted on springs projecting from the wallpaper, and the boy bouncing happily on his bed, banging a drum, and then pouring tea for his teddies. A picture of Pinocchio with an extremely long nose implies the fictitious nature of his explanations. In the pictures of his room, the walls often appear tilted, in contrast to the more orderly arrangement of the rest of the house. Levert's implication is that the child's world and responses to it are different from those of adults. Interestingly, Mrs Ming is not seen in his room; Jeremiah's place of imagination is private from the reader as well.

In *When Jeremiah Found Mrs. Ming*, the boy comes upon the adult, who is busy doing chores, and offers to help. His assistance is brief, as he becomes bored and suggests that the two play, using broomsticks to ride on, cans of vegetables to make a dangerously leaning tower, and junk found when cleaning the attic to play dress-up. In this story, Mrs Ming, who is very practical (she fixes her own car), enters into the child's world, although what they both do is accepted as make-believe. Levert's illustrations indicate the woman's playful, somewhat eccentric nature. She bounces happily on the bed she has made, grins slyly as she topples the tower of cans she has just erected, and makes shadow figures on the garage wall. Details of her house also reveal her somewhat eccentric character. Her sheets are festooned with banana patterns, her Volkswagen is painted like a ladybug, and she keeps a small teddy bear in the pocket of her apron. She seems to share the playful spirit of Jeremiah.

Like the first book, *Sleep Tight, Mrs. Ming* deals with the boy's excuses for being unable to get to sleep and the sense of security she provides as she chases away things that bother him. He identifies the source of his problems as 'something'—that pushed him out of bed, took his bear and blanket, scared him, and wet his bed. Levert's illustrations identify these somethings: a giant turtle, huge bear, large wolf, Goldilocks and the Three Bears, and a painting of the sea leaking water onto the floor. The artist also reveals the real nature of these objects: a toy turtle, the picture, his own teddy, and two books, *Little Red Riding Hood* and *The Story of the Three Bears*. Mrs Ming does not dismiss his worries as fantasies, but soothes the child, accepting them and dealing with them as if they were real. Three double-spreads show her in Jeremiah's bedroom. In the first, she stands at the edge of the room, looking astonished at the giant turtle. In the second, she moves towards the boy's bed to rescue him from the wolf; while in the third, she is at the edge of the bed, treading water in the flooded room. She has entered Jeremiah's world. Because they are now equals, Jeremiah is able to offer comfort when she is frightened by a real thunderstorm. In the book's final illustration, he has his arm protectively around her while she sleeps, hugging his teddy.

Rose by Night, the first story both written and illustrated by Levert, gives a new twist to a familiar theme: a child's frightening night-time fantasies. When she has to go to the bathroom in the middle of the night, a little girl uses a magic spell and her quick wits to escape from a witch, a vampire, and an ogre, all of whom wish to devour her. Levert's brightly coloured, cartoon-like pictures, which reveal the influence of Gay and Sendak, make a potentially frightening narrative funny and emphasize the heroism of the girl. Like Sendak's in *Where the Wild Things Are*, Levert's illustrations increase in size from a small single-page picture showing the girl preparing to go to bed, to a double-spread after she has escaped the monsters, and, on the final page, as she falls asleep feeling safe and secure, to a single-page picture that just fits onto the page. Details in the opening picture suggest a reason for the appearance of the frightening beings: her magic, pre-bedtime drink is concocted of wine, milk, pop, eggs, salt, pepper, and food colouring. When the monsters appear, their figures extend beyond the borders, an indication of both their power and the fact that they are fantastic creatures from the girl's imagination. As Rose defeats them, she increases in size while they diminish. When she arrives in the bathroom, escaping both her final attacker and the pressure on her bladder, the double-spread is dominated by bright greens, oranges, and yellows, a contrast to the darker colours of earlier pages. She sits on the toilet, a relieved smile on her face.

In order to dissipate any fears that children might experience when hearing the text of *Little Red Riding Hood*, Levert creates humorous, often foolish-looking characters. As the wolf, on his hind legs, walks behind the girl, the potential alarm of his great size is offset by his sagging belly and non-threatening pose. He looks ridiculous donning Grandmother's nightgown, and, when the hunter comes to the rescue, the human beings look larger than the unconscious animal stretched on the bed. The girl looks more puzzled than frightened during the dangerous moments, while the rescuing hunter looks silly in a cap with earflaps sticking out to each side.

Particularly in the Jeremiah stories and *Rose by Night*, Mireille Levert has established herself as an important visual interpreter of the imaginative and imaginary worlds of children. Her use of bright colours and exaggerated cartoon-like characters dispel fear from the fantasies children create as they deal with what are, to them, important, stressful situations.

Ron Lightburn

Born: 24 June 1954, in Cobourg, Ont.

Principal Residences: Cobourg; Vancouver; Victoria, BC; Annapolis Valley, NS.

Education: Alberta College of Art.

Career: window display artist; commercial artist; illustrator.

Major Awards: Amelia Frances Howard-Gibbon Medal (1992); Governor-General's Award for Illustration (1992); Elizabeth Mrazik Cleaver Award (1992); Mr Christie's Book Award, ages 7 and under, with Nan Gregory (1995).

Works for Children

Works illustrated by Ron Lightburn

Waiting for the Whales, by Sheryl McFarlane (Victoria, BC: Orca, 1991). **Rev:** *BiC* 21 (Feb. 1992): 31; *CCL* 69 (1993): 68; *CM* 19 (Nov. 1991): 339; *EL* 20 (Mar. 1993): 72; *HB* 68 (Sept. 1992): 621; *QQ* 57 (Dec. 1991): 25; *SLJ* 39 (June 1993): 83.

I Can't Sleep, by Patti Farmer (Victoria, BC: Orca, 1992). **Rev:** *CCL* 69 (1993): 92; *QQ* 58 (Dec. 1992): 27.

Eagle Dreams, by Sheryl McFarlane (Victoria. BC: Orca, 1994). **Rev:** *CBRA* (1994): 459; *QQ* 60 (Sept. 1994): 69; *RT* 50 (Dec. 1996): 343; *SLJ* 41 (June 1995): 91.

How Smudge Came, by Nan Gregory (Red Deer, Alta: Red Deer College Press, 1995). **Rev:** *CBRA* (1995): 470; *QQ* 62 (Feb. 1996): 41.

Driftwood Cove, by Sandra Lightburn (Toronto: Doubleday, 1997).

Ron Lightburn had been working for several years as a commercial artist in Victoria before he showed his portfolio to the staff at Orca Books. As a result of the visit, he was commissioned to create illustrations for Sheryl McFarlane's story *Waiting for the Whales*. Although a rookie at the age of 36, Lightburn brought considerable background, in addition to his commercial art experience, to the task. As a child growing up in Vancouver, he spent much time in the outdoors responding to the sights and colours of the west coast, and he devoured comic books, studying their techniques of narrative art. As a student, he fell under the influence of the French Impressionists, particularly their subtle use of delicate colour and shading to evoke mood. Because he has applied their techniques to realistic images, he has been called a 'photographic impressionist'.

The realism of his illustrations derives from his practice of modelling his drawings after photographs of people and scenes. Their impressionistic atmosphere comes from his use of coloured pencils to manipulate intensity and hue, particularly of the backgrounds, thereby suggesting the sensitive emotions of his characters and reflecting the many tones of the narratives.

Sheryl McFarlane's *Waiting for the Whales* celebrates the relationship between an old man and his granddaughter. Their companionship is centred on the activities they share around his home overlooking the ocean: planting in the garden, walking in the woods, but, most importantly, watching for the annual return of the migrating Orca whales. After his death, the girl is disconsolate until her mother suggests that his spirit has joined the whales, and, when the pod swims past, she notices a small calf, a symbol of the renewal of life. Ron Lightburn divides the illustrations into three groups: the first, depicting the old man alone, is generally monochromatic, representing the dullness of his life; the second, in which many of the activities are repeated, includes his granddaughter and employs a full spectrum of colour; the third, portraying the old man's last days and the girl's grieving, emphasizes browns and oranges, which relate back to those of the first section but foreshadow the dominant orange and gold tones of the final illustrations in which the girl looks out to sea and the new calf is discovered. Colour celebrates both the richness of the grandfather's life and of the girl's memories of their shared experiences. Composition is deft as well. In the first section, the old man's face is never seen; either he is facing the background or his hat covers his eyes. When daughter and granddaughter arrive, driving away his loneliness, his face is seen for the first time. Only as he sits on his porch, knowing he will soon die, is his hat removed and his face fully revealed. His life has reached fulfilment in his relationship with the young girl. It should be noted that each illustration is framed by a brown border, giving the impression of a photograph preserving memories and also of looking through a window, just as the old man and the child frequently looked out across the waters from the windows of his home.

In *Eagle Dreams*, McFarlane again examines the relationship between a child and adult as both consider an animal. In this case, however, the two human beings are in conflict about the animal: a father does not believe his son has the time or responsibility necessary to care for a wounded eagle. During the opening part of the story, when the boy finds the bird and his father reveals his anger, dark clouds glower overhead and brown dominates the fall landscape. The father stands away from the boy and, in one scene in which the mother, the boy, and the veterinarian care for the bird, only his legs are in the illustration as he looks on at the trio. When the boy is permitted to keep the eagle, the light of the setting sun breaks through the clouds, and the boy, in silhouette, raises his arms in joy as his mother and the veterinarian face him. In the distance, the father walks away. Although much of the tending of the bird takes place in late fall and winter, the illustrations contain shades of green, symbolizing the hope for the eagle's recovery. Robin kneels by a stream with evergreens in the background; an evergreen is seen next to a silo in the farmyard, and the pale green of rushes contrasts with the dark brown walls of the barn. The stages by which the eagle, fully healed, regains its freedom are shown in three illustrations in which the bird becomes increasingly the dominant figure. It is seen first perched on a log in the barnyard; then, its head and neck stare forward in fierce determination. Finally, in the book's only double-spread, it flies out of the barn, while, in the background, the family and vet look on in awe. As the bird returns to the wilds, the father and son are reconciled. For the first time, the man becomes part of the group watching the eagle. In the following illustration, the two sit together on a green hillside, looking up into a blue sky laced with white clouds, searching for the eagle. The white space that borders the illustrations creates a sense of openness that parallels the eagle's need for freedom and the boy's need to have the freedom to exercise his responsibility.

The friendship between a lost puppy and a girl living in a group home is the subject of Nan Gregory's *How Smudge Came*. The conflict arises when the supervisors of the home tell the Down's Syndrome child that she cannot keep the animal. With the exception of the walls of rooms, Lightburn does not present backgrounds, thus emphasizing the heroine's focus on the people with whom she interacts and the dog she befriends. These define the limits of her world. Only once, when she looks out the window of the hospice in which she works, is a large scene presented. In the distant city she views is the SPCA shelter to which she must take the animal. However, when she waits at the bus stop for transportation to the shelter, the background is white: she is heading into a completely unknown territory. When the dog seems lost to her forever, her desolation is illustrated for the sentence, 'There's No Place to Go But Home.' The back of a small figure, her shoulders slouched, is walking into a white background: the future seems to hold no hope for her. However, when the people of the hospice finally bring the dog there, she is surrounded by loving people.

Driftwood Cove, which Lightburn wrote with his wife, Sandra, tells of the friendship between Matthew and Katelyn, camping with their grandparents, and Salena, a girl who lives with her parents in a tree house on the west coast of Vancouver Island. When the brother and sister are trapped in the fog, Salena, who is walking along the beach looking for her goat, takes the two back to her home. There the mother and father describe their simple life and, that evening, prepare a meal for the brother and sister and their grandparents. The girls agree to meet again the next summer. The gentle emotions evoked by the almost lyrical prose are enhanced by Ron Lightburn's coloured-pencil illustrations, each of which occupies one-and-a-half pages. The world of Katelyn and her family is dominated by blues, reds, and yellows in their clothing and around their campsite; that of Salena's family, by browns, oranges, and golds, colours of the earth and the sun, the natural world in which they live. The siblings travel from the former to the latter. However, both take something back to their own world: she has a pendant carved by Salena, he carries a load of wood to carve. The children's body language and expressions illustrate their changing emotions. Exploring an old shack, Matthew and Katelyn crouch to look with curiosity under a loose floorboard; lost in the fog, they creep over the rocks on all fours, looking anxiously over their shoulders; and, in the tree house, they lean forward in fascination as Salena's father carves a whale from a piece of driftwood.

Lightburn's illustrations have the crispness of coloured photographs. However, through his delicate use of colour and shading in individual illustrations and changes of these between illustrations, he subtly communicates the great range of emotions his characters experience in their relationships with each other and their responses to the natural worlds in which they live.

See also: *SATA* 91; *WSMP*.

Jean Little

Born: 22 January 1932, in Taiwan.

Principal Residences: Taiwan; Guelph, Ont.

Education: University of Toronto (BA 1955); Institute of Special Education, Salt Lake City.

Career: special education teacher; university lecturer; writer.

Major Awards: Canada Council Children's Literature Prize (1977); Canadian Library Association Book of the Year Award (1985); Ruth Schwartz Award (1985); Vicky Metcalf Award (1974); IODE Violet Downey Children's Book Award (1996).

Works for Children

Mine for Keeps (Toronto: Little, Brown, 1962). **Rev:** *CBRA* (1995): 510; *HB* 88 (Oct. 1992): 484.

Home From Far (Toronto: Little, Brown, 1965). **Rev:** *HB* 41 (Aug. 1965): 387; *SLJ* 30 (Feb. 1984): 30.

Spring Begins in March (Toronto: Little, Brown, 1966). **Rev:** *CBRA* (1996): 482; *IR* (Winter 1967): 35.

Take Wing (Toronto: Little, Brown, 1968). **Rev:** *IR* (Winter 1969): 28; *RT* 37 (Feb. 1984): 506.

When the Pie Was Opened (Toronto: Little, Brown, 1968). **Rev:** *IR* 2 (Aug. 1968): 13; *CCL* 42 (1986): 56.

One to Grow On (Toronto: Little, Brown, 1969). **Rev:** *CCB-B* 23 (Nov. 1969): 49; *HB* 45 (June 1969): 308; *IR* 3 (Summer 1969): 15.

Look Through My Window (Toronto: Fitzhenry & Whiteside, 1970). **Rev:** *CCB-B* 24 (Jan. 1971): 76: *HB* 46 (Dec. 1970): 620; *IR* 4 (Autumn 1970): 24.

Kate (Toronto: Fitzhenry & Whiteside, 1971). **Rev:** *CCB-B* 25 (Dec. 1971): 59; *HB* 48 (Feb. 1972): 49; *IR* 6 (Summer 1972): 30; *NYTBR* (16 Jan. 1972): 18.

From Anna (Toronto: Fitzhenry & Whiteside, 1972). **Rev:** *CCB-B* 26 (Jan. 1973): 78; *HB* 48 (Oct. 1972): 467; *IR* 7 (Winter 1973): 25; *SLJ* 34 (Winter 1978): 189.

Stand in the Wind (Toronto: Fitzhenry & Whiteside, 1975). **Rev:** *BiC* 25 (May 1996): 20; *CCB-B* 29 (Mar. 1976): 114; *IR* 10 (Summer 1976): 57; *SLJ* 22 (Mar. 1976): 48.

Listen for the Singing (Toronto: Clarke, Irwin, 1977). **Rev:** *CCB-B* 31 (Nov. 1977): 50; *HB* 53 (Oct. 1977): 532; *IR* 12 (Winter 1978): 57; *SLJ* 24 (Sept. 1977): 132.

Mama's Going to Buy You a Mockingbird (Toronto: Penguin, 1984). **Rev:** *CCL* 42 (1986): 89; *Language Arts* 63 (Jan. 1986): 88; *TES* (14 Feb. 1986): 28.

Lost and Found (Toronto: Penguin, 1985). **Rev:** *CCB-B* 40 (Oct. 1986): 30; *CCL* 45 (1987): 94; *EL* 14 (May 1987): 49; *QQ* 51 (Aug. 1985): 37; *SLJ* 33 (Oct. 1986): 163.

Different Dragons (Toronto: Penguin, 1986). **Rev:** *BiC* 15 (Dec. 1986): 16; *CCB-B* 40 (July 1987): 214; *CCL* 45 (1987): 91; *CL* 116 (Spring 1988): 167; *EL* 14 (Mar. 1987): 28; *SLJ* 33 (June 1987): 98; *TLS* (15 May 1987): 529.

Hey World! Here I Am! (Toronto: Kids Can Press, 1986). **Rev:** *CCB-B* 42 (July 1989): 279; *CCL* 50 (1988): 76; *CM* 16 (1988): 35; *EL* 14 (Jan. 1987): 47; *HB* 65 (Sept. 1989): 622.

Little by Little: A Writer's Education (Toronto: Penguin, 1987). **Rev:** *BiC* 17 (Apr. 1988): 36; *CCB-B* 41 (July 1988): 33; *CCL* 50 (1988): 56; *CM* 16 (July 1988): 121; *EL* 15 (Mar. 1988): 86; *HB* 64 (Sept. 1988): 645; *SLJ* 34 (June 1988): 112.

Stars Come Out Within (Toronto: Penguin, 1990). **Rev:** *CCB-B* 45 (Dec. 1991): 98; *CCL* 67 (1992): 80; *EL* 18 (Jan. 1991): 52; *HB* 68 (Jan. 1992): 93; *QQ* 56 (Nov. 1990): 13; *VOYA* 15 (Apr. 1992): 58.

Once Upon a Golden Apple, with Maggie De Vries, illus. Phoebe Gilman (Toronto: Penguin, 1991). **Rev:** *CCL* 69 (1993): 88; *CM* 19 (Sept. 1991): 230; *EL* 19 (Mar. 1992): 15; *QQ* 57 (Feb. 1991): 22; *SLJ* 37 (Aug. 1991): 151.

Jess Was the Brave One, illus. Janet Wilson (Toronto: Penguin, 1992). **Rev:** *CCL* 72 (1993): 69; *CM* 20 (Mar. 1992): 82; *EL* 19 (Mar. 1992): 17; *QQ* 57 (Aug. 1991): 24.

Revenge of the Small Small, illus. Janet Wilson (Toronto: Penguin, 1992). **Rev:** *CBRA* (1995): 475; *QQ* 58 (Oct. 1992): 31; *RT* 47 (Oct. 1993): 148.

Bats About Baseball, with Claire Mackay, illus. Kim LaFave (Toronto: Penguin, 1995). **Rev:** *BiC* 24 (Sept. 1995): 50; *CBRA* (1995): 76; *CCL* 87 (1997): 66; *EL* 23 (Mar. 1996): 24; *QQ* 61 (Mar. 1995): 78.

His Banner Over Me (Toronto: Viking, 1995). **Rev:** *BiC* 24 (Oct. 1995): 50; *CBRA* (1995): 509; *CCL* 79 (1995): 71; *EL* 23 (Mar. 1996): 25; *HB* 72 (Mar. 1996): 231; *QQ* 61 (Apr. 1995): 41.

Jenny and the Hanukkah Queen, illus. Suzanne Mogensen (Toronto: Viking, 1995). **Rev:** *CBRA* (1995): 475; *CCL* 87 (1997): 85; *QQ* 61 (Dec. 1995): 38.

Gruntle Piggle Takes Off, illus. Johnny Wales (Toronto: Viking, 1996). **Rev:** *CBRA* (1996): 448; *CCB-B* 50 (May 1997): 328; *EL* 24 (Mar. 1997): 27; *QQ* 62 (Sept. 1996): 72; *SLJ* 43 (June 1997): 96.

The Belonging Place (Toronto: Viking, 1997). **Rev:** *BiC* 26 (June 1997): 33; *CCB-B* 51 (Jan. 1998): 164; *SLJ* 43 (Nov. 1997): 120.

Emma's Magic Winter (Toronto: HarperCollins, 1998).

What Will the Robin Do Then? Winter Tales (Toronto: Viking, 1998). **Rev:** *BiC* 27 (Oct. 1998): 27.

Other

'A Long Distance Friendship', *CCL* 34 (1984): 23–30.

'Secret Garden', *CCL* 53 (1989): 25–32.

'A Writer's Social Responsibility', *New Advocate* 3 (Spring 1990): 79–88.

'Homecoming: Stories of Weary Wanderers Seeking Home', *HB* 67 (May 1991): 286–94.

'My Historical Fictions', *CCL* 83 (1996): 94–7.

Selected Discussions

Frazer, Frances. 'Something on Jean Little', *CCL* 53 (1989): 33–9.

Ross, Catherine. 'An Interview with Jean Little', *CCL* 34 (1984): 6–22.

Zola, Meguido. 'Profile: Jean Little', *Language Arts* 58 (Jan. 1981): 86–92.

'What I am trying to say through my books is that there is humanity in other kids and in parents, and that all these people are real. And then I am trying to share with them some of my own feelings of excitement about living. That living is a Yes thing rather than a No thing.' In her children's novels, picture-book texts, poetry, and autobiographies, Jean Little celebrates this joyous optimism. In coping with physical handicaps, emotional strains, and social pressures, her young characters grow in understanding and appreciation of themselves, their families, and their friends.

Shortly after her birth in Formosa (Taiwan), Jean Little was discovered to have severely limited vision. Her emotional and physical struggles, which she described in her autobiography *Little by Little*, influence her perceptive treatment of the physically disabled characters in several of her novels. As a young child, Little discovered the joys of reading and writing fiction: 'I lived in a world in which I was constantly making up stories. I wrote my first book in grade five, filling a whole scribbler. . . . The first real pull to write came from the fact that I found that I could escape through writing just as well as by reading.' Such childhood favourites as L.M. Alcott's *Little Women* and L.M. Montgomery's *Anne of Green Gables* are often mentioned in her own novels, and their influence in Little's own presentation of events and portrayal of character are evident in her works. Assisted by a very encouraging father, she had her work first published when she was 17 years old—two poems in the Canadian periodical *Saturday Night*. However, it was not until she heard American children's writer Virginia Sorensen speak that she decided to write her own children's books. *Mine for Keeps*, her first novel, the story of a girl with cerebral palsy, was written for the special-education children she taught in Guelph.

Most of Little's novels are set in Guelph, called Riverside in the stories, and Toronto. They deal with boys and girls who must find their places among family and friends, cope with physical handicaps, and face the traumas occasioned by household moves, adults, prejudice, and death. Several of the novels can loosely be called sequels. *Spring Begins in March* deals with Meg, sister of the heroine of *Mine for Keeps*. Members of the Solden family are the central figures in *From Anna* and *Listen for the Singing*; the title heroine of Kate is the best friend of Emily, the heroine of *Look Through My Window*.

'Often a book starts with a problem that interests me', Jean Little has said. Although the problems of Sal Copeland in *Mine for Keeps* and Anna Solden in *Listen for the Singing* are physical, they are also symbolic of the emotional problems faced by many children. Thus, Sal's father tells her: 'The real you, the you that matters, has nothing to do with crutches.' Like many of Jean Little's characters, 'she was shutting herself behind a high wall.' Upset at leaving the security of a residential school, the girl worries about adjusting to her family and an ordinary school. Visually impaired, Anna faces a similar problem: her family does not seem to understand her difficulties as she moves with them from Germany to Canada and enters a new school. For others, the problems are emotional. In *Spring Begins in March*, Sal's sister Meg is unhappy about being the youngest in the family. In *One to Grow On*, Jane must learn to tell the truth if she is to earn the trust of her family. In *Look Through My Window*, Emily, a solitary child, must establish friendships with peers. Jeremy, hero of *Mama's Going to Buy You a Mockingbird*, hides behind his sorrow and anger over the death of his father. Ben Tucker, in *Different Dragons*, must overcome his fear of dogs. What his father tells him is true for Little's other characters as well: 'Everyone has to fight a dragon some time. . . . You have different dragons to fight.'

In order to mature, these boys and girls must move from behind the walls they have built and must face their dragons. To dramatize this movement, Little often has her characters change residences. In *Mine for Keeps*, Sally Copeland is frightened as she looks out the window of the airplane taking her back to her family: 'It meant leaving the life you were used to and beginning a new one full of unfamiliar places and people.' For Anna Solden, in *From Anna*, the move is even more traumatic, as her father decides that the family must leave strife-torn pre-World War II Germany: 'Overnight, Anna's sometimes happy, often unhappy, but always familiar world turned upside down.' At the beginning of *Lost and Found*, Lucy Bell feels lost. It is Saturday of Labour Day weekend, and the family has moved to a new town; however, as the weekend progresses, Lucy makes new friends and acquires a sense of belonging. In *Different Dragons*, Ben makes a temporary move to his aunt's home, where he faces his fear of dogs.

Of course, the greatest moves are internal: the central characters must achieve new interior balance and new relationships with others. Early in *Kate*, the title heroine says to herself, 'I think I've been moving toward a new place.' She arrives at this new place by coming to a fuller understanding of her father and the long-standing quarrels he had with his own father. Anna Solden grows in sympathy towards her brother, in *Listen for the Singing*; she becomes aware of the tensions he feels when preparing to fight in the Canadian armed forces against his homeland, Germany. In *Look Through My Window*, Emily Blair's mother explains that her daughter understands prejudice because she has a quality that others lack: she can consider the point of view of her friends: 'It's not obvious to everyone. It's only obvious to you because you've looked through Kate's window.'

Achieving an understanding of others is not always easy for Little's characters; they are often so wrapped up in their own problems that they fail to appreciate those who wish to be their friends. Because of her unhappiness over the family's move, Lucy Bell, in *Lost and Found*, often feels angry towards her neighbour Nan. Grieving over his father's death, Jeremy Talbot, in *Mama's Going to Buy You a Mockingbird*, does not want to associate with Tess, thinking angrily to himself: 'Who'd want to be friends with a girl, anyway, especially a weird, snooty girl like that?'

Hey World, Here I Am!, a collection of poems; the texts for several picture books; and the short stories in *What Will the Robin Do Then?* repeat many of the themes of Little's novels of social realism. The poems, presented as the creations of the central character of the novel Kate, embody the girl's thoughts about herself and her attempts to define herself. 'Everything's changed', she observes. 'I suddenly have a million unanswered questions.' *Jess Was the Brave One*, in which a timid girl puts her overactive imagination to good use, rescuing her sister from bullies, and *Revenge of the Small Small*, about a youngest child's asserting herself, focus on sibling relationships. *Bats About Baseball*, written with Claire Mackay, and *Gruntle Piggle Takes Off* deal with child-grandparent interactions. In *Jenny and the Hanukkah Queen*, a mother helps her daughter overcome unhappiness at not celebrating Christmas, as her friends do; and in *Emma's Magic Winter*, a shy girl faces her fears about reading aloud in class.

Little has drawn on her own and her family's and ancestors' experiences in two autobiographies and two historical novels. *Little by Little* depicts the author's childhood in Taiwan, Hong Kong, and then Canada; her growing problems with her vision; her love of reading and writing; and her studies at the University of Toronto. *Stars Come Out Within* portrays her adult life. With blindness threatening to end her career as a writer, the author displays courage and stubbornness to confront and deal with not only her physical limitations, but also long periods of depression. In addition to portraying the many supportive friendships she developed, Little discusses the sometimes difficult relationship with the companion dog she acquired. Many characters and incidents reappear in the novels in fictionalized form.

His Banner Over Me, a fictionalized account of her mother's life, first with missionary parents in China and later in Canada, and *The Belonging Place*, relating to her Scottish ancestors' move to Canada, although based on facts, present many of the themes and conflicts of Little's earlier novels. Gorrie, heroine of *His Banner Over Me*, must deal with four major moves before she enters university—from Taiwan, to western Ontario, to Regina, and to Toronto—and must learn to relate to new relatives and friends. The deaths of her brother during World War I and of a close friend test the feistiness and resolve of the heroine, who, like other Little characters, often finds solace and encouragement in such children's classics as *Anne of Green Gables* and Francis Hodgson Burnett's *The Secret Garden*. Orphaned at age four, Elspet, the central character narrator of *The Belonging Place*, lives first with neighbours and then with relatives who move from Scotland to Upper Canada in the 1840s. The love of her aunt, uncle, and cousins, whom she considers parents and siblings, the adopting of an abandoned kitten, and the acquisition of a best friend help to transform their wilderness cabin into a home, a 'belonging place'.

Critics of Little's works have emphasized the often overt moralizing of her books and the forced resolutions to many of the conflicts. Others remark that her characters are too nice; seldom is there real malice, only misunderstanding. However, the most significant criticism is that her books are only bibliotherapeutic exercises; that is, in showing the characters overcoming major problems, they appear to indicate that readers can also find similar solutions. While there may be some truth to these criticisms, many are overstated. On the other hand, Little has been praised for her realistic portrayal of character, particularly in depicting tensions within families and between close friends. Undoubtedly these are her greatest gifts as a writer, as can be seen by looking more closely at two of her novels, *Listen for the Singing* and *Mama's Going to Buy You a Mockingbird*.

Listen for the Singing is organized around a series of tensions. Anna worries about her ability to cope at a new high school, away from friends who had been with her at the special education school. As World War II breaks out, the family feels torn in its loyalties between its German homeland and the adopted country of Canada. Their anxieties increase when they learn that Aunt Tania has been taken away by the German police and when Rudi leaves his university studies to enlist. Although Anna soon makes new friends, she is aware of prejudice both at school and in the neighbourhood, where the family's grocery business falls off. The crisis occurs when Rudi is blinded in a maritime accident and Mrs Solden goes into a state of depression. However, the family survives because of its love and because, in the midst of calamity and disaster, its members have continued to 'listen for the singing', have continued to find love and joy in their relationships.

Mama's Going to Buy You a Mockingbird centres on Jeremy Talbot's difficult struggle to accept the death of his father. During summer vacation at the family's lake cottage, Jeremy feels anger when he thinks he is being kept away from his ailing father. However, he does spend special moments with his father before the latter's death, when they watch an owl perched in a tree and when his father asks him to take care of Tess Medford, a lonely student he had taught. The statue of an owl, the father's last gift to his son, becomes one of the major symbols in the novel. At first, Jeremy is very protective of it, for it represents the special relationship he felt with his father; but by the end of the narrative, he is able to give it to his mother as a Christmas gift. He is, as well, able to share his memories with other people and to let go of the anger that has been a large part of his life since his father's death. Tess Medford is the person most responsible for helping Jeremy to accept his father's death. At first, the boy is hesitant to establish a friendship, fearing peer-group ostracism. However, he begins to understand Tess's sensitivity, loyalty, and courage, and learns about her unhappy background: she was the unwanted child of an unwed teenage mother. Learning about Tess helps him to overcome the selfishness that has characterized his life since his father's death.

Although *Mama's Going to Buy You a Mockingbird* deals with a common theme of contemporary children's literature—the death of a parent—it achieves levels of excellence not often found in such books. Perhaps the most tightly structured of Little's novels, it clearly presents Jeremy's struggles. Little is also extremely successful in introducing and developing symbols. Finally, in this novel Little makes the best use of one of her favourite devices, literary allusion. Reading such works as Kipling's *Kim*, Dennis Lee's 'Prayer to Ookpik', and Katherine Paterson's *The Great Gilly Hopkins* helps Jeremy understand the reality of his father's death, the continuing life of the family, and the troubled background of Tess Medford.

As a writer of stories about children with physical handicaps, Jean Little is a pioneer, presenting her characters honestly and unsentimentally. As a writer of the modern family story, she has created a number of novels of considerable excellence. Most important, her presentation of the difficult problems children and adolescents must all face as they grow and mature has earned her a major position in the history of Canadian children's literature.

See also: *CAFR* 21–4; *CANR* 42, 66; *CLR* 4; *Junior* 4; *Profiles*; *SAAS* 17; *SATA* 2, 68; *TCCW*; *WSMP*.

Celia Barker Lottridge

Born: 1 April 1936, in Iowa City, Iowa.

Principal Residences: Iowa City; San Diego; New York; Toronto.

Education: University of California (BA); Columbia University (MA, Library Science).

Career: librarian; book buyer; storyteller; writer.

Major Awards: Canadian Library Association Book of the Year (1993); Geoffrey Bilson Award for Historical Fiction (1993); IODE (Toronto) Book Award (1993); IODE Violet Downey Book Award (1998); Ruth Schwartz Children's Book Award, with Harvey Chan (1999).

Works for Children

The Juggler, illus. Ariadne Ochrymovych (Richmond Hill, Ont.: Scholastic, 1985). **Rev:** *EL* 13 (Mar. 1986): 15; *QQ* 51 (Dec. 1985): 27.

Prairie Dogs (Toronto: Grolier, 1985).

Mice (Toronto: Grolier, 1985).

One Watermelon Seed, illus. Karen Patkau (Toronto: Oxford UP, 1986). **Rev:** *BiC* 15 (Nov. 1986): 37; *CCL* 47 (1987): 96; *CM* 16 (June 1988): 7; *EL* 14 (Mar. 1987): 27; *QQ* 52 (June 1986): 28.

The Name of the Tree, illus. Ian Wallace (Toronto: Groundwood, 1989). **Rev:** *BiC* 18 (Dec. 1989): 19; *EL* 17 (Mar. 1990): 85; *HB* 66 (Mar. 1990): 213; *QQ* 55 (Oct. 1989): 13; *SLJ* 36 (Mar. 1990): 209.

Ticket to Curlew (Toronto: Groundwood, 1992); published in the US as *A Ticket to Canada.* **Rev:** *EL* 20 (Mar. 1993): 14; *QQ* 58 (Oct. 1992): 35; *SLJ* 40 (June 1994): 122.

Ten Small Tales (Toronto: Groundwood, 1993). **Rev:** *CBRA* (1994): 518; *CCB-B* 47 (May 1994): 293; *HB* 70 (1994): 112; *QQ* 59 (Oct. 1993): 37; *SLJ* 40 (June 1994): 122.

Something Might Be Hiding, illus. Paul Zwolak (Toronto: Groundwood, 1994). **Rev:** *CBRA* (1994): 458; *CCL* 81 (1996): 45; *CM* 22 (Nov. 1994): 208; *QQ* 60 (Oct. 1994): 41.

The Wind Wagon (Toronto: Groundwood, 1995). **Rev:** *CBRA* (1995): 510; *CCL* 89 (1998): 62; *EL* 3 (Mar. 1996): 25; *QQ* 61 (June 1995): 58; *SLJ* 41 (Aug. 1995): 125.

Wings to Fly (Toronto: Groundwood, 1997). **Rev:** *CCL* 93 (1999): 83; *CM* 4 (16 Jan. 1998): on-line; *EL* 25 (Mar. 1998): 28; *QQ* 63 (June 1997): 66.

Music for the Tsar of the Sea, illus. Harvey Chan (Toronto: Groundwood, 1997).

Works edited by Celia Lottridge

Mythic Voices, with Alison Dickie (Toronto: ITP Nelson, 1991).

The Moon Is Round: and Other Rhymes to Play with Your Baby (Toronto: Vermont Square, 1992).

Mother Goose: A Canadian Sampler (Toronto: Groundwood, 1994). **Rev:** *CCL* 81 (1996): 90.

Letters to the Wind: Classic Stories and Poems for Children (Toronto: Key Porter Books, 1995). **Rev:** *CCL* 86 (1997): 74.

Other

'Folktales as a Source for Writing', in *Writers on Writing: Guide to Writing and Illustrating Children's Books*, ed. David Booth (Markham, Ont.: Overlea House, 1989), 116–19.

In Celia Lottridge's life there have been two constants: frequent moves and storytelling. She lived in five different states as a child and, as an adult, has called New York state, Rhode Island, California, and Ontario home. In all these residences, she has been an avid consumer and creator of stories. Her parents told her stories of their childhood; she made up fairy tales for her younger sister; and she has spent much of her adult life as a professional teller of traditional tales. Not surprisingly, these two constants figure largely in the picture books, folktale collections, and novels she has written for children. Her characters are frequently travelling to new places and are often involved in remembering, discovering, and telling stories.

Lottridge had written two picture books—*The Juggler*, about a handicapped boy and his circus community, and *One Watermelon Seed*, a counting book in which a brother and a sister work together in a garden—before she achieved national recognition with the publication of *The Name of the Tree*, a Bantu tale illustrated by Ian Wallace. In it, a group of animals travelling in a time of drought discover a tree, the fruit of which is beyond their reach. As in her own life, the author emphasizes the importance of remembering stories told by old people. Because Turtle recalls his great-great-great-grandmother's narrative about how to gather the harvest, she is able to help her friends survive in this new country. Lottridge's style reproduces the rhythms of oral storytelling with frequent repetitions and variation. *Music for the Tsar of the Sea* is a retelling of a traditional Russian tale about a poor orphan whose wonderful musical activities make him a prisoner of a supernatural being. The story also offers an explanation for the origin of the Volkov River.

Co-operation and individual resourcefulness are the main themes of *Ten Small Tales*, a collection of stories from cultures around the world. By sleeping together, a boy and his father avoid being devoured by a tiger; by working as a group, a turtle, snake, rabbit, and elephant are able to move a rock that covers their picnic spot; a family plants, cultivates, and harvests a giant turnip. By thinking carefully, several characters are able to resolve their conflicts: a greedy fox is outwitted by a family who puts a vicious dog in his sack; a grandmother finds a simple way to defeat the strange noises scaring a child at night—she oils the bedroom door hinges; and an old woman uses delaying tactics to escape animals that want to eat her. Selfish and foolish characters suffer: the increasing greed of a fox results in his losing his tail to a dog, while a monkey who will not heed warnings barely escapes from a village. Several of the stories picture child-adult relationships: the father and son sleeping together in the forest, the grandmother comforting her frightened grandson. A sense of the importance of family unity, seen again in the novels, is stressed. Honed over several years of telling in schools and libraries, these short tales, intended for younger children, capture in print the characteristics of oral telling: frequent refrains, variation with repetition, and short, precise presentation of action.

Lottridge's realistic fiction focuses on people moving into new homes or territories. In the picture book *Something Might Be Hiding*, Jenny explores the house into which the family has just moved and becomes frightened that things might hide in the hall closet, or under the stairs, or in the bedroom. With the help of her mother, father, and brother, she overcomes her fears and, having explored the house and become more familiar with it, falls asleep. *The Wind Wagon*, told in the style of a tall tale, begins in 1859 when Sam Peppard alights from a train at his new home, a small town in Kansas, carrying his bag of tools. With the aid of his friends, he builds a wind-propelled wagon that they drive to Colorado during the silver rush. Along the way they are surrounded by Indians, who only want to race them, not scalp them, and are carried away by a tornado. Years later, he delights in telling the story to whichever grandchild will listen. A humorous story about people co-operating in a new territory has become part of family lore.

The novels *Ticket to Curlew* and *Wings to Fly*, Lottridge's best-known works, recount three years in the lives of the Ferriers, a pioneer family that moved from Iowa to central Alberta in 1915. Like *The Wind Wagon*, *Ticket to Curlew* opens at a railroad station, as another Sam and his father, who also brings his tools, arrive at their new home. The narrative describes their first year on the Prairies, first building a small home, then learning to adapt to the long winter and experiencing the joy of the arrival of spring. The book contains almost no conflict and is, instead, a record not only of the living conditions of the family, but also of the 11-year-old boy's exploring the new countryside, developing an understanding of and feeling of belonging in the Prairies. Although Sam begins to discover his own individuality, he learns the importance of co-operation, too. Indeed, much of the book describes the Ferriers' relationships with other new neighbours, all of whom need each other to survive in their new homes. Characterization is relatively slight. However, Lottridge gives a good sense of pioneer life, particularly of the daily activities. One such activity describes the family gathered around the Eaton's catalogue, looking at the wonderful items and making careful selections of things they want, need, and can afford.

Wings to Fly also describes a prairie year in the life of the Ferriers. It is three years later and Sam's sister, now 11, responds not only to daily life around her, but currents of change from the outside world that effect her life and those of the scattered prairie community. A more complex novel, with the character of Josie more fully developed than Sam's was, *Wings to Fly* focuses on the ways several female characters define their own lives in relation to their families, the land, and society at large. Josie learns from her mother about the difficulties that moving to a new land caused her, and, in observing the mother of her best friend, sees how easily a major move can sap a person's spirit. The girl also learns how difficult it is for a young woman to define her own adult life. However, the examples of Angela Barnett, a young teacher who wants to go to university to study astronomy, considered a man's profession, and Katherine Stinson, a professional aviatrix who, because of her gender, was not allowed to fly during World War I, give her the determination to struggle and never to take 'no' for an answer. Josie acquires this knowledge because she 'liked to know about people and she always wanted to know their whole story.' In addition to presenting the daily activities of the girl's life, times with her best friend, events at school, and visits to an abandoned home she sees on the way to school, Lottridge movingly portrays the influenza epidemic that swept North America in 1918 and 1919. During the height of the outbreak, members of the family work together to help their stricken neighbours, just one of the many examples of co-operative activities throughout the book.

Lottridge's work as an adaptor of traditional stories and as a historical novelist have established her as an important writer for Canadian children. In her two major novels, she has given a vivid and fresh look at a relatively ignored experience in western Canadian history: the lives of people who settled the land in the early twentieth century. Not only has she detailed the daily activities and hardships they faced, she has examined how events influenced the lives of a young boy and girl as they defined themselves in their new homes. In *Wings to Fly*, she has also presented a complex picture of the lives of girls and women as they struggled with their socially defined gender roles.

See also: *TCCW*; *WSMP*.

Janet Lunn

Born: 28 December 1928, in Dallas, Texas.

Principal Residences: Montclair, NJ; Ottawa; Kingston; Toronto; Hillier, Ont.

Education: attended Queen's University (1947–50).

Career: children's editor; freelance editor; writer.

MAJOR AWARDS: IODE (Toronto) Book Award (1979, 1992); Canadian Library Association Book of the Year for Children (1982, 1987); Vicky Metcalf Award (1982); Canada Council Children's Literature Prize (1986); Canadian Library Association Young Adult Canadian Book Award (1987); IODE Violet Downey Book Award (1987); Ruth Schwartz Children's Book Award (1989); Mr Christie's Book Award, ages 9-14, with Christopher Moore (1992); Governor-General's Award for Children's Literature (1998).

WORKS FOR CHILDREN

Double Spell (Toronto: Peter Martin, 1968); republished as *Twin Spell* (New York: Harper, 1969). **Rev:** *CCB-B* 23 (Feb. 1970): 101; *CBRA* (1981): 3258; *CCL* 15 (1980): 29; *HB* 45 (Dec. 1969): 675; *IR* 15 (Oct. 1981): 42; *QQ* 48 (June 1982): 5.

The Twelve Dancing Princesses, illus. Laszlo Gal (Toronto: Methuen, 1979). **Rev:** *BiC* 8 (Dec. 1979): 13; *CBRA* (1979): 3265; *CCL* 15 (1980): 140; *EL* 10 (Sept. 1982): 22; *IR* 14 (Apr. 1980): 51; *Maclean's* 92 (17 Dec. 1979): 49; *NYTBR* 85 (11 May 1980): 25; *QQ* 48 (June 1982): 3; *RT* 34 (Nov. 1980): 235, and 34 (Jan. 1981): 482; *SLJ* 26 (Mar. 1980): 131.

Larger than Life (Victoria, BC: Press Porcepic, 1980). **Rev:** *BiC* 8 (Dec. 1979): 14; *CCL* 20 (1980): 76; *IR* 14 (Apr. 1980): 50.

The Root Cellar (Toronto: Lester & Orpen Dennys, 1981). **Rev:** *CBRA* (1981): 228; *Fantasy Review* 7 (Aug. 1984): 48; *HB* 59 (Oct. 1983): 575; *Language Arts* 61 (Feb. 1984): 179, and 61 (Apr. 1984): 422; *JR* 27 (Jan. 1984), 375; *RT* 37 (Feb. 1984): 528; *SLJ* 30 (Sept. 1983): 124.

Shadow in Hawthorn Bay (Toronto: Lester & Orpen Dennys, 1986). **Rev:** *BiC* 16 (June 1987): 37; *CCB-B* 40 (June 1987): 192; *CCL* 46 (1987): 60; *CM* 16 (Jan. 1988): 5; *EL* 15 (Nov. 1987): 65, and 19 (Nov. 1991): 61; *HB* 63 (Sept. 1987): 618; *SLJ* 34 (Sept. 1987): 197; *VOYA* 10 (Aug. 1987): 122.

Amos's Sweater, illus. Kim LaFave (Toronto: Groundwood, 1988). **Rev:** *APBR* 15 (Nov. 1988): 9; *Booklist* 86 (15 June 1990): 200; *BYP* 2 (Oct. 1988): 15; *CBRA* (1988): 276; *CCL* 57 (1990): 115; *EL* 16 (Mar. 1989): 21, 46.

Duck Cakes for Sale, illus. Kim LaFave (Toronto: Groundwood, 1989). **Rev:** *CBRA* (1989): 301; *CCL* 59 (1990): 83; *CM* 18 (Mar. 1990): 66; *QQ* 55 (Nov. 1989): 14.

One Hundred Shining Candles, illus. Lindsay Grater (Toronto: Lester & Orpen Dennys, 1990). **Rev:** *CBRA* (1990): 297; *EL* 18 (Mar. 1991): 24; *QQ* 56 (Oct. 1990): 14; *SLJ* 37 (Oct. 1991): 31.

The Hollow Tree (Toronto: Alfred A. Knopf Canada, 1997). **Rev:** *CM* 4 (17 Oct. 1997): on-line; *CBRA* (1997): 516; *EL* 25 (Mar./Apr. 1998): 27; *QQ* 64 (Jan. 1998): 36.

Come to the Fair, illus. Gilles Pelletier (Toronto: Tundra, 1997). **Rev:** *CBRA* (1997): 481; *SLJ* 44 (Feb. 1998): 88.

Charlotte, illus. Brian Deines (Toronto: Tundra, 1998).

The Umbrella Party, illus. Kady MacDonald Denton (Toronto: Douglas & McIntyre, 1998).

Other

The Story of Canada, with Christopher Moore, illus. Alan Daniel (Toronto: Lester Publishing and Key Porter Books, 1992; updated, 1996).

The Unseen: Scary Stories, ed. (Toronto: Lester, 1994).

'The Doppelgänger of *Shadow in Hawthorn Bay*', *The Voice of the Narrator in Children's Literature: Insights from Writers and Critics*, ed. Charlotte F. Otten and Gary D. Schmidt (New York: Greenwood, 1989), 276–7.

Selected Discussions

Garner, Barbara Carman. 'Lost and Found in Time: Canadian Time-slip Fantasies for Children', *ChLQ* 15 (Winter 1990): 206-11.

Jones, Raymond E. 'Border Crossing: Janet Lunn's *The Root Cellar*', *ChLQ* 10 (Spring 1985): 43-4.

Nikolajeva, Maria. 'A Typological Approach to the Study of *The Root Cellar*', *CCL* 63 (1991): 53-60.

'I honestly believe', says Janet Lunn, 'that writing stories is magic. It either comes to you or it doesn't.' Lunn has chosen to concentrate on children's fiction because it provides 'the excitement of pure magic' and affords her a direct way of expressing her ideas: 'I don't like subtleties; I like to get to the bone, to the marrow.'

Lunn also admits that she 'can't leave history alone'. In fact, her first book, *The County*, written with her late husband, was a Centennial Project history of Prince Edward County, Ontario. This concern with the past is a major element in Lunn's children's books. It is evident in *Larger than Life*, 10 stories of such Canadian heroes as Madeleine de Vercheres, Alexander Mackenzie, Crowfoot, and John A. Macdonald. Lunn wrote it because, having herself grown up with such American heroes as George Washington, she became 'quite irked that there were no heroes here' for her Canadian children. Extensively researched to ensure authenticity, the book is anecdotal history, re-creations of how characters responded under special circumstances. Lunn, who became a Canadian citizen in 1963, acknowledges that the book does not generally treat acts of overt grandeur celebrated in the stories of American history she grew up with: 'I now feel because I've become a Canadian in more than just a slip of paper that maybe that isn't our way.' Recently Lunn collaborated with Christopher Moore on *The Story of Canada*, a sweeping history of the country that tries to inject drama into events and to give personality to historical figures.

A different kind of concern for the past, a respect for tradition, is apparent from *The Twelve Dancing Princesses*, Lunn's first picture book. After studying a number of versions of the tale, she took that by the Brothers Grimm and a French version and 'sifted them through myself'. Although some reviewers severely criticized her for departing from the German version, Lunn places herself in a living tradition of storytelling by insisting that 'Every generation brings fairy tales up to date.'

Lunn's most creative use of research and her most significant presentation of her concern for the past have come, however, in her novels. For her first, *Double Spell*—more appropriately titled *Twin Spell* in its US edition—she did considerable research in the Royal Ontario Museum to give authenticity to her story of twins beset by an unshriven ghost, whose guilt terrifyingly pulls them back into Toronto's past. Only by forgiving the ghost do the twins dispel its malignancy and come to some understanding of their own family's history.

Even more impressive in showing the continuing force of the past on the present, however, is *The Root Cellar*. This time-shift fantasy explores issues of adolescent and national identity by following the adventures of Rose Larkin, an American orphan living with Canadian relatives, who enters an abandoned root cellar and is transported into the nineteenth century. Disguised as a boy, she sets off to find Will Morrissay, a Canadian who has run off to fight on the Union side in the American Civil War. Because the fantasy is confined to events in the twentieth century, the scenes of the past are as realistic as those in any historical novel, and Lunn uses them to paint a horrifying vision of the Civil War and its aftermath. Many of the soldiers sent off as heroes return to face scorn; many, including the mutilated, are forced to steal because they can find no work. When Rose finds Will and he tells of his grim experiences, Lunn creates a powerful anti-war statement, revealing herself to be, as she says, 'quite a violent pacifist'.

Like *The Twelve Dancing Princesses*, *The Root Cellar* shows Lunn's sense of belonging to a tradition of storytelling that she can update for her purposes. She has said that one of her favourite childhood books was Frances Hodgson Burnett's *The Secret Garden* (1910). In *The Root Cellar*, Lunn refers to it, and she makes characters and situations parallel Burnett's. Will Morrissay, like Burnett's Dickon Sowerby, plays a flute and tries to talk to birds with it. To Rose he thus suggests the simplicity and harmony of nineteenth-century life. Will is also like Colin Craven because he is temporarily 'sick' with delusions and must be cured by a girl who has transformed her own character. In this novel the secret garden that is restored is internal; Rose, fulfilling the hope her symbolic name suggests, blooms into love. Lunn also uses parallels to one of the twentieth century's most successful time fantasies, Philippa Pearce's *Tom's Midnight Garden* (1958). Like Tom, Rose makes a number of journeys to the past, never aging, although those she meets continue to get older. Like Tom, she at first wants to remain in the world of the past. In both books, a storm that destroys a tree marks a significant turning point in events.

Shadow in Hawthorn Bay, a historical novel, has a simpler plot than *The Root Cellar*, but it explores similar questions of personal and national identity. Furthermore, like all of Lunn's work, it mixes a number of elements: it combines a comparative study of manners and beliefs in the Old and New Worlds, a Gothic romance with an unusual wilderness setting, and a gripping psychological investigation. Mairi Urquhart, a young Scots girl possessing 'second sight' travels to Canada in 1815 after she hears within her a call for help from her beloved cousin, Duncan Cameron, who had emigrated four years earlier. Instead of bringing happiness, however, her journey tests Mairi when she discovers that Duncan is dead. Mairi comes to understand and value the customs of the settlers among whom she lives. Her burdensome gift of second sight, however, alienates her from the community, which does not share Mairi's beliefs in fairies and the spirit world. Furthermore, she fears the land, believing that evil resides in its dark woods.

Lunn has said of Catharine Parr Traill's observation that the Irish and Scots left their superstitions behind when they settled in Canada, 'She was right; myths don't travel well.' That observation forms the basis for Mairi's development. When she is in Scotland, Mairi is alert to the world of spirits and conscious of myth. In Canada, she must accept a more mundane reality. Once she realizes that it was not the fairies but Luke Anderson who helped her, and once she understands that Duncan, who continues to call her, has committed suicide and now wants to bind her to him in death, she shakes off the hold of the Old World and its beliefs. In a richly symbolic scene, both Mairi and her homestead are transformed. No longer haunted by the black despair of the Old World, symbolized by the corpse of Duncan, the transformed Mairi accepts her new land for the first time by walking into the woods she had always feared. She also accepts her own personal destiny, which she had strenuously denied, when she agrees to be Luke's wife.

Like both *The Root Cellar* and *Shadow in Hawthorn Bay*, *The Hollow Tree* develops themes of identity and belonging by focusing on a girl who comes from another country and eventually recognizes that Canada is her home. Set during the American Revolution, it traces the maturation of 15-year-old Phoebe Olcott, who does not know what she is because she is neither a rebel nor a Tory. Circumstances soon force her to take stock of her inner resources and values. First, her father is killed fighting for the rebel cause, leaving her an orphan, and then, two years later, her beloved cousin Gideon, a Loyalist soldier, is hanged as a spy. The grief-stricken Phoebe decides that, because it might prevent innocent people from suffering, she must deliver to the British at Fort Ticonderoga a coded message that Gideon had hidden in a hollow tree. She therefore undertakes alone a perilous wilderness journey, only to find that the British have abandoned the fort. Luckily, she encounters young Jem Morrissay, who leads her to a party of Loyalist refugees heading for safety in Canada. Improbably, Gideon's family, with whom Phoebe had been living, is part of this group.

Gideon's sister, Anne, bitterly accuses Phoebe of being a rebel responsible for Gideon's death, but Phoebe earns the respect of the others by tending the children. After the refugees capture a young man they believe to be a spy, however, Phoebe, remembering the horror of Gideon's hanging, frees the prisoner and again sets off alone. Eventually, she delivers the coded message to a British fort and is reunited with Jem and her relatives. Phoebe then realizes that her experiences have given her a new confidence, maturity, and independence. Knowing who and what she is, Phoebe remains in Canada, which has become her home because her friends are there, and eventually marries Jem.

As a political novel, *The Hollow Tree* makes an exceptionally strong case for each side, showing clearly why people would rebel against the King and why they would support him. Its preoccupation, however, is the sufferings of Loyalists, and it portrays many Patriots as opportunistic and intolerant bullies. Without idealizing the Loyalists, it shows villains on both sides, balancing a robbery by starving Patriots, for example, with one by starving British deserters. Such scenes of victimization undercut the romance of war and suggest that Phoebe's ethic of compassion, her motive for releasing the prisoner, is more laudable than any ideological fervour. Furthermore, the novel suggests that relationships are more important than politics: Phoebe elects to stay in Canada because the presence of friends makes it feel like a home, not because she accepts its allegiance to the King. As an adventure, *The Hollow Tree* is somewhat strained. The inclusion of a cat and a bear cub, which insist on following Phoebe, weakens tension because their presence is improbable and the tone of their presentation is inappropriately light. Nevertheless, they reveal Phoebe's character. Like the children of the refugees who later cling to Phoebe, these animals symbolize by their affection the fundamental magnetism of Phoebe's innocence and natural compassion. Furthermore, the departure of the bear tests Phoebe's maturity because she needs to accept inevitable change, both in her relationships with the animals and in her social relationships and political allegiances. In addition to establishing her determination, Phoebe's journey effectively forces her to choose her own course of conduct, the author's point being that people need to be independent in their personal lives. Finally, in concluding as a love story, *The Hollow Tree* may be predictable, but it offers Lunn's readers the satisfaction of learning about the settlement of Hawthorn Bay, prominent in the geography of Lunn's earlier novels.

To the concern for the past, Lunn's novels add strong moral concerns, displayed especially through images of redemption or restoration. *Double Spell* treats the healing power of forgiveness: the twins are freed from psychological terror when they forgive the guilty ghost. In *The Root Cellar*, which began as a Christmas story, Lunn uses the Christmas dinner that appears from the past, she says, as 'an allegory' to convey the 'sense of redemption'. Rose's experiences in nineteenth-century Canada and the United States teach her that she belongs to the twentieth century, to Canada, and to her new family. Having pretended to be a boy for many of her adventures, she now accepts herself. The dinner from the past is a tangible sign of traditional values—it literally nourishes family life. Rose determines to restore the old house in which her adoptive family lives, thus ensuring a perpetuation of those loving values. The climax of *Shadow in Hawthorn Bay* is thematically like that in *Double Spell*. Mairi wades naked into the black water of the bay but realizes in time that Duncan was a man of black despair who only wanted to bind her to him. She demonstrates the redemptive power of love when she attempts to forgive him, setting his spirit at peace and freeing herself from the hold of the land of her birth. In *The Hollow Tree* Phoebe, believing that the refugees will hang her because she has released their prisoner, threatens to kill herself. While doing so, Phoebe not only declares that killing people because of their political ideas is evil, but she also advances the idea that true morality does not depend on social conventions. Consequently, she not only lives because Jem allows her to escape, but she is transformed into a person who understands herself and her own powers.

Particularly concerned about the way the past influences the present, Lunn has created novels that do not focus on magnificent historical deeds but on the moral and psychological heroism that enables individuals to establish their identities. Her books thus use the personal identity crises of adolescent girls to explore the ways in which alienated individuals accept themselves and their country. Lunn has said that she accepts that her focus on girls has made her a girls' novelist. Perhaps her books do appeal more to girls than boys, but the questions of identity and morality that her heroines face transcend issues of gender.

In addition to her sophisticated and challenging novels, Lunn has produced six original picture books. Three of these show Lunn's characteristic concern with the past. *One Hundred Shining Candles*, set in Upper Canada in 1800, is about 10-year-old Lucy Jamieson's efforts to give her pioneer family a special Christmas by making and lighting 100 candles. After Lucy becomes bossy and carelessly spills all her tallow, her brother gallantly offers his only penny to buy more. Co-operating, the children produce only five candles, but their joyful light seems to come from 100. This simple story idealizes sharing and togetherness, but it is too predictable and stilted to be genuinely moving. In contrast, *Charlotte*, based on events in the life of Charlotte Haines, the grandmother of one of Canada's Fathers of Confederation, is genuinely affecting. When 10-year-old Charlotte decides to say farewell to her cousins, Loyalists leaving New York for exile in Nova Scotia, her father, a stern rebel, forever bans her from his house, thereby forcing Charlotte into exile with her cousins. Although more anecdote than tale, this powerful account of dispossession succeeds as a portrait of destructive political passion. *Come to the Fair* also is short on plot, but it affectionately catalogues the pleasures of a farm family, the Martins, when they travel to the country fair during the first half of the twentieth century. Gilles Pelletier's bright, primitive illustrations, which are busy with details (including a mouse to be found in every one), are a perfect complement to the narrator's nostalgic account of activities at the fair.

Lunn's other picture books are humorous contemporary stories. In *Amos's Sweater*, Amos, an old sheep, becomes cold after he has been shorn and repeatedly attacks the sweater that Aunt Hattie has knit from his wool. One day, after Amos the sheep becomes tangled in the sweater, Hattie and Uncle Henry decide that they will let him wear it. An even more absurd situation is central to *Duck Cakes for Sale*. After an old woman moves to the country and obtains two ducks for her creek, she finds herself overrun with ducks and duck eggs. Changing her house into a tea shop in which she sells her baking, she soon finds herself as overrun by tourists as by ducks. The ducks themselves soon solve her problem, however, flying away from her crowded house. *The Umbrella Party* is the story of Christie, who wants only umbrellas for her birthday. During her party at the beach, a big wind sends all of her umbrellas flying. The children who run about retrieving them, and then huddle under them when it begins to rain, come to learn that umbrellas can provide fun and be useful. Because of its feeble plot, strained attempt at manic comedy, and weak theme, *The Umbrella Party* is disappointing.

Janet Lunn is most notable as a historical novelist. *The Root Cellar*, *Shadow in Hawthorn Bay*, and *The Hollow Tree* are not only good historical novels, but they are among the finest books written for Canadian children. Their vivid historical scenes provide more than gripping entertainment or educational insights into the past: they also advance important themes of identity.

See also: *CA* 33–6R; *CANR* 22; *CLR* 18; *MAICYA*; *Profiles*; *SATA* 4, 68; *SAAS* 12; *TCCW*.

Sheryl McFarlane

Born: 20 January 1954, in Pembroke, Ont.

Principal Residences: Pembroke; Arizona; Vancouver; BC.

Education: University of British Columbia (B.Ed. 1985).

Career: child-care worker; research technician; writer.

Major Awards: IODE Violet Downey Book Award (1992).

Works for Children

Waiting for the Whales, illus. Ron Lightburn (Victoria, BC: Orca, 1991). **Rev:** *BiC* 21 (Feb. 1992): 31; *CCL* 69 (1993): 68; *CM* 19 (Nov. 1991): 339, and 20 (Jan. 1992): 23; *EL* 20 (Mar. 1993): 72; *HB* 68 (Sept. 1992): 621; *QQ* 57 (Dec. 1991): 25; *SLJ* 39 (June 1993): 83.

Jessie's Island, illus. Sheena Lott (Victoria, BC: Orca, 1992). **Rev:** *CCL* 76 (1994): 85; *CM* 20 (Sept. 1992): 208; *QQ* 58 (May 1992): 32.

Eagle Dreams, illus. Ron Lightburn (Victoria, BC: Orca, 1994). **Rev:** *CBRA* (1994): 459; *QQ* 60 (Sept. 1994): 69; *RT* 50 (Dec. 1996): 343; *SLJ* 41 (June 1995): 91.

Moonsnail Song, illus. Sheena Lott (Victoria, BC: Orca, 1994). **Rev:** *CBRA* (1994): 459; *CCL* 87 (1997): 67; *CM* 22 (Sept. 1994): 13; *QQ* 60 (Mar. 1994): 80; *RT* 48 (Apr. 1995): 606, and 49 (Fall 1996): 396.

Tides of Change: Faces of the Northwest Coast, illus. Ken Campbell (Victoria, BC: Orca, 1995). **Rev:** *CBRA* (1995): 538; *CCL* 89 (1998): 84; *EL* 23 (Mar. 1996): 24; *QQ* 61 (Sept. 1995): 72.

Going to the Fair, illus. Sheena Lott (Victoria, BC: Orca, 1996). **Rev:** *CBRA* (1996): 450; *CCL* 86 (1997): 94; *QQ* 62 (Apr. 1996): 38.

Sheryl McFarlane uses the picture book to educate young readers about the environment. Her texts are notable for their poetic qualities, rhythm and repetition evoking a sense of wonder at the beauties of the natural world.

Four of McFarlane's books are essentially loving catalogues. *Tides of Change: Faces of the Northwest Coast* repeatedly asks the reader, 'Do you know the Northwest Coast?' It then offers brief statements or questions about the history, peoples, and ecology of the region. Ken Campbell's bright paintings perfectly complement this respectful celebration of a region. *Jessie's Island* provides a narrative hook for its catalogue. When Jessie receives a letter saying that life must be boring on her island, she writes to invite her cousin for a visit, listing all the things to see and do. Supplemented by Sheena Lott's watercolours, McFarlane's listing of the wildlife, scenic beauties, and numerous activities that a child can enjoy along the coast creates an image of a childhood Eden. An even stronger narrative line structures *Going to the Fair*, a list of the sights one can see at a small exhibition fair. The narrative line has Erin, who has put her entry into the pumpkin growing contest, join friends and visit a number of displays before she learns that she has won third prize. Although Sheena Lott's illustrations are appropriately multicultural in picturing two of Erin's friends as Oriental, their static nature, evident in the omission of the crowds and confusion typical of modern fairs, gives the story an atmosphere of quaint nostalgia. *Moonsnail Song* differs from the other catalogue books in that its text is not only poetic but is actually a poem. Using a dreamy girl's attachment to a moonsnail shell, the text describes various natural elements of coastal and sea life from dawn to nightfall. A refrain, 'In and out./Out and in', stresses the tidal rhythms governing this life. Sheena Lott's watercolours are generally pale, reinforcing the dreamy nature of the text.

McFarlane's other books are narratives that connect human relationships and animal life. *Waiting for the Whales* is a symbolic tale in which the relationship between an old man and his granddaughter provides the context for a theme about acceptance of the cycle of life. The story is divided into three parts, each describing an emotion and a phase of the cycle. The first stage of the story concentrates on loneliness and on old age. Here the orca, the central symbol in the book, represents life's longings, and the leaping and cavorting of the whales suggest the joys that life brings. The lonely old man thus feels happy only in the summer when these whales come close to shore, where he can watch them. They provide temporary companionship, and their inevitable departure intensifies his sadness. He thus returns to his solitary occupations of planting more than he can eat, gathering clams and seaweed, or gathering herbs and firewood. The second phase concentrates on childhood and the joys of companionable sharing. The transformation occurs on an archetypically symbolic spring day: the old man's daughter arrives with his granddaughter, giving him a companion who shares and therefore makes meaningful the very activities that seemed lonely, dull, and pointless in the first stage of the story. The brief third stage, in which the old man dies, begins with sadness, cycling back to the mood of the opening. In the story's joyful conclusion, however, the granddaughter, who has been told that the old man's spirit is swimming with the whales, is ecstatic to see within a pod of orcas a young calf, the symbol of life's renewal. The story also suggests that life will continue to offer hope and joys to the living. Neither sentimental nor didactic, the text suggests that death is part of the cycle of life but that the life of the deceased continues in the memories of those who knew and loved them. Ron Lightburn's Governor-General's Award-winning illustrations deftly use colour and viewpoint to underscore the meaning of each stage.

In *Eagle Dreams*, the story of a boy who finds a wounded eagle and nurtures it back to health, the eagle is the symbolic animal that affects the relationship between a boy and his father. For Robin, the eagle symbolizes the freedom he dreams of attaining. For his father, it is a nuisance, another distraction that will keep his day-dreaming son, who has a history of neglecting his duties, from doing chores. The eagle thus becomes a test for Robin. By doing his chores even while nurturing the eagle, he proves that he is a responsible boy. Furthermore, Robin's dedication to both the eagle and his chores earns his father's respect. Having given his son the freedom to prove his character, the father gradually loses his stern pragmatism. He thus comes both to admire the wild beauty of the eagle and to form a closer relationship with his son. The conclusion, which indicates that Robin continues to dream about flying with the eagles, suggests that he has been able to mature into a responsible person while holding onto the imaginative sympathy that inspired him to save the eagle. As in *Waiting for the Whales*, Ron Lightburn's manipulation of colour and point of view in the pictures makes this simple story a moving account of a profound moment of change in a child's life.

The euphony, imagery, and poetic, even hypnotic, cadences of McFarlane's texts express a deep love of the natural world. Without resorting to overt didacticism, she establishes that human lives are better when they are connected to and respect nature. Blessed with illustrators capable of giving complementary graphic expression to her ecological vision, she has produced picture books that educate and inspire.

See also: *SATA* 86.

Claire Mackay

Born: 21 December 1930, in Toronto.

Principal Residences: Toronto; Vancouver; Sarnia, Ont.; Regina.

Education: University of Toronto (BA 1952); University of British Columbia; University of Manitoba (Certificate in Rehabilitation Counselling 1971).

Career: librarian; medical social worker; writer.

Major Awards: Ruth Schwartz Children's Book Award, with Marsha Hewitt (1982);Vicky Metcalf Award (1983).

Works for Children

Mini-Bike Hero (Richmond Hill, Ont.: Scholastic, 1974; rev. 1991). **Rev:** *BiC* 20 (Dec. 1991): 38; *CCL* 7 (1977): 36; *CM* 20 (Jan. 1992): 12; *EL* 19 (Jan. 1992): 60; *IR* 9 (Aug. 1975): 38.

Mini-Bike Racer (Richmond Hill, Ont.: Scholastic, 1976; rev. 1991). **Rev:** *BiC* 20 (Dec. 1991): 38; *CCL* 7 (1977): 36; *EL* 19 (Jan. 1992): 60; *IR* 11 (Winter 1977): 36.

Exit Barney McGee (Richmond Hill, Ont.: Scholastic, 1979). **Rev:** *CCL* 20 (1980): 67; *CL* 138 (Fall 1993): 172; *IR* 16 (Feb. 1982): 45.

One Proud Summer, with Marsha Hewitt (Richmond Hill, Ont.: Scholastic, 1981). **Rev:** *BiC* 10 (1981): 5; *CCL* 29 (1983): 45; *IR* 16 (Feb. 1982): 39.

Mini-Bike Rescue (Richmond Hill, Ont.: Scholastic, 1982; rev. 1991). **Rev:** *BiC* 20 (Dec. 1991): 38; *EL* 19 (Jan. 1992): 60; *QQ* 49 (May 1983): 12.

The Minerva Program (Toronto: James Lorimer, 1984). **Rev:** *BiC* 13 (Aug. 1984): 32; *CCL* 43 (1986): 47.

Pay Cheques and Picket Lines: All About Unions in Canada (Toronto: Kids Can Press, 1987). **Rev:** *BiC* 17 (Apr. 1988): 36; *CM* 16 (July 1988): 76; *EL* 15 (Mar. 1988): 26.

The Toronto Story (Willowdale, Ont.: Firefly Books, 1991). **Rev:** *CCL* 64 (1991): 80; *QQ* 56 (Nov. 1990): 13.

Touching All the Bases: Baseball for Kids of All Ages (Richmond Hill, Ont.: Scholastic, 1994). **Rev:** *CBRA* (1994): 540; *CM* 22 (Nov. 1994): 224; *EL* 22 (Jan. 1995): 56.

Bats About Baseball, with Jean Little, illustrated by Kim LaFave (Toronto: Viking, 1994). **Rev:** *BiC* 24 (Sept. 1995): 50; *CBRA* (1995): 76; *CCL* 87 (1997): 66; *EL* 23 (Mar. 1996): 24; *QQ* 61 (Mar. 1995): 78.

Laughs: Funny Stories Selected by Claire Mackay (Toronto: Tundra, 1997). **Rev:** *BiC* 26 (June 1997): 35; *EL* 25 (Mar. 1998): 27; *QQ* 63 (Mar. 1998): 27.

Other

'Real Plums in Imaginary Cakes', *CCL* 54 (1989): 26–30.

'What's in a Name: Selecting Names for Your Characters', *Writers on Writing: Guide to Writing and Illustrating Children's Books*, ed. David Booth (Markham, Ont.: Overlea House, 1989), 82–7.

Selected Discussions

Jenkinson, Dave. 'Claire Mackay: Mini-Bikes, Strikes and Mini-Computers', *EL* 15 (Nov. 1987): 59–64.

Michasiw, Barbara. 'An Interview with Claire Mackay', *CCL* 64 (1991): 6–25.

When Claire Mackay was eight years old, she wrote and published her own newspaper; but it was not until over 30 years later that she became a professional writer of children's books. Born and raised in a politically active and radical family, she was a social worker before she wrote what became her first book, *Mini-Bike Hero*, for her son. It is the story of Steve MacPherson, who must hide his passionate interest in mini-bikes from his father. With the aid of a kindly motorcycle shopkeeper, he learns the skills of cross-country racing and is instrumental in saving a group of campers from a flash flood. In addition to the exciting events, the book is noteworthy for its presentation of the moral dilemmas Steve faces and for its communication of the joys of riding.

Two sequels are less successful. In *Mini-Bike Racer*, Steve is kidnapped by an escaped convict and then rescued by his best friend. Although the tensions of friendship are well portrayed, the adventure story is somewhat sensational and contrived. In *Mini-Bike Rescue*, Julie Brennan is sent to Ontario for the summer so that she can become more ladylike. The girl wins her family's respect when she solves the mystery of a series of robberies and rescues an old man from a forest fire and an angry bear. Although Julie's character growth is clearly delineated, it sometimes seems secondary to the plot.

In *Exit Barney McGee*, the 13-year-old hero feels abandoned after his mother remarries and has a child. He runs away to Toronto, where he finds his father, an alcoholic living in a rundown boarding house. He comes to understand the good points of the man who ran out on his mother and himself, but more important, he realizes that his true home is back with his mother, stepfather, and stepsister. The book is very strong in its portrayal of the conflicting emotions and loyalties Barney experiences, and it reflects Mackay's understanding, gained during her years as a social worker, of the emotional difficulties faced by many young people today.

One Proud Summer, co-authored with Marsha Hewitt, is based on events surrounding the Quebec Textile Workers' Strike of 1946. Thirteen-year-old Lucille Laplante becomes involved in the labour dispute and joins the strikers. Frightened and insecure at the beginning, she develops courage as she fights the ruthless attempts to suppress the walkout. The book, which expresses the author's radical leanings, has been carefully researched, but reads at times like a historical tract, with the characters generally portrayed as good if they support the workers and bad, or misled, if they do not.

When the insecure 14-year-old heroine of *The Minerva Program* is chosen to be a member of a special computer class, she feels that she has found her niche. However, her happiness does not last: she is accused of using the computer to alter her grades. In her search for the culprit, she learns that she has been guilty of misunderstanding several of her classmates and teachers. She also develops a much closer relationship with her working mother.

In her three books of non-fiction, Mackay combines the results of her painstaking, objective research with her emotional involvement in the subjects to create works that combine fact and interpretation in a style that is witty and relaxed, but does not trivialize the material presented. *Pay Cheques and Picket Lines: All About Unions in Canada*, an outgrowth of her lifelong contact with labour movements, explains the origins, functions, and future of these organizations along with accounts of major Canadian strikes. Quotations from participants, photographs, sketches, and short boxes of related material create an immediacy to material that could otherwise overwhelm her intended audience. *The Toronto Story*, about her hometown, and *Touching All the Bases: Baseball for Kids of All Ages*, about her favourite sport, use similar techniques and formats with equal success.

In her fiction, Claire Mackay exhibits a tremendous sensitivity to the feelings of young adolescents. She understands the conflicts and uncertainties they experience, the joy they take in activities they love, and their painful realization of the difficulties faced by the adults who seem to control their lives. In her non-fiction, she respects her audiences' attitudes towards factual material and communicates her respect for her subjects in a manner that is both educational and entertaining.

See also: *CA* 105; *CLR* 43; *CANR* 22, 50; *SAAS* 25; *SATA* 40, 97; *TCCW*; *WSMP*.

Janet McNaughton

Born: 29 November 1953, in Toronto.

Principal Residences: Toronto; St John's, Nfld.

Education: York University (BA 1978); Memorial University of Newfoundland (MA 1983, Ph.D. 1989).

Career: freelance writer.

Major Awards: IODE (Toronto) Book Award (1997); Geoffrey Bilson Award for Historical Fiction for Young People (1997); IODE Violet Downey Book Award (1997); Ann Connor-Brimer Award (1997, 1999).

Works for Children

Catch Me Once, Catch Me Twice (St John's, Nfld: Tuckamore, 1994). **Rev:** *BiC* 23 (Sept. 1994): 58; *CBRA* (1994): 491; *CCL* 84 (1996): 113; *CM* 22 (Oct. 1994): 179; *QQ* 60 (Apr. 1994): 40.

To Dance at the Palais Royale (St John's, Nfld: Tuckamore, 1996). **Rev:** *BiC* 26 (May 1997): 33; *CBRA* (1996): 484; *QQ* 62 (Aug. 1996): 42.

Make or Break Spring (St John's, Nfld: Tuckamore Books, 1998). **Rev:** *BiC* 27 (May 1998): 34; *QQ* 64 (May 1998): 34.

Publishing three novels in four years, Janet McNaughton has quickly established herself as a distinguished author of historical novels for young adults. In each novel, McNaughton combines insightful examinations of complex adolescent lives with an exploration of various social types.

McNaughton's first novel, *Catch Me Once, Catch Me Twice*, contains both historical realism and fantasy. Set in St John's, Newfoundland, during the fall and winter of 1942, it focuses on 12-year-old Evelyn (Ev) McCallum. Having moved from her outport home to the house of her grandparents, Ev is unhappy: her father, serving with the military in North Africa, has not replied to her weekly letters; her pregnant mother, wallowing in self-pity, ignores her; her grandmother is cold and snobbishly decorous. Fortunately, her grandfather is sensitive to her needs and encourages her friendship with Peter Tilley, a boy from a poorer section of town afflicted with a severe limp. Through her sometimes uneasy relationship with Peter, Ev forms bonds with Peter's grandmother and 'Uncle' Chesley Barrett, two elderly people who become confidants and mentors. The major crisis in Ev's development occurs after a fairy promises that he will give Ev her heart's desire if she can catch him again. Ev sets out to catch the fairy, but she is uncertain whether to wish for the safety of her father, who has been reported as missing in action, or that of her mother, who is in hospital facing a severely complicated delivery. Because Ev does not again catch the fairy, however, she learns that magic will not resolve her anxieties and that she must face life's problems realistically.

The fantasy section complements the social realism by introducing folk beliefs. Furthermore, because the fairy wants to make off with Ev, he symbolizes the psychological dangers Ev faces, paralleling the physical and social dangers afforded by the soldiers and sailors stationed in the city. These physical dangers are particularly apparent in the unresolved subplot of Millie, Ev's grandparents' maid, who refuses to continue seeing an American soldier named Gerry: subsequently, he harasses Millie, accosts Ev at night, and may be responsible for burning a dance hall. Nevertheless, the brief fantasy section weakens the credibility of the dominant realism, adding to the ungainliness of a novel that attempts to develop too many subplots.

The sequel, *Make or Break Spring*, eschews fantasy and succeeds in integrating its various plot strands into a coherent coming-of-age story. Set in 1945, it recounts how Ev overcomes a series of emotional tribulations and discovers what she wants to become. One plot thread has Ev nursing resentment of Dr John Thorne, who seems to be courting her mother. A second has her torn by her feelings for two boys. Ev enjoys studying with Peter Tilley, with whom she shares her deepest feelings and secrets, but she is physically attracted to handsome, athletic Stan Dawe, a rich boy with absolutely no sense of humour. A third plot line has Ev consumed by hatred after a returning soldier reveals that he may have accidentally caused the death of Ev's father. All three plot lines are resolved because of a dramatic crisis. After Ev screams that Dr Thorne is not his father, Ian, her two-and-a-half-year-old brother, runs away and tumbles down a hill, knocking himself into a coma. Dr Thorne saves Ian's life, thereby making Ev realize that he is a good man who will make her mother happy and that she, too, wants to be a doctor. Because Peter, from whom she became estranged when she began dating Stan, secretly visits Ian in the hospital, Ev realizes that he has the depth of character missing in the superficial Stan, and she soon reconciles with him. Finally, after hearing her grandfather declare that hatred of Germany after World War I created the conditions that caused World War II, Ev matures into a realization that she cannot allow herself to be consumed by hatred for the Germans or for the soldier who may have caused her father's death. Although in outline it seems like a melodramatic and conventional love story in which a girl learns to value substance over appearance and to accept positive attitudes over negative ones, in *Make or Break Spring* the presentations of the social milieu and of the inner life of Ev and of Peter are so vivid that it succeeds as a plausible account of adolescent development during turbulent times.

Even more successful, however, is *To Dance at the Palais Royale*, in which an immigrant's experiences offer revealing vignettes of social history while developing a story of personal maturation. Agnes (Aggie) Maxwell has grown up in a poor, coal-mining community in Scotland, in a large household dominated by her stern father. On her seventeenth birthday, Aggie, like her sister Emma before her, is to leave for Canada to work as a domestic servant in order to earn enough money to bring over the rest of her family. Discrete episodes illustrate social attitudes and conditions. The initial scenes in Scotland show the bleak outlook for those living in the dirty coal town that has claimed the life of Aggie's brother. They also establish her father's harsh and joyless moralism, evident in a whipping he gives to her younger siblings for stealing from the church collection. Aggie's journey by ship and train details some of the hardships immigrants suffered.

The bulk of the novel, however, introduces characters typifying attitudes of those living in Toronto in the two years prior to the stock market crash of 1929. Aggie's wealthy employers, the Stockwoods, display the class bias that unfairly judges those of lower station when they accuse Aggie of stealing. By proving that Aggie is innocent, however, their son, Rodney, shows that some members of the privileged classes reject the stereotypes that condemn the lower classes as prone to immorality. Rose Chandler, Rodney's fun-loving friend, represents those who develop attitudes from books instead of from observation. Addicted to romantic novels in which true love dissolves class barriers, Rose introduces Aggie to some of the joys of social life, taking her dancing at the Palais Royale. Bobby Chandler, Rose's brother, illustrates the absurdity of the class bias that actually dominates social relationships. Thinking that Aggie is wealthy when he meets her at the Palais Royale, he becomes infatuated. On a later occasion, discovering that Aggie is only a servant, he angrily storms away. (A lawyer, he eventually marries a secretary, someone occupying a socially acceptable position.) Rachel Mendorfsky, a Russian Jew to whom Aggie teaches English, illustrates the experiences of minority immigrant groups and provides a way of revealing the bigotry of the Anglo-Christian majority. Finally, the men dating Aggie and her sister show that people of the same class can be radically different. Stuart, an arrogant lower-class dandy, threatens to end their relationship unless Emma satisfies his sexual demands. (The novel implies that Emma gives in and becomes pregnant.) Will Collins, the Newfoundlander who courts Aggie, on the other hand, aware of his own bitter experiences as an illegitimate child, is respectful of Aggie. Aggie herself begins as an innocent—she doesn't learn how babies are made until she is 18—but she matures, finally facing her father without fear when he arrives in Canada. She thus symbolizes the independent spirit fostered by experiences in Canada.

To Dance at the Palais Royale is a historical romance, but its uncompromising realism makes it anti-romantic in that it eschews the social and psychological distortions of sentimentality. McNaughton's other novels are more conventional in resolving their plots, but all of her novels illuminate the biases that unfairly affected many Canadians whose social position, ethnic background, accent, or physical disabilities set them apart from the majority. What makes these novels compelling, however, is not their implicit social messages but the complex characters at their centre.

Kevin Major

Born: 12 September 1949, in Stephenville, Nfld.

Principal Residences: Stephenville; Eastport, Nfld; St John's, Nfld.

Education: Memorial University of Newfoundland (B.Sc. 1973).

Career: high school teacher; substitute teacher; writer.

Major Awards: Canada Council Award for Children's Literature (1978); Ruth Schwartz Children's Book Award (1979); Canadian Association of Children's Librarians Book of the Year Award (1979, 1992); Canadian Library Association Young Adult Book Award (1981); Vicky Metcalf Award (1992); Ann Connor Brimer Award (1992, 1998); Mr Christie's Book Award, ages 8–11 (1997).

Works for Children

Hold Fast (Toronto: Clarke Irwin, 1978). **Rev:** *APBR* 10 (Nov. 1983): 2, 18; *CCB-B* 33 (June 1980): 196; *CCL* 14 (1979): 81; *HB* 60 (Feb. 1984): 99; *IR* 12 (Summer 1978): 70; *Maclean's* 102 (17 Apr. 1989): 61; *SLJ* 26 (May 1980): 78.

Far From Shore (Toronto: Clarke Irwin, 1980). **Rev:** *BiC* 9 (Dec 1980): 21; *CCL* 22 (1981): 50; *CL* 93 (Summer 1982): 154; *CM* 9 (1981): 93; *IR* 15 (Feb. 1981): 42; *Maclean's* 93 (15 Dec. 1980): 56.

Thirty-Six Exposures (Toronto: Delacorte, 1984): **Rev:** *BiC* 14 (Jan.-Feb. 1985): 16/17; *CCL* 43 (1986): 56; *CL* 106 (1985): 118; *CM* 13 (Mar. 1985): 67; *QQ* 50 (Nov. 1984): 18.

Dear Bruce Springsteen (Toronto: Doubleday, 1987). **Rev:** *BiC* 16 (Dec. 1987): 11; *CCB-B* 41 (May 1988): 183; *CCL* 51 (1988): 78; *CM* 16 (Sept. 1988): 172; *EL* 16 (Mar. 1989): 22; *Maclean's* 102 (17 Apr. 1989): 61; *QQ* 53 (Aug. 1987): 4.

Blood Red Ochre (Toronto: Doubleday, 1989). **Rev:** *BYP* 3 (Apr. 1989): 14; *CCB-B* 42 (Apr. 1989): 200; *CCL* 61 (1991): 59; *HB* (Sept.-Oct. 1989): 659.

Eating Between the Lines (Toronto: Doubleday, 1991). **Rev:** *CM* 20 (Jan. 1992): 26; *QQ* 57 (Sept. 1991): 57.

Diana: My Autobiography (Toronto: Doubleday, 1993). **Rev:** *BiC* 22 (Oct. 1993): 57; *CCL* 76 (1994): 91; *EL* 21 (Mar. 1994): 17; *QQ* 59 (Apr. 1993): 31.

The House of Wooden Santas, illus. Imelda George, photos by Ned Pratt (Red Deer, Alta: Red Deer College Press, 1997). **Rev:** *CBRA* (1997): 481; *CM* 4 (13 Mar. 1998): on-line; *QQ* 63 (Oct. 1997): 40.

Other

Doryloads: Newfoundland Writings and Art, ed. (Portugal Cove, Nfld: Breakwater Books, 1974).

'My Life and Letters', *CCL* 54 (1989): 6–25.

No Man's Land (Toronto: Doubleday, 1995) [adult novel].

Gaffer: A Novel of Newfoundland (Toronto: Doubleday, 1997) [adult novel].

Selected Discussions

Brown, Lloyd. 'Kevin Major: Newfoundland's Problem Novelist', *CCL* 66 (1992): 23–34.

Duffy, Mary. 'A Sense of Truth', *CM* 17 (Dec. 1989): 255–6.

Jenkinson, Dave. 'Kevin Major', *EL* 19 (Jan.-Feb. 1992): 66–70.

Jones, Raymond E. 'Local Color, Universal Problems: The Novels of Kevin Major', *ChLQ* 10 (Fall 1985): 140–1.

McNaughton, Janet. 'Major's Moves', *QQ* 59 (Apr. 1993): 1, 30.

Posesorski, Sherie. 'Kevin Major', *BiC* 13 (Dec. 1984): 24–5.

Variety is the hallmark of Kevin Major's career. Constantly changing his narrative approach, style, or subject matter, he is perpetually 'reinventing' himself as author, he says, in order to keep both the writer and the audience interested in each new work. In the early stages of his career, Major achieved success and notoriety as a problem novelist. Critics praised his honest representations of adolescent life, but several school boards and libraries banned his books because of their blunt language and frank discussions of sex, alcohol, and drugs. In his fifth novel, *Blood Red Ochre*, Major took the problem novel in new directions by combining it with a historical narrative. Since then, he has made a radical break from what he calls the 'high realism' of his early books, showing himself adept as a comic novelist in *Eating Between the Lines*, a fantasy, and in *Diana: My Autobiography*, a farce with a female narrator. With *No Man's Land*, Major has reinvented himself as author of serious adult historical fiction.

Major's first novels—*Hold Fast*, *Far from Shore*, *Thirty-six Exposures*, and, to a lesser degree, *Dear Bruce Springsteen*—reflect his Newfoundland heritage. In fact, his work as a teacher in the outports focused Major's writing ambition: 'I saw that there were very few novels that had characters in any way like the students in my classes. The settings were very foreign, the plots of little relevance to their lives.' Having decided to write a novel from the viewpoint of a Newfoundland teenager, he gave up full-time teaching and became a substitute teacher. Major's first three novels, *Hold Fast*, *Far from Shore*, and *Thirty-six Exposures*, are distinctive blends of Newfoundland local colour and the universal problems of adolescence. He had, he says, two main objectives in writing them: 'to say something about growing up generally (the problems, joys, frustrations that are universal) and to portray life in present-day Newfoundland outport society'.

The presentation of Newfoundland life in these novels focuses on destructive changes. In *Hold Fast*, the outport of Marten, presented through the eyes of 14-year-old Michael, is idyllic. He identifies life there with family ties and a closeness to nature gained through such traditional practices as squidding with his father and grandfather. Sent to live with his dictatorial uncle after his parents are killed by a drunk driver, he discovers what modern concerns have done to traditional Newfoundland values. Obsessed by possessions and the desire to dominate others, his uncle alienates both his own children and Michael. Furthermore, Michael's outport habits of speech and interest in nature mark him as a 'baywop', an outsider continually scorned by urban teenagers. Only by running back to Marten does he find meaning: he realizes that he can 'hold fast' to himself through memories of his father and grandfather and by living with caring relatives in the outport.

The traditional life that provides solace in *Hold Fast* is a victim of modern economic conditions in *Far from Shore*. Christopher Slade changes when his father, a chronically unemployed man whose heavy drinking threatens the survival of the family, heads to Calgary to search for work. Left without guidance and the visible signs of love, Chris loses interest in school, fails, and begins running around with a heavy-drinking, rowdy group. He eventually gets into legal trouble. Furthermore, his mother comes close to having an affair with her boss. Only the return of the father restores order. The novel implies, however, that unless the father finds work soon, the family will have to leave Newfoundland to avoid destruction.

Thirty-six Exposures is not as detailed in its look at Newfoundland life, but it is permeated with the despair of young people who feel that they will have to leave the island to have any chance of securing employment or leading meaningful lives. The death of Trevor in a car crash on graduation night symbolizes the self-destruction of the island's youth, who have lost hope of a future. The young protagonist's departure for Europe suggests that youth must look elsewhere for meaning.

Dear Bruce Springsteen marked a significant and somewhat disappointing departure for Major: its generic setting and its references to Springsteen, an enormously popular American singer when the novel was published, suggest a deliberate attempt to capture an American readership. The high unemployment caused by a mill closure links the novel to the portraits of Newfoundland in the previous books, but nothing else, not even Terry Blanchard's frequently ungrammatical statements, suggests that the novel is set in Newfoundland, or even Canada: Terry's unnamed hometown could be almost anywhere in eastern North America.

Although social conditions are important in these books, Major is not merely a regionalist or a social realist. He emphasizes psychology instead of sociology, and character instead of topical problems: 'the problems are never the focus of the novels. My emphasis is on how individual characters cope with the problems.' To achieve this emphasis, he adopted a different narrative approach for each work. *Hold Fast* employs a typical device of problem novels, an adolescent first-person narrator. But Michael is not merely a conventional narrator. Speaking in outport dialect, he seems to be a plausible and unique individual. Some reviewers even compare him to Huck Finn and Holden Caulfield, first-person narrators who also have undertaken journeys that lead to self-discovery and who have, albeit somewhat naïvely at times, honestly and clearly presented a vision of adult society.

Major felt that much fiction teenagers read is 'one-sided' because 'we see everything from one point of view.' A reading of Faulkner shortly before he began his second novel provided a way for Major to expand the characters and story. In *Far from Shore* he uses the Faulknerian device of multiple narrators—Chris Slade is the central narrator, but four more narrators provide additional perspectives. This narrative device successfully conveys Chris's confusion of motives and the difficulty that others have in understanding him. A similar attempt at stylistic innovation is apparent in *Thirty-six Exposures*, which is divided into 36 sections, each like a frame of film snapped by Lorne, a student whose passion is photography. Each chapter, that is, presents a dominant feeling or an episode important to Lorne. Furthermore, Lorne's poems, interspersed throughout the third-person narrative, provide a sense of first-person intimacy. Unfortunately, Major does not accompany the formal experimentation with an equally good plot. He resolves the central problem of student rights and the morality of revenge by falling back on an improbable love story that causes the entire novel to lose thematic focus.

Dear Bruce Springsteen returns to a single uncomplicated viewpoint. The novel consists of letters that Terry Blanchard, a 14-year-old boy trying to come to terms with his parents' separation, sends to Bruce Springsteen. Springsteen provides Terry with a therapeutic outlet for his feelings about his father, his mother's new boyfriend, his problems at school, and his fears about dating. Furthermore, Springsteen's biography and lyrics help Terry to cope with his own situation, leading him to a sympathetic understanding of the feelings and needs of both his father and his mother. Although its plot is too predictable, this novel conveys an understanding of the powerful emotional role music plays in the lives of teens, and it provides a convincing portrait of a boy working through fears of inadequacy to maturer feelings of acceptance.

A daring departure from these early works, *Blood Red Ochre* alternates third-person and first-person viewpoints, and it also combines three genres: adolescent problem novel, historical fiction, and time-shift fantasy. The third-person chapters are set in the present and focus on 15-year-old David, who has discovered that his mother's husband is not his biological father. David eventually meets his real father but does not think much of the man. Attracted to Nancy, a mysterious new classmate, David works with her on a school project about the extinction of Newfoundland's Beothuk Indians. Alternate chapters are set in the past and are narrated by Dauoodaset, a 15-year-old Beothuk valiantly trying to save his starving people. A time-shift fantasy links the stories. Nancy, in her own first-person chapter, reveals that she is actually Shanawdithit, Dauoodaset's betrothed. She takes David into the past in the hope that his awareness of the Beothuks' condition will somehow prevent the extinction of her people. Tragically, a white hunter kills Dauoodaset, and Shanawdithit, knowing that she is the last of her people, paddles away. Having seen senseless destruction in the past, David reconciles himself to the present, going 'back to his home and his family'.

Blood Red Ochre is not entirely successful. Its best parts are the tense and emotionally gripping historical sections. The present-day problem novel is neither dramatically nor thematically satisfying because it lacks a sharp focus and a clear resolution. The linking time-shift fantasy is logically weak, failing to explain the magic that enables Shanawdithit/Nancy to travel in time or to make sufficiently clear her plans in bringing David back with her. Its dramatic events, however, bring historical attitudes alive and develop the personalities of the three protagonists.

In *Eating Between the Lines*, which employs conventional third-person narration, Major spices standard ingredients of adolescent fiction with comic fantasy. Sixteen-year-old Jackson is the centre of a double plot in which he tries to break up one romantic relationship and save another. In love for the first time, Jackson tries to convince Sara, the girl of his dreams, that she should break up with Adam, her almost-perfect boyfriend, and go out with him. He also tries to rejuvenate his parents' disintegrating marriage: his mother has announced that she is going to leave in two weeks unless her dull, spiritless husband changes. With magical help, Jackson succeeds in both quests. He discovers that the gold pizza token he won at the grand opening of Masterpizza can transport him into any book that he reads. His adventures in *The Odyssey*, *Huckleberry Finn*, and *Romeo and Juliet* bring him the understanding to solve his difficulties with school work and to make Sara fall in love with him. By using the token with his mother's diary, he takes his parents back into the time of his own birth, thereby rekindling their romance. Showing true maturity and insight, Jackson ultimately gives up the magic token because he realizes that he doesn't need magic to make his life more satisfying. Amusing episodes, witty social satire, sly sexual references, and a naïve yet forceful protagonist make *Eating Between the Lines* an accomplished comic novel.

The naïvety of the narrator is more pronounced in *Diana: My Autobiography*, a spoof of both the public's excessive fascination with the British Royal Family and a typical pre-teen's egocentric absorption with her identity. Here, Major experiments with yet another approach, having a female provide two narratives in each chapter. Inspired by reading Andrew Morton's *Diana: Her True Story*, Diana Major, fictional daughter of the author, writes her autobiography, rendered in italics at the beginning of every chapter. It is an inflated, self-aggrandizing account burlesquing the pomposity of Morton's book. Following each autobiographical entry is Diana's equally blinkered narration of her current adventures, rendered in roman type. When an English family visits Newfoundland for the summer, Diana, who once believed that she was a princess adopted by ordinary Canadians, becomes convinced that they are aristocrats and that the son, Will Smith, is attracted to her. After numerous comic mistakes trying to win his affection, Diana overhears Will talking with his mother and realizes that he is not interested in her. Because of this painful revelation, Diana matures, putting aside her childish obsession with the British aristocracy and reconciling with her best friend, from whom she became estranged because of her infatuation with Will.

Motifs of perception form the thematic core of *Diana: My Autobiography*, with comical misperceptions indicating immaturity. In the end, differences in perception hone the comic edge: Diana, appearing in makeup, upswept hair, and a gown, giggles uncontrollably, showing that she is not entirely ready to abandon childhood; her confused father and her brother are relieved by the familiar girlish laugh, but her mother praises her for being 'positively royal'. By eschewing an overly dramatic change in character and by presenting contrasting visions of Diana, this coming-of-age farce avoids slipping into sentimentality.

The House of Wooden Santas, Major's first picture book, is something like an Advent calendar: each chapter focuses on one of the 24 days leading up to Christmas, presenting the reader with both a lavish photograph of an unusual carved Santa and a narrative event linked to that figure. Each day, nine-year old Jesse's mother carves a new Santa that represents an element of her son's feelings or activities. Unfortunately, no one buys her carvings, so she is unable to pay the rent. When Jonathan, an obnoxious boy at school, begins teasing him and their landlady says that they have to move, Jesse loses faith in Santa Claus. Other people also have troubles: Jonathan is obnoxious because his father has turned surly after being injured at work, and Mrs Wentzell, the landlady, has suffered such loneliness after the death of her husband that she has become an intolerant and bitter old woman. Eventually, Jesse and Jonathan become friends and try to bring the Christmas spirit to Mrs Wentzell. Nothing goes according to plan, but Mrs Wentzell and the rest of the characters gain renewed faith and hope for the future. *The House of the Wooden Santas* mixes social realism with a touch of sentiment—but not sentimentality—to produce a warm-hearted tale that respects probability yet celebrates the concern for others that underlies the true significance of Christmas.

Kevin Major's novels are significant for their frankness, for their willingness to tackle significant themes with honesty and humour, and for the respect that they have always shown to young adults. Several years ago, however, Major expressed frustration with responses to his work: 'Many reviewers have the notion that anyone who writes novels that appeal to young people must in some way be less of a writer than, say, someone who writes purely "adult" fiction. I want my work to be judged on its quality, on how well it works as a piece of fiction. A well-written book is a well-written book, no matter who it appeals to.' *No Man's Land* (1995) and *Gaffer: A Novel of Newfoundland* (1997), two adult novels, may be signs that Major now demands the respect that comes to successful writers of adult books. Those who believe that young adults deserve well-written books and that someone who succeeds in doing something different for them each time is an artist worthy of respect can only hope that he will not permanently reinvent himself as an adult novelist.

See also: *CA* 97–100; *CANR* 21, 38; *CLC* 26; *CLR* 11; *DLB* 60; *MAICYA*; *MCAI*; *Profiles* 2; *SATA* 32; *TCYAW*; *WSMP*.

Markoosie

Born: 19 June 1942, in Port Harrison, Que.

Principal Residences: Port Harrison; Yellowknife, NWT; Inukjuak, Que.

Career: aviator; translator; civil administrator; writer.

Works for Children

Harpoon of the Hunter, illus. Germaine Arnaktauyok (Montreal: McGill-Queen's UP, 1970). **Rev:** *CCB-B* 24 (May 1971): 141; *Canadian Forum* 51 (June 1971): 33; *Canadian Geographical Journal* 83 (Aug. 1971) 4; *IR* 5 (Summer 1971): 34.

Harpoon of the Hunter, the first novel to be written by a Canadian Inuk, is the work of a northern bush pilot, Markoosie, who began writing after reading an Inuk autobiography published in a Canadian government magazine. His adventure-survival saga first appeared in the Inuit periodical *Inuttituut* and was later translated into English. It has since been published in several languages, receiving high critical acclaim. *Harpoon of the Hunter* is the story of 16-year-old Kamik who joins his father and a party of hunters searching for a rabid polar bear. Although the animal is finally killed, so too are all the other hunters. The youth, alone and without dogs, makes a long, difficult journey back to his people. Reunited with them, he joins his small village in its move to a larger community located across a wide, dangerous river. During the crossing, his mother and new wife are drowned, and Kamik, drifting on a loose ice floe, kills himself in despair.

The book is a consciously, although somewhat roughly crafted and structured novel. When Kamik finally kills the bear, he proves his manhood by avenging the death of his father. Although his suicide shocks many non-Inuit readers, careful rereading of the novel in the light of the ending reveals many statements, implicit ironies, and foreshadowings that show that Markoosie never intended a conventional happy ending, that his novel is a study of grim fortitude in the face of ever-present death. The harpoon with which Kamik gathers food, slays the polar bear, and finally kills himself symbolizes the confrontation between life and death. At one point the author notes, 'By his side is his harpoon, which can mean life or death. The harpoon which is so small, yet holds such power.' Although descriptions of Kamik's relationship with the young woman he marries read a little like a Hollywood romance, *Harpoon of the Hunter* has deservedly achieved the status of a minor Canadian classic.

See also: *CLR* 23; *CA* 101; *Profiles*; *TCCW*.

Michael Martchenko

Born: 1 August 1942, in Carcassone, France.

Principal Residences: Carcassone; Toronto.

Education: Ontario College of Art, Toronto (Associate, 1966).

Career: advertising agency art director; illustrator; author.

Works for Children

Written and Illustrated by Michael Martchenko

Birdfeeder Banquet (Toronto: Annick, 1990). **Rev:** *CCL* 67 (1992): 107; *QQ* 57 (Jan. 1991): 22.

Illustrated by Michael Martchenko

The Paper Bag Princess, by Robert Munsch (Toronto: Annick, 1980). **Rev:** *BiC* 9 (Dec. 1980): 19; *CBRA* (1979): 211; *CCL* 22 (1981): 56, and 26 (1982): 92; *EL* 9 (Sept. 1981): 28, and 9 (Nov. 1981); 35; *IR* 15 (Apr. 1981): 49, and 16 (Feb. 1982): 47; *QQ* 47 (Feb. 1981): 47, and 48 (May 1982): 37, and 48 (June 1982): 3; *TES* (21 May 1982): 31.

Jonathan Cleaned Up, Then He Heard a Sound; or, Blackberry Subway Jam, by Robert Munsch (Toronto: Annick, 1981). **Rev:** *BiC* 10 (Oct. 1981): 33; *CBRA* (1981): 229; *EL* 9 (Nov. 1981): 35; *IR* 15 (Oct. 1981): 46; *QQ* 47 (Aug. 1981): 29; *SLJ* 28 (Apr. 1982): 60.

The Boy in the Drawer, by Robert Munsch (Toronto: Annick, 1982). **Rev:** *BiC* 11 (Aug.-Sept. 1982): 39; *CBRA* (1982): 240; *CCL* 30 (1983): 88; *QQ* 48 (Aug. 1982): 28.

Murmel, Murmel, Murmel, by Robert Munsch (Toronto: Annick, 1982). **Rev:** *BiC* 11 (Dec. 1982): 8; *CBRA* (1982): 241; *CCL* 30 (1983): 88; *Maclean's* 95 (13 Dec. 1982): 56-68.

Angela's Airplane, by Robert Munsch (Toronto: Annick, 1983; rev. edn, 1988). **Rev:** *BiC* 12 (May 1983): 31; *CBRA* (1988): 277; *CCL* 30 (1983): 88; *EL* 11 (Nov. 1983): 37; *QQ* 49 (Aug. 1983): 34.

David's Father, by Robert Munsch (Toronto: Annick, 1983). **Rev:** *CBRA* (1983): 280; *BiC* 12 (Dec. 1983): 13; *CCL* 39/40 (1985): 125; *QQ* 49 (July 1983): 10, and 49 (Nov. 1983): 23; *SLJ* 30 (May 1984): 68.

The Fire Station, by Robert Munsch (Toronto: Annick, 1983). **Rev:** *CBRA* (1991): 317; *CCL* 30 (1983): 88; *EL* 11 (Nov. 1983): 37; *QQ* 49 (July 1983): 10, and 57 (June 1991): 25.

Mortimer, by Robert Munsch (Toronto: Annick, 1983). **Rev:** *BiC* 12 (May 1983): 31; *CBRA* (1985): 253; *CCL* 30 (1983): 88; *EL* 11 (Nov. 1983): 37; *QQ* 49 (July 1983): 10.

Matthew and the Midnight Tow Truck, by Allen Morgan (Toronto: Annick, 1984). **Rev:** *CCL* 39-40 (1985): 125–30.

Matthew and the Midnight Turkeys, by Allen Morgan (Toronto: Annick, 1985).

Thomas' Snowsuit, by Robert Munsch (Toronto: Annick, 1985). **Rev:** *BiC* 14 (Nov. 1985): 37, and 20 (Oct. 1991): 26; *CBRA* (1985): 254; *CM* 14 (Jan. 1986): 30; *EL* 13 (Mar. 1986): 15, and 15 (Sept. 1987): 19; *Maclean's* 98 (9 Dec. 1985): 44; *QQ* 51 (Dec. 1985): 30; *SLJ* 32 (Apr. 1986): 77.

50 Below Zero, by Robert Munsch (Toronto: Annick, 1986). **Rev:** *CCL* 44 (1986): 95; *EL* 14 (Mar. 1987): 47; *QQ* 52 (Apr. 1986): 26; *SLJ* 33 (Mar. 1987): 148.

Hurrah for the Dorchester, by Anne Fotheringham (Montreal: Conceptus Renaissance, 1986).

I Have to Go!, by Robert Munsch (Toronto: Annick, 1986). **Rev:** *CBRA* (1987): 228; *CCL* 46 (1987): 108: *EL* 14 (Mar. 1987): 47; *SL* 38 (Aug. 1990): 104; *SLJ* 34 (Jan. 1988): 68.

Matthew and the Midnight Money Van, by Allen Morgan (Toronto: Annick, 1987). **Rev:** *CCL* 47 (1987): 96.

Moira's Birthday, by Robert Munsch (Toronto: Annick, 1987). **Rev:** *BiC* 16 (Dec. 1987): 12; *BYP* 1 (Dec. 1987): 6; *CBRA* (1995): 479; *CM* 16 (May 1988): 100; *EL* 15 (Mar. 1988): 23.

One Sock, Two Socks, by Judy Owens (Toronto: Gage, 1987).

Pigs, by Robert Munsch (Toronto: Annick, 1989). **Rev:** *BYP* 3 (June 1989): 8; *CBRA* (1995): 479; *CM* 17 (July 1989): 190.

Jeremy's Decision, by Ardyth Brott (Toronto: Oxford UP, 1990). **Rev:** *CBRA* (1990): 288; *CCL* 64 (1991): 73.

Something Good, by Robert Munsch (Toronto: Annick, 1990). **Rev:** *BiC* 19 (June 1990): 16; *CBRA* (1991): 301, and (1995): 479; *CCL* 61 (1991): 104; *CM* 18 (July 1990): 181; *EL* 18 (Mar. 1991): 24; *QQ* 56 (June 1990): 16.

Show and Tell, by Robert Munsch (Toronto: Annick, 1991). **Rev:** *BiC* 20 (Dec. 1991): 37; *CBRA* (1991): 317; *CCL* 69 (1993): 87; *CL* (Autumn 1992): 164; *CM* 19 (Nov. 1991): 354; *QQ* 57 (Oct. 1991): 36; *RT* 45 (Apr. 1992): 639.

Zoomerang a Boomerang: Poems to Make Your Belly Laugh, ed. Caroline Parry (Toronto: Kids Can Press, 1991). **Rev:** *CBRA* (1992): 312.

The Magic Hockey Skates, by Allen Morgan (Toronto: Oxford UP, 1991). **Rev:** *CCL* 67 (1992): 82.

A Rhyme for Me: A Big Poetry Book, ed. Caroline Parry (Toronto: Houghton, 1992).

Portus Potter Was Loose!, by Patricia Seeley (Toronto: Doubleday Canada, 1992).

Alison's House, by Maxine Trottier (Toronto: Oxford UP, 1993). **Rev:** *CBRA* (1993): #6090.

Counting My Friends, by Selma Hooge (Toronto: Gage, 1993).

Anna Takes Charge, by Ted Staunton (Bramalea, Ont.: Bramalea City Centre, 1993).

Frogs, by Andrea Wayne-von Konigslow (Toronto: HarperCollins, 1993). **Rev:** *CBRA* (1993): #6092.

Wait and See, by Robert Munsch (Toronto: Annick, 1993). **Rev:** *CBRA* (1993): #6065; *CCL* 78 (1995): 79; *CM* 22 (Mar. 1994): 48; *QQ* 59 (Oct. 1993): 37.

Where There's Smoke, by Janet Munsil (Willowdale, Ont.: Annick, 1993). **Rev:** *CBRA* (1993): #6066.

Jessica Moffat's Silver Locket, by Allen Morgan (Toronto: Stoddart, 1994). **Rev:** *CBRA* (1994): 460; *QQ* 60 (Nov. 1994): 34.

From Far Away, by Robert Munsch and Saoussan Askar (Toronto: Annick, 1995). **Rev:** *CBRA* (1995): 480; *EL* 23 (Mar. 1996): 24; *QQ* (July 1995): 61; *SLJ* 42 (Mar. 1996): 190.

Spuzzles: The Game Book of Comic Clues and Secret Answers, by Michael Furey (Toronto: Penguin, 1995).

Silver Threads, by Marsha Forchuk Skrypuch (Toronto: Viking, 1996).

Stephanie's Ponytail, by Robert Munsch (Toronto: Annick, 1996). **Rev:** *BiC* 25 (Oct. 1996): 32; *CBRA* (1996): 452; *EL* 24 (Mar. 1997): 26; *QQ* 62 (Oct. 1996): 45; *SLJ* 42 (Nov. 1996): 89.

Matthew and the Midnight Ball Game, by Allen Morgan (Toronto: Stoddart, 1997). **Rev:** *CBRA* (1997): 483.

Matthew and the Midnight Pilot, by Allen Morgan (Toronto: Stoddart, 1997). **Rev:** *CBRA* (1997): 483.

Pocketful of Stars: Rhymes, Chants and Lap Games, by Felicity Williams (Toronto: Annick, 1997). **Rev:** *CBRA* (1997): 546.

Alligator Baby, by Robert Munsch (Richmond Hill, Ont.: North Winds, 1997). *CCB-B* 51 (Oct. 1997): 63; *CBRA* (1997): 484; *QQ* 63 (Sept. 1997): 72; *SLJ* 43 (Nov. 1997): 96.

The Dark, by Robert Munsch (Toronto: Annick, 1997; rev. edn). **Rev:** *CBRA* (1997): 484; *CM* 4 (31 Oct. 1997): on-line.

Andrew's Loose Tooth, by Robert Munsch (Richmond Hill, Ont.: North Winds, 1998).

Matthew and the Midnight Flood, by Allen Morgan (Toronto: Stoddart Kids, 1998).

Matthew and the Midnight Pirates, by Allen Morgan (Toronto: Stoddart, 1998).

Matthew and the Midnight Hospital, by Allen Morgan (Toronto: Stoddart, 1999).

We Share Everything!, by Robert Munsch (Markham, Ont.: Scholastic, 1999).

Selected Discussions

Nodelman, Perry. 'The Illustrators of Munsch', *CCL* 71 (1993): 5–25.

Vanderhoof, Ann. 'Michael Martchenko', *QQ* 51 (Oct. 1985): 12.

Undoubtedly, one reason for the enormous popularity of Robert Munsch's books is that many of them have illustrations by Michael Martchenko, whom the author has praised as 'definitely crazy'. Martchenko himself says about his illustrations that he tries 'to make them fun: a bit goofy, bizarre even'. To a significant degree, he has succeeded, fusing scenes of comic chaos to the text of Allen Morgan's 'Matthew's Midnight Adventure Series' as well as many of Munsch's best stories. Like John Tenniel's pictures for *Alice in Wonderland* or E.H. Shepard's pictures for *The Wind in the Willows*, Martchenko's seem to be definitive: they shape our responses and linger in memory. In fact, a good deal of the humour in these books is directly attributable to them.

Although Martchenko can make effective drawings in a basically realistic style, as he shows in Morgan's *Jessica Moffat's Silver Locket*, his most notable illustrations owe much to those in the comic books he avidly read in his native Carcassone, France. In these, his characters are relatively simple, outlined in black, and often identifiable by a salient feature, such as the curly red hair of Morgan's Matthew. Bright watercolours make his pictures visually exciting. Martchenko enhances this excitement in two distinct ways. To focus on foreground action, he frequently keeps backgrounds simple, often eliminating them entirely. To create a general sense of excitement or chaos, he fills the pictures with mood-creating details, such as the jumbled mess of the bedroom in the opening picture of *Matthew and the Midnight Turkeys* or the crowds of animals coping in various ways with the flooded city in *Matthew and the Midnight Flood*.

Martchenko's cartoon-like drawings do not, however, simply depict what the text describes. Especially in his pictures for Munsch's books and in the dream adventure sequences of Morgan's 'Matthew's Midnight Adventure Series', they are humorous expansions of the text. One way pictures expand the words is by presenting details not mentioned in the text. For example, in *The Paper Bag Princess*, Martchenko creates an absurd anachronism by picturing the haughty Prince Ronald holding a racquet and dressed in a crown, tights, medieval boots, and a tennis sweater. Similarly, in *The Boy in the Drawer*, he shows only the tail and ears of the cat in the flooded kitchen, and in *Thomas' Snowsuit*, he graphically indicates the principal's increasing frustration by making his hair grow progressively whiter.

Martchenko also frequently employs what he calls a 'little visual vignette', a graphic addition to the story's conclusion. The final illustration of *Matthew and the Midnight Flood*, for example, portrays a scene not mentioned or implied in the text: Matthew's mother squints in concentration as she kneels over the basement drain holding a piece of string. Martchenko thus implies that she is realizing finally that Matthew caused the flooding of their basement when he used the string to lower a toy robot down the drain. Similarly, the last picture of Munsch's *Stephanie's Ponytail* provides a conclusion not mentioned in the text: Stephanie, who has fooled the entire class into shaving their heads, runs laughing as the angry mob of bald children chase her. The vignette in *Jonathan Cleaned Up* is slightly different. It shows the mayor's office becoming a subway stop, something implied by, but not definitely stated in, the text. In *David's Father*, the picture of a giant, hairy leg makes humorously concrete Munsch's punchline about meeting the grandmother. The picture of Megan examining the lock on an elephant's cage intensifies the irony of Munsch's concluding statement in *Pigs* that Megan never again let out any more pigs. Similarly, Martchenko's picture of the zoo animals smashing down the family's door in Munsch's *Alligator Baby* explains why Kristen can say that her parents do not need to do anything about returning the baby animals they have mistakenly brought home from the zoo. The end of Munsch's *The Fire Station* extends the story in still another way: the picture of Sheila dragging Michael to a police station implies that they will have more comical trouble and shows that Sheila is undaunted by her adventure.

In his only effort as both author and illustrator Martchenko has created a text that combines elements evident in tales by the two authors with whom he has most often collaborated. *Birdfeeder Banquet* contains Allen Morgan's manic fantasy and Robert Munsch's exaggeration and satire. When Jennie invents a new feed, the birds like it so much that they become enormous. Because the birds terrorize cats and dogs, and divebomb people and cars, the townspeople demand that Jennie take care of the problem. When she discovers that they are too heavy to migrate, Jennie cleverly tricks them into getting on to a plane headed for a health spa. In a manner reminiscent of the way in which he creates the bizarre world of Matthew's midnight dreams, Martchenko enhances the comedy in his illustrations. Thus, as the birds get larger and more troublesome, he makes them increasingly human, showing them with clothing and even golf clubs. The ending may be a bit flat, but *Birdfeeder Banquet* shows that Martchenko can, if he so desires, create entertaining books entirely on his own.

Martchenko has said that he considers his audience, always asking when he begins an illustration, 'If I were a kid what would I want to see? What would appeal to me?' He is Canada's pre-eminent comic illustrator because his answers have been both popular and consistently amusing.

See also: *MCAI*; *SATA* 50, 95; *WSMP*.

Suzanne Martel

Born: 8 October 1924, in Quebec City.

Principal Residences: Quebec City; Toronto; Montreal.

Education: University of Toronto.

Career: sales representative; editor; writer.

Major Awards: Vicky Metcalf Award (1976); Canada Council Children's Literature Prize (French, 1981); Governor-General's Award for Children's Literature (French, 1994); Ruth Schwartz Children's Book Award (1981).

Works for Children

The City Under Ground, trans. Norah Smaridge (New York: Viking, 1964). **Rev:** *CCL* 33 (1984): 81; *EL* 12 (Nov. 1984): 22; *IR* 10 (Aug. 1976): 51; *QQ* 49 (Mar. 1983): 66; *SLJ* 23 (Dec. 1976): 31.

The King's Daughter, trans. David Homel and Margaret Rose (Toronto: Groundwood, 1980). **Rev:** *BYP* 2 (Apr. 1988): 6; *CCL* 30 (1983): 80; *QQ* 48 (June 1982): 4.

Peewee, trans. John Fleming (Richmond Hill, Ont.: Scholastic, 1982).

Robot Alert, trans. Patricia Sillers (Toronto: Kids Can Press, 1985). **Rev:** *EL* 13 (Mar. 1985): 15; *QQ* 51 (Oct. 1985): 22.

Selected Discussions

Jenkinson, Dave. 'Portrait: Suzanne Martel', *EL* 12 (May 1985): 49–51.

Suzanne Martel is a born storyteller. When she was a little girl, she, together with her sister, author Monique Corriveau, created a long series of fantasies about an imaginary kingdom that resembled the India of Rudyard Kipling, one of the girls' favourite authors. After she was married and began raising a family, Martel began writing stories for her six boys, often using them as central characters.

In *The City Under Ground*, two pairs of brothers living in a subterranean world built after a nuclear war discover the wonderful world above ground and are instrumental in bringing their people into a new life. In *The King's Daughter* a French orphan girl comes to New France, finds a husband, and proves her courage. *Peewee* is the story of a small boy who earns a place on the local hockey team. In *Robot Alert*, an English girl living in Vancouver and a French-Canadian boy living in Montreal are instrumental in preventing the destruction of Earth by a death star.

Although Martel's stories encompass a variety of genres—science fiction, the historical novel, and the sports story—they reveal common themes and patterns. In each, there are a number of parallel characters and situations. In

The City Under Ground, people of the below- and above-ground worlds are, at first, ignorant of each other's existence, but finally come to understand their need for each other. Jeanne, the King's Daughter (a term applied to poor orphan girls), must leave Old France and her dreams of marriage to a wonderful knight for the realities of working with a stern husband in a rugged and dangerous land. Peewee learns, like Jeanne, to adapt; he is able to succeed against bigger opponents when he uses teamwork. In *Robot Alert*, English and French children discover that they have common problems and that, by working together, they can prevent impending disaster.

In order to reach fulfilment, the central characters must cross frontiers and enter strange and wonderful new worlds. For Luke, Paul, Eric, and Bernard, this means leaving the womb-like security of the underground city and walking in a world erroneously believed to be filled with poisonous gases. Jeanne faces the wilderness of Canada; Peewee, the roughness of the hockey rink. Adam and Eve do not leave the environs of their home cities, but they communicate with alien beings. During their adventures, Martel's heroes discover not only their inner strengths, but also the value of friendship and love. Working together and learning to accept outsiders—people of different backgrounds and cultures—they are able to grow as individuals. Although these heroes' adventures are generally outside the experiences of their readers, their inner development is not unlike that of all young people. Within the exciting, action-filled plots of her stories, Suzanne Martel has captured the enduring themes of growing up.

See also: *CA* 160; *SATA* 99; *WSMP*.

Carol Matas

Born: 14 November 1949, in Winnipeg.

Principal Residences: Winnipeg; London, Ont.; London, England; Toronto.

Education: University of Western Ontario (BA 1969); graduate of Actor's Lab, London, England (1972).

Career: actor; writing instructor; playwright; novelist.

Major Awards: Geoffrey Bilson Award for Historical Fiction for Young Readers (1988).

Works for Children

The DNA Dimension (Toronto: Gage, 1982). **Rev:** *BiC* 12 (Feb. 1983): 33; *CBRA* (1982): 251; *CCL* 34 (1984): 92.

The Fusion Factor (Saskatoon: Fifth House, 1986), republished as *It's Up to Us*

(Toronto: Stoddart, 1991). **Rev:** *BYP* 1 (June 1987): 9; *BiC* 16 (Mar. 1987): 37; *CCL* 50 (1988): 79; *CL* 116 (Spring 1988): 143.

Zanu (Saskatoon: Fifth House, 1986). **Rev:** *BYP* 1 (June 1987): 9; *BiC* 16 (Mar. 1987): 37; *CCL* 50 (1988): 79; *CL* 117 (Summer 1988): 158.

Lisa (Toronto: Lester & Orpen Dennys, 1987); republished in the US as *Lisa's War* (New York: Scribner's, 1989). **Rev:** *BYP* 1 (Dec. 1987): 6; *BiC* 17 (Apr. 1988): 36; *CBRA* (1988): 291; *CCB-B* 43 (Sept. 1989): 12; *CCL* 50 (1988): 79; *EL* 16 (Mar. 1989): 22, and 16 (May 1989): 53; *HB* 65 (May 1989): 377; *NYTBR* 94 (21 May 1989): 30; *SLJ* 35 (May 1989): 127; *VOYA* 12 (June 1989): 104, and 14 (Dec. 1991): 349.

Me, Myself, and I (Saskatoon: Fifth House, 1987) **Rev:** *BYP* 2 (Feb. 1988): 10; *CM* 16 (July 1988): 130.

Jesper (Toronto: Lester & Orpen Dennys, 1989); republished in the US as *Code Name Kris* (New York: Scribner's, 1990). **Rev:** *BiC* 18 (Dec. 1989): 21; *CCL* 59 (1990): 85; *CM* 18 (May 1990): 129; *HB* 67 (Jan.-Feb. 1991): 74; *SLJ* 36 (Dec. 1990): 121.

Adventure in Legoland (Toronto: Scholastic, 1991). **Rev:** *CM* 20 (Sept. 1992): 204; *QQ* 58 (July 1992): 49.

The Race (Toronto: HarperCollins, 1991). **Rev:** *CCL* 73 (1994): 79; *CM* 20 (May 1992): 168; *QQ* 57 (Oct. 1991): 35.

Sworn Enemies (Toronto: HarperCollins, 1993). **Rev:** *BiC* 22 (Summer 1993): 30; *CBRA* (1993): #6166; *CCB-B* 46 (Apr. 1993): 258; *CCL* 75 (1994): 70; *CM* 21 (Sept. 1993): 153; *NYTBR* 98 (11 Apr. 1993): 30; *QQ* 59 (Jan. 1993): 30; *SLJ* 39 (Feb. 1993): 94; *VOYA* 16 (June 1993): 92.

Safari Adventure in Legoland (Richmond Hill, Ont.: Scholastic,1993): **Rev:** *CBRA* (1993): #6165; *CM* 22 (May-June 1994): 76; *QQ* 59 (Oct. 1993): 43.

Daniel's Story (New York: Scholastic, 1993). **Rev:** *BiC* 22 (Oct. 1993): 57; *CBRA* (1993): #6164; *CCB-B* 46 (May 1993): 289; *CM* 21 (Sept. 1993): 153; *EL* 21 (Mar. 1994): 58; *NYTBR* 98 (5 Sept. 1993): 17; *QQ* 59 (Feb. 1993): 35; *SLJ* 39 (May 1993): 107; *VOYA* 16 (Aug. 1993): 153.

The Lost Locket (Richmond Hill, Ont.: Scholastic, 1994). **Rev:** *BiC* 23 (Summer 1994): 58; *CBRA* (1994): 490; *CCL* 86 (1997): 56; *CL* (Spring 1996): 198; *CM* 22 (Oct. 1994): 179; *QQ* 60 (Feb. 1994): 39.

The Burning Time (Toronto: HarperCollins, 1994). **Rev:** *CBRA* (1995): 512; *CCB-B* 48 (Dec.1994): 139; *QQ* 61 (Feb. 1995): 37; *VOYA* 17 (Oct. 1994): 210

Of Two Minds, with Perry Nodelman (Winnipeg: Bain & Cox, 1994). **Rev:** *BiC* 23 (Dec. 1994): 57; *CBRA* (1994): 491; *CCL* 86 (1997): 82; *QQ* 60 (Dec. 1994): 33; *SLJ* 41 (Oct. 1995): 136, and 41 (Dec. 1995): 22; *VOYA* 19 (Apr. 1996): 23, 40, and 19 (June 1996): 88

The Primrose Path (Winnipeg: Bain & Cox, 1995). **Rev:** *BiC* 25 (Oct. 1996): 30; *CBRA* (1995): 512; *QQ* 61 (Nov. 1995): 45.

After the War (Richmond Hill, Ont. Scholastic, 1996). **Rev:** *CBRA* (1996): 483; *CCB-B* 49 (Apr. 1996): 271; *CM* 4 (13 Feb. 1998): on-line; *QQ* 62 (Oct. 1996): 49; *SLJ* 42 (May 1996): 135; *VOYA* 20 (June 1997): 86.

More Minds, with Perry Nodelman (New York: Simon & Schuster, 1996). **Rev:** *CCB-B* 50 (Feb. 1997): 214; *SLJ* 42 (Oct. 1996): 148; *VOYA* 20 (June 1997): 119.

The Freak (Toronto: Key Porter, 1997). **Rev:** *CBRA* (1997): 518; *QQ* 63 (Mar. 1997): 79.

The Garden (Toronto: Scholastic, 1997). **Rev:** *CBRA* (1997): 519; *CM* 4 (27 Feb. 1998): on-line; *QQ* 63 (Sept. 1997): 77; *SLJ* 43 (May 1997): 137; *VOYA* 20 (June 1997): 110.

Greater than Angels (New York: Simon & Schuster 1998). **Rev:** *VOYA* 21 (Oct. 1998): 275.

Telling (Toronto: Key Porter Kids, 1998).

Out of Their Minds, with Perry Nodelman (New York: Simon & Schuster, 1998).

Cloning Miranda (Toronto: Scholastic, 1999).

In My Enemy's House (Toronto: Scholastic, 1999).

Selected Discussions

Nodelman, Perry. 'Good, Evil, Knowledge, Power: A Conversation between Carol Matas and Perry Nodelman', *CCL* 82 (1996): 57–68.

In claiming that 'the greatest pleasure is to read a book that is compelling *and* substantive', Carol Matas places herself within a tradition in which books for children exist 'to teach and to delight'. In fact, Matas has identified both purposes as goals of her writing. First, she has said, she wants to provide children with the delight of 'a wonderful reading experience' by creating 'a story that is unputdownable'. Second, she wants her material to teach by providing intellectual challenges: 'I'm trying to open a question, a dialogue, give my reader food for thought, challenge assumptions.' Although she sometimes falls into preaching, Matas has tried to make ideas integral to her books by letting them arise naturally from dramatic situations: 'Often I place my characters in a situation where their assumptions are challenged, or where they are forced to challenge others.' Matas has been particularly concerned with challenging ideas about conformity and about the obligation for and possibilities of individual resistance to abuses of power. Whether writing science fiction, historical fiction, contemporary realism, or fantasy, she repeatedly returns to the idea that the individual has the power to affect the community as a whole and therefore must make decisions that reflect more than narrow self-interest. Combining tensely gripping plots with questions about morality, authority, and individual identity, her best work puts a modern spin on the classic purpose of children's books by pleasing and provoking.

Matas began her career with the avowed purpose of using a series of science fiction novels to change children by making them think. The four 'Rebecca Lepidus' novels explore alternative worlds or alternative futures in order to emphasize that even one individual can profoundly affect society. In the first, *The DNA Dimension*, four children from contemporary Winnipeg fall into Pred, a world in another dimension. Through genetic and social engineering, the dictator, Kard, has programmed citizens to be efficient and complacent. One of the children, Norman, overthrows Kard, becomes the new dictator, and declares that people must now work only to please him. Eventually, Rebecca Lepidus (a character named after and inspired by the author's own daughter) deposes Norman and brings him home. Norman, rather than rejecting dictatorships as evil, now decides to study science so that he can become a dictator. His decision means that Rebecca and the others must be vigilant if they are to prevent a future in which selfish scientists enslave society. Although marred by a preposterous plot and crude stereotypes (Norman, for example, repeatedly responds with an evil chuckle), *The DNA Dimension* is substantive in warning of the potential abuses of genetic and social engineering.

Rebecca's subsequent adventures reveal the dangers of nuclear proliferation and of unchecked consumerism. In *The Fusion Factor*, survivors of a nuclear holocaust kidnap Rebecca and bring her to the year 2040 to participate in their plan to repopulate their shattered world. As an adventure, the tale again focuses on Rebecca's efforts to rescue other kidnapped children from a dictatorship that may have noble ends but that denies them choice. Didacticism becomes overly prominent when Rebecca learns that the future is not to be determined. When she escapes, therefore, she decides to make other children aware that they can prevent disaster by coming together, by educating themselves about the causes of war, and by opposing the proliferation of nuclear weapons. In *Zanu*, Rebecca is accidentally transported to 2080 and yet another possible future. This time Zanu, the only corporation remaining in the world, exerts an absolute dictatorship that requires all citizens to be avid consumers. Learning that she will be executed because she might adversely affect this future if she returned to her own time, Rebecca escapes and joins a revolutionary movement. Although its adventure sequences are only slightly less hackneyed than those in previous novels, this story profoundly challenges attitudes to business and consumerism. By showing how Zanu imposes conformity, pollutes the environment, and executes those who rebel, it suggests that the profit motive may lead to corporate control of government, the abolition of individualism, and the environmentally destructive excesses of consumerism. As with the previous novel, however, it holds out the hope that individual action can be instrumental in preventing such a future.

Me, Myself and I concludes the series with another instance of the importance of individual action, but it has a humorous edge absent in earlier instalments. Returning from Zanu, Rebecca discovers that she has returned home before she had left so that two of her now exist. Her efforts to avoid her other self and to respond to those confused by her dual presence are humorous. The serious element begins to dominate when Rebecca, in order to become a single, whole person, returns to the year 2080. She discovers a world in which Zanu did not develop because she was active in her own time. She also realizes that this world seems idyllic but that, in order to prevent conflicts, it discourages individuality. After meeting the person she will be in the future, an archetypally wise grandmother who provokes her into thinking about her future, Rebecca returns to her own time determined to preserve her individuality while working to make the world better.

Although they contain too many amateurish science fiction clichés and permit preaching to dominate their conclusions, the Rebecca novels successfully use adventure to raise significant social and ethical questions. When Matas returned to science fiction more than a dozen years later, she showed a more mature artistry when raising such questions. The simple plot of *Cloning Miranda* focuses on an almost perfect teen. After contracting a seemingly fatal genetic disease, Miranda makes the horrifying discovery that she is a genetically improved clone of a sister who died of cancer. Furthermore, she learns that her wealthy parents employ a scientist who has created another clone to provide body parts in case she becomes ill. The well-drawn teen characters are consistently plausible. In addition, Miranda's suspenseful efforts to save her clone and to prevent her parents from engaging in more experiments generate intriguing questions about the ethics of genetic engineering, the nature of identity, the basis of relationships based on deception, and the moral and psychological consequences of creating legal troubles for one's parents.

After the Rebecca series, Matas took a new direction, achieving both artistic success and critical recognition as an author of historical novels about World War II and its aftermath. This period is compelling, Matas has said, because it 'offers an incredible wealth of dramatic stories' and the 'life and death situations where moral dilemmas have to be faced'. Matas, who is herself Jewish, has also noted that 'the Holocaust is evil, and to study it is to study the very worst in human nature.' Thoroughly researched, her historical novels show the extent of evil while making the Jewish victims plausible individuals with flaws and doubts. Her obviously improved ability to create such characters may be attributable to her switch to first-person narration, which requires a strong and consistent sense of an individual's social, psychological, and moral qualities.

Her first historical novels, *Lisa* (US title *Lisa's War*) and its sequel, *Jesper* (US title *Code Name Kris*), focus on the German occupation of Denmark, which Matas heard about through the stories her husband told about his Danish father and grandfather. Of the more than 7,000 Jews living in Denmark, only 475 were captured by the Germans. Most of the Danish Jews escaped in 1943 on the eve of Rosh Hashanah, the Jewish New Year. Warned that the Germans planned to round them up while they celebrated in their homes and aided by non-Jewish

Danes, they made their way to the coast and escaped to Sweden. *Lisa* covers a three-year period, from the morning of the German invasion in 1940 to the night of this massive exodus. Narrated by Lisa, it tells of how she first overcomes the prejudice against her as a girl to win acceptance by the Danish resistance. Insisting that she, like her older brother, Stefan, is capable of contributing to the resistance, Lisa begins distributing propaganda leaflets. Her habit of throwing up when she is nervous, a trait that stops her from being an idealized hero but that also stretches plausibility, makes her initial assignment comical. Fearing that she will be detected while distributing leaflets on a streetcar, she vomits on a pair of German soldiers. Later, after she has participated in the bombing of a factory her nervousness is life-saving: her companions point to Lisa's vomiting to convince a German patrol that they are rushing her to the hospital. *Lisa* is most notable for showing the pressure of circumstances on ordinary people. Lisa is convincingly ordinary: she worries about her appearance and daydreams about Jesper, a young resistance fighter. She also worries about the way violence has changed everyone, possibly making them descend to the level of the Nazis. Nevertheless, in the novel's most powerful scene, she herself kills a German guard so that a group of Jews can safely board the boats taking them to Sweden.

Jesper, which concentrates on the period after Lisa escapes to Sweden, is more dramatic and exciting. It ripples with tension because Jesper, having been captured, tortured, and told that he is going to be executed, recounts his adventures in the resistance in order to prevent himself from going crazy or from giving in to despair. His tale traces his development from a defiant child putting sugar in German gas tanks, through to a young adult member of the underground gathering stories and printing a resistance newspaper, bombing factories, and even killing soldiers. Jesper realistically displays a mixture of feelings, expressing confusion and guilt, for instance, because, while yet thinking about Lisa, he begins to love an older girl working for the resistance. More significantly, Jesper, like Lisa, shows moral sensitivity, worrying about the way hatred and violence shape his own life. This last concern comes into particularly sharp focus when Jesper, whose fingernails have been pulled out by his captors, discovers that the battle between good and evil is not as simple as he once imagined. He realizes that the Gestapo officer supervising his torture, a boyhood friend, is not an undercover agent but an idealist who believes in the Nazi cause. An intriguing moral dilemma arises because this officer, understanding that the defeat of Germany is imminent, offers Jesper the opportunity to live if he and Stefan, also a prisoner, will help him to escape. While Jesper ponders whether the offer is a trick to get him to expose other resistance fighters or whether he can accept this offer but then give into his hatred and kill his former friend, Allied planes bomb the prison. The officer is killed by falling rubble, but Jesper and Stefan escape. This contrived episode short-circuits the intriguing moral dilemma, but the novel plausibly dramatizes an interesting mixture of danger, fear, sorrow, and confusion in a time filled with unspeakable brutality and memorable heroics.

Because of the power and success of *Lisa* and *Jesper*, the US Holocaust Memorial Museum commissioned Matas to write a novel that would complement a photographic exhibition. Matas has said that 'it was the most painful and difficult book I've ever had to research.' *Daniel's Story* employs a young boy as a representative of the millions of Jews who suffered under the Nazi regime. Its device of beginning each section of the novel with its young narrator riding on a train and either looking at or thinking about photographs that recount the previous stage of his life may seem self-consciously artistic to some readers; in fact, some reviewers complained that it distanced the subject, robbing it of immediacy. By making Daniel look back on what has been taken from him, however, this device emphasizes that each of Daniel's enforced journeys brings greater losses. It also effectively foregrounds memory, a kind of knowledge Matas suggests is necessary if we are to prevent another holocaust. The story itself is rather straightforward, and, despite some reviewers' complaints about the absence of concrete details, it is chilling and gruesome. It begins with an account of family life in Frankfurt and the devastation and hatred that Daniel's family feel when the Nazis progressively strip them of rights and property. Forced to move to the ghetto of Lodz, Poland, Daniel's family shows that it is resourceful in the midst of increasing hardships. Daniel even falls in love with a Polish girl. His life becomes more nightmarish, however, when his family is sent to Auschwitz, where his mother is killed, and then to Buchenwald. Throughout this journey, images of Nazi atrocities show the bland heart of human evil: in one scene, for instance, a Nazi officer, having just sat for a photograph that shows him as a loving family man with his wife and children, callously tortures and kills a Jewish boy. Such horrifying scenes are complemented by those portraying the Jews as both victims and resourceful survivors sabotaging the plans of their tormentors. The conclusion, in which Daniel returns to Poland, finds the girl he loves, and proposes to her, may strike some readers as too sentimental, a romantic cliché, but this conclusion also provides an appropriately optimistic note by suggesting that the heart of the Jewish people survived their unprecedented horrors.

Matas shows yet another side of the Jewish experience in *Greater than Angels*, the story of a 15-year-old girl, Anna Hirsch, deported from Mannheim to a displaced-persons camp in Vichey, France. Although Anna's family is shipped to Poland and perishes, she is among a fortunate group of adolescents saved by Swiss humanitarians and the villagers of Le Chambon-sur-Lignon. After one perilous failure to escape to Switzerland, Anna succeeds in crossing to safety with friends, but she contemplates returning later as a resistance fighter. The focus in *Greater than Angels* is on the psychological and spiritual reactions of the young people who have lost home and family to the Nazis. Unfortunately, although it presents a variety of responses to serious questions as to how a God of love could allow atrocities, too much of the theme depends on staged classroom debates among the young people. Furthermore, the characterization of

Anna as a spirited and talented music-hall performer who constantly tells jokes to inspire people (a device also characterizing Zvi in *The Garden*) is awkward and artificial. In spite of her religious doubts, her growing understanding of her romantic feelings for a boy, and her deep desire to wage battle against the Nazis, Anna is seldom more than a device for presenting vignettes of wartime France. Finally, the novel's ending is somewhat anticlimactic: the second attempt to reach Switzerland lacks the dramatic tension of the first one.

Written earlier than *Greater than Angels*, *After the War* and its sequel, *The Garden*, treat a later period, the postwar exodus of Jews from Europe and their attempt to create a safe homeland in Israel. *After the War* traces the journeys of 15-year-old Ruth Mendenberg after her release from Buchenwald. Believing that she has lost all of her relatives, Ruth is numb and devoid of hope, believing in neither God nor a meaningful future. Nevertheless, she agrees to smuggle a group of children into Palestine. As part of her duties, Ruth records the children's experiences. By doing so, she learns how to remember her own horrifying past and to let her heart thaw. On the ship to Palestine, Ruth discovers her brother and becomes filled with joy and hope. Although captured on the very shore of Palestine, Ruth and her brother escape and complete their quest. The narrative has disturbing and exciting moments, but it suffers from its diffuseness: accounts of too many experiences and too many conversations portraying conflicting attitudes make it difficult to gain a clear sense of Ruth's psychological transformation. Because it tells about, rather than shows, most of the characters, settings, and events, *After the War* is more of a documentary account than a gripping novel.

Similar problems are evident in *The Garden*, about the adventures of Ruth, her brother, and her boyfriend, Zvi, in the months leading up to the creation of an independent Israel. Ruth longs for the peace and beauty symbolized by a garden that she plants, one that the British troops symbolically destroy during a search for illegal weapons. Ruth is caught also between conflicting religious views about the will of God and opposing political attitudes about the proper way to establish a Jewish state. Events drag her into increasingly violent conflicts, causing her to question her own values and those of her friends. The political background nearly overpowers both plot and characterization, but *The Garden* has notable highlights. For one, it successfully dramatizes some starkly gruesome moments, especially a commando raid in which Ruth shoots 16 Arabs, and a sickening, botched attack on an Arab village by zealous but incompetent Jewish fighters. For another, although the characters are sometimes puppets articulating differing positions, the multiplicity of views is provocative. *The Garden* may stumble into melodrama at the end, when the wise-cracking Zvi, having been wounded, breaks down and expresses his pent-up sorrows while Arab planes strafe a hospital, but it successfully communicates the fervour many Holocaust survivors felt about creating a homeland.

Matas has also written historical novels about two other eras in which repression and injustice challenged the faith and spirit of individuals. *Sworn Enemies*, which is set in nineteenth-century Russia, is an attempt, Matas has said, 'to explore the issues of faith, idealism and religion' and to 'ask a larger question: how does one live morally in an immoral world?' The novel proceeds through two intertwined first-person narratives: that of Aaron, a brilliant yeshiva student deeply in love with Miriam, and that of Zev, a poor boy jealous that Aaron has won Miriam's hand. When Aaron is captured by Zev, a *khapper*, a Jew who kidnaps Jewish boys to fill the Russian conscription quota, Aaron undergoes a crisis of faith. Brutally forced to convert to Christianity, he wrestles with questions about the letter and spirit of the Jewish law and about the validity of hatred and revenge. Ironically, Zev is also kidnapped and sent to the same Russian military camp, but he follows the letter of the Jewish law, refusing to convert. Furthermore, he refuses to see himself as culpable, blaming his misfortunes on Aaron. These contrasting narratives suggest that both morality and true religion lie in a humane heart, rather than in formal observations or rules. Although it has an intriguing theme, presents interesting and brutal historical scenes, and ends with an escape that makes it a hopeful adventure, *Sworn Enemies* is not completely involving. The villains are flat, and neither the complex and sensitive Aaron nor the patently evil Zev is a convincing, psychologically complex individual.

Because the villains are even more prominent in *The Burning Time*, about the witch trials in late sixteenth-century France, the one-dimensional characterization of them turns it into a strident declaration about the injustices of patriarchal oppression of females instead of chilling drama. Each of the villains is a male motivated by greed, lust, or both. In contrast, the central females are reasonable and exceptionally talented. Trouble arises when Madame Rive, a widow noted for her talent as a healer and a midwife, frustrates three men. The doctor is angry because she safely delivers a baby after he declares that both mother and infant will die; a relative becomes vengeful after she resists his sexual advances and refuses to turn over her property to him; the village priest harbours resentment because she laughs when he suggests that she become his mistress. All three accuse her of witchcraft to a travelling judge, whose venality is evident in his continual talk about the profitability of witch hunting. Although Matas has said that she left out much of what was done to women during the period, the description of Madame Rive being tortured while Rose, her 15-year-old daughter, watches from a hiding place is horrifying. Rose, herself accused of witchcraft after rejecting a peasant's marriage proposal, is central to one of the moral dilemmas Matas characteristically dramatizes: she helps her mangled mother to commit what is technically the sin of suicide, but in doing so, she is more humane and moral than the church officials who follow the law that says that only a confession arising from torture is valid. *The Burning Time* is earnest, showing that women were brutalized and demonized whenever they frustrated male desires, but it lacks both the drama and the nuances of character that would make it more than an illustrated polemic.

In her forays into contemporary realism, Matas has written problem novels that characteristically insist that individuals must involve themselves in social and ethical issues. The subjects of *The Primrose Path* are pedophilia, hypocrisy, and abuse of authority. Fourteen-year-old Debbie becomes involved with a new group of friends and a new way of life when she is enrolled in an orthodox Jewish school. When she becomes disturbed that the charismatic rabbi repeatedly touches in inappropriate ways, the novel convincingly portrays the agonizing conflict between her desire to fit in and her sense that the rabbi is violating her. Debbie's confusion, the confusion of her mother, who has an affair with the rabbi, and the hypocrisy of the rabbi, who maintains a loyal following in spite of a plethora of accusations, make this novel a realistically complex account of serious moral failures. Hypocrisy is also central to *The Race*, an unusual young adult novel for its intensive look at Canadian politics. Set during a weekend when the mother of 14-year-old Ali Green is vying for the leadership of the Liberal Party, it combines normal teenage anxieties about appearance and dating, family problems arising from the teenager's feeling that her mother both overprotects and ignores her, and ethical dilemmas arising from political corruption. The central dilemma for Ali comes when she overhears her mother's chief rival, the father of her new boyfriend, accepting a bribe. The scene in which Ali confronts the corrupt politician may be implausible, but the novel shows that individuals who care can make a significant difference.

A variety of problems surface in *Telling*, an engaging slice of life about three adolescent sisters who share their experiences in a nightly 'telling' ritual. Alex, the middle sister and narrator, tells of how she failed to get her friends to put on a play that was a more historically accurate account of the witchcraft trials in France. The youngest sister reveals how her association with a wild group given to 'partying' with alcohol and drugs led her to betray the privacy of a boy who is homosexual. The oldest sister explains how she lied about her background to make a boy interested in her and then had a sexual experience that she now regrets. Although the morality is clear because each sister realizes that she has a lesson to learn about personal responsibility, the novel is honestly open-ended. In particular, it is not at all certain that the youngest sister, who resolutely refuses to give up her association with a group that leads her into increasing social, moral, and perhaps legal dangers, will be able to act on her new understanding. *The Lost Locket*, a chapter book for younger readers, touches on the issue of schoolyard bullies. When Curtis refuses to give Roz an heirloom locket that has gone missing from her desk, Roz must confront the bully. The resolution, in which she uses a karate move to defend herself, will seem too pat to adult readers, and it avoids the problem about how to handle bullies if one truly believes that violence is not appropriate and if one also lacks skill in the martial arts. Nevertheless, *The Lost Locket* shows that Matas can make even works for the very young both entertaining and provocative.

Matas is most celebrated for her realism, but she has also written fantasy. *The Freak* qualifies as fantasy only because its central character discovers that she has psychic abilities. For the most part, it is a combination of psychological realism and detective romance. After contracting meningitis, 15-year-old Jade begins hearing people's thoughts and seeing visions of future events. Because Jade has trouble understanding and accepting her new condition, Matas is able to raise questions about God, free will, and determinism. The drama comes when Jade, partly because of her psychic abilities, saves a synagogue from a bomb planted by neo-Nazis. A weak mystery adventure and the rather forced philosophical discussions prevent *The Freak* from realizing the potential inherent in its premise. Matas has also written two magical quest adventures for young readers, *Adventure in Legoland* and *Safari Adventure in Legoland*. Aaron, visiting the Danish Legoland factory with his family, discovers that it comes alive at night. In the first story, he rescues a fairy, Prince Aryeh, from Bad Bart, and in the second, he aids Prince Aryeh in recovering a lost trophy. Younger readers may find these tales entertaining, but neither the characters nor the quest plots are notable.

Teaming up with Perry Nodelman, a literary critic whom she has thanked for advice in nearly all of her books, Matas has produced a comical fantasy series that combines undisciplined inventiveness and intellectual playfulness. The series introduces the wilful Princess Lenora, from a kingdom where people can make real whatever they imagine, and the reticent Prince Coren, from a kingdom where people can live in their imaginations and can read other people's minds. Lenora is forbidden use of her power because changing reality might destroy the balance of the world. Naturally, Lenora insists on using her imagination to make her life more interesting. *Of Two Minds*, the best book in the series, uses third-person narration, but the viewpoint alternates entertainingly between that of Lenora and that of Coren, adding depth to both characters. Lenora and Coren, whose families have arranged for them to marry, are mysteriously pulled out of their world into one of conformity and mindless obedience. The dictator, Hevak, is conspiring to take over the universe. The plot develops ideas about freedom and the abuse of authority evident in Matas's early science fiction, but it also introduces more complex concepts about the nature of identity and the ethical dimensions of choice. In an ironic conclusion, Lenora thus learns that she herself has created Hevak, that he is something of a Jungian shadow created when she imagined herself as a hero jumping into other worlds to have adventures forbidden at home. Because she herself is the source of the evil, she is able to make Hevak vanish.

The second volume, *More Minds*, works towards a similar ironic discovery. When her people begin to lose their power and a clumsy giant appears in the kingdom, Lenora rashly sets out to discover the cause. To avoid detection, however, she imagines a blandly obedient copy of herself and, when Prince Coren follows her, one of him. Eventually, Lenora, seeking the roots of the chaos, goes into the mythic past, where she herself, mistaken for a goddess, decrees the very balance that she finds intolerable in her own life. The meeting of the independent originals and their vacuous copies generates amusing moments, and the typographic tricks showing Lenora's mental confusion are interesting, but the plot collapses under the weight of an excessive number of surreal episodes. The relatively more controlled plot of *Out of Their Minds* takes place in Prince Coren's kingdom, where the couple have gone to be married. When people again lose their powers and Lenora begins to have disturbing dreams about Hevak, she again sets out with Coren. They discover that Coren's kingdom contains Skwoes, a completely unimaginative people who perform all the utilitarian tasks that the courtiers neglect by imagining better circumstances. Although the episodes with the Skwoes are belaboured and repetitive, they raise valid questions about balancing imagination and utilitarianism, and about intellectual snobbery. Once again, however, the main issues arise because Lenora proves to be the real author of the chaos. In her desire to make the world perfect, she has provided a way for Hevak to return from oblivion and thus to suck the power away from others. Hevak's reappearance leads to a questioning of the nature of choice: Coren wonders whether a life devoid of the choice of doing good or evil can actually be good. Belaboured or unnecessary inventions too frequently crowd out the comedy or confuse the plot, but the *Two Minds* series is frequently witty and intellectually challenging. One can hope that the authors strike a more satisfying balance when they release their fourth volume, tentatively titled *A Meeting of the Minds*.

Carol Matas has become one of the most important Canadian writers for youth because she respects the intelligence of her audience. She may be too overtly polemical at times, but she never offers easy answers to difficult questions and never falls back on moralistic clichés. As a result, in spite of some of her limitations with characterization or plotting, she succeeds admirably in her goal of entertaining and challenging young people.

See also: *AAYA* 22; *CA* 158; *CLR* 52; *Junior* 7; *MCAI*; *SATA* 93; *WSMP*.

O.R. Melling

(pen name of Geraldine Whelan)

Born: c. 1952, in Dublin, Ireland,

Principal Residences: Bray, Ireland; Toronto; Malaysia; Ballinamore, Ireland; Dublin.

Education: University of Toronto (BA in Celtic Studies, MA in Medieval History).

Career: barmaid; waitress; bank clerk; sub-lieutenant in the Canadian Naval Reserve; publisher's assistant; writer.

Major Awards: Canadian Library Association Young Adult Book Award (1984); Ruth Schwartz Young Adult Book Award (1994).

Works for Children:

The Druid's Tune (Markham, Ont.: Viking Kestrel, 1983). **Rev:** *BiC* 12 (Dec. 1983): 16; *CCL* 38 (1985), 105–9; *QQ* 49 (Nov. 1983): 24; *TES* (6 July 1984): 28.

The Singing Stone (Markham, Ont.: Viking Kestrel, 1986). **Rev:** *APBR* 13 (Nov. 1986): 1; *BiC* 15 (Dec. 1986): 18; *CCB-B* 41 (Dec. 1987): 71; *CCL* 47 (1987): 71; *QQ* 52 (Oct. 1986): 20; *RT* 41 (Jan. 1988): 467; *SLJ* 34 (Sept. 1987): 198.

The Hunter's Moon (Toronto: HarperCollins, 1993). **Rev:** *BiC* 22 (Oct. 1993): 57; (CCL 86 (1997): 82; *QQ* 59 (May 1993): 33.

My Blue Country (Toronto: Viking Penguin, 1996). **Rev:** *CBRA* (1996): 485; *CM* 2 (28 June 1996): on-line.

Other

[as Geraldine Whelan] 'World Wise: CWY—Malaysia', *Miss Chatelaine* 11, 1 (1974): 54, 66, 77–82.

[as Geraldine Whelan] 'Barmaiding in an Irish Pub', *Miss Chatelaine* 12, 2 (1975): 44.

When she came to publish her first novel, Geraldine Whelan decided that her name lacked the 'ring' possessed by those of such fantasy authors as C.S. Lewis and J.R.R. Tolkien. She also decided that knowledge of personal information, such as her date of birth, could lead readers to form preconceptions about her book. To limit such preconceptions and to preserve her privacy, she therefore adopted a *nom de plume*, that of her childhood friend, Orla Melling. Perhaps not surprisingly, given this deliberate construction of an authorial persona, issues of identity dominate her fiction. Melling, as we call her throughout this essay, uses time-shift fantasy as the basis for exploring this staple theme of young adult fiction. In each of her fantasies, one or more adolescents mysteriously shift from mundane twentieth-century life into mythic time. Perilous journeys and encounters with figures from Celtic mythology test their inner resources and ultimately lead them to develop a deeper understanding of themselves.

Incorporating a vivid retelling of an Irish epic *The Táin bó Cúailnge* ('The Cattle Raid of Cooley'), *The Druid's Tune* recounts the adventures of two Canadian adolescents who magically join the legendary raid on Ulster. Because her father disapproves of her choice of friends, 17-year-old Rosemary Redding and her 15-year-old brother, Jimmy, are sent from Toronto to spend the summer in Ireland with relatives. The siblings meet a mysterious farmhand, Peter Murphy, a Druid who needs them so that he can complete the development of his character. Peter takes them to Ireland's mythic past, where they join Queen Maeve's camp during her cattle raid. Jimmy soon deserts Maeve to serve as charioteer for her enemy Cuculann, the ferocious Hound of Ulster. Enraged, Maeve plots to kill Rosemary, but Peter helps her to escape and rejoin Jimmy. The siblings then attend Cuculann, but Peter, to ensure their safety, transforms them into birds who watch Maeve defeat the forces of Ulster. After the battle, they find themselves again in modern Ireland feeling transformed by their adventures.

Although it won the CLA Young Adult Book Award, *The Druid's Tune* is decidedly an apprentice author's work. In particular, it suffers from flat, artificial characterization. Rosemary and Jimmy lack engaging personalities, speak in a stilted manner jarringly at odds with the speech of the Iron-Age Celts, and learn complex skills, such as driving a chariot into combat with implausible ease and rapidity. Furthermore, although they witness diplomatic deceit, Cuculann's terrifying blood rage, and the slaughter of an army of children, their adventures have only the slightest impact on their self-understanding. Rosemary supposedly learns that there is more than the shallow, modern world, and Jimmy learns to be more considerate of loved ones, but these lessons are hardly commensurate with their elaborate experiences. The anti-war theme is far stronger, but it is ironically at odds with the novel's attempt to celebrate mythic heroism, which depends on war and violence. The role of their companion and guide, Peter Murphy, is also problematic. At the beginning, his quest to understand his own identity initiates the plot, but he is absent during most of the adventures, and his successful completion of his quest is merely reported, not adequately dramatized. In spite of such obvious weaknesses, however, *The Druid's Tune* vividly evokes the mythic past.

The identity theme is more overt, more focused, and more complex in *The Singing Stone*. Kay Warrick, abandoned at an orphanage when she was an infant, is intent on learning who she is and from where she came. Having mysteriously received a bundle of books containing stories about standing stones, especially the Singing Stone that holds answers for heroes, she journeys to Ireland to seek her own answers. Locating the Singing Stone, she passes under it and finds herself in Iron-Age Ireland, where she meets Aherne, a girl who has no memory of her own past, and Fintan the Mage, who gives them a quest. Fintan tells them to bring together the lost treasures of the Tuatha De Danaan in order to restore harmony to the troubled land. During the course of this archetypal treasure quest, Aherne discovers her identity, learning that she is actually Eriu, the Rising Queen of the Tuatha De Danaan. Overcoming a plot to kill her, Eriu wins a contest that confirms her as queen. She then informs her people that their defeat by invaders is inevitable and that honourable surrender is preferably to a futile and bloody war. Her people then pass under the Singing Stone to become Ireland's fairy folk, but Eriu marries one of the invaders to signal the need for compromise and peace, and her husband names the country Eire in her honour. For her part, Kay learns that she is both a Mage who possesses significant psychic powers and Eriu's daughter, whom Fintan sent to the future so that she could come back and help her mother bring peace. Now knowing who she is and confident in her powers to decide her own destiny, Kay returns to the twentieth century to decide how and where she will live.

The diffuse plot is packed with exciting episodes, but its complexity vitiates the unity of its quest. Furthermore, the symbolic meanings of the objects of the quest—the Spear of Truth, the Cauldron of Generosity, the Stone of Destiny, and the Sword of War—are poetic, not dramatic: their acquisition seems less a moral necessity than a contrivance to present Kay with opportunities for testing her character and for developing the psychic powers that enable her to read minds and control others. Nevertheless, the repeated claims that the Tuatha De Danaan became a cruel people who sealed their doom by relying on the Sword, to the exclusion of the qualities represented by the other objects, advance an anti-war theme that is integral to the main plot. Eriu, upon discovering her identity as Rising Queen thus must overcome her traditional respect for fighting to save her people by arranging an honourable surrender. Just as significantly, Kay's discovery that she is Eriu's daughter allows her to overcome her feelings of alienation and to understand that she is a person of power, a Mage, who can choose her own destiny.

The journeys in Melling's third fantasy, *The Hunter's Moon*, are even more frenetic than those in her previous books. Gwen Woods, a 16-year-old from Canada, goes to Ireland to visit her cousin, Findabhair, called Finn. Because both share a love of fantasy, they set off in search of adventure among Ireland's ancient ruins. When they spend the night in a mound, the fairies kidnap Finn, forcing Gwen to undertake an elaborate series of journeys to rescue her. During her travels from one ancient site to another, Gwen receives help from people who believe in fairies. Eventually, she learns that Finn, who loves Finvarra, King of the Fairies, has agreed to save his kingdom by sacrificing herself to Crom Cruac, the Great Worm, also called the Hunter. Gwen therefore gathers her helpers, and they manage to kill the thousand-eyed beast. To their dismay, however, it rises up fully restored and demands a sacrifice of someone more than mortal. Finvarra immediately offers himself, and the monster pulls him beneath the surface of a lake. On their way home, though, Gwen and Finn meet the restored Finvarra, now a mere mortal with no memory of his previous life, but with a deep attraction to Finn.

The Hunter's Moon suffers from the overly complex plotting characteristic of Melling's previous fantasies with many events seeming extemporized, but the characterization and dialogue are far better. The minor characters, those who help Gwen on her quest, are particularly well-realized. Gwen herself is not implausibly heroic, and although warned not to eat at their banquet, succumbs to temptation. In spite of her failure to control her appetites, one that parallels her cousin's failure to resist the sexual allures of the King of the Fairies, Gwen grows in confidence and ability, learning a new sense of self-respect. Still, the novel hints at psychological and symbolic meanings that it does not fully articulate. Melling sets up an opposition between the timid Gwen and wilder Finn, for instance, and then takes pains to point out that Gwen's name, Gwyenhyvar is the Welsh version of the Irish Findabhair. Whether they are shadow versions of the same personality or symbols of elements of the psyche remains a mystery that is further complicated by the fact that Finn's lover, Finvarra, also has a name like hers. In spite of obvious intellectual limitations, *The Hunter's Moon* smoothly blends the mythic and the mundane, producing a fast-paced, generally entertaining adventure.

In addition to her young adult fantasies, Melling has also written an adult fantasy, *Falling Out of Time* (1989), and a fictionalized version of her experiences working in Malaysia as a member of the Canada World Youth program. Like her *Miss Chatelaine* article on this subject, *My Blue Country* is written as diary entries. As in the fantasies, the identity theme is prominent because 17-year-old Jesse McKinnock joins the project with the hope that she will 'discover who I really am'. Jessica does not arrive at a final answer, but she grows in understanding as she learns about differences among citizens in her own country and in Malaysia, and as she comes to understand something about the prejudices various people harbour. Her account of the training camps and her life in Malaysia honestly reports the arguments, drinking, and sexual activities of the young volunteers, it provides interesting glimpses of Malaysian culture, and it is earnest in attacking prejudice, but the absence of both dramatic tension and thematic focus make this novel little more than a mildly interesting travelogue.

Melling's fantasies are conventional in theme and in their use of the quest structure. The central characters are rather hollow for novels delving into issues of identity, but the overly elaborate plots do provide some intense and intriguing visions of figures from Irish legend.

Tololwa M. Mollel

Born: 25 June 1952, in Arusha, Tanzania.

Principal Residences: rural Tanzania; Dar-es-Salaam; Edmonton; Minneapolis.

Education: University of Dar-es-Salaam (BA 1972); University of Alberta (MA 1979).

Career: children's theatre director; actor and university lecturer (Tanzania, 1979–86); writer, storyteller, and lecturer since 1986.

Works for Children

Rhino's Boy: A Maasai Legend (Aukland, New Zealand: Outriggers, 1988).

The Orphan Boy, illus. Paul Morin (Toronto: Oxford UP, 1990). **Rev:** *BiC* 19 (Dec. 1990): 31; *CCB-B* 44 (Apr. 1991): 201; *CM* 19 (Jan. 1991): 29; *EL* 18 (Jan. 1991): 52, and 19 (Sept. 1991): 51, and 18 (May 1991): 50; *NYTBR* 96 (11 Aug. 1991): 1; *QQ* 56

(Oct. 1990): 14; *RT* 47 (Feb. 1994): 382; *SL* 39 (Nov. 1991): 142; *SLJ* 37 (July 1991): 70.

Rhinos for Lunch and Elephants for Supper!, illus. Barbara Spurll (Toronto: Oxford UP, 1991). **Rev:** *CCL* 69 (1993): 63; *CM* 19 (Nov. 1991): 339, and 20 (Jan. 1992): 24; *EL* 19 (Mar. 1992): 15, and 21 (Sept. 1993): 59; *QQ* 57 (Aug. 1991): 24; *SLJ* 38 (July 1992): 70.

A Promise to the Sun: An African Story, illus. Beatriz Vidal (Toronto: Little, Brown, 1992). **Rev:** *EL* 21 (Jan. 1994): 61; *QQ* 58 (June 1992): 34; *RT* 47 (Sept. 1993): 53; *SLJ* 38 (July 1992): 62.

The Princess Who Lost Her Hair: An Akamba Legend, illus. Charles Reasoner ([Mahwah, NJ]: Troll Associates, 1993). **Rev:** *CCB-B* 46 (Jan. 1993): 142; *SLJ* 39 (Feb. 1993): 85.

The King and the Tortoise, illus. Kathy Blankley (Toronto: Lester, 1993). **Rev:** *BiC* 22 (May 1993): 31; *CCL* (1995): 55; *CM* 21 (Sept. 1993): 147; *EL* 21 (Jan. 1994): 61; *HB* 69 (May 1993): 340, and 70 (May 1994): 363; *QQ* 59 (Mar. 1993): 58; *SLJ* 39 (Aug. 1993): 160.

The Flying Tortoise: An Igbo Tale, illus. Barbara Spurll (Toronto: Oxford UP, 1993). **Rev:** *BiC* 23 (May 1994): 58; *CCB-B* 48 (Oct. 1994): 58; *CM* 22 (Sept. 1994): 133; *QQ* 60 (Apr. 1994): 36; *SLJ* 40 (Sept. 1994): 210.

Big Boy, illus. E.B. Lewis (Toronto: Stoddart, 1995). **Rev:** *BiC* 24 (Nov. 1995): 40; *CBRA* (1995): 478; *CCB-B* 48 (Mar. 1995): 244; *HB* 71 (July 1995): 453; *QQ* 61 (Aug. 1995): 33; *RT* 49 (Oct. 1995): 156; *SLJ* 41 (June 1995): 93.

Ananse's Feast: An Ashanti Tale, illus. Andrew Glass (New York: Clarion, 1997). **Rev:** *SLJ* 43 (May 1997): 122.

Dume's Roar, illus. Kathy Blankley Roman (Toronto: Stoddart Kids, 1997). **Rev:** *CCB-B* 51 (Apr. 1998): 289; *QQ* 64 (Feb. 1998): 48.

Kele's Secret, illus. Catherine Stock (Toronto: Stoddart Kids, 1997). **Rev:** *CCL* 23 (1996): 59.

Kitoto the Mighty, illus. Kristi Frost (Toronto: Stoddart Kids, 1998).

Shadow Dance, illus. Donna Perrone (New York: Clarion, 1998).

Song Bird, illus. Rosanne Litzinger (New York: Clarion, 1998).

Selected Discussions

Jenkinson, Dave. 'Tololwa Mollel: "Eater of Words," Storyteller and Picturebook Author', *EL* 21 (Jan.-Feb. 1994): 61–4.

Saldanha, Louise. 'Bordering the Mainstream: The Writing of Tololwa Mollel', *CCL* 81 (1996): 24–30.

Internationally praised for his retellings of African tales, Tololwa Marti Mollel places himself within two narrative traditions. 'I see myself', he says, 'as both a storyteller and an author.' As a storyteller, Mollel is part of an ancient oral tradition, one that he calls 'the continuum of storytellers' who pass on tales from various African cultures. Mollel also belongs, however, to the tradition of writers, a literary tradition in which originality is a virtue. Therefore he does not merely repeat his sources: 'I add my own themes or amplify the themes of the original tales.' In fact, in addition to retelling tales, Mollel writes original stories, some of which employ the narrative structures and motifs of folktales. In Mollel's best works, the storyteller and author are inseparable: the storyteller provides a sense of immediacy through such oral devices as rhythm, repetition, and African terms; the author provides clarity, polish, and thematic focus.

Mollel began his career with retellings of three ironic Maasai tales. The first, *Rhino's Boy*, a monograph published in New Zealand, is a dark tale of tragic destiny. When villagers kill an attacking rhino, a boy, who has lived under a prophecy that only the rhino can kill him before he becomes a man, jubilantly dances around its corpse. The subsequent action suggests, however, that one cannot escape fate: the boy slips in the rhino's blood, falls on its horn, which points up towards the prophetic spirits, and dies.

Mollel's second ironic work, *The Orphan Boy*, is rich in pathos. Based on a *pourquoi* tale about the planet Venus, which the Maasai call Kileken, or the orphan boy, it illustrates both the happiness of love and the pain of betrayal. The initial section of the story focuses on the magic power of love. A lonely old man, whose good heart is evident because he loves the stars as if they were his children, takes in Kileken, a mysterious orphan boy seeking a home. Kileken soon changes the man's fortunes, making him happy and wealthy. Even when drought strikes, Kileken mysteriously keeps the man's cattle fat. The old man thus comes to love Kileken as a son. In the second part of the tale, uncontrolled curiosity leads to a destructive betrayal of trust. Kileken, explaining that his father told him never to reveal the secret of his magic power, warns the curious old man that he will lose his good fortune if he learns that secret. Nevertheless, urged on by his shadow, the symbol of rational curiosity, the old man violates the trust that Kileken demands. When Kileken goes out with the cattle, the old man follows and sees the boy transform the parched land into a verdant pasture. Kileken catches sight of the old man, however, and explodes into a star that ascends into the sky.

The Orphan Boy reflects the values of Maasai society, which decree that it is not proper to seek some kinds of knowledge—children, for example, are not supposed to listen to the talk of their elders—but this cautionary tale transcends cultural specifics. No knowledge of Maasai culture is necessary to appreciate that the old man shows weakness by putting his curiosity ahead of the boy's request for secrecy. He clearly violates the trust between parent and child, a trust that Kileken demonstrates by obeying his own father. The old man thus destroys the love and happiness that depend on trust, and he once again becomes poor and lonely. Paul Morin amplifies the poignancy of this tale with pictures that won three major illustration awards: the Governor-General's Award for

Children's Literature (Illustration), 1990; the Elizabeth Mrazik-Cleaver Canadian Picture Book Award, 1991; and the Amelia Frances Howard-Gibbon Illustrator's Award, 1991.

Mollel's third ironic Maasai tale, *Rhinos for Lunch and Elephants for Supper!*, is different in mood: it is a comic cumulative tale about the discrepancy between appearance and reality. When a voice within little hare's cave booms out that it is a monster that eats rhinos for lunch and elephants for supper, the frightened hare seeks help. In turn, increasingly larger animals approach the cave, but the voice frightens away each. Finally, a little frog shouts that she eats monsters for supper. Absurdly, what emerges is a caterpillar that used the echoes within the cave to make itself sound like a monster. The humour comes, first, from the marked contrast between the proud certainty of each animal as it approaches the cave and its blind panic when it hears the voice. Second, it comes from a double irony: the smallest character and the one least likely to combat a monster, a female frog, is the only successful animal, and she succeeds by using the caterpillar's own trick of boasting. This humour establishes two themes: that appearances can deceive and that wit is more effective than brawn in solving problems.

Wit is, of course, the province of the trickster, a figure Mollel constantly employs because 'Something has to make things happen in a children's story, and the trickster makes things happen, for better or worse.' One of his best trickster tales is *Ananse's Feast*, a revenge tale that uses parallel episodes to show that people reap what they sow. In the first, Ananse the Spider slyly insists that politeness demands that Akye the Turtle wash his hands before sharing a feast. Because Akye walks on all fours and therefore dirties his hands immediately after washing them, Ananse repeatedly sends him away. Consequently, greedy Ananse manages to consume the entire feast himself. The second episode reverses the situation. Inviting Ananse for a feast in his underwater home, Akye insists that polite manners require that Ananse remove his robe. Because Ananse loaded his pockets with stones in order to remain submerged, he immediately floats to the surface and never gets a share of Akye's feast. *The King and the Tortoise*, which also focuses on two tricksters, is lighter in mood. The first trickster, a proud king, uses his wit in the service of vanity. Insisting that he is the smartest person in the world, the king challenges his subjects to prove that they are cleverer than he is by making him a robe of smoke. After everyone else fails in this obviously impossible test, Tortoise exacts a promise that the king will provide whatever he needs to complete the robe. When Tortoise then asks for thread of fire, the outwitted king, unwilling to confess his own inability to perform a task, laughingly declares that the kingdom holds the two cleverest beings in the world. A kind of trickster also appears in *Song Bird*, a modified version of a traditional tale that preserves the quality of African oral tales through its use of numerous songs in Swahili. Shortly after the family's cows disappear, Mariamu finds a bird that has made weeds overrun the family's freshly tilled field. In exchange for Mariamu's promise not to clear the field again, the bird magically provides her family with gourds of milk. Mariamu's parents are greedy, however, and put the bird in a cage to extort more milk from it. After she again shows kindness by releasing the bird, it takes her to Makucha, a cow-stealing monster, and helps her by tricking Makucha into blunting its nails, the source of its strength. With their cattle returned, the family allows the field to remain in weeds. This trickster quest tale thus establishes the need to respect nature and to avoid greediness.

Two other trickster tales rank among Mollel's best work. *Shadow Dance*, an original story presented in the manner of a folktale, presents an outwitted trickster of a far more sinister character. Stranded in a gully after flood waters recede, Crocodile gets little Salome to free him and escort him to the river, where he seizes and threatens to eat her. Salome then tricks him into proving to a curious pigeon that he had been trapped and was not feigning his predicament. When Crocodile then foolishly strands himself to prove his claims, Salome wisely abandons him to his fate. The central section of the story, in which the girl seeks the help of various elements in nature, introduces extraneous thematic elements. Nevertheless, it generates meaningful irony: the ineffective aid of the boastful pigeon teaches Salome to rely on her own wit to survive. In addition to its surface theme about using wit to survive, the story also delivers an indirect lesson in 'streetproofing', suggesting that children must be careful about trusting strangers. *Dume's Roar*, another original tale, has a much more controlled plot. Kobe the tortoise becomes a true hero by using his wits to save the kingdom in two ways. First, when hunters threaten the forest, Kobe tricks the frightened Dume, King of the Forest, into saving everyone. Kobe, pretending that he cannot hear Dume's roar, tells the lion that he must roar mightily to dislodge something stuck in his throat. Dume roars, and the hunters flee in panic. Afterwards, when the grateful Dume offers to reward Kobe for restoring his roar, Kobe gets the lion to reform his tyrannical ways and to boast that he will be both good and wise. The tale thus shows that the true benefactors of society are not always the ones who receive the greatest credit.

Mollel's other books include two *pourquoi* tales, *The Flying Tortoise*, an Igbo story explaining why the tortoise has a dull shell, and *A Promise to the Sun*, an original tale explaining why bats avoid daylight. The former, although not especially distinguished, is interesting for its presentation of Mbeku the tortoise as a greedy trickster; the latter has an awkward, overly contrived, and unsatisfying plot. Similar problems of construction beset *The Princess Who Lost Her Hair*, a commissioned retelling of an Akamba story about a vain princess who loses all her hair after refusing to let a magical bird have a strand for its nest. According to the author's note, the tale shows the importance of all living things, but the text itself passes too quickly over the crucial events in which Muoma, a beggar boy who seeks the bird so that he can restore the princess's hair, unwittingly passes tests of his virtues by showing kindness to ants, a flower, and a mouse.

Kitoto the Mighty, a highly modified version of a traditional tale, is a much better constructed quest tale. Kitoto, a mouse, sets out to find a strong friend to protect him from the hawk. After learning that the river, the sun, the wind, and the mountain have weaknesses, Kitoto meets a mountain mouse, whose ability to chomp tunnels in the mountain gives him title to the most powerful being in the world. *Kitoto the Mighty* lacks dramatic tension and a convincing plot resolution, but it amusingly presents the ironic notions that the smallest being may have the greatest power and that one must learn to appreciate one's own seemingly small abilities.

Mollel has also experimented with African stories that do not imitate folk tales. According to its author's note, *Big Boy* uses the African motif of the prodigious child. Its plot, however, relies on the familiar therapeutic dream journey. Little Oli, who is always told that he is too small to do what his big brother does, sneaks out of the house to have an adventure. After a magic bird transforms him into a giant, he travels around the country, becomes tired, and falls asleep. When he awakens, he is again a small boy, who is surrounded by his worried family. Because his mother carries him home while his brother must walk, Oli cheerfully decides that being small has advantages. *Big Boy* has a clear theme about self-acceptance, and it cleverly maintains ambiguity by never declaring that Oli has been dreaming, but its plot is weak because Oli's travels are devoid of dramatic interest. *Kele's Secret*, inspired by Mollel's experiences on his grandfather's farm, is far more satisfying. A simple first-person account, it focuses on the pride of a little boy who helps his family by discovering where Kele the hen has been hiding her eggs. Representing a new direction for a writer known for adapting traditional materials, both of these contemporary stories suggest that Mollel can point to universal meaning in African experience without sacrificing its exotic qualities.

See also: *CA* 137; *SATA* 88; *WSMP*.

L.M. Montgomery

Born: 30 November 1874, in Clifton, PEI.

Died: 24 April 1942, in Toronto.

Principal Residences: Cavendish, PEI; Charlottetown, PEI; Prince Albert, Sask.; Halifax; Leaskdale, Ont.; Norval, Ont.; Toronto.

Education: Price of Wales College, Charlottetown (teacher's certificate, 1894); Dalhousie College, Halifax.

Career: teacher; newspaper reporter; writer.

Works for Children

Anne of Green Gables (Boston: Page, 1908).

Anne of Avonlea (Boston: Page, 1909).

Kilmeny of the Orchard (Boston: Page, 1910).

The Story Girl (Boston: Page, 1911).

Chronicles of Avonlea (Boston: Page, 1912).

The Golden Road (Boston: Page, 1913).

Anne of the Island (Boston: Page, 1915).

Anne's House of Dreams (New York: Stokes, 1917).

Rainbow Valley (Toronto: McClelland & Stewart, 1919).

Further Chronicles of Avonlea (Boston: Page, 1920).

Rilla of Ingleside (Toronto: McClelland & Stewart, 1921).

Emily of New Moon (New York: Stokes, 1923).

Emily Climbs (New York: Stokes, 1925).

The Blue Castle (Toronto: McClelland & Stewart, 1926).

Emily's Quest (New York: Stokes, 1927).

Magic for Marigold (Toronto: McClelland & Stewart, 1929).

A Tangled Web (New York: Stokes, 1931).

Pat of Silver Bush (New York: Stokes, 1933).

Mistress Pat: A Novel of Silver Bush (New York: Stokes, 1935).

Anne of Windy Poplars (New York: Stokes, 1936).

Jane of Lantern Hill (Toronto: McClelland & Stewart, 1937).

Anne of Ingleside (New York: Stokes, 1939).

The Road to Yesterday (Toronto: McGraw-Hill Ryerson, 1974).

The Doctor's Sweetheart and Other Stories (Toronto: McGraw-Hill Ryerson, 1979).

Akin to Anne: Tales of Other Orphans (Toronto: McClelland & Stewart, 1988).

Along the Shore: Tales by the Sea (Toronto: McClelland & Stewart, 1989).

Among the Shadows: Tales from the Darker Side (Toronto: McClelland & Stewart, 1990).

Other

The Selected Journals 1: 1889–1910; 2: 1910–1921; 3: 1921–1929; 4: 1929–1935, eds Mary Rubio and Elizabeth Waterston (Toronto: Oxford UP, 1985, 1987, 1992, 1998).

The Alpine Path: The Story of My Career (Don Mills, Ont.: Fitzhenry & Whiteside, 1974).

Selected Discussions

Canadian Children's Literature 65 (1992). (Special L.M. Montgomery issue.)

Gillen, Mollie. *The Wheel of Things: A Biography of L.M. Montgomery* (Don Mills, Ont.: Fitzhenry & Whiteside, 1975).

Reimer, Mavis, ed. *Such a Simple Little Tale: Critical Responses to L.M. Montgomery's Anne of Green Gables* (Metuchen, NJ: Scarecrow Press, 1992).

Rubio, Mary. *Writing a Life: L.M. Montgomery* (Toronto: ECW Press, 1995).

'I cannot remember when I was not writing, or when I did not mean to be an author. To write has always been my central purpose toward which every effort and hope and ambition of my life has grouped itself.' So wrote the creator of Canada's most famous literary heroine, Anne of Green Gables. As a child, Lucy Maud Montgomery led a relatively quiet life in rural Prince Edward Island. However, she lived a richly imaginative one. She gloried in the scenery of the Island and in her mind she transformed it into a rich fairyland. 'I had, in my vivid imagination', she was to write, 'a passport to the geography of fairyland.' At age nine, she showed her father a blank-verse poem she had composed and was upset when he replied that it was very blank indeed. In an ironic turn of events, while she was living briefly with him in Prince Albert, Saskatchewan, 'On Cape LeForce', her first published poem, based on a Prince Edward Island legend, was published in the *Charlottetown Daily Patriot*.

During her time as a teacher, she steadfastly pursued her literary career, getting up at six o'clock and writing for an hour in an unheated room. In 1895, she received her first payment: five dollars for a story accepted by an American magazine. Her works appeared regularly, and she wrote that, by 1904, she had earned nearly $600 from her writings. In 1904, reading over one of the notebooks she had been keeping, she came across an entry about a couple who had applied to an orphanage for a boy and had, by mistake, been sent a girl. Writing in her spare time over the next year, she created *Anne of Green Gables*, which was published in 1908 and which, along with its numerous sequels, made Montgomery one of Canada's best-known authors. In spite of the novel's success and the popularity of the heroine, the demands of publishers and readers for further Anne stories caused the author to become tired of her creation; Montgomery spoke of feeling a prisoner of her heroine.

The opening sentence of *Anne of Green Gables* epitomizes in the symbol of the brook the life of Anne Shirley and, in many ways, the lives of Montgomery's other heroines: 'Mrs. Rachel Lynde lived just where Avonlea main road dipped down into a little hollow, fringed with alders and ladies' eardrops and traversed by a brook that had its source way back in the woods of the old Cuthbert place; it was reputed to be an intricate, headlong brook in its earlier course through those woods, with dark secrets of pool and cascade; but by the time it reached Lynde's Hollow it was a quiet, well-conducted little stream, for not even a brook could run past Mrs. Rachel Lynde's door without due regard for decency and decorum.' The stream, lively, independent, and somewhat impulsive, slowing down as it nears civilization, is like the heroines, who mature and accept the social values represented by Mrs Lynde.

For Anne Shirley, the lonely, talkative, and insecure Nova Scotia orphan, maturity makes her an established member of her Prince Edward Island community, wife of a doctor and mother of a big, usually happy family. However, the road to maturity is not easy for Anne. The early books treat the stages of her development, recounting the setbacks she experiences and the ways in which she learns to understand herself and her community. When, early in *Anne of Green Gables*, Marilla Cuthbert agrees to keep her, the girl begins her socialization process. She starts to make friends for the first time in her life, calling them 'kindred spirits'; she frequently disagrees both with adults and children; and often finds herself in trouble because of her active imagination, her impulsiveness, and her fiery temper. However, Anne doesn't always blunder; she is good, honest, loyal, and generally responsible, and her noblest act takes place after Matthew's death, when she gives up a college scholarship so that she can help Marilla keep their home. Some people feel that in making the heroine grow to a responsible young adult, the author was compromising, giving in to accepted attitudes towards fiction for girls: she replaced the imaginative, spontaneous little girl with a much more ordinary, socially acceptable young woman.

Chronicles of Avonlea presents a year in the life of the 17-year-old teacher. Idealistic and full of theories at the beginning of the year, Anne is still prone to mishaps. Gone, however, is the spontaneous, ingenuous heroine of the first novel. Her adventures seem contrived, and her good-natured altruism seems almost too good to be true. The same criticism can be leveled against *Anne of the Island*, the account of her time at college. In *Anne's House of Dreams* the long-awaited marriage to Gilbert Blythe occurs. However, before it there are many conflicts and delays which the author seems to have employed to prolong the suspense before the great event. When Anne and Gilbert move into their new home, he begins his medical practice, and she cultivates 'kindred spirits'. During the story, she is able to pave the way for unhappy Leslie Moore to marry author Owen Ford and helps Captain Jim publish his book, which becomes the sensation of the season. Montgomery's increasing dislike for writing sequels perhaps accounts for the lessening power of the later stories.

Montgomery's second-best-known heroine, Emily Byrd Star, central character of *Emily of New Moon*, *Emily Climbs*, and *Emily's Quest*, bears some resemblance to Anne: orphaned as a young child, she must move to a new home where, with pride and determination, she achieves happiness. At the end of the third book, after many misunderstandings she finally marries the man she has long been interested in. Like her creator, Emily is an author, struggling to achieve success in spite of the obstacles she faces as a Canadian writer and a woman.

The Prince Edward Island landscape has a great influence on the heroines. On the drive from the station with Matthew, Anne reacts imaginatively to each locale, giving each a new name that, for her, captures its spirit. Emily comes to realize how important New Moon is for her. Early in *Pat of Silver Bush*, the central character names all the fields and groves around Silver Bush and announces: 'I don't want to love anyone or anything but my own family and Silver Bush.' The dreariness of Toronto's misnamed Gay Street depresses the title heroine of *Jane of Lantern Hill*; happiness comes for her only after she has left Toronto to spend a summer with her father on Prince Edward Island.

Montgomery's heroines do not mature in isolation. They have best friends who are very important and, although it may take them time to realize it, each, with the exception of Jane, finds a male companion for whom she is ideally suited. The heroines are also surrounded by older people who influence them and who, in turn, are influenced. The crusty Marilla and shy Matthew are, as it were, brought to life by the little girl they have adopted. Emily gradually wins the heart of her aloof Aunt Elizabeth.

In spite of the large number of books Montgomery wrote, she is best remembered for one book and its title character. In *Anne of Green Gables* she undoubtedly created her finest work. Mark Twain called Anne 'the dearest, and most lovable child in fiction since the immortal Alice', and the book's admirers are found in many countries, including Japan, where young school children annually delight in reading it. The success in the United States and Canada of a 1985 television special attests to its continued popularity and vitality. Reasons for its success are easily discovered. The central character is fresh and original; she is unconventional, unlike the prim and proper girls who peopled the majority of late nineteenth- and early twentieth-century children's books. The events she becomes involved in are often funny and always moving. The characters she encounters are deftly, vividly portrayed. In addition, beneath the realistic portrayal of Anne and her Prince Edward Island setting is one of the most enduring plot structures of children's literature: the search for security and self-fulfilment. Like the orphans of so many fairy tales, Anne earns her right to a 'happy ever after' ending. It is not just the structure of the orphan story that makes the book so appealing; it is also the skill with which the author has dressed the framework, fleshed out the skeleton. In developing the character of Anne, giving her a full life in a fully realized social and geographical setting, Montgomery has created the only book of Canadian children's literature that has a secure, established position as an international classic.

See also: *AAYA* 11; *CA* 108, 137; *CLR* 8; *DLB* 11; *SATA*; *TCCW*; *WSMP*.

Allen Morgan

Born: 29 September 1946 in New York City.

Principal Residences: New York City; Vancouver; Toronto.

Education: attended but did not graduate from Swarthmore College, New York University, and Carnegie-Mellon University Drama School; University of British Columbia (B.Ed.)

Career: kindergarten teacher; storyteller; writer.

Works for Children

Molly and Mr. Maloney, illus. Maryann Kovalski (Toronto: Kids Can Press, 1981). **Rev:** *BiC* 11 (Aug. 1982): 39; *CCL* 34 (1984): 73; *QQ* 48 (June 1982): 3, and 48 (Dec. 1982): 25; *SLJ* 29 (Jan. 1983): 63.

Beautiful Dreamer (Toronto: Kids Can Press 1982). **Rev:** *CCL* 33 (1984): 52.

Christopher and the Elevator Closet, illus. Franklin Hammond (Toronto: Kids Can Press, 1982). **Rev:** *BiC* 11 (Aug. 1982): 39; *CCL* 34 (1984): 73.

Barnaby and Mr. Ling, illus. Franklin Hammond (Toronto: Annick, 1984). **Rev:** *BiC* 13 (May 1984): 31: *CCL* 39/40 (1985): 115; *QQ* 50 (Apr. 1984): 16; *SLJ* 31 (Sept. 1984): 107.

Matthew and the Midnight Tow Truck, illus. Michael Martchenko (Toronto: Annick, 1984). **Rev:** *CCL* 39/40 (1985): 125, and 44 (1986): 94; *EL* 12 (Jan. 1985): 45; *QQ* 50 (Nov. 1984): 13; *SLJ* 31 (Apr. 1985): 81.

The Kids From B.A.D. (Richmond Hill: Scholastic-TAB, 1984).

Christopher and the Dream Dragon, illus. Brenda Clark (Toronto: Kids Can Press, 1984). **Rev:** *CCL* 43 (1986): 70; *SLJ* 31 (May 1985): 80.

Matthew and the Midnight Turkeys, illus. Michael Martchenko (Toronto: Annick, 1985). **Rev:** *BiC* 14 (Nov. 1985): 37; *QQ* 51 (Dec. 1985): 30; *SLJ* 32 (Apr. 1986): 77.

Sadie and the Snowman, illus. Brenda Clark (Toronto: Kids Can Press, 1985). **Rev:** *EL* 13 (Mar. 1986): 15, and 21 (May 1994): 55; *QQ* 51 (Aug. 1985): 37.

Daddy-Care, illus. John Richmond (Toronto: Annick, 1986). **Rev:** *EL* 14 (Mar. 1987): 47; *QQ* 52 (Apr. 1986): 26; *SLJ* 33 (Dec. 1986): 93.

Nicole's Boat: A Good-Night Story, illus. Jirina Marton (Toronto: Annick, 1986). **Rev:** *APBR* 13 (Nov. 1986): 6; *QQ* 52 (Aug. 1986): 36; *SLJ* 33 (May 1987): 90.

Matthew and the Midnight Money Van, illus. Michael Martchenko (Toronto: Annick, 1987). **Rev:** *BYP* 1 (June 1987): 5; *CCL* 47 (1987): 96; *SLJ* 34 (Jan. 1988): 68.

Search for the New-Moon Stones (Toronto: Annick, 1987). **Rev:** *BYP* 2 (Feb. 1988): 8.

Ellie and the Ivy, illus. Steve Beinicke (Toronto: Oxford UP, 1989). **Rev:** *CBRA* (1989): 303; *CCL* 62 (1991): 98.

Andrew and the Wild Bikes, illus. Steve Beinicke (Toronto: Annick, 1990). **Rev:** *BiC* 19 (Dec. 1990): 33; *CBRA* (1990): 300; *CCL* 64 (1991), 73; *CM* 19 (Jan. 1991), 29; *HB* 67 (Jan. 1991): 108; *QQ* 56 (July 1990): 36.

Sam and the Tigers, illus. Christina Farmilo (Toronto: Oasis, 1990). **Rev:** *CBRA* (1990): 300; *CCL* 63 (1991), 97; *CM* 18 (Nov. 1990): 270; *EL* 18 (Nov. 1990): 61.

Brendon and the Wolves, illus. Christina Farmilo (Toronto: Oasis, 1991). **Rev:** *BiC* 20 (May 1991): 53; *CCL* 67 (1992): 82; *CM* 19 (May 1991): 17.

The Magic Hockey Skates, illus. Michael Martchenko (Toronto: Oxford UP, 1991). **Rev:** *BiC* 21 (Apr. 1992): 44; *CCL* 67 (1992): 82; *CM* 19 (Nov. 1991): 354, and 20 (Jan. 1992): 13; *RT* 45 (Apr. 1992): 639.

Ryan's Giant, illus. Marian Buchanan (Toronto: Oxford UP, 1992). **Rev:** *CCL* 69 (1993): 86; *CM* 20 (Sept. 1992): 209.

Megan and the Weather Witch: Two Stories, illus. Vladyana Krykorka (Toronto: Oasis, 1992). **Rev:** *CBRA* (1992): 299; *CCL* 76 (1994): 85; *CM* 21 (Sept. 1993): 137; *QQ* 59 (Apr. 1993): 35.

Celebrate the Season—Fall: A Story Collection, illus. Vladyana Krykorka (Toronto: Oasis, 1994). **Rev:** *CBRA* (1994): 494; *CM* 22 (Oct. 1994): 180.

Jessica Moffat's Silver Locket, illus. Michael Martchenko (Toronto: Stoddart, 1994). **Rev:** *CBRA* (1994): 460; *QQ* 60 (Nov. 1994): 34.

Celebrate the Season—Winter: A Story Collection, illus. Vladyana Krykorka (Toronto: Oasis, 1995). **Rev:** *CBRA* (1995): 514.

Matthew and the Midnight Ball Game, illus. Michael Martchenko (Toronto: Stoddart, 1997). **Rev:** *CBRA* (1997): 483.

Matthew and the Midnight Pilot, illus. Michael Martchenko (Toronto: Stoddart, 1997). **Rev:** *CBRA* (1997): 483.

Matthew and the Midnight Flood, illus. Michael Martchenko (Toronto: Stoddart, 1998).

Matthew and the Midnight Pirates, illus. Michael Martchenko (Toronto: Stoddart, 1998).

Matthew and the Midnight Hospital, illus. Michael Martchenko (Toronto: Stoddart, 1999).

Selected Discussions

Granfield, Linda. 'Allen Morgan: Waiting for the Midnight Hour', *QQ* 51 (Aug. 1985): 32.

The major motif and the central plot device in many of Allen Morgan's books is the dream. Sometimes he creates pleasing ambiguity or irony by refusing to state definitely that fantastic events occur during a dream, but the meaning of the stories remains constant. Through dreams or fantasy, Morgan's young protagonists resolve their problems or come to a new sense of self-worth.

After coming to Canada in 1968, Morgan helped to found Theatre Passe Muraille and wrote for adults several plays and one novel, *Dropping Out in 3/4 Time* (1972). Since 1980, when he gave up his job as a kindergarten teacher to devote himself to full-time writing, he has concentrated on producing children's books and on performing as a children's storyteller.

Morgan's children's books include easy readers, short fantasies that combine fairy-tale elements and contemporary settings, novels, and picture-story books. The easy readers, part of the Kids-Can-Read series, are limited by a controlled vocabulary. All three use the dream motif to depict a child's understanding of his or her relationship to the world. *Christopher and the Elevator Closet* and its sequel, *Christopher and the Dream Dragon*, are structured around dream journeys. Both resemble *pourquoi* tales because they explain such natural phenomena as rain, thunder, lightning, and the phases of the moon. *Molly and Mr. Maloney*, a series of three connected stories, presents life from the viewpoint of a child for whom fantasy is real.

Designed for adult storytellers or accomplished child readers, Morgan's short fantasies contain the words and music to songs that perform a magical role in the tales. These tales also contain such fairy-tale elements as archetypal giants and witches. The first of the three loosely connected tales forming *Ryan's Giant* has a promising premise: a boy learns to control his bad dreams by selling them to a giant. The idea that imagination, which can be the source of fears, may also be used to control imaginary fear is the most notable feature of the tale. Like the decidedly inferior tales that follow it, it suffers from ineffective plotting, forced humour, and erratic characterization. *Megan and the Weather Witch* contains two tales about a Toronto girl who meets a weather-controlling witch. In the first tale, Megan helps the Witch and her bats to round up the clouds and bring much-needed rain to Toronto. In the second, the Witch takes Megan to watch the statues on a Toronto street come alive at midnight and form a raucous Victoria Day parade. They contain some amusing word play, but these tales are awkward, failing to make the fantastic episodes meaningful. Similar problems beset both of Morgan's *Celebrate the Season* collections. The tales present both literary myth—the personification of the seasons to explain why they come one at a time—and the adventures of two children, Michael and Megan, who play with the personified seasons and with such other personified elements as Windman and Iceman. Occasionally, the tales operate as *pourquoi* myths. The fall collection thus explains the presence of summer-like weather during autumn by recounting an episode during which Summer, seeking the socks he needs to wear in order to dream, returns during the time that Fall is supposed to rule the land. Similarly, the winter collection contains a tale that explains the phases of the moon by describing Megan's adventures with a dragon that constantly eats the moon. In the absence of gripping and memorable events, these tales rely on weak contrivances, such as Summer's socks, that make them awkward as adventures and negligible as literary myths.

Morgan has written three novel-length books. *The Kids from B.A.D.* links six stories about the Barton Avenue Detectives, a group of children who solve a number of crimes. The stories are implausible escapist fiction—the stuff of childish daydreams—but one, the story of a boy who steals so that he can have money to bribe people into liking him, contains both crisp characterization and thematic focus absent in the other stories. *Beautiful Dreamer* is a problem novel about a 12-year-old girl who feels alienated because she is unable to make significant financial contributions to her family. Using dream sequences to conclude all but the first and last chapters, the novel successfully explores Katie's feelings of frustration and inadequacy. Less successful but more ambitious is *Search for the New-Moon Stones*, an unstable mixture of zany characters, slapstick comedy, fairy-tale situations, dreams, secondary-world quest fantasy, animal fantasy, and the problem novel. When Jennifer and her mother move in with the girl's eccentric great-grandfather, she discovers a world of magic in the ravine next to the house. Falling up into the moon, which is really a hole in the sky, Jennifer has a mystical experience of oneness with the universe, overcomes her fears about the future, and locates a stone that gives her the confidence that, in spite of any future changes, things will work out for her and her mother. *Search for the New-Moon Stones* is interesting as an exploration of the power of perception, arguing that even the mundane contains the magical, but it does not adequately sustain this significant theme or satisfactorily develop Jennifer's growing confidence. Instead, its uncontrolled and crowded inventiveness prevents the characters and plot from blending into a satisfying unity.

Morgan's most popular and successful works are his 'Matthew's Midnight Adventure' picture books, which use to good advantage the dream journey structure. Each book follows the same pattern. During the day, something happens to Matthew Holmes that inspires a series of adventures that occur 'just after midnight', the time of dreaming and magic in all of Morgan's texts. The next morning, Matthew tells his beleaguered and puzzled mother about his adventures, providing her with some physical sign of them. The first in the series, *Matthew and the Midnight Tow Truck* is the most tightly plotted. Matthew, having lost a toy van and having been refused red licorice for dessert, goes out after midnight with a tow-truck driver who believes that licorice builds muscles. When Matthew awakens the next morning, he has his van, and his mother, hearing of the need for red licorice, takes him to the store. In *Matthew and the Midnight Turkeys*, Matthew, having been called a turkey for his behaviour during the day, at midnight joins a group of turkeys, whose silly manner of playing and eating satirizes adult-imposed rules of decorum. Matthew leaves an unusually messy kitchen for his mother to discover the next morning. In *Matthew and the Midnight Money Van*, he goes to a midnight mall to buy a Mother's Day present, which he discovers the next day hidden in a box of cereal.

Matthew's dual concern about a toy plane that has become lodged in a tree and his mother's concern about a package that she is expecting leads to the dream adventure in *Matthew and the Midnight Pilot*. Invited to accompany a pilot who has landed on his roof, Matthew eventually delivers his mother's package and recovers his lost toy. *Matthew and the Midnight Flood* has the little boy creating waking-world chaos when he has a toy robot explore the basement drain during a rainstorm. The toy becomes stuck, and the basement floods. Matthew, who has wondered where water goes when one pulls the bathtub plug, then goes on a midnight adventure with a plumber, whom he helps to save the city from flooding. *Matthew and the Midnight Ball Game* has a more direct and harmless connection between the daylight and night-time worlds: Matthew, who was playing ball during the day and listening to the World Series at bedtime, joins the Toronto Turkeys just after midnight for a wacky world championship game against the Montreal Posties.

The adventure in *Matthew and the Midnight Pirates* develops from two concerns. First, Matthew is worried that the library board is going to change the rates and that he will have to pay a big fine for an overdue book about pirates. Second, inspired by the book, Matthew has hidden his mother's earrings, drawing a treasure map showing their location, but he has now forgotten where he hid the map. Around about midnight, therefore, he has a wild adventure involving pirates, librarians, and the ubiquitous midnight turkeys, and they convince the library board not to increase fines and to extend the loan period for Matthew's book. The next morning, Matthew turns over the card in the pocket of his library book and finds a stamp indicating that his book is not overdue. Furthermore, he finds his treasure map in the card pocket and is therefore able to return his mother's earrings. *Matthew and the Midnight Hospital* also combines two plot threads. After Matthew scrapes his knee performing a circus act for his mother and she places a bandage on it, they rescue and place in their garage a squirrel that has kocked itself out falling from a tree. That night, in a wild satire of medicine, Matthew goes to the Midnight Hospital where he has a transplant—of his bandage—and the staff heals the squirrel. Performing a fantastic circus trick by being shot out of a cannon, Matthew returns home, releasing the squirrel from his garage. The series is formulaic, but each book humorously supports Matthew's sense of empowerment because he returns from every adventure in the midnight world convinced of his ability to succeed at tasks or to alter events for the better. Much of the pleasure in these stories comes, however, from the reader's superior understanding of events: readers, unlike Matthew, realize that adventures occur during dreams and that Matthew fails to understand that his proofs of their reality actually have mundane explanations.

Morgan has had mixed success in his other picture books. The early ones lack the sustained wit and energy that make the 'Matthew's Midnight Adventure' stories memorable. *Daddy-Care* is simply an extended joke reversing the normal pattern of adult-child relationships. *Sadie and the Snowman* is an uninspired and predictable story of a girl who saves some melted snow from a snowman to form the basis of a new snowman the following year. *Barnaby and Mr. Ling*, designed as a kind of fairy tale about an elephant and a peanut man who run away from a circus to live their dreams, falters on the sentimentality inherent in its open-ended conclusion, an overt invitation for the reader to join the characters in their dream. *Nicole's Boat: A Good-Night Story* suffers from the same problem. Its initial sections are folkloric in structure as, in turn, a crow, a cow, and some kittens join Nicole on her boat sailing 'to the end of the day'. Each makes a contribution to the boat (the illustrations show it altering size and changing in design), which eventually reaches the sea. The book ends with the narrator-father inviting the sleeping Nicole to bring back to him stories of all that she sees on the sea of night. Obviously designed as a soporific to lure children into sleep, the book lacks a plot that would invite rereading or make it satisfying outside of bedtime.

When he eschews open-ended conclusions and sentimentality, Morgan has relatively more success. *Andrew and the Wild Bikes*, in which a boy whose family cannot afford to buy him a bicycle discovers a herd of bikes and tames one, shares some of the zaniness of the Matthew books. *Ellie and the Ivy*, a contemporary fairy tale about a lonely girl who convinces the well-behaved ivy at her father's hotel to rebel, has considerable wit. The personified ivy is obviously the little girl's alter ego. Unfortunately, although it shows that children can be wittier than adults in solving problems, the story retreats from a solution to its central problem, Ellie's loneliness, by having her happily cavort with the ivy at night. Although the story overtly suggests that Ellie must learn to consider the feelings of others by exercising self-control, the covert message, probably an unintended one, is that lonely children can find happiness only in the escape of dream adventures. The message of *Sam and the Tigers* is far clearer and more satisfying. When three tigers come in sequence to his house and threaten him on his fifth birthday, the terrified Sam offers them whatever they want. Sam eventually overcomes his terror, however, and turns the tigers into tiger butter. Using the repetitive structure of folktales, this tale succeeds as a didactic illustration of the idea that confident people can overcome fear and as a comical explanation for the source of crunchy peanut butter (Sam believes that the peanuts are tiger teeth).

The textual elements are more substantial in Morgan's other picture books. *Brendon and the Wolves* tells of a little boy who sleeps in a tent at his cottage, wanders off in the night, is transformed into a wolf, spends what he thinks is a year away from home, and returns to his parents. It gives some sense of a wolf's life, evokes an aura of mystery, and creates ambiguity about whether Brendon dreamed the entire adventure, but it has little else to commend it. Both of Morgan's other picture books explore special objects. *The Magic Hockey Skates* effectively employs ambiguity within a contemporary fairy-tale structure. When little Joey, disappointed at receiving a used pair of skates instead of the new ones that he covets, is told that the skates are magical and will grant him three wishes, he wishes to be a better skater, to be able to skate like the big kids, and, when his brother is injured in a championship game, to be as good in goal as his brother. Joey receives each of his wishes, but the power of the tale resides in its ambiguity, its implication that positive thinking and constant practice are the true magic behind Joey's achievements. The special object central to *Jessica Moffat's Silver Locket* is an old locket bequeathed to a girl by her grandmother. When Jessica's father runs into financial trouble, Jessica dreams that she goes back in time and sees her grandmother putting a valuable stamp that her war-bound fiancé has given her inside the locket. After waking up and retrieving the stamp, Jessica decides to keep the locket empty until she finds something that is a key to her own character. The story touchingly connects the generations by having the grandmother appear in the dream as Wise Woman who offers advice and who guides Jessica back into the past. Unfortunately, the mundane and contrived result of Jessica's dream quest, purchase of new computers for her father's business, blunts the force of the idea that Jessica is learning from her grandmother's example that each person cherishes different keys to life and character.

Allen Morgan's books are uneven: they strain after novelty, crowd in highly contrived episodes, lack thematic depth, and succumb to sentimentality. His reputation depends on his best books, the formulaic 'Matthew's Midnight Adventure' series, in which the wild invention is genuinely amusing.

See also: *WSMP*.

Paul Morin

Born: 14 January 1959, in Calgary.

Principal Residences: Calgary; Toronto; Rockwood, Ont.

Education: Grant McEwen College (Edmonton); Sheridan College (Oakville, Ont.); Ontario College of Art (Toronto).

Career: freelance artist; illustrator; writer.

Major Awards: Governor-General's Award for Illustration (1990); Amelia Francis Howard-Gibbon Illustrators Award (1991, 1993); Elizabeth Mrazik-Cleaver Canadian Picture Book Award (1991).

Works for Children

Written and Illustrated by Paul Morin

Animal Dreaming: An Aboriginal Dreamtime Story (Toronto: Stoddart, 1998). **Rev:** *QQ* 64 (July 1998): 41; *SLJ* 44 (Mar. 1998): 236.

Illustrated by Paul Morin

The Orphan Boy, by Tololwa Mollel (Toronto: Oxford UP, 1990). **Rev:** *BiC* 19 (Dec. 1990): 31; *CCB-B* 44 (Apr. 1991): 201; *CM* 19 (Jan. 1991): 29; *EL* 18 (Jan. 1991): 52; *NYTBR* (11 Aug. 1991): 16; *QQ* 56 (Oct. 1990): 14; *RT* 45 (Feb. 1992): 458; *SLJ* 37 (July 1991): 70.

The Dragon's Pearl, by Julie Lawson (Toronto: Oxford UP, 1992). **Rev:** *BiC* 21 (Nov. 1992): 37; *CCB-B* 46 (May 1993): 287; *CCL* 75 (1994): 47; *CM* 20 (Oct. 1992): 264; *EL* 21 (Sept. 1993): 49; *QQ* 58 (Aug. 1992): 24; *SLJ* 39 (July 1993): 62.

Fox Song, by Joseph Bruchac (Toronto: Oxford UP, 1993). **Rev:** *CCB-B* 47 (Oct. 1993): 40; *CM* 21 (Oct. 1993): 186; *EL* 21 (Mar. 1994): 16; *HB* 69 (Nov. 1993): 771; *QQ* 59 (Sept. 1993): 66.

The Mud Family, by Betsy James (Toronto: Oxford UP, 1994). **Rev:** *EL* 22 (Mar. 1995): 18; *QQ* 60 (Nov. 1994): 34; *RT* 49 (Dec. 1995): 328; *SLJ* 69 (Apr. 1995): 110.

The Ghost Dance, by Alice McLerran (Toronto: Stoddart, 1995). **Rev:** *CCB-B* 49 (Nov. 1995): 100; *QQ* 62 (Feb. 1996): 41.

The Vision Seeker, by James Whetung (Toronto: Stoddart, 1996). **Rev:** *BiC* 25 (Dec. 1996): 35; *EL* (Mar. 1997): 27; *QQ* 62 (Aug. 1996): 43.

Lasting Echoes: An Oral History of Native American People, by Joseph Bruchac (San Diego: Harcourt, Brace, 1997). **Rev:** *CCB-B* 51 (Mar. 1998): 237; *HB* 74 (Jan. 1998): 90; *SLJ* 44 (Mar. 1998): 229.

Flags, by Maxine Trottier (Toronto: Stoddart, 1999).

For Paul Morin, illustrating a children's book entails more than visually rendering the written text or even expanding on narrative meanings. Deeply interested in traditional religions and music, he has visited the countries of the cultures whose stories he illustrates, immersing himself in their mundane and spiritual lives as well as sketching and photographing settings and artifacts. As a result, he has said, he is transformed by the illustration process; he cannot depict a culture unless he has taken part of it into himself. Tanzania, China, Australia, and rural areas of Canada and the United States figure in his works as both physical locations and spiritual presences.

The illustrations for Morin's first book, Tololwa Mollel's *The Orphan Boy*, a Maasai star myth, accurately depict the artifacts and landscapes of these African peoples, repeat visually the main events of the narrative, subtly expand on the emotions of the characters, and communicate the spiritual significance of the story. The tale of a friendship between an old man and a mysterious orphan who, it is discovered, is a star-being, explains the nature of the morning/evening star, or Kileken, as the Maasai call it. The opening and closing illustrations depict the old man in the foreground, with the blue-black night sky behind him. However, there are two significant differences. At the beginning, the old man faces forward, looking anxiously because the evening star is missing from the sky, in which the thin crescent of the new moon is the most noticeable object. At the end, he faces towards the background, his left hand raised in a slight wave towards the evening star shining brightly above him. In both, he is the sole human being; however, the nature of his aloneness has changed. He has discovered and then lost the star-being, Kileken.

Three illustrations depict cows being herded. In all of them, the orange and brown hues emphasize the drought conditions that make Maasai life so difficult. However, in the first two, the boy, who is Kileken, drives fat, healthy cattle from the distance, while in the last one, the old man, having betrayed his trust to the star-boy, walks despondently into the hills with his now emaciated herd. The companionship and prosperity associated with the orphan boy have been replaced by sadness, loneliness, and poverty. The bond between man and boy and its later loss are seen in two night-time illustrations. In the first, the boy stands, his hand on the knee of the sitting man; a circle of light highlights their physical contact; each looks affectionately at the other. When the man breaks his trust, he hides behind a bush, while the boy, his arms raised high, stands alone, absorbing a circle of light. Now he faces away from the man. This illustration has been preceded by three in which increasing amounts of shadow symbolize the old man's yielding to the temptation to disobey the boy's request not to try to discover the source of his mysterious powers. Morin, in addition to depicting accurately the semi-arid landscape of the Maasai people, along with their simple houses and clothing, suffuses each of his pictures with a brightness, a luminescence that evokes a sense of the mysterious powers operative not only in this story, but also in the daily lives of the traditional Maasai.

The power of dragons to bring rain to the agricultural peoples of central China underlies the plot of Julie Lawson's *The Dragon's Pearl* and Morin's accompanying illustrations. Oranges and browns dominate the first two of four landscape paintings; in the third, greens become more noticeable; whereas in the fourth, after the boy hero is transformed into a dragon because of his kindness and rain begins to fall, lush green vegetation appears on the banks of the river and is reflected in its blue waters. Xiao Scheng's metamorphosis is prefigured in paintings of a magical pearl he discovers and later swallows, as it contains the blood-red shape of an embryonic dragon. Although Morin communicates the characters' emotions through facial expressions more fully than he did in *The Orphan Boy*, he does, as in the first book, suffuse his detailed, realistic paintings with a luminescence that suggests the supernatural powers presented through the legend. He also creates photographic arrangements of actual objects—stalks of grass, gold coins, and a pearl—that are important objects in the plot.

Morin has also created pictures for stories from several Native North American cultures. Two, *Fox Song*, by Abenaki author Joseph Bruchac, and *The Mud Family*, by Betsy James, focus on family relationships. The other two, *The Ghost Dance*, by

Alice McLerran, and *The Vision Seeker*, by Anishnabeg (Ojibway) writer James Whetung, deal with the importance of visions in the lives of the people. In *Fox Song*, six-year-old Jamie keeps alive the memories of her recently deceased grandmother, in part by dreaming of the activities she shared with the old woman. In the opening illustration, a dream-catcher hung on the wall and a birch basket on the child's bedside table indicate the importance of dream and memory for the girl. In most of the pictures, the girl and the woman are together outdoors. However, near the conclusion, Jamie stands alone beneath an autumn tree, where only recently her grandmother had given her a traditional song of greeting. Moments later, she sees a fox, whose red colouring, similar to that of the leaves, and whose very presence reminds the girl of the grandmother's gift.

In *The Mud Family*, a member of an Anasazi family living 600 years ago in the cliff dwellings of the American Southwest feels excluded from the rest of the family, especially when she is not permitted to take part in ceremonies designed to end a drought. Morin contrasts paintings that reveal her loneliness in the village with those that portray the happiness she experiences alone in the valley creating and playing with mud figures. However, the unity with her family that she discovers at the conclusion is emphasized by the circle made of the family's hands as they leave imprints on the cave wall. Throughout the book, Morin carefully and accurately depicts the landscape and housing of the people, along with reproductions of the stylized rock designs that expressed their spiritual beliefs.

The Ghost Dance combines textual and visual accounts of the destruction of the buffalo herds, relocation of Native peoples, and rise of the visionary, revivalist movement of the Ghost Dance—a movement that ended tragically at the Wounded Knee Massacre of 1890. Morin combines realistic paintings depicting the Plains landscape and the activities of the people, with paintings in the style of the vision art of the plains peoples and assemblages, photographs of found objects and traditional artifacts, to complement the simple, poetic text. Photographs of a sacred buffalo skull, a turtle-shell rattle, and shields decorated with their owners' sacred visions contrast a double-spread containing a rifle, bullets, and army map of Indian Territory. The former items are reminders of the vital links between spiritual and physical life; the latter, of the forces that destroyed the holistic lifestyle of the Native peoples. The vision paintings accompanying the discussions of the Native prophets who believed that the Ghost Dance would cause the departure of the white people and the return of the buffalo are dominated by circles that symbolize the concept of unity among human, animal, and spiritual worlds and by pictographs of hunters and buffalo. Pictures of two modern scenes, a clear river flowing past green banks and smokestacks polluting the air, reflect the author and illustrator's mixed hopes and fears for the future of the land that the Native people had revered.

The Vision Seeker is an account of the origins of the sacred sweat lodge of the Ojibway people of the northern woodlands. At a time when family members are fighting among themselves and villages and nations make war, a boy undertakes a vision quest to find the wisdom to help his people towards peace. Travelling into the land of the seven supernatural grandfathers, he is instructed in the ways the people must behave and returns home with his message. The configuration and adornments of the sweat lodge celebrate his mythic journey. The darkness that parallels the darkness of the people's lives is replaced by the green of trees and grass, symbols of revival. As the boy sits on 'the high place' where he receives his vision, the forms of a bear, frog, beaver, and wolf appear in the rocks, an indication, perhaps, that he has entered a world in which the spirits of animal powers are present. Figures from vision paintings adorn the walls of the lodge of the seven grandfathers, indicating the boy's having reached a plane of heightened spiritual awareness. The vision itself is dominated by a series of interrelated circles and radiating sun symbols. In the depiction of the boy after his return home, Morin repeats the circle patterns and includes seven rocks symbolizing the grandfathers and the green cedar of renewed life that the boy's journey has made possible. Whereas Morin's depictions of vision in *The Ghost Dance* emphasized the tragedy, those in *The Vision Seeker* focus on the positive results.

Animal Dreaming, the first work Morin both wrote and illustrated, deals with subjects similar to those of the earlier books: the relationship between human beings and the natural and supernatural worlds in which they live and the importance of visions in the lives of individuals. Mirri, a young boy, accompanies an elder to a remote region of the Australian outback. Beside a cliff adorned with vision paintings, the old man tells the legend of the Dreamtime, when the ancestral kangaroo, long-necked turtle, and emu sought visions to help them end the battles various land, sea, and earth animals waged for power. The elder explains that the paintings portray this great myth that 'we keep . . . alive by listening, passing on our story, and by leaving our mark on this rock.' In order to indicate the two levels of existence, Morin uses different styles. Realistic pictures of the boy, the man, and the landscape they pass through are contrasted to highly stylized representations, based on traditional designs Morin studied during a 1996 visit to northern Australia of the visions the animals experience. Contrasts between illustrations indicate the movement toward a resolution of conflicts and the establishment of harmony as a result of the three animals' wisdom. The double-spread of the land across which the boy and man walk early in the story contains only traces of green; yellow-coloured rocks dominate. That of the harmonious world after the three animals' intervention balances blue sky and water, green grass and trees, an indication of the peaceful, interrelated lives of the animals from the three realms. Whereas each of the vision paintings of the three animals' dreams had contained only one animal, the one of the time after the war of the animals depicts many animals from each of the three areas. The final illustration, showing the shadow of the boy's hand against the rock wall and the light emanating from it, indicates that, through his initiation journey and learning the story told him by the elder, he has become one with the land and the world of the Dreamtime.

Morin's illustrations of traditional stories and customs are triply accurate. They depict key aspects of the narratives, they correctly represent the landscapes and cultural artifacts associated with the people originally telling the stories, and they embody the sense of spiritual power present in the original stories. In the afterword to *The Ghost Dance*, Morin spoke of a 'sacred connection' that he wished to embody in his illustrations. In presenting this sacred connection in his pictures, he has enhanced and expanded the many levels of meaning of the written texts.

See also: *WSMP*.

Farley Mowat

Born: 12 May 1921, in Belleville, Ont.

Principal Residences: Belleville; Trenton, Ont.; Windsor; Richmond Hill, Ont.; Toronto; Saskatoon; Palgrave, Ont.; various Newfoundland outports; Cape Breton, NS; Port Hope, Ont.

Education: University of Toronto (BA 1949).

Career: naturalist; writer.

Major Awards: Governor-General's Award for Juvenile Literature (1956); Canadian Association of Children's Librarians Bronze Medal (1958); Boys' Clubs of America Award (1962, for *Owls in the Family*); Vicky Metcalf Award (1971).

Works for Children

Lost in the Barrens (Boston: Little, Brown, 1956).

Owls in the Family (Boston: Little, Brown, 1961).

The Black Joke (Toronto: McClelland & Stewart, 1962).

The Curse of the Viking Grave (Boston: Little, Brown, 1966).

Other

People of the Deer (Boston: Little, Brown, 1952; rev. edn Toronto: McClelland & Stewart, 1975).

The Dog Who Wouldn't Be (Boston: Little, Brown, 1957).

Never Cry Wolf (Toronto: McClelland & Stewart, 1963).

The Boat Who Wouldn't Float (Toronto: McClelland & Stewart, 1969).

A Whale for the Killing (Toronto: McClelland & Stewart, 1972).

The World of Farley Mowat: A Selection, ed. Peter Davison (Boston: Little, Brown, 1980).

A Farley Mowat Reader, ed. Wendy Thomas (Toronto: Key Porter Kids, 1997).

Selected Discussions

Ford, Mary. 'The Wolf as Victim', *CCL* 7 (1977): 5–15.

Goddard, John. 'A Real Whopper', *Saturday Night* 111 (May 1996): 46–50, 52, 54, 64.

Jones, Raymond E. 'Heroes in the Perilous Land: Pattern and Meaning in Arctic Fiction for Children', *CCL* 31/32 (1983): 30–40.

Lucas, Alex. *Farley Mowat.* Toronto: McClelland & Stewart, 1976.

——. 'Farley Mowat: Writer for Young People', *CCL* 5/6 (1976): 40–51.

Orange, John. *Farley Mowat: Writing the Squib* (Toronto: ECW, 1993).

Rotert, Richard. 'Farley Mowat in the Wilderness', *Triumphs of the Spirit in Children's Literature*, ed. Francelia Butler and Richard Rotert (Hamden, Conn.: Library Professional Publications, 1986): 21–6.

Farley Mowat is unique in being a writer almost as popular with children as he is with adults. An internationally successful author who has cultivated a reputation for being colourful and controversial, he approaches the task of writing for children with a distinctly moral attitude: 'A good book for youngsters can influence the whole future life of the young reader.... I happen to believe that it is an absolute duty for good writers to devote a significant part of their time and talent to writing for young people.' For Mowat, the task is 'of absolutely vital importance if basic changes for the good are ever to be initiated in any human culture.' Although obviously concerned with conveying a message, Mowat is not forbiddingly didactic. In fact, on numerous occasions he has insisted that he is, first and foremost, a storyteller: 'In another time I might have been a Saga-man. Perhaps that's really what I am today.'

Mowat has written four books expressly for children, but at least two others have found an audience among them, and several others have a readership among young adults. His books suitable for young readers fall into three groups. First, are three children's adventure novels: *Lost in the Barrens*, *The Black Joke*, and *The Curse of the Viking Grave*. Filled with perilous and exciting adventures that inspire deeds of heroism, they obviously suit Mowat's sense of saga. Next are two stories of domesticated animals, *Owls in the Family*, a children's book, and the adult work upon which it is based, *The Dog Who Wouldn't Be*. The third group, best represented by *Never Cry Wolf*, concerns wild animals and man's relation to them. In these books Mowat's skilful storytelling advances the ecological, anthropological, and historical themes found throughout his work.

Mowat's concern for nature developed naturally during his well-travelled childhood, especially in the time he spent in Saskatoon, where he came to know the prairie and its wildlife. By the time he was 13, he was writing a regular newspaper column on birds. When he was 14, his great-uncle, Walter Farley, an amateur ornithologist, took him along on a field trip to The Pas to study Arctic birds, introducing Mowat to the northern setting of *Lost in the Barrens* and igniting in him a lifelong passion for the North. After serving with the Canadian army during World War II, Mowat returned to Canada and began studying biology at the University of Toronto. While working towards his degree, he was hired by the federal government to study the wolf and caribou situation in Keewatin. Fired for becoming involved in the problems of the Native peoples of the area, Mowat began work on a short story that formed the basis for his first book, *People of the Deer*, a controversial chronicle of the vanishing Ihalmiut, the inland Inuit of the Barrens.

Concern for the North underpins two conventional Arctic survival stories, *Lost in the Barrens* and its sequel, *The Curse of the Viking Grave. Lost in the Barrens* is by far the more successful artistically and thematically. A maturation tale, it is the story of Jamie Macnair, a white orphan, and Awasin Meewasin, the son of a Cree chief, who are forced to spend the winter on the Barrens after they foolishly become separated from a hunting party. In order to survive, they must understand themselves, each other, and the resources of the seemingly hostile land. They discover, as Awasin makes clear, that, if man humbly submits to Nature, even Arctic nature will nurture him: 'If you fight against the spirits of the north you will always lose. Obey their laws and they'll look after you.' In addition to the ecological theme, the novel treats themes of racial prejudice and tolerance. Jamie, at first impatient of some Native beliefs, becomes more mature and more capable of survival as he comes to accept traditional Native wisdom.

Lost in the Barrens relies on conventional characterization and events, but it is still exciting and meaningful. *The Curse of the Viking Grave*, which Mowat has called a 'potboiler' and 'a really bad piece of work', uses the same materials, but lacks a meaningful narrative. Threatened with being sent to the south for schooling, Jamie, accompanied by Awasin, Peetyuk, and Angeline, Awasin's sister, flees from the police (we learn at the end that they do not want, as he thinks, to put him in an orphanage) and heads north to find a Viking treasure. The novel contains speculation about the Norse discovery of Canada, discussion of the plight of the Ihalmiut, and even a denunciation of white treatment of the Natives, but none of this is well integrated into the plot. Even the curse in the title, which has no effect on anyone, weakens the book by making the traditional Inuit seem somewhat foolish.

In his other adventure, *The Black Joke*, Mowat eschewed the attempt at packing the tale with relevance and created a gripping tale of piracy during the Depression. Three boys with different ethnic backgrounds heroically recover a ship that a wily businessman has taken away from an honest Newfoundland fisherman.

Mowat's tales of domesticated animals lean to humorous narrative. *The Dog Who Wouldn't Be* is an episodic biography of Mutt, a mongrel who 'concluded that there was no future in being a dog'. An eccentric animal who learned to walk fences like a cat, proved to be a 'Prince Albert retriever' who would even bring back stuffed birds from the hardware store, and rode happily in the rumble seat while wearing driving goggles, Mutt is a source of joy and hilarious consternation for his owners. *Owls in the Family* highlights the amusing antics of two owls. The more outgoing one, Wol, receives most attention: he contributes a dead skunk to the family dinner, frightens a minister, and follows Billy (the Farley Mowat persona in this version) to school. Central to the book is a nostalgic look at boyhood when one could be close to nature and find in it friendship and happiness that one thought could never end.

Somewhere between the fictional adventure tales and the fictionalized animal autobiographies is *Never Cry Wolf*, an account of the wolf study that changed Mowat's life. An attempt to deflate the myth of the wolf as a ferocious killer, the book uses both realistic reporting of animal behaviour and pointed satire to make its case. The account of wolf behaviour, realistic and closely observed in the tradition of Roberts and Seton, shows that wolves do not wantonly kill but actually keep the caribou stock healthy by removing its weaker members. The satire is double-pronged. Part of it is directed at governments and bureaucracies that foster the wolf myth and refuse to accept the lessons of observation. Part of it is directed at Mowat himself as a naïve believer in the myth. His change of attitude in the face of the government's resistance to change is a powerful appeal for men to respect nature for what it actually is instead of fearing it for what is imagined to be.

As an adventure writer, Mowat relies on the trusted formula of the journey into troubles that test and mature young boys. His characters are not psychologically deep, but they do work well as vehicles for communicating Mowat's love of nature and his respect for the rights of all people, but especially Natives. Mowat's non-fiction has often been attacked as exaggeration, but it is undeniably entertaining and often educational. Furthermore, Mowat has added to Canadian literature animal characters who linger in the memory, and he has been instrumental in making many adults and children sensitive to the claims of nature. Above all, by showing that adventure is everywhere, Mowat has achieved his goal of bringing to young readers 'the feeling that life is very much worth living'.

See also: *AAYA* 1; *CA* 1-4R; *CANR* 4, 24, 42; *CLC* 26; *CLR* 20; *DLB* 68; *Junior* 3; *MAICYA*; *Profiles* 2; *SATA* 3, 55; *TCCW*; *TCYAW*; *WSMP*.

Robin Muller

Born: 30 October 1953, in Toronto.

Principal Residences: Toronto.

Education: Algonquin College, Ontario (BFA 1979).

Career: editorial illustrator; set designer; writer; artist.

Major Awards: Governor-General's Award (1989).

Works for Children

Written and Illustrated by Robin Muller

Mollie Whuppie and the Giant (Richmond Hill, Ont.: Scholastic, 1982). **Rev:** *BiC* 11 (Dec. 1982): 9; *CCL* 35 (1984): 109; *QQ* 49 (Feb. 1983): 35.

Tatterhood (Richmond Hill, Ont.: Scholastic, 1984). **Rev:** *CCL* 39 (1985): 145; *QQ* 51 (Feb. 1985): 10.

The Sorcerer's Apprentice (Toronto: Kids Can Press, 1985). **Rev:** *QQ* 51 (Dec. 1985): 29; *SLJ* 33 (Feb. 1987): 72.

The Lucky Old Woman (Toronto: Kids Can Press, 1987). **Rev:** *BiC* 16 (Dec. 1987): 14; *CM* 16 (May 1988): 25.

Little Kay (Richmond Hill, Ont.: Scholastic, 1988). **Rev:** *BiC* 18 (Apr. 1989): 37; *BYP* 3 (Feb. 1989): 9; *CCL* 57 (1990): 116.

The Magic Paintbrush (Toronto: Doubleday, 1989). **Rev:** *BiC* 19 (June 1990): 16; *CCL* 63 (1991): 83; *CL* (Winter 1992): 165; *CM* 18 (Mar. 1990): 67; *EL* 17 (Mar. 1990): 23; *QQ* 55 (Nov. 1989): 15; *SLJ* 36 (July 1990): 78.

The Nightwood (Toronto: Doubleday, 1991). **Rev:** *BiC* 21 (Apr. 1992): 44; *CCL* 73 (1994): 88; *CM* 20 (May 1992): 161; *QQ* 57 (Aug. 1991): 24.

Row, Row, Row Your Boat (Richmond Hill, Ont.: Scholastic, 1993). **Rev:** *CCL* 87 (1997): 93; *CM* 22 (Jan. 1994): 23; *QQ* 59 (Sept. 1993): 68; *RT* 49 (Feb. 1996): 397.

Little Wonder (Richmond Hill, Ont.: Scholastic, 1994). **Rev:** *CBRA* (1994): 461; *QQ* 60 (Sept. 1994): 69.

The Angel Tree (Toronto: Doubleday, 1997). **Rev:** *BiC* 26 (Dec. 1997): 35; *CM* 4 (12 Dec. 1997): on-line; *QQ* 64 (Feb. 1998): 42.

Written by Robin Muller

Hickory, Dickory, Dock, illus. Suzanne Duranceau (Richmond Hill, Ont.: Scholastic, 1992). **Rev:** *CM* 20 (Oct. 1992): 265; *QQ* 58 (July 1992): 45; *SLJ* 40 (May 1994): 109.

When Robin Muller was a teenager, he took a summer job and discovered his calling. Working in a publisher's warehouse, he spent hours browsing among the books and realized that he would like to write and illustrate stories. Before 1982, when he published his first children's book, *Mollie Whuppie and the Giant*, he built a career as a successful artist, exhibiting paintings in Canada, the United States, and Europe. Like most of Muller's books, *Mollie Whuppie and the Giant* is an adaptation of a traditional tale. Although his stories come from different cultures and each deals with a different type of central character, his books share several characteristics. None rigidly follows sources, Muller often supplying original plot material and characterization. Most focus on the growth to maturity of a young person who must pass tests. Often the resolution of conflicts involves the hero's overcoming adults who seek to impose their power over others. Muller's heroes are frequently strong girls and women who must, in addition to their own inner struggles, confront powerful adult males. Finally, in all of the books Muller's illustrations contribute significantly to tone and characterization.

In portraying the British folktale heroine Mollie Whuppie, Muller emphasizes her cleverness and courage. However, she is not just a witty trickster; she has other people's interests at heart and willingly exposes herself to danger so that her sisters can have fine husbands. The 20 full-page, black-and-white illustrations emphasize Mollie's heroic qualities. Although in nearly every picture she is the smallest figure, she is by no means the meekest: her facial expressions, body language, and position in relation to others indicate her leadership.

The title hero of the Finnish tale *Tatterhood* is also a strong heroine. Born to a mother who had disobeyed a witch's instructions, the girl is wild and boisterous, riding a goat around the palace, banging with a huge wooden spoon, and yelling. But she is devoted to her younger sister, and when, because of the mother's foolishness, a group of witches replaces her sister's head with a cow's head, she fearlessly sets out to rectify the situation. At the conclusion of the story, she has earned the love of a prince. Muller's full-colour illustrations are major vehicles of characterization. The ineffectual mother wanders around with melancholy, fearful, or distraught looks. Belinda, lovely, good, and passive, is generally seen smiling gently. In each illustration a different expression reveals the heroine's changing emotions. At first she is merely wild looking, a very large and uncontrolled baby. But she smiles happily at her baby sister, an indication of the love that will take her on her dangerous voyage. Along the way she is angry, determined, pensive, and, when she first sees her prince, intrigued. At the end, she is pictured as a beautiful, radiant young woman. She no longer wears the green hood that inspired her nickname; she has donned a royal-blue gown, and her shining black hair cascades over her shoulders.

The Sorcerer's Apprentice bears little similarity to the German tale from which it takes its name. Although it deals with a poor boy who seeks work from a sorcerer and is warned not to read the books of magic spells, it is, as Muller has remarked, really about the value of learning to read and write. In the opening paragraph, readers are told that Robin, although he was poor and had no trade, 'was clever and brave and, what was more, he could read and write.' When he learns that the sorcerer plans to take over the neighbouring kingdom, Robin uses his skills, risking terrible punishment to thwart his master's scheme. Once again, a strong heroine is instrumental in the resolution of the conflict. The wizard's dove, who is a princess transformed by the wizard to keep her from claiming the throne, helps Robin and gives the advice necessary for him to develop into the mature young man he is at the end. Muller's ink and pencil-crayon pictures represent one of his best uses of illustration to enhance mood, theme, and characterization. For example, the first and last pictures are in sharp contrast. As he wanders through a dark, terrifying forest at the story's beginning, Robin is small, vulnerable, and somewhat bewildered. Finally, as he stands at the edge of a bright meadow looking towards the palace, he is a stronger, wiser individual.

The troubles of the title heroine of *The Lucky Old Woman* begin as she walks home alone at night, oblivious to her friends' warnings about the fearful Grumpleteaser. Muller, who has stated it is important that he like his story characters, reports, 'I was drawn to her optimism.' When a lump of gold she discovers turns into silver, then iron, then stone, she keeps her good spirits and, because of her good nature, is rewarded by and becomes a friend of the supernatural imp. Based on 'The Hedley Kow', an Irish folktale collected by Jacob Josephs, the story contains illustrations dominated by warm yellow colours that reflect the central character's optimism and the inner riches of her character.

In *Little Kay*, as in *Mollie Whuppie*, it is the youngest of three sisters who is the heroine. When the Sultan demands that every family must send a son to court to serve as a knight, the magician father of three girls finally agrees to the request of his youngest daughter that she be allowed to go in disguise. Dressed as a boy and wearing armour made from a tea-kettle and other kitchen objects, she becomes the best knight in the court and, using trickery rather than force, defeats a terrifying ogre. Her gender discovered, she demands that the Sultan allow daughters as well as sons to serve in his court. Thus Kay has freed members of her sex from imprisoning stereotypes. The illustrations reveal the broad humour of the situations: Kay dressed in tea-kettle and stew-pot armour, the Sultan's supposedly brave warriors draping themselves in delicate silks, and the purple ogre ignominiously fleeing a swarm of hornets. In the court scenes, Kay seems out of place in the opulent settings; although she is the one pretending, it is the courtiers who look pretentious. In several full-page illustrations, the scenes extend beyond the borders, a reflection of Kay's beliefs and actions extending the boundaries the Sultan had created for women and girls.

The Magic Paint Brush, based on an old Chinese tale, focuses on the power of art to bring about either good or evil. Nib, a street-urchin with a talent for drawing, lives in a large nineteenth-century European city. He rescues an old man and is rewarded with a brush that brings to life whatever the boy paints. Captured by a king who wishes to use the boy's talent to achieve his evil goals,

Nib paints a tunnel through which he escapes. However, he can now only create pictures of darkness and sorrow, reflections of the effect of the king's power on the country. When he learns to paint from the heart, he is able to revive a dying friend and to cause the king's disappearance. Muller's most powerful narrative about the unlikely child hero, *The Magic Paint Brush* develops fully the themes of courage, selflessness, freedom, and power seen in his earlier works. The grim city landscape, which is a product of the king's evil, the vulnerability of the street children, the wonder the boy feels about his new talents and his despair at their loss, and the power of adults all are illustrated. The darkest of Muller's works, the illustrations also contain small elements of light, foreshadowings of the understanding and happiness the hero eventually achieves.

The old Scottish ballad 'Tamlynne' forms the basis of *The Nightwood*, the story of Elaine, a restless young woman who, to escape her repressive father, ignores warnings not to sneak into an enchanted forest, in which place she courageously rescues a young man who has been imprisoned by the Elfin Queen. As in *The Magic Paint Brush*, there is no humour in this story and an intensity permeates the narrative, as Muller delineates the coming of age of the central character. Strong-willed, impetuous, and rebellious, she is ready to break the ties to her imperfect father; without a mother, she must define herself in relation to three other women: her old nurse, who does little more than offer warnings that are ignored; another old woman, whom she meets in the forest, who had failed to rescue her own lover from the Elfin Queen; and the Queen herself, who uses her magic to control others. The first would keep her in a state of childhood; the second is an example of what she might become; the third is all that a mature woman should not be.

The maturing of Elaine is intricately presented in three illustrations of her sitting by a castle window. In the first, she looks happily out at a blue sky, safe within her home. However, her embroidery of a young man and the tapestry behind her of a girl running through a forest suggest that she will not remain long in the world of her childhood. After she has been forbidden to attend a magnificent ball, she sits mournfully in the darkened room. Her embroidery has become the image of a knight, and, in the tapestry, a pair of hands are drawing her deeper into the woods. The forest is illuminated clearly by a full moon. A new realm of experience lies outside her room. In the third, after she has visited the Nightwood and met the entrapped young man, she looks emaciated and her nurse sorrowfully grasps her hand. In a stained glass window, an angel holds a broken heart. In another window is the face of a young man who looks at her with alarm. Outside, under the full moon, another man wanders about calling. There is no tapestry or embroidery figure: the man of her imaginings and the forest that entraps him are real. Elaine is in actual danger of death; if she is to live and be transformed from a child into a woman, she must again enter into the dangerous woods and rescue the lonely man who calls to her.

The misuse of power is the theme of *The Angel Tree*, a traditional story that Muller sets in the Old West. Once again an apprentice must struggle against an evil master, in this case a blacksmith. When the hero discovers an angel in a dying tree outside of the smithy, he helps her save it from the blacksmith. Later he plants seeds from its fruit, thus ensuring that it will continue its life in a new form. During the events, the young man displays not only his courage, but also his compassion. In planting the seeds, he is fulfilling a dream of the angel, who during her life on earth had been the girl who planted the tree. Without her guidance, he, like Robin in *The Sorcerer's Apprentice*, could not have succeeded.

Muller has also created three books for younger readers. *Little Wonder*, the story of a timid little pup that displays his hidden talent—the ability to howl very loudly—to scare away burglars, also deals with the heroism of an unlikely hero, here literally an 'underdog'. *Row, Row, Row Your Boat* and *Hickory, Dickory, Dock* provide humorous extensions of well-known children's songs.

Robin Muller has established a firm reputation as one of the important later-twentieth-century retellers of traditional stories. As do all good adaptors of these narratives, he is able to present them in ways that emphasize both their timeless themes and their contemporary relevance. Although the illustrations set the stories in long-ago eras, as is typically the case for folktales, his treatment of character, particularly of young women, emphasizes the modern theme of the importance of individuals asserting their individuality over those who use their power to control and diminish others. Whether the evil adult is a giant, a wizard, a foolish sultan, an elfin queen, a grumpy imp, or a blacksmith, the Muller hero uses cleverness, courage, and concern for others in his or her successful quest for well-being and self-reliance.

See also: *CANR* 52; *SATA* 86; *TCCW*; *WSMP*.

Robert Munsch

Born: 11 June 1945, in Pittsburgh.

Principal Residences: Pittsburgh; Boston; Coos Bay, Oreg.; Guelph, Ont.

Education: Fordham University (BA 1969); Boston University (MA 1971); Tufts University (MA in Early Childhood Education 1973).

Career: day-care worker; Head Teacher at Family Studies Preschool, Guelph University; storyteller; writer.

Major Awards: Ruth Schwartz Children's Book Award (1986); Vicky Metcalf Award (1987).

Works for Children

Mud Puddle, illus. Sami Suomalainen (Toronto: Annick, 1979; rev. edns 1982, 1995). **Rev:** *BiC* 8 (Dec. 1979): 12; *CBRA* (1979): 211, (1982): 240, and (1996): 452; *CCL* 15/16 (1980): 115; *IR* 14 (Feb. 1980): 53.

The Dark, illus. Sami Suomalainen (Toronto: Annick, 1979; rev. edn 1984); rev. edn illus. Michael Martchenko (Toronto: Annick, 1997). **Rev:** *BiC* 8 (Dec. 1979): 12, and 10 (Dec. 1981): 5; *CBRA* (1979): 211, (1984): 319, and (1997): 484; *CCL* 15/16 (1980): 115; *CM*: 4 (31 Oct. 1997): on-line; *EL* 14 (Mar. 1987): 47; *HB* 61 (May 1985): 343.

The Paper Bag Princess, illus. Michael Martchenko (Toronto: Annick, 1980). **Rev:** *BiC* 9 (Dec. 1980): 19; *CBRA* (1979): 211; *CCL* 22 (1981): 56, and 26 (1982): 92; *EL* 9 (Sept. 1981): 28, and 9 (Nov. 1981); 35; *IR* 15 (Apr. 1981): 49, and 16 (Feb. 1982): 47; *QQ* 47 (Feb. 1981): 47, and 48 (May 1982): 37, and 48 (June 1982): 3; *TES* (21 May 1982): 31.

Jonathan Cleaned Up, Then He Heard a Sound; or, Blackberry Subway Jam, illus. Michael Martchenko (Toronto: Annick, 1981). **Rev:** *BiC* 10 (Oct. 1981): 33; *CBRA* (1981): 229; *EL* 9 (Nov. 1981): 35; *IR* 15 (Oct. 1981): 46; *QQ* 47 (Aug. 1981): 29; *SLJ* 28 (Apr. 1982): 60.

The Boy in the Drawer, illus. Michael Martchenko (Toronto: Annick, 1982). **Rev:** *BiC* 11 (Aug.-Sept. 1982): 39; *CBRA* (1982): 240; *CCL* 30 (1983): 88; *QQ* 48 (Aug. 1982): 28.

Murmel Murmel Murmel, illus. Michael Martchenko (Toronto: Annick, 1982). **Rev:** *BiC* 11 (Dec. 1982): 8; *CBRA* (1982): 241; *CCL* 30 (1983): 88; *Maclean's* 95 (13 Dec. 1982): 56.

Angela's Airplane, illus. Michael Martchenko (Toronto: Annick, 1983; rev. edn 1988). **Rev:** *BiC* 12 (May 1983): 31; *CBRA* (1988): 277; *CCL* 30 (1983): 88; *EL* 11 (Nov. 1983): 37; *QQ* 49 (Aug. 1983): 34.

David's Father, illus. Michael Martchenko (Toronto: Annick, 1983). **Rev:** *CBRA* (1983): 280; *BiC* 12 (Dec. 1983): 13; *CCL* 39/40 (1985): 125; *QQ* 49 (July 1983): 10, and 49 (Nov. 1983): 23; *SLJ* 30 (May 1984): 68.

The Fire Station, illus. Michael Martchenko (Toronto: Annick, 1983). **Rev:** *CBRA* (1991): 317; *CCL* 30 (1983): 88; *EL* 11 (Nov. 1983): 37; *QQ* 49 (July 1983): 10, and 57 (June 1991): 25.

Mortimer, illus. Michael Martchenko (Toronto: Annick, 1983). **Rev:** *BiC* 12 (May 1983): 31; *CBRA* (1985): 253; *CCL* 30 (1983): 88; *EL* 11 (Nov. 1983): 37; *QQ* 49 (July 1983): 10.

Millicent and the Wind, illus. Suzanne Duranceau (Toronto: Annick, 1984). **Rev:** *CBRA* (1984): 319; *CCL* 39/40 (1985): 125; *QQ* 50 (July 1984): 8, and 50 (Nov. 1984): 10; *SLJ* 32 (Sept. 1985): 122.

Thomas' Snowsuit, illus. Michael Martchenko (Toronto: Annick, 1985). **Rev:** *BiC* 14 (Nov. 1985): 37, and 20 (Oct. 1991): 26; *CBRA* (1985): 254; *CM* 14 (Jan. 1986): 30;

EL 13 (Mar. 1986): 15, and 15 (Sept. 1987): 19; *Maclean's* 98 (9 Dec. 1985): 44; *QQ* 51 (Dec. 1985): 30; *SLJ* 32 (Apr. 1986): 77.

50 Below Zero, illus. Michael Martchenko (Toronto: Annick, 1986). **Rev:** *CCL* 44 (1986): 95; *EL* 14 (Mar. 1987): 47; *QQ* 52 (Apr. 1986): 26; *SLJ* 33 (Mar. 1987): 148.

I Have to Go!, illus. Michael Martchenko (Toronto: Annick, 1986). **Rev:** *CBRA* (1987): 228; *CCL* 46 (1987): 108: *EL* 14 (Mar. 1987): 47; *SL* 38 (Aug. 1990): 104; *SLJ* 34 (Jan. 1988): 68.

Love You Forever, illus. Sheila McGraw (Toronto: Firefly, 1986). **Rev:** *BYP* 1 (Feb. 1987): 10; *CBRA* (1986): 140; *CCL* 55 (1989): 77; *CM* 15 (Mar. 1987): 78; *NYTBR* 99 (13 Nov. 1994): 48, and 102 (16 Nov. 1997): 26.

Moira's Birthday, illus. Michael Martchenko (Toronto: Annick, 1987). **Rev:** *BiC* 16 (Dec. 1987): 12; *BYP* 1 (Dec 1987): 6; *CBRA* (1995): 479; *CM* 16 (May 1988): 100; *EL* 15 (Mar. 1988): 23.

A Promise Is a Promise, illus. Vladyana Krykorka (Toronto: Annick, 1988). **Rev:** *BiC* 17 (Aug. 1988): 36; *CCL* 53 (1989): 55; *CM* 16 (Nov. 1988): 228; *EL* 16 (Mar. 1989): 22, and 18 (Sept. 1990): 53; *QQ* 57 (Feb. 1991): 21; *SLJ* 35 (Feb. 1989): 74.

Pigs, illus. Michael Martchenko (Toronto: Annick, 1989). **Rev:** *BYP* 3 (June 1989): 8; *CBRA* (1995): 479; *CM* 17 (July 1989): 190.

Giant; or, Waiting for the Thursday Boat, illus. Gilles Tibo (Toronto: Annick, 1989). **Rev:** *BiC* 19 (June 1990): 15, and 20 (Oct. 1991): 26; *CBRA* (1989): 303; *CCL* 61 (1991): 104; *CM* 18 (Mar. 1990): 67; *QQ* 56 (Jan. 1990): 17.

Something Good, illus. Michael Martchenko (Toronto: Annick, 1990). **Rev:** *BiC* 19 (June 1990): 16; *CBRA* (1991): 301, and (1995): 479; *CCL* 61 (1991): 104; *CM* 18 (July 1990): 181; *EL* 18 (Mar. 1991): 24; *QQ* 56 (June 1990): 16.

Good Families Don't, illus. Alan Daniel (Toronto: Doubleday, 1990). **Rev:** *BiC* 19 (Dec. 1990): 32; *CBRA* (1990): 301; *CCL* 64 (1991): 64; *EL* 18 (Jan. 1991): 31.

Show and Tell, illus. Michael Martchenko (Toronto: Annick, 1991). **Rev:** *BiC* 20 (Dec. 1991): 37; *CBRA* (1991): 317; *CCL* 69 (1993): 87; *CL* (Autumn 1992): 164; *CM* 19 (Nov. 1991): 354; *QQ* 57 (Oct. 1991): 36; *RT* 45 (Apr. 1992): 639.

Get Me Another One!, illus. Shawn Steffler (Toronto: Doubleday Canada, 1992). **Rev:** *CBRA* (1992): 300.

Purple, Green and Yellow, illus. Hélène Desputeaux (Toronto: Annick, 1992). **Rev:** *BiC* 22 (Feb. 1993): 37; *CCL* 76 (1994): 85; *CBRA* (1992): 300; *CM* 21 (Jan. 1993): 23; *EL* 20 (Mar. 1993): 13; *QQ* 58 (Aug. 1992): 26; *SL* 41 (May 1993): 57.

Wait and See, illus. Michael Martchenko (Toronto: Annick, 1993). **Rev:** *CBRA* (1993): #6065; *CCL* 78 (1995): 79; *CM* 22 (Mar. 1994): 48; *QQ* 59 (Oct. 1993): 37.

Where is Gah-ning?, illus. Hélène Desputeaux (Toronto: Annick, 1994). **Rev:** *BiC* 23 (Oct. 1994): 58; *CBRA* (1995): 479; *CCL* 87 (1997): 69; *CM* 22 (Oct. 1994): 184; *QQ* 60 (Oct. 1994): 40; *SLJ* 41 (Jan. 1995): 90.

From Far Away, with Saoussan Askar, illus. Michael Martchenko (Toronto: Annick, 1995). **Rev:** *CBRA* (1995): 480; *EL* 23 (Mar. 1996): 24, and 24 (Mar. 1997): 46; *QQ* 61 (July 1995): 61; *SLJ* 42 (Mar. 1996): 190.

Stephanie's Ponytail, illus. Michael Martchenko (Toronto: Annick, 1996). **Rev:** *BiC* 25 (Oct. 1996): 32; *CBRA* (1996): 452; *EL* 24 (Mar. 1997): 26; *QQ* 62 (Oct. 1996): 45, and 63 (Sept. 1997): 72; *SLJ* 42 (Nov. 1996): 89.

Alligator Baby, illus. Michael Martchenko (Richmond Hill, Ont.: North Winds, 1997). **Rev:** *CBRA* (1997): 484; *CCB-B* 51 (Oct. 1997): 63; *QQ* 63 (Sept. 1997): 72; *SLJ* 43 (Nov. 1997): 96.

Andrew's Loose Tooth, illus. Michael Martchenko (Richmond Hill, Ont.: North Winds, 1998).

Ribbon Rescue, illus. Eugenie Fernandes (Toronto: Scholastic, 1999).

We Share Everything!, illus. Michael Martchenko (Markham, Ont.: Scholastic, 1999).

Other

'Whatever You Make of It', *CCL* 43 (1986): 22–5.

Selected Discussions

Kondo, David. 'Robert Munsch: An Interview', *CCL* 43 (1986): 26–33.

McDonough, Irma. 'Profile: Robert Munsch', *IR* 16 (Feb. 1982): 13–14.

Vanderhoof, Ann. 'The Weird and Wonderful Whimsy of Robert Munsch', *QQ* 48 (May 1982): 37.

Although he is one of the most successful authors of children's books in Canada, Robert Munsch is not really a writer. Munsch does not, that is, sit down to compose literary works for publication. From conception to final publication, his books have roots deep in the oral tradition of storytelling, beginning as tales delivered to audiences of children. He does not always plan these tales before telling them. He often responds during performances to children's requests for tales involving particular objects or settings. By observing his listeners' reactions to these spontaneous compositions, Munsch modifies his tales, removing things that fail and refining things that work. Eventually, he commits the most successful to writing. Not surprisingly, given this genesis, Munsch insists that his books 'always have to be read aloud'.

Munsch has said that he began telling tales in daycare centres while working on his MA but that he really learned his craft when working at a child-care centre in Coos Bay, Oregon, where he told stories without using books in order to keep the children on their cots at nap time. He learned to be inventive because the children constantly demanded new tales. In 1976, he moved to Canada and taught in the Department of Family Studies at the University of Guelph before he decided to devote himself full-time to practising his art in books, recordings, and, of course, appearances as a storyteller. His popularity is evident in the fact that a number of his tales have been adapted for television in animated musical versions.

Munsch is acutely aware of the difference between storytelling and writing. 'When you story tell', he says, 'you have your presence there and it's possible to keep kids interested in a story that isn't publishable.' The appeal of many of Munsch's stories, in fact, depends heavily on facial expressions, body movement, and, strange noises: 'A lot of my oral style', he says, 'is sound effects.' Furthermore, such recordings as *Robert Munsch: 'Favourite Stories'* (1983) and *Murmel Murmel Munsch: More Outrageous Stories* (1984) reveal that storytelling is for him something of a communal performance. By lingering over the initial sounds of the words 'yes' and 'no' or by cueing his audience to repeated phrases with a slow, drawn-out mouthing of the first part of the phrase, he gets children to participate in the telling.

Munsch admits that 'you lose a lot of that in the translation to book form.' He tries, however, to give some sense of the language in a few books. The speech of the giant in *David's Father* is thus presented in italicized capital letters to suggest his volume. When he yells, the letters are dark, large, and slightly distorted, as if they were shaking on the page. Similar typographical devices appear to indicate Amy's deep snoring in *Get Out of Bed!*, both the boy's pain when he bites an apple and the explosiveness of his sneeze in *Andrew's Loose Tooth*, and the sickening rocking of the boat in *Get Me Another One!* Munsch also occasionally stretches words to indicate their importance. In *Thomas' Snowsuit*, for example, the stretched out 'NNNNNO' typographically indicates childish defiance. For the most part, however, Munsch's texts are without signs of the various voices, cries, and sounds he adds when telling the tales himself.

What survives translation to the printed page is a style owing much to traditional folktales. In particular, Munsch uses repetition of phrase and episode as the primary building blocks of his stories. In *Mortimer*, for instance, he characterizes the obstreperous Mortimer by giving him a memorable chant, 'Bang-bang, rattle-ding-bang, goin' to make my noise all day!' Another conventional element of folklore, episodic repetition, with the last episode being a climactic variation, is evident in *50 Below Zero*, in which Jason finds his sleepwalking father on the refrigerator, then on the car, and finally outside and frozen. A final twist comes when Jason, having thawed and secured his father, ends up sleepwalking himself.

The secret of Munsch's appeal is not, however, in his use of repetition but in his development of plots that comically exaggerate a child's dilemmas. Munsch told a television interviewer that children identify with his stories because 'my stories are about everyday experiences for kids—going to bed, getting new clothes, getting dirty, having a new baby, cleaning up their own rooms—they're about everyday experiences, only the kids win.'

The very best of his stories are hero tales in which the child achieves victory through bravery and wit. *Mud Puddle*, his first published book, shows the pattern. By personifying a mud puddle, this story makes hilariously literal the kind of excuse children fearful of punishment offer for getting dirty so often. Jule Ann is bathed by her mother and dressed in clean clothes again and again, but a mud puddle always leaps on her. The story is completely satisfying in technique and theme. Repetition of the basic episode suggests both Jule Ann's growing frustration and the power of her antagonist. Cumulative repetition—the mother adds a new body part for special washing each time—indicates the extended time required to restore Jule Ann to cleanliness after each attack. The conclusion is symbolically appropriate. It shows that Jule Ann has matured enough to learn that soap destroys dirt and that she no longer has to rely on Mother to keep her clean. Munsch quietly revised this story, one of his best, in 1982, making the prose flow better, but the book continued to suffer from extremely poor illustrations. Although Sami Suomalainen revised his pictures for a 1995 edition, the book remains visually crude, an unfortunate situation given the high quality of the text.

Perhaps the most engaging of his hero tales and one likely to become a Canadian classic is *The Paper Bag Princess* (1980), a witty, feminist variation of the traditional dragon tale. Elizabeth, a princess wearing a paper bag because a dragon burned all her clothes, becomes a trickster hero. She tracks down the dragon, tricks it into fatiguing itself, and rescues her captured fiancé, Prince Ronald. The conclusion, a twist on romantic fairy tales, provides a significant statement about appearance and reality. When Prince Ronald arrogantly tells her to come back when she is not so messy, she rejects him as a 'bum' and decides not to marry him. In stressing the girl's heroic determination and wit, the story amusingly shows that a person's worth is not obvious from appearance.

A successful trickster hero also appears in *A Promise Is a Promise*, on which Munsch collaborated with the Inuit author Michael Kusugak. When Allushua disobeys her mother's orders to stay away from the dangerous spring ice and is captured by the Qallupilluit, she selfishly offers to bring her siblings in exchange for her freedom. Fortunately, her mother tricks the Qallupilluit into dancing with her while Allushua fulfils her promise of taking her brothers and sisters to the sea ice. One of the few tales in which Munsch presents competent adult figures, this adaptation of a cautionary tale shows both the value of traditional Inuit culture and the ability of parents to help their children overcome mistakes. A contemporary urban trickster hero appears in *Jonathan Cleaned Up, Then He Heard a Sound, or Blackberry Subway Jam*, a satire on bureaucracies. Jonathan outwits the mayor after the city declares that Jonathan's house is a subway stop. Other hero stories, such as *The Dark*, about a child's fear of the dark, *The Boy in the Drawer*, about a tiny boy who grows when people attack him and completely disappears when they express love for him, and *Murmel Murmel Murmel*, about a girl who tries to give away a baby that has mysteriously appeared in her sandbox, do not succeed: their humour is forced, and the points they are making with their bizarre episodes are not clear.

Silliness and exaggeration of common childhood events are central to many of Munsch's tales. Typically in these, adults, unable to maintain composure, end up running around in frenzied circles when opposed or confused. Children maintain perfect control. Bedtime is the focus of one of Munsch's most entertaining tales, *Mortimer*, in which a sequence of adults unsuccessfully tries to get Mortimer to be quiet and go to sleep. In the comparatively bland *Get Out of Bed!*, Munsch reverses the situation, showing adults as unable to wake up Amy after she stays up late watching television. School provides the setting for three stories. *Thomas' Snowsuit*, a superb story that has been attacked and even banned because it mocks authority figures, has a teacher and a principal try to get Thomas to wear a snowsuit, only to end up wearing each other's clothes. Cross-dressing also generates the comedy in *We Share Everything!* After repeatedly insisting to the quarrelling Amanda and Jeremiah that children in kindergarten share everything, their idealistic teacher loses her composure when they interpret her words literally and dress in each other's clothes. *Show and Tell*, about Benjamin, who takes his baby sister to school for show-and-tell, similarly makes fun of incompetent and flustered adults, but its humour is far more forced. *Stephanie's Ponytail* successfully satirizes fads and mindless conformity. When her classmates repeatedly copy each hair style that she tries, Stephanie teaches them a lesson about foolishly following trends. She announces that she is going to shave her head, but she shows up the next day with a ponytail and is able to laugh at the rest of the class, all of whom have shaved their heads.

Both adults and children recognize the situation in *I Have To Go!*, in which young Andrew, who has to pee at the most awkward times on a trip to grandmother's, insists he doesn't need to go to the bathroom at bedtime and ends up wetting the bed. (Perhaps for space constraints the Annick version ends at this point, whereas the large-format edition has Andrew calling for his grandfather, going to the bathroom with him, and not wetting the bed again.) Also familiar are the child's desires in *Moira's Birthday*, in which a party gets wildly out of control when Moira, against her parents wishes, invites everyone in her school. Unlike her parents, however, Moira proves to be perfectly capable of coping. Children's bragging about their parents receives a novel twist in *David's Father*, in which the father is actually a giant. Disobedience leads to unpredictable chaos in *Pigs*, in which a girl's failure to heed a warning about not opening the gate to a pig pen frees the intelligent pigs to overrun her home, the school, and even the school bus. In one of his refreshingly original tales, *Purple, Green and Yellow*, Munsch combines a satire of make-up and a child's tendency to paint herself with her coloured markers. When Brigid proves herself responsible by not colouring on the walls or herself, her mother buys her 'super-indelible-never-come-off-till-you're-dead-and-maybe-even-later colouring markers'. Predictably, Brigid covers herself hideously. She has to go to the doctor, who gives her pills to remove the colours, but she then becomes invisible and has to use flesh colours to make herself even better looking than she was before. The punch-line is that she previously coloured her father, who will look very good until he gets wet and the flesh tones wash away to reveal the rainbow colours beneath. Appearance plays a slightly different role in *Ribbon Rescue*. Jillian, a Mohawk girl, helps various members of a wedding party to get to the church on time, giving them ribbons from her traditional dress to tie shoes, wrap parcels, and solve other problems. The bride and groom are so grateful that they insist that Jillian, who was refused entry into the church because she was dirty and dishevelled, be their flower girl. *Ribbon Rescue* is not distinctive Munsch because its episodes are not wildly funny, but it ably develops its theme that character is more important than clothing.

The often inspired silliness of these books contrasts with the mechanical plotting of such stories as *Angela's Airplane*, about how Angela accidentally flies a plane, and *The Fire Station*, about how Michael and Sheila, on a visit to a fire station, are accidentally taken to a fire. Lacking satisfying resolutions to conflict, these stories merely stop instead of concluding. In other books, the silliness is so forced that the tale falls flat. Such is the case in *Something Good*, in which a girl is mistaken for a doll and her father has to buy her to prove his love, and *50 Below Zero*, in which a father repeatedly sleepwalks outside during winter. Similarly, *Where Is Gah-ning?*, about a disobedient girl who repeatedly runs away to go shopping in Kapuskasing, has a punchline but no adequate joke. *Wait and See* is a strained fantasy in which a girl's success at wishing for impossible conditions culminates in her wishing for her parents to have three babies, a wish that lacks adequate thematic preparation. The mystery of the origin of babies is also the premise of another contrived manic comedy, *Alligator Baby*, in which Kristen's parents go to the zoo, instead of the hospital, when her mother is about to give birth to another child. Her parents mistakenly bring home a baby alligator, and repeatedly fail to get their own child until Kristen saves the day. Unfortunately, this tale about accepting new siblings does not succeed as either a hero tale or a zany satire because the attempts at manic comedy are too predictable. Much the same can be said of *Andrew's Loose Tooth*, in which a boy's tooth is so firmly stuck in his mouth that not even a rope tied to an automobile can extract it. By far the weakest of these tales, however, is *Get Me Another One!*, about a fisherman who sends his daughter into the sea to grab big fish. This tale about child exploitation and subsequent family squabbles lacks both invention and humour.

Munsch's only book to go out of print is a failure of a different sort. *Giant; or Waiting for the Thursday Boat* aroused controversy because it presented God as a little girl. This story of a giant who is angry at St Patrick for driving out of Ireland all the elves, snakes, and giants actually has a more serious thematic flaw. By having God, in the form of a little girl, get St Patrick, who hangs church bells, and the giant, who tears them down, uncritically accept each other's habits, Munsch denies moral responsibility and development. Instead, he presents the universe as mindlessly deterministic. Neither the saint nor the giant, after all, is able to behave in any other way. *Giant* is not a failure because it presents God as female: it is a moral and aesthetic disaster because it makes a grotesque parody of the philosophy of accepting differences.

Munsch has also written three books that are deliberately without humour. *From Far Away*, based on letters from Saoussan Askar about her experiences as an immigrant, shows a child from a war-torn country gradually learning to understand and accept Canadian customs. *Millicent and the Wind*, the story of a lonely child who gets the wind to bring her a playmate, is a hackneyed, sentimental tale. Munsch's best-selling book, *Love You Forever*, has had a mixed reception. Many adults have warmly embraced this attempt to show the continuity of parental love over the generations. A good number of critics, however, feel that the text and illustrations are grotesquely literal in having a man rock his elderly mother and that the repetitive song about love is cloyingly sentimental. By negative example, this book clearly demonstrates that Munsch needs humour to save his exaggeration of basic human feelings and situations from becoming mawkish.

At his best, Munsch is entertaining. His hero tales and silly tales satirizing adult-child relationships amuse both children and adults. Memorable in language and structure, they invite further readings.

See also: *CA* 121; *CANR* 37; *CLR* 19; *MAICYA*; *MCAI*; *Profiles* 2; *SATA* 48, 50, 83; *TCCW*; *WSMP*.

Frank Newfeld

Born: 1 May 1928, in Brno, Czechoslovakia.

Principal Residences: Brno; London, England; Toronto.

Education: Central School of Arts and Crafts, London, England (Diploma 1952).

Career: teacher; lecturer; art designer; book designer; publishing administrator.

Works for Children

Written and Illustrated by Frank Newfeld

Simon and the Golden Sword (Toronto: Oxford UP, 1976). **Rev:** *CCL* 15 (1980): 123; *IR* 10 (Autumn 1976): 54.

Creatures: An Alphabet for Adults and Worldly Children (Toronto: Groundwood, 1998). **Rev:** *BiC* 27 (Nov. 1998): 45; *QQ* 64 (Aug. 1998): 36.

Illustrated by Frank Newfeld

The Princess of Tomboso, ed. Marius Barbeau (Toronto: Oxford UP, 1960).

Alligator Pie, by Dennis Lee (Toronto: Macmillan, 1974). **Rev:** *CCB-B* 29 (Mar. 1976): 113; *CCL* 1 (1975); 68; *HB* 51 (Dec. 1975): 608; *IR* 9 (Winter 1975): 35; *SLJ* 22 (Dec. 1975): 47.

Nicholas Knock and Other People, by Dennis Lee (Toronto: Macmillan, 1974). **Rev:** *CCL* 1 (1975): 68; *HB* 53 (Dec. 1977): 675; *IR* 9 (Winter 1975): 35; *NYTBR* (13 Nov. 1977): 47; *SLJ* (Feb. 1978): 59.

Garbage Delight, by Dennis Lee (Toronto: Macmillan, 1977). **Rev:** *BiC* 9 (Feb. 1979): 140; *CCL* 12 (1978): 72; *IR* (Winter 1978): 55; *RT* 33 (Oct. 1979): 92; *SLJ* (Jan. 1979): 55.

The Night the City Sang, by Peter Desbarats (Toronto: McClelland & Stewart, 1977). **Rev:** *CCL* 12 (1978): 56; *IR* 12 (Summer 1978): 57.

Selected Discussions

Ghan, Linda. 'An Interview with Frank Newfeld', *CCL* 17 (1980): 3–19.

Kelly, Terry. 'Escape Artist', *BiC* 6 (Nov. 1977): 9–11.

Stott, Jon C. 'The Marriage of Pictures and Text in *Alligator Pie* and *Nicholas Knock*', *CCL* 39 (1985): 72–9.

'When I first consider a book I'm going to design or illustrate, I don't think page by page. Instead, I visualize a concertina—I see all the pages stretched out one after the other. I make thumbnail sketches on long strips of paper, trying to find the overall rhythm of the book. Each illustration has to be seen in terms of all those that come before or after it.' This is the approach of Frank Newfeld, one of Canada's foremost book designers and the illustrator of two of the most popular of all Canadian children's books, Dennis Lee's *Alligator Pie* and *Nicholas Knock*.

The Princess of Tomboso, an adaptation of a French-Canadian folktale, was Newfeld's first children's book and reveals the essentials of his art, but in undeveloped form. Often several illustrations appear on a page, providing a visual parallel to the repetitive language of the narrative. However, in abridging the text of this story about a youngest son who outwits a clever and greedy princess, Newfeld omits important elements of characterization: the two older brothers' desire for wealth and power and the princess's greed for apples, a trait that leads to her undoing. The highly stylized illustrations do not reveal the personalities of the characters.

The design and illustrations for *Alligator Pie* and *Nicholas Knock* reveal Newfeld's art at its finest. He did not see the poems until they were in their final form and, with one or two exceptions, in the sequences in which they were to appear in the published volumes. He began his task with a basic premise: 'The book is the author's, not the illustrator's.' Thus, in dealing with individual poems, he did not try to extend the meanings. 'I didn't want to interrupt the poem. I wanted to let the poet finish the poem and then let the children look at the picture. In many ways, what I was trying to do in the illustrations was to present a reaction to the poems, not an interpretation.'

For *Alligator Pie*, Newfeld saw his job as responding to the play of the young child, the joys of youthful imagination, and the sense of security in the familiar world—all elements found in the poems. The cover depicts a gaily coloured balloon carrying four passengers: an alligator, two children, and a Mountie. Their happiness as they float upward hints at the sense of liberation found in the book. The green of the endpapers is not only appropriate for alligators, but also for the natural vitality of the child's spirit. The continuity of the themes in the book is reinforced by the visual patterns of circles and arcs. The dominant circle is the sun, which illuminates the children's achievements, their escapes from limitations. Many of the arcs are rainbows of happy colours.

Although *Nicholas Knock* is a companion volume, its tone is a contrasting one: in many of the poems, repression and restriction stand in the way of the speakers' searches for fulfilment. The visual differences to *Alligator Pie* are immediately apparent. Instead of a full-colour, full-page cover illustration, there is an orange cloth cover with a hooded executioner standing in the corner, his arms folded over an enormous ax. Beside him, the chopping block reads, 'For Nicholas'. The endpapers are a dull brown rather than a lively green, and brown is the dominant colour of many of the illustrations. We find nowhere the gaiety, the sense of discovery, or the idea of children controlling their own destiny. Instead, there are hints of punishment, containment, and dullness. While the motifs of circles and arcs are also found in *Nicholas Knock*, the circles most often create impressions of confinement. The sense of loneliness found in many of the poems is emphasized by the fact that 17 of the illustrations depict only a single living creature.

Simon and the Golden Sword, for which Newfeld created both words and pictures, is a folktale about a youngest son who, in spite of being scorned and mistreated by his older brothers, passes a series of dangerous tests, rescues a princess, earns a golden sword, and inherits his father's farm. Because he had complete control of visuals and verbals, Newfeld was, he remarked 'able to balance the pictures and text as I pleased. I made the illustrations tell more of the story, and I could leave elements out of the words.' The book is more successful than *The Princess of Tomboso* in embodying the stylized quality of folktales. Contrast in facial expressions and body language reveal the differences between the brothers. The opulence of the castle is balanced against the poverty of the little farm. The opening and closing illustrations are particularly effective. As Simon and his brothers leave the farm, they are placed at opposite sides of the picture. Simon, wearing plain clothes and carrying a bundle on a stick, smiles at his brothers, who look disdainfully at him over their shoulders. They wear foppish, eighteenth-century clothing. The illustration is bare of other details. At the conclusion the brothers occupy the same positions on the page. However, Simon is now in the foreground, embracing his father, who points at the other brothers as they slouch away. Between the two groups is a sunflower plant whose bright colour epitomizes Simon's new prosperity and happiness.

In 1998, Newfeld published *Creatures: An Alphabet for Adults and Worldly Children*. Each double-spread contains a large, full-colour illustration containing an elaborately drawn object, the name of which begins with the appropriate letter and a smaller, related painting. For the letter 'G' a golden and green gryphon walks on the ground near clumps of grass. In the smaller accompanying picture, a grandmother in a little garden paints a picture of the beast's head; beside her lies a ginger-coloured cat. There are no words accompanying the illustrations; viewers must turn to a glossary at the back of the book to find a list of the applicable words for each letter.

Although Newfeld as the illustrator of others' texts acknowledges his responsibility to the author, he feels his greatest responsibility is to the child who is the reader/viewer. 'You could say', he has noted, 'that there are four books in every volume I have worked on. One is by the creator of the words; another, by the illustrator; a third results from the marriage of the pictures and the text. But the most important is the fourth one which is created by the reader. I have to give the children who read the books freedom to react and to add to the pictures in their own minds. Only when they can and do accomplish this do I really feel I've been successful.'

See also: *CA* 105; *Profiles*; *SATA* 26; *WSMP*.

bp Nichol

Born: 30 September 1944, in Vancouver.

Died: 25 September 1988, in Toronto.

Principal Residences: Vancouver; Port Coquitlam, BC; Toronto.

Education: University of British Columbia (Elementary Basic Teaching Certificate 1963).

Career: teacher; 'theradramist'; poet; scriptwriter; performer.

Works for Children

Moosequakes and Other Disasters, illus. Anthony LeBaron (Windsor, Ont.: Black Moss, 1981).

The Man Who Loved His Knees, illus. bp Nichol (Windsor, Ont.: Black Moss, 1983). **Rev:** *CCL* 41 (1986): 70.

ONCE: A Lullaby, illus. Ed Roach (Windsor, Ont.: Black Moss, 1983; illus. Anita Lobel, New York: Greenwillow, 1986). **Rev:** *CCL* 39/40 (1985): 100; *EL* 14 (Mar.

1987): 27; *NYTBR* 92 (8 Mar. 1987): 31; TLS (3 Apr. 1987): 356; *SLJ* 33 (Oct. 1986): 165.

To the End of the Block, illus. Shirley Day (Windsor, Ont.: Black Moss, 1984). **Rev:** *CCL* 39/40 (1985): 100.

Giants, Moosequakes & Other Disasters, illus. Maureen Paxton (Windsor, Ont.: Black Moss, 1985). **Rev:** *BiC* 14 (Nov. 1985): 37; *CCL* 42 (1986), 69; *QQ* 52 (Feb. 1986): 22.

A Number of Numbers, illus. Michele Nidenoff (Windsor, Ont.: Black Moss, 1991). **Rev:** *CCL* 74 (1994): 89.

Recipient of the 1971 Governor-General's Award for his poetry for adults, Barrie Phillip Nichol played with and explored the physical, aural, and syntactical properties of language. Although they are not experimental, bp Nichol's children's books display the same love of sound and rhythm that is characteristic of his adult works and his membership in the Four Horsemen, a poetry performance group. The concern for sound is particularly evident in *Giants, Moosequakes & Other Disasters*, an enlarged and slightly revised edition of his first children's work, *Moosequakes and Other Disasters*. Heavily dependent on rhyme and alliteration, many of the poems are reminiscent of the bouncy schoolyard chants in Dennis Lee's *Alligator Pie*. The poems here, however, are aimed at a much wider range of ages, and their nonsense humour is sometimes awkwardly forced. Still, the collection has some bright moments and contains some works that demand reading aloud.

Nichol's other children's books are single, unified works. *ONCE: A Lullaby*, a repetitive, rhythmic bedtime book in which a number of animals make characteristic sounds before falling asleep, has been issued twice. The 1983 Canadian edition, with simple, spare drawings by Ed Roach, pales before the lavish 1986 American edition, which contains richly detailed, full-colour pictures by Anita Lobel. *The Man Who Loved His Knees* is an unusual prose fable crudely illustrated by bp Nichol himself. It tells of George, a man who learned to love his knees—and, by association, himself—even more once he discovered that he could put his knees to use helping a stationary flower move around and be happy. The posthumously issued *A Number of Numbers*, a counting book in which a bouncy, rhythmic poem describes the silliness of a group of children, falters because its final poem is syntactically awkward and too intellectually complex, requiring the child to understand that multiplication by zero results in zero. Nichol's most successful children's book, *To the End of the Block*, is a simple rhymed poem about a father and daughter taking a walk. In this unified work, the pictures complement the text, illustrating actions not mentioned by the words and thereby adding humour to the situations. The conclusion is open-ended: the text ends in mid-sentence, and the picture shows the tired but happy father sitting to think about whether he will again walk 'one more block' with his indefatigable daughter. This ending emphasizes the rhythmic, repetitive action of the story as well as the characters of both father and daughter.

In his work for children past the second grade Nichol strains to be funny or meaningful. He is far more successful in writing for preschoolers. His strength is his sensitivity to the sounds and rhythms of language: his books are a pleasure to read aloud.

See also: *CA* 53–6; *CLC* 18; *DLB* 53; *SATA* 66.

Ruth Nichols

Born: 4 March 1948, in Toronto.

Principal Residences: Toronto; Vancouver; Hamilton; Ottawa.

Education: University of British Columbia (BA 1969); McMaster University (MA 1972, Ph.D. 1977).

Career: writer.

Major Awards: Canadian Library Association Book of the Year for Children (1973).

Works for Children

A Walk Out of the World (Toronto: Longman, 1969). **Rev:** *CCB-B* 22 (July 1969): 180; *HB* 45 (Aug. 1969): 412; *IR* 3 (Autumn 1969): 23.

The Marrow of the World (Toronto: Macmillan, 1972). **Rev:** *IR* 7 (Spring 1973): 47; *QQ* 48 (June 1982): 5.

Song of the Pearl (Toronto: Macmillan, 1976). **Rev:** *CCB-B* 30 (Mar. 1977): 110; *CCL* 12 (1978): 47; *HB* 53 (Feb. 1977): 59; *IR* 11 (Winter 1977): 39; *SLJ* 23 (Oct. 1976): 120.

The Left-Handed Spirit (Toronto: Macmillan, 1978). **Rev:** *BiC* 8 (Feb. 1979): 21; *CCB-B* 32 (Jan. 1979): 85; *SLJ* 25 (Oct. 1978): 158.

Other

'Fantasy and Escapism', *CCL* 4 (1976): 20–7.

'Something of Myself', *Ocean*, 189–94.

'Fantasy: the Interior Landscape', *Proceedings of the Fifth Annual Conference of the Children's Literature Association* (Villanova, Penn.: ChLA Publications, 1979), 41–7.

Selected Discussions

Stott, Jon C. 'An Interview with Ruth Nichols', *CCL* 12 (1978): 5–19.

When she was a young child, Ruth Nichols created a series of fantasy/adventure cycles about her dolls; when she was 14, she received a Government of India prize for a 100-page biography of Catherine de Medici. These juvenilia introduce the main subject of the four novels she wrote for children and young adults: the quest journey of a strong woman.

A Walk Out of the World, a fantasy that reveals the influence of J.R.R. Tolkien and C.S. Lewis, whom Nichols later studied in her Ph.D. dissertation, is the story of Judith and Tobit, a lonely and unhappy sister and brother who are transported into another world. They engage in a dangerous and important quest to help restore the rightful rulers to the throne. Judith takes the initiative, announcing, 'I do not know how we were brought here, but I know why. It is we who must end Hagerrak's reign. Only so will the circle be made complete.' During their successful adventure, the children mature and grow in self-knowledge. Judith, who for much of the novel had wanted to remain in the alternate universe, realizes that her place is back in this world, with parents who love her.

Like *A Walk Out of the World*, *The Marrow of the World* deals with children transported into an alternate universe. However, the characters are older and the problems they face are more complex. Linda and Philip are teenage cousins who spend their summers at a northern Ontario lake. The boy admires his cousin's strength of character and wonders about her identity—she is an adopted orphan. When they are transported into the world of Linda's birth, the girl's supernatural powers grow, and Philip is virtually powerless to control or help her as she struggles to define her identity and her loyalties. At the conclusion, she has resolved her conflicts and Philip has learned an important lesson: 'No human being can possess another.' Even though he loves her, he must allow her to choose her own identity.

In *Song of the Pearl*, Nichols departs from the conventions of high fantasy used in the first two books. Writing for older readers about a heroine who must confront her complex and conflicting attitudes to her personality, Nichols needed a looser form of fantasy, one that allowed deeper analysis of character. The heroine, Margaret Redmond, dies early in the novel. Seventeen years old, she is filled with anger and hatred towards herself and her uncle, whose lustful advances she had encouraged. The action of the novel takes place in her afterlife, when Margaret is told, 'You must read the riddle of yourself.' She encounters earlier reincarnations of herself and faces her responsibility for her actions and attitudes in those lives. When she is reborn at the end of the novel, she has the self-knowledge necessary to lead a fulfilling life. The book marks a significant advance in Nichols's writing because she deals with difficult emotions and conflicts and gives new depths to themes she has been treating since her earliest works.

In *The Left-Handed Spirit*, which also traces a young woman's growth to maturity, Nichols uses a different genre, the historical novel. Set during the reign of Emperor Marcus Aurelius, it is the story of Mariana, an orphan who has no knowledge of her parents or her exact age. When she learns that she possesses healing powers, a gift of the god Apollo, Mariana is both frightened and angry. Only when she is captured by Paulus, an ambassador from the Chinese court, and taken to China does she realize that her gifts are not for herself alone and that she is responsible for the consequences of her actions. Although the book is not literally fantasy, it employs many elements found in the earlier works: the influence of powerful supernatural forces, the journey through strange exotic lands, and the confrontation with earlier states of existence.

In her essay 'Fantasy: the Interior Landscape', Nichols makes several observations that cast light on the techniques, themes, and characters of her works. Writers of fantasy, she states, have a special ability; they have somehow 'preserved a habit of access to the subconscious which has become unfortunately rare in modern culture'. As a result, they are able to draw on powers that the rationalistic, mechanistic, modern world has repressed or ignored, powers that must be used if the individual is to be healthy and complete. Fantasy embodies these forces and thus 'can provide an instructive correction . . . to the excesses of the dominant culture'. In reading a fantasy, one is sharing the author's awareness of 'the essential coherence, wonder, and loving energy which he perceives to permeate existence'. Reading has the result of awakening the reader's awareness of those forces within themselves.

An examination of the characters, actions, and settings of Nichols's four novels for children and young adults indicates the basic nature of the inner qualities that must be faced and understood if human fulfilment is to be achieved. Each of Nichols's major characters is young, isolated, and lacking in self-knowledge. She has said, 'The youth of my heroes has always been merely a guise for the questing soul.' Their ages are also symbolic of their states of being. Even Margaret, who in earlier incarnations has been married several times, is not yet mature, a state symbolized by the fact that, when she dies, she is only 17 years old. Only after her long journey across the Near and Far East does Mariana of *The Left-handed Spirit* achieve true adulthood. The incompleteness of these characters is partly indicated by the fact that they are exiles from their homes. Tobit and Judith have literally descended from an exiled king; Linda has been transported to our world by her evil half-sister; Margaret is a wanderer; and Mariana feels rootless during her long absence from Rome. As a result of their long, arduous, and dangerous quests, the characters discover their true homes.

Particularly in *A Walk* and *The Marrow*, the events in Nichols's novels are exciting and even dangerous; but, as Margaret is told, 'the journey lies within', and the events provide characters with opportunities for inner growth. Judith and Tobit, playing instrumental roles in the restoration of the rightful king, learn to respect each other's differences and to acknowledge responsibilities to other people. Linda's task is more difficult; in searching for the marrow that will give health to her wicked half-sister, she discovers and controls the tremendous power she has over others. Before she can exorcise the hatred and anger that she possessed when she died, Margaret must realize that 'power enthralled her. Its existence seemed sufficient for its use.' With it she had made herself and the men in her lives miserable; yet she had refused to acknowledge her responsibility for her and their situations. Mariana does not wish to be a healer, and she responds to her gift with fear, anger, and bitterness. Love for Paulus (who in *Song of the Pearl* had appeared as Paul) is an ennobling experience that Mariana accepts gradually and reluctantly. Only when the characters finally confront the depths of their realities, only when they are in touch with and recognize the powers of the subconscious can they achieve fulfilment and completeness. In telling their stories, Nichols, like the fantasists she so admires, is telling the universal story, the story of discovering who one is and where one belongs.

See also: *CA* 25–8R; *CANR* 16, 37; *DLB* 60; *Junior* 4; *Profiles*; *SATA* 15; *TCCW*.

Ken Nutt (a.k.a. Eric Beddows)

Born: 29 November 1951, in Woodstock, Ont.

Principal Residences: Woodstock; Stratford, Ont.

Education: York University.

Career: artist; illustrator.

Major Awards: Amelia Frances Howard-Gibbon Illustrator's Award (1984, 1986); Elizabeth Mrazik-Cleaver Canadian Picture Book Award (1989); Governor-General's Award for Illustration (1996).

Works for Children

*Illustrated by Ken Nutt (*illustrated as Eric Beddows)*

Zoom at Sea, by Tim Wynne-Jones (Toronto: Groundwood, 1983). **Rev:** *EL* 12 (Nov. 1984): 19; *QQ* 50 (Mar. 1984): 72.

Zoom Away, by Tim Wynne-Jones (Toronto: Groundwood, 1985). **Rev:** *EL* 13 (1986): 16; *HB* 63 (May 1987): 378; *QQ* 51 (Aug. 1985): 38.

I Am Phoenix: Poems for Two Voices (New York: Harper & Row, 1985). **Rev:** *RT* 39 (Mar. 1986): 720.

The Emperor's Panda, by David Day (Toronto: McClelland & Stewart, 1986)*. **Rev:** *BiC* 15 (Dec. 1986): 18; *CCL* 47 (1987): 73; *CM* 16 (Mar. 1988): 132; *QQ* 52 (Dec. 1986): 16; *SLJ* 33 (Aug. 1987): 81.

The Cave of Snores, by Dennis Hasley (New York: Harper & Row, 1987)*. **Rev:** *BYP* 1 (Dec. 1987): 8; *CM* 16 (Sept. 1988): 182; *SLJ* 33 (Apr. 1987): 82.

Joyful Noise: Poems for Two Voices, by Paul Fleischman (New York: Harper & Row, 1988)*. **Rev:** *CCB-B* 41 (Feb. 1988): 105; *EL* 16 (Jan. 1989): 56; *HB* 64 (May 1988): 366; *VOYA* 11 (Aug. 1988): 145.

Night Cars, by Teddy Jam (Toronto: Groundwood, 1988)*. **Rev:** *BiC* 17 (Dec. 1988): 16; *CCL* 60 (1990): 108; *EL* 16 (Mar. 1989): 21; *SLJ* 35 (Oct. 1989): 88.

Shadow Play, by Paul Fleischman (New York: Harper & Row, 1990)*. **Rev:** *CCB-B* 44 (Jan. 1991): 117; *EL* 18 (Mar. 1991): 24; *HB* 69 (July 1990): 64; *NYTBR* (11 Nov. 1990): 52; *QQ* 56 (Dec. 1990): 19.

Who Shrank my Grandmother's House? Poems of Discovery, by Barbara Juster Esbensen (New York: HarperCollins, 1992)*. **Rev:** *CCB-B* 45 (Apr. 1992): 204; *CM* 20 (Sept. 1992): 210; *QQ* 58 (June 1992): 37.

Zoom Upstream, by Tim Wynne-Jones (Toronto: Groundwood, 1992)*. **Rev:** *EL* 21 (Mar. 1994): 16; *SLJ* 40 (Aug. 1994): 148.

The Rooster's Gift, by Pam Conrad (Toronto: Groundwood, 1996)*. **Rev:** *CBRA* (1996): 438; *EL* 24 (Mar. 1997): 27; *HB* 72 (Nov. 1996): 721; *QQ* 62 (July 1996): 57; *SLJ* 42 (Sept. 1996): 177.

Selected Discussions

Jenkinson, Dave. 'Eric Beddows: Award Winning Children's Illustrator', *EL* 20 (May 1993): 68.

Ken Nutt was enjoying a successful career as an artist in Stratford, Ontario, when his friend Tim Wynne-Jones suggested that they collaborate on a book for children. The result, *Zoom at Sea* and its sequel, *Zoom Away*, made Nutt one of Canada's most sought-after children's book illustrators.

In the 'Zoom' books, both Wynne-Jones and Nutt wanted to capture the strange fantasy world experienced by the title hero, a small, rather ordinary cat. To achieve the desired effect, Nutt created black-and-white drawings not unlike those used in the fantasy picture books of American artist Chris Van Allsburg, using graphite, with occasional watercolour washes beneath and acrylics to highlight. As a result, the firmly realized physical details found in the pictures radiate a strangeness that suggests magical power. In the books, both words and pictures create a mixture of the homey and familiar with the unusual and fantastic. Opening illustrations depict the feline hero in the ordinary world of his home. In *Zoom at Sea*, he is playing with the water in his kitchen sink; in *Zoom Away*, he lies on his back in his easy chair, knitting. However, when he enters the house of Maria, his human friend, he moves into a strange new world. Nutt's illustrations are of a very large house filled with mysterious shadows and passageways. From the house, Zoom goes to the sea or the North Pole, and, as he does, enters into a world of bright light and distant horizons. Nutt implies that the passage through Maria's house is from the ordinary to the fabulous. His adventures over, the cat returns to his own house in the first book and to Maria's in the second. Nutt's drawings are a perfect complement to Wynne-Jones's slender text, providing visual details and, more important, emphasizing the sense of wonder and magic inherent in the plot. In a third book, *Zoom Upstream*, published several years later, Nutt pictures the Egyptian landscape and the interior of the pyramids through which the cat searches for the abducted Maria. His finished art was based on sketches he made on a research trip to Egypt.

Nutt created pencil drawings for Paul Fleischman's *I Am Phoenix* and *Joyful Noise*, companion volumes of poetry about birds and insects, respectively. In illustrating poems rather than narratives, Nutt faced a different challenge: he had to capture the rhythm and symbolism of the language of individual pieces and the entire collection. In the first book, the pictures for the opening and closing poems show a bird at a window; the first, a finch with a grey light behind it; the last, an owl with a cloudy, moonlit sky beyond. The design of each of the pictures parallels the pattern of the corresponding poem. For example, that for 'Sparrows' has 16 birds on the faces of playing cards, with each card showing a different activity. The poem suggests the variety and vitality of sparrows and their movements. The humorous tone of many of the insect poems in *Joyful Noise* is enhanced by Nutt's drawings in which anatomical accuracy and subtle human details are combined. For example, a pair of book lice, despite their literally different taste in books, have their arms around each other as they look through two holes they have eaten. A queen bee reclines luxuriantly on a couch while a sweating worker carries heavy buckets. And a bedraggled moth with woeful eyes serenades a light bulb.

Under the name Eric Beddows, Nutt has also illustrated Fleischman's story *Shadow Play*, extending the meanings of the written narrative far more than he did in the 'Zoom' books. The story of two children at an old-time carnival who attend the shadow play of M. Legrand and Family has a limited text. The boy announces that they have only 20 cents and hopes that the famous puppeteer will grant autographs. A brief narrative, spoken by Legrand, provides the basic plot of 'Beauty and the Beast' up to the point when the heroine's father plucks a rose and, at the end of the performance, provides a moral: 'appearances are as thin and deceptive as shadows.' Sixteen of Nutt's 28 black-and-white pencil illustrations are without accompanying written text. In them, the well-known fairy tale is given a new twist; the silhouette of the beast that charges the merchant resembles Stupendo, the 1,500-pound bull being exhibited in the carnival's next tent. Various members of the Legrand family appear to come on the stage in unsuccessful attempts to control it; the youngest, a little girl, tames it, at which time the father announces to the audience that, indeed, a beauty (his daughter) has tamed a beast. But when members of the audience are invited backstage, the illustrations give the written moral about appearances a new twist: the Legrands are not puppeteers, but stick puppets themselves, shadows on a screen. Nutt's careful research into late nineteenth- and early twentieth-century carnivals gives a realistic quality to the carnival settings, while his use of silhouettes enhances the apparent magic and mystery of the shadow play.

At a time when the large majority of children's picture books were published in full colour, Ken Nutt achieved his first great success with monochromatic illustration. His subtle use of design, details, and light and shade catches the spirit of the texts with which he is working and adds his own sensitive interpretations. More recently he has begun to illustrate in full colour and with equal success. The double-spread illustrations that accompany Teddy Jam's simple, rhythmic lullaby in *Night Cars* present activities on a night street as seen by a baby looking from the bedroom window of a second-floor walkup. While the background of buildings remains the same, the vehicles passing on the road and activities on the sidewalk change according to the time of night and the weather conditions. Nutt's angle of vision is from above, as is that of the baby, who looks into the illustrations from the surrounding white borders. At the book's conclusion, the child enters the pictures; with his father, he goes downstairs and into the coffee shop across the street from his apartment. In addition to the crisply rendered architectural details of the buildings, Nutt also subtly changes the intensity and hue of lights and shadows to indicate the passage of time.

Nutt's full-colour illustrations for *The Rooster's Gift*, Pam Conrad's animal fable about the false pride of a barnyard fowl who believes his call brings up the sun each day, encompass the full spectrum to enhance character and theme. As in *Joyful Noise*, the basically realistic birds also show human emotions and character flaws. Body language and positions and very subtly delineated facial expressions reveal the central character's pride, self-doubt, satisfaction, and shame. Nutt also presents three groups of parallel pictures using the small differences between them to indicate the rooster's pride and fall. Three pictures of the dawn contain different hues and intensities, with the pinks, oranges, and yellows of the last one reflecting the rooster's recognition of his true accomplishment, the ability to announce, not create, the coming of the day. Several of the pictures present the hero and his friend, Smallest Hen, against a white background. The absence of background detail focuses attention on the positions of each bird on the page and its postures. At the end, having overcome his false pride, the rooster stands beside his friend and facing her, a position of equality indicative of his having abandoned his condescending attitude. Finally, two double-spreads show the rooster crowing against a black background. At first, the two look identical. Closer examination reveals two small, but significant, differences. In the first picture, he tilts his head higher, as if he does not deign to acknowledge the world around him. In the second, he looks straight ahead, seeing the world that he lives in. Moreover his body is larger on the double-spread. Because of his greater humility and more accurate assessment of his gift, he has exhibited positive character growth.

Unlike many illustrators, Nutt does not possess an easily recognizable style. Although he skilfully uses lights and shadows, whether working in black and white or full colour, carefully depicts interiors and exteriors of buildings, and varies the angle from which his main scenes are viewed, all to enhance tone and complement and expand on written text, he does not impose a style on the works he illustrates; rather, he adapts his style to the needs of the texts, enhancing their unique qualities.

See also: *Junior* 7; *SATA* 97; *WSMP*.

SEAN O HUIGIN

(born John Higgins)

Born: 27 June 1942, in Brampton, Ont.

Principal Residences: Brampton; Caledon East, Ont.; Toronto; Cobh, Ireland.

Career: performance artist; poet, visiting poetry reader, performer, and instructor in schools; writer.

Major Awards: Canada Council Children's Literature Prize (1983).

Works for Children

The Trouble With Stitches, illus. Anthony LeBaron (Windsor, Ont.: Black Moss, 1981). **Rev:** *CCL* 42 (1986): 58; *IR* 16 (Feb. 1982): 48.

Scary Poems for Rotten Kids, illus. Anthony LeBaron (Windsor, Ont.: Black Moss, 1982). **Rev:** *CCL* 42 (1986): 58, and 57 (1990): 111; *CM* 17 (Jan. 1989): 18; *SLJ* 30 (Dec. 1983): 68.

Pickles, Street Dog of Windsor, illus. Phil McLeod (Windsor, Ont.: Black Moss, 1982).

The Ghost Horse of the Mounties (Windsor, Ont.: Black Moss, 1983). **Rev:** *BYP* 1 (Oct. 1987): 8; *CCB-B* 44 (July 1991): 269; *CCL* 42 (1986): 58; *EL* 19 (Mar. 1992): 50; *NYTBR* 96 (19 May 1991): 32.

Well, You Can Imagine, illus. John Fraser (Windsor, Ont.: Black Moss, 1983).

The Dinner Party, illus. Maureen Paxton (Windsor, Ont.: Black Moss, 1984). **Rev:** *BiC* 14 (June 1985): 39; *CCL* 42 (1986): 62.

Blink (a strange book for children), illus. Barbara Di Lella (Windsor, Ont.: Black Moss, 1984). **Rev:** *BiC* 13 (Dec. 1984): 12; *CCL* 42 (1986), 62–4; *QQ* 50 (Nov. 1984): 13.

Atmosfear, illus. Barbara Di Lella (Windsor, Ont.: Black Moss, 1985). **Rev:** *CCL* 42 (1986): 62.

I'll Belly Your Button in a Minute!, illus. Barbara Di Lella (Windsor, Ont.: Black Moss, 1985).

Pickles and the Dog Nappers, illus. Phil McLeod (Windsor, Ont.: Black Moss, 1986).

Monsters He Mumbled, illus. John Fraser and Scott Hughes (Windsor, Ont.: Black Moss, 1989). **Rev:** *CM* 18 (Mar. 1990): 67; *EL* 17 (May 1990): 59; *QQ* 55 (Dec. 1989): 22.

King of the Birds, illus. Tim Dixon (Windsor, Ont.: Black Moss, 1991). **Rev:** *CM* 20 (Oct. 1992): 268; *QQ* 58 (Jan. 1992): 33.

A Dozen Million Spills and Other Disasters: Poems New and Old, illus. John Fraser (Windsor, Ont.: Black Moss, 1993). **Rev:** *BiC* 23 (Mar. 1994): 48; *CCL* 75 (1994): 55; *CM* 22 (Sept. 1994): 136; *QQ* 60 (Feb. 1994): 38.

Other

Poe-Tree: A Simple Introduction to Experimental Poetry (Windsor, Ont.: Black Moss, 1978).

Selected Discussions

McGillis, Roderick. 'Lyric Poetry Is for Heroes: It Makes Heroes', *CCL* 42 (1986): 44–50.

Sean o huigin is a vocal proponent of experimental poetry. In *Poe-Tree: A Simple Introduction to Experimental Poetry*, an essay reprinted in *Well, You Can Imagine*, he argues that experimental poetry is both serious and playful because it teaches people to see language as something that they can manipulate and enjoy. Consequently, it removes their fear of reading and writing, and it also encourages them to explore poetic techniques and forms used in former ages. His own poetry for children employs such elements as short lines, internal rhyme instead of end rhyme, repetition, and parataxis (lines that can connect meaningfully to either a previous or a following line). Furthermore, it lacks punctuation and capitalization, elements of conventional grammar that o huigin believes will prevent children from engaging with language and from exploring the various meanings a single poem may suggest.

Despite its experimental surface, however, much of o huigin's work is relatively conventional light verse. Most of the poems in *The Trouble with Stitches* and *A Dozen Million Spells* (which reprints the better poems from o huigin's first collection), for example, are humorous presentations of such common childhood experiences as the urgent need to go to the bathroom and the fear of getting a vaccination. None of these poems is especially clever or memorable. In other works, however, the experimental verse is effective. *Blink (a strange book for children)* employs parallel columns of poetry to present the experiences of a girl who imagines herself simultaneously in two places: the left column describes the city scenes she sees with one eye, and the right column describes corresponding country scenes that she observes with the other eye. After the girl ceases to imagine that she is in two places, the columns become identical in wording. The form thereby supports the theme, suggesting that, while the girl accepts her upcoming vacation in the country, she does not suffer a loss of identity.

O huigin has achieved his greatest popularity with poems about bizarre creatures and monsters. Some, such as *I'll Belly Your Button in a Minute!*, in which a strange little person crawls out of a boy's navel, are rather strained nonsense poems. Others, filled with absurd violence and comical warnings, belong to the tradition of Hilaire Belloc's cautionary verses. In *Scary Poems for Rotten Kids*, for example, 'The Day the Mosquitoes Ate Angela Jane' warns against meanness by describing mosquitoes sucking dry a bad girl and then dying themselves because her blood is too nasty. Most of these poems, however, gently mock childhood fears. Thus, in *Monsters He Mumbled*, the narrator of 'My Monster' warns children away from his house by declaring that a gruesome, child-eating monster is hiding under the floorboards. These poems provide a safe scare, but they also subvert conventional aesthetic ideas about poetry through grotesque and disgusting images. *The Dinner Party*, for example, describes a meal that begins with 'with bits of / skin / the type you'd / find a / rat within'.

O huigin's other books are mixed in subject and quality. *Atmosfear* is a didactic poem that awkwardly combines a myth about a monster frozen in the ice and a warning against pollution. *King of the Birds*, an agonizingly long *pourquoi* tale in verse with an unnecessary narrative frame, explains why wrens fly close to the ground. Two prose tales, *Pickles, Street Dog of Windsor* and *Pickles and the Dog Nappers*, are about a dog who speaks in free verse. The former lacks a substantial plot, whereas the latter meanders, becomes embarrassingly inept in its introduction of a science fiction theme, and then collapses in the trivial ambiguity of whether all of the episodes were dreams. *The Ghost Horse of the Mounties*, the first poetry book to be awarded the Canada Council Children's Literature Prize, is based on events in 1874, when a day-long thunderstorm stampeded the horses of the first Mounties in Manitoba. Creating a dream-like state, the narrator instructs the reader alternately to imagine himself a horse and a Mountie. The poem succeeds in evoking pathos when describing the separate deaths of the horse and a Mountie, but the apotheosis, when the horse carries the rider into the sky, is too brief and too muted for a triumphant mythic conclusion.

When *Scary Poems for Rotten Kids* was widely popular, some adults objected that o huigin's poems were assaulting conventional standards in both taste and poetics. His work now seems relatively tame, and such experimental elements as his extremely short lines appear more quirky than syntactically meaningful. Although he has failed to make poetry designed for oral presentation work well on the printed page, o huigin has shown that free verse presents no obstacles to children. It can, as it does in the monster poems, entertain, and it can, as it does in *The Ghost Horse of the Mounties*, arouse complex feelings.

See also: *WSMP*.

Kenneth Oppel

Born: 31 August 1967, in Port Alberni, BC.

Principal Residences: Port Alberni; Victoria, BC; Halifax; Toronto; Oxford, England; Corner Brook, Nfld.

Education: University of Toronto (BA 1989).

Career: typist; editor; screenwriter; author.

Major Awards: Canadian Authors' Association Air Canada Award for Most Promising Canadian Writer under age 30 (1995); Mr Christie's Book Award, ages 12 and up (1997); Canadian Library Association Book of the Year Award for Children (1998).

Works for Children

Colin's Fantastic Video Adventure (New York: E.P. Dutton, 1985). **Rev:** *CCB-B* 39 (Oct. 1985): 34; *SLJ* 32 (Oct. 1985): 175.

The Live-Forever Machine (Toronto: Kids Can Press, 1990). **Rev:** *CCL* 65 (1992): 106; *CM* 19 (Jan. 1991): 35; *QQ* 56 (Nov. 1990): 14.

Cosimo Cat, illus. Regolo Ricci (Richmond Hill, Ont.: North Winds, 1990). **Rev:** *APBR* 18 (Sept. 1991): 13; *BiC* 20 (June 1991): 58; *CCL* 71 (1993): 87; *CM* 19 (May 1991): 174; *QQ* 57 (Mar. 1991): 20.

Dead Water Zone (Toronto: Kids Can Press, 1992). **Rev:** *CCL* 81 (1996): 89; *CM* 20 (Nov. 1992): 312; *EL* 20 (Mar. 1993): *HB* 69 (Nov. 1993): 747; *JR* 37 (Fall 1994): 438; *SLJ* 39 (May 1993): 32; *VOYA* 16 (June 1993): 104.

A Bad Case of Ghosts (London: Hamish Hamilton, 1993). **Rev:** *QQ* 61 (Apr. 1995): 41; *SL* 41 (Aug. 1993): 109.

A Bad Case of Magic (London: Hamish Hamilton, 1993).

Cosmic Snapshots (London: Hamish Hamilton, 1993). **Rev:** *CCL* 71 (1993): 87.

Galactic Snapshots (London: Hamish Hamilton, 1993).

A Bad Case of Dinosaurs (London: Hamish Hamilton, 1994).

A Bad Case of Robots (Toronto: Penguin, 1994). **Rev:** *QQ* 61 (May 1995): 48.

Follow That Star, illus. Kim LaFave (Toronto: Kids Can Press, 1994). **Rev:** *CBRA* (1994): 461; *CCL* 87 (1997): 85; *QQ* 60 (Aug. 1994): 33.

Emma's Emu (Toronto: Penguin, 1995).

A Bad Case of Super-Goo (Toronto: Penguin, 1996).

Silverwing (Toronto: HarperCollins, 1997). **Rev:** *CCB-B* 51 (Jan. 1998): 51; *CCL* 86 (1997): 52; *HB* 73 (Nov. 1997): 684; *QQ* 63 (Apr. 1997): 37; *VOYA* 21 (Apr. 1998): 14, 58.

Kenneth Oppel published his first book while he was still a teenager, and he received the Canadian Authors' Association Air Canada Award for the most promising Canadian writer under the age of 30 in 1995. Prolific and versatile, he has written comic fiction for newly proficient readers, two picture books, and novels for adolescents, as well as a number of unproduced film scripts. His books are notable for their careful plotting, for archetypal symbolism, and for themes that promote imaginative sympathy over cold rationality and relationships with people over connections to things.

Oppel drafted his first novel when he was only 14. A year later, he sent a revised version of it to Roald Dahl, who recommended it to his agent. By the time Oppel was 18, he was the published author of *Colin's Fantastic Video Adventure*, a comic fantasy that develops a strong moral. Colin Filmore is addicted to an arcade game, Meteoroids. One day two tiny spacemen, Snogel and Drogel, emerge from Colin's favourite machine and reveal that they actually control the video spaceship. Realizing an opportunity to win money in tournaments, Colin convinces them to fly the video spaceship while he pretends to control it. The plan succeeds, but Colin realizes that he is cheating. At the national championships, therefore, he refuses Snogel and Drogel's assistance. Although he is a loser in the tournament, he is morally a winner. The novel has obvious weaknesses—Crazy Rick, an arcade owner, is neither comically zany nor essential to the plot—but the constant arguments between Snogel and Drogel make it occasionally amusing.

Oppel has also written fast-paced and amusing chapter books, brief novels divided into short sections so that newly proficient readers can comfortably graduate from tales and picture books. In *Emma's Emu*, comic chaos erupts after delivery men mix up Emma's address with that of a Safari Park. Completely ignored by the adults, Emma enlists the help of her friend Howie to get the emu, which has 'pooped enthusiastically' on her carpet, over to the Safari Park. In *Galactic Snapshots*, Ian befriends an alien, whom he names William because the alien has studied Shakespeare. With the help of Sean, a friend and rival spectacularly adept at trading, Ian gets the parts William needs to repair his spaceship, permitting William to fly away just before the police arrive. In the sequel, *Cosmic Snapshots*, William returns to Earth and takes Ian on a trip into space, where Ian hopes to take pictures that will win a photography contest. Problems mount, however, after Sean, who has managed to sneak aboard, presses a button that turns off the ship's gravity. The humour in Oppel's 'Bad Case' chapter-book series generally depends on a pair of child eccentrics, Tina and Kevin Quark, who are self-proclaimed 'local geniuses'. Tina constantly transforms such household appliances as toasters into machines that, in spite of her unrestrained hubris, never perform quite as she intends. In contrast, Giles Barnes displays a practical wisdom, or common sense, that enables him to solve the problems that defeat Tina. In *A Bad Case of Ghosts*, for instance, Giles rids his house of both ghost birds and their ghostly mistress because his sensitivity enables him to understand how to end the unhappiness that makes them haunt the place they occupied when alive. *A Bad Case of Magic* similarly comically juxtaposes Tina's inept scientific logic and Giles's pragmatic sympathy. When a magician is unable to make himself visible after performing a trick, Tina builds a visibility machine, but it destroys or alters everything at which she aims it. In contrast, Giles succeeds because he understands that the magician remains invisible only because he has no confidence in his skill. Although light and comical, the stories in this series repeatedly indicate that sensitivity and compassion are more valuable than cold logic.

Both of Oppel's picture books are quest stories. The quest in *Cosimo Cat* shows the variety of life in a city, revealed by Regolo Ricci's beautiful illustrations of Toronto. After reading that Cosimo, a cat with cobalt-blue eyes, is missing, Rowan sets out to find it. Each time he approaches Cosimo, the cat moves away, and strangers must point out where it has gone. Perhaps significantly, only a shopkeeper, who is convinced that a cat would never be in a mall, fails to offer guidance. Because others help, however, Rowan follows the cat into an office building, down the subway, through an underground mall, and into the museum, where Cosimo perches next to an Egyptian statue of a cat with green eyes. For his efforts in returning Cosimo, who turns out to be a female, Rowan receives the reward of a kitten. In spite of its simple plot, *Cosimo Cat* resonates with implications: in having Rowan abandon an electronic cat detector and follow the advice of strangers, the tale subtly suggests that fondness for animals brings people together; by having the cat virtually go back in time by passing through the modern city and into the Egyptian room of the museum, it implies that cats embody an attraction that is ancient and mysterious; by making the cat a quest object, it transforms Cosimo into a symbol of desire and reciprocal affection.

The boy hero in *Follow that Star* also needs the aid of strangers, but their significance is far more pointed in the story's conclusion. Zach, who has never believed in angels, is angered when he discovers a note from his fellow shepherds claiming that they had seen angels and were off to Bethlehem. Noticing angel mist, Zach decides that he, too, will go to Bethlehem, but being a dutiful shepherd, he sets off with his sheep. Frustrated by the flock's stupidity, Zach periodically needs help from strangers. The first is an old man who guides him when he is lost by pointing out the star he should follow. Subsequent strangers help in different ways—a carpenter builds a bridge so that the sheep can cross a river, an armed man fights off thieves who try to rob Zach, and a boy helps him to slingshot the sheep to the top of the hill—but all reiterate the instruction to follow the star. Only with Bethlehem in sight does Zach realize that all of his helpers are angels. With the exception of the inappropriately absurd slingshot episode, this is a moving and meaningful Christmas tale. It stresses that a practical person, one who tends his sheep, can still be a person of faith, and that the heavenly, in the form of those who do us good turns, is right in front of us.

Oppel's two young adult novels are almost mathematical in their numerous and carefully balanced plot elements, but they are still tense and intellectually provocative. In *The Live-Forever Machine*, teenager Eric Sheppard is attracted by the past, in the artifacts in the museum and a game of memorizing dates that he and his father play. Although his father encourages an interest in the cultural and political past, he does not provide Eric with information about his personal past, refusing to discuss Eric's mother, who died when Eric was small. (Only later does his bitter father reveal to Eric she committed suicide.) The intellectual Eric also frequently finds himself arguing with his athletic friend Chris, a lover of all things modern and technological. Eric becomes involved in another conflict about the past between two bitter enemies who discovered a way to become immortal in AD 391. One of the men, Alexander, resembles Eric: he treasures the past and has a personal hoard of artifacts. The other, Coil, is an extreme version of Chris: he despises the past and wants to destroy it to build the future. When Coil plots to destroy both Alexander and the museum, Eric and Chris become partners in a quest to stop him. Descending beneath the city, a descent reminiscent of archetypal heroes' journeys to the nether world and rife with symbolic suggestiveness as a descent into the personal and cultural unconscious, the two boys manage to destroy Coil. In keeping with the classical symbolism, Eric emerges transformed, recognizing that his concern with the past had more to do with people than artifacts. As a result, he feels respect and affection for Chris, and he establishes a new relationship with his father. The transformation of Eric's relationship with his father occurs so rapidly that it is not entirely convincing, but *The Live-Forever Machine*, in raising issues such as the desirability of immortality, the value of the past, and the modern worship of machines and change, shows that young adult fiction can be both exciting and intellectually stimulating.

The characters in *Dead Water Zone* also fit into patterns that develop provocative themes. Questions about protection and betrayal, the wisdom of trust, and the dangers of dreams of perfection arise through the deadly interaction of three pairs of siblings. Paul Berricker, a middle-class boy proud of his muscular physique, is searching for his brother, Sam, a genius who suffers from a stunting congenital disease. Sam has asked him to come to Watertown, a polluted area inhabited by social outcasts. Paul meets Monica Shanks and her brother, Armitage, whose emaciated appearance belie their dexterity and strength. Paul eventually learns that Sam has discovered a secret about the addictive dead water that makes those who drink it thin and strong before killing them. The elaborate plot has Paul hunted by gang members in the hire of a corrupt corporation that wants to sell refined dead water as an addictive drug. Ironically, Sam, who discovered the refining process and who hopes that the dead water will give him the physical strength he has admired in his brother, is helping the corporation. Paul also encounters a third pair of siblings: David Sturm is a horrifyingly skeletal man who lives only because of transfusions of dead water, whereas his brother, Decks, wants to protect others from the fatal effects of the water. Further twists have all three sets of siblings deceiving or betraying each other, calling into question the value of trust. After a violent escape from those who want to use him as a guinea pig by injecting him with the addictive dead water, Paul realizes, however, that people complement and need each other. Hence, he refuses to judge Sam for seeking physical perfection through the dead water. He also realizes that he loves Monica and therefore must trust her. Filled with ironic reversals and revelations, *Dead Water Zone* succeeds both as a science fiction thriller and as a study of the moral and psychological complexities of relationships.

Silverwing, a talking animal fantasy, is just as densely plotted and thematically rich as Oppel's first two young adult novels. Using again the heroic journey as the basis for a series of conflicts and revelations, this fantasy explores such issues as the value of tradition and stories in shaping conduct, the competition between religious dogmas, the justice of inflexible laws, the nature of life as a power struggle, and the relationship of groups who hold competing ideas of their rights and responsibilities. Shade, the runt in a colony of Silverwing bats, is a misfit because of his curiosity. Unlike other young bats, who believe their mother's stories about turning to dust if they view the sun, Shade questions what he has been told. When he actually looks at the sun, however, he violates an ancient law, thereby giving the owls and other birds an excuse to launch a war against the bats. The owls retaliate by burning the bats' ancient roost, forcing them to migrate. Shade, however, becomes separated from the others during a storm.

During his subsequent lengthy struggle to rejoin the colony, he meets a number of significant characters. Marina, a female Brightwing bat banished from her community because humans have banded her, raises the issue of competing beliefs: unlike Shade's colony, which regards banded bats as being privileged with the sign of a divine promise, her group believes that banding kills a bat. Zephyr, an albino bat, follows the archetype of the divine seer: he gives Shade the hope that his father, long thought to be dead, is alive. Scirocco, a bat who believes that banding is the beginning of a transformation that will turn bats into humans, represents irrational cults. Goth and Throbb, giant bats from the southern jungles, worship the cannibal bat Cama Zotz and thus represent those who believe power is the only true value. Goth displays his evil nature when he eats Scirocco and his followers and when he tries to get Shade to show him where the colony hibernates so that he can eat the bats while they sleep. Two rats also illustrate the struggle of competing ideologies. Remus is an arrogant and cruel ruler of a kingdom within a garbage dump; his brother, Romulus, deposed as ruler because Remus declared him mad, shows the folly of judging by appearances when he helps Shade and Marina escape from the death sentence imposed by Remus.

With its deft use of such plot elements as the journey to the underworld, richly developed mythologies and religions, and fully rounded characters who grow with each conflict, *Silverwing* is a notable literary achievement. If the same combination of intellectual substance and exciting adventures appears in *Sunwing*, a sequel announced for publication in late 1999, Oppel will stake his claim as a new major writer for Canadian children.

See also: SATA 99; *WSMP*.

MYRA (GREEN) PAPERNY

BORN: 19 September 1932, in Edmonton.

PRINCIPAL RESIDENCES: Edmonton; Vancouver; New York City; Calgary.

EDUCATION: University of British Columbia (BA 1953); Columbia University (M.Sc. in Journalism 1954).

CAREER: reporter; creative writing instructor; writer.

MAJOR AWARDS: Canada Council Children's Literature Prize (1976); Little, Brown Children's Literature Award (1976).

WORKS FOR CHILDREN

The Wooden People (Boston: Little, Brown, 1976). **Rev:** *CCL* 10 (1977–8): 68, and 50 (1988): 66; *CM* 16 (May 1988): 89; *EL* 12 (Nov. 1984): 14, and 19 (Nov. 1991): 62; *SLJ* 23 (Mar. 1977): 147.

Take a Giant Step (Toronto: Overlea House, 1987). **Rev:** *BYP* 1 (Feb. 1987): 8; *CCL* 50 (1988): 66.

Nightmare Mountain (Markham, Ont.: Overlea House, 1988). **Rev:** *CCL* 54 (1989): 91; *CM* 17 (Jan. 1989): 18.

SELECTED DISCUSSIONS

Vickers, Reg. 'Myra Paperny: Trying To Practise What You Preach', *QQ* 43 (Jan. 1977): 18–19.

Although she has published only three books for children, Myra Paperny has secured a place in Canadian children's literature because her distinguished first novel, *The Wooden People*, won both the Canada Council Prize and the Little, Brown Children's Literature Award. The daughter of a Jewish Russian emigrant, Paperny has used childhood memories, the experiences of her parents and in-laws, and careful research to present graphically the Alberta of earlier eras in her first two novels. For her third, a contemporary story, she turned to her own experiences in the nearby Rockies.

Paperny's historical novels develop variations on the theme of an artistic son and the stern, domineering father. In *The Wooden People*, which opens in the year 1927, Teddy Stein is the sensitive, artistic child whose father seems a 'tyrant' because he forbids his son all things associated with the theatre. Teddy defies his father by secretly developing his 'own private world', a puppet theatre. The novel is very slow in developing the tense confrontation between Teddy and his father, and it depends on a contrived resolution, but it pictures historical conditions clearly and portrays with sensitivity a lonely child seeking refuge in his imagination.

Take a Giant Step reverses the situation presented in *The Wooden People* by having a child reject the world of art. Buzz Bush, a violin prodigy, wants to do what ordinary boys do, but his domineering father, afraid Buzz will injure his hands, won't let him play ball or ride a bike. Again, the device setting up the resolution to the problem is implausible and awkward. After an abortive effort at running away, Buzz comes to terms with his talent and his unique individuality when his father shows him how he can use the instrument to express himself. A denser novel than *The Wooden People*, *Take a Giant Step* paints more fully its social world, the early years of World War II, with its polio scares, scarlet fever quarantines, and the upheaval in families who lost relatives in combat.

Paperny's third novel, *Nightmare Mountain*, combines a mystery, a wilderness adventure, lessons about ecological respect, and a complex family story. Its focus is on two children from divorced families, Cassandra Fox and Jordan Scott-Brown, whose parents have married. While on a family camping trip in the Rockies, the children try to discover the identity of a ring of big-game poachers. The mystery depends on overly eccentric characters as red herrings, and it relies on a chestnut of such stories, implausible efforts to scare away the inquisitive child detectives. Nevertheless, the poachers' subsequent efforts to dispose of the children through a fatal 'accident' provide tension, the novel then becoming a wilderness survival adventure. The basic mystery-adventure also contributes to the family-problem strand, helping Cassie and Jordie, who initially do not like each other, develop a respectful friendship and come to understand that both will have roles in the new, blended family.

Although *Nightmare Mountain* is readable, Paperny's reputation will ultimately depend on *The Wooden People* and *Take a Giant Step*. Both have weaknesses as family stories, falling into sentimentality near the end, but they succeed as historical novels because they recreate historical periods that exacerbated the problems affecting relationships between adults and their children.

See also: *CA* 69–72; *Profiles* 2; *SATA* 33, 51.

William Pasnak

Born: 19 October 1949, in Edmonton.

Principal Residences: Edmonton; Banff; Calgary; Tokyo, Japan; Vancouver.

Education: University of Alberta (BA 1969).

Career: teacher of conversational English in Japan; freelance magazine writer, editor, and educational scriptwriter; children's author.

Major Awards: R. Ross Annett Award for Children's Literature (1984, 1988).

Works for Children

In the City of the King (Vancouver: Douglas & McIntyre, 1984). **Rev:** *BiC* 13 (Aug. 1984): 31; *CBRA* (1984): 341; *CCL* 43 (1986): 75; *QQ* 50 (Oct. 1984): 35.

Exit Stage Left (Toronto: James Lorimer, 1987). **Rev:** *BYP* 2 (Apr. 1988): 8; *CBRA* (1987): 235; *CCL* 55 (1989): 76; *CM* 16 (July 1988): 130; *VOYA* 11 (Oct. 1988): 185.

Mimi and the Ginger Princess (Toronto: James Lorimer, 1988). **Rev:** *CBRA* (1988): 294; *CCL* 56 (1989): 81; *CM* 17 (May 1989): 127.

Under the Eagle's Claw (Vancouver: Douglas & McIntyre, 1988). **Rev:** *CBRA* (1988): 294; *CCL* 56 (1989): 74.

Sink or Swim (Toronto: James Lorimer, 1995). **Rev:** *CBRA* (1995): 516; *QQ* 61 (July 1995): 61.

William Pasnak twice won the R. Ross Annett Award for Children's Literature, presented by the Writers' Guild of Alberta, for his fantasy books set in the kingdom of Estria. In the first, *In the City of the King*, young Elena and her guardian, Ariel, save the king of Estria from the sinister Black Priests, who control him. Ariel and Elena are travelling jugglers and entertainers, but on their way to the City of the Kings, Ariel reveals that he is part of the mysterious Brotherhood of the Silent Heart, a group charged with protecting the king. Elena herself not only discovers that she is a member of the Brotherhood, but she is also initiated into another mysterious group, the Daughters of Ismay. *In the City of the King* does not make adequate use of the secret societies and special identities it laboriously introduces, so atmosphere overwhelms action. Once Ariel and Elena reach the City of the King, however, the pace and intensity quicken. Because of her efforts to save the King from the spell of the Black Priests, Elena is condemned to a fiery death. Unfortunately, Ariel's efforts, not her own newly discovered talents, are responsible for her salvation. Furthermore, the final confrontation, in which Ariel destroys the head priest in a contest of light against dark, lacks earlier exposition that would make the magical duel meaningful. This novel contains numerous archetypes and motifs—the wise old man, the giving of three pieces of advice, magical spells, and the discovery that a seemingly ordinary person has a special destiny—but the mixture is imperfectly blended. Both those who help the heroes and their enemies lack sufficient development. The priests, for example, are stereotypes of diabolical villainy in both appearance and gestures, but their evil purposes are not entirely clear. *In the City of the King* has numerous flaws, but some readers may find its pseudo-Persian atmosphere and its feisty, questioning heroine sufficient reason to excuse them.

If the lack of adequate exposition weakens Pasnak's first novel, the opposite harms its sequel, *Under the Eagle's Claw*. Too much of the novel explains and prepares for a ceremony said to be vital to the continuing well-being of the kingdom. Nevertheless, much more happens in the sequel, and Elena is far more important than she was in the first adventure. Adding interest to the sequel is the fact that Elena has to leave Ariel behind when she goes to the site of the ceremony. Accompanied by Welf, a boy whose presence tests her will and patience, Elena discovers a conspiracy to disrupt the ceremony and to steal a sacred jewel that will bring power to an evil merchant. Although Ariel again plays a role in the climax, Elena's efforts in foiling the plot are far more important than they were in her first adventure; indeed, her wit and insight are essential in preventing the theft of the jewel. As with the previous book, the presentation of magic, secret societies, and cryptic warnings lacks clarity and directness, but the characters are developed far more fully, allowing Elena to emerge as a bright and compelling heroine. The stronger plotting and characterization enhance the themes of avoiding shallow judgement by appearances and of gaining self-confidence.

In addition to these award-winning fantasies, Pasnak has written three realistic stories. *Exit Stage Left* is a spin-off from the *Degrassi Junior High* television series. Although it is an original story, the need to remain faithful to characterization developed by the show and to avoid resolutions dramatically at odds with the show's stories somewhat limits the novel's possibilities. Furthermore, because it was the first in the series of books based on the show, it must also devote considerable attention to introducing all the series characters and their situations. The cancellation of the television series means that the novel can no longer attract readers fond of the television characters. Nevertheless, this novel is still an interesting story about a group of teens who face problems at home and school while preparing to put on their first big school play. *Mimi and the Ginger Princess*, a 'chapter book' for junior readers, is also workmanlike and readable. It includes an account of the Japanese story of Momotaro, the Peach Boy, that inspires its young protagonist to take action. When nine-year-old Mimi Kiguchi, a Japanese Canadian who is fond of cats but cannot own one because of her father's allergy, learns that a neighbour boy plans to send a cat up in a balloon as part of a science experiment, she decides to become a heroic Momotaro and rescue the cat from the boy 'ogres'. The chaotic rescue does not go according to plan, but it shows that heroic girls can defeat bullying boys. Mimi becomes an even greater hero, however, when she gives the rescued cat to an ailing neighbour and thereby gives the elderly gentleman a reason to continue living. Pasnak's third realistic novel, *Sink or Swim*, is part of a series of sports stories. Set at a summer camp that specializes in teaching water skills, it tells of how 12-year-old Dario Cavalito overcomes the fear of water that has

The Singing Basket, illus. Ann Blades (Toronto: Groundwood, 1990). **Rev:** *CCL* 65 (1992): 97.

Looking at the Moon (Toronto: Viking, 1991). **Rev:** *CCB-B* 45 (June 1992): 273; *CCL* 69 (1993): 42; *CL* 134 (Autumn 1992): 162; *CM* 20 (Mar. 1992): 92; *EL* 19 (Mar. 1992): 18; *QQ* 57 (Nov. 1991): 24; *SLJ* 38 (Aug. 1992): 156; *VOYA* 15 (Oct. 1992): 228.

The Lights Go On Again (Toronto: Viking, 1993). **Rev:** *CCB-B* 47 (June 1994): 331; *EL* 21 (Nov. 1993): 46; *HB* 70 (Sept. 1994): 590; *QQ* 59 (Sept. 1993): 68; *SLJ* 40 (July 1994): 103.

Awake and Dreaming (Toronto: Viking, 1996). **Rev:** *BiC* 26 (Feb. 1997): 32; *CCB-B* 50 (May 1997): 332; *CCL* 86 (1997): 77; *QQ* 63 (Feb. 1997): 51.

Other

'Balancing Past and Present', *CCL* 84 (1996): 89–91.

The Land: A Cross Country Anthology of Canadian Fiction for Young Readers, ed. (Toronto: Viking, 1998).

Selected Discussions

Day, Karen. 'Connections in Prairie Fiction: Paradigms of Female Adolescent Development', *CCL* 67 (1992): 33–47.

Flick, Jane. '"Writing is the Deepest Pleasure I Know": An Interview with Kit Pearson', *CCL* 74 (1994): 16–29.

Jenkinson, Dave. 'Kit Pearson: Boarding Schools, Beaches and Bombs', *EL* 17 (Sept. 1989): 65–9.

In her six novels, Kit Pearson combines her memories of childhood experiences, emotions, and reading with her adult knowledge of children's books and reading interests. Summers at an Alberta lake cabin and winters as a boarding school student in Vancouver provide bases for scenes and events in *A Handful of Time* and *The Daring Game*, respectively. References to Sheila Burnford's *The Incredible Journey*, Arthur Ransome's *Swallows and Amazons*, Sidney Lanier's *The Boys' King Arthur*, Kenneth Grahame's *The Wind in the Willows*, and L.M. Montgomery's *Emily of New Moon* help to cast light on Pearson's fictional characters. Emily, a particular childhood favourite of the author, resembles both the author and her characters. Pearson has said that she often felt like Montgomery's heroine, displaced and frequently insecure away from her home and family, and these feelings frequently enter into her novels.

Pearson's first novel, *The Daring Game*, reveals her knowledge of children's books and use of personal memory. Set in a Vancouver boarding school like the one she attended in the early 1960s, it belongs to the schoolgirl genre popular in England in the first half of the twentieth century. When her family must spend a year in Toronto, 11-year-old Eliza moves to Vancouver, where she learns to overcome her shyness and to understand the inner natures of her four dormmates. In addition to presenting descriptions of daily life and major school events, the novel focuses on the dares the girls carry out under the direction of the rebellious and troubled Helen. When faced with choosing between loyalty to a roommate or honesty to the headmistress, Emily gains a fuller understanding of herself, her friends, and the adults who control the girls' outer lives.

A Handful of Time, set in both the mid-1980s and the mid-1950s, is a time-shift fantasy that bears a resemblance to *Tom's Midnight Garden*, a work by Philippa Pearce mentioned in the epigraph. Twelve-year-old Patricia, who is sent from Toronto to the family's Alberta lake cabin while her parents work out their divorce settlement, at first feels lonely and alienated among cousins whom she has not seen for many years and who exclude her from their activities. Playing alone, she discovers and winds an old watch, which transports her to the time when her mother was the same age. Invisible in the past, Patricia learns about the tensions and hostilities that existed between her now famous and glamorous mother and her grandmother, an autocratic woman who favoured her sons in their frequent quarrels with their sister. With her new knowledge, Patricia is able to understand herself, her mother, and her grandmother more fully and to achieve a better relationship with her cousins. Her new maturity is signalled at the end of the summer when she freely and happily makes her own decision about whether to live with her mother or father.

The Sky is Falling, *Looking at the Moon*, and *The Lights Go On Again* form a trilogy about a brother and sister who are sent to live in Toronto during the German bombing of London during World War II. The books present new versions of an established genre, the war-evacuation novel, and a new focus on the author's portrayals of lonely, displaced girls. Norah Stoakes is forced to leave her English village during the German bombing. However, unlike Pearson's earlier displaced heroines, she is not alone, for her five-year-old brother, Gavin, accompanies her. The first book of the trilogy presents Norah's reactions to events taking place between August and December 1940. As she and her brother prepare to leave England, she promises her father that she will take care of Gavin, which she does, insisting that the two be 'adopted' by the same Canadian family. However, unhappy with their domineering guardian's favouritism to her brother and feeling alienated at her new school, Norah becomes less attentive to him, barely noticing his unhappiness and excessive quietness. Only as her discontent increases and she prepares to run away does she understand that she 'had never taken care of him'. Although she takes him with her when she leaves the house, she soon realizes her irresponsibility and returns to the home of her guardian, with whom she establishes an uneasy peace.

Two years later, at the beginning of *Looking at the Moon*, Norah has turned 13 and, like Eliza of *The Daring Game*, does not want to grow up. However, when her guardians take her for a vacation to their family summer home, which to Norah's delight is on an island, as is the house in her favourite book, *Swallows and Amazons*, many things change. She is conscious of the physical and emotional differences between herself and her slightly older cousins, feels excluded from the close-knit extended family group, and laments 'it wasn't much fun to flounder in between [childhood and adolescence].' Inevitably, the changes she resists arrive: she begins her menstrual cycles, develops a crush on her 19-year-old cousin Andrew, and discovers the terrible difficulty of choosing between personal beliefs and family values, when Andrew, a pacifist, upholds family tradition by enlisting in the army. This summer-vacation novel presents an in-between time, as the Norah who returns to the city at the end of August is much different from the one who had arrived on the island five weeks earlier.

In the third book, *The Lights Go On Again*, Norah, now 15, plays a much smaller role; the focus is on Gavin. Whereas Norah had been filled with memories of the home she had left behind, he hardly remembers England, considers himself a Canadian, and treats his guardians as his parents. When news arrives in Canada of his mother and father's deaths in a bomb strike, he feels virtually no emotion, and, as the Allied victory draws near, announces that he wishes to remain in Canada. However, he becomes filled with guilt at his decision to stay in his adopted country and finds himself remembering more and more of his life in England. When he remembers his promise to his father to stick with Norah, he makes the difficult choice to return home. Five years after it began, the Stoakes children's evacuation saga is completed. However, their futures are less bright than Eliza's and Patricia's were at the end of their stories. Their country has been devastated by war, their own home has been demolished, and they are orphans. Their courage and their love for each other and for their grandfather and two older sisters back home will support them when, as Gavin remarks, 'I don't know what's going to happen.'

Early in *Awake and Dreaming*, nine-year-old Theo is sent to Victoria by her young, irresponsible, unwed mother to live with an aunt. A lonely child who finds her happiness reading about and dreaming of becoming a member of the families in such books as L.M. Alcott's *Little Women* or Sydney Taylor's *All-of-a-Kind Family*, her wishes appear to have come true when, after fainting on the ferry to Vancouver Island, she is adopted by the Kaldors, whose children she had been playing with before she collapsed. However, her perfect life in this family proves to have been only a dream, induced by both her longing and that of Cecily Stone, a ghost who had died before she could write a novel about a lonely girl adopted by a happy family. Theo must learn to live in the real world into which she awakens, while still keeping alive her rich, imaginative inner life: she must be able to live fully both 'awake and dreaming'. The novel is Pearson's most complex analysis of a girl's character development as it takes place in relation to adult women. None of the women can be the mother Theo wishes. Rae, only 25, is not much more mature than her daughter; Aunt Sharon has her own life as a single career woman; the real Mrs Kaldor, whom Theo meets after awakening from her dream, has her own children to raise. The closest to a real mother the heroine encounters is a restless ghost, Cecily Stone, an author who died unfulfilled, but who is able to provide Theo with the encouragement and advice she needs to achieve her own sense of fulfilment and well-being.

Even in her fantasies, Pearson's novels are marked by a strong realism. The author brings to each story a full understanding of the nature of the times and places in which her characters live and the importance these have in their lives. She has remarked about the centrality of setting in her work. Each location in her novels is fully realized through careful selection and precise description of details. However, the settings are more than backdrops for actions; they also symbolize the characters' emotions and conflicts. Significantly, several of them shift to 'new' locales that highlight the characters' loneliness and sense of being outsiders. Their abilities to move successfully toward adulthood are reflected by their capacities for understanding and responding to the alien environments in which they find themselves. The major settings are, in a sense, transitional places, half-way houses on the way to maturity.

Pearson has said that the phase of childhood she most clearly remembers and most fully relates to occurs between the ages of 10 and 12, what she calls 'the peak of childhood'. Beyond it lies a period that her characters do not look forward to. As an old woman tells Norah in *Looking at the Moon*, 'I'd never want to be thirteen again—a miserable, muddled age.' Eliza is embarrassed that she is the only girl at the boarding school who doesn't wear a bra. Norah feels different from her slightly older cousins. However, Pearson's heroines mature significantly, not only as to wearing bras or beginning menstrual cycles, but developing greater confidence in themselves, inner responsibility, and fuller understanding and often sympathy for their peers and the sometimes tyrannical older people in their lives. The words 'safety' and 'freedom' occur frequently in the novels and represent polarities between which the girls move. With their arrivals at new places, the safety of childhood is shattered and then replaced by freedom through responsible action and growing self-knowledge.

Despite their excellencies in presentation of character, setting, conflict, and theme, Pearson's books have been criticized. *A Handful of Time*, considered by many to be one of her strongest novels, has been accused of showing prejudice towards Native peoples, while *The Daring Game* has been termed limited because of its focus on middle- to upper middle-class girls living in a privileged environment. These observations, however, seem to be motivated as much by the political sensitivities of the reviewers as by elements in the stories themselves. Pearson's greatest strengths far outweigh these supposed limitations. Chief of her virtues as a writer is her clear-sighted, in-depth portrayal of the insecurities, sensitivities, and growing moral consciousness of her female characters, particularly as these are related to their interaction with the adult females of their lives, whether mothers, grandmothers, guardians, headmistresses, or ghosts.

See also: *CA* 145; *CLR* 26; *SATA* 77; *TCCW*; *WSMP*.

Stéphane Poulin

Born: 6 December 1961, in Montreal.

Principal Residences: Montreal.

Education: College Ahunstic, Montreal.

Career: illustrator.

Major Awards: Canada Council Children's Literature Prize, French (1986); Elizabeth Mrazik-Cleaver Canadian Picture Book Award (1988); Vicky Metcalf Award (1989); Governor-General's Award for Children's Literature, French (1989); Mr Christie's Book Award, French (1991, 1996).

Works for Children (in English)

Written and Illustrated by Stéphane Poulin

Ah! belle cité! A Beautiful City ABC (Montreal: Tundra, 1985). **Rev:** *CCB-B* 39 (Mar. 1986): 135; *CCL* 44 (1986): 79; *CM* 14 (May 1986): 137; *EL* 13 (Mar. 1986): 16; *QQ* 51 (Dec. 1985): 24; *SLJ* 32 (Apr. 1986): 78.

Have You Seen Josephine? (Montreal: Tundra, 1986). **Rev:** *CCL* 46 (1987): 108; *CM* 16 (Jan. 1988): 7; *QQ* 52 (Dec. 1986): 16; *SLJ* 33 (Aug. 1987): 74; *TES* (3 June 1988): 46.

Can You Catch Josephine? (Montreal: Tundra, 1987). **Rev:** *Bic* 16 (Dec. 1987): 13; *BYP* 1 (Oct. 1987): 18; *CCL* 47 (1987): 96; *CM* 16 (May 1988): 101; *EL* 15 (Mar. 1988): 23; *TES* (3 June 1988): 46.

Could You Stop Josephine? (Montreal: Tundra, 1988). **Rev:** *BiC* 17 (Dec. 1988): 11; *CCL* 57 (1990) 105; *CM* 17 (Jan. 1989): 35; *EL* 17 (Sept. 1989): 57.

Benjamin and the Pillow Saga (Willowdale, Ont.: Annick, 1989). **Rev:** *CCL* 61 (1990): 96; *CM* 18 (Jan. 1990): 14; *EL* 17 (Mar. 1990): 60; *QQ* 55 (July 1989): 31.

My Mother's Loves: Stories and Lies from My Childhood (Willowdale, Ont.: Annick, 1990). **Rev:** *BiC* 20 (Apr. 1991): 37; *CCL* 63 (1991): 87; *CM* 19 (Jan. 1991): 30; *HB* 67 (Sept. 1991): 632; *QQ* 57 (Feb. 1991): 22.

Travels for Two: Stories and Lies from My Childhood (Willowdale, Ont.: Annick, 1991). **Rev:** *BiC* 21 (Feb. 1992): 31; *CCL* 70 (1993): 84; *CM* 20 (Mar. 1992): 84; *EL* 19 (Mar. 1992): 17; *QQ* 57 (Dec. 1991): 24.

Illustrated by Stéphane Poulin

Leonardo for Children Young and Old, by Helene Lamarche, trans. Judith Terry (Montreal: Montreal Museum of Fine Arts, 1987).

The Christmas Elves, by Henriette Major, trans. Alan Brown (Toronto: McClelland & Stewart, 1988). **Rev:** *CCL* 54 (1989): 76; *CM* 17 (May 1989): 138.

Teddy Rabbit, by Kathy Stinson (Willowdale, Ont.: Annick, 1988). **Rev:** *CCL* 51 (1988): 100; *CM* 17 (Jan. 1989): 35.

Family Album, by Michel Quintin, trans. Alan Brown (Waterloo, Que.: Quintin Editions, 1991). **Rev:** *CCL* 69 (1993): 65; *CM* 20 (May 1992): 76.

Animals in Winter, by Michel Quintin, trans. Alan Brown (Waterloo, Que.: Quintin Editions, 1992). **Rev:** *CCL* 69 (1993): 65; *CM* 20 (Mar. 1992): 76.

Dinosaurs, by Michel Quintin, trans. Alan Brown (Waterloo, Que.: Quintin Editions 1992). **Rev:** *CM* 21 (Jan. 1993): 19; *QQ* 58 (Dec. 1992): 28.

Endangered Animals, by Michel Quintin, trans. Alan Brown (Waterloo, Que.: Quintin Editions, 1992). **Rev:** *CCL* 72 (1993): 88; *CM* 21 (Jan. 1993): 19; *QQ* 58 (Nov. 1992): 34.

The King's Giraffe, by Mary Jo Collier and Peter Collier (New York: Simon & Schuster, 1996). **Rev:** *CCB-B* 49 (Mar. 1996): 222; *SLJ* 42 (Mar. 1996): 167.

Other

'L'Illustration pour enfants / Illustrating for Children', *Writers on Writing: Guide to Writing and Illustrating Children's Books*, ed. David Booth (Markham, Ont.: Overlea House, 1989), 20–7.

During the 1980s, Stéphane Poulin quickly established himself as one of Canada's foremost creators of children's books. Only in his twenties, he won major English and French awards for stories that combine tall-tale humour with realism, precise depictions of setting with exaggerated characters and action. He has, he stated, worked in his picture books to join what he calls 'fantastic or poetic books' with 'realistic story books' so that the settings offer infinite possibilities for imaginary elements. Whether describing the escapades of a runaway cat or the adventures of a shy man who makes magical pillows, Poulin, mainly through his vivid and detailed oil paintings, draws on memories of his childhood as these are filtered through a richly creative imagination.

Ah! belle cité!/A Beautiful City, the first book Poulin both wrote and illustrated, reveals many of the elements developed more fully in later works. The simple bilingual texts, with French and English words for each letter of the alphabet, accompany complex and subtle paintings. Although primitive in style, they evoke the cosmopolitan, multicultural characteristics of Montreal as these would be perceived by children. In each picture are unobtrusively included other objects, the words for which begin—in one or other of the official languages—with the letter being illustrated on the page. There is frequent humour. For example, for the letter 'L', as children skate on the lake, a boy wearing glasses is so intent on reading his book ('le livre') that he is about to walk into a tree. The main word for the letter 'N' is 'navel/nombril': a girl laughs as a boy pulls up his sweater to look at his own navel.

Three books use both pencil sketches and full-page oil paintings to depict the chases on which an elusive cat leads its master. Early in *Have You Seen Josephine?*, a sketch depicts a cat playing with a wind-up mouse toy. In the pages that follow, the animal will be playing a reverse cat-and-mouse game with Daniel, letting the boy almost catch up with it as the two run through east Montreal, the area, incidentally, in which Poulin grew up. In several of the pictures, Josephine is about to disappear—around a corner, over a fence—just as the boy reaches to grab her. At the beginning of *Can You Catch Josephine?*, the cat is missing as Daniel prepares to leave for school. As the illustrations reveal, she has hidden in his backpack and is only discovered at school, where she leads her master on a chase through the building, to the delight of the other children and the annoyance of the teachers. The illustrations capture people's differing emotions and the unusual places, such as the janitor's bucket in the girls' washroom, where Josephine tries to hide. The crisis in *Could You Stop Josephine?* is precipitated when the cat crawls into the trunk of the car just as Daniel and his father leave to visit relatives on their farm. Her encounters with a snorting bull, runaway piglets, and frightened chickens are hilariously depicted. Critic Elizabeth Waterston, in *Children's Literature in Canada*, suggests that the visual and verbal humour is created by the fact that the cat's antics embody a kind of wild and forbidden activity that children would not be permitted to indulge in and thus offer a vicarious release for young readers, who also laugh at the annoyance and anger that pompous adults express.

While the Josephine books could be categorized as exaggerated realism, *Benjamin and the Pillow Saga*, is pure fantasy. The story of a shy man whose habit of humming while he works gives the pillows he sews a magical sleep-inducing quality, the crisis arrives when Benjamin accepts an offer to hum at an Italian opera house and the pillows the factory now manufactures have no magic. The humorous absurdity of the narrative premise is reflected in Poulin's oil paintings. On the cover, Benjamin in the bathtub, his father on the toilet, and his mother perched on the basin happily make music together. In the last illustration, they are performing the same activity, but are wearing formal attire on the stage of an opera house. In the audience, people clutch the pillows they have brought to be charged with the magic of the humming. In all the pictures, the hero beams shyly and good naturedly, appearing happiest when surrounded by his loving parents, either in the bathroom or on stage.

My Mother's Loves and *Travels for Two*, both subtitled *Stories and Lies from My Childhood*, are tall tales that implicitly pay tribute to Poulin's mother, who raised a large family alone. *My Mother's Loves* recounts the activities that take place in and around 'a house that was almost as small as me'. The text is simple, merely statements about the inconveniences created by the large size of the family and the tininess of the dwelling. 'Sometimes,' the text states, 'even the yard was too small.' In the accompanying illustration, furniture is stacked precariously on the roof, so that the family can play baseball; the pitcher throws from the yard through the window into the single room, where the batter stands and the mother crouches, a sieve for a catcher's mask and an oven mitt for a glove. In *Travels for Two*, Mother has won a vacation cruise for two, and, in order to bring all the children along, hides them in a trunk. A series of absurd, slapstick misadventures are pictured, from the ride to the airport to the family's capture by and escape from pirates.

Poulin has also illustrated a series of nature books for young readers, each one designed to emphasize significant aspects of the animal world. *Family Album* deals with zoological categories; *Animals in Winter*, with seasonal behavior; *Dinosaurs*, with an extinct species, and *Endangered Animals* with those that may soon be extinct. The illustrations and facts are scientifically accurate; however, Poulin's sense of humour, especially his satire of the foolish and absurd, is evident throughout. Each book is presented as a collection of photographs taken by Mr Click, a timid, walrus-mustached man who takes his old-fashioned diaphragm camera and tripod to various locations and time periods. He is seen suspended from a cliff, clinging to the neck of a brontosaurus, and being attacked by a poodle, as he attempts to perform his duties.

In his own books, along with those he has illustrated for others, Poulin has created pictures that, in their details, colours, and depiction of exaggerated actions, extend the meanings of the often brief texts, communicating the vitality of human life, especially in the city, and the frequent absurdity of people's activities, especially as these are perceived by children.

See also: *CA* 165; *CLR* 28; *SATA* 98; *WSMP*.

James Reaney

Born: 1 September 1926, in South Easthope, Ont.

Principal Residences: Toronto: Winnipeg; London, Ont.

Education: University of Toronto (BA 1948, MA 1949, Ph.D. 1958).

Career: university professor; writer.

Works for Children

Plays

Let's Make a Carol: A Play with Music for Children, music by Alfred Kunz (Waterloo, Ont.: Waterloo Music Company, 1965).

All the Bees and All the Keys, music by John Beckwith (Erin, Ont.: Press Porcépic, 1973).

Apple Butter and Other Plays for Children (Vancouver: Talonbooks, 1973) [Contents reissued separately as *Apple Butter: A Play*, *Geography Match: A Play*,

Ignoramus: A Play, and *Names and Nicknames: A Play* (Vancouver: Talonbooks. 1978)]. **Rev:** *CCL* 8/9 (1977): 98, and 21 (1981): 69.

Lewis Carroll's Alice through the Looking Glass (Erin, Ont.: Porcupine's Quill, 1994).

FICTION

The Boy with an R in His Hand: A Tale of the Type-Riot at William Lyon Mackenzie's Printing Office in 1826 (Toronto: Macmillan, 1965). **Rev:** *CCL* 23/24 (1981): 96; *EL* 9 (Sept. 1981): 29; *QQ* 46 (June 1980): 36.

Take the Big Picture (Erin, Ont.: Porcupine's Quill, 1986). **Rev:** *BiC* (Oct. 1986): 38; *CCL* 44 (1986): 56.

OTHER

Colours in the Dark (Vancouver: Talonplays with Macmillan of Canada, 1969).

Listen to the Wind (Vancouver: Talonbooks, 1972).

'Ten Years at Play', *CL* 41 (Summer 1969): 53–61.

SELECTED DISCUSSIONS

Dragland, Stan, ed. *Approaches to the Work of James Reaney* (Downsview, Ont.: ECW Press, 1983).

Lee, Alvin, and Eleanor R. Goldhar. 'James Reaney', *Profiles in Canadian Literature 4* (Toronto: Dundurn Press, 1982), 17–28.

Parker, Gerald D. *How to Play: The Theatre of James Reaney* (Toronto: ECW Press, 1991).

Ross, Catherine, and Catherine Sheldrick Ross. 'An Interview with James Reaney', *CCL* 29 (1983): 4–24.

Three times the winner of the Governor-General's Award for his adult writings—twice for poetry and once for drama—James Reaney has said about drama that 'you've got to have an underlying legend or myth or pattern that makes the whole thing work dynamically.' Believing that children can absorb even complex material as long as it is contained within a powerful story, he has used folktale patterns or the conventions of Greek comedy to produce some of the most unusual and stimulating plays ever written for Canadian children. Although not as successfully, he has also exercised his mythic and pattern-making tendencies in two novels.

Reaney wrote the four plays in *Apple Butter and Other Plays for Children* as 'a set which should guide a child's imaginative and community development through to the end of high school'. These plays show two approaches to children's stories. The two for younger children are more heavily patterned, exhibiting the repetition of words and episodes typical of folktales. In *Apple Butter*, an amusing puppet play for preschoolers first produced in 1965, the title hero shows his respect for nature through his kindness to a tree and a cow. He thus receives the protection of the Wuzzles (Fairies) and eventually becomes mythically identified with the ripening of fruit and the solving of human problems. *Names and Nicknames*, a play for a slightly older audience first produced in 1963, uses a transformation legend: spite and envy turn mean old Grandpa Thornberry, who ruins children's lives with derogatory nicknames, into an actual thornberry. Filled with poetic repetitions and catalogues, this play effectively uses a chorus to celebrate the beauty of naming.

Because two of Reaney's adult plays, *Listen to the Wind* (first produced in 1966) and *Colours in the Dark* (first produced in 1967), are accessible to high school students, they are frequently listed with his works for young people. In the former, some children stage a drama that enables them to come to terms with their feelings. In the latter, which Reaney's prefatory note describes as 'a play box' because it includes disparate elements, a free-flowing story explores the identity theme.

Reaney's other theatrical works include two musical works for children: *Let's Make a Carol: A Play with Music for Children*, with music by Alfred Kunz, and *All the Bees and All the Keys*, a folkloric tale with accompanying music by John Beckwith. Commissioned by the Stratford Festival, he wrote *Lewis Carroll's Alice Through the Looking-Glass*, a stage adaptation of Carroll's dream fantasy that involves use of magical special effects.

The two approaches to storytelling evident in his plays are also apparent in Reaney's novels. In *The Boy with an R in His Hand*, a fictional account of the smashing of William Lyon Mackenzie's printing press in 1826, Reaney's excessive reliance on patterns weakens the novel. Parallel scenes, such as the poor man being hanged for stealing a cow and the influential Tories being merely fined for wrecking the press, advance the theme, but other patterns, such as Alec's accidental fall into the water and the preposterous story of the bear who saves the boy who had freed him, violate the historical realism developed in much of the novel. *Take the Big Picture*, a bolder and freer comic novel for slightly older readers, uses the story-within-a-story technique of *Listen to the Wind* to mix a number of elements. These include a pattern based on that of Scheherazade's uncompleted tales, a mythic transformation of the Sasquatch into a god of retribution, a farcical comedy about uncontrollable triplets known as the Terrible Three, a family comedy about generational relationships and the meaning of home, and a crime story. Attempting too much, the novel does not quite hang together, but it has fine comic moments and is especially successful in celebrating the gripping power of story.

Because Reaney takes chances, he sometimes goes to extremes in the use of repetition and mythic patterning. Nevertheless, all of his works have stimulating sections. Breaking new ground with his exuberant, rhythmic language, his use of the chorus, and his loose structures that encourage improvisation, he is a major force in Canadian children's drama. Although his fiction is less successful, it nevertheless shows him to be a writer who combines a playful intelligence with a strong ethical sense.

See also: *CA* 41–4; *CANR* 42; *CLC* 13; *DLB* 68; *SATA* 43; *TCCW*; *WSMP*.

Karen Reczuch

Born: 4 July 1956, in Woodstock, Ont.

Principal Residences: Woodstock; Ivory Coast, Africa; Acton, Ont.

Education: Sheridan College, Oakville, Ont. (Diploma in Illustration 1977).

Career: graphic artist; illustrator.

Major Awards: Amelia Frances Howard-Gibbon Illustrator's Award (1996); IODE (Toronto) Book Award, with David Booth (1996).

Works for Children

Illustrated by Karen Reczuch

The Auction, by Jan Andrews (Toronto: Groundwood, 1990). **Rev:** *CCB-B* 44 (Feb. 1991): 135; *CCL* 64 (1991): 92; *CM* 19 (Mar. 1991): 96; *EL* 18 (Mar. 1991): 50; *QQ* 56 (Dec. 1990): 18; *SLJ* 37 (May 1991): 74.

Sure as Strawberries, by Sue Ann Alderson (Red Deer, Alta: Red Deer College Press, 1992). **Rev:** *CM* 21 (Jan. 1993): 19; *EL* 21 (Mar. 1994): 16; *QQ* 58 (Dec. 1992): 27.

Just Like New, by Ainslie Manson (Toronto: Groundwood, 1995). **Rev:** *CBRA* (1995): 477; *CCB-B* 50 (Jan. 1997): 180; *CCL* 84 (1996): 121; *QQ* 61 (Aug. 1995): 33; *SLJ* 42 (Dec. 1996): 100.

The Dust Bowl, by David Booth (Toronto: Kids Can Press, 1996). **Rev:** *BiC* 25 (Dec. 1996): 36; *CCB-B* 51 (Oct. 1997): 43; *CBRA* (1996): 434; *EL* 24 (Mar. 1997): 27; *QQ* 63 (Sept. 1996): 73; *SLJ* 43 (Dec. 1997): 81.

Harvest Queen, by Joanne Robertson (Red Deer, Alta: Red Deer College Press, 1996). **Rev:** *CBRA* (1996): 455.

Morning on the Lake, by Jan Bourdeau Waboose (Toronto: Kids Can Press, 1997). **Rev:** *CM* 4 (7 Oct. 1997): on-line; *EL* 25 (Mar. 1998): 26; *QQ* 63 (July 1997): 50; *SLJ* 44 (May 1998): 127.

This New Baby, by Teddy Jam (Toronto: Groundwood, 1998).

Melted Star Journey, by Nancy Hundal (Toronto: HarperCollins, 1999). **Rev:** *QQ* 65 (Jan. 1999): 43.

When she was a girl, Karen Reczuch left pictures of ballerinas around the house, hinting to her parents that she would like to take dancing lessons. However, they were so impressed with her drawings that they enrolled her in art classes. She studied commercial art in high school and college and worked in advertising before travelling to the Ivory Coast in Africa, where she illustrated children's textbooks. Although she continued that activity for several years after her return to Canada, she wished to create more challenging pictures and began illustrating children's stories.

With one exception, Ainslie Manson's *Just Like New*, the texts Reczuch has illustrated deal with the relationships between a child and an adult: a boy and his grandfather in *The Auction*, *The Dust Bowl*, and *Morning on the Lake*; a girl and her uncle in *Sure As Strawberries*; a girl and her grandmother in *Harvest Queen*; and a newborn baby and its mother in *This New Baby*. Reczuch's pencil and watercolour illustrations sharply and crisply detail settings of the stories, and her representations of characters disclose their emotional reactions to events and other people. A detailed examination of four of these titles will indicate the nature of her artistic achievement.

David Booth's *The Dust Bowl* describes the struggles of three generations of wheat farmers to save their land in times of drought. After his discouraged father has gone outside, Matthew listens to his grandfather recount the struggles he and his wife had during the Depression, when dust storms and grasshopper plagues drove many farmers off their land. Based on her visit to the prairies and extensive background research, Reczuch's watercolour and graphite-pencil illustrations both portray the events of the 1930s and early 1990s and communicate the emotions of the farmers. The story's conflicts are summed up in the cover illustration. In the foreground, Matthew and his father lean their heads to one side, shielding themselves from wind and dust; behind them brown grass and grey dirt stretch to the horizon. Significantly, the direction of movement is from right to left, the opposite of normal eye movement in reading. Just as the movement on the cover impedes the usual visual patterns of reading, so, too, the wind is an obstacle to the farmers' happiness. With the exception of the boy's sweatshirt, there is no green in the illustration, just as there is no growth on the land and little happiness and hope in the characters' hearts.

Until near the end of the story, little green appears in the illustrations; yellow-oranges, browns, and greys—the colours of drought, dust, and despair—dominate. Grey clouds tower on the horizon, as the farmer tries to control a rearing horse; children turn their backs against the wind as it blows through the pale yellow grass of the schoolyard; yellow lights shine from the farm house as the dust obscures a noonday sun that casts an orange hue over the land. Ironically, the green stalks of a promising crop are devoured by grasshoppers whose large brown shapes loom in the foreground of an illustration. There is one significant exception: a picture of Matthew and his deceased mother is set in a green frame and the woman is holding a pot containing a small green plant. This detail foreshadows a later scene in which Matthew's father tends a garden his wife had planted shortly before her death. Green tomato plants, a green bucket, and green trim around the window suggest that the farmer's hope and courage will continue.

On one level, Ojibway author Jan Waboose's *Morning on the Lake* is a simple description of a day and night spent in nature by a boy and his grandfather. On a deeper level, it is an account of the old man's introducing the child to the natural and spiritual powers that guide the Ojibway people. Travelling quietly in the canoe, the two observe a family of loons, birds associated with shamans, early in the morning; an eagle, emblem of power and wisdom, at midday high on a hill; and a pack of wolves, symbols of freedom, at night in the forest. Like the written text, Reczuch's illustrations can be read literally and spiritually. Each picture depicts natural objects, animals, and actions. However, the sharp rendering of detail and the intensity of the graphite pencil, prismacolour, and watercolour illustrations suggest that the two human beings are in the presence of powerful spiritual forces. The only three double-spread illustrations reveal important moments of the day: grandfather and grandson paddling out of the mist encounter the loons; each looks out over the landscape experiencing, just before the eagle's arrival, the majesty and grandeur of the natural world; and, finally, the old man embraces the boy in the dark woods as both look in awe at the departing wolf pack.

Three generations of women are the focus of Joanne Robertson's *Harvest Queen*. After Bridgit and her grandmother build a Harvest Queen effigy out of a pumpkin and garden vegetables, the girl joins the harvest dance with a fairy prince before returning to the kitchen to join her mother and grandmother. Reczuch's illustrations emphasize the closeness between the girl and the old woman as the latter initiates her into an old custom; the pictures also capture the emotions the girl experiences during her magical adventure. The grandmother, whose green sweater links her to the nature myth she teaches the girl, smiles thoughtfully at the child as the two work together. As she enters the kitchen, Bridgit looks pensively over her shoulder at the night skies, while the grandmother and mother exchange knowing glances. The implication of this final illustration is that they recognize that she has entered the mystical realm that they have also experienced.

Reczuch's illustrations for Ainslie Manson's *Just Like New* reveal at their fullest her talents for using colours and depicting facial expressions and body language to communicate themes, conflicts, and emotional tones. Set in Montreal during World War II, the narrative presents the inner struggles Sally goes through before she gives up one of her favourite dolls, sending it as a 'Just Like New' Christmas gift for a child in England. Her emotional conflicts are compounded by the actions of a teasing, often mean, older brother. The artist has carefully researched the styles of clothing, furniture, and other objects of the early 1940s, along with the appearance of the bombed areas of London, to provide historical accuracy. She has also executed her coloured illustrations in more muted colours than those of her other works, simulating the faded pictures from an earlier time. The muted colours also emphasize the sombre emotions that permeated daily life during the war. Until the final two pages, colour is used only for pictures relating to Sally's activities in Canada; those depicting England are black-and-white. The contrast between the lives in the two countries is thus reinforced. The picture of the English girl opening her gift employs colour for the first time in the English scenes; the gift from Canada brings joy. However, the colours used in this illustration are even more muted than those in the Canadian scenes, as Sally's present offers only partial relief from the stresses of war. Sally experiences various emotional reactions to the idea of giving a gift and then letting a favourite doll go. Walking home from church, she looks thoughtfully ahead of her; she gasps in horror when her brother gleefully talks about tanks and bombs, stares angrily at him when he decides to send as his gift a book that he doesn't like, gazes longingly at the doll she is about to relinquish, and stares sadly out of the window on Christmas day.

Although she has illustrated only a few books, Karen Reczuch's reputation as an important new children's book artist is well deserved. She has combined her skill with colour and design with her sensitive responses to the characters in stories she is working with to create memorable visual narratives of children's responses to adults and to the physical and emotional worlds in which they live.

Barbara Reid

Born: 16 November 1957, in Toronto.

Principal Residences: Toronto.

Education: Ontario College of Art (Diploma 1980).

Career: writer; illustrator.

Major Awards: Canada Council Children's Literature Prize for Illustration (1986); IODE (Toronto) Book Award (1986); Ruth Schwartz Children's Book Award (1987); Amelia Frances Howard-Gibbon Illustrator's Award (1995, 1998); Elizabeth Mrazik-Cleaver Canadian Picture Book Award (1987, 1993); Governor-General's Award for Children's Literature (1997); Mr Christie's Book Award (1991).

Works for Children

Written and Illustrated by Barbara Reid

Playing With Plasticine (Toronto: Kids Can Press, 1988). **Rev:** *CM* 17 (Jan. 1989): 23; *SLJ* 35 (May 1989): 121.

Zoe's Rainy Day; Zoe's Sunny Day; Zoe's Windy Day; Zoe's Snowy Day (Toronto: Kids Can Press, 1991). **Rev:** *CCL* 69 (1993): 90; *CM* 29 (Mar. 1992): 84; *EL* 19 (Mar. 1992): 15; *QQ* 57 (Oct. 1991) 36.

Two by Two (Richmond Hill, Ont.: Scholastic, 1992). **Rev:** *BiC* 21 (Nov. 1992): 36; *CM* 20 (Oct. 1992): 265; *EL* 21 (Mar. 1994): 48; *QQ* 58 (July 1992): 16.

First Look Board Books: Acorn to Oak Tree, Seed to Flower, Caterpillar to Butterfly, Tadpole to Frog (Richmond Hill, Ont.: Scholastic, 1997).

The Party (Richmond Hill, Ont.: North Winds, 1997). **Rev:** *CM* 4 (4 Dec. 1997): on-line; *EL* 25 (Mar. 1998): 26; *QQ* 63 (Nov. 1997): 46.

Fun with Modelling Clay (Toronto: Kids Can Press, 1998). **Rev:** *QQ* 64 (Mar. 1998): 72.

Illustrated by Barbara Reid

Mustard, by Betty Waterton (Richmond Hill, Ont: Scholastic, 1983). **Rev:** *CCL* 30 (1983): 69; *CM* 20 (Oct. 1992): 267; *QQ* 49 (Aug. 1983): 35.

It's Tough to be a Kid, by Mary Blakeslee (Richmond Hill, Ont.: Scholastic, 1983). **Rev:** *CCL* 42 (1986): 52.

Jenny Greenteeth, by Mary Alice Downie (Toronto: Kids Can Press, 1984). **Rev:** *CCL* 41 (1986): 56; *QQ* 50 (Nov. 1984): 13; *SLJ* 31 (May 1985): 72.

The New Baby Calf, by Edith Newlin Chase (Richmond Hill, Ont: North Winds, 1984). **Rev:** *CCL* 42 (1986): 66; *HB* 64 (Jan. 1988): 102; *QQ* 51 (Feb. 1985): 14.

Have You Seen Birds?, by Joanne Oppenheim (Richmond Hill, Ont: North Winds, 1986). **Rev:** *CCL* 52 (1988): 26; *CM* 16 (Jan. 1988): 7; *EL* 17 (Jan. 1990): 52; *HB* 64 (Jan. 1988): 103; *QQ* 52 (Dec. 1986):16; *SLJ* 33 (June 1987): 88.

How to Make Pop-Ups, by Joan Irvine (Toronto: Kids Can Press, 1987). **Rev:** *BiC* 16 (Nov. 1987): 39; *CM* 16 (Nov. 1988): 204; *EL* 15 (Mar. 1988): 24.

Have Fun with Magnifying, by Carol Gold (Toronto: Kids Can Press, 1987). **Rev:** *CM* 16 (July 1988): 150; *EL* 16 (Mar. 1989): 24.

Sing a Song of Mother Goose (Richmond Hill, Ont.: North Winds, 1987). **Rev:** *CCL* 52 (1988): 23; *EL* 16 (Mar. 1989): 22.

Effie, by Beverley Allinson (Toronto: Summerhill, 1990). **Rev:** *CCL* 72 (1993): 64; *CM* 19 (Sept. 1991): 226; *EL* 18 (Mar. 1991): 24; *QQ* 56 (Sept. 1990): 19; *SLJ* 37 (July 1991): 52.

Gifts, by Jo Ellen Bogart (Richmond Hill, Ont.; North Winds, 1994). **Rev:** *CBRA* (1994): 443; *CCL* 78 (1995): 77; *CM* 22 (Nov. 1994): 208; *EL* 22 (Nov. 1994): 45, and 22 (Mar. 1995): 18, and 25 (Jan. 1998): 45; *QQ* 60 (Sept. 1994) 70; *SLJ* 42 (Mar. 1996), 166.

Just Desserts and Other Treats for Kids to Make, by Marilyn Linton (Toronto: Kids Can Press, 1998).

When she was a child, Barbara Reid enjoyed reading picture books and playing with plasticine modelling clay. But it was not until she attended a presentation at her high school's career day that she decided to attend art school, where she rediscovered plasticine. In one of her classes she was required to copy a well-known work of art in another medium. After several attempts at recreating Botticelli's 'The Birth of Venus' using tissue paper, she tried plasticine, and the results pleased both her fellow students and her instructor. It wasn't until she had illustrated three children's books the conventional way that she returned to plasticine. Her work for *The New Baby Calf* brought her national attention, and her pictures for her next book, Joanne Oppenheim's *Have You Seen Birds?*, earned her the Canada Council Prize for Illustration.

The 14 full-page illustrations that accompany Edith Chase's poem in *The New Baby Calf* were, as with Reid's other books, first framed in a box to prevent crushing and then photographed with strong light that caused shadows and created a three-dimensional effect. The focus is on the newly arrived animal, but there are also representations of the loving environment into which the calf has been born. In 10 of the pictures the mother is present, licking the calf clean, feeding him, and watching anxiously as he takes his first tentative steps and then begins to explore the world. The emphasis is on new life, and often there are other young animals. Presiding over the farm is the benevolent farmer, who cares for all the animals as the cow does for her calf.

Reid's illustrations for *Have You Seen Birds?* make a far greater contribution to the total effect of the book than do those of *The New Baby Calf.* Joanne Oppenheim's poem begins with the question of the title and then invites the reader to consider the tremendous variety of birds in the world. The book is superbly designed: the individual pages and the relationships between the pages contribute to the overall effect. Different sizes, numbers, and arrangements of birds on a double-spread suggest the size of individual birds and the relationships between them. Page design is constantly varied so that viewers become aware of the differences between the types of birds and their habitats. In every illustration a part of the bird—leg, beak, wing—extends beyond the blue plasticine border. These are not museum specimens, dead and rigid in glass cases, but living birds that cannot be tied down or contained within the picture frames. The book opens and closes with a visual joke, one not mentioned in the poem. A cat is looking out the window as the text says, 'Have you seen birds?' He is not seen again until the end of the book, when he must back from the window into the safety of the room. He has seen birds, but he has not caught any. Perhaps their numbers and variety, along with the size of some of them, have frightened him away.

Reid has illustrated two well-known traditional works, the Mother Goose rhymes and the Biblical tale of Noah. In each, she uses her plasticine pictures to provide a humorous perspective on very familiar material. In *Sing a Song of Mother Goose*, each page has a top and bottom lattice border on which are placed details important to the rhyme: a tipping pail for 'Jack and Jill', three bags of wool for 'Baa Baa Black Sheep'. There is also a humorous illustration of the main character in a significant action. Humpty Dumpty is depicted in mid-air, a startled look on his face; the little girl with the curl frowns, sticks out her tongue, and waves a paint brush at her fleeing cat; the pig being taken home from the market looks at the sweating farmer pushing the wheelbarrow in which it reclines, fanning itself. The animals are humorously anthropomorphized: a lady bug with a flowered hat, purple gown, and lace handkerchief runs home, a look of alarm on her face; Old Mother Hubbard's dog rolls on its back clutching its stomach and laughing.

In *Two by Two*, Reid first presents the people who 'turned to evil ways' in the city before showing Noah working on his farm. The majority of the book is devoted to the people and animals entering the ark from 'one by one' up to 'ten by ten'. Not all the animals mentioned are depicted. For example, the only evidence of the fleas is the agitated scratching of one monkey. Two jumping animals—frogs and kangaroos—enter together, the humour arising from the fact that the smaller creatures leap the highest over a startled Noah. Noah, in fact, is often in the way after he has finished his construction work: he is nearly trampled by the elephants and is almost knocked off the gangplank as the rain begins and the last animals charge into the ark. Although there is much comedy throughout the book, the final scene, in which Noah and his wife plant seeds at their new farm and a rainbow signals God's blessing, is one of peace and joy and, as such, a contrast to the urban wickedness of the beginning.

In the illustrations for Beverley Allinson's *Effie*, an animal fantasy about an ant whose booming voice makes her first an outcast but later a hero, the title character tries unsuccessfully to befriend a dopey-eyed blue caterpillar who wears flip-flops, a butterfly dressed in a ballerina outfit, a spider who has a bib tied around its neck, and a beetle with saddle-oxford shoes. Each of these characters reveals a very human reaction to Effie's vocal peculiarity. Although Reid's illustrations do not expand on the meanings of the written text, they enhance the humour of the situations in which the unlikely heroine finds herself.

By contrast, her illustrations for *Gifts*, by Jo Ellen Bogart, are essential for indicating the nature of the relationship between the narrator and her grandmother. In the simple, repetitive text, the grandmother, before leaving on vacations to such places as Africa, Australia, and China, asks 'What would you have me bring?' and the girl makes simple requests. At the end, the narrator explains to her unnamed audience, 'And everything she gave to me / I'm going to give to you.' The pictures reveal the lengths to which the woman goes to honour her granddaughter's requests. In Australia, for example, she is pictured wading through mud, a tape recorder on her shoulders, collecting both the sounds of a didgeridoo and some billabong goo. She paints the sun rising over a Mayan temple so that the girl can hang it on her bedroom wall. The loving, active grandmother takes along a backpack on which an increasing number of travel patches are sewn. But, in later pictures, she shows signs of increasing age, and, in the last scene, she is being pushed around England in a wheelchair. When her granddaughter receives a letter from her, the girl is now a young woman. Her audience, as the final illustration reveals, is her own child, whom she is pushing in a stroller to which is attached the grandmother's backpack. She is sharing both the grandmother's gifts and her memories of the old woman with her child.

Reid's text for *The Party* is simple: a rhyming account of a family reunion in honour of grandmother's ninetieth birthday. She expands the meanings of her words through her illustrations, revealing the changing emotions of two sisters who reluctantly attend the event, depicting the activities they engage in, and satirizing the adults. At first, the girls wear clean dresses and unhappy expressions, and they lean backward to resist entering the party scene. But their unhappiness disappears; several double-spreads show the children racing around the yard, leaping off the picnic table, and gorging themselves. In the car on the way home, they slump contentedly in the back seat of the car, their faces and party dresses smeared with food, their mouths curved in sleepy grins. Not only do Reid's illustrations capture the children's emotions and actions, but they also present the adults as they are seen by the girls. Aunts and uncles loom over them, lips puckered for kisses; the sisters walk past a sea of adult legs to reach their cousins; and they creep up on a fat uncle, asleep in a lawn chair, potato chip crumbs on his ample stomach.

Reid's success as a children's book illustrator is not merely a result of her using a novel medium but of her skilled and witty application of plasticine to give added dimensions of meaning to short and relatively simple texts.

See also: *SATA* 93; *WSMP*.

Mordecai Richler

Born: 27 January 1931, in Montreal.

Principal Residences: Montreal; Paris; London, England.

Education: Sir George Williams University.

Career: screenwriter; writer.

Major Awards: Canadian Library Association Book of the Year for Children (1976); Mr Christie's Book Award (1995); Ruth Schwartz Children's Book Award (1976).

Works for Children

Jacob Two-Two Meets the Hooded Fang (Toronto: McClelland & Stewart, 1975). **Rev:** *BiC* 19 (Apr. 1981): 28; *CCB-B* 28 (July 1985): 184; *CCL* 3 (1975): 96; *SLJ* 22 (Sept. 1975): 90; *TLS* (2 Apr. 1976): 376.

Jacob Two-Two and the Dinosaur (Toronto: McClelland & Stewart, 1985). **Rev:** *BiC* 16 (Aug. 1987): 35; *BYP* 1 (Apr. 1987): 19; *CCB-B* 40 (June 1987): 194; *CCL* 49 (1988): 43; *SLJ* (Apr. 1987): 102.

Jacob Two-Two's First Spy Case (Toronto: McClelland & Stewart, 1995). **Rev:** *BiC* 24 (Dec. 1995): 34; *CBRA* (1995): 518; *CCL* 86 (1997): 79; *EL* 23 (Mar. 1996): 25; *QQ* 61 (Nov. 1995): 45; *SLJ* 43 (Aug. 1997): 139.

Other

'Writing *Jacob Two-Two*', *CL* 78 (Autumn 1978): 6–8.

Selected Discussions

Nodelman, Perry. 'Jacob Two-Two and the Satisfactions of Paranoia', *CCL* 15 (1980): 31–7.

Paterson, Gary H. 'Hooded Fang and Jabberwock: The Richler-Carroll Connection', *CCL* 76 (1994): 48–54.

'Isn't there something of yours we aren't too young to read?' This question, asked by the children of Canadian novelist Mordecai Richler, provided the impetus for writing one of the best-loved Canadian children's novels of the last half of the twentieth century: *Jacob Two-Two Meets the Hooded Fang*. In answer to their requests, he created a story that drew on their personalities and their life in London, England, where the family lived in the 1960s and early 1970s.

The title hero, who is loosely based on the author's youngest son, suffers from feelings of inadequacy and says things twice to gain attention. Running away from an unfriendly grocer, he falls asleep and dreams he is instrumental in releasing thousands of inmates from the children's prison and in revealing that the dreaded Hooded Fang, a wrestler turned prison warden, is a soft-hearted person. The narrative takes the form of the circular dream journey in which the central character's waking problems are confronted and overcome during the dream. Richler's achievement lies in the vitality of characterization and in the humour he infuses into his narrative. He is adept at capturing Jacob's view of the world, particularly of the adults in it. They are overwhelming, unreasonable, and tyrannical, treating him at best with benign neglect, or at worst with bullying nastiness. The plot moves quickly; the presentation of the hero's development is clear. The story is marred by some inconsistency, most notably in the viewpoint of two chapters from which the dreamer is absent. Generally, younger children can identify with Jacob, older ones can enjoy the mocking of adults, and grownups can recognize in the older characters elements of their less desirable selves.

Although Richler frequently stated that he had no plans for a sequel, one appeared in 1987: *Jacob Two-Two and the Dinosaur*. The hero, now eight years of age, receives the gift of a lizard brought back from Africa by his parents. The new pet is really a dinosaur and grows to monstrous size. Although the boy and his pet are devoted to each other, the rest of society is outraged, and the two flee across the country to the Rocky Mountains where they hope to find a mate for the reptile. The book disappoints, lacking the élan and sparkling satire of the first book. Jacob, who seems to have lost the respect he had gained at the end of the earlier story, undergoes little character development; the satire of various adults, including the prime minister, is gratuitous; and elements of the plot are forced.

A second sequel, which appeared in 1995, *Jacob Two-Two's First Spy Case*, is much closer in tone and theme to the first book, of which there are many echoes. The hero, who seems only slightly older than in *The Hooded Fang*, still feels insignificant: 'the older he got . . . the more difficult and complicated his life became. Once he had been appreciated, but not any longer.' His major troubles begin when Mr I.M. Greedyguts, the new headmaster at Jacob's exclusive private school, installs Leo Louse as chief caterer. With the help of X. Barnaby Dinglebat, a spy who quotes Mick Jagger and dons outlandish disguises, Jacob fights against the school official's evil plans, regains his confidence, and wins the approval of family and friends.

Unlike *Jacob Two-Two and the Dinosaur*, *First Spy Case* does not include much satire of Canadian institutions, but it does capture the child's view of mean, petty adults. Greedyguts and Louse, the two villains, seek power over children, but are seen to be childish themselves. By contrast, Dinglebat accepts Jacob as an equal, and Jacob's father, whom the boy considers a pal, stands up for him in the headmaster's office. The hero is more fully delineated that he was in the preceding book. Insecure, 'because he was still a little boy who never got anything right', he bravely carries out his role in liberating his classmates from the misery of life at the school.

Although his juvenile satire, a milder form of the often biting commentary of society found in his adult works, will appeal to older children, Richler's success with younger readers lies in his sensitive, accurate portrayal of children developing a stronger sense of self-confidence and in his humorous portrayal of the underlying foolishness, pettiness, and insecurity of adults who, for selfish reasons, seek, like many of Charles Dickens's adults, to control those less powerful than themselves.

See also: *CA* 65–8; *CANR* 31, 62; *CLR* 17; *DLB* 53; *SATA* 44, 98; *TCCW*.

Sir Charles G.D. Roberts

Born: 10 January 1860, in Douglas, NB.

Died: 26 November 1943, in Toronto.

Principal Residences: Douglas, NS; Windsor, NS; New York City; London, England; Toronto.

Education: University of New Brunswick (BA 1879, MA 1881).

Career: headmaster; editor; professor; writer.

Works for Children

The Raid from Beausejour, and How the Carter Boys Lifted the Mortgage: Two Stories of Acadie (New York: Hunt and Eaton, 1894).

Reube Dare's Shad Boat: A Tale of the Tide Country (New York: Hunt and Eaton, 1895).

Around the Campfire (New York: Crowell, 1896).

Earth's Enigmas: A Book of Animal and Nature Life (Boston: Lamson Wolffe, 1896).

The Kindred of the Wild: A Book of Animal Life (Boston: Page, 1902).

The Watchers of the Trails: A Book of Animal Life (Boston: Page, 1904).

Red Fox: The Story of His Adventurous Career in the Ringwaak Wilds, and of His Final Triumph over the Enemies of His Kind (Boston: Page, 1905).

In the Deep of the Snow (New York: Crowell, 1907).

The House in Winter: A Book of Animal Life ((Boston: Page, 1908).

The Backwoodsmen (New York: Macmillan, 1909).

Kings in Exile (London: Ward Lock, 1909).

Neighbours Unknown (London: Ward Lock, 1910).

More Kindred of the Wild (London: Ward Lock, 1911).

Babes of the Wild (New York: Cassell, 1912).

The Feet of the Furtive (London: Ward Lock, 1912).

Hoof and Claw (London: Ward Lock, 1913).

The Secret Trails (London: Ward Lock, 1916).

Jim: The Story of a Backwoods Police Dog (New York: Macmillan, 1919).

Wisdom of the Wilderness (London: Dent, 1922).

They Who Walk in the Wild (New York: Macmillan, 1924).

Eyes of the Wilderness (New York: Macmillan, 1933).

Further Animal Stories (London: Dent, 1935).

Thirteen Bears, ed. Ethel Hume Bennett (Toronto: Ryerson, 1947).

Forest Folk, ed. Ethel Hume Bennett (Toronto: Ryerson, 1949).

King of the Beasts and Other Stories, ed. Joseph Gold (Toronto: Ryerson, 1967).

Eyes of the Wilderness and Other Stories: A New Collection, ed. Brian Carter (London: Dent, 1980).

The Lure of the Wild: The Last Three Animal Stories, ed. John C. Adams (Ottawa: Borealis, 1980).

Selected Discussions

Gold, Joseph. 'The Precious Speck of Life', *CL* 26 (Autumn 1965): 22–32.

Hornyanski, Michael. 'Roberts for Children', *CCL* 30 (1983): 33–41.

McCord, David. 'Introduction to a New Edition', *HB* 48 (June 1972): 255–8.

Murray, Tim. 'Charles Roberts' Animal Stories', *CCL* 2 (1975): 23–37.

Charles G.D. Roberts spent much of his childhood in rural New Brunswick reading and observing the wildlife around his home, activities that provided valuable background for the books that later established his reputation as one of the major creators, along with Ernest Thompson Seton, of realistic animal fiction. In his 'Prefatory Note' to *The Watchers of the Trails*, he referred to his childhood: 'The present writer, having spent most of his boyhood on the fringes of the forest, with few interests save those which the forest afforded, may claim to have had the intimacies of the wilderness as it were thrust upon him.' It wasn't, however, until several years as a headmaster, college professor, and journalist that he published the first of his over two dozen books for children. A prolific writer, he also published 20 books of poetry, four collections of short stories, and several novels, and has been called 'The Father of Canadian Literature' as a result of both the quality and quantity of his output.

Underlying Roberts's animal stories are a carefully thought out philosophy and methodology, which he explained in detail in the prefaces to several of his books. In 'Introductory: The Animal Story', the preface to *The Kindred of the Wild*, he explained that the modern animal story is the product of an evolutionary process extending back to primitive times. Cavemen, he hypothesized, must have frequently recounted their hunting exploits and perilous escapes from savage beasts. However, with greater sophistication, human beings developed a literary tradition in which the animals came to symbolize human characteristics and moral concerns. Domestic animal stories of the nineteenth century, combined with growing scientific studies, rekindled an interest in detailed, precise observation of wild animals, observation that was brought to a high degree of accuracy and artistic skill in the stories of Seton. Roberts went far beyond giving accurate descriptions of his animal characters: 'Having got one's facts right,—and enough of them to generalize from safely,—the exciting adventure lies in the effort to "get under their skins" . . . to discern their motives, to understand and chart their simple mental processes.' Although he did not think that the mental faculties of animals were anywhere as fully developed as those of human beings, he did believe that they possessed powers of rational thought.

He was most interested in studying and portraying the superior members of each species, the 'kings' or 'masters' as he often refers to them in book or story titles. In the 'Preface' to *Red Fox*, he states of the title hero: 'He simply represents the best, in physical and mental development, of which the tribe of the foxes has shown itself capable. . . . Once in a while such exceptional strength and such exceptional intelligence may be combined in one individual. This combination is apt to result in just such a fox as I have made the hero of my story.' Roberts's animal characters were every bit as heroic to him as are human actors in adventure stories.

Because Roberts repeatedly dealt with the same types of characters and actions in his animal stories, an understanding of his themes, characters, and techniques can be gained from reading one representative collection, *The Kindred of the Wild*, and his best-known animal biography, *Red Fox*.

In *The Kindred of the Wild*, his greatest interest is in superior animals: 'The Lord of the Air', 'the great bald eagle who ruled supreme over all the aerial vicinage'; Hushwing, an owl of 'tameless spirit'; and 'The King of the Mamozekel', a magnificent bull moose. Each possesses great size, strength, and skill, and overall daring, courage, and wisdom. Roberts also admires animal mothers, whose role is not only to give birth and thus to ensure the continuity of life, but also to protect and train their young so that they can grow to adulthood. 'Wild Motherhood' is an account of a cow moose who, in spite of the presence of stalking wolves, leaves the herd to protect a calf who has fallen into a pit. Although she is successful at keeping her enemies at bay, she is later shot by a hunter who needs fresh meat for his wife and baby. Roberts suggests that the greatness of the King of the Mamozekel results not only from his inherent superiority, but also from the benefit he received from his mother's careful tutelage.

For each of Roberts's noble animals, the most dangerous enemy is man: 'Whenever any individual of the wild kindreds, furred, feathered, or finned achieves the distinction of baffling man's efforts to undo him, his doom may be considered sealed.' The backwoodsmen, as Roberts calls his hunters, stalk their prey for three reasons: they need fresh meat for their families; they wish to prove their 'woodcraft', their cunning, against animals whose cleverness challenges them; and they respond to their hunting instincts. Although admiring the skill and determination of human hunters, Roberts shows greatest respect for people who prefer to study nature without killing. A recurrent character is 'the Boy', a solitary individual who quietly and sympathetically observes the wild kindred.

In *Red Fox*, Roberts combines character types and themes found in his short stories into a tightly unified biographical narrative. The novel opens with a scene that illustrates the interrelatedness of life and death. To save his newborn pups, a wily old fox, 'a very Odysseus of his kind for valor and guile', leads a pair of dogs on a long and devious chase away from the den before being killed. One of the pups early shows his superiority, combining instinct, native intelligence, and the ability to learn survival skills from his mother's teachings and his own experience. He quickly learns about the danger from human beings and about ways either to avoid or outwit them. The two people who most interest Roberts are Jeb Smith, a backwoodsman who prides himself on his skill as a hunter, and a youngster, 'the Boy', who prefers to use his woodcraft to study the creature.

The central portion of the novel focuses on the mature life of Red Fox as he mates with a vixen who, like him, has superior mental abilities, protects his young, proves his cleverness in surviving a particularly harsh winter, and leads his family and other animals to safety during a forest fire. However, his superiority creates problems. He develops 'that self-confident pride which so often proves a snare to its possessor'. Moreover, his skill in raiding barnyards and evading human and canine trackers increases the determination of Jeb Smith to shoot him: 'It was inconsistent with his reputation as a woodsman to let the wily and audacious fox go any longer triumphant over gun and dog and trap.' The Boy convinces Smith that it would be better to trap than shoot the fox, and the two work together to capture him. Released in the American South, Red Fox becomes the prey in a fox hunt and must summon all his cleverness and strength to escape with his life.

Extremely popular during the earlier decades of the twentieth century, Roberts's animal stories are not widely read today. As the dominant interests of young readers have changed, the relative simplicity of his plots, characters, and themes seem old-fashioned. There are also limitations inherent in Roberts's treatment of his subjects. Although he emphasizes the animals' cleverness and heroism, he cannot engage in overly complex characterization without running the danger of humanizing them. Not surprisingly, the reader of several of his stories soon sees the formula underlying each one. Nevertheless, in *Red Fox* and his best short stories, Roberts's achievement is considerable. The New Brunswick settings are fully realized; his heroic beasts become three-dimensional characters; and the life-and-death nature of the conflicts in which they become involved raise the plots to the level of high, sometimes tragic, drama.

See also: *CA* 105; *CLR* 33; *DLB* 92; *SATA* 29, 88; *TCCW*.

Nazneen Sadiq

(Nazneen Sheikh, her maiden name, since 1992)

Born: 19 June 1944, in Srinigar, Kashmir, India.

Principal Residences: Srinigar, India; Lahore, Pakistan; Dallas, Texas; Karachi, Pakistan; Thornhill, Ont.; Toronto.

Education: Punjab University, Lahore, Pakistan (BA 1964).

Career: freelance correspondent; writer.

Works for Children

Camels Can Make You Homesick and Other Stories (Toronto: James Lorimer, 1985). **Rev:** *BiC* 14 (1985): 12; *CBRA* (1985); 272; *CL* 111 (Winter 1986): 166; *CM* 14 (Jan. 1986): 19; *QQ* 51 (Oct. 1985): 17.

Heartbreak High (Toronto: James Lorimer, 1988). **Rev:** *CBRA* (1988): 298; *CCL* 56 (1989): 84; *CM* 17 (Mar. 1989): 74.

Lucy (Toronto: James Lorimer, 1989). **Rev:** *CBRA* (1989): 326; *CCL* 62 (1991): 80; *CM* 18 (May 1990): 130.

Selected Discussions

Jenkinson, Dave. 'Nazneen Sadiq', *EL* 17 (Mar.–Apr. 199): 65–71.

Having immigrated to Canada in 1964, Nazneen Sadiq (now Nazneen Sheikh) understands the dual allegiances of the immigrants who make up a large part of Canada's cultural mosaic. As a mother, she also understands that the children of immigrants sometimes feel torn between the claims of their parents' traditional culture in the home and those of the culture that they experience at school and with friends. In two of her books for young people, Sadiq has portrayed the competing cultural claims with such sensitivity and understanding that these books will appeal both to immigrants who want to see literature reflect their lives and to those willing to look at lives that are at least partially different from their own.

Sadiq's first book, *Camels Can Make You Homesick*, a collection of stories about children of South Asian heritage, was published as part of the 'Time of Our Lives' multicultural series. Each of its five stories focuses on a young person coming to terms with his or her position as a child of two cultures. 'Peacocks and Bandaids' represents the two worlds of second-generation immigrants through Jaya Gopal's love of classical Indian dance and her desire to perform at a school recital. Hostility to immigrant culture appears when someone deliberately destroys a fan of feathers that Jaya is to wear during her performance. A boy's ingenious use of Band-Aids to repair the fan testifies that not all members of the majority culture are prejudiced. In 'Who Needs Heroes', the weakest of the tales, Raj Dhillon, a Sikh boy, is on a wilderness survival trip. Frightened, he gains such courage from a dream about Ranjit Singh, a Sikh hero, that he decides to share some of his cultural traditions with his non-Sikh friends. The title story places emphasis on the child's discovery of feelings for Canada. During a trip to Pakistan, Zorana is thrilled to experience some of the things that her mother has lovingly talked about over the years. Nevertheless, a much-anticipated camel ride leads her to realize that, although she enjoys the exotic culture of Pakistan, Canada is her true home. The strongest story in the collection, 'Shonar Arches', presents a common experience: a New World child's sense of both frustration and embarrassment because relatives cling to traditional ways. When Amit's grandmother comes to visit from Calcutta, he does not like her domineering ways or the very spicy food she insists on preparing. When he finally convinces her that she must try fast food at McDonald's, Amit becomes embarrassed that she has dressed in her finest sari and insists on sitting in the centre of the restaurant, where she can watch everyone. Nevertheless, the meal becomes a genuine communion, as they share feelings. Amit is thus pleased that his grandmother likes the food and that the restaurant workers find his grandmother charming. The final tale, 'Figs for Everyone', is the only one with unresolved tensions. After she allows a woman to draw intricate designs on her hand as part of the celebration of a Muslim festival, Shanaz Ali becomes embarrassed because the henna designs will not wash off. Teased by some insensitive members of her class, Shanaz is initially so upset that she never wants to return to school. Her principal's request that she share some Muslim traditions with the rest of the class, however, offers hope that education will make others more tolerant. These stories may be overly optimistic and may be too restrained in presenting the conflicts and hostilities that cultural differences often create, but they offer pleasing sketches of cultures seldom portrayed in Canadian writings for young people.

Such conflicts are overt in *Heartbreak High*, in which the dizzying rapture of first love incites age-old cultural hostilities. When Rachel Steiner, a Jew, meets Tariq Khan, a Muslim, they become so infatuated that they give absolutely no thought to their religious differences. Their families, especially their tradition-minded mothers, however, oppose their relationship. Although the novel stretches plausibility by having the children seem completely unaware of their parents' traditions and feelings, it effectively develops the conflict between children and parents. It thus shows that the children, raised in a multicultural community, feel anger and frustration because their parents seem to be intolerant bigots. It is especially effective in creating parallel scenes in which the children refuse to eat with their families, thus showing how much alike they are. A rather stale contrivance offers partial resolution: when Tariq is injured in an accident, the two mothers meet at the hospital and make the first steps to tolerance, if not complete acceptance. Furthermore, Rachel decides to spend the summer at a kibbutz in Israel to learn more of her Jewish heritage, and Tariq not only listens to his father's recording of the Muslim call to prayer but is deeply moved by it. The strength of *Heartbreak High* is its characterization, which evokes the stormy emotional life of teens experiencing first love, parental demands, and a growing understanding of culture.

In addition to her two books about immigrant experiences, Sadiq has also written a novel based on characters from the *Degrassi Junior High* television series. *Lucy* focuses on Lucy Fernandez, who feels so alienated from friends and her busy parents that she decides to escape by using her mother's credit card to book a vacation to the Bahamas. The facile ending and the need to maintain characterization and relationships developed on television and in other books in the series deprive this novel of any notable qualities and leave it unappealing to anyone unfamiliar with the television show.

Sadiq seems to have abandoned juvenile fiction to concentrate on writing for adults, an unfortunate circumstance for Canadian children's literature because she has given glimpses of lives and subjects that have received scant attention. Her published books are more than mirrors in which minority children can view their experiences: requiring no prior knowledge of minority cultures, they are accessible to all readers and may therefore make them aware of and sensitive to important cultural issues.

See also: *SATA* 101.

Margaret Marshall Saunders

Born: 13 April 1861, in Milton, NS.

Died: 15 February 1947, in Toronto.

Principal Residences: Berwick, NS; Halifax; Edinburgh; Boston; Toronto.

Career: author; social reformer.

Works for Children

Beautiful Joe: The Autobiography of a Dog. (Philadelphia: C.H. Banes, 1894).

Charles and His Lamb: Written for the Little Ones of the Household (Philadelphia: C.H. Banes, 1895).

For the Other Boy's Sake, and Other Stories (Philadelphia: C.H. Banes, 1896).

For His Country and Grandmother and the Crow (Boston: L.C. Page, 1900).

'Tilda Jane, An Orphan in Search of a Home; A Story for Boys and Girls (Boston: L.C. Page, 1901).

Beautiful Joe's Paradise: A Sequel to Beautiful Joe (Boston: L.C. Page, 1902).

The Story of the Gravelys: A Tale for Girls (Boston: L.C. Page, 1903).

Nita, the Story of an Irish Setter; Containing Also Uncle Jim's Burglar and Mehitable's Chicken (Boston: L.C. Page, 1904).

Princess Sukey: The Story of a Pigeon and Her Human Friends (New York: Eaton and Mains, 1905).

Alpatok: The Story of an Eskimo Dog (Boston: L.C. Page, 1906); republished as *The Story of an Eskimo Dog* (London: Hodder and Stoughton, 1906).

'Tilda Jane's Orphans (Boston: L.C. Page, 1909).

Pussy Black-Face; or, The Story of a Kitten and Her Friends (Boston: L.C. Page, 1913).

The Wandering Dog; Adventures of a Fox-Terrier (New York: Doran, 1916); also published as *'Boy' the Wandering Dog; Adventures of a Fox-Terrier* (New York: Grosset & Dunlap, 1916).

Golden Dicky: The Story of a Canary and His Friends (Toronto: McClelland & Stewart, 1919).

Bonny Prince Fetlar: The Story of a Pony and his Friends (Toronto: McClelland & Stewart, 1920).

Jimmy Gold-Coast; or, The Story of a Monkey and His Friends (Toronto: Hodder and Stoughton, 1923).

Esther de Warren: The Story of a Mid-Victorian Maiden (New York: Doran, 1927).

Selected Discussions

Blakely, Phyllis. 'Margaret Marshall Saunders: The Author of *Beautiful Joe*', *Nova Scotia Historical Quarterly* 1 (1971): 225–38.

McMullen, Lorraine. 'Marshall Saunders and the Mating Game in Victorian Scotland', *CCL* 34 (1984): 31–40.

Although she published close to 30 novels, a large number of which she directed at children, Margaret Marshall Saunders is today remembered for only one, *Beautiful Joe*, the autobiography of a dog. The winning entry in a contest sponsored by the American Humane Association, *Beautiful Joe* was immensely popular: it is frequently cited as the first Canadian book to sell over a million copies. Although Saunders wrote other animal stories, including *Beautiful Joe's Paradise: A Sequel to Beautiful Joe*, neither they nor her girls' stories focusing on human protagonists achieved significant popularity.

Beautiful Joe is the last historically significant work in a style of animal writing that was to be superseded by the more realistic animal stories of Ernest Thompson Seton and Charles G.D. Roberts. Written in imitation of Anna Sewell's *Black Beauty* (1877), it is narrated by Beautiful Joe, a dog who has been mutilated by his cruel master. Episodic rather than tightly plotted, the story is relentlessly didactic: Joe faithfully reports long discussions about the proper methods of keeping a variety of pets and about the need for respect for wild animals. The story also links the causes of abstinence and animal rights: the villains who abuse animals are drinking men who come to bad ends.

Beautiful Joe is stiff and artificial in its dialogue, weak in characterization, and conventional in its episodes, unabashedly sentimental in its expression, but it is undeniably earnest in its respect for 'dumb animals'. Now mostly a historical curiosity, it represents an outmoded way of treating animals and of addressing children.

See also: *DLB* 92.

Ernest Thompson Seton

(born Ernest Evan Thompson)

Born: 14 August 1860, in South Shields, County Durham, England.

Died: 23 October 1946, in Santa Fe, New Mexico.

Principal Residences: South Shields, England; Lindsay, Ont.; Toronto; London, England; Carberry, Man.; Santa Fe.

Education: Ontario College of Art (1877–9); Royal Academy School of Painting and Sculpture, London, England (1881); Art Students' League, NY (1884); Académie Julian, Paris (1891).

Career: artist; illustrator; author; lecturer; naturalist for Manitoba government; founder of Woodcraft Indians (later Woodcraft League); founding member and Chief Scout of the Boy Scouts of America (1910–15).

Works for Children

Wild Animals I Have Known, Being the Personal Histories of Lobo, Silverspot, Raggylug, Bingo, The Springfield Fox, The Pacing Mustang, Wully, and Redruff (New York: Scribner, 1898).

Lobo, Rag, and Vixen and Pictures (New York: Scribner, 1899).

The Trail of the Sandhill Stag (New York: Scribner, 1899).

The Biography of a Grizzly (New York: Century, 1900).

The Wild Animal Play for Children, with Alternate Reading for Very Young Children (Philadelphia: Curtis/New York: Doubleday, Page, 1900).

Lives of the Hunted: A True Account of the Doings of Five Quadrupeds and Three Birds (New York: Scribner, 1901).

Krag and Johnny Bear (New York: Scribner, 1902).

Two Little Savages; Being the Adventures of Two Boys Who Lived as Indians and What They Learned (New York: Doubleday, Page, 1903).

Monarch, The Big Bear of Tallac (New York: Scribner, 1904).

Animal Heroes, Being the Histories of a Cat, a Dog, a Pigeon, a Lynx, Two Wolves, and a Reindeer (New York: Scribner, 1905).

Woodmyth and Fable (Toronto: Briggs, 1905; New York: Century, 1905).

The Natural History of the Ten Commandments. (New York: Scribner, 1907); republished as *The Ten Commandments in the Animal World* (New York: Doubleday, Page, 1907).

The Biography of a Silver Fox; or, Domino Reynard of Goldur Town (New York: Century, 1909).

Rolf in the Woods; The Adventures of a Boy Scout with Indian Quonab and Little Dog Skookum (Garden City, NY: Doubleday, Page, 1911).

Wild Animals at Home (Toronto: Briggs, 1913; New York: Doubleday, 1913).

The White Reindeer, Arnaux, and the Boy and the Lynx (London: Constable, 1915).

The Slum Cat, Snap, and The Winnipeg Wolf (London: Constable, 1915).

Wild Animal Ways (Garden City, NY: Doubleday, Page, 1916).

The Preacher of Cedar Mountain: A Tale of the Open Country (Garden City, NY: Doubleday, Page, 1917).

Woodland Tales (Garden City, NY: Doubleday, Page, 1921).

Bannertail: The Story of a Gray Squirrel (New York: Scribner, 1922).

Katung the Snow Child (Oxford: Blackwell, 1929).

Krag, the Kootenay Ram, and Other Animal Stories (London: U of London P, 1929).

Johnny Bear, Lobo, and Other Stories (New York: Scribner, 1935).

The Biography of an Arctic Fox (New York: Appleton-Century, 1937).

Great Historic Animals: Mainly about Wolves (New York: Scribner, 1937).

Santana, the Hero Dog of France (Los Angeles: Phoenix Press, 1945).

Selected Discussions

Keller, Betty. *Black Wolf: The Biography of Ernest Thompson Seton* (Vancouver: Douglas & McIntyre, 1984).

MacDonald, Robert H. 'The Revolt against Instinct: The Animal Stories of Seton and Roberts', *CL* 84 (Spring 1980): 18–29.

Magee, William H. 'The Animal Story: A Challenge in Technique', *Dalhousie Review* 44 (1964): 156–64.

McMullen, Lorraine. 'Ernest Thompson Seton', *Profiles in Canadian Literature* 5, ed. Jeffrey M. Heath (Toronto: Dundurn, 1986), 65–71.

Poirier, Michel. 'The Animal Story in Canadian Literature: E. Thompson Seton and Charles G.D. Roberts', *Queen's Quarterly* 34 (Jan.-Apr. 1927): 298–312.

Polk, James. *Wilderness Writers: Ernest Thompson Seton, Charles G.D. Roberts, Grey Owl* (Toronto: Clarke, Irwin, 1972).

Read, S.E. 'Flight to the Primitive: Ernest Thompson Seton', *CL* 13 (Summer 1962): 45–57.

'If there be one man, since St. Francis of Assisi, whom all the kindreds of the wild have cause to bless', declared Sir Charles G.D. Roberts, 'it is Ernest Thompson Seton.' According to Roberts, Seton was 'chiefly responsible for the vogue of the modern "Animal Story"', a form that 'resulted in a more sympathetic and understanding humane attitude toward our inarticulate kin.' Seton did not number himself among the saints, but throughout his long career as an artist, naturalist, lecturer, and writer, he tried to share his passion for nature to educate people about the ways of wild creatures and thereby to interest them in the cause of conservation.

Seton's celebrated animal stories are the most notable and enduring legacy of his lifelong passion for nature. In his prefaces to them, he articulated both his philosophic premises and his artistic methods. He announced his central tenet in *Wild Animals I Have Known*: '. . . we and the beasts are kin.' He concluded: 'Since, then, the animals are creatures with wants and feelings differing in degree only from our own, they surely have their rights.' Once a hunter himself, Seton was particularly concerned with the right of wild creatures to live without being wantonly hunted by men. Consequently, he took more and more to portraying hunters as villainous or deranged. For example, in 'The Winnipeg Wolf', included in *Animal Heroes*, Fiddler Paul kills the mother and siblings of

Garou, the wolf of the title, in order to collect a bounty. Abusive humans subsequently cruelly exploit Garou. Ironically, Garou eventually kills Paul, thereby suggesting that nature is a moral force that exacts retribution from man. Similarly, in 'Krag, the Kootenay Ram', a haunting tale from *Lives of the Hunted*, Old Scotty, who obsessively stalks and kills the magnificent Krag, is himself killed by an avalanche.

Seton recognized, nevertheless, that violence and death were inevitable in the lives of all wild creatures. He said in *Wild Animals I Have Known* that 'The life of a wild animal *always has a tragic end*.' In *Lives of the Hunted*, he added that 'There is only one way to make an animal's history untragic, and that is to stop before the last chapter.' He implied that violence in nature was part of the Darwinian process by which the fittest survived and transmitted their genes to their offspring. He thus describes the death of Molly Cottontail in 'Raggylug', one of the tales included in *Wild Animals I Have Known*, by pointing to her son: 'She lives in him, and through him transmits a finer fibre to her race.' In another story in that collection, 'Redruff', he says of the death of some young partridges, 'The weakest, by inexorable law, dropped out.'

To evoke sympathy for animals as tragic victims, Seton concentrates on the animal hero, which he defined in *Animal Heroes* as 'an individual of unusual gifts and achievements'. As an individual, the animal is not simply a type of its species. Possessing a discrete personality and superior abilities, usually because of its superior size, it is a natural leader, a suitable protagonist for a tragic fate. Animals with such characteristics are evident, for example, throughout the stories in *Wild Animals I Have Known*: the 'Poor old hero', Lobo the Wolf, 'King of the Currumpaw', is larger and more cunning than all others; Silverspot the Crow is the wisest, strongest, and bravest of his band; Molly Cottontail is 'a true heroine' because she sacrifices her life to save her son; the Pacing Stallion is 'an image of horse perfection and beauty, as noble an animal as ever ranged the plains' and is more powerful and elusive than any other horse; Redruff the partridge is 'the biggest, strongest, and handsomest of the brood'. Seton also ensures the tragic stature of these animals by ennobling their behaviour. The 'inevitable tragedy' comes for the outlaw Lobo because he is loyal to his mate. Silverspot and Molly Cottontail are dedicated teachers who pass on their wisdom. Although 'Good fathers are rare in the grouse world', Redruff is an exemplary parent. Vixen the Fox poisons her captive young because she cannot endure to see it deprived of rightful freedom. Similarly, the Pacing Mustang so values his freedom that, once he is captured, he commits suicide by going over a cliff.

In *Wild Animals I Have Known*, Seton insisted that his stories were true. He admitted, however, that to develop the character of his tragic heroes and to intensify the drama of their lives, he 'pieced together some of the characters' from the exploits of a number of individuals. The admission that his stories are composite portraits has given an opening to critics who question the authenticity of other elements. In particular, they point Seton's occasional tendency to report animal conversations. In his own defence, Seton has noted that on such occasions he has not actually invented details: his lengthy observations of animal behaviour, he declares, enable him to act as a translator of their sounds and actions.

Although frequently charged with anthropomorphizing animals, Seton never went to the extremes evident in Anna Sewell's *Black Beauty* (1877) or Margaret Marshall Saunders's *Beautiful Joe* (1893), in which the animal narrators possess remarkable vocabularies, an ability to transcribe human speeches, and a tendency to moralize about human and animal behaviour. Seton's third-person narration convinces most readers that he is portraying real animals, not costumed people. His presentation of animal psychology stresses basic feelings of hatred, loneliness, hunger, and pain, not emotions or ideas more suitable to humans. He avoids the generalized nature study by making his characters interesting as individuals and their stories gripping as struggles for survival. Although he occasionally slips into stridency when pleading for animal rights or when preparing for the tragic climax of a story, for the most part he uses a simple, direct style that is equally effective in communicating information and tense drama. As a result, his stories have a continuing freshness absent in those by Roberts. As Roberts himself said, Seton is still 'the King of the craft of the wild kindred'.

See also: *DLB* 92; CA 109; *SATA* 18; *TCCW*.

Lois Simmie

Born: 11 June 1932, in Edam, Sask.

Principal Residences: Edam; Saskatoon.

Education: attended University of Saskatchewan, did not graduate.

Career: writer; creative writing instructor.

Works for Children

Auntie's Knitting a Baby (Saskatoon: Western Producer Prairie Books, 1984). **Rev:** *CCL* 42 (1986): 59; *HB* 62 (May 1986): 355; *NYTBR* (26 Mar. 1989): 19; *QQ* 50 (1984): 8; *RT* 42 (Jan. 1989): 331.

An Armadillo Is Not a Pillow (Saskatoon: Western Producer Prairie Books, 1986). **Rev:** *CCL* 46 (1987): 99; *EL* 14 (Jan. 1987): 47; *QQ* 52 (Dec. 1986): 15.

What Holds up the Moon? (Regina: Coteau Books, 1987). **Rev:** *BYP* 2 (Feb. 1988): 9; *CM* 15 (July 1988): 147.

Who Greased the Shoelaces? (Toronto: Stoddart, 1989). **Rev:** *CCL* 61 (1991): 77; *CM* 17 (Dec. 1989): 268.

Oliver's Chickens (Toronto: Groundwood, 1991). **Rev:** *QQ* 58 (Aug. 1992): 27.

Mister Got to Go: The Cat That Wouldn't Leave (Red Deer, Alta: Red Deer College Press, 1995); published in the US as *No Cats Allowed.* **Rev:** *BiC* 24 (Nov. 1995): 40; *CBRA* (1995): 485; *QQ* 61 (Aug. 1995): 36; *SLJ* 43 (Apr. 1997): 117.

A respected author of short stories for adults, Lois Simmie approached writing for children with the beliefs that entertaining young readers is, in itself, a worthy goal and that, although a humorous tone is appropriate, a poet must approach the writing with a serious attitude, respecting both the audience and subject matter. In three collections of poems and three short picture-book stories, she has achieved her goal. She is able to make children laugh as she depicts the world as they see it.

The short poems that constitute the collections *Auntie's Knitting a Baby*, *An Armadillo is Not a Pillow*, and *Who Greased the Shoelaces?* deal with four main subjects: children's everyday world, the creations of their imaginations, odd and eccentric people and animals, and questionings about life. Frequently written in the voice of a child of middle-elementary age, the works use a variety of rhyme schemes, from couplets and ballad stanzas to irregular rhyme patterns. Lines generally contain three or four strong stresses. The result is that the speaker seems amused or bemused by the imaginary or real people, creatures, objects, or events being contemplated. Even such poems about frightening creatures of the imagination as 'Kitchen Witch', in which a decoration is believed to fly around at night, or 'The Sock Monster', about the being who steals only one of a pair of stockings, are whimsical. Eccentric adults, like the Auntie whose unsuccessful attempts to create articles of clothing for a new baby are chronicled in several poems, or a father who has become a poetry fanatic, are the objects of the speaker's gentle laughter. On a more thoughtful note, the speaker in 'Sunday Night' laments that 'Monday is ruining Sunday again.' Another child, in 'Mean', asks 'Why do I feel mean today?'

The three picture books continue themes frequently found in the poetry collections. In *What Holds Up the Moon?*, Roberta Muldoon asks that question of a number of adults, all of whom give answers that relate to their professions: the carpenter, for example, suggesting nails; the candy store lady, toffee. The conflict is resolved when the heroine realizes that although she doesn't know the answer to her question, the adults in her life don't either. *Oliver's Chickens* deals with a child's coming to terms with his imaginary world. The young hero finally decides that he must let his pretend pets go, as they are old enough to fend for themselves. He, of course, is leaving one stage of his own life, continuing the process of growing up. In *Mister Got to Go*, Simmie sensitively responds to real pets, recounting the life of a stray cat that wandered into a residential hotel and gradually worked its way into the affections of the crusty manager.

Through her skilful use of language, Simmie is able to arouse a variety of emotions in her young readers. From gentle fear to broad humour, from real to imaginary worlds, she sensitively communicates the many aspects of life to which children respond.

See also: *CA* 165.

Barbara Smucker

Born: 1 September 1915, in Newton, Kansas.

Principal Residences: Newton, Kan.; Manhattan, Kan.; Harper, Kan.; Lake Forest, Ill.; Lombard, Ill.; New York City; Chicago; Princeton, NJ; Cambridge, England; Waterloo, Ont.

Education: Bethel College (1932–3); Kansas State University (BS 1936); Rosary (Illinois) Library School (1963–5); Waterloo University (1975–7).

Occupations: teacher; reporter; bookseller; librarian; writer.

Major Awards: Canada Council Children's Literature Prize (1979); Ruth Schwartz Children's Book Award (1980); Brotherhood Award, National Conference of Christians and Jews (1980, for *Underground to Canada*); Vicky Metcalf Award (1988); IODE Violet Downey Book Award (1991).

Works for Children

Henry's Red Sea (Scottdale, Penn.: Herald Publishing, 1955). **Rev:** *CCL* 25 (1982): 19; *JR* 25 (Jan. 1982): 357.

Cherokee Run (Scottdale, Penn.: Herald Publishing, 1957).

Wigwam in the City (New York: Dutton, 1966); reissued as *Susan* (New York: Scholastic, 1970).

Underground to Canada (Toronto: Clarke Irwin, 1977); reissued as *Runaway to Freedom* (New York: Harper and Row, 1979). **Rev:** *CM* 19 (May 1991): 156; *EL* 19 (Nov. 1991): 61; *NYTBR* (30 Apr. 1978): 52; *RT* 32 (Feb. 1979): 606, and 33 (Oct. 1979): 48, and 45 (Apr. 1992): 638; *SLJ* 24 (Apr. 1978): 89, and 27 (Sept. 1980): 43.

Days of Terror (Toronto: Clarke Irwin, 1980). **Rev:** *BiC* 8 (Dec. 1979): 14; *CCL* 25 (1982): 18, and 35 (1984): 140; *IR* 14 (Feb. 1980): 58; *Maclean's* 92 (17 Dec. 1979): 49; *QQ* 48 (Feb. 1982): 16, and 48 (June 1982): 4; *RT* 45 (Apr. 1992): 638; *SLJ* 27 (Sept. 1980): 43.

Amish Adventure (Toronto: Clarke Irwin, 1983). **Rev:** *CM* 11 (Nov. 1983): 249; *RT* 45 (Apr. 1992): 638.

White Mist (Toronto: Irwin Publishing, 1985). **Rev:** *BiC* 14 (Dec. 1985): 12; *CCL* 44 (1986): 57, and 45 (1987): 55; *CL* 111 (Winter 1986): 169; *CM* 14 (Mar. 1986): 65; *EL* 13 (May 1986): 44; *QQ* 51 (Dec. 1985): 30.

Jacob's Little Giant (Markham, Ont.: Viking Kestrel, 1987). **Rev:** *BiC* 16 (Dec. 1987):

12; *CCL* 56 (1989): 99; *CM* 16 (Mar. 1988): 47, and 17 (Jan. 1989): 7; *EL* 15 (Mar. 1988): 24; *RT* 45 (Apr. 1992): 638; *SL* 36 (Aug. 1988): 103; *TLS* (19 Feb. 1988): 200.

Incredible Jumbo (Toronto: Viking Penguin, 1990). **Rev:** *CCL* 62 (1991): 107; *CM* 8 (July 1990): 181; *EL* 18 (Mar. 1991): 23; *NYTBR* (3 Mar. 1991): 29; *QQ* 56 (Mar. 1990): 21; *RT* 45 (Apr. 1992): 638; *SL* 40 (Nov. 1992): 148; *SLJ* 37 (Apr. 1991): 123.

Garth and the Mermaid (Toronto: Penguin, 1992). **Rev:** *QQ* 58 (Aug. 1992): 25.

Selina and the Bear Paw Quilt, illus. Janet Wilson (Toronto: Lester, 1995). **Rev:** *CBRA* (1995): 487; *EL* 23 (Mar. 1996): 24; *QQ* 61 (Dec. 1995): 38; *SLJ* 42 (July 1996): 74.

Selina and the Shoo-Fly Pie, illus. Janet Wilson (Toronto: Stoddart, 1998). **Rev:** *QQ* 65 (Jan. 1999): 43.

Other

'An Adventure with Time Travel', *CCL* 67 (1992): 32–4.

The fiction of Barbara Claasen Smucker is concerned with history, traditions, social justice, and conflicts involving minority groups or the lower classes. Smucker herself belongs to a minority, the New Order Mennonites, a group that values tradition but does not believe in the complete withdrawal from the world practised by Old Order Mennonites. She thus understands both how outsiders view minorities and how tensions can develop between those who seem to have much in common.

Before she and her husband, a Mennonite minister and professor of sociology, came to Canada in 1969, Smucker published three novels focusing on minority groups. She wrote *Henry's Red Sea*, describing the escape of Mennonites from Russia to Paraguay after World War II, and *Cherokee Run*, recounting the Mennonite migration from Kansas to Oklahoma, to teach Mennonite children their history. *Wigwam in the City* (republished as *Susan*), about a Native family moving from a reservation to Chicago, was her first attempt to deal with contemporary social problems and with people outside of the Mennonite community.

Since taking up residence in Canada, Smucker has published seven novels and two picture books. Her first two Canadian books established her reputation as an author of powerful historical novels: *Underground to Canada* is a dramatic account of blacks escaping from slavery in the southern states to freedom in Canada, and *Days of Terror* is a tense account of the persecution and emigration of Russian Mennonites after the Revolution. *Amish Adventure* is a contemporary story about a boy spending time on an Amish farm after he is injured in an auto accident.

Smucker maintains her historical interests in her two fantasies, which employ the device of time shifts. In *White Mist*, two Natives travel back to the nineteenth century to discover and accept their relationship with the exiled Natives of Michigan and to learn reverence for the land. In *Garth and the Mermaid*, a twentieth-century boy resolves his personal problems and gains hope for the future by travelling back to fourteenth-century England. Animals are prominent in two novels. *Jacob's Little Giant* is a gentle tale about a small Mennonite boy who matures and gains respect when he successfully raises some giant Canada geese. *Incredible Jumbo* combines a historical account of Barnum's famous circus elephant with the story of a poor boy who tries both to care for his widowed mother and to achieve his dream of becoming a circus clown. With *Selina and the Bear Paw Quilt*, Smucker returns to the subject of her first works, Mennonite migrations, this time telling of the flight to Canada from Civil War America. The emphasis in this picture book, however, is not on the tribulations of journeys but on the emotional significance of quilts as repositories of family memories. In its sequel, *Selina and the Shoo-Fly Pie*, set a year later, a relocated American family welcomes a troubled Mennonite boy with food and fellowship, helping him to see that he can regain in Canada the peace and security he lost in the Civil War.

Smucker structures her novels to investigate beliefs and values. 'I like my story heroes to have difficult goals to win', she has said, 'and to strive for values that are the very best in our society.' Thus, in most of her novels, child heroes undertake journeys that lead to new understanding of themselves or their group, and to a symbolic affirmation of Christian or democratic values.

The pattern is clear in *Underground to Canada*, which, she says, was partly inspired by a speech in which Martin Luther King talked about the coded language of slaves: 'Heaven was the word for Canada.' Jullily, a black slave, journeys from the earthly hell of the American South to the earthly heaven of Canada, which represents the opportunity for freedom and human dignity. While testing her courage and compassion, her journey includes strengthening grace, in the form of the assistance she receives along the way. Smucker shows Christian charity, one of her primary values, by contrasting the good deeds of the saintly Abolitionists, who risk their own freedom and lives, with the mindless brutality of Sims, the slave hunter and overseer, who, as even Smucker admits, is a 'sort of a stereotype bad man'. Jullily's successful journey to freedom also symbolizes the journey of life, implying Smucker's belief that God watches over believers. Smucker does not, however, allow the pattern to violate historical accuracy. She points out, for example, that Canada is only relatively a heaven for the escaped slaves because they are not welcome in white schools and their lack of education makes them unfit for many jobs.

A similar journey pattern is evident in *Days of Terror*, in which Canada, the goal of the Mennonite migration, stands for political and religious freedom and, thus, happiness and godliness. In this case, however, Smucker conducts a much more complex study of the effect of beliefs and values. Although she does not excuse the racism of the Russians who hated the German-speaking Mennonites, she shows how Mennonite aloofness exacerbated the prejudice. Wise old Grandfather Penner thus expresses Smucker's New Order belief in the coexistence of religious values and participation in the state: he says that, once in Canada, 'We must not withdraw from the native people as we have done in

Russia.' Furthermore, Smucker uses the story of Otto Neufeld, a member of a Mennonite Self-Defence League that took up arms to defend the community, to show how the pressure of circumstances affects principles. She also contrasts the moral inflexibility of the community with the sensitivity and devotion to private conscience displayed by Otto's brother, Peter. After the group ostracizes the prodigal Otto, Peter is the only one who keeps in touch and remains true to him.

In *Amish Adventure*, Smucker varies the journey pattern. Ian McDonald journeys from Chicago to an Amish farm near Waterloo, Ontario. There, the hardships of daily farm life test him, and the kindness of his Amish hosts opens his eyes, helping him to discover his own abilities and inspiring him with a desire to become a farmer. Because he is not Amish, he continues his journey beyond the farm, returning to his own community. Counterbalancing this pattern is the circular journey of John Bender, who has left his Amish home for adventures in the outside world but returns to accept it as the ideal place for him. The climactic, community barn-raising symbolizes the solidarity of the group. The fact that John Bender 'seemed to be holding the whole structure together' shows that only the voluntary participation of young people will ensure the survival of the group. Still, Smucker's plot indicates problems with inflexible adherence to rules. John returns, after all, only because an outsider, Ian McDonald, tells him about his father's misfortunes. Furthermore, John's sister, who left the community to be a nurse, continues to be shunned because she does not repent. By presenting issues from the perspectives of both the Amish and the outsider, Ian, Smucker makes us feel the hard steel of faith and the pain it occasions for both sides.

In *White Mist*, Smucker uses the journey of two outsiders to explore values. May Apple Appleby, who denies her obvious Native ancestry, and Lee Pokagon, a Native bitter about the way whites have treated both Natives and their lands, are mysteriously shifted into the nineteenth century. Their adventures enable them to witness the expulsion of Natives and the wasteful logging practices of white settlers. They are unable to alter the course of history, but, they gain pride in their ancestry. When they return to their own time, they therefore offer white people the ecological vision of the Natives: 'If we destroy the earth, we destroy ourselves. We are one with the earth.' *White Mist* lacks a satisfyingly dramatic conclusion because the teenagers are limited to making speeches, which may or may not affect their twentieth-century listeners. The novel's pattern, however, suggests that people must go deeply into their heritage, into their identities, if they are to face the modern world with confidence and purpose, and that individuals must stand up for their beliefs.

Smucker's second foray into time-shift fantasy, *Garth and the Mermaid*, is disappointing because the presentation of twentieth-century characters and problems is too superficial to make the parallels between present and past more than tenuous. Garth Merriman dislikes Hawk Goderich, the dour businessman his widowed mother plans to marry. While saving a classmate nicknamed Mermaid from being hit by a truck, Garth is knocked unconscious. Awakening in the fourteenth century as a villein, or peasant, Garth finds himself persecuted by Hawkin, a cruel steward who resembles Hawk. Garth escapes and joins the crew building a cathedral so that he can become a freeman and realize his dream of working as a stone mason. The novel is unsuccessful in trying to establish a dual consciousness for Garth, and his interest in carving a mermaid, an idea suggested by his fondness for a twentieth-century girl, is a plot device unwarranted by his characterization in the fourteenth century. Even more contrived is the conclusion: after saving the master mason's daughter, whom he calls Mermaid, from a crumbling wall, Garth awakens in the twentieth century. He now accepts that Hawk is more like Goderic, his fourteenth-century stepfather, than the cruel Hawkin. Although Garth's journey through time advances a theme about the desirability of social equality, the main journey, his melodramatic and implausible escape from his feudal home, does not satisfactorily resolve the psychological themes. Garth's recognition that he has been wrong in his perception of Hawk is more contrivance than insight.

Jacob's Little Giant, a novel for younger children, lacks the dramatic journeys of Smucker's other books and does not explore their large moral or social issues. Jacob Snyder, a Mennonite boy small for his age, tires of being 'Little Jakie', a name suggesting incompetence and insignificance. Although heavy-handed in repeatedly identifying Jacob with Little Giant, the smallest of the goslings he raises, the novel succeeds in using Jacob's journeys between the pond and other settings, particularly his home, to show how he gains maturity and acceptance. By beginning and ending with the migratory journeys of geese and by presenting significant stages of their life cycle, the novel also conveys a reverence for nature. Smucker's other novel about the affection of animals and people, *Incredible Jumbo*, fails in both characterization and plot. It unsuccessfully blends the true account of Jumbo, an enormous circus elephant, with the fictional tale of a poor English boy, Tod Tolliver, who runs away to work in the circus and to become a clown. Not even the pathos of the elephant's accidental death can leaven the cloying sentimentality of Tod's dedication to his consumptive mother or make more acceptable the contrivances that enable Tod simultaneously to achieve his dreams of becoming a clown and of being reunited with his mother.

Most of the weaknesses in Smucker's writing are attributable to the didacticism that has been a prominent part from the beginning. Her dialogue, for instance, is often contrived: instead of conversing naturally and in language appropriate to their age and social station, characters present information as if they were lecturing from the pulpit. Furthermore, to establish a clash of values, Smucker lacks deftness in portraying villains, making Sims, the slave trader in *Underground to Canada*, Mahkno, the anarchist in *Days of Terror*, Pete Moss, the teenage troublemaker in *Amish Adventure*, and Hawkin the steward in *Garth and the Mermaid* speak and behave implausibly. Smucker also has difficulty making characters other than the Mennonites and Amish seem psychologically plausible. In *Amish Adventure*, for example, she attempts to contrast characters who accept responsibility and tolerate differences with those who fail to do so.

Neither Ian McDonald's obsessive guilt for being in the car that crippled Ezra Bender nor the cowardice of the driver in hiding afterwards, however, seem more than awkward and mechanical thematic devices.

Smucker has compensating strengths nevertheless. She is, as the bibliographies appended to some of her novels suggest, a meticulous researcher who can skilfully reconstruct history. Thus, even her weakest novels, the fantasies *White Mist* and *Garth and the Mermaid*, are redeemed by vivid portrayals of a nineteenth-century logging camp and a fourteenth-century village, respectively. It is *Underground to Canada* and *Days of Terror*, however, that support her belief 'that there are so many exciting things happening in history and that it doesn't have to be dull.' At her best, Smucker is a Christian novelist. Eschewing narrow sectarianism, she advocates tolerance and compassion in the treatment of all peoples. Her sympathetic glances at lives not normally treated in Canadian children's literature show that Canada's cultural mosaic can provide fitting material for intelligent fiction.

See also: *CA* 106; *CANR* 23; *CLR* 10; *MAICY*; *MCAI*; *Profiles* 2; *SAAS* 11; *SATA* 29, 76; *TCCW*; *WSMP*.

Kathy Stinson

Born: 22 April 1952, in Toronto.

Principal Residences: Etobicoke, Ont.; Toronto.

Education: attended Lakeshore Teachers College; University of Toronto.

Career: mail sorter; teacher; waitress; preschool instructor; writer.

Major Awards: IODE (Toronto) Book Award (1982).

Works for Children

Red Is Best, illus. Robin Baird Lewis (Toronto: Annick, 1982). **Rev:** *APBR* 10 (Nov. 1983): 15; *BiC* 11 (Dec. 1982): 8; *CCL* 30 (1983): 78; *EL* 10 (May 1983): 29; *QQ* 49 (Aug. 1983): 34; *SLJ* 29 (Aug. 1983): 58.

Big or Little?, illus. Robin Baird Lewis (Toronto: Annick, 1983). **Rev:** *BiC* 12 (May 1983): 31; *CCL* 30 (1983): 78; *EL* 11 (Sept. 1983): 40; *QQ* 49 (Aug. 1983): 34.

Mom and Dad Don't Live Together Anymore, illus. Nancy Lou Reynolds (Toronto: Annick, 1984). **Rev:** *BiC* 13 (Dec. 1984): 10; *CCL* 31 (1985): 125; *QQ* 50 (Nov. 1984): 10; *SLJ* 31 (Apr. 1985): 83.

Those Green Things, illus. Mary McLoughlin (Toronto: Annick, 1985); rev. edn, illus. Deirdre Betteridge (Toronto: Annick, 1995). **Rev:** *BiC* 14 (Nov. 1985): 37; *CBRA* (1995): 88; *CCL* 44 (1986): 91; *QQ* 52 (Feb. 1986): 22; *SLJ* 32 (Apr. 1986): 80.

The Bare Naked Book, illus. Heather Collins (Toronto: Annick, 1986). **Rev:** *APBR* 13 (Nov. 1986): 6; *BiC* 15 (Dec. 1986): 15; *BYP* 1 (Feb. 1987): 3; *CCL* 45 (1987): 95; *EL* 14 (Jan. 1987): 47; *SLJ* 33 (Apr. 1987): 90.

Seven Clues in Pebble Creek (Toronto: James Lorimer, 1987). **Rev:** *BYP* 2 (Feb. 1988): 8; *CCL* 51 (1988): 73; *CM* 16 (July 1988): 132.

Teddy Rabbit, illus. Stéphane Poulin (Toronto: Annick, 1988). **Rev:** *BYP* 2 (Oct. 1988): 14; *CCL* 51 (1988): 100; *CM* 17 (Jan. 1989): 35; *EL* 18 (Mar. 1991): 59.

The Dressed Up Book, illus. Heather Collins (Willowdale, Ont.: Annick, 1990). **Rev:** *CCL* 62 (1991): 95; *CM* 18 (July 1990): 182; *EL* 18 (Mar. 1991): 24; *QQ* 56 (July 1990): 36; *RT* 45 (Apr. 1992): 639; *SL* 40 (Aug. 1992): 99.

Who Is Sleeping in Auntie's Bed?, illus. Robin Baird Lewis (Toronto: Oxford UP, 1991). **Rev:** *CCL* 67 (1992): 84; *CM* 19 (Nov. 1991): 355; *EL* 19 (Mar. 1992): 17; *QQ* 59 (Oct. 1991): 36.

Fish House Secrets (Saskatoon: Thistledown, 1992). **Rev:** *BiC* 21 (Nov. 1992): 38; *CM* 20 (Oct. 1992): 272; *EL* 20 (Mar. 1993): 30; *QQ* 58 (July 1992): 47.

Steven's Baseball Mitt: A Book About Being Adopted, illus. Robin Baird Lewis (Willowdale, Ont.: Annick, 1992). **Rev:** *BiC* 21 (Sept. 1992): 45; *CCL* 79 (1995): 82; *CM* 20 (Oct. 1992): 266; *EL* 20 (May 1993): 30; *QQ* 58 (June 1992): 37.

The Fabulous Ball Book, illus. Heather Collins (Toronto: Oxford UP, 1993). **Rev:** *QQ* 59 (Oct. 1993): 43; *CM* 20 (Mar. 1992): 98; *QQ* 57 (Dec. 1991): 27.

The Great Pebble Creek Bike Race (Toronto: James Lorimer, 1994). **Rev:** *CBRA* (1995): 519; *CM* 22 (Nov. 1994): 223; *QQ* 60 (July 1994): 61.

Writing Your Best Picture Book Ever (Markham, Ont.: Pembroke, 1994).

One Year Commencing (Saskatoon: Thistledown, 1997). **Rev:** *QQ* 63 (July 1997): 49.

Other

Writing Picture Books: What Works and What Doesn't (Markham, Ont.: Pembroke, 1991). **Rev:** *CBRA* (1994): 538.

Kathy Stinson first came to prominence as an author who used her experiences as a teacher and a parent, along with her own memories of childhood, to create picture books for preschool children. In recent years she has shown herself adept as a novelist, producing books for both middle-school readers and young adults.

Stinson's picture books present children's simple but nonetheless significant responses to various situations. In the award-winning *Red Is Best*, based on Stinson's daughter's preference for red socks, the narrator steadfastly refuses her mother's suggestions that she choose clothes of different colours. The speaker in *Big or Little?* experiences the common dilemma of being in between: he is big enough to do up zippers and tie shoes, but he is too little to ring doorbells. In *Mom and Dad Don't Live Together Any More*, a small child pondering her parents' separation concludes that she loves them both and that both still love her. *Steven's Baseball Mitt* is similar. Although he feels different because, unlike the other children, he doesn't know his birth mother, Steven concludes that, although he may one day find his birth mother, he truly belongs with his adoptive family.

Three of Stinson's books are built upon questions. The most elaborate, *Those Green Things*, is a question-and-answer session between a child and her mother. Every time the young speaker asks what something is and receives a factual answer, she replies that she had thought that the object was something imaginary and fantastic. In mock frustration, the mother finally creates a fantastic answer herself, claiming that the green things on the porch are Martians ready to take her away so that her child will not ask any more questions about green things. Amusingly, the mother's extravagant answer fails to silence her curious child. *The Bare Naked Book* discusses various parts of the body, including genitals, each time asking the child reader, 'Where is your . . .?' A sequel, *The Dressed Up Book*, shows children dressing up in various costumes and asks questions about their choices, such as what does a person see with mad scientist eyes.

Two of Stinson's picture books have more fully developed stories. *Teddy Rabbit* focuses on Tony's worry that his stuffed companion, Rabbit, won't be welcome at the Teddy Bears' Picnic. On the day of the big event, Tony is devastated when someone knocks Rabbit out of his arms and onto the subway tracks. An understanding guard rescues Rabbit, and Tony proceeds to the picnic, where he is relieved to find children with lion teddies and monkey teddies. Completely different from all of her other pictures books, *Who Is Sleeping in Auntie's Bed?* is a domestic farce. When Meg, her sister, Nicole, and their parents visit Auntie, Meg gets to sleep with Auntie. Because Auntie snores, Meg joins her parents, thus setting off an amusing round of bed roulette as each new companion disturbs somebody already in that bed. Adding to the humour is the final joke: the father is completely unaware of how many times people have changed beds during the night.

In addition to the illustrations, which are excellent complements to the texts, Stinson's picture books succeed because of the sensitive use of simple language to capture children's emotions. Even in *The Bare Naked Book*, which seems at first glance to be merely a listing of body parts, the words build a rhythm that expresses the child's joy of exploring various body parts and the pleasure of repeating words that describe them. The adjectives preceding the repeated nouns suggest that people may look different but that all possess the same body parts. As her revision of *Those Green Things* shows, Stinson is also aware of how word placement and the turning of pages affect a story. In her revised version, she creates comic emphasis by dividing the child's statement so that the reader must turn the page to read the child's conjecture about the green things, which appears alone on a two-page spread.

Stinson's two novels for middle-school readers develop themes about appearances. *Seven Clues in Pebble Creek* is a mystery, but it includes no crime. Matt Randall, bored because his friends are away on vacation, receives a postcard that launches him on a treasure hunt. Needing help, he enlists the aid of David Varvarikos, whom he has previously dismissed as a brainy wimp. They eventually discover that Mr Grubb, whom Matt has regarded as the Boogey Man of Booth Street, has set up the treasure hunt so that the boys will come to his house and play with his computer. Matt's discovery that neither David nor Mr Grubb is what he appears to be and that he can be friends with both adds thematic depth to a fast-paced and interesting adventure. The *Great Pebble Creek Bike Race*, set a week later, is more elaborate, adding ethical dimensions to the theme of judging by appearances. When Matt's best friend, Mike Lennox, returns from vacation, he makes it known that he detests David. Matt must therefore choose whether to remain loyal to his new friend or to resume his relationship with Mike. Matt passes this test of integrity by asserting his friendship with David. He then becomes instrumental in helping Mike to see that both David and Mr Grubb are worthwhile friends. The story of these relationships fits within a plot focusing on Matt's desire to win the bicycle that is the prize in a race. Mike loses to another new friend, the deaf Amanda Pirie, whose handicap proves no barrier to accomplishments or friendships. He realizes his wish, however, when Mr Grubb, who at Matt's suggestion entered his antique bicycle in a contest, turns over to Matt the bicycle he has won. *The Great Pebble Creek Bike Race* portrays the determination of athletes and the excitement of competing in a sports event, but the focus of this appealing story is not entirely on athletic prowess. The training, the climactic race, and the subsequent bicycle contest reveal the ethical and psychological qualities of the characters, and they advance the novel's theme by demonstrating the meaning of friendships.

Stinson's two novels for young adults are also about relationships. Both focus on artistic children whose family lives have been disrupted by death or by divorce. In each, the child redefines the parent-child relationship to establish an independent identity. *Fish House Secrets*, which contains two alternating first-person narratives, describes a three-day period during which both narrators come to important realizations about themselves and their families. Chad Merrill, who blames himself because the accident that killed his mother occurred when she was coming to pick him up, struggles with his sense of loss and his feelings that his father is smothering him with attention. Jill Croft is running away because her father is a crook who stole money at work and who gambled away the money set aside for her dance lessons. When she and Chad meet, they are both transformed for the better. Chad, who has been afraid to let his father know that he, like his mother, is a painter, reveals his secret and insists on having more freedom; Jill, deciding that she will not run away even though home life is not perfect, becomes determined to find a way to keep up her dancing. *Fish House Secrets* places the changing perceptions of these artistically sensitive and emotional young people in a context that reveals how people of all ages suppress their desires and identities. Chad, for example, discovers that his father is smothering him because he had, in his grief for his late wife, wished that Chad had died. He also discovers that his grandfather, who chose a financially safe career as a lawyer, is secretly writing a book. Chad's story is dominant, and ends happily; Jill's contains less dramatic discoveries, and its resolution remains in doubt. Nevertheless, *Fish House Secrets* celebrates the courage of honestly facing one's situation.

One Year Commencing, a simpler book, also touches on the issue of honest relationships. Al (Alison) Gaitskill, raised in Alberta by her divorced mother, is required by a court order to spend a year in Toronto with her father before she chooses the parent with whom she will live permanently. At first Al hates her new home and tries to devise ways to let her father know that she wants to go back to live with her mother. After a year, during which she discovers her father's feelings, confronts him about the ethics of his job and his insensitivity to the plight of the poor, and realizes that, in spite of his philistine taste, he will do all in his power to help her develop her artistic talent, she decides to live with her father. The idea of change and the acceptance of it is clear throughout, but the novel disappointingly implies that Al's decision to stay with her father is based on the material and cultural advantages she enjoys in Toronto. However true to life the decision is, it is not clearly connected to the issues of honesty and social responsibility raised earlier.

In addition to her fiction, Stinson has also written three works of non-fiction. *The Fabulous Ball Book* looks at every form of ball, from those used in games to the moon and the planets. *Writing Picture Books: What Works and What Doesn't* is an adult guide to writing that is accessible to older children; *Writing Your Best Picture Book Ever* aims similar writing advice specifically at children.

Stinson's picture books have made her a significant author for preschoolers. In them, she has used sensitive, poetic language to present the world as they experience it. Her middle-school novels succeed in developing themes about appearances while remaining fast-paced entertainment. Her young adult novels mark another stage in her career. Both, but especially *Fish House Secrets*, respect the intelligence of young people by developing significant emotional and ethical themes.

See also: *WSMP*.

Patti Stren

Born: 8 August 1949, in Brantford, Ont.

Education: University of Toronto (BA 1971); Ontario College of Art (1972–4); School of Visual Arts, New York (BFA 1977).

Principal Residences: Brantford; Toronto; Tel Aviv; New York City; Connecticut.

Career: author; illustrator; cartoonist.

Works for Children

Picture Books Written and Illustrated by Patti Stren

Hug Me (New York: Harper & Row, 1977). **Rev:** *CCB-B* 31 (Feb. 1978): 102; *IR* 12 (Summer 1978): 80; *NYTBR* (16 Oct. 1977): 47; *SLJ* 24 (Jan. 1978): 82.

Bo, the Constrictor Who Couldn't (Toronto: Green Tree, 1978). **Rev:** *IR* 12 (Autumn 1978): 79.

Sloan & Philamina; Or How To Make Friends with Your Lunch (New York: Dutton, 1979). **Rev:** *CCB-B* 33 (Nov. 1979): 59; *CCL* 25 (1982): 48; *IR* 13 (Oct. 1979): 57; *Maclean's* 92 (17 Dec. 1979): 49; *SLJ* 26 (Sept. 1979): 22.

I'm Only Afraid of the Dark (at Night!!) (Toronto: Fitzhenry & Whiteside, 1982). **Rev:** *BiC* 11 (Dec. 1982): 9; *CCL* 34 (1984): 73; *Maclean's* 95 (13 Dec. 1982): 57; *QQ* 49 (1984): 73; *SLJ* 29 (Jan. 1983): 68.

Mountain Rose (Toronto: Clarke Irwin, 1982). **Rev:** *CCL* 27/28 (1982): 180; *QQ* 48 (July 1982): 62; *SLJ* 28 (Mar. 1982): 140.

For Sale: One Brother (Richmond Hill, Ont.: North Winds, 1993). **Rev:** *CM* 22 (Nov. 1994): 209; *NYTBR* 99 (30 Jan. 1994): 27; *QQ* 59 (Sept. 1993); *SLJ* 39 (Nov. 1993): 95.

Novels

There's a Rainbow in My Closet (Toronto: Fitzhenry & Whiteside, 1979). **Rev:** *BiC* 9 (Feb. 1980): 21; *CCB-B* 33 (Feb. 1980): 120; *CCL* 22 (1981), 68; *IR* 14 (Apr. 1980): 56; *QQ* 46 (Feb. 1980): 44; *RT* 34 (Oct. 1980): 104; *SLJ* 26 (Sept. 1979): 149.

I Was a 15-Year-Old Blimp (Toronto: Irwin, 1985). **Rev:** *CCL* 46 (1987): 84.

Illustrated by Patti Stren

Yaay Crickets!, by Rosemary Allison (Toronto: Flying Rabbit Press, 1971).

I Never Met a Monster I Didn't Like Colouring Book, by Rosemary Allison (Toronto: Flying Rabbit Press, 1976).

Wings, by Mary Kennedy (New York: Scholastic, 1980).

Eating Ice Cream with a Werewolf, by Phyllis Green (New York: Harper & Row, 1983).

My First Day at School, by Ronnie Sellers (New York : Caedmon, 1985). **Rev:** *SLJ* 32 (Mar. 1986): 152.

I Hate School: How To Hang In and When To Drop Out, by Claudine G. Wirths and Mary Bowman-Kruhm (New York: Crowell, 1986).

Your New School, by Claudine G. Wirths and Mary Bowman-Kruhm (New York: Twenty-first Century Books, 1993).

Your Power with Words, by Claudine G. Wirths and Mary Bowman-Kruhm (New York: Twenty-first Century Books, 1993).

Your Circle of Friends, by Claudine G. Wirths and Mary Bowman-Kruhm (New York: Twenty-first Century Books, 1993).

Selected Discussions

Loder, Karen. 'The Prolific Art of Patti Stren', *QQ* 45 (Oct. 1979): 8.

Patti Stren has won critical respect for her blend of urbane wit and sentiment in books illustrated with appealingly quirky, cartoon-like drawings. She has illustrated works for other writers, but she is at her best when she is both author and illustrator because she then controls the interplay between her idiosyncratic, unconventional drawings and her relatively simple, straightforward text.

All of Stren's work explores some facet of the related themes of friendship and self-acceptance. In *Hug Me*, Elliot Kravitz, the first of Stren's heroes who must adjust to being different from the crowd, is a porcupine who longs for a friend to hug and finally meets Thelma Claypits, a female porcupine. *Hug Me* is a minor classic because it presents a universal theme and because the combination of clear, direct prose and witty illustrations saves it from its inherent sentimentality. Seemingly constructed out of the least possible number of lines and enhanced with only a single colour, the deceptively child-like drawings concentrate attention on Elliot and develop his personality. As in her later books, Stren's pictures here work in one of two ways. Sometimes they illustrate the action directly, picturing exactly what is written, with words from the text included, cartoon-fashion, in the drawing. At other times, the drawings amplify the text with commentary. For instance, one picture shows Elliot trying to hug a flower, an act not mentioned in the main text. This flower explains to another that Elliot is lonely, while yet another, separated from all the rest, says, 'I know how he feels.'

For Sale: One Brother focuses on Molly, who dreams of being an only child because she finds her four-year-old brother, David, a pest. When Molly puts up a sign offering to sell David, her angry mother punishes Molly by ordering her to spend an entire week with him. Although Molly is initially annoyed by everything that David does, she eventually discovers that she really likes him and wants to keep her brother. The brightly coloured pen-and-watercolour illustrations of this first-person narrative are crowded with captions and images made by rubber stamps (Stren markets her own line of rubber stamps). As with those in *Hug Me*, these pictures complement and expand the tale. Because they have supposedly been produced by Molly herself, however, they become an additional agent of characterization. The multitude of details and words in various orientations force the reader to linger over the pictures, skipping around to find all their jokes and sentiments. By thus breaking the normal linear flow of the story, these comical illustrations increase the reader's understanding of Molly and her feelings of frustration.

Stren's other picture books more closely follow the pattern of *Hug Me*, although none is quite as successful in blending elements. *Bo, the Contrictor Who Couldn't*, an early work illustrated with colourful watercolours, explores peer pressure and individuality through the story of a snake who would rather kiss his enemies than squeeze and eat them. In *Sloan & Philamina; Or How To Make Friends with Your Lunch*, an anteater and an ant become friends. In *I'm Only Afraid of the Dark (at Night!!)*, Harold, an Arctic owl, and Gert, a girl owl, help each other overcome their debilitating fear of the dark. *Mountain Rose* is the tale of a girl who is teased for being big but who finds happiness and identity as a world champion wrestler. Weak in focus, it lacks the clear development of theme and the sharp wit that distinguishes the other books.

Stren has pursued her theme of the search for identity in two novels. In *There's a Rainbow in My Closet*, Emma Goldberg, a girl with a passion for painting, is brought to a deeper appreciation of her artistic talent, and hence, her own individuality, when her unconventional grandmother comes to take care of her. Dialogue and characterization, particularly of the impossibly ideal grandmother, are weak, the thematic strands never quite fuse, and the story occasionally succumbs to sentimentality. Nevertheless, this novel is humorous, and it also provides unusual insight into a child's artistic sense.

I Was a 15-Year-Old Blimp is Stren's only book without illustrations. It is a conventional problem novel treating bulimia, an eating disorder suffered by girls who vomit and purge themselves with laxatives in order to control their weight. Gabby Finklestein, a fat girl, dreams of romance, but she endures humiliating mockery. Sentimental and predictable, this novel has obvious flaws, but it is readable because of its simple, conversational prose and because Stren extends the identity crisis theme beyond the issue of obesity.

Although only partially successful as a novelist, Stren is a significant and original picture-book artist. Her offbeat blending of textual and graphical elements, in combination with her characteristically comic approach to serious themes, has enabled her to create several memorably entertaining books.

See also: *CA* 117, 124; *CLR* 5; *SATA* 41, 88; *WSMP*.

George Swede
(born Juris Purins)

Born: 20 November 1940, in Riga, Latvia.

Principal Residences: Riga; rural Fraser Valley, BC; Vancouver; Toronto.

Education: University of British Columbia (BA 1964); Dalhousie University (MA 1965); Greenwich University, Norfolk Island, Australia (Ph.D. in Creative Writing 1996).

Career: college psychology instructor; psychologist; professor; writer.

Works for Children

Quillby, The Porcupine Who Lost His Quills, with Anita Krumins, illus. Martin Lewis (Toronto: Three Trees, 1979). **Rev:** *BiC* 9 (1980): 19; *IR* 14 (Dec. 1980): 54.

The Case of the Moonlit Gold Dust (Toronto: Three Trees, 1979; rev. edn without chapter divisions, 1981). **Rev:** *CCL* 22 (1981): 85; *IR* 14 (Aug. 1980): 63; *QQ* 47 (Apr. 1981): 34.

The Case of the Missing Heirloom (Toronto: Three Trees, 1980). **Rev:** *CCL* 22 (1981): 85; *IR* 15 (Apr. 1981): 53.

The Case of the Seaside Burglaries (Toronto: Three Trees, 1981). **Rev:** *IR* 15 (Oct. 1981): 55; *QQ* 47 (Dec. 1981): 30; *SLJ* 28 (Aug. 1982): 108.

The Case of the Downhill Theft (Toronto: Three Trees, 1982). **Rev:** *APBR* 10 (Nov. 1983): 12; *BiC* 11 (Dec. 1982): 10; *EL* 11 (Nov. 1983): 37.

Undertow (Toronto: Three Trees, 1982). **Rev:** *BiC* 12 (May 1983): 32; *EL* 11 (Nov. 1983): 38.

Tick Bird: Poems for Children (Toronto: Three Trees, 1983). **Rev:** *CCL* 42 (1986): 92.

Time Is Flies: Poems for Children (Toronto: Three Trees, 1984). **Rev:** *BiC* 13 (Dec. 1984): 12; *CBRA* (1984): 346; *CCL* 41 (1986): 87; *EL* 12 (Mar. 1985): 46.

Dudley and the Birdman, illus. Mary McLoughlin (Toronto: Three Trees, 1985). **Rev:** *CBRA* (1985): 274; *CCL* 44 (1986): 92; *EL* 13 (Mar. 1986): 44; *QQ* 52 (Feb. 1986): 19.

Dudley and the Christmas Thief, illus. Allan and Deborah Drew-Brook-Cormack (Toronto: Three Trees, 1986). **Rev:** *CCL* 55 (1989): 84.

High Wire Spider: Poems for Children (Toronto: Three Trees, 1986). **Rev:** *BYP* 1 (June 1987): 10; *EL* 15 (Nov. 1987): 53.

Leaping Lizard (Stratford, Ont.: Three Trees, 1988). **Rev:** *BiC* 18 (Apr. 1989): 37; *CBRA* (1988): 219; *CM* 17 (Jan. 1989): 36.

Holes in My Cage: Poems for Young Adults (Stratford, Ont.: Three Trees, 1989). **Rev:** *CCL* 59 (1990): 101.

I Want To Lasso Time (Toronto: Simon and Pierre, 1991). **Rev:** *CCL* 67 (1992): 97; *CM* 20 (May 1992): 163.

Other

The Modern English Haiku (Toronto: Columbine Editions, 1981). **Rev:** *CBRA* (1982): 235.

The Universe Is One Poem: Four Poets Talk Poetry, ed. and contributor (Toronto: Simon and Pierre, 1990). **Rev:** *CBRA* (1990): 264; *CCL* 59 (1990): 101.

George Swede, a poet best known as an advocate of English haiku, has also published poetry and prose for children. Swede's most notable prose works are the four mysteries in the series 'Sherlock, The Bloodhound Detective (With Watson, The Cat)'. These short mysteries focus on the adventures of Inspector Holmes of the Halifax Police Force, a devoted reader of Sherlock Holmes fiction. Inspector Holmes has a fat, white cat named Watson and a bloodhound named Sherlock, who are instrumental in solving each of his cases. Watson and Sherlock think but do not talk, so the humans they encounter regard them merely as ordinary animals. In *The Case of the Moonlit Gold Dust*, the two pets help Holmes to capture a ring of gold smugglers. Sherlock helps by discovering evidence of the smuggling and, later, by saving Holmes from an attack by one of the dogs used to transport gold dust. Watson helps by finding evidence that the smugglers threw away. *The Case of the Missing Heirloom* is a much slighter story about the theft of a valuable necklace. Just as Holmes is about to arrest a chauffeur with a prison record, Sherlock realizes that a crow, attracted to shiny things, is the real culprit. *The Case of the Seaside Burglaries* has the Inspector trying to solve a crime wave at a resort. With the help of Sherlock, who sees one thief in the act, and Watson, who finds a brooch with the finger-prints of the other, Holmes is able to prove that two gallery owners were stealing so that they could buy paintings for their business. In their final adventure, *The Case of the Downhill Theft*, the animals help Holmes to prove that the operator of a ski lodge restaurant, who has fallen into financial trouble, has been pretending that he is the victim of robbery.

Swede's other prose works include a mystery adventure and three picture books. *Undertow* uses changing points of view to present a taut adventure about teens who, having retrieved a toy motorboat containing heroin, are pursued by smugglers. The crudely illustrated *Quillby, The Porcupine Who Lost His Quills*, written with his wife, Anita Krumins, is the tale of a porcupine who writes books. Quillby is soon nearly naked because he uses his own quills to write them. After his neglected wife leaves, Quillby sets out to find her, escaping the jaws of a dog only because it laughs to see him covering his nakedness with a checkered tablecloth. Swede's other picture books are about a boy named Dudley, who shows sensitive awareness of the needs of others. In *Dudley and the Birdman*, Dudley comes across an old man who is trapping birds so that he can hear their songs during the winter. Dudley, who has received two tape recorders as birthday presents, gives one to the man so that he can record the bird songs and let the birds stay free. *Dudley and the Christmas Thief* has Dudley witness a theft and then locate the poor boy who committed the theft so that he could have gifts for his family. After the thief returns the stolen gifts, Dudley gets his father to play Santa and bring the poor family presents.

Swede has made his most significant contribution to children's literature as a poet and presenter of poetry workshops. Ironically, the poems in his first two collections for children, *Tick Bird* and *Time Is Flies*, had all been previously published in journals for adults. Their brevity and relative simplicity, however, allowed children to comprehend and enjoy them. In his books, *High Wire*

Spider, *Leaping Lizard*, *Holes in My Cage*, and *I Want To Lasso Time*, Swede avoids nearly all rhyme because it is associated with traditional poetics. He also tends to avoid simile and even metaphor, preferring the directness of early twentieth-century imagism or the suggestiveness of his favourite form, the haiku, which he defines loosely as a brief poem. In *Time Is Flies*, for example, a one-line poem connects a season to an immediately perceptible object: 'All of winter in this one long icicle.' The title poem of *I Want To Lasso Time* evokes a more elaborate image of a cowboy roping a calf when the narrator proclaims that he wants to lasso time and wave his hat at the sky. In addition to providing images that force readers to make comparisons, Swede also plays with the physical design of poems. Some of these playful works are shaped poems: *High Wire Spider*, for example, contains a poem shaped like an icicle and composed only of the letters forming the word 'icicle'. Others are playful concrete poems in which the word or letter placement creates the meaning. In *Time Is Flies* Swede thus writes the word 'skiing' so that the 'ing' slopes downward from 'ski', with the 'g' inverted as if a skier has had an accident. Another poem in the same book arranges the words to resemble the side of a mountain. The reader can make sense of the poem, however, only by reading some words from bottom to top and the remainder from top to bottom, a process that replicates both a climber's ascent and his metaphoric slide back into prehistory. The design of some poems creates a witty joke. The first line of a poem in this same collection, to cite one example, consists of the word 'MISSING' but with the vowels missing, thus making the word reinforce its signification. Adding to the humour is the second line, in which the word 'Thief' contains two extra 'i's. The design of a poem about a leaking tap in *I Want To Lasso Time*, to cite a second example, not only arranges the words to look as if water is dripping from a tap, but spaces the word 'clouds' to emphasize the internal word, 'loud', as a way of indicating what annoys people about dripping taps. Even when he does not use typographical tricks, Swede is often witty. Sometimes the wit is situational, as in the satire of love poets in *I Want To Lasso Time*: the poet writing a poem of longing is annoyed when the very one for whom he longs interrupts him with a telephone call. At other times the wit is purely verbal, as in the closing poem of *High Wire Spider*, in which he uses the roots of the word 'universe' to create a punning definition: 'The universe is one poem.'

Swede himself has written one of the best introductions to his poems. 'The Universe Is One Poem', his contribution to the collection of essays by the same name, describes how he conducts poetry workshops with children. His description of his procedure for involving children in poetic thinking and his analysis of sample poems makes this superb introduction to experimental poetry a practical guide to pedagogy that will be welcomed by elementary teachers of language arts.

See also: *CA* 113; *CANR* 32; *SATA* 67; *WSMP*.

Shizuye Takashima

Born: 12 June 1928, in Vancouver.

Principal Residences: Vancouver; New Denver, BC; Toronto.

Education: Ontario College of Art (AA 1953).

Career: painter; writer.

Major Awards: Amelia Francis Howard-Gibbon Illustrator's Award (1972).

Works for Children

A Child in Prison Camp (Montreal: Tundra, 1971). **Rev:** *CCB-B* 28 (Nov. 1974): 55; *CCL* 7 (1977): 69; *IR* 6 (1972): 41; *NYTBR* (5 May 1974): 20; *SLJ* 27 (Sept. 1980): 43.

'Rambo-type, violence-oriented stories are doing great harm to the young. If we as adults wish to have a better world with fewer wars, with less of the usual human failures to care for one another, then we should all make greater efforts to expose our young to beautifully illustrated books, well-written ones which will set their hearts on fire so that they will aspire to excellence all through their lives.' These thoughts of Vancouver-born artist Shizuye Takashima could well serve as an introduction to her own book, *A Child in Prison Camp*, in which she draws on her experiences as a Japanese Canadian during World War II. Like thousands of her people, she was interned in central British Columbia, denied her rights as a Canadian citizen, and treated as a prisoner.

A Child in Prison Camp is loosely autobiographical: Takashima was two years older than she portrays herself in the book, and she had four brothers, not one. She is thus presented as the vulnerable youngest child of three, a more generally recognizable character type. The story becomes a universal one of loss and restoration. The narrator, expelled from a place of security, survives a journey through an unknown land supported by a loving family and community, her own hopeful personality, and the beneficent forces of nature.

The events are carefully structured to emphasize three major themes: the injustice of the historical events and the bitterness they caused; the strong sense of family and community that gave the displaced people the strength to endure; and the abiding, restorative power of nature. Takashima's verbal and visual artistry give her presentation of these themes the status of a Canadian classic. Events are perceived through the eyes of the young narrator, and the reader/viewer experiences her bewilderment, hopes, and fears. There is little authorial comment; instead, sensitively chosen and presented details evoke the various emotions. Vignettes, such as the visit to the Exhibition Grounds where the Japanese are housed in animal barns, the confusion and anger at the railway station, the terror at watching a family's house consumed by fire, and the preparations for the O-bon festival, give readers a clearer sense of events and emotions than generalized statements would. The eight watercolours reinforce the themes. The frontispiece illustration of the O-bon festival held against the backdrop of the Rocky Mountains introduces the ideas of community and nature; the picture of the bucket brigade vainly fighting the house fire emphasizes the hazards of their lives. The concluding illustration underscores the theme of love and joy that dominates: as Shichan and her mother stand in the shallow waters of the lake doing their laundry there for the final time, the sun shines down on them through a break in the clouds; the rainbow hues are symbolic of the new hope they feel as they prepare to leave their temporary home for a new life in Ontario.

See also: *CA* 45–8; *Profiles* 2; *SATA* 13.

C.J. Taylor

Born: 31 August 1952, in Montreal.

Principal Residences: Eastern Townships of Quebec; Montreal; Chateauguay, Que.

Career: waitress; artist; radio host; author.

Works for Children

How Two-Feather Was Saved from Loneliness: An Abenaki Legend (Montreal: Tundra, 1990). **Rev:** *BiC* 20 (Apr. 1991): 36; *CCL* 61 (1991): 57; *CL* (Winter 1992): 190; *CM* 19 (Jan. 1991): 31; *EL* 18 (Mar. 1991): 22; *QQ* 56 (Sept. 1990): 19; *RT* 46 (Feb. 1993): 413.

The Ghost and Lone Warrior: An Arapaho Legend (Montreal: Tundra, 1991). **Rev:** *CCB-B* 45 (Feb. 1992): 170; *CCL* 72 (1993): 60; *CM* 20 (Mar. 1992): 76; *EL* 19 (Mar. 1992): 16; *QQ* 57 (Nov. 1991): 26; *SLJ* 38 (Feb. 1992): 84.

Little Water and the Gift of the Animals: A Seneca Legend (Montreal: Tundra, 1992). **Rev:** *CCB-B* 46 (Feb. 1993): 193; *CCL* 72 (1993): 84; *CM* 21 (Jan. 1993): 17; *QQ* 58 (Sept. 1992): 72.

How We Saw the World: Nine Native Stories of the Way Things Began (Montreal: Tundra, 1993). **Rev:** *BiC* 22 (Dec. 1993): 56; *CCL* 75 (1994): 59; *CM* 21 (May 1993): 94; *EL* 21 (Mar. 1994): 18; *QQ* 59 (Apr. 1993): 34; *SLJ* 40 (Feb. 1994): 98.

The Secret of the White Buffalo: An Oglala Legend (Montreal: Tundra, 1993). **Rev:** CL 146 (Fall 1995): 146; *CM* 22 (Mar. 1994): 49; *QQ* 59 (Oct. 1993): 39; *SLJ* 40 (Feb. 1994): 99.

Bones in the Basket: Native Stories of the Origin of People (Montreal: Tundra, 1994).

Rev: *CBRA* (1994): 520; *EL* 22 (May 1995): 16; *QQ* 60 (Sept. 1994): 70; *RT* 49 (Feb. 1996): 398; *SLJ* 41 (Jan. 1995): 131.

The Monster from the Swamp: Native Legends of Monsters, Demons, and Other Creatures (Montreal: Tundra, 1995). **Rev:** *BiC* 24 (Dec. 1995): 18; *QQ* 61 (Nov. 1995): 46.

The Messenger of Spring (Toronto: Tundra, 1997). **Rev:** *EL* 25 (Mar. 1998): 48; *QQ* 63 (Nov. 1997): 46.

Like many artists whose works have been published by Tundra Books, C.J. Taylor entered the field of children's literature as a result of a Montreal exhibition of her paintings. After viewing her work, publisher May Cutler asked Taylor if she would consider writing and illustrating a book based on a Native myth. She chose the Abenaki story of the origin of corn, which was published as *How Two-Feather Was Saved From Loneliness*. The creation of this and her other books celebrates Taylor's rediscovery of the culture she had moved away from as a child. When she began to paint portraits in her late teens, many of her subjects were relatives from the Kahnawake reserve near Montreal. 'The Native theme naturally came out', she recalled. 'I was meant to do what I do.'

The stories Taylor adapts frequently deal with central figures who undertake quests during which their worthiness to help their people is tested. Two-Feather, for example, searches for a friend to end the loneliness he feels in a world with only a few, scattered human beings in it. Because he obeys a spirit woman, following where she leads, making fire, and trusting her when she commands him to drag her through hot ashes, he is given the gift of corn and founds a village where people find companionship in their new agricultural life. Taylor's oil paintings reinforce the thematic and emotional elements of the legend. The opening illustration of a bleak winter landscape devoid of people is a contrast to the concluding scene of villagers celebrating the corn harvest in the brightly coloured late summer settings. Green pervades the illustrations in the middle of the story, symbolizing both the corn goddess and the vitality of life she embodies.

Little Water and The Gift of the Animals is set in the myth time when people and animals could talk together. When a mysterious illness strikes his people at harvest time, the hero, who is a good friend of the animals, especially Wolf, goes to the forest to ask them to share their healing powers. Knocked unconscious in a fall, he is rescued by the animals, who communicate to him while he dreams. The cures they give him quickly heal the people and are still practiced by the Little Water Society of the Iroquois Confederacy. This *pourquoi* legend illustrates not only the importance of hunters respecting the game, but also the spiritual kinship that exists between human beings and animals. Taylor's oil paintings emphasize this spirituality, particularly in the scene in which the helping animals are depicted in a vortex swirling about the head of the unconscious youth and in the final illustration where the healthy villagers gathering their harvest are seen opposite the ghostly faces of the animals who have shared their healing magic.

In *The Ghost and Lone Warrior*, set in a time when horses had not yet arrived on the northern plains, a group of hunters travels to distant mountains in search of buffalo to feed their hungry village. When his ankle is injured, Lone Warrior must stay alone. His courage and determination are rewarded as he is able to shoot a buffalo; but his good fortune seems to be short-lived when a ghost arrives at his camp. The visitor is the spirit of a famous chief, an ancestor who has been testing the young man's worthiness to be the leader of his people. In many ways, the narrative parallels the stages of the vision quest, the journey of initiation taken by young men in most traditional Plains cultures. As a member of a hunting culture, Lone Warrior's selflessness, his generosity, and his reverence (he thanks the slain animal) make him an appropriate leader. Taylor's oil paintings evoke both the physical landscape and the spiritual dimensions of the tale.

The Secret of the White Buffalo: An Oglala Legend is a retelling of the account of the origin of the sacred rites of the Sioux people. When starvation threatens a quarrelling tribe, a worthy hunter, who has acted with respect to a buffalo that had transformed itself into a woman, is given instructions for the building of a sacred tipi. Because the village agrees to work co-operatively, it is visited by Buffalo Woman who gives the sacred pipe and the rituals that are practised to this day. Like *The Ghost and Lone Warrior*, this myth reflects the deep spirituality of the hunting cultures of the northern Plains and the belief that success in the hunt depends as much, if not more, on the goodness of the hunter as on his technical skills. In the illustrations, the vastness of the Prairies, with their overarching blue skies, is the realistic backdrop against which this mythic drama is enacted. The brilliance of the woman's white dress, the shadowy presence of a white buffalo in the background, and the lines of power radiating from her dominate the picture of her encounter with the hunter. Later, as she lays her gift before the chiefs, light from the smoke hole shines down on her. As she returns to her animal form, her white garments blend with the buffalo's hide and luminous vapours arise from the grasses. As the illustrations reveal, a union among the human, natural, and supernatural spheres has been achieved.

The Messenger of Spring is an adaptation of the Ojibway *pourquoi* myth about the changing of the seasons. A young man, arriving at the wigwam of an old man, listens to the tale of the power of winter and then performs a dance and song that bring spring back to the land. Unlike many Native seasonal myths, Taylor's rendering of this story emphasizes friendship and balance. The two men do not quarrel or fight; each accepts his role. Taylor's illustrations illustrate this friendship and the gradual shift from winter to spring. The opening picture balances the two characters and the colours of the seasons they represent. As Winter tells the story of his rule, blues and whites dominate, and he is the largest figure on the page. However, his size diminishes with the arrival of the

Messenger of Spring, who becomes larger in the increasingly brighter, more colourful pictures. In the final illustration, he smiles from the sky at the human beings gathering the bounty he has provided.

Taylor has also published three thematic collections of short tales from a variety of Native cultures. Each of the stories is illustrated with a full-page picture that depicts a central episode and indicates the relationships among the human, natural, and spiritual worlds. The nine tales in *How We Saw the World* are designed to reinforce the need to show 'love and respect for our Mother Earth'. *Bones in the Basket: Native Stories of the Origin of People* continues the theme, stating in the preface, 'All see the earth as a gift given to us, prepared for us ahead of our arrival.' *The Monster from the Swamp: Native Legends of Monsters, Demons, and Other Creatures* focuses on beings who use their size and power to hurt or kill people, thus upsetting the balance of the world. The heroes in each story are brave individuals who selflessly risk themselves to help others.

Although C.J. Taylor's stories come from a variety of Native cultures, each of which the author has carefully researched, a common theme underlies each: the need for human beings to live in balance and harmony with the rest of creation. They teach, as she has said, 'the value of life, of the Earth, of the individual'. This is seen particularly in her treatment of women: while the active, physical roles are usually taken by men, females, both natural and supernatural, have profound influences on events. This is as it should be for a writer who emphasizes our responsibility to 'our Mother the Earth'. Her paintings, in acrylic, pencil, watercolour, and oil, reflect not only her deep reverence for the numinous aspects of the world, but also for the spirituality inherent in the stories she tells and in traditional Native life.

See also: *WSMP*.

Cora Taylor

Born: 14 January 1936, in Fort Qu'Appelle, Sask.

Principal Residences: Carlton, Sask.; Edmonton; Winterburn, Alta.

Education: University of Alberta (BA 1973).

Career: medical secretary; teacher; writer.

Major Awards: Canada Council Children's Literature Prize (1985); Canadian Library Association Book of the Year for Children (1986, 1995); Ruth Schwartz Children's Book Award (1988).

Works for Children

Julie (Saskatoon: Western Producer Prairie Books, 1985). **Rev:** *BiC* 14 (Nov. 1985):

36; *CCL* 44 (1986): 75; *CM* 14 (Mar. 1986): 66; *EL* 14 (Mar. 1987): 27; *HB* 62 (Sept. 1986): 628; *QQ* 51 (Oct. 1985): 16.

The Doll (Saskatoon: Western Producer Prairie Books, 1987). **Rev:** *BiC* 16 (Dec. 1987): 11; *BYP* 1 (Aug. 1987): 11; *CCL* 52 (1988): 76; *CM* 16 (Mar. 1988): 48; *EL* 15 (May 1988): 55; *HB* 64 (May 1988): 391.

Julie's Secret (Saskatoon: Western Producer Prairie Books, 1991). **Rev:** *CCL* 66 (1992): 91; *CM* 19 (Sept. 1991): 240; *EL* 19 (Mar. 1992): 18; *QQ* 57 (Apr. 1991): 18; *RT* 45 (Apr. 1992): 640.

Ghost Voyages (Richmond Hill, Ont.: Scholastic, 1992). **Rev:** *CCL* 76 (1984): 60; *CM* 20 (May 1992): 153; *QQ* 58 (Apr. 1992): 32.

Summer of the Mad Monk (Toronto: Groundwood, 1994). **Rev:** *CBRA* (1994): 503; *QQ* 61 (Jan. 1995): 41.

Vanishing Act (Red Deer, Alta: Red Deer College Press, 1997). **Rev:** *CM* 4 (13 Mar. 1998): on-line.

Other

'I'd Like to Thank . . .', *School Libraries in Canada* 15 (Summer 1995): 9–11.

Selected Discussions

Jenkinson, Dave. 'Profile: Cora Taylor—Teacher, Student, Playwright, Author of *Julie*', *EL* 14 (Mar. 1987): 51, 53–6.

'I'd written a short story for my creative writing class at the University of Alberta', Cora Taylor remembered. 'During a roundtable discussion, I began to see that I had too complex a theme and more characters than I could handle in a short story. Over a period of years, it evolved into my first novel, *Julie*.' This first novel had its roots in her own childhood on the Prairies. But it wasn't until her husband gave her a copy of *Who Has Seen the Wind*, by W.O. Mitchell, that she first came into contact with an author whose work was to influence her writing profoundly and from whom, in the 1970s, she was to take a creative writing course.

'Julie had been different from the beginning.' This statement, early in Chapter One, expresses both the character of the title heroine and her central conflict. Julie Morgan is a seer. At an early age, she amazes her family with the involved stories she tells, her unusual sensitivity to nature, and her ability to discuss scenes that happened long before she was born. Warned by her mother that she must distinguish between the real and the imaginary and partially rejected by her brothers and sister, Julie is forced to face her special talents by Granny Goderich, an aging family friend who also has psychic powers. At her deathbed, the old woman tells the girl, 'That's how it is with us, Julie. We're not sure what to do. . . . we're afraid. We don't know what to do and so we do nothing, nothing at all. Sometimes that's right, there's nothing we can do, sometimes . . . there comes a time when we have to act. . . . You have to decide and that's when the gift can be terrible.' Although Julie tries very hard to be normal at school, she cannot deny her powers; and when she sees an Egyptian Ship of the Dead sailing in the clouds above the farm, she realizes that her father is in grave danger and then courageously saves him. She accepts her differences, along with the joys and the tremendous burden of responsibilities these will give her.

Like Mitchell's *Who Has Seen the Wind*, *Julie* is more than a prairie novel. Although, like Mitchell's novel, it captures a sense of the mystic powers of the prairie skies and lands, it uses this sense to reinforce its theme: the great difficulties faced by the individual who is different because of special powers. The work is also about 'sisterhood', for, although Julie feels closest to her father, the most intricate relationships are between the female characters. Julie has been visited in dreams by her paternal grandmother, a woman who was also reputed to have had special powers; at school, the librarian, Miss Johnson, encourages the girl to read special books; Granny Goderich is the wise old woman leading her into her role.

Julie's Secret traces the heroine's life from shortly after her rescue of her father to the end of the following summer. Trapped with her sister in an abandoned barn during a late spring snowstorm, she discovers, to her distress, that she still possesses her powers. In the barn, she feels the presence of evil, has visions of a fire and an upside-down cross, and hears screaming. Later, she is able to help police discover the skeleton of a long-buried murder victim. When her brother Billy is captured by cultists who plan to make him a ritual sacrifice, Julie's visions lead to his rescue. While the sequel is more dramatic than the first book and relies more heavily on plot, it nonetheless continues the perceptive analysis of the title heroine that had made *Julie* such a strong work. She must confront her difference once again, accept her powers, and use them to save others. Yet she fears that, should others learn of her secret, she will be more lonely and isolated than she is. Gifted with extraordinary abilities, she will never be able to experience the happiness of ordinary people.

Two of Taylor's novels, *The Doll* and *Ghost Voyages*, are time-shift fantasies. In the former, a 10-year-old contemporary urban girl is transported into the nineteenth century, where she becomes one of her ancestors; in the latter, a boy is able to transport himself onto the old ships depicted on stamps that had been part of his grandfather's collection. When she began to write *The Doll*, Taylor had not been consciously trying to write within the form, but, instead, felt that she was dealing with reincarnation, given the fact that Meg was and, in her time-shifts backward becomes, Morag, who had died in her childhood. Sent to her grandmother's farm to recover from rheumatic fever and to allow her parents to settle their divorce, Meg falls asleep clutching an old doll rumoured to have healing powers and awakens on a Red River cart as Morag, the ill daughter of a pioneer family travelling to Fort Carleton, Saskatchewan. As she defines her role in the nineteenth-century family, she is able to come to terms with the conflicts of her modern life. Significantly, she is a preserver of life, helping to bring a newborn calf back to the family camp and rescuing her little sister from a prairie fire. Unlike Julie, Meg is an ordinary child who finds herself in extraordinary circumstances and rises to the occasion. Having discovered the meaning of her family's past and her links to and role in it, she will be able to face her future in a single-parent family.

Jeremy, the 10-year-old hero of *Ghost Voyages*, is also an ordinary child and a member of a single-parent family. When he looks at the stamps through a magnifying glass, he finds himself on the various ships. However, he is invisible; while Meg becomes a person from the past, he does not. But like her, he has an influence on it, saving what turns out to be an ancestor from a bullet fired on the ship during the Riel uprising of the nineteenth century. This novel does not have the complexity of character development of *The Doll*, but does present the theme of a young person's defining himself through coming to understand earlier generations of his family.

Summer of the Mad Monk is set in rural Alberta during the Dust Bowl era of the 1930s. It focuses on the difficult struggles of 12-year-old Pip as he deals with the inhospitable landscape and the tough moral decisions he must make in his relationships with his family and with other children and adults, some of whom are evil. Based, in part, on the boyhood experiences of her husband, the novel is a tribute to young people's ability, in times of great difficulty, to hope and dream: 'Having a dream is simply having hope and having the imagination to make it something of your own', the young hero muses. With the family farm failing, his mother in a state of depression, and his father displeased with him for having taken an old gun without permission, Pip finds hope in fantasizing that the village's foreign blacksmith is Rasputin, the pre-Revolutionary Russian leader, and that his injured friend is the son of the Tsar. As he learns the less glorious but equally important reality about the two, Pip also comes to a greater understanding of these two men, his parents, and even the town bully, who is fatally injured by a gun he has stolen. Focusing on the relationships between the 12-year-old boy, his father, and the two other men, this work marks a significant departure for the author. Placing its character on the edge of adolescence, emphasizing his character development in relation to his future adult life, also marks a shift in focus. It is also completely within the bounds of realistic historical fiction, capturing precisely and concretely the physical, emotional, and social climate of rural Alberta of the 1930s.

In *Vanishing Act*, Taylor combines the fantasy convention of a spell of invisibility with elements of the spy thriller to tell the story of identical twins' search for their missing father. Thirteen-year-old Maggie and Jennifer are similar in looks only. The former is a calm and orderly person; the latter is impulsive and messy. When Jennifer learns how to control the spell of invisibility discovered in a library book, she uses the power to help find her father, an airline pilot who has been captured by Middle Eastern terrorists. While the novel presents an interesting study of the contrasting and often conflicting personalities of the girls, the plot, with its complications, surprises, and cliff-hanging chapter endings, is elaborate to the point of confusion. The idea of invisibility, which might have been developed as a symbol of Jennifer's character development, remains a gimmicky plot device and, sometimes, a source of forced humour.

Of her works, Taylor has remarked, 'My novels are all character driven.' The central characters try to define themselves in the face of major problems within themselves and surrounding them: Julie's awareness of her difference; Meg's dealing with her parents' divorce and the dangers of the past; Pip, helping a morally stern, but loving father and a shattered mother; the twins' search for a dearly loved father. Some of the conflicts involve the children and their parents. The children feel separated and, as a result, the security and continuity of their lives is threatened. It is through the contact with older people that they are able to establish links with family history and, with awareness of their pasts, to establish new relationships within their families. Even in *Summer of the Mad Monk*, which does not deal with direct links to a family past, Pip, by understanding the true rather than imagined pasts of the mysterious foreigners in his town, can better deal with the difficult realities of his family life.

In addition to her skilful portrayal of her protagonists' difficult inner lives, Cora Taylor creates a strong impression of the prairie landscapes and cultures, past and present, in which her stories take place. From her grandmother came her awareness of the lives of nineteenth-century settlers depicted in *The Doll*, and from her husband, understanding of the struggles and hopes of those living in the Depression. She also draws on her own childhood memories of growing up in rural Saskatchewan. The historical and physical landscapes she creates are more than just backdrops; they are forces that influence the lives of the characters. Writing about conflicts of childhood that may be common to children of many times and places, she roots them in particularities of time and space, creating novels of wide appeal that are also specifically of the Canadian Prairies.

See also: *CA* 124; *SATA* 64; *TCCW*; *WSMP*.

Mark Thurman

Born: 27 September 1948, in Toronto.

Principal Residences: Toronto.

Education: Central Technical School, Toronto (1966).

Career: designer and sign letterer; animation painter; designer and illustrator; comic strip designer and artist; teacher; writer; book illustrator.

Works for Children

Written and Illustrated by Mark Thurman

The Elephant's Cold (Toronto: NC Press, 1979; rev. 1981). **Rev:** *CCL* 17 (1980): 73; *IR* 14 (June 1980): 60; *QQ* 48 (May 1982): 39.

The Elephant's New Bicycle (Toronto: NC Press, 1980; rev. 1985). **Rev:** *CCL* 22 (1981): 43; *IR* 15 (Apr. 1981): 54; *QQ* 47 (Apr. 1981): 34; *QQ* 48 (May 1982): 39.

The Birthday Party (Toronto: NC Press, 1981; rev. 1985). **Rev:** *BiC* 10 (Dec. 1981): 3; *CCL* 25 (1982): 51; *IR* 15 (Oct. 1981): 55; *QQ* 48 (May 1982): 39.

The Lie that Grew and Grew (Toronto: NC Press, 1981; rev. 1985). **Rev:** *APBR* 10 (Nov. 1983): 15; *BiC* 10 (Dec. 1981): 3; *CCL* 25 (1982): 51; *QQ* 8 (May 1982): 39.

Mighty Mites in Dinosaurland, with Emily Hearn, illus. Mark Thurman (Toronto: Greey de Pencier, 1981).

Who Needs Me? (Toronto: NC Press, 1981).

Two Pals on an Adventure (Toronto: NC Press, 1982; rev. as *Two Pals*, 1985).

City Scrapes (Toronto: NC Press, 1983; rev. 1985).

You Bug Me (Toronto: NC Press, 1984; 2nd edn 1985). **Rev:** *QQ* 51 (Feb. 1985): 17.

Old Friends and New Friends (Toronto: NC Press, 1985).

Two Stupid Dummies (Toronto: NC Press, 1986). **Rev:** *BiC* 16 (Mar. 1987): 39.

Cabbage Town Gang (Toronto: NC Press, 1987). **Rev:** *BiC* 16 (Mar. 1987): 38.

Some Sumo (Toronto: NC Press, 1988). **Rev:** *EL* 17 (Jan. 1990): 53.

One Two Many (Toronto: Penguin, 1993). **Rev:** *CCL* 86 (1997): 65; *QQ* 59 (Oct. 1993): 39.

Illustrated by Mark Thurman

Belinda's Ball, by Joan Bodger (Toronto: Oxford UP, 1981). **Rev:** *CCL* 25 (1982): 51; *IR* 16 (Feb. 1982): 30; *QQ* 48 (Feb. 1982): 36; *SLJ* 29 (Sept. 1982): 104.

Good Morning Franny, Good Night Franny, by Emily Hearn (Toronto: Women's Educational Press, 1984). **Rev:** *BiC* 13 (Dec. 1984): 11; *EL* 12 (Jan. 1982): 45; *QQ* 50 (1984): 13.

Race You Franny!, by Emily Hearn (Toronto: Women's Educational Press, 1986).

Franny and the Music Girl, by Emily Hearn (Toronto: Second Story Press, 1989). **Rev:** *CCL* 59 (1990): 105; *CM* 18 (Mar. 1990): 64; *EL* 17 (Mar. 1990): 60; *QQ* 56 (Feb. 1990): 14.

Primary Rhymerry, by Sonja Dunn (Markham, Ont.: Pembroke, 1993). **Rev:** *CCL* 75 (1994): 55.

I Want To Lasso Time, by George Swede (Toronto: Simon and Pierre, 1991). **Rev:** *CCL* 67 (1992): 97; *CM* 20 (May 1992): 163.

Cookie Magic, by Geraldine Mabin and Lynn Seligman (Toronto: Oxford UP, 1994). **Rev:** *BiC* 23 (May 1994): 58; *QQ* 60 (Mar. 1994): 80.

Gimme a Break, Rattlesnake!: Schoolyard Chants and Other Nonsense, by Sonja Dunn (Don Mills, Ont.: Stoddart, 1994). **Rev:** *QQ* 60 (Dec. 1994): 35.

Fearless Jake, by Margaret Haffner (Richmond Hill, Ont.: North Winds, 1995). **Rev:** *CCL* 86 (1997): 65.

Ivan and the All-Stars, by Kathleen Cook Waldron (Toronto: Boardwalk Books, 1995). **Rev:** *QQ* 61 (Sept. 1995): 73.

Other

Draw and Write Your Own Picture Book, with Emily Hearn (Markham, Ont.: Pembroke, 1990). **Rev:** *CCL* 60 (1990): 128; *QQ* 56 (July 1990): 38.

Helping Kids Draw and Write Picture Books, with Emily Hearn (Markham, Ont.: Pembroke, 1990).

Illustration Ideas for Creating Picture Books, with Emily Hearn (Markham, Ont.: Pembroke, 1990).

Fun-Tastic Collages (Markham, Ont.: Pembroke, 1992). **Rev:** *QQ* 58 (Sept. 1992): 70.

How to Plan Your Drawings (Markham, Ont.: Pembroke, 1992).

Any sketch of Mark Thurman would probably have to be subtitled 'A Portrait of the Artist as Educator'. Thurman has taught weekly classes at the Toronto School of Art and conducted workshops for elementary school students in which he demonstrated how they can express their ideas and feelings through drawings. Outgrowths of these workshops are the three books on writing and illustrating picture books that he and Emily Hearn have produced. *Draw and Write Your Own Picture Book*, *Helping Kids Draw and Write Picture Books*, and *Illustration Ideas for Creating Picture Books* are practical guides that offer concise advice on everything from storyboarding to the use of perspective in picture books.

Thurman is probably best known for his work on the 154 instalments of *Owl* magazine's 'Mighty Mites' series, which was designed to make natural science interesting to children. Together with Emily Hearn, who wrote the text, Thurman researched the topics, then devised the adventures of three children who can shrink to explore many facets of the natural world. Thurman illustrated these adventures in the comic-book style of pen-and-ink panels. In *Mighty Mites in Dinosaurland*, a similar book-length adventure, the children visit Alberta's Badlands, where they go back in time and learn about the dinosaurs that once roamed the region.

The Mighty Mites opened the door for Thurman to illustrate other educational books. Joan Bodger's *Belinda's Ball* is designed to teach Piaget's concept of object constancy in space, and Thurman's illustrations support the idea that the ball continues to exist even when Belinda cannot see it, either by picturing it in a cartoon-like 'thought bubble' or by placing it where the reader, unlike Belinda, can clearly see it. Thurman has also illustrated Emily Hearn's *Good Morning*

Franny, Good Night Franny and *Race You Franny*, books teaching children about the humanity of the physically disabled. His paper-cutout illustrations for the first of these are particularly clever in their use of perspective. It is only in the fourth picture that readers get a sign that Franny is in a wheelchair, allowing children to develop an identification with her before they realize that she is disabled. The fifth drawing, showing the world from Franny's viewpoint, intensifies this identification.

The books that Thurman has written and illustrated himself show a similar concern for instruction. *Who Needs Me?* is designed to teach children about interdependency. A simple concept book, it invites them to make up sentences showing relationships and to colour the line drawings. Far more substantial are Thurman's animal-tale picture books for children aged three to eight. Both the 'Douglas the Elephant' series (*The Elephant's Cold*, *The Elephant's New Bicycle*, *The Lie that Grew and Grew*, and *The Birthday Party*) and the 'Two Pals on an Adventure' series (*Two Pals on an Adventure*, revised as *Two Pals*, *City Scrapes*, *You Bug Me*, *Old Friends and New Friends*, *Two Stupid Dummies*, and *Some Sumo*) use simple stories to teach children such concepts as sharing, accepting disappointments, and learning to believe in oneself even when people say mean things. In *The Elephant's New Bicycle*, for example, Douglas the Elephant at first refuses to let anyone ride on the bicycle he received for his birthday, but he eventually realizes that sharing increases fun. In *The Lie that Grew and Grew*, Douglas seeks attention by bragging about his brave deeds but then shows genuine courage by confessing that he has lied. In *Some Sumo*, which is basically a travelogue teaching children about Japanese life and customs (it includes instructive illustrations for two origami projects), Douglas learns the folly of judging people by their appearance. Having met the gigantic Sumo-San, Douglas has nightmares in which he and Albert encounter Sumo-San in the sumo ring. The next day, however, Douglas is relieved to learn that Sumo-San is a champion at origami, at folding paper, not people. Thurman has revised titles in both series to make the morals slightly less awkward and heavy-handed. Thurman illustrates these gentle and often amusing tales in vibrant watercolours. To keep the focus on the antics of the characters, he frequently omits the backgrounds. At other times, he adds details designed to amuse adults: in *Two Stupid Dummies*, for example, Doctor Zighound Froid the Fourth reads a book entitled *Id Did It*.

In addition to his animal picture books, Thurman has produced a complex symbolic picture book employing a fairy-tale quest pattern. In *One Two Many*, the unhappy Jan believes that no one understands him. Staring into his reflection in the river, a symbolic act of self-contemplation, he foolishly wishes that there were someone just like him. Magically, a second Jan emerges from the water. Because each claims ownership of Jan's possessions, they soon begin fighting. The Keeper of the Keys, an archetypal wise woman, tells them that Jan can become one again only if his two selves undergo a perilous journey to the cove of the Double Isle. Co-operating and using three objects given to them, the two Jans get to the centre of the cave, a journey symbolizing a descent into the psyche, where they answer a riddle that unites them. The tale ends with the suggestion that Jan has dreamed the entire adventure, a suggestion amplified by the fact that a dream-like rosy hue dominates Thurman's pencil drawings. Unfortunately, in spite of its symbolic potential as a story about achieving psychological integrity, it is not thematically satisfying because the final liberating riddle lacks a connection to concepts about accepting both self and differences.

Thurman has written one longer work, *Cabbage Town Gang*, an illustrated, partly autobiographical novel about growing up in a housing project in the 1960s. Slow-paced and with too many trivial episodes receiving belaboured attention, its best moment is a tense scene in which the hero decides not to cheat on a test.

Thurman is unapologetically didactic, describing himself as 'a philosopher who paints'. His moralizing is sometimes heavy-handed and simplistic, but his animal tales bring an amusing light to bear on the problems that all young children encounter.

See also: *CA* 131; *SATA* 63; *WSMP*.

Gilles Tibo

Born: 18 July 1951, in Nicolet, Que.

Principal Residences: Longueuil, Que.; Montreal.

Education: Self-taught artist.

Career: author and illustrator.

Major Awards: The Owl Prize, Japan (1989, for *Simon and the Snowflakes*); Governor-General's Literary Award for illustration in a French book (1992, for *Simon et la ville de carton*, trans. as *Simon and His Boxes*); Governor-General's Literary Award for best French text (1996, for *Le Secret de Madame Lumbago*).

English Language Works for Children

Written and Illustrated by Gilles Tibo

Simon and the Snowflakes (Montreal: Tundra, 1988). **Rev:** *APBR* 15 (Nov. 1988): 9; *BiC* 17 (Dec. 1988): 12; *BYP* 2 (Dec. 1988): 8; *CBRA* (1988): 311; *CCL* 61 (1991): 96; *CM* 17 (Mar. 1989): 89; *Maclean's* 101 (26 Dec. 1988): 60; *SLJ* 35 (Apr. 1989): 92.

Simon and the Wind (Montreal: Tundra, 1989). **Rev:** *APBR* 15 (Nov. 1989): 12; *CBRA* (1989): 311; *CCL* 60 (1990): 138; *CM* 18 (Mar. 1990): 68; *EL* 17 Mar. 1990): 23.

Simon Welcomes Spring (Montreal: Tundra, 1990). **Rev:** *CBRA* (1990): 309; *CM* 19 (Jan. 1991): 31; *EL* 18 (Mar. 1991): 24; *QQ* 56 (Nov. 1990): 12.

Simon in Summer (Montreal: Tundra, 1991). **Rev:** *BiC* 20 (Sept. 1991): 52; *CCL* 66 (1992): 94; *CM* 19 (Sept. 1991): 233; *EL* 19 (Mar. 1992): 15; *QQ* 57 (June 1991): 25.

The King of Sleep, trans. Sheila Fischman (Toronto: Doubleday Canada, 1991). **Rev:** *BiC* 21 (Mar. 1992): 50; *CM* 20 (May 1992): 162; *EL* 19 (Mar. 1992): 58; *QQ* 57 (Oct. 1991): 36.

Santa Takes a Tumble, trans. Sheila Fischman (Toronto: Doubleday Canada, 1991). **Rev:** *BiC* 21 (Mar. 1992): 50; *CM* 20 (May 1992): 162; *EL* 19 (Mar. 1992) 58; *QQ* 57 (Oct. 1991): 36.

Mr. Clark's Summer Holiday, trans. Sheila Fischman (Toronto: Doubleday Canada, 1991). **Rev:** *CBRA* (1992): 309; *EL* 19 (Mar. 1992): 58; *QQ* 58 (Aug. 1992): 28.

Simon and His Boxes (Montreal: Tundra, 1992). **Rev:** *CBRA* (1992): 309; *CM* 20 (Nov. 1992): 309; *QQ* 58 (Oct. 1992): 33; *SLJ* 39 (Mar. 1993): 187.

Simon in the Moonlight (Montreal: Tundra, 1993). **Rev:** *CBRA* (1993): #6088; *CM* 22 (Mar. 1994): 50; *EL* 21 (Mar. 1994): 16; *QQ* 59 (Oct. 1993): 40.

Mr. Patapoum's First Trip, with François Vaillancourt (Willowdale, Ont.: Annick, 1993). **Rev:** *CBRA* (1993): #6087; *CCL* 78 (1995): 79; *CM* 21(Oct. 1993): 189; *QQ* 59 (Aug. 1993): 36.

Simon Finds a Feather (Montreal: Tundra, 1994). **Rev:** *CBRA* (1994): 468; *EL* 22 (Mar. 1995); *QQ* 60 (Oct. 1994): 44; *SL* 43 (May 1995): 60.

Simon Makes Music (Montreal: Tundra, 1995). **Rev:** *CBRA* (1995): 488; *CCL* 88 (1997) 84; *QQ* 61 (Nov. 1995): 46.

Simon Finds a Treasure (Toronto: Tundra, 1996). **Rev:** *BiC* 26 (May 1997): 33; *CBRA* (1996): 458.

Simon at the Circus, trans. Sheila Fischman (Toronto: Tundra, 1997). **Rev:** *CBRA* (1997): 492.

Illustrated by Gilles Tibo

Annabel Lee: The Poem, by Edgar Allan Poe (Montreal: Tundra, 1987). *APBR* 14 (Nov. 1987): 3; *BiC* 16 (Nov. 1987): 37; *BYP* 1 (Oct. 1987): 18; *CCL* 52 (1988): 56; *CM* 16 (May 1988): 101; *EL* 16 (Mar. 1989): 22; *SLJ* 34 (Dec. 1987): 108.

Giant; or, Waiting for the Thursday Boat, by Robert Munsch (Toronto: Annick, 1989). **Rev:** *BiC* 19 (June 1990): 15, and 20 (Oct. 1991): 26; *CBRA* (1989): 303; *CCL* 61 (1991): 104; *CM* 18 (Mar. 1990): 67; *QQ* 56 (Jan. 1990): 17.

The Beast, by Alice Bartels (Willowdale, Ont.: Annick, 1990). **Rev:** *CCL* 63 (1991): 83; *CM* 18 (July 1990): 177; *QQ* 56 (July 1990): 36.

Paper Nights, with Pierre Filion (Willowdale, Ont.: Annick, 1992). **Rev:** *CBRA* (1992): 310; *CCL* 75 (1994): 81; *EL* 20 (May 1993): 50; *QQ* 58 (Oct. 1992): 38.

The Magic Powder, by Jean-Pierre Guillet, trans. Sheila Fischman (Waterloo, Que.: Quintin Publishers, 1992). **Rev:** *CM* 21 (Jan. 1993): 18; *QQ* 58 (Dec. 1992): 28.

Castle Chaos, by Jean-Pierre Guillet, trans. Frances Morgan (Waterloo, Que.: Quintin Publishers, 1993). **Rev:** *CM* 21 (Nov. 1993): 217; *QQ* 59 (Oct. 1993): 37.

The Bubble Machine, by Jean-Pierre Guillet, trans. Frances Morgan (Waterloo, Que.: Quintin Publishers, 1994). **Rev:** *CBRA* (1994) 453; *CCL* 81 (1996): 50; *QQ* 60 (Dec. 1994): 35.

Pikolo's Night Voyage, by Pierre Filion (Willowdale, Ont.: Annick, 1994). **Rev:** *CBRA* (1994): 450; *CCL* 81 (1996): 50; *CM* 22 (Oct. 1994): 184; *QQ* 60 (Sept. 1994): 73.

Selected Discussions

Sybesma, Jetske. 'Illustrated Children's Books as Art: The Art of the Lobster Quadrille', *CCL* 60 (1990): 8–24.

An avid reader of comics when he was a child, Gilles Tibo was always interested in drawing, and he was determined to make his own books. Even so, it is remarkable that he published his first book, a 40-page black-and-white comic, in 1970, when he was only 18. He then went on to produce numerous drawings and daily cartoon strips for magazines and newspapers throughout Quebec. In 1975 he collaborated on his first book for children. Nevertheless, English-language readers did not become aware of his remarkable talent until 1987, when he produced an illustrated version of Poe's *Annabel Lee* that was nominated for the Governor-General's Award for Illustration. Since that time, Tibo has published French and English versions of many of his books, earning the admiration of readers across Canada. As an illustrator, he is known particularly for his deft manipulation of light. As an author, he likes to blend reality and imagination, producing a world that he describes as 'something like the world inhabited by children when they play'. His dominant themes celebrate the joy of friendship and the glory of nature.

Tibo has said that 'light is the most important part of my illustration.' Working with an airbrush and transparent ink, he can blend shades smoothly into each other, giving his pictures depth and variations in lighting that suggest mood. To add solidity to his pictures and to define their details, Tibo completes them with pencil crayons. The technique is central to *Annabel Lee*. The pictures begin with a bright and airy spring scene, one that, although it pictures the Gaspé coast, seems nearly pastoral in its idyllic evocation of natural beauty and human love. As the mood becomes sombre with the illness and death of Annabel Lee, Tibo darkens the pictures, suppressing many of the background details. He adds a supernatural aura by eliminating some foreground details: the ship that carries away the girl's body, for instance, is entirely white, only the subtlest shading giving it dimensionality. Tibo's handling of the people is similarly notable. Although the faces of the lovers at first may seem cartoonish because their features are simply circles and lines drawn with pencil, the technique establishes the childlike innocence of the young lovers; like the masks in some forms of drama, these stylized faces also universalize the lovers. Tibo heightens the reader's identification with the sorrowing male in the later drawings by positioning him in such a way that his face does not show at all.

In Tibo's most popular series, his books about an inquisitive little boy named Simon, the pictures complement a simple text. The elaborate backgrounds and glowing textures make the world of the round-faced Simon magical. The stories in the Simon books follow a quest pattern: Simon seeks either a physical object or the answer to a question. During his quest, he also seeks advice, questioning various adult surrogates. Because these surrogates are inanimate objects (a snowman, a scarecrow), elements of nature (the moon, the sun), animals (a rabbit, a cow), archetypal humans (a miner), or supernatural agents (a ghost), the text complements the pictures in transforming Simon's world from the mundane to the magical world of fairy tales. Although Simon does not always succeed in the way he intended, he is always satisfied. Part of the satisfaction comes because Simon, who always begins alone, ends up with at least one friend, a movement that suggests that friendship is the real magic of life.

The first four Simon books focus on the seasons. *Simon and the Snowflakes*, the first and possibly the best in the series, is set in winter. It begins, as do Paulette Bourgeois's Franklin books, with a statement of ability and then a statement of failure. In this case, Simon, who loves to count, finds that he cannot count the snowflakes. He tries various ingenious methods, such as counting the flakes on a bird and then counting all the birds, but he simply cannot count everything. He then seeks wisdom from both elements in his world, a snowman and the moon, but the 'easy' solutions they suggest do not work for him. Finally, Simon realizes that the world contains many things that he cannot count, but that it also contains things that he can. The text here is hollow, but the accompanying picture fills it with meaning. It illustrates this moment of understanding by showing Simon in the forest surrounded by animals, friends, and decorated trees. Constructed like an oral tale in that it is aggregative instead of analytical, the understated text of *Simon and the Snowflakes* suggests to children that, although many things are beyond their comprehension and their control, the world is still full of wonderful things that they can understand and that they can count on.

Simon Welcomes Spring also subtly explores a child's sense of his powers and place in the world. Simon loves spring so much that he tries to make it come: he ties balloons to sprouts, for example, to help them grow into the flowers because he has been told that flowers bring spring. All of his efforts fail, but when spring does come on its own, Simon joins his friends in ecstatically welcoming it. He thus sees that he may not have the power to control the environment, but that he can enjoy with others what nature gives. Simon also finds compensation for his limitations in *Simon and the Wind*, a book about his love of the autumn wind. Although he cannot learn to fly himself, Simon happily realizes that he and his friends can make kites fly. In *Simon in Summer*, Simon learns about the inevitable passage of time because he fails to make summer stay. As with the other seasonal stories, he finds compensation: he knows that with the end of summer his friends will return. The final picture shows Simon and his friends celebrating each other's company by playing in the moonlight with balls that mysteriously glow like lanterns. The fifth book, *Simon in the Moonlight*, continues his lesson about the passage of time through a 'mystery' of nature. In this case, Simon learns that although the moon gets smaller and although he cannot find its missing pieces, the moon will inevitably grow bigger in time. Again, he moves from lonely curiosity to communal joy: he and his friends celebrate the coming of the full moon by releasing hundreds of bright balloons into the sky.

The Simon books also present several other themes. Two express ecological lessons. In *Simon and His Boxes*, Simon tries to get a number of animals to make their homes in his cardboard boxes. Although he fails to provide homes for citizens of nature, he learns that he and his friends can do something worthwhile: they pick up litter and put it in the boxes. In *Simon Finds a Feather*, Simon's quest to find the owner of a missing red feather leads to the discovery of a cardinal with a broken wing. He and the companion of most of his adventures, Marlene, nurse the cardinal to health, and then all of their friends celebrate its departure. Two of the weaker titles in the series, both of which use awkward rhyming couplets, make overt the theme of friendship that is implicit in all the other titles. In *Simon Makes Music*, Simon fails to get the animals to pay attention to him when he plays various instruments. When he joins together with his friends, however, their music becomes so enchanting that the birds join in a chorus. In *Simon Finds a Treasure*, Simon begins searching for a mysterious treasure. Each person he encounters has a different idea of what a treasure is, but when Simon gets lost and his friends find him, he realizes that friendship is the only meaningful treasure. As laudable as the sentiment is, the story is mechanical; furthermore, a ghost, which is the last of the advisers Simon consults, claims so anti-climactically that bats are a treasure that the tale loses the magical quality of fairy-tale quest. Finally, in a much more satisfying book, *Simon at the Circus*, Tibo celebrates the strength of imagination. When Simon tries to get the goats and pigs to play circus with him, he ends up smashing the boxes and umbrella that make up his circus. After imagining himself as a successful circus performer, Simon makes his dreams come alive by gathering with his friends to cut out a new circus and animals from paper and cardboard.

The other books that Tibo has both written and illustrated contain interesting, nearly three-dimensional cartoons, but they are inferior to the Simon series because their humour is decidedly forced and their plots are more elaborate than meaningful. *The King of Sleep* is a futuristic fairy tale about King Roger 37, so-called because of his habit of sleeping 37 days straight. While sleeping, King Roger is repeatedly disturbed by a sheep. (The pictures, but not the words, indicate that the sheep is pink; obviously the colour supplements other absurdities in the story, but whether this colour is also supposed to indicate that the sheep is a dream creature is never clear.) In order to get peace, Roger gives his crown to the sheep, which thus becomes king and forces Roger to wait on him. Eventually, both sheep and Roger fall asleep, but Roger alone wakens when a spaceship of multicoloured children arrive for a picnic. This elaborate story simply fails to cohere. A similar point can be made about several other books. In *Mr. Clark's Summer Holiday* a zoo keeper, tired of taking the same vacation every year is pleasantly surprised when many of his animals join him at the seaside. Unfortunately, the plot continues with an unnecessary automobile crash and concludes in an open ended, anti-climactic fashion: Mr Clark thinks about the travels of the one animal who has not returned from vacation. *Santa Takes a Tumble* tries to suggest that Santa may be anyone and may be living anywhere by telling an elaborate tale about Santa falling from his sleigh because he can't control his mechanical reindeer. Santa lands in a city, where his coat is stolen; because hundreds of people are dressed in Santa suits, he is unable to convince people of his identity, so he supports himself at various trades. The idea of the skilled craftsperson and the kind citizen being Santa is noble, but the plot is so haphazard that the story lacks Christmas magic.

In collaboration with others, Tibo has produced slightly more successful quest tales. *Mr. Patapoum's First Trip* is notable primarily because he and François Vaillancourt illustrated the tale with photographs of figures constructed of modelling clay and posed in miniature three-dimensional settings. The tale itself is a cumulative journey story that, like the Simon books, takes its central character from solitary isolation to communal joy. Mr Patapoum, a pig with a talent for building things, decides to take a stranded duckling south to its parents. Along the way, he asks directions of various animals, all of whom join the journey. With each meeting Mr Patapoum also constructs a slightly more elaborate mode of transportation, finally cobbling together a plane that flies the friends to a southern beach. The two Pikolo books, *Paper Nights* and *Pikolo's Night Voyage*, written by Pierre Filion from ideas devised by Tibo, treat another kind of journey, a child's dream adventures. In both a little boy named Pikolo enters a dream world by going into his closet. In *Paper Nights*, Pikolo, who has been cutting out paper animals and a paper man at bedtime, follows a paper man named Max through the closet and into a world entirely made of paper. Pikolo has such a good time that he doesn't want to return by dawn and therefore has to be carried by some paper men back to his bed. The theme is more substantial in *Pikolo's Night Voyage*. Uncle Roger gives Pikolo a train that he says is special because it has been made out of wood from a tree that grew from a sapling from the Treasure Tree at the end of the earth. That night Pikolo rides the train to Wooden City, plays with many other children who have come there, finds the Treasure Tree, and brings back a sapling that he will plant with Uncle Roger. The story thus conveys the idea that nature is a magical treasure. The pictures in both books are detailed and elaborate. Both books also use a device reminiscent of the rumpus in Maurice Sendak's *Where the Wild Things Are*: four wordless double-page spreads convey the joy that Pikolo feels when playing in the dream cities. Although neither story rivals Sendak's classic dream journey, Tibo's pictures invite readers to linger over their details and to dream themselves.

Tibo's pictures are the highlights of other collaborations. His manipulation of light gives an appropriate mystical feeling to Alice Bartels' *The Beast*, an elaborate dream fable about a lost girl's near-death discovery of the beauty of life. Tibo's luminescent colours make the girl's new appreciation of beauty almost palpable and do as much as the text to explain why she awakens after accidentally being thrown from a snowmobile on the frozen tundra. Tibo's pictures also effectively convey mood in Jeanne-Pierre Guillet's overly didactic 'Clementine's Kingdom' series. Each book uses a fairy-tale setting to teach an ecological lesson: *The Magic Powder* warns about insecticides and chemical poisons; *Castle Chaos* cautions about upsetting the balance of nature through elimination of wetlands; and *The Bubble Machine* shows the destruction brought on by air pollution. Tibo's drawings give the impish Clementine an engaging personality. More significantly, the scenes of ecological destruction contain sickening colours and a dullness that contrast with the glowing brilliance and vibrancy of the scenes of ecological health and succeed better than the heavy-handed text in advancing the idea that ecological sensitivity and awareness are necessary if we are to save the earth.

It is as an artist that Tibo is most notable. His blend of comic-book faces, nearly three-dimensional settings, and brilliantly evocative colouration of lighting effectively communicate mood and meaning. Although the texts they support are frequently weak, the pictures are pleasing and invite repeated study.

See also: *CA* 136; *MCAI*; *SATA* 67; *WSMP*.

Catharine Parr Traill

Born: 9 January 1802, in Kent, England.

Died: 26 August 1899, in Lakefield, Ont.

Principal Residences: rural Suffolk, near Bungay and then Reydon; Otonabee River area, near present-day Peterborough and Lakefield, Ont.

Career: writer; pioneer.

Works for Children (Selected)

The Tell Tale: An Original Collection of Moral and Amusing Stories (London: Harris, 1818).

Little Downy; or, The History of a Field Mouse: A Moral Tale (London: Dean & Munday, 1822).

The Young Emigrants; or, Pictures of Life in Canada (London: Harvey & Darton, 1826).

The Canadian Crusoes: A Tale of the Rice Lake Plains (London: Hall, Virtue, 1852); republished as *Lost in the Backwoods: A Tale of the Canadian Forest* (London: Nelson, 1882).

Other

The Backwoods of Canada: Being Letters from the Wife of an Emigrant Officer, Illustrative of the Domestic Economy of British America (London: Knight, 1836).

The Female Emigrant's Guide, and Hints on Canadian Housekeeping, 2 vols (Toronto: Maclear, 1854); republished in one vol. as *The Canadian Settler's Guide* (Toronto: Old Countryman, 1855).

Selected Discussions

Maclulich, T.D. 'Crusoe in the Backwoods: A Canadian Fable', *Mosaic* 9 (1976): 115–26.

Peterman, Michael. 'Catharine Parr Traill', *Profiles in Canadian Literature* 3, ed. Jeffrey M. Heath (Toronto: Dundurn, 1982): 25–31.

The first significant example of a form considered to be quintessentially Canadian, the outdoor adventure tale, was Catharine Parr Traill's *The Canadian Crusoes: A Tale of the Rice Lake Plains* (later retitled *Lost in the Backwoods*). Mrs Traill was a member of an immigrant family that made a significant contribution to Canadian letters. Her brother, Samuel Strickland, was author of *Twenty-seven years in Canada West* (1853) and her younger sister, Susanna Moodie, published numerous works, including *Roughing It in the Bush* (1852). Before moving to Canada in 1832, Mrs Traill had written *The Tell Tale*, a collection of children's tales, and several didactic and pious works, the most notable of which is *The Young Emigrants; or, Pictures of Canada* (1826), an epistolary novel based on the Canadian experiences of family friends.

An accomplished botanist as well as a pioneer who endured many hardships, Mrs Traill wrote a number of adult works instructing others in the natural wonders of Canada and showing them how to turn the wilderness to use. Her most famous adult works were *The Backwoods of Canada* and *The Female Emigrant's Guide* (later retitled *The Canadian Settler's Guide*). The combination of accurate description of wilderness conditions and practical advice for survival found in these books also appears in *The Canadian Crusoes*. An attempt to use an entertaining survival tale to impart practical instruction, this novel shows how two boys and a girl survive in the forest for three years because of their previous knowledge, the instruction in survival techniques provided by a friendly Mohawk princess, and their sustaining Christian faith. The children, who became lost because they were careless and did not think sufficiently of others, are changed by their adventures, becoming both wiser and more thoughtful.

The story suffers from overt didacticism evident in the cataloguing of the flora of the region, complete with Latin names in the footnotes; from stilted, pious dialogue; and from an explicit attempt to make the wilderness adventure an allegory of life. It is, however, notable for its symbolic marriages between a Scot and a French Canadian and between the Mohawk princess and a white boy. Through these marriages, Mrs Traill signals her hope that Canada will be a land of united aspirations and domestic harmony. It is also notable for establishing a pattern carried on by such modern Canadian wilderness novelists as Farley Mowat and James Houston: the circular journey into a wilderness that becomes the testing ground of courage and character.

See also: *DLB* 99.

Jan Truss

Born: 3 May 1925, in Stoke-on-Trent, England.

Education: Goldsmiths' College, University of London (Teacher's Certificate 1945); University of Alberta (B.Ed. 1962); University of Calgary (graduate study 1965–8).

Principal Residences: Stoke-on-Trent; London, England; Liverpool, Winchester, Peterborough, and Basildon, Essex, England; Edmonton; Calgary; Water Valley, Alta.

Career: schoolteacher in England and Alberta; school administrator; school art consultant in rural Alberta; university lecturer; writer.

Awards: Ruth Schwartz Award for Children's Fiction (1983).

Works for Children

Plays

Attack (Edmonton: Alberta Dept of Culture, Youth and Recreation 1971).

Ooomerahgi Oh! and A Very Small Rebellion: Two Plays for Children (Toronto: Playwrights Canada, 1978).

The Judgement of Clifford Sifton (Toronto: Playwrights Canada, 1979).

Cornelius Dragon, in *Eight Plays for Young People*, ed. Joyce Doolittle (Edmonton: NeWest Press, 1984): 29–56.

Novels

Bird at the Window (Toronto: Macmillan, 1974).

A Very Small Rebellion, with Jack Chambers (Edmonton: Lebel, 1977). **Rev:** *CCL* 14 (1979): 75, and 31/32 (1983): 63; *SLJ* 27 (Sept. 1980): 43.

Jasmin (Vancouver: Douglas & McIntyre, 1982). **Rev:** *CBRA* (1982): 255; *CCL* 27/28 (1982): 187.

Summer Goes Riding (Toronto: Groundwood, 1987). **Rev:** *CCL* 50 (1988): 60; *CM* 20 (Jan. 1992): 13.

Red (Toronto: Groundwood, 1988). **Rev:** *CCL* 57/58 (1990): 146.

Picture Books

Peter's Moccasins, with Nancy Mackenzie, illus. Philip Spink (Edmonton: Reidmore, 1987). **Rev:** *EL* 16 (Mar. 1989): 21.

Other

'Soliloquy by One Who Writes for Children's Theatre', *CCL* 8/9 (1977): 70–3.

Rocky Mountain Symphony, photographs by George Brybycin (Calgary: GB Publishing, 1983).

Selected Discussions

Davis, Marie. 'Jan Truss: An Interview', *CCL* 68 (1992): 50–1.

——. '"The Big Adventure Is Close-in": An Interview with Jan Truss', *CCL* 69 (1993): 6–16.

Reimer, Mavis. 'Ice Women, Earth Mothers and Fairy Godmothers: Woman as Metaphor in Two Recent Canadian Children's Novels', *CCL* 49 (1988): 6–13.

At the age of 45, Jan Truss, who had been teaching in Alberta since coming to Canada in 1957, felt exhausted and burned out. Looking for something to invigorate her, she turned to writing, producing a novel, *Bird at the Window*, that won the first Search for a New Alberta Novelist Award in 1972. Truss has since written a number of stories for radio and magazines, and even the libretto for a chamber opera, but her published work for children consists of five plays, one picture book, and five novels.

Two of the plays explore moral issues in Canadian history. *A Very Small Rebellion*, first produced in 1974, presents sympathetically the struggle of Louis Riel and his Métis followers to defend their lands and rights against the encroachments supported by the federal government. *The Judgement of Clifford Sifton*, also produced in 1974, uses a device similar to that popularized in Charles Dickens's *A Christmas Carol* to examine anew the settlement of the West. After his death, Sir Clifford Sifton (1861–1929), a politician often celebrated for his aggressive promotion of immigration, hears the voices of Conscience, Truth, and History challenge his accomplishments. The play concludes by asking the audience to judge whether Sifton was justified in making some immigrants pay a high price in suffering so that people like those in the audience could benefit. Truss has said that of all her works, she is happiest with *Cornelius Dragon*, which was presented in a workshop in 1983 but has yet to receive a full production. Although this highly theatrical play seems to blend various historical periods, it is concerned with the immigrant experience and with the psychology of outsiders. The central character, Cornelius Horatio Dragon (the surname is shortened from Dragonoffskiwitch), is an immigrant mocked by the inhabitants of a frontier town. After running away and being robbed by a cowboy, another wandering outsider, Cornelius works as a clown in a children's circus until he finds love with a female outsider and thereby acquires self-acceptance. Her other drama, *Ooomerahgi Oh!*, a fantasy for preschoolers first produced in 1974, shows Mimi, the youngest of three children, maintaining her love of home in the face of enticements to wander into the wide world with the Traveller, an evil magician who enslaves the rest of the family.

Given her interest in the treatment of minorities in Canadian history, it is not surprising that Truss agreed to do the text for a picture book that would give contemporary Native children a positive vision of their culture. Truss was so frustrated with producing a book acceptable to educators and bureaucrats, however, that she insisted that the editor who changed her text share cover credit. In its published form, *Peter's Moccasins* is insipid. Peter Cardinal, a Native boy, is embarrassed because the other children have brought old sneakers to put on when they are in their classroom, but he has brought moccasins that his grandmother made. Eventually, everyone admires his beautiful moccasins, so the teacher suggests that all the children bring moccasins or slippers. *Peter's Moccasins* clearly demonstrates that admirable social values do not alone guarantee a meaningful literary experience.

In her novels, Truss treats social and moral difficulties faced by young people, generally focusing on the way characters handle the pressure of severe problems and thereby discover their identities and their relationship to others. Because it combines a historical essay and fiction, *A Very Small Rebellion* is an unusually powerful outgrowth of the play with the same title. Sections of the essay, an account of the Riel rebellion written by Jack Chambers, alternate with Truss's fictional account of the efforts of some Métis and Natives to resist being evicted from their homes. The fact that the youths who are the focus of the story are staging Truss's play about Riel intensifies our sense of the continuity of historical conditions. Although the protesters lose their battle, as did the followers of Riel, the youthful Métis acquire a new pride in their heritage.

Truss's other books are problem novels, three of them focusing on the difficulties of talented young girls. *Bird at the Window* is a frank account of teenage pregnancy that straddles the border between adolescent and adult fiction. Eighteen-year-old Angela Moynahan, a lonely 'brain' at school, refuses to allow her unexpected pregnancy to interfere with a long-planned trip to Europe. After the baby is stillborn, she returns to Canada, where her father has just died, and tries to gain control of her life. A tense psychological study that weaves throughout themes of death, rebellion, liberation, and identity, it does not judge Angela. Instead, it shows how she gradually comes to understand herself, her mother, and the social pressures that often control lives.

Jasmin, Truss's most impressive novel, uses the familiar pattern of the journey into the wilderness to show a young girl's growth in identity. Jasmin Marie Antoinette Stalke, oldest of seven children living in a squalid two-room farmhouse, runs away to live in the woods when she can no longer bear the burden of looking after her siblings and the noise and lack of privacy that prevents her from doing her homework. During her journey, she learns that she is a talented artist and that her ability can gain her acceptance outside of her family. The presentation of events from the point of view of several characters is notably successful in providing a rich understanding of Jasmin and the conditions against which she rebels.

Summer Goes Riding attempts to give sociological and psychological depth to the conventional horse story. Charlotte Mauney, a Nebraska farm girl who longs for a horse so that she can become a championship rider, matures as she learns to deal with jealousy and thwarted ambition. The novel suffers from strained symbolism in the mechanical Gothicism of Charlotte's identification with an ancestor killed by a horse and in the implausibility and heavily veiled eroticism of Charlotte's transforming immersion in a river. Nevertheless, it contains some powerful sequences, especially its presentation of Charlotte's shock after a tornado destroys her home and all chances of obtaining her horse. A note of realistic hope prevents undue pessimism at the conclusion: Charlotte's friends provide her with opportunities to be around horses, and she determines to continue working for her dream.

Whereas a female's desire is convincingly central to *Summer Goes Riding*, a male's desire for acceptance by females awkwardly dominates the sequel, *Red*. Red Wallinger, Charlotte's 12-year-old friend, gains a more mature sense of relationships when he journeys from Nebraska to Calgary to visit his mother, whom he has not seen in more than four years. During the visit, Red learns that, even though his mother insists on her freedom, she loves him and wants him to visit again. Red also becomes deeply attracted to Celeste, a girl who is so beautiful that he considers her perfect. Only after Charlotte comes to stay with him and points out that Celeste is different does he see beneath her beauty and realize that she is mentally slow. *Red* shows that males too often rashly and foolishly judge females of all ages, and concludes with the boy gaining understanding and tolerance. Unfortunately, to establish that Red can be bravely considerate, it also relies on an implausible and ironic melodramatic conclusion: Red rushes to rescue a baby from drowning, only to discover that he has saved a child's doll. The scene of Red's immersion may deliberately parallel Charlotte's, but its symbolism is not as meaningful. In spite of a few touching and insightful moments, *Red* is not particularly satisfying, being a rather unconvincing portrait of male maturation.

Truss is an uncompromising artist whose best works tackle tough social and moral issues without preaching or resorting to blatant didacticism. Her greatest strength is her ability to create convincing characters and to make their problems both socially and psychologically interesting.

See also: *CA* 102; *Profiles* 2; *SATA* 35; *TCCW*; *WSMP*.

Deborah Turney-Zagwÿn

Born: 14 August 1953, in Cornwall, Ont.

Principal Residences: Cornwall; Harrison Hot Springs, BC.

Education: attended Fraser Valley College.

Career: artist; illustrator; writer.

Works for Children

Written and Illustrated by Deborah Turney-Zagwÿn

Mood Pocket Mud Bucket (Markham, Ont.: Fitzhenry & Whiteside, 1988). **Rev:** *CCL* 57/58 (1990): 114.

The Pumpkin Blanket (Markham, Ont.: Fitzhenry & Whiteside, 1990). **Rev:** *CCL* 64 (1991): 96.

Long Nellie (Victoria, BC: Orca, 1993). **Rev:** *CCL* 78 (1995): 79; *CM* 22 (Mar. 1994): 50; *QQ* 59 (Oct. 1993): 40.

Hound Without Howl (Victoria, BC: Orca, 1994). **Rev:** *CBRA* (1994): 469; *QQ* 60 (Oct. 1994): 42.

Illustrated by Deborah Turney-Zagwÿn

A Winter's Yarn, by Kathleen Waldron (Red Deer, Alta: Red Deer College Press, 1986). **Rev:** *CCL* 52 (1988): 56.

Deborah Turney-Zagwÿn is a writer-illustrator who searches for subjects that are different from both those of other artists and those in her previous books. Nevertheless, her stories tend to focus on unusual characters and the affections others develop for them. Her pictures also have a resemblance, being somewhat primitive stylistically and using colours to suggest both a homey warmth and vibrancy.

Turney-Zagwÿn began her career by illustrating Kathleen Cook Waldron's *A Winter's Yarn*, a poem in rhyming couplets about a zoo keeper who spends the winter knitting garments for her animals. Her whimsical depictions of the animals wearing clothes are the highlights of this overly long poem.

The title of the first book that she both wrote and illustrated, *Mood Pocket Mud Bucket*, emphasizes two unusual characters who have a strong bond of affection. The first is Sonia, a changeable child patterned after Turney-Zagwÿn's daughter of the same name. Sonia has a face for every mood, and she stores the faces in her pocket until she needs them. The second unusual person is Laslo, an old man who lives on what a sign in one picture calls a 'Wreck Ranch', a farm filled with old televisions, refrigerators, and tires. Laslo owns Bucket, an unreliable, moody backhoe, that is sometimes perky and at others cranky. When a spring storm threatens to flood the pastures of Sonia's farm, Laslo rescues the cows and puts them in his litter-filled basement. He and Sonia then use Bucket to drive them to a high pasture and to scoop up mud to fill in a dyke. The episode ends with Sonia, who had begun the day moodily and with a worried face, wearing a tired-but-happy one. More a character study than a well-defined tale, the book uses colours and shading to emphasize mood. Pictures of the storm and Sonia's troubled parents are thus darker than those showing the contented Sonia at the end. In addition, Turney-Zagwÿn shifts from single-page illustrations to double-page spreads for emphasis on two occasions. In the first, when Laslo volunteers to use Bucket for the round-up, the right-hand page of the spread is devoid of background detail, thus emphasizing Laslo's energy and humour. The second spread, the picture of the round-up, provides a panorama of the farm showing both its beauty and the effort required to drive the cattle from one area to another.

A fight against the elements also features prominently in *The Pumpkin Blanket*, a more tightly plotted tale. When Clee was born, the Northern Lights 'shook their folds', producing a blanket that the wind tossed into Clee's house. Her father called this blanket the pumpkin blanket because Clee, when wrapped in it, resembles a pumpkin. As the illustrations show, this blanket's twelve squares comprise both celestial and earthly parts of nature, thus symbolizing the child's closeness to nature. For Clee, it becomes a great source of comfort and an element in all of her games. When frost threatens her father's pumpkins, however, Clee must give up her blanket, one square each night, to protect them. On the night before Halloween, when Clee's father harvests these pumpkins, the wind takes the squares up to the sky, where the stars stitch them together and wrap them around the moon, a mother-of-pearl pumpkin in the sky. Because of its mystical origins and its delivery by the wind, a conventional symbol of imaginative energy, the blanket symbolizes youthful imagination, which comforts and makes happy the growing child. The shift from double-page to single-page illustrations graphically underscores the fact that giving up the blanket marks a significant transition in her life. Symbolically and graphically, that is, the book implies that the maturing Clee, in giving up the blanket to protect the pumpkins, is experiencing the pragmatism that inevitably brings an end to the carefree delights of childhood. The story does not, however, emphasize loss and sadness. Because the stars stitch up the blanket on an autumn night almost identical to the one on which Clee was born, Turney-Zagwÿn suggests that Clee is entering a new stage of life. By picturing Clee in the final wordless picture, in which Clee clutches a remnant of the blanket, she reassures us that Clee will retain at least a bit of her childhood wonder as she grows. Its graphic design, its beautiful use of colour, and its thoughtful symbolism make *The Pumpkin Blanket* a significant work of picture-book artistry.

The theme of *Long Nellie* is acceptance of social differences and the need for companionship. Long Nellie is a scavenger who lives alone in a cluttered trailer. The plastic that covers her windows so that she can't see out and others can't see in symbolizes her isolation as one of society's invisible minorities. When Jeremy finds a kitten but can't keep it because of his father's allergies, he decides that it would make a perfect pet for Long Nellie. In a scene of comic disasters, Jeremy places the kitten by a dumpster, but he so frightens Nellie that she falls and twists her foot. Jeremy thereafter takes her home and befriends her, deciding that he will later help her by providing real windows so that the light will make her world within the trailer more beautiful. One critic has criticized the tale because the middle-class Jeremy saves someone of a lower class, thus suggesting class superiority and a desire to make other classes more like the middle class. Another way of seeing the book, however, is to recognize that neither age nor sex are barriers to friendships and that true friends do whatever is necessary to make the lives of others better. Graphically, the book is interesting both for the way in which the pictures at the end are lighter than those at the beginning, colourfully emphasizing the joys of a true home, and for the change from double-page to single-page illustrations at two points to signal transitions in the plot.

Hound without Howl, another story of an eccentric, is decidedly tongue-in-cheek. Howard, an opera-loving bachelor, buys Clayton, a basset hound, because he wants a pet who will be a musical companion. Disappointed when Clayton makes no sounds, Howard goes to various comical measures to make the dog bay: he puts a bay window in the dog house, he makes dog food with bay leaves, he takes him shopping at The Bay, and he even moves the doghouse to the backyard to give it a view of the bay. Nothing works; contented Clayton remains silent. On a walk one night, however, they see the rising moon reflected in the water of the bay, and Clayton yowls and then bays, becoming a perfect companion for Howard. With its puns on 'bay' and its implicit joking about opera as the howling of dogs, *Hound without Howl* is an amusing story of wish fulfilment. Cartoon drawings in the bottom corners of the pictures and graphic details, such as a booklet titled 'Soppy Opera: Singing in the Rain', reinforce the humour.

Her thematic concern with loving relationships, her subtle use of symbolism, her gentle humour, her skilful variation of graphic format to emphasize changes in plot or theme, and her evocative use of colour have made Turney-Zagwÿn one of the more interesting author-illustrators to emerge in the 1990s.

See also: *SATA* 78.

Ian Wallace

Born: 31 Mar. 1950, in Niagara Falls, Ont.

Principal Residences: Niagara Falls; Toronto.

Education: Ontario College of Art (AA 1974).

Career: information officer; writer; illustrator.

Major Awards: IODE (Toronto) Book Award (1984, 1997); Amelia Frances Howard-Gibbon Illustrator's Award (1985); Mr Christie's Book Award (1989); Elizabeth Mrazik-Cleaver Picture Book Award (1990).

Works for Children

Written and Illustrated by Ian Wallace

Julie News (Toronto: Kids Can Press, 1974). **Rev:** *IR* 9 (Summer 1975): 45.

The Sandwich, with Angela Wood (Toronto: Kids Can Press, 1975). **Rev:** *CM* 19 (May 1991): 156; *EL* 13 (Nov. 1985): 43; *IR* 9 (Autumn 1975): 45; *RT* 41 (Dec. 1987): 361.

The Christmas Tree House (Toronto: Kids Can Press, 1976). **Rev:** *CCL* 14 (1979): 46; *IR* 11 (Autumn 1977): 63

Chin Chiang and the Dragon's Dance (Toronto: Groundwood, 1984). **Rev:** *BiC* 13 (Dec. 1984): 14; *HB* 60 (Apr. 1984): 190; *QQ* 50 (Sept. 1984): 80; *RT* 14 (1987): 361; *SLJ* 30 (May 1984): 74; *TLS* (29 Mar. 1985): 352.

The Sparrow's Song (Toronto: Viking, 1986). **Rev:** *BiC* 15 (Nov. 1986): 35; *CCL* 57 (1990): 35; *CM* 15 (Jan. 1987): 35; *QQ* 52 (Aug. 1986): 39; *SLJ* 34 (Jan. 1988): 71.

Morgan the Magnificent (Toronto: Groundwood, 1987). **Rev:** *BiC* 17 (June 1988): 37; *BYP* 1 (Oct. 1987): 24; *CCB-B* 41 (June 1988): 218; *CCL* 60 (1990): 108; *CL* 122 (Autumn 1989): 246; *EL* 15 (Mar. 1988): 23; *SLJ* 34 (Apr. 1988): 92.

Mr. Kneebone's New Digs (Toronto: Groundwood, 1991). **Rev:** *CCL* 67 (1992): 74; *CL* (Autumn 1992): 161; *CM* 20 (Mar. 1992): 85; *EL* 20 (May 1993): 54; *QQ* 57 (Nov. 1991): 26; *RT* 45 (Apr. 1992): 639.

A Winter's Tale (Toronto: Groundwood, 1997). **Rev:** *CCB-B* 51 (Jan. 1998): 180; *CM* 4 (2 Jan. 1998): on-line; *EL* 25 (Jan. 1998): 52; *QQ* 63 (Dec. 1997): 36; *SLJ* 43 (Dec. 1997): 102.

Boy of the Deeps (Toronto: Groundwood, 1999).

Illustrated by Ian Wallace

Very Last First Time, by Jan Andrews (Toronto: Groundwood, 1985). **Rev:** *CCB-B* 40 (Sept. 1986): 1; *CCL* 45 (1987): 82; *EL* 13 (Mar. 1986): 15; *NYTBR* (15 June 1986): 38; *QQ* 51 (Dec. 1985): 24; *SLJ* 32 (May 1986): 67.

Architect of the Moon, by Tim Wynne-Jones (Toronto: Groundwood, 1988). **Rev:** *CCL* 60 (1990): 108.

The Name of the Tree: A Bantu Folktale, by Celia Barker Lottridge (Toronto: Groundwood 1990). **Rev:** *BiC* 18 (Dec. 1989): 19; *EL* 17 (Mar. 1990): 85; *HB* 66 (Mar. 1990): 213; *QQ* 55 (Oct. 1989): 13; *SLJ* 36 (Mar. 1990): 209.

The Year of the Fire, by Teddy Jam (Toronto: Groundwood, 1992). **Rev:** *BiC* 21 (Dec. 1992): 36; *EL* 20 (Mar. 1993): 13; *NYTBR* (17 Oct. 1993): 33; *QQ* 58 (July 1992): 46; *SLJ* 39 (May 1993): 86.

The Mummer's Song, by Bud Davidge (Toronto: Groundwood, 1994). **Rev:** *EL* 21 (Nov. 1993): 47; *HB* 70 (May 1994): 364; *QQ* 59 (Sept. 1993): 67; *SLJ* 40 (Nov. 1994): 96.

Hansel and Gretel, by the Brothers Grimm (Toronto: Groundwood, 1994). **Rev:** *CBRA* (1996): 521; *CCL* 83 (1996): 132; *CM* 22 (Nov. 1994): 208; *EL* 22 (Mar. 1995): 17; *QQ* 60 (Oct. 1994): 40; *SLJ* 42 (May 1996): 104.

Sarah and the People of Sand River, by W.D. Valgardson (Toronto: Groundwood, 1996). **Rev:** *BiC* 25 (Oct. 1996): 30; *CBRA* (1996): 460; *CCB-B* 50 (Dec. 1996): 154; *EL* 24 (Mar. 1997): 27; *QQ* 62 (Oct. 1996): 43; *SLJ* 42 (Dec. 1996): 108.

Other

'The Emotional Link', *Writers on Writing: Guide to Writing and Illustrating Children's Books*, ed. David Booth (Markham, Ont.: Overlea House, 1989), 9–11.

'One Author's Tour: Children's Book Festival November 18–25, 1978', *IR* 13 (Apr. 1979): 11–14.

Selected Discussions

Steig, Michael. 'The Importance of the Visual Text in *Architect of the Moon*', *CCL* 70 (1993): 22–33.

Stott, Jon C. 'Profile: Ian Wallace', *Language Arts* 66 (Apr. 1989): 443–9.

Walker, Ulrike. 'A Matter of Thresholds', *CCL* 60 (1990): 108–16.

'My books all seem to deal with "Very Last First Times." But I wasn't conscious of this until a librarian drew it to my attention.' So spoke Ian Wallace about the visual and verbal content of his children's books. In them, he combines his artistic talents, love of story, sensitivity to the problems children face as they grow up, and respect for the courage of vulnerable individuals as they confront the challenges in their lives. Primarily through his illustrations, he is able to expand on the written texts of the narratives to reveal the emotional dimensions and cultural backgrounds of his central characters.

Wallace's first two books were part of the Kids Can Press series about children of diverse cultures living in contemporary urban settings. In *The Sandwich*, Vincenzo eats his lunch at school for the first time and is mocked by his classmates for his powerfully smelling mortadella and provolone sandwich. His father explains, 'Your friends laughed because it was different. . . . It was new to them.' And he tells the boy, 'You are who you are and you have nothing to be ashamed of.' For Nick, the hero of *The Christmas Tree House*, 'every Saturday would begin quite routinely, but once he closed the front door of his house, anything could happen.' Just before Christmas, he and his new friend Gloria discover a treehouse that has been built by the dreaded local eccentric, Don Valley Rose, and learn that she is really a friendly and kind person. While these stories are relatively simple, they explore the themes of self-worth, understanding of others, and friendship that are developed more fully in Wallace's later works.

Chin Chiang and the Dragon's Dance reveals the insecurities of the title character as he prepares to participate with his grandfather in his first dragon's dance. Fleeing to the roof of the nearby public library, he meets Pu Yee, an old lady who, without his realizing it, helps him to practise the intricate steps of the dance. The illustrations, with their formalized designs, inclusion of several traditional religious symbols, and representation of contemporary Chinese-Canadian life, imply the importance of the community to which the boy belongs. The text simply states the importance of the dance. The illustrations reveal the conflict through which he goes before he accepts this fact. At first, he stands apart from his grandfather; but the process of his integration is indicated in the illustration of Chin and the old lady dancing; the figures are in harmony as they perform the intricate steps on the library roof. The integration is completed as the family celebrates. Chin is no longer set apart from other people in the illustrations; he is in the midst of his family in a room gorgeously decorated in traditional Chinese style.

Very Last First Time is the first work of another writer that Wallace illustrated. However, the theme is certainly a congenial one, dealing as it does with a young person's engaging in an activity that integrates her into her culture. Eva Padlyat makes her first solitary journey under the sea ice to gather mussels. In planning the illustrations, Wallace deliberately chose a different style: '*Very Last First Time* could not have been painted with the same intricate detailing as *Chin Chiang*. The very nature of the culture it was portraying demanded a style that was much looser and freer to accurately reflect the Inuit society.' The words and pictures of the book transform an unusual northern activity into a universal journey of maturation. The movement from village to seashore and under the ice is one away from the known and secure. When she finds herself in darkness and hears the tide beginning to flood, Eva has reached the turning point of her journey; relighting her candle, she moves towards the hole, the light, her mother, and finally, the village.

Wallace's illustrations reinforce and expand on the meaning of the narrative, both in the structural patterns and in specific details. Two colours dominate: yellow, representing the known and secure world, and purple, representing the realm Eva enters alone for the first time. Visually the reader moves from yellow to purple and back to yellow; similarly, Eva leaves and then returns to her home. In the second structural pattern, Wallace moves from single-page illustrations for the scenes above ice to double-spreads for those under the ice, and back to single-page illustrations as Eva rejoins her mother. The details of individual pictures reflect the nature of Eva's experiences. Her home is ordinary, with a refrigerator, a picture of Michael Jackson taped to it, and a box of cornflakes on the table. But once Eva has entered the world under the ice, she is in a place of darker hues and threatening shapes of animals and spirit creatures. Psychologically, she is confronting her fears of the unknown. The relighting of the candles, the return of yellow into the pictures, signals the beginning of her return to the human world. The final illustration, in which she sits at the kitchen table, contains the purple mussel shells that she has brought back from the under-ice world. She has also brought the memories of her experiences back to her daily life.

In *The Sparrow's Song*, Wallace draws on the Niagara Falls area in which he grew up, but sets the story near the beginning of the twentieth century. When a mother sparrow is killed by Charles, his sister Katie cares for the orphaned fledgling. Finally agreeing to forgive Charles for his cruel deed, she joins with him in gathering food for the bird and teaching it to fly. Wallace deals with a familiar theme: the chance for children to grow in understanding their world and the people in it. However, he deepens his concerns as the children confront the mysteries of life and death and the need of nature's children to become free. Katie becomes a caregiver; Charles accepts responsibility for his actions; and the two grow in their love for each other.

The book's opening and closing illustrations deal with the themes of birth, growth, and death. The title page depicts an empty nest: the mother will never return, for she has been killed by Charles's slingshot. The baby has left the nest in the first stage of growth. In the concluding picture, the sparrow and its mate stand above their nest, proudly guarding three speckled eggs; the cycle of life is beginning anew. The illustrations also trace the changing relationships between Katie and Charles. In the early pictures, she is seen alone or in confrontational situations with her brother. The transition is depicted in a double-spread without text. In order to teach the sparrow to fly, they dance together, twigs and grass woven into their clothes and hair. In the background are the gorge and Niagara Falls, the spiritual power of which, it is implied, is influencing the children.

In *Morgan the Magnificent*, Wallace combines his love of the circus with the fruits of a research trip to Baraboo, Wisconsin, home of the Circus World Museum, to study the art of traditional costumes, wagons, and posters, all of which he used to enhance the visual dimensions of his story. The title heroine, who lives with her father, sneaks away to the circus, enters the tent of star aerialist Anastasia, dons her costume, and climbs to the highwire. Terrified when the reality of her situation shatters her imaginings, she must be rescued by the star. Her adventure is another 'Very Last First Time'. In her loneliness, Morgan had taken to walking on the beams of the barn, fantasizing that she was a circus star. Only after she is rescued is she able to balance reality and imagination. Like Chin Chiang and Eva, she grows through her experiences and with the guidance of a wise older person.

Wallace makes use of different angles of vision to reflect the heroine's emotional, as well as physical, situations. Early in the story, as Morgan fantasizes, and later, when she first walks across the highwire, viewers look down on the scenes; Morgan is happily on top of her world. However, as the reality of the situation dawns on her, the paintings locate viewers on the ground, looking upward and realizing the peril of her situation. Pictures in which the viewer looks directly at events show the reality of Morgan's daily life: milking cows; travelling to the circus and entering the dressing tent; being guided to safety by Anastasia; and, with her father, watching the circus wagons leaving town. In each illustration, there is a small silent observer: an angel resembling the bas-relief ornaments on circus wagons registers a variety of emotions as she views Morgan's actions.

After *Morgan*, Wallace illustrated four books by other writers, adding dimensions to their relatively short, simple narratives through his pictures. In Tim Wynne-Jones's *Architect of the Moon*, David Finebloom, 'brave block builder', takes his toys into the sky where he restores the waning moon to its full size and returns home in time for breakfast with his mother. The illustrations raise an interesting question: is the adventure a dream or a real trip? The paintings and toys seen in the boy's room suggest that the journey takes place in his imagination. Before he leaves, however, the date on the tear-away calendar is 23 September; when he returns, it reads 12 October. Has he actually spent three weeks at his labours? *The Name of the Tree*, a Bantu tale adapted by Celia Lottridge, deals with a common theme of African folklore, drought and famine and the success of the most unlikely of the animals in finding a solution to their problem. The colours of the illustrations reflect the conflict. The brown, dingy colours of a dusty landscape pervade during much of the story, with a miraculous fruit tree the only green object to be seen. After the green-coloured tortoise has helped end the animals' thirst, the green leaves and colourful fruits of the tree dominate the pictures. In Teddy Jam's *The Year of the Fire*, a grandfather's reminiscence of a major event of his childhood, oranges and reds are seen on the old man's vest, as well as in the raging flames. At the conclusion, more green appears in the landscape's rebirth both after the time of the fire and during the spring making of maple syrup when the old man tells his story. Bud Davidge's *The Mummer's Song* celebrates an old Newfoundland Christmas custom, while Wallace's illustrations depict its renaissance in recent times. A grandmother and two small children eagerly await the arrival of the revellers at their home. The children, who have been reading *In The Night Kitchen*, experience a night-time revelry as rambunctious and jolly as that in Sendak's book. The illustrations are a mix of both double-spreads and a series of smaller panels, the former giving a panoramic view of the festivities, the latter, close-ups of the individuals. At the beginning, the children are in their beds, sitting up, looking out the window in eager anticipation. The revels over, they lie back contentedly, on the edge of sleep, thinking back over the night's activities and looking ahead to those of next year.

Mr. Kneebone's New Digs returns to the theme of *The Christmas Tree House*: the plight of the adult homeless in a large city. April Moth and her dog, Mr Kneebone, leave their rat-infested rooming house in an unsuccessful hunt for better lodgings. The new digs turn out to be a tiny cave among the rocks in a large park. The story is both a tribute to the courage of the old lady and an indictment of the slum landlords and, by extension, a society that allows such conditions to exist. The outdoor backgrounds contain the office towers and shopping centers where the more fortunate work, shop, and play; indoor scenes reflect the squalor of the unfortunate. Small details relate to characterization. A poster of a Tom Thompson painting in the heroine's apartment foreshadows her happiness in finding a home in nature. A small replica of the Statue of Liberty signifies her independent spirit. The oversized slippers of a nasty person are decorated with a monster face and teeth, appropriate for her personality. In the final two illustrations the woman and her dog at their cave demonstrate the ambiguity of the conclusion. In the first she throws her battered hat joyously into the air, while the dog prances. In the second the two are huddled at the mouth of the cave. Green dominates both pages. While it is appropriate for the natural setting, it is muted almost to a grey tone. April Moth has her freedom and a new home. But she and her dog, who are very small in these pictures, appear lonely and vulnerable. How long will their present happiness last? What will happen to them when summer is over?

Wallace's adaptation of the Grimm Brothers' *Hansel and Gretel* may well be his most ambitious book. With so many illustrated retellings of one of the best-known European folktales, the creator of a new version faces the challenge of providing pictures that both enhance the traditional meanings of the story and communicate new ones. Wallace succeeds admirably on both counts. The text follows the Grimm Brothers' closely, even to the point of making the wife the children's own mother, something the Grimms had changed in later editions of their folktale collection. Wallace modernizes the story with contemporary Canadian implications: the father is an impoverished Atlantic Coast fisherman.

The illustrations are the darkest of any in Wallace's books. Sombre browns and black dominate until the final illustration, when, as the children joyously race home, the light dawn sky breaks overhead. In the foreground, in a nearby graveyard, the statues of a lamb and of Jesus, arms out in welcoming poses, are seen. Details of the parents' and witch's houses emphasize the contemporary setting. The tattered furniture and sensational tabloids the wife reads suggest the physical and spiritual poverty of the children's home. Adorned with M & M candies and wall lights shaped like soft ice creams, the witch's dwelling offers quick, but not lasting, nourishment, as well as soon-extinguished hope. One detail indicates a major shift in interpretation. The white dove who had finally helped the children in the Grimms' version is here closely associated with the witch and disappears from the illustrations after the evil one's death. There is no help from nature here; the children must depend on their own inner strengths.

W.D. Valgardson's *Sarah and the People of Sand River* is the story of an Icelandic-Canadian girl who, mistreated by the woman with whom she is sent to live by her widowed father, is aided by a raven and the spirit of a Cree woman in her escape to her home. Although Valgardson's long text conveys much of the story's meaning, Wallace's illustrations, in addition to depicting realistically the historical settings, embody the symbolism and mystic aura of the narrative. Warm golds and browns suffuse the pictures of her country home and surround the spirit woman when she appears to the girl. The physical proximity of father and daughter reflect their deep love, while the heartlessness of the landlady is seen in the dominating posture she assumes around Sarah. The raven, realistically portrayed or symbolically presented in stars, looks down from the skies offering assistance.

In *A Winter's Tale*, nine-year-old Abigail makes her first winter camping trip with her father and brother and plays an important role in freeing a fawn trapped in the ice. Like Eva and Morgan, she leaves the security of a familiar place, and, like Katie, she helps a creature of nature regain its freedom. Although the dominant colours are brown, for the dead vegetation and the fawn, and blue, for the clear day, the snow, and Abigail's parka, small patches of red—on her mittens, her father's snow jacket, and the lining of her brother's parka—highlight human warmth: the family's love for each other and the tenderness the people feel for the trapped animal. The majority of the illustrations are single-paged, facing the text. However, five double-spreads emphasize important moments of the girl: standing on a rock surveying the wilderness, preparing camp, discovering the fawn on the ice, seeing it spring free, enjoying the sunset over the ice, and feeling that 'she had never been so happy.' Significantly, in the final double-spread, the browns and blues of the landscape are tinged with the reds and oranges of the sunset, as if the inner warmth of the family has been projected into the natural world.

The careful planning and meticulous execution of the total design and specific illustrations for stories he and others have written have earned Ian Wallace the reputation of one of Canada's major picture-book artists. His books present a significant and strong vision of life. They emphasize not only the individual's successful quest for self-worth, but also the importance of individuals understanding themselves in relation to family, friends, community, tradition, and the powerful world of nature of which they are a part.

See also: *CA* 107; *CANR* 25, 38, 50; *CLR* 37; *Junior* 6; *SATA* 53, 56; *TCCW*; *WSMP*.

Betty Waterton

Born: 31 August 1923, in Oshawa, Ont.

Principal Residences: Oshawa; Vancouver; Sidney, BC.

Education: Vancouver School of Art.

Career: newspaper artist; writer.

Works for Children

A Salmon for Simon, illus. Ann Blades (Vancouver: Douglas & McIntyre, 1978) **Rev:** *CCB-B* 33 (July 1980): 225; *CCL* 21 (1981): 58; *IR* 13 (Apr. 1979): 64; *SLJ* 26 (Aug. 1980): 58.

Pettranella, illus. Ann Blades (Vancouver: Douglas & McIntyre, 1980). **Rev:** *BiC* 10 (Oct. 1981): 33; *CCL* 35 (1984): 25; *IR* 15 (Apr. 1981): 56; *QQ* 47 (June 1981): 34; *SLJ* 27 (Aug. 1981): 72.

Mustard, illus. Barb Reid (Richmond Hill, Ont.: Scholastic, 1983). **Rev:** *CCL* 30 (1983): 69; *CM* 20 (Oct. 1992): 267; *QQ* 49 (Aug. 1983): 35.

The Cat of Quinty (Toronto: Thomas Nelson, 1984).

The White Moose (Scarborough, Ont.: Ginn, 1984).

Orff, 27 Dragons (and a Snarkel!), illus. Karen Kulyk (Willowdale, Ont.: Annick, 1984). **Rev:** *CCL* 39 (1985): 158; *QQ* 50 (Nov. 1984): 13.

Quincy Rumpel (Toronto: Groundwood, 1984). **Rev:** *BiC* 13 (Oct. 1984): 11; *CCL* 42 (1986): 95; *SLJ* (Apr. 1987): 106.

The Dog Who Stopped the War (Toronto: Groundwood, 1985). **Rev:** *EL* 13 (Mar. 1986): 16.

Starring Quincy Rumpel (Toronto: Groundwood, 1986). **Rev:** *CCL* 46 (1987): 81; *QQ* 52 (Oct. 1986): 24.

Quincy Rumpel, P.I. (Toronto: Groundwood, 1988).

Plain Noodles, illus. Joanne Fitzgerald (Toronto: Groundwood, 1989); published in the US as *Baby Boat*. **Rev:** *BiC* 18 (Dec. 1989): 23; *CCL* 59 (1990): 83; *CM* 18 (Mar. 1990): 69; *QQ* 55 (Dec. 1989): 22.

Morris Rumpel and the Wings of Icarus (Toronto: Groundwood, 1989). **Rev:** *CCL* 61 (1991): 91; *QQ* 60 (Mar. 1994): 86.

Quincy Rumpel and the Sasquatch of Phantom Cove (Toronto: Groundwood, 1990). **Rev:** *CCL* 76 (1994): 66; *CM* 19 (Sept. 1971): 220.

Quincy Rumpel and the Woolly Chaps (Toronto: Groundwood, 1992). **Rev:** *QQ* 58 (Sept. 1992): 74.

Quincy Rumpel and the Mystifying Experience (Toronto: Groundwood, 1994). **Rev:** *BiC* 23 (Sept. 1994): 58; *CBRA* (1994): 504; *CM* 22 (Sept. 1994): 125; *QQ* 60 (Apr. 1994): 40.

Quincy Rumpel and the All-Day Breakfast (Toronto: Groundwood, 1996). **Rev:** *CBRA* (1996): 494; *CCL* 86 (1997): 93; *QQ* 60 (Mar. 1996): 75.

The Lighthouse Dog (Victoria, BC: Orca, 1997). **Rev:** *QQ* 63 (Sept. 1997): 73.

Betty Waterton had her first work, a poem, published in the *Vancouver Sun* when she was 12 years old. She also worked as a newspaper reporter and television artist for many years. However, her first children's book, *A Salmon for Simon*, did not appear until 1978. Since then she has published many books, most of them reflecting her humorous view of the predicaments into which people can precipitate themselves.

Waterton's stories can be divided into two groups. The first deals with young characters overcoming problems in their lives. In *A Salmon for Simon*, the title hero feels inadequate because he is the only person in his west coast Native village unable to catch a fish. In *Pettranella*, a young girl is unhappy because she has lost the flower seeds her grandmother had given her to take from their Old World home to a new homestead in Manitoba. The central figure in *Orff, 27 Dragons (and a Snarkel!)* is the only member of his group of dragons who cannot fly. The characters resolve their conflicts by helping others: Simon liberates a salmon trapped in a tidal pool; Pettranella discovers that the seeds she lost have bloomed in the wilderness and is happy that they will give joy to passing travellers; Orff finds happiness with a school of fish he has rescued from the dreaded Snarkel.

The second group of stories deals with the humorous adventures and misadventures of zany characters. In *Mustard*, an oversized and wild puppy with a penchant for trouble finds a home after he rescues a kitten from the sea. *The Lighthouse Dog* deals with a huge dog that is given a home by a woman but who turns out to be a big nuisance until he rescues a drowning man. *Plain Noodles* is another story of a lighthouse keeper's wife. When Mrs Figg, who misses her now grown children, discovers a boatload of babies, she takes care of them until, to her relief, their mothers come looking for them. *Quincy Rumpel* and its many sequels focus on the escapades of the 11-year-old girl and her unpredictable family. In the first book, the heroine, her brother, her sister, her mother, and her father, an impractical inventor, pile into their old station wagon to travel across the country to a new home in Vancouver. Quincy is disaster prone: she locks herself on the balcony of the new house, breaks through the attic floor, cracks her brand new glasses, and gives herself a new perm, which turns out horribly. In *Starring Quincy Rumpel*, she wants to appear on television so that she can help her father sell his latest invention: home trampolines called Rumpel Rebounders. In later books, she longs to become a private investigator so that she can find a lost treasure, searches the forest for a sasquatch, and helps her mother to run a very chaotic bed-and-breakfast. The accounts of the Rumpels' frequently disorganized but loving family life are told in a lively, fast-paced, and humorous fashion.

In her sensitive portrayals of the problems faced by her insecure characters and her humorous depictions of Quincy and the oversized dogs, Betty Waterton has created books that are widely enjoyed by middle- and upper-elementary readers.

See also: *CA* 111; *CANR* 28, 56; *SATA* 34, 37; *WSMP*.

DIANA WIELER

BORN: 14 October 1961, in Winnipeg.

PRINCIPALRESIDENCES: Winnipeg; Calgary; Saskatoon.

EDUCATION: Southern Alberta Institute of Technology, Calgary.

CAREER: advertising copy writer; freelance editor.

MAJOR AWARDS: Max and Greta Ebel Award (1987); Governor-General's Award for Children's Literature (1989); Canadian Library Association Young Adult Book Award (1990); Ruth Schwartz Children's Book Award (1990); Mr Christie's Book Award, ages 12 and up (1993).

WORKS FOR CHILDREN

A Dog on His Own: A Short Story for Boys and Girls [as Diane J. Wieler], illus. Wieler (Winnipeg: Prairie Publishing Company, 1983).

Last Chance Summer (Saskatoon: Western Producer Prairie Books, 1986). **Rev:** *CCL* 46 (1987): 86; *VOYA* 13 (Feb. 1991): 360; *Wilson Library Bulletin* (May 1991): 6.

Bad Boy (Toronto: Groundwood, 1989). **Rev:** *CCL* 57/58 (1990): 147.

RanVan the Defender (Toronto: Groundwood, 1993).

RanVan: A Worthy Opponent (Toronto: Groundwood, 1995). **Rev:** *CCL* 82 (1996): 95.

To the Mountains by Morning, illus. Ange Zhang (Toronto: Groundwood, 1995). **Rev:** *CCL* 86 (1997): 63.

RanVan: Magic Nation (Toronto: Groundwood, 1997). **Rev:** *CCL* 93 (1999): 100.

Drive (Toronto: Groundwood, 1998). **Rev:** *CCL* 93 (1999): 100.

SELECTED DISCUSSIONS

Cherland, Meredith Rogers. 'A Postmodern Argument Against Censorship: Negotiating Gender and Sexual Identity through Canadian Young Adult Novels', *CCL* 80 (1995): 41–54.

Easun, Sue. '"The Ice Is Its Own Argument": A Canadian Critic Takes a Second Look at *Bad Boy* and Her Own Modest Ambitions', *CCL* 87 (1997): 5–14.

Harker, Mary J. 'Tweaking the Canon: Diana Wieler's Bad Boys', *CCL* 76 (1994): 22–30.

Jenkinson, Dave. 'Diana Wieler: Delinquents and Other Bad Boys', *EL* 17 (May-June 1990): 63–6.

Nodelman, Perry. 'Bad Boys and Binaries: Mary Harker on Diana Wieler's *Bad Boy*', *CCL* 80 (1995): 34–40.

Because she passed high school English with a grade of only 55 per cent, Diana Jean Wieler did not immediately consider a writing career. After she graduated from the television, stage, and radio arts program at the Southern Alberta Institute of Technology, however, a Calgary radio station hired her to write advertising copy. This job proved valuable, she has said, because it taught her the importance of rewriting and made her aware of how words fit together and sound when spoken. Wieler soon began writing stories for adults, but she was unable to get them published. Learning that an American children's magazine needed stories, she decided to try her hand at writing for a younger audience. She not only sold a story, but discovered while writing it, she says, that she could remember precisely what it felt like to be a child. She continued writing for children, but she now concentrates on novels that communicate the intense feelings and emotional confusions of adolescence.

Two of Wieler's short stories, both anthropomorphic animal tales treating the theme of freedom, have been published as books. *A Dog on His Own*, which she illustrated, contains parallel stories. Dog believes, because no one owns him, that he is free. Exhausted and starving, Dog wanders to the cabin of Lori and her embittered Papa, who resembles Dog because he dislikes people. When Lori becomes ill enough to require hospitalization, Papa realizes that he truly needs people. Seeing Papa's change in mood, Dog decides that true freedom comes from relationships, not from avoiding people, and he happily accepts the cabin as home. *To the Mountains by Morning*, an illustrated version of a story that won the 1984 CBC Literary Competition and was used as a Grade 3 reader, reverses this plot pattern. Old Bailey, a 10-year-old quarter horse living on a guest ranch, is gentle with humans and kind to other horses. Only Stocking, a young horse, dislikes Old Bailey. When she courageously decides to escape to the mountains because the ranch's new owner is going to send her to the slaughter house, Old Bailey finally earns Stocking's admiration. First freeing himself from his unwarranted hatred, Stocking joins Old Bailey in a successful quest for physical freedom.

Finding a true home, a theme in both of these stories, is also a theme in Wieler's first novel, *Last Chance Summer*. Twelve-year-old Marl Silversides, a victim of fetal alcohol syndrome, repeatedly runs away from foster homes. Warning him that he will be kept in closed custody in a juvenile facility if he runs away again, his sympathetic social worker gives Marl one last chance in a group home in Alberta's Badlands. Among the nine other boys on this farm are

Goat, a boy physically scarred by abuse, and Topo, a lonely bully who resents Marl's friendship with Goat. Although Topo deviously gets Marl to sniff typewriter fluid where Carleton Jenner, owner of the farm, is certain to catch him, Marl does not take revenge. In fact, when Jenner later decides to send Topo to the detention centre, Marl, who accepts the farm as a good home, compassionately convinces Jenner to let Topo stay.

Last Chance Summer communicates the confusion and longings of alienated boys and the frustrations of the adults who try to help them. By presenting events from the viewpoint of too many characters, however, Wieler softens the focus on Marl and his problems. Furthermore, her heavy-handed references to his unusual eyes constantly remind readers that Marl is the victim of a social problem, fetal alcohol syndrome, but Wieler does not supplement this description with an adequate explanation of the physical and psychological consequences of his condition. In addition to these weaknesses, *Last Chance Summer* suffers from a sentimental, improbable conclusion—because of her affection for Marl, for instance, Cecile Martin, his social worker, quits her job to work with Jenner. Nevertheless, this novel succeeds as a moving and intelligent presentation of social problems and as a sympathetic portrait of troubled adolescents.

Wieler's next book, *Bad Boy*, a combination of the problem novel and the sports story, treats issues of sexual identity and acceptance of differences. The narrative alternates between the viewpoints of two teens, A.J. (Allan James) Brandiosa and his best friend, Tully (Tulsa) Brown, to emphasize their different attitudes and problems. After they make the Triple-A Moose Jaw Cyclones hockey team, A.J. is devastated to discover that Tully is gay. Angry and confused by his feelings for his friend, A.J. becomes vicious on the ice, earning the nickname 'Bad Boy'. At home, A.J. is surly because his father, whose wife left him, is going out with a young woman who often sleeps over. Feeling that his heterosexuality has been challenged by the taunting of some acquaintances, A.J. nearly assaults Summer, Tully's sister. After fighting with the enraged Tully, he gets into an honest discussion in which he learns that his crush on Tully does not make him a homosexual. Accepting that Tully's sexual identity is not a betrayal of friendship, A.J. shows maturity by reconciling with Tully, Summer, his father, and his father's girlfriend.

Bad Boy is tactful yet honest in treating controversial issues. The sports sequences are thematically integrated, becoming part of A.J.'s identity crisis: he begins as a 'marginal' player, earns an identity as a goon, and then deliberately leaves that identity behind. A.J. plausibly overcomes problems at home, at school, and at the hockey rink. Tully doesn't receive equal attention, so he is less successfully developed. Nevertheless, Wieler's portrait is honest and non-judgemental: he is both a successful athlete in a 'macho' sport and a popular person who is not ashamed of and does not come to grief because of his homosexuality.

With the publication of the RanVan trilogy, Wielder added hints of fantasy to the familiar ingredients of the problem novel, creating a series about inner and outer power. Rhan Van, a bespectacled 15-year-old orphan, thinks of himself as RanVan, a knight of the Magic Nation (a childish mispronunciation of imagination). His adventures are described in terms of the mazes and traps of the video universe. Although he tries to battle evil, RanVan is rash and naïve, frequently making errors in judgement. In *RanVan the Defender*, a bitter and confused girl lures him into vandalizing a school and a house. In *RanVan: A Worthy Opponent*, he moves from Vancouver to Thunder Bay, where he competes in a destructive real-world contest with a video player who possesses similar inner power. RanVan also heroically prevents a murder. In both volumes, RanVan performs such extraordinary physical deeds as stopping a robbery at a convenience store by throwing a can that knocks out the robber. In the final volume, *RanVan Magic: Nation*, 18-year-old Rhan goes to school in Calgary to become a television cameraman. This novel incorporates an account of school life and his developing love for a girl, but the fantasy element is belaboured: Rhan prevents an assassination by pointing a camera that is equated with a knight's two-handed sword. The trilogy does not explain RanVan's extraordinary physical prowess, his uncanny premonitions, or the neon-blue light that he sees when he becomes powerful. Nevertheless, the inner glow of chivalry adds nobility to the gritty portrayals of working-class life.

Drive marks a return to Wieler's hard-edged realism. The title reflects the values of its narrator, 18-year-old Jens Friesen. His dedication to hard work made him a success in high school football, earned him the title of Chocolate King because he set a record selling chocolates as a school fund-raiser, and opened up a position for him selling cars when he dropped out of school and moved away from home. Convinced that a meaningful identity comes through material success, Jens is devastated when he loses his job and must sneak away from his apartment because he owes back rent. When his younger brother, Daniel, a talented, moody, socially inept musician and songwriter informs him that he needs to raise $5,000 dollars because of a bad musical contract he signed, Jens applies his drive to extricate him. Together, the two set out on a journey to raise money by getting people to buy copies of Daniel's demo tape. Their weekend sales journey soon becomes a psychological one to the heart of their fears, resentments, and affections. During this journey, it becomes evident that Jens is more driven than driving, that doubts about his birth, his identity, and his self-worth have made him into a person he believes to be unlovable. Jens does, however, find redemption when his brother prevents him from committing suicide. What makes *Drive* notable is that neither brother initially seems likeable or admirable, yet the story makes us care for and sympathize with both because well-placed flashbacks put their traumatic weekend journey into a meaningful context.

Wieler does not portray the comfortable middle-class life that dominates too many books for young people. Instead, she portrays a coarser, raunchier world that resembles the one that many adolescents actually inhabit. The success of her novels does not depend, however, solely on her ability to capture the surface features of young adult experience. While she clearly pictures the bravado of strutting adolescent males, she is adept at penetrating their social façades to reveal the uncertainty and suppressed fears that actually dominate them and make their lives so stressful.

See also: *WSMP*.

Budge (Margery) Wilson

Born: 2 May 1927, in Halifax.

Principal Residences: Halifax; Toronto; Wolfville, NS; Peterborough, Ont.; North West Cove, NS; Hubbards, NS.

Education: Dalhousie University (BA 1949, Teaching Certificate 1953); graduate study at University of Toronto (1941–51).

Career: teacher; artist; photographer; editor; librarian; fitness instructor; writer.

Awards: Canadian Library Association Young Adult Book Award (1991); Ann Connor Brimer Award (1993).

Works for Children

The Worst Christmas Present Ever (Richmond Hill, Ont.: Scholastic-TAB, 1984). **Rev:** *CBRA* (1984): 347; *CM* 13 (May 1985): 117; *EL* 13 (Mar. 1986): 16.

A House Far from Home (Richmond Hill, Ont.: Scholastic-TAB, 1984). **Rev:** *APBR* 15 (Nov. 1988): 10; *BYP* 1 (June 1987): 10; *CM* 15 (Mar. 1987): 64; *EL* 14 (May 1987): 50.

Mr. John Bertrand Nijinsky and Charlie, illus. Terry Roscoe Boucher (Halifax: Nimbus, 1986). **Rev:** *APBR* 13 (Nov. 1986): 4; *BiC* 15 (Dec. 1986): 16; *CCL* 44 (1986): 16; *EL* 14 (Jan. 1987): 47; *QQ* 52 (Oct. 1986): 20.

Mystery Lights at Blue Harbour (Richmond Hill, Ont.: Scholastic-TAB, 1987). **Rev:** *BYP* 1 (Dec. 1987): 10; *CCL* 51 (1988): 73; *CM* 15 (May 1988): 55; *EL* 16 (Mar. 1988): 48.

Breakdown (Richmond Hill, Ont.: Scholastic-TAB, 1988).

Going Bananas (Richmond Hill, Ont.: Scholastic-TAB, 1989). **Rev:** *CBRA* (1989): 328.

Thirteen Never Changes (Richmond Hill, Ont.: Scholastic-TAB, 1989). **Rev:** *BiC* 18 (Dec. 1989): 20; *CBRA* (1989): 329; *CCL* 62 (1991): 88; *CM* 18 (May 1990): 131; *QQ* 56 (Mar. 1990): 22.

Madame Belzile and Ramsay Hitherton-Hobbs (Halifax: Nimbus, 1990). **Rev:** *APBR* 18 (June 1991): 17; *CM* 19 (Oct. 1991): 300.

Lorinda's Diary (Toronto: General, 1991). **Rev:** *CM* 20 (May 1992): 169.

Oliver's Wars (Toronto: Stoddart, 1992). **Rev:** *CCL* 81 (1996): 65; *CM* 20 (Oct. 1992): 256; *EL* 20 (Nov. 1992): 59; *QQ* 58 (May 1992): 33.

Cassandra's Driftwood (Lawrencetown Beach, NS: Pottersfield Press, 1994). **Rev:** *BiC* 23 (Sept. 1994): 56; *CBRA* (1994): 505; *CM* 22 (Sept. 1994): 126; *QQ* 60 (July 1994): 60.

Harold and Harold (Lawrencetown Beach, NS: Pottersfield Press, 1995). **Rev:** *CBRA* (1995): 521; *CCL* 89 (1998): 62.

Sharla (Toronto: Stoddart, 1997). **Rev:** *CBRA* (1997): 532; *CCL* 89 (1998): 62.

Duff the Giant Killer (Halifax: Formac, 1997). **Rev:** *CBRA* (1997): 532; *CM* 4 (19 Sept. 1997): on-line; *QQ* 63 (July 1997): 50.

The Long Wait, illus. Eugenie Fernandes (Toronto: Stoddart, 1997). **Rev:** *CBRA* (1997): 496; *CCL* 93 (1999): 54; *QQ* 63 (Mar. 1997): 79.

The Cat that Barked (Lawrencetown Beach, NS: Pottersfield Press, 1998).

Works for Adults and Young Adults

The Leaving (Toronto: House of Anansi, 1990). **Rev:** *APBR* 18 (Dec. 1991): 9; *CCB-B* 45 (June 1992): 284; *CBRA* (1990): 205; *CM* 19 (Nov. 1991): 343; *EL* 19 (Nov. 1991): 64; *HB* 68 (July 1992): 456; *SLJ* 38 (Dec. 1992): 23; *VOYA* 15 (Aug. 1992): 170.

Cordelia Clark (Toronto: Stoddart, 1994). **Rev:** *CBRA* (1994): 505.

The Courtship: Stories (Toronto: House of Anansi, 1994). **Rev:** *CBRA* (1994): 198.

The Dandelion Garden and Other Stories (New York: Philomel, 1995). **Rev:** *CCB-B* 48 (June 1995): 363; *SLJ* 41 (June 1995): 132; *VOYA* 18 (Aug. 1995): 166.

Mothers and Other Strangers (New York: Harcourt Brace, 1996).

Selected Discussions

Jenkinson, Dave. 'Budge Wilson', *EL* 23 (Nov. 1995): 61–4.

Budge (Margery) Wilson did not begin writing until she was 50 years old, but she quickly proved herself to be both prolific and versatile. Her works include a picture book, chapter books for beginning readers, children's novels, and short story collections for adults that have generally been treated as 'cross-over' fiction, adult literature that also speaks comprehensibly to adolescents. In many respects, Wilson is a local colourist: she provides a vivid sense of life in small-town Nova Scotia and the effects of both fog and sunshine on the emotions of its inhabitants. She does not, however, simply depict quaint landscapes. She indicates the social and economic conditions that shape regional attitudes while developing themes about family life and the ways that various relationships affect character, both positively and negatively.

Wilson's first book, *The Worst Christmas Present Ever* (almost always cited, even by the author, as *The Best/Worst Christmas Present Ever* because of the way the title is displayed on the cover), launched a series of books about the Dauphinee family of Blue Harbour, Nova Scotia. The series includes a number of concerns, but it concentrates on the oldest child, Lorinda, and her relationships within and outside the family. In the first book, Lorinda is determined to buy a $35 red vase as a Christmas present for her mother. With the aid of her brother, James, and a group of friends, she devises a series of money-making schemes that go disappointingly awry. Eventually, however, she raises enough money, only to discover that nasty and wealthy Reginald Corkum, knowing her plans, has purchased the vase for his mother. The amusingly ironic twist is that Lorinda's mother, having seen the vase, reveals that she thinks it is hideous. Lorinda and James, realizing that their mother never has money to take advantage of post-Christmas sales, make a money book by taping dollar bills to pages of an album. Brimming with appropriate seasonal spirit and goodwill, *The Worst Christmas Present Ever* is an amusing, fast-paced tale that contains interesting, likeable, and plausible characters.

Although the subsequent Blue Harbour books present interesting glimpses of family life, none are as cohesive and original as the first volume. In *A House Far from Home*, which takes place a week after the first book, Mr Dauphinee's health has deteriorated so much that he has to go to Texas to recuperate. Lorinda and James are therefore sent to live with Aunt Marian (unaccountably called Marion in later books) and Uncle Harry. In a conventional story about loving and lively children reviving the ossified emotions of an older person, Lorinda transforms rigid Aunt Marian into an affectionate and understanding woman who eventually decides to adopt a baby. In addition to the domestic story, the novel includes a two-pronged school story. One part involves the nasty Mildred, who insinuates that Lorinda is a thief, and the other involves a sports story in which Lorinda, having been kept off the hockey team by a sexist coach, becomes a star in a crucial playoff game. A third story, about a businessman who fears flying, aids the theme but stretches plausibility even more than the sports story. The next in the series, *Mystery Lights at Blue Harbour*, is the weakest, combining a predictable story about changes in Mildred and Hank, two students from Peterborough, Ontario, who visit James and Lorinda in Nova Scotia, and a rather feeble mystery about lights in the harbour and the disappearance of Mr Dauphinee.

The final two volumes use diaries to convey the emotions of adolescent girls. In *Thirteen Never Changes*, Lorinda, reading the diaries bequeathed by her late grandmother, becomes drawn into her grandmother's adolescence during World War II, when her family hosted an English Guest Child. Reading about her grandmother's friendships and first love, Lorinda discovers a girl who was very much like herself. The diary entries are generally effective in making the story both a historical novel and a contemporary story of a girl discovering herself through the discovery of her roots. As a result of reading her grandmother's diaries, Lorinda begins writing her own, presented in *Lorinda's Diary*.

When Lorinda's grandfather comes to visit for six months, he proves to be bitter and lonely (a male type common in Wilson's fiction). Feeling that he has never been of first importance to anyone, even to his late wife, he broods and demands attention. As she did with Aunt Marian, Lorinda eventually reconnects her grandfather to life and gives him a new sense of purpose. In addition to this story of youth teaching the elderly lessons about life, the novel also includes stories about Lorinda's friendship with a fat girl who becomes jealous of the time Lorinda spends practising basketball and about Lorinda's confused feelings when she discovers that, although in distinctly different ways, she likes the two boys who like her. Unfortunately, in spite of the effort to show that Lorinda is deliberately incorporating a larger vocabulary into her entries, the first-person narration does not ring true, making the novel decidedly artificial.

Wilson's other children's novels include embittered males and disruptions in family life, although the focus in each is different. In *Breakdown*, a father's collapse creates problems for his children. Mr Collicut, overworked in a job he hates, becomes surly and domineering. Having had his own promising track-and-field career terminated by an accident, he insists that his oldest son, Daniel, concentrate on making the track team and on winning a provincial championship. He therefore forbids him to take a part in a school play. He also lashes out at Katie, his musically talented daughter, demanding that she stop her constant practising. Katie eventually plays a major role in her father's recuperation, convincing him to try music, which he had given up as a youth when he devoted himself to track and field. Mr Collicut also comes to accept that Daniel has a right to determine his own course in life. He therefore not only accepts Daniel's decision to be an actor, but he also begins running with him, a non-competitive activity that Daniel loves. The presentation of the breakdown and the subsequent disturbances to family life are somewhat sanitized, but the novel adopts the positive attitude that breakdowns permit the building of a stronger identity in both the patient and those who love him. Rounding out the main story is another one about identity: Katie helps an overweight girl to slim down and thus to feel good about herself.

Equally rich in the diversity of conflicts is *Oliver's Wars*, winner of the 1993 Ann Connor Brimer Award. The surly male in this novel is Oliver Kovak's grandfather, who has lost his sense of purpose after retirement. When Oliver and his mother move in with his grandparents because her husband's medical unit is serving in the Gulf War, Oliver finds that his grandfather is domineering and inflexible. At school, Oliver endures taunts from Gus, a bully, who mocks him because his father is a nurse, and sarcasm from his gym teacher, who accuses the unco-ordinated Oliver of being lazy. When Gus copies Oliver's report, the teacher accuses Oliver of being the cheater. Communication eventually solves all problems: Oliver and his grandfather begin sharing walks that bring them together; Oliver first confronts and then comforts Gus when he learns that Gus is worried about his father, a gunner wounded in combat; Oliver lets the teacher know that he has tried his best at sports, and the teacher, having realized that Oliver did not cheat, becomes tolerant and understanding. Except for the reformation of Gus, *Oliver's Wars* successfully packs plausible difficulties into a story that shows the transformative power of sympathetic understanding.

In *Sharla*, the surly male is more of a background figure, but the force of his anger is evident in its effect on his daughter. Because her father has lost his high-paying job in Ottawa, Sharla Dunfield finds herself living in Churchill, Manitoba, the polar bear capital of the world. Bitter about the move and the unhappy conditions at home, Sharla performs poorly at school. The only bright spot in her life comes when an American photographer hires her to help him. Sharla begins fantasizing about him. When he foolishly imperils her life by baiting a polar bear in order to photograph it, Sharla realizes that he is a selfish, nasty person who values a picture more than human relationships. Having also learned that he has a daughter, Sharla condemns him for ignoring people, an act that has a positive reformative effect on him. Her realization of the photographer's true character and her encounter with the majestic polar bears also enable Sharla to take hold of her own emotions. In spite of its good intentions, however, *Sharla* suffers from two problems. First, its belaboured efforts to work in local colour make it sound too much like an old-fashioned travelogue. Second, too much of the dialogue is sermonizing about anger management and the restorative wonders of counselling. Preaching and wooden characterization thus make *Sharla* a disappointing and unconvincing problem novel.

In addition to children's novels, Wilson has also written shorter works for beginning readers. Several of these focus on cures for loneliness. *Mr. John Bertrand Nijinsky and Charlie* features another of Wilson's embittered men. John Bertrand Nijinsky, a 65-year-old man who has given up on life and friendships, is transformed into his old fun-loving self when Charlie, the ugly outcast in a litter of attractive kittens, makes himself at home in his house. The story continues too long after its climax, but succeeds as an unsentimental presentation of the idea that life's frustrations can change personalities for the worse, whereas the active concern for others can cause positive transformation. A similar transformation occurs in *Madame Belzile and Ramsay Hitherton-Hobbs*. When fat, shy Ramsay moves in next door to Madame Belzile, a lonely widow without interests, she gains a purpose. Seeing that Ramsay is miserable because he is behind his classmates in French and because everyone taunts him about his weight, she puts him on a diet and instructs him in French. By transforming Ramsay into a thin, confident, and likeable boy, Madame Belzile gains other interests and ceases to be a bored and lonely recluse. The lonely people in three chapter books are children. In *Cassandra's Driftwood*, Cassandra Westhaver, a shy girl living by the sea, turns a large piece of driftwood into a friend she names Amos. When teenagers take Amos to use in a beach fire, Cassandra overcomes her shyness and fear, demanding that they return Amos to her. Her success gives her new confidence in solving problems that had previously frustrated her. *The*

Cat That Barked is less satisfying as a narrative. After Stephanie Henderson moves from Peterborough, Ontario, to Halifax, her only friend seems to be her cat, Fido. When Stephanie says that Fido is six-coloured and barks, students at her new school come to her house because they don't believe her. Even after the cat loses his bark, the result of a temporary trauma, Stephanie is satisfied with her new life because the children have become genuine friends. *Harold and Harold*, about a lonely boy whom everyone ignores, has an even more implausible and weaker plot. Harold's only friend is a heron, with whom he identifies so completely that he gives it his own name. When people think that Harold the boy is missing during a storm, they realize that they should have made him part of their lives, and they do so after he is discovered to have been safe in bed all the time.

For readers just graduating to chapter books, Wilson has written a couple of fast-paced, action-filled farces based on the unintentional chaos created by a pair of energetic and engaging friends. In *Going Bananas* (which Wilson has indicated she will issue in a revised version as *Duff's Monkey Business*), Duff Dooley and Simon Abrams discover a chimp in Duff's barn, but no one believes them because they are known to have wild imaginations. Comic troubles follow until they learn that the chimp has escaped from a travelling circus. *Duff the Giant Killer*, based on an episode in *Going Bananas*, has Duff and Simon cause chaos when they decide to act out 'Jack the Giant-Killer'. A woman, mistaking their improvised drama for a real killing, calls the police. Both stories are improbable but entertaining. Unfortunately, *The Long Wait*, a picture book based on a true experience of a cat lost during a move, has little to recommend it as a narrative. The lost cat does nothing remarkable, and neither the people who lost it nor those who find it do anything to compel interest. The only real interest lies in Eugenie Fernandes's pictures, which offer reassuring glimpses of the playful cat while the text describes the anxieties of those searching for it.

Wilson accidentally moved into the area of young adult fiction when *The Leaving*, which was written and published as a collection of stories for adults, won the Canadian Library Association Young Adult Book Award in 1991. Subsequently, it was republished in the United States as a book specifically for young adults. The book is appealing to adolescents because it concentrates on significant events that altered or illuminated a girl's relationship with her parents, friends, or boys. It appeals to adults because, with a single exception, its stories are retrospective, having adults look back on childhood and adolescence. The single exception is the concluding story, 'The Pen Pal'. Narrated through the letters of Edna Publicover to an Australian named Hilary, this story expresses a girl's feelings about the onset of puberty and her joy in knowing that she is a woman. In the hilariously ironic conclusion, Edna, who has used her letters to explore her most intimate feelings, learns that Hilary is a boy, not a girl. Other moments of transformation are far from comic. In 'The Diary', entries apparently addressed to a psychiatrist help a woman assess the role of her hypocritical and repressive father, a minister whom she discovered to be having an affair. Able to see clearly the patriarchal repression that limited her own life, she frees herself from its constrictions by encouraging her own son, in spite of her husband's desires, to follow his heart in marriage and in finding a new career. A young girl makes an even more startling discovery about her parents in the touching 'My Mother and Father'. Born after her father had drowned, the narrator tells of how she developed an image of her father as a handsome hero. After discovering that her father was a domineering, self-centred fool, she is reconciled to her mother. Simultaneously, her mother, no longer needing to maintain a patriarchal myth that made her a secondary figure in her daughter's life, is rejuvenated. In the title story, 'The Leaving', a woman leaves her family for a brief period, and then adopts a practical course for making the males in her family treat her with some degree of respect. Males are not, however, the villains in all of these stories. 'Be-ers and Doers' focuses on a son, constantly criticized by his mother, who, after proving that he is intelligent and heroic, rejects his mother and decides to live life on his own terms. 'The Waiting' explores the ironic shifts in affection when a talented girl, her mother's favourite, discovers that her twin sister's quiet beauty exerts more power than all of the accomplishments upon which she, a chubby and egotistical girl, prided herself. Of the remaining stories, the most notable is 'The Metaphor', about a flamboyant elementary teacher who gives the narrator a love of language but then becomes the butt of jokes and intolerance when she becomes a high school teacher.

With their subtle evocation of the painful self-consciousness of adolescence and the power of memories of childhood events to haunt one long into adulthood, the stories in *The Leaving* offer youthful readers a chance to take a mature look at their own lives. Although not quite as distinguished, Wilson's subsequent collections (some of which repeat stories included in previous volumes) also contain intelligent and unsentimental accounts of life-shaping moments. They are particularly notable for developing the sometimes uneasy relationship between children and parents.

The Nova Scotia landscape and weather are prominent features of Budge Wilson's work, and her novels conclude with happy endings (in spite of some tales of bitterness or defeat, the stories are also generally optimistic), but she does not offer regional idylls. Primarily a problem novelist exploring psychological and social difficulties, she focuses on the often prickly relationship between young and old, showing how each can make the other's life better. Except in her books for early readers, which frequently belabour points, she succeeds in packing several conflicts into each book, in making them come alive through interesting characters, and in developing intelligent, thought-provoking conclusions.

See also: *CA* 121; *SATA* 51, 55; *WSMP*.

Eric Wilson

Born: 24 November 1940, in Ottawa.

Education: University of British Columbia (BA 1963, teacher's certificate, 1964).

Principal Residences: Ottawa; Winnipeg; St John's, Nfld; Montreal; Saskatoon; Regina; Kitimat, BC; Vancouver; London, England; White Rock, BC; Campbell River, BC; Nanaimo, BC; Powell River, BC; Blubber Bay, BC; Nelson, BC; Victoria, BC.

Career: teacher; writer.

Works for Children

Murder on the Canadian (Toronto: Clarke, Irwin/Bodley Head, 1976). **Rev:** *CBRA* (1976): 244; *CCL* 7 (1977): 56.

Susie-Q (Richmond Hill, Ont.: Scholastic, 1978). **Rev:** *CBRA* (1978): 189; *CCL* 14 (1979): 58.

Vancouver Nightmare (Toronto: Clarke, Irwin/Bodley Head, 1978). **Rev:** *CBRA* (1978): 187, and (1982): 257.

Terror in Winnipeg (Toronto: Clarke, Irwin/Bodley Head, 1979). **Rev:** *CCL* 20 (1980): 73.

The Lost Treasure of Casa Loma (Toronto: Clarke, Irwin/Bodley Head, 1980). **Rev:** *CBRA* (1980): 171; *CCL* 22 (1981): 61.

The Ghost of Lunenburg Manor (Toronto: Clarke, Irwin, 1981). **Rev:** *CBRA* (1981): 235; *CCL* 30 (1983): 83; *QQ* 47 (Aug. 1981): 28.

Disneyland Hostage (Toronto: Clarke, Irwin, 1982). **Rev:** *BiC* 11 (Dec. 1982): 11; *CBRA* (1982): 256; *QQ* 48 (Dec. 1982): 25.

The Kootenay Kidnapper (Toronto: Collins, 1983). **Rev:** *BiC* 13 (Mar. 1984): 29; *CBRA* (1983): 298; *CM* 13 (July 1985): 164; *QQ* 50 (Apr. 1984): 17.

Vampires of Ottawa (Toronto: Collins, 1984). **Rev:** *CBRA* (1984): 348; *CCL* 48 (1987): 91; *CM* 13 (May 1985): 117; *QQ* 51 (Feb. 1985): 18.

Summer of Discovery (Toronto: Collins, 1984). **Rev:** *CBRA* (1984): 347; *CCL* 48 (1987): 92.

Spirit in the Rainforest (Toronto: Collins, 1984). **Rev:** *CBRA* (1985): 275; *CCL* 48 (1987): 91; *CM* 14 (May 1986): 118.

The Unmasking of 'Ksan (Toronto: Collins, 1986). **Rev:** *CCL* 48 (1987): 91; *CM* 15 (Mar. 1987): 64.

The Green Gables Detectives (Toronto: Collins, 1987). **Rev:** *APBR* 14 (Nov. 1987): 4; *CM* 16 (Mar. 1988): 48.

Code Red at the Supermall (Toronto: Collins, 1988). **Rev:** *CBRA* (1988): 300; *CM* 17 (Jan. 1989): 22.

Cold Midnight in Vieux Québec (Toronto: Harper & Collins, 1989). **Rev:** *CBRA* (1989): 329; *CM* 18 (May 1990): 132; *QQ* 56 (Mar. 1990): 22.

The Ice Diamond Quest (Toronto: HarperCollins, 1990). **Rev:** *CCL* 69 (1993): 50; *CM* 19 (Mar. 1991): 90; *QQ* 57 (May 1991): 22.

The Prairie Dog Conspiracy (Toronto: HarperCollins, 1992). **Rev:** *CCL* 76 (1994): 66; *CM* 20 (Sept. 1992): 21; *QQ* 58 (Aug. 1992): 28.

The Hole in Tommy's Pocket, illus. Joel Reid (Edmonton: Donovan Publishing, 1993). **Rev:** *CM* 22 (Oct. 1994): 186.

The St. Andrews Werewolf (Toronto: HarperCollins, 1993). **Rev:** *CBRA* (1993): #6194; *CM* 21 (Nov. 1993): 21; *QQ* 59 (July 1993): 56.

The Case of the Golden Boy (Toronto: HarperCollins, 1994). **Rev:** *CBRA* (1994): 505; *CCL* 87 (1997): 73.

The Inuk Mountie Adventure (Toronto: HarperCollins, 1996). **Rev:** *CBRA* (1995): 521; *CCL* 89 (1998): 50.

Escape from Big Muddy (Toronto: HarperCollins, 1997). **Rev:** *QQ* 64 (Feb. 1998): 49.

Selected Discussions

Jones, Raymond E. 'Popular Books, the Responsibilities of the Reviewer, and Literary Nationalism: The Case of Eric Wilson', *ChLQ* 8 (Summer 1983): 34, 44–5.

Eric Hamilton Wilson, author of the popular Tom and Liz Austen mysteries, began writing for children while he was teaching slow learners in White Rock, BC. Having purchased numerous books for his class, Wilson watched in dismay as the students repeatedly tossed them aside as boring. He therefore decided to write something his class would willingly read all the way through. Although his students enjoyed the stories he subsequently wrote for them, publishers were less impressed, rejecting five manuscripts in five years. Only after Margaret Clark, a British children's editor for Bodley Head, showed him some of the problems with his fiction did Wilson succeed in devising a formula for publishable books that would capture the interest of his intended readers.

Wilson's formula, based on his observations of the way his students responded to books, is relatively simple. First, he decided, a book must be short so that students for whom reading is difficult and long books are threatening would not immediately discard it. Next, the story had to start instantly. *Murder on the Canadian*, for example, begins with 'The package was ticking.' Most of his subsequent books have similar dramatic openings because reluctant readers, Wilson believes, need the lure of narrative hooks. Although Wilson also felt that a story's language had to be simple and straightforward, he rejected the concept of a controlled vocabulary because, he says, 'I don't believe that an unfamiliar word is a roadblock in a good story.' In addition, Wilson felt that abundant dialogue was essential for three reasons: to add interest because conversation is itself dramatic and active; to add realism; and to create 'a lot of white space' to break up the dense blocks of text that frighten reluctant readers. Finally, through his belief that reluctant readers need continuing enticements to keep them turning pages, he decided to end each chapter with a cliff-hanger that forces the reader on to the next chapter, where, of course, the action builds to another suspenseful situation.

Wilson's Austen mysteries attempt to combine the adventure of the Hardy Boys or Nancy Drew with the true detection of an Agatha Christie novel in order to make the reader an active participant. Not surprisingly, the first in the series, *Murder on the Canadian*, contains references to both the Hardy Boys and Agatha Christie, and its setting and title echo Christie's *Murder on the Orient Express*. In many of the other titles, Tom and Liz mention either the Hardy Boys or Nancy Drew. The distinguishing feature of the series, however, is their settings. Wilson consciously gives the books Canadian settings, all of which he has visited. By filling the novels with historical data and interesting facts about each setting, he hopes to educate and excite his readers about Canada. His one non-Canadian title, *Disneyland Hostage*, was intended to launch a series of international novels presenting other parts of the world through Canadian eyes, those of Liz Austen, but he appears to have abandoned the project.

Although all of Wilson's mysteries contain both adventure and educational information, they emphasize these in different proportions. Some are primarily traditional adventure-mystery stories in which Tom, Liz, or both land in threatening or mysterious circumstances that demand detection and luck to survive. The emphasis is on thrilling adventure and red-herring mysteries. These include *Murder on the Canadian*, *The Lost Treasure of Casa Loma*, *The Ghost of Lunenburg Manor*, *Code Red at the Supermall*, *Vampires of Ottawa*, *The Green Gables Detectives*, *The Prairie Dog Conspiracy*, *The Case of the Golden Boy*, and *Escape from Big Muddy*. Other books, although not neglecting adventure, use the settings and the mystery formula to provide information that enables the books to function as teaching vehicles or springboards for discussions in classrooms. In these, issues from the evening news become important thematic elements. Thus, *Terror in Winnipeg* and *Spirit in the Rainforest* express environmental concerns, the former about industrial pollution and Minimata disease, and the latter about the devastation of clear-cut logging. *Terror in Winnipeg* and *Disneyland Hostage* show terror as a misguided instrument of social reform. *Vancouver Nightmare*, *Disneyland Hostage*, and *The Kootenay Kidnapper* are efforts to streetproof children. The first shows the sordid world of drugs that often claims runaways. The second tries to show that quiet compliance with the demands of terrorists, not hostile opposition, is necessary when one is held ransom. *The Kootenay Kidnapper*, inspired by the grisly Clifford Olson case of kidnap-murders in British Columbia, seeks to teach children the necessity of avoiding strangers, even those who seem like figures of authority. It shows some of the tricks that Olson and others used to lure unsuspecting children. *The St. Andrews Werewolf* has a subplot encouraging victims of sexual abuse to tell others about assaults and reassuring them that they are not bad people if someone does molest them. Its dominant plot shows the tension between those who want a mall built because of its economic benefits and those who fear that such development will spoil the quality of life they enjoy in their picturesque town. *The Inuk Mountie Adventure* raises the issues of Canadian identity through a plot involving an arrogant and unscrupulous Prime Minister's proposal to have Canada merge with the United States. Set primarily in the Arctic, it also provides information about Inuit culture.

Wilson's plots are improbable. In *Cold Midnight in Vieux Québec*, for instance, Tom, who is supposed to be playing in a hockey tournament, becomes instrumental in preventing an assassination of world leaders gathered in Quebec City. In *The St. Andrews Werewolf* the Gothic elements—a number of people believe that a werewolf is responsible for a series of arsons—strain credibility to the breaking point. Nevertheless, Wilson balances the improbability by ensuring that his young detectives are not outrageously heroic or infallible. Tom, for example, constantly jumps to false conclusions and repeatedly makes mistakes in identifying the villains. Wilson claims that young people more readily identify with Tom because he is an ordinary boy who blunders around and worries that his sister may discover something important and get glory before he does. Liz is generally more competent, but she is also less than ingenious in solving crimes.

Although he has not varied his formula, Wilson has added additional wrinkles to a couple of his Austen books. *The Prairie Dog Conspiracy* is a frame story in which Tom, sitting in Petty Harbour, Newfoundland, after winding up the events recounted in *The Ice Diamond Quest*, tells his cousin about his very first case. The framed tale, about the kidnapping of wealthy Dianne Dorchester in Winnipeg, is among Tom's most improbable adventures. Its major interest lies in comparing it with the first mystery about Tom Austen that Wilson wrote, *The Case of the Golden Boy*, an earlier version of the same story that is even more improbable and that Wilson's introductory note says that he is publishing as 'an artifact'. *Escape from Big Muddy*, the second Austen mystery attempting some novelty, resembles *The Prairie Dog Conspiracy* in being a retrospective frame tale. In this case, however, the frame is set in the future, and 60-year-old Liz Austen, by means of a two-way computer display, recounts to a fan the details of her first case. This adventure involves a quest that takes Liz to various places in Saskatchewan in an effort to locate a stolen statue before members of a motorcycle gang can get to it. Wilson adds an extra dimension to the tale by overt allusions to Robert Louis Stevenson's *Treasure Island*. The echoes come from the names of characters or places: Billy Bones, Blind Pew, Smollett, Squire, Arrow, and Benbow Farm. Wilson also alludes to episodes in Stevenson's novel, having the female villain, like Long John Silver, become engaged as a cook during the treasure-hunting expedition; having the members of the motorcycle gang, who are like the pirates, slip each other the black spot that signals death; and having Liz, like Jim Hawkins, overhear a conversation while hiding in an apple barrel. Unfortunately, the parallels are little more than gimmicky allusions, making an insubstantial contribution. When Liz hides in the barrel, for instance, she does not, as Jim did when he hid, receive information that causes her to lose innocence, a loss that makes an apple barrel an appropriately symbolic location for Jim.

In addition to the Austen mysteries, Wilson has written one without them, *The Unmasking of 'Ksan*, about the theft of a valuable Native mask. Primarily an adventure in which Graham, the narrator, aids his Aboriginal friend, Dawn, in solving the mystery of the theft and in recovering the artifact, the novel gives some attention to the issue of the Gitksan people's pride in their culture. In addition, Wilson has published two problem novels, *Susie-Q*, a tough-minded exploration of class bias and teenage pregnancy, and *Summer of Discovery*, which contains two parallel stories of independence, one involving a handicapped boy and the other an able-bodied one. Finally, for beginning readers, Wilson has published *The Hole in Tommy's Pocket*, an amusing fantasy about a boy who finds a talking hole that helps him to solve several problems.

Because he did not allow his publishers to indicate in any way that his first books were written for reluctant readers, Eric Wilson became enormously popular with both his intended audience and a much younger group of accomplished readers. Although he talks more now about exciting children about Canada than about appealing to reluctant readers, his recent works differ little from his earlier ones. None of his books are what he calls capital 'L' literature, and all have obvious flaws. Some of these flaws are endemic to mysteries, in which the need for action weakens effective characterization. Other flaws arise from Wilson's educational agenda. In his efforts to introduce geographical, cultural, and historical information, Wilson too often resorts to stilted dialogue that seems as if it has come from a bad documentary film. Nevertheless, his books, even when they are improbable, are carefully plotted, swift in movement, and interesting in setting. Wilson also plays the mystery game fairly: he provides all the clues necessary to solve the case even before his detectives do. He thus rewards careful readers with information, entertainment, and a sense of accomplishment.

See also: *CA* 101; *CANR* 20; *MCAI*; *Profiles* 2; *SATA* 32, 34; *WSMP*.

Janet Wilson

Born: 20 November 1952, in Toronto.

Principal Residences: Toronto; Eden Mills, Ont.

Education: Ontario College of Art (AA 1985).

Career: illustrator.

Major Awards: Elizabeth Mrazik-Cleaver Picture Book Award (1996); IODE (Toronto) Book Award, with Linda Granfield (1995).

Works for Children

Illustrated by Janet Wilson

Danny's Dollars, by Susan Green and Sharon Siamon (Toronto: Gage, 1986).

The Laughing Cake, by Sharon Siamon (Toronto: Gage, 1987).

Break Out, by Martyn Godfrey (Toronto: Maxwell Macmillan, 1988).

Kid's Games: How to Have Great Times with Your 3 to 6 Year Old, by Elaine Martin (Toronto: Random House, 1989).

Jump Start, by Sylvia McNicoll (Toronto: Maxwell Macmillan, 1989).

Daniel's Dog, by Jo Ellen Bogart (Richmond Hill, Ont.: Scholastic, 1990). **Rev:** *CCB-B* 43 (June 1990): 233; *CCL* 59 (1990): 81; *CM* 18 (May 1990): 117; *EL* 18 (Sept. 1990): 52; *QQ* 56 (Mar. 1990): 20; *SLJ* 36 (Mar. 1990): 188.

The Math Whiz, by Betsy Duffey (New York: Viking, 1990). **Rev:** *SLJ* 36 (Dec. 1990): 76.

Let's Find Out About Cats, by Barbara Hehner (Toronto: Random House, 1990).

We Both Have Scars, by Paul Kropp (Toronto: Maxwell Macmillan, 1990).

Secret of the Lunchbox Criminal, by Alison Lohans (Richmond Hill, Ont.: Scholastic, 1990).

The Gadget War, by Betsy Duffey (New York: Viking, 1991). **Rev:** *CCB-B* 45 (Sept. 1991): 8; *SLJ* 37 (Nov. 1991): 116.

Let's Find Out About Dogs, by Barbara Hehner (Toronto: Random House, 1991). **Rev:** *QQ* 57 (Apr. 1991): 20.

Jess Was the Brave One, by Jean Little (Toronto: Penguin, 1991). **Rev:** *CCL* 72 (1993): 69; *CM* 20 (Mar. 1992): 82; *EL* (Mar. 1992): 17; *QQ* 57 (Aug. 1991): 24.

Hello, Hello, by Jenifer McVaugh (Toronto: Maxwell Macmillan, 1991).

Benny and the Crazy Contest, by Cheryl Zach (New York: Bradbury Press, 1991). **Rev:** *SLJ* 37 (May 1991): 96.

Buried in Ice, by Owen Beattie and John Geiger (Toronto: Madison Press, 1992). **Rev:** *CCB-B* 45 (Mar. 1992): 174; *SLJ* 38 (Apr. 1992): 138.

Revenge of the Small Small, by Jean Little (Toronto: Penguin, 1992). **Rev:** *CBRA* (1995): 475; *QQ* 58 (Oct. 1992): 31; *RT* 47 (Oct. 1993); 148.

Germy Johnson's Secret Plan, by Alison Lohans (Richmond Hill, Ont.: Scholastic, 1992).

Benny and the No-Good Teacher, by Cheryl Zach (New York: Bradbury Press, 1992). **Rev:** *SLJ* 38 (Sept. 1992): 262.

Gopher Takes Heart, by Virginia Scribner (New York: Viking, 1992). **Rev:** *CCB-B* 46 (Mar. 1993): 224; *SLJ* 34 (Jan. 1993): 103.

Howard's House is Haunted!, by Maureen Bayless (Richmond Hill, Ont: Scholastic, 1993). **Rev:** *CM* 21 (Sept. 1993): 135; *QQ* 59 (Feb. 1993): 36.

How to be Cool in the Third Grade, by Betsy Duffey (New York: Viking, 1993). **Rev:** *CCB-B* 47 (Oct. 1993): 42; *SLJ* 39 (Sept. 1993): 206.

Heather Come Back, by Dayle Gaetz (Toronto: Maxwell Macmillan, 1993).

The Trail of the Chocolate Thief, James Heneghan (Richmond Hill, Ont.: Scholastic, 1993).

Tiger Flowers, by Patricia Quinlan (Toronto: Stoddart, 1993). **Rev:** *CBRA* (1994): 463; *CCB-B* 47 (July 1994): 371; *CCL* 79 (1995): 82; *CL* (1995): 205; *HB* 71 (May 1995): 204; *QQ* 60 (Apr. 1994): 36; *SLJ* 40 (July 1994): 87.

Baby Games: The Joyful Guide to Child's Play from Birth to Three Years, by Elaine Martin (Toronto: Stoddart, 1994).

Gopher Draws Conclusions, by Virginia Scribner (New York: Viking, 1994). **Rev:** *CCB-B* 48 (Mar. 1993): 224; *SLJ* 40 (Nov. 1994): 107.

The Baritone Cat, by Mora Skelton (Toronto: Stoddart, 1994). **Rev:** *BiC* 23 (Summer 1994): 57; *CBRA* (1994): 466; *CM* 22 (Sept. 1994): 134; *QQ* 60 (Apr. 1994): 38.

Rachel Carson, Writer and Scientist, by Carol Alexander (Columbus, Ohio: Modern Curriculum Press, 1995).

What's He Doing Now?, by Patti Farmer (Richmond Hill, Ont.: Scholastic, 1996). **Rev:** *CBRA* (1996): 441; *QQ* 62 (Nov. 1996): 46.

In Flanders Fields: The Story of the Poem by John McCrae, by Linda Granfield (Toronto: Stoddart, 1996). **Rev:** *CBRA* (1995): 536; *CCL* 84 (1996): 99; *EL* 23 (Mar. 1996): 26; *QQ* 61 (Dec. 1995): 38; *RT* 51 (Nov. 1997): 243; *SLJ* 42 (Dec. 1996): 129.

Selina and the Bear Paw Quilt, by Barbara Smucker (Toronto: Stoddart, 1996). **Rev:** *CBRA* (1995): 487; *CCL* 84 (1996): 121; *EL* 23 (Mar. 1996): 24; *QQ* 61 (Dec. 1995): 38; *SLJ* 42 (July 1996): 74.

At Grandpa's Sugarbush, by Margaret Carney (Toronto: Kids Can Press, 1977). **Rev:** *QQ* 63 (Jan. 1997): 38; *SLJ* 44 (Apr. 1998): 114.

Amazing Grace: the Story of the Hymn, by Linda Granfield (Toronto: Tundra, 1997). **Rev:** *CCL* 87 (1997): 89; *CM* 4 (19 Sept 1997): on-line; *EL* (Mar. 1998): 28; *QQ* 63 (Jan. 1997): 37; *SLJ* 43 (Aug. 1997): 167.

Lucy Maud and the Cavendish Cat, by Lynn Manuel (Toronto: Tundra, 1997). **Rev:** *CM* 4 (10 Apr 1998): on-line; *HB* 73 (Nov. 1997): 706; *QQ* 63 (Sept. 1997): 74.

Sarah May and the New Red Dress, by Andrea Spaulding (Victoria, BC: Orca, 1998). **Rev:** *QQ* 64 (Nov. 1998): 44.

Selina and the Shoo-Fly Pie, by Barbara Smucker (Toronto: Stoddart, 1998). **Rev:** *QQ* 65 (Jan. 1999): 43.

Other

The Worm Song (And Other Tasty Tunes), comp. and illus. Cory Wilson (Richmond Hill, Ont.: Scholastic, 1993).

By 1990, when *Daniel's Dog*, the first picture book she illustrated, was published, Janet Wilson had established a solid reputation as an illustrator of non-fiction and chapter books. Her black-and-white pencil illustrations for such works as Martyn Godfrey's novel *Break Out* and Barbara Hehner's *Let's Find Out About Cats* depicted clearly key events or concepts and objects. However, in picture books, she found an avenue for an expansion of her talents. In realistic stories of children confronting major and minor conflicts in their lives, historical narratives, and historical non-fiction, Wilson's full-colour oil paintings evoke mood and suggest aspects of character and conflict not contained within the words.

Wilson has said that she is 'fascinated by reality' and has expressed her admiration for the American realist painters Winslow Homer, Norman Rockwell, and Andrew Wyeth. She uses realistic styles in her illustrations for three picture books about modern families. The illustrations for Jo Ellen Bogart's *Daniel's Dog*, in which a little boy invents an imaginary pet after the arrival of his baby sister, use bold colours and sharply outlined figures. The body language, facial expressions, and positioning of characters on the page indicate the hero's shifting attitudes towards his sibling. In two instances, Wilson breaks from the realistic style: she represents the anger Daniel feels with an impressionistic background of red and yellow flames, and the imaginary pet is a semi-visible dog sitting beside the sharply defined boy. Their facial expressions and their changing positions in the pictures indicate the contrasts between two sisters in Jean Little's *Jess Was the Brave One*, in which the timid older girl must overcome her fears to rescue the younger, usually fearless one from local bullies. Wilson uses similar techniques to picture the conflicts between the youngest member of the family and her often thoughtless and mean older brothers and sisters in Little's *Revenge of the Small Small.*

For Patricia Quinlan's *Tiger Flowers*, about a small boy's grieving over the death from AIDS of a favourite uncle; Patti Farmer's *What's He Doing Now?*, the account of a boy's questions during his mother's pregnancy; and *At Grandpa's Sugar Bush*, Margaret Carney's presentation of a boy and his grandfather's celebration of an annual spring ritual, Wilson employs a more impressionistic style, emphasizing the emotions evoked by events. Lights, shadows, and splashes of different colours highlight illustrations in which Joel remembers activities shared with his recently deceased uncle. The colours of the final illustrations reveal his movement from grief to acceptance. Purple dominates the pictures in which the boy, waking at night, decides to go outside to the tree house he and the man had built. The yellow-gold of the rising sun streaming through the green tree and the vibrant orange of the lilies they had both loved indicate the joy he feels thinking that, in spirit, his uncle is still with him. Pastel borders decorated with teddy bears, toy ducks, and other objects associated with the unborn baby about whom Lewis asks questions in *What's He Doing Now?* surround impressionistic crayon drawings of the boy, his mother, father, and, later, newborn baby sister. The young narrator in *At Grandpa's Sugar Bush* describes the activities he shares with his grandfather during spring break. The bright patches of colour on the clothing of the two, who are pictured working together in each illustration, contrast with the browns, greys, and whites of the winter woods where they gather sap and boil it into syrup, emphasizing their feelings of love and companionship.

The oil paintings accompanying Linda Granfield's texts for *In Flanders Fields: The Story of the Poem by John McCrae* and *Amazing Grace: The Story of the Hymn* combine the results of Janet Wilson's research into the backgrounds of these famous older poems with her sensitive responses to the emotions involved in their creation. For the former, Wilson travelled to northeastern France to study the World War I settings. Double-spreads of battlefields, bombed and burning villages, and a makeshift hospital are contrasted with single-page close-ups of poppies blooming amid coils of barbed wire, a woman weeping in the bedroom of a slain soldier, and modern children observing a wreath-laying ceremony in Canada. Wilson's depictions evoke the emotions of pity and sadness that are conveyed by the words of the poem. The paintings illustrating the account of the life of Captain John Newton, who composed 'Amazing Grace', also emphasize contrast; in this case the brutality of his life as a slave trader and the quiet religiosity of his later years. Pictures of shanghaied sailors; slaves being led in chains through their homelands or crouching in terror in the squalid holds of ships; a slave auction in which they are displayed like animals; and their labours under hot suns on southern plantations attest to the cruelty he helped perpetuate. Retired, he is pictured sitting in his study writing religious tracts. He is elegantly dressed and wears a powdered wig; outside the window is a quiet springtime countryside. In the final double-spread, he is part of a choir of men and women, children and adults, blacks and whites, presumably all singing the words of his song. In the aggregate, Wilson's illustrations reinforce the sense of Granfield's words of a contradictory and paradoxical life.

In the historical picture books she has illustrated, Wilson combines her skill at delineating historical settings and costumes with her ability to present tender emotional relationships. In Barbara Smucker's *Selina and the Bear Paw Quilt*, a Mennonite girl must leave her grandmother behind when, during the American Civil War, she and her pacifist parents move from Pennsylvania to Canada. The quilt she brings with her is made from scraps of family members' clothing and symbolizes the links between past and present, old and new lives. It figures prominently in the illustrations. Each single-page oil painting is surrounded by a quilt-like border and features pieces of cloth that will be in the completed quilt. The three generations of females—grandmother, mother, and daughter—wear Mennonite garments and work in a home furnished in the old ways.

Although Selina is alone in the opening and closing illustrations, generally she is seen with her family, most often with her grandmother. Her facial expressions reveal her changing emotions—joy, contemplativeness, sadness, worry, pride, and shyness—as she prepares for and then undertakes the journey. In *Selina and the Shoo-Fly Pie*, Wilson's illustrations communicate the girl's happiness when her grandmother visits her in Upper Canada.

In illustrating Lynn Manuel's *Lucy Maud and the Cavendish Cat*, an account of the relationship between the famous author and her pet, Wilson accurately reproduces clothing, architecture, and objects from early twentieth-century Prince Edward Island. Moreover, many of the oil paintings of Montgomery are in the portrait style of late nineteenth-century Impressionist Edgar Degas, further reinforcing the period atmosphere. Wilson's compositions also confirm the feelings between the pet and its mistress. The cat curls around her neck as the author sits at her writing desk; a yellow-orange glow spread by a coal-oil lamp provides a warm, cosy atmosphere. Subdued blues and greys dominate the painting in which Montgomery, tears running down her cheeks, embraces the cat from which she has been separated for many months. In the final illustration, the author sits contentedly at her writing desk, the cat cradled in her arms; spring plants brighten the window sill.

Janet Wilson has illustrated a wide variety of children's books: novels, concept books, poems, and picture books about contemporary life and earlier eras. Her illustrations realistically depict settings, clothing, and objects as they are or were in the times in which the narratives are set. Perhaps more important, the details and colours of her pictures convincingly communicate emotions that, no matter what period in which the books are set, can be recognized and experienced by modern readers.

Tim Wynne-Jones

Born: 12 August 1948, in Bromborough, England.

Principal Residences: Kitimat, BC; Vancouver; Ottawa; Toronto.

Education: University of Waterloo (BFA 1974); York University (MA 1978).

Career: rock musician; lyricist; book designer; university instructor; author; book critic.

Major Awards: IODE (Toronto) Book Award (1983); Ruth Schwartz Award (1984); Governor-General's Award (1993, 1995); Canadian Library Association Book of the Year for Children (1994, 1999); Canadian Library Association Young Adult Book Award (1996); Vicky Metcalf Award (1997).

WORKS FOR CHILDREN

Madeline and Ermadello, illus. Lindsey Hallam (Toronto: Before We Are Six, 1977). **Rev:** *IR* 12 (Winter 1978): 70.

Zoom at Sea, illus. Ken Nutt (Toronto: Groundwood, 1983). **Rev:** *CCL* 60 (1990): 108; *EL* 12 (Nov. 1984): 19; *QQ* 50 (Mar. 1984): 72.

Zoom Away, illus. Ken Nutt (Toronto: Groundwood, 1985). **Rev:** *CCL* 60 (1990): 109; *EL* 13 (Mar. 1986): 16; *HB* 63 (May 1987): 378; *QQ* 51 (Aug. 1985): 38.

I'll Make You Small, illus. Maryann Kovalski (Toronto: Groundwood, 1986). **Rev:** *BiC* 15 (Dec. 1986): 15; *CCL* 54 (1989): 66; *QQ* 52 (Oct. 1986): 16.

Mischief City, illus. Victor Gad (Toronto: Groundwood, 1986). **Rev:** *BiC* 15 (Dec. 1986): 15; *CCL* 54 (1989): 66; *QQ* 52 (Oct. 1986): 15.

Architect of the Moon, illus. Ian Wallace (Toronto: Groundwood, 1988). **Rev:** *CCL* 60 (1990): 108.

The Hour of the Frog, illus. Catharine O'Neill (Toronto: Groundwood, 1989). **Rev:** *CCL* 60 (1990): 138; *HB* 66 (May 1990): 332; *QQ* 55 (Dec. 1989): 22; *SLJ* 36 (Aug. 1990): 136.

Zoom Upstream, illus. Eric Beddows (Ken Nutt) (Toronto: Groundwood, 1992). **Rev:** *BiC* 22 (Feb. 1993): 37; *EL* 20 (Mar. 1993): 13; *QQ* 58 (Nov. 1992): 33; *SLJ* 40 (Aug. 1994): 148.

Mouse in the Manger, illus. Elaine Blier (Toronto: Penguin, 1993). **Rev:** *BiC* 25 (Dec. 1996): 33; *CCL* 87 (1997): 85; *EL* 21 (Nov. 1993): 47; *QQ* 59 (Nov. 1993): 38.

The Last Piece of Sky, illus. Marie-Louise Gay (Toronto: Groundwood, 1993). **Rev:** *BiC* 22 (Dec. 1993): 56; *QQ* 59 (Oct. 1993): 38.

Some of the Kinder Planets (Toronto: Groundwood, 1993). **Rev:** *BiC* 23 (Mar. 1994): 47; *CCB-B* 48 (May 1995): 328; *CM* 22 (Jan. 1994): 4; *EL* 21 (Mar. 1994): 17; *QQ* 59 (Dec. 1993): 34; *SLJ* 41 (Apr. 1995): 138.

Rosie Backstage, with Amanda Lewis, illus. Bill Slavin (Toronto: Kids Can Press, 1994).

The Book of Changes (Toronto: Groundwood, 1994). **Rev:** *CBRA* (1995): 522; *CCB-B* 49 (Oct. 1995): 75; *CCL* 80 (1995): 81; *CM* 22 (Nov. 1994): 210; *HB* 71 (Jan. 1995): 99; *QQ* 60 (Oct. 1994): 38.

The Maestro (Toronto: Groundwood, 1995). **Rev:** *BiC* 25 (May 1996): 20; *CBRA* (1995): 522; *CCB-B* 50 (Oct. 1996) 81; *CCL* 81 (1996): 58; *EL* 23 (Mar. 1996): 25; *QQ* 61 (Dec. 1995): 36; *VOYA* 20 (Apr. 1997): 35.

The Hunchback of Notre Dame, illus. Bill Slavin (Toronto: Key Porter, 1996). **Rev:** *BiC* 25 (Oct. 1996): 32; *QQ* 62 (Oct. 1996): 43; *SLJ* 44 (Apr. 1998): 132.

Dracula, illus. Laszlo Gal (Toronto: Key Porter, 1997). **Rev:** *CM* 4 (16 Jan. 1998): on-line; *QQ* 63 (Dec. 1997): 38.

Stephen Fair (Toronto: Groundwood, 1998). **Rev:** *CCL* 91/92 (1998): 141; *HB* 74 (July 1998): 502; *QQ* 64 (Mar. 1998): 73; *SLJ* 44 (May 1998): 150.

On Tumbledown Hill, illus. Dusan Petriciv (Red Deer, Alta: Red Deer College Press, 1998). **Rev:** *CCL* 93 (1999): 57.

Lord of the Fries (Toronto: Groundwood, 1999).

Other

'To Pass on the Good News: Reviewing Books for Children', *Writers on Writing: Guide to Writing and Illustrating Children's Books*, ed. David Booth (Markham, Ont.: Overlea House, 1989), 164–8.

'The Isle of Diamonds Does Not Exist', *School Libraries in Canada* 11 (Spring 1991): 17–21.

'The Sad J(y)oke of Cultural Appropriation', *CCL* 68 (1992): 87–98.

'Some of the Kinder Planets', *Horn Book* 71 (Jan. 1996): 35–7.

Selected Discussions

Jenkinson, Dave. 'Tim Wynne-Jones', *EL* 15 (Jan. 1988): 56–62.

'His research into the history of the Mafia was a fairy tale, but like any fairy tale, it was peppered with very real aspects; reality observed through a distorted glass, no less real for the distortion.' This comment in Tim Wynne-Jones's adult novel, *The Knot*, could well be applied to the author, especially as a creator of children's literature. In his picture books, poetry, short story collections, and novels, he mixes reality and fantasy to create characters and situations that, although sometimes make-believe, reflect experiences and emotions true to human nature.

Wynne-Jones's first book, *Madeline and Ermadello*, an outgrowth of an Ontario Government Opportunities for Youth grant project, is a relatively slight story about the relationship between a little girl and her imaginary friend. The book anticipates two themes of Wynne-Jones's later stories: the creative power of imagination and the importance of love and friendship.

Three books about the cat Zoom grew out of the author's observations of his own water-loving cat and a desire to do a book with his friend, artist Ken Nutt. It seemed logical, the author later recalled, to send the hero to the seashore. However, that seemed to be a fairly trivial approach: 'And then I thought of the enclosed quality of Ken Nutt's drawing and realized that Zoom would have to find the sea inside a magical house.' In the house, Zoom meets Maria, a woman who is a kind of Jungian mother figure, a fact Wynne-Jones admits but did not think of while writing. In *Zoom at Sea*, Maria lets the sea into her house and permits the hero to take a wonderful raft ride. In *Zoom Away*, he goes upstairs with her, walks through a dark passage to the North Pole, and discovers his Uncle Roy's ship, stuck in the winter ice. In *Zoom Upstream*, he rescues Maria, who has gone in search of his uncle, before he is reunited with the sea captain. The uncle and nephew then search for the source of the Nile River. Although the cat's adventures are relatively simple, one can see their appeal to younger children. Zoom is small and inquisitive, and, when he leaves his familiar home, he is discovering a new world, in his case a world of magic and adventure. He must explore alone, but nearby is the adult Maria, providing security and, if needed, help. She is like the fairy godmother of folktales, helping the hero to help himself. His ultimate search is for a father figure, whom he discovers only after crossing several thresholds and passing a series of tests, like the quester in folktales. When he joins his uncle, he does so as an equal partner, prepared to face the unknowns of an adult world.

The texts written by Wynne-Jones for several other picture books deal with the journeys of the central characters. *I'll Make You Small*, like the Zoom books, sends a young person into the world of an adult; however, both the tone of the story and the significance of the child's adventure are much different. Redemption, a theme found in Wynne-Jones's novels, is important in this story: the boy hero is the agent of that redemption, courageously and thoughtfully entering into an unknown and frightening house to help Mr Swanskin escape from his self-imposed isolation. In addition to presenting the boy's heroic qualities, the author successfully portrays a child's view of many adults. *Architect of the Moon*, *The Hour of the Frog*, and *The Last Piece of Sky* describe the imaginary night journeys of young heroes. David Finebloom travels into the sky to rebuild the disintegrating moon; a girl confronts a frog who nightly leaves its swamp to invade her home; and a brother must go to the bottom of a swamp to recover the last piece of his sister's jigsaw puzzle that he had thoughtlessly scattered about. The simple texts focus on the characters' actions and the inner courage they reveal in dangerous situations. The successful completions of their quests signal their discovery of their own inner strengths. *On Tumbledown Hill* is the first-person narration of a man who, on a walk with his dog, encounters 26 monsters. Each of the narrative's 26 sentences contains one word less than its predecessor.

Mischief City is a collection of poems in the tradition of A.A. Milne's *Now We Are Six* and Dennis Lee's *Alligator Pie*. Based on the author's observations of his son and his memories of his own childhood, the 25 poems focus on the two worlds of young Winchell: one containing his parents and baby sister and another created from his imagination. In the former, he laments the difficulty of communicating with his sister and discusses the problems of adjusting to her. His imaginary world, realized in the pictures he draws, contains monsters over which he exercises control and his imaginary friend Maxine. 'I Wasn't Angry When I Thought About Maxine', the focal poem of the collection, describes the wonderful day when he drew the girl into existence and received the praises of the baby and of his parents.

The short stories in *Some of the Kinder Planets* and *The Book of Changes* expand Wynne-Jones's explorations of his main themes to include the experiences of older children and young adults. In the former, a girl's star-gazing expedition with an old woman makes her science project more meaningful than the elaborate creations of other students; a bewildered teenager entering a high-tech futuristic home during a winter storm mistakes the residents for alien invaders; reluctantly writing a mundane account of a summer vacation experience, a boy begins to appreciate his friend's love of *Alice in Wonderland*; and a boy angry at having to move to the country with his parents encounters the ghost of his neighbour's dead son. Each of these encounters, mundane or supernatural, presents the central characters with the opportunities of stepping outside their familiar and comfortable lives. The title of *The Book of Changes*, from an ancient Chinese book of wisdom, emphasizes the significance of the character's encounters. Dan wins over the bully in his new school; Sally, who thinks that 'if I put my whole family in the dryer, they'd come out regular', sees the value of the life she has. The reasons for the moroseness of a high school hockey player become clear when his classmates meet the woman his father had run off with. Barnsey, on a bus trip to northern Ontario, meets an eccentric English girl whose wisdom helps him to confront his parents' impending divorce.

The themes and conflicts of these short pieces are expanded in the young adult novel *The Maestro*. Running into the forest to escape his abusive father, Burl enters a strange house and befriends the occupant, an eccentric musician. During much of the story, the boy compares his situation to that of a questing hero in a traditional story. For example, knocking on the door of various houses, he thinks of parallel events in folktales and seeks to make his story end happily ever after. However, the death of the musician, his father's return, and the destruction of the forest home require him to adjust his storying to take painful realities into account.

The 15-year-old title hero of *Stephen Fair* thinks that 'he is not a whole person . . . only a collection of disconnected bits.' During early spring, he must come to terms with his older brother's and father's having left the family, his mother's emotional problems, and his own nightmares. With the support of his friend Virginia, whose family is also experiencing troubled times, and the guidance of a wise old woman rumoured to practise witchcraft, he learns the significance of his dreams about climbing a ladder to a tree house and the truth about his past. His parents had kidnapped him from an uncaring hippie couple with whom they had been living in a California tree-house commune. Stephen, with this knowledge, is able to accept the actions of his brother and now remarried step-father, to help his mother face her guilt about the abduction, and to become reconciled with all members of his family.

Like *The Maestro*, *Stephen Fair* examines an adolescent's coming of age in relation to peers and adults. However, unlike *The Maestro*, which focuses on Burl's physical activities and interactions with adult males, *Stephen Fair* places greater emphasis on peer-group relationships and the link between dreams and unresolved emotional conflicts. Each book uses setting symbolically, with an unusual home set in the woods the focal point of the narratives. The musician's home is as out of place in its natural setting as he has been throughout his life. The Ark, alternative housing built by Stephen's family in the middle of the woods, is, like its Biblical namesake, supposed to offer sanctuary in times of disaster. Only after the Fairs have faced their difficulties does it become a real home, not just an odd building in the forest.

Wynne-Jones has also dealt with the confrontations between ordinary people and lonely recluses in his abridgements of two nineteenth-century classics, Bram Stoker's *Dracula* and Victor Hugo's *The Hunchback of Notre Dame.*

Tim Wynne-Jones's success in a wide range of genres has established him as a major Canadian children's author. His writing displays a delicate sensitivity for the sounds and meanings of words. More important, he uses language to capture the truth of the emotional experiences of his characters in their real and imagined worlds. He is able to explore the significance of the thresholds his characters cross and their relationships with the people they encounter, making his stories accurate reflections of the complex realities of childhood and adolescence.

See also: *CA* 105; *CANR* 39; *CLR* 21; *SATA* 67, 96; *TCCW*; *WSMP*.

PAUL YEE

BORN: 1 October 1956, in Spalding, Sask.

PRINCIPAL RESIDENCES: Vancouver; Toronto.

CAREER: archivist; teacher; policy analyst; writer.

EDUCATION: University of British Columbia (BA 1978, MA 1983).

MAJOR AWARDS: IODE Violet Downey Book Award (1990); Sheila A. Egoff Children's Book Prize (1990); Ruth Schwartz Award (1992, 1997); Governor-General's Award (1996).

WORKS FOR CHILDREN

Teach Me to Fly, Skyfighter! and Other Stories (Toronto: James Lorimer, 1983).

The Curses of Third Uncle (Toronto: James Lorimer, 1986). **Rev:** *BiC* 15 (Dec. 1986): 18; *CL* 116 (Spring 1988): 167; *CM* 19 (May 1991): 156; *EL* 14 (May 1987): 51; *QQ* 52 (Dec. 1986): 14.

Tales from Gold Mountain: Stories of the Chinese in the New World, illus. Simon Ng (Toronto: Douglas & McIntyre, 1989). **Rev:** *CCB-B* 43 (Mar. 1990): 178; *BiC* 18 (Dec. 1989), 19; *CL* (Autumn 1991): 142; *CM* 18 (Mar. 1990): 72, and 19 (May 1991): 156; *HB* 66 (July 1990): 45; *JR* 35 (Mar. 1992): 509; *QQ* 55 (Dec. 1989), 23; *RT* 44 (Apr. 1991): 587; *SLJ* 36 (May 1990): 121.

Roses Sing on New Snow: A Delicious Tale, illus. Harvey Chan (Toronto: Macmillan, 1992). **Rev:** *APBR* 19 (Apr. 1992): 13; *CCL* 70 (1993): 92; *EL* 19 (Mar.

1992): 17; *HB* 68 (Mar. 1992): 196; *SLJ* 38 (May 1992): 95; *NYTBR* 98 (11 Apr. 1993): 30; *QQ* 57 (Aug. 1991): 24; *RT* 46 (Dec. 1992): 331, and 47 (Feb. 1994): 385.

Breakaway (Toronto: Groundwood, 1994). **Rev:** *CM* 22 (Sept. 1994): 139; *QQ* 60 (Apr. 1994): 39.

Ghost Train, illus. Harvey Chan (Toronto: Groundwood, 1996). **Rev:** *CCL* 83 (1996): 130.

Other

Saltwater City: An Illustrated History of the Chinese in Vancouver (Vancouver: Douglas & McIntyre, 1988).

Struggle and Hope: The Story of Chinese Canadians (Toronto: Umbrella Press, 1996).

Selected Discussions

Davis, Marie C. '"A Backward Way of Thanking People": Paul Yee on his Historical Fiction', *CCL* 83 (1996): 50–68.

Jenkinson, Dave. 'Paul Yee', *EL* 22 (May-June 1995), 61–4.

Shklanka, Diana. 'Oriental Stereotypes in Canadian Picture Books', *CCL* 60 (1990): 81–96.

The major themes of his works for children, Paul Yee has said, are 'history, identity and the acceptance of who one is'. These concerns arise naturally from his experiences as a member of a visible minority and from his education. Born in Spalding, Saskatchewan, but raised in the Strathcona and Chinatown districts of Vancouver, Yee studied history at the University of British Columbia, graduating with a BA in 1978 and an MA in 1983. He began his professional career as an archivist, preserving and ordering documents from Vancouver's past. Because he also worked as a volunteer with Chinatown organizations, he realized that his community was ignorant of its history: fearful that tales of suffering and injustice would scar their children, Chinese Canadians did not speak about the past. Yee believes, however, that knowledge of history empowers people to control their destinies. Therefore he has written fiction to make the past emotionally meaningful, and two histories, *Saltwater City: An Illustrated History of the Chinese in Vancouver* for adults and *Struggle and Hope: The Story of Chinese Canadians* for children, to provide broader factual overviews of Chinese Canadians.

Yee initially wrote poetry, short fiction, and articles for adults. He turned to juvenile audiences when a publisher who had launched a series on ethnic communities asked him for a book about Vancouver's Chinatown. Deciding he had an invaluable opportunity 'to portray accurately how kids lived in that neighbourhood and to give them an accurate mirror to help them grow', Yee wrote *Teach Me To Fly, Skyfighter! and Other Stories*. These four loosely linked stories portray working-class life in contemporary Chinatown, but their focus is not local colour. Each story concentrates on the psychology of the protagonists and explores identity problems of children in an ethnic community. Without resorting to unrealistic events, each story works to a significant climax, usually involving acceptance by the group. For example, in the title story, Canadian-born Sharon Fong symbolically comes to terms with her heritage by flying a kite made by an old Chinese man.

Yee wrote the first of two historical novels, *The Curses of the Third Uncle*, 'to immortalize and thank those who raised me and to celebrate the strengths that enable common people to overcome adversities'. Inspired by stories that his aunt had told him about her childhood, Yee erected a framework of adventure and mystery to explore the relationship between Old World culture and New World potential, the question of female identity, and the possibility of individual heroism. The novel is set in British Columbia in 1909, during a conflict between those seeking to overthrow the Chinese emperor and those trying to prevent a revolution. It focuses on the development of Lillian Ho, who represents the possibilities of the New World. Steeped in the sword tales of the Orient and taught the ancient medical art of 'breath fighting', she becomes both warrior and healer, thus using Old World knowledge to preserve her family in Canada. Her evil 'third uncle' represents the worst side of Chinese feudalism, constantly threatening to send her back to China, where girls are, as he says, 'garbage'. Physically courageous in exposing her third uncle's schemes, Lillian also demonstrates maturity by teaching her mother that China means fear and Canada means hope.

Breakaway, his other historical novel, is both a sports story about a soccer team that was the pride of Chinatown during the Depression and a tense problem novel. Set in 1932, it explores questions of identity and belonging by detailing conflicts between generations and cultures. Eighteen-year-old Kwok-Ken Wong dreams of escaping his dreary life on the family farm by earning a soccer scholarship to university. He resents his tradition-bound father, who wants Kwok to take over the farm. Disappointments test Kwok's character: he does not receive the scholarship, a white bigot prevents him from joining an all-star soccer team, and his father refuses to sell the farm to a white developer. Kwok is also dismayed that his sister, whom the novel uses to illustrate the constraints traditional Chinese society imposes on females, agrees to an arranged marriage to earn 'bride money' for the family. Kwok himself undergoes an epiphany after playing for the Chinese soccer team that beats the all-stars in the climactic championship game. Feeling pride in his race and a sense of cultural solidarity for the first time, he dedicates himself to saving the farm and the values it represents. This conclusion is contrived, but *Breakaway* sympathetically dramatizes the generational, economic, cultural, and racial conflicts Chinese Canadians faced.

In addition to writing standard historical fiction, Yee has attempted 'to pull together history and mythology' by casting events in the form of folktales. The eight narratives gathered in *Tales from Gold Mountain* and his two picture books, *Roses Sing on New Snow* and *Ghost Train*, evoke the social, moral, spiritual, and emotional attitudes of immigrants to 'Gold Mountain', the name impoverished Chinese gave to North America because they envisioned it as a land of plenty. The stories are varied in topic and effect. Two ghost stories, 'Spirits of the Railway' and *Ghost Train*, convey loss and sacrifice: in each, a child's search for a long-absent father ends with the discovery that the father died while building the railroad and now needs his child to honour his spirit before he can be at rest. Another ghost tale, 'Rider Chan and the Night River', contrasts the destructive greed of some Chinese miners with the nobility and respect for tradition shown by others. The stories about lovers are stark contrasts. The devoted lovers of 'Ginger for the Heart' overcome their disagreement about following traditional ways in the New World and happily marry. The lovers in 'Forbidden Fruit' have a sadder fate: a mercenary farmer, exercising his patriarchal power, refuses to allow his daughter to marry her industrious but impecunious suitor, thereby killing her. This tale and 'Gambler's Eyes', in which both Chinese and whites ostracize a man of mixed blood, illustrate Yee's refusal to idealize the Chinese. Especially entertaining are the revenge tales, 'The Friends of Kwan Ming' and 'The Revenge of the Iron Chink', in which victimized Chinese workers cleverly gain victories over their callous employers.

Finally, two tales treat the issue of female worth in traditional societies. In 'Sons and Daughters', a merchant who wants to pass on his family name sells his infant daughters and buys twin boys to raise as his own. When his adopted sons decide to marry his actual daughters, he is forced to tell the truth, ironically ensuring that his name will be lost. *Roses Sing on New Snow* extols the New World sense of individualism that enables a girl to gain fame for wisdom and talent. Maylin cooks delicious food in her father's restaurant, but her father publicly gives the credit to his lazy sons. For a banquet for a visiting Chinese governor, Maylin creates a culinary masterpiece, 'Roses Sing on New Snow'. When the governor demands the recipe so that the emperor may taste it, Maylin's father and brothers take credit, but they fail to duplicate the dish. When the truth emerges, Maylin demonstrates that she is an artist of the kitchen, and also proves that, because each person is different, no one can duplicate her dish.

Because he intends to concentrate on writing for adults, Yee may never produce another work for young people. In spite of the small number of his works, he has already made a notable contribution to Canadian children's literature. By fusing the unique details of ethnic experiences with the universal concerns for identity and love, Yee has created works that can instil pride in Chinese Canadians and can make others more sensitive to a people who, for more than a hundred years, have been an important part of the Canadian cultural mosaic.

See also: *CA* 135; *SATA* 67; *TCCW*; *WSMP*.

Leo Yerxa

Born: 1947, at Little Eagle Reserve, Ont.

Principal Residences: Little Eagle Reserve; Ottawa.

Education: Algonquin College, Ottawa; University of Waterloo.

Career: artist; designer; writer.

Major Awards: Mr Christie's Book Award (1993); Amelia Frances Howard-Gibbon Illustrator's Award (1994); Elizabeth Mrazik-Cleaver Picture Book Award (1994).

Works for Children

Last Leaf First Snowflake to Fall (Toronto: Groundwood, 1993). **Rev:** *BiC* 22 (Nov. 1993): 58; *CBRA* (1994): 514; *EL* 22 (Nov. 1994): 45; *QQ* 59 (Sept. 1993): 66; *SLJ* 40 (Dec. 1994): 92.

A Fish Tale, or The Little One That Got Away (Toronto: Groundwood, 1995). **Rev:** *CBRA* (1995): 491; *CCB-B* 50 (Sept. 1996): 39; *QQ* 61 (Sept. 1995): 72; *TES* (8 Dec 1995): 12.

The desire to preserve a memory of his own childhood for his young son led Leo Yerxa to write the story that became his first picture book. He recalled walking with his father along a winter trapline located on the Ojibway Little Eagle Reserve and, thinking about the joy of that experience, created the words and, many years later, the illustrations for *Last Leaf First Snowflake to Fall.* An account in free verse of a parent and child's late autumn day and night presents a sequence of simple events and emphasizes the harmony among all elements in nature. As the day breaks, the parent and child leave their cabin, walk through the forest, and then fall asleep. They awaken to find the season's first snow covering the carpet of leaves they had crossed the previous day. The child expresses his feeling of new life, both in himself and in the forest: 'I arose from the earth / and walked into the light / of a new season.'

The words and pictures combine to present the theme of continuity and interrelationship: the cycles of the seasons and of the day and night and the links between the natural and human spheres. The written text begins with a reverential hymn to creation. Then father and son become a part of the natural world into which they enter. The clouds reflected in the water give a sense of 'our canoe . . . drifting across the sky'. The ripples made by a falling leaf become a circle that embraces the entire pond. In his play, the child becomes a leaf, and the pair 'mingled' their footprints with those of 'the other animals'. Yerxa creates the accompanying pictures from dyed pieces of tissue paper combined with ink sketches and watercolours. These reinforce the idea of a unified world. The human figures don't dominate the forest; they are most frequently the smallest objects in the pictures, and their buckskin garments make them blend with the autumn landscape. Circle designs, symbolizing harmony, are placed in many of the pictures, some of which are themselves shaped as circles or ovals. Not only does the book embody traditional Native themes, but it also treats such universal topics as the relationship between an adult and child and a child's sense of wonder at a marvellous natural event: the season's first snowfall.

In *A Fish Tale, or The Little One that Got Away*, Yerxa employs a different artistic technique and moves away from the autobiographical subject matter of his first book. The narrative of a small walleye who, unhappy with life at 'darting school', searches for answers to large questions that puzzle him, it resembles moralistic animal fables frequently told to children. However, the fish, who is now very old and who tells his tale of long ago to young fish, will not give simple answers to the questions he once raised. In examining the importance of telling a story about his past, the old fish may, in fact, be presenting some of the author's own thoughts about narratives. A lover of the 'fantastic tales' told by old fish, the narrator, when young, wonders if they are true or simply lies told to warn the children. 'One school of thought was that the stories could come true if you believed.' The hero, after he is taken to the water's surface by a guileful, evil pike, is caught and then released by a fisherman. He makes it back home a wiser, more mature fish. Yerxa's watercolour washes, in various hues, depict the shifting light patterns of the water world and suggest the changing emotions of the hero, a tiny, often solitary figure in many of the book's double-spreads.

Yerxa's native Ojibway heritage is certainly an influence on his artistic style and his use of the journey pattern. However, his books are not specifically within the Native tradition. His central characters are on voyages of discovery that lead them to new awareness of themselves and the worlds around, as is the case in many Native vision quests. However, the experiences of the first snow recall the experiences of the child in Ezra Jack Keats's *The Snowy Day*, and the travels of the fish are like those in Leo Lionni's animal fables, especially *Swimmy*. Yerxa speaks from his Native heritage, but to the interests and concerns of children from many cultures.

See also: *TCCW*.

Scott Young

Born: 14 April 1918, in Glenboro, Man.

Principal Residences: Glenboro; Winnipeg; Toronto; Cavan, Ont.

Education: Delvin Technical High School, Winnipeg.

Career: journalist; columnist; broadcaster; author.

Works for Children

Scrubs on Skates (Boston: Little, Brown, 1952); rev. edn (Toronto: McClelland & Stewart, 1985). **Rev:** *CBRA* (1985): 276; *IR* 14 (June 1980): 27.

Boy on Defence (Boston: Little, Brown, 1953); rev. edn (Toronto: McClelland & Stewart, 1985). **Rev:** *CBRA* (1985): 275; *IR* 14 (June 1980): 27.

A Boy at the Leafs' Camp (Boston: Little, Brown, 1963); rev. edn (Toronto: McClelland & Stewart, 1985). **Rev:** *IR* 14 (June 1980): 27.

The Clue of the Dead Duck (Boston: Little, Brown, 1962). **Rev:** *CCL* 29 (1983): 65; *IR* 15 (Aug. 1981): 64.

Face-off in Moscow (St Paul, Minn.: EMC, 1973).

Learning To Be Captain (St Paul, Minn.: EMC, 1973).

The Moscow Challengers (St Paul, Minn.: EMC, 1973).

The Silent One Speaks Up (St Paul, Minn.: EMC, 1973).

Bobby Hull, Superstar (St Paul, Minn.: EMC, 1974).

Frank Mahovlich, the Big M (St Paul, Minn.: EMC, 1974).

Gil Perreault Makes It Happen (St Paul, Minn.: EMC, 1974).

Stan Mikita, Tough Kid Who Grew Up (St Paul, Minn.: EMC, 1974).

One of Canada's top sports journalists and broadcasters, Scott Young has shown himself to be the quintessential hockey writer. In numerous books for adults and children, he has captured the personalities of the coaches and players, explained both the basic strategies and the nuances of the game, and, most importantly, conveyed the excitement of and passion for a sport Canadians call their own. His hockey books for children include the 'Hockey Heroes' series, four brief biographies celebrating the dedication and skills of professional players, and two series of novels about high school hockey. In addition, he has published a mystery, *The Clue of the Dead Duck*, in which his interest in sports is reflected in the extensive descriptions of boating and duck hunting.

Young's 'Face-off' series consists of four short, action-filled novels designed to appeal to both avid readers and those who usually don't enjoy books. Each is an independent story focusing on one member of the Northwest High School hockey team, but together they tell the story of a dramatic season. *Learning To Be Captain*, chronologically first in the series, begins with the team feeling resentment at Norm Dennison, a new player. No one associates with Norm, a high-scoring star forward, because everyone thinks he is aloof. Billy Amherst, the captain, unites the team when he realizes that even a superstar needs friendship and encouragement. Billy Burdett, a goalie who has trouble expressing himself, is the focus of *The Silent One Speaks Up*. After suggesting the idea of playing a series of games against a Russian team, Billy overcomes his fear of public speaking to deliver a speech that convinces the school board to give the team financial support. In *Face-off in Moscow*, defenceman Mac Rutland, billeted with a Russian player's family during the first part of the tournament, learns that he can be friends with someone who is his rival on the ice. *The Moscow Challengers* concludes the series with the Russian team coming to North America to conclude the tournament (the novel is vague about whether the Northwest team is American or Canadian). The theme, again, is friendship and team solidarity. A Russian player whose teammates shun him because the boy's father once was exiled for engaging in political protest learns how to fit in with his team after Billy Amherst offers him friendship and encouragement.

Originally published in 1952, 1953, and 1963, Young's novels about Winnipeg high school hockey players proved so popular that he updated their topical references in 1985 to make them more accessible and appealing to new generations of readers. This trilogy is notable not only for its exciting descriptions of hockey action but also for themes that assert the positive value of sports in developing personal discipline, teamwork, loyalty, camaraderie, and understanding of others. In *Scrubs on Skates*, star player Pete Gordon is angry that he must play at a new school on a team of inferior players, or 'scrubs'. The other players, all of whom try their best, resent Pete, whose lack of school spirit prevents him from using his talent to the fullest. Only after he examines his actions and begins displaying a positive attitude to the other players does Pete become a true part of the team. Bill Spunska, a Polish immigrant whose determination provides a counterpoint to Pete's early lack of effort, is the central character in *Boy on Defence*. Bill and Cliff Armstrong, a star player who has transferred to Northwest, develop an intense dislike for each other. The hostility becomes physical when Bill, angered by Cliff's arrogance and lack of respect for other players, hits him with a bone-rattling check during a practice game. Embittered, Cliff returns to play for his old school, setting up an exciting championship game in which Bill and Cliff oppose each other. In *A Boy at the Leafs' Camp*, Bill tries to make the difficult transition from high school to professional hockey. After unintentionally injuring a player in an exhibition game, Bill learns to develop the mental toughness professionals need. He doesn't make the Maple Leafs, but he is successful, earning a scholarship to university and a chance to be on the Olympic team.

See also: *CA* 9–12R; *CANR* 5, 20; *SATA* 5.

Ludmila Zeman

Born: 23 April 1947, in Gottwadlov, Czechoslovakia.

Principal Residences: Gottwadlov; Vancouver; Montreal.

Education: Palacky University, Czechoslovakia.

CAREER: film-maker; art instructor; writer; illustrator.

MAJOR AWARDS: Governor-General's Award for Illustration (1995).

WORKS FOR CHILDREN

Gilgamesh the King (Montreal: Tundra, 1992). **Rev:** *CCB-B* 46 (Jan. 1993): 160; *CCL* 73 (1994): 865; *CM* 21 (Jan. 1993): 20; *EL* 20 (Mar. 1993): 12; *QQ* 58 (Sept. 1992): 72; *SLJ* 39 (June 1993): 124.

The Revenge of Ishtar (Montreal: Tundra, 1993). **Rev:** *CCB-B* 47 (Jan. 1994): 172; *CCL* 77 (1995): 55; *EL* 21 (Mar. 1994): 18; *QQ* 59 (Sept. 1993): 67; *SLJ* 40 (June 1994): 52.

The Last Quest of Gilgamesh (Montreal: Tundra, 1995). **Rev:** *BiC* 24 (Oct. 1995): 48; *CCL* 83 (1996): 132; *EL* 22 (Mar. 1995): 17; *QQ* 61 (June 1995): 56.

The First Red Maple Leaf (Toronto: Tundra, 1997). **Rev:** *CCL* 86 (1997): 51; *CM* 4 (27 Feb. 1998): on-line.

Sinbad: Tales of the Thousand and One Nights (Toronto: Tundra, 1999).

In three picture books, *Gilgamesh the King*, *The Revenge of Ishtar*, and *The Last Quest of Gilgamesh*, Ludmila Zeman has selected and adapted important episodes from the long, complex Sumerian epic of King Gilgamesh. In the first book, the hero—part god, part human—rules despotically over the city of Uruk until he is defeated in combat by Enkidu, a gentle man who has lived in the forest with animals. When Enkidu spares the king's life, Gilgamesh becomes humanized and a wise and kind ruler. The second book deals with the friends' struggles against the goddess Ishtar after Humbaba, one of her creatures, kills the beloved and beautiful maiden Shamhat. After Gilgamesh spurns the goddess's offer of immortality as her husband, Ishtar achieves revenge by killing the gentle Enkidu, and, at the end of the book, the king pledges to seek and destroy death. Gilgamesh's adventures on this quest provide the plot for the final volume, in which, in spite of his courage and determination, he fails. However, the spirit of Enkidu returns him to Uruk, telling the king: 'Here . . . is the immortality you sought. . . . The city you built, the courage you showed, the good you have done.'

In reducing the text of one of the world's longest and most complex epics to fit into three 24-page picture books, Zeman faced a considerable challenge. The afterword to the final volume indicates her approach: 'He is the first hero of western literature, embodying all the virtues we associate with heroes. . . . all our heroes owe their appeal to the standards of legendary heroism set by Gilgamesh.' Zeman focuses on episodes that illustrate these standards: the reform of the despot, the loyalty of his friend, the courage the two display in their various battles, and the sense of determination and responsibility the king reveals in rejecting the offers of the goddess and, during his journey, promises of a life of ease. In order to do this, Zeman has had to excise several important aspects of the original narrative: the facts that the king abducted daughters and wives, that the woman he sent to lead Enkidu to the city was a harlot who did not fall deeply in love with the wild man, and that Gilgamesh began his quest in terror and panic in the face of his own mortality. Finally, the adaptation transforms the pessimistic ending of the epic—when the spirit of Enkidu tells his friend of the deeply sorrowful nature of life after death—into one of honour and hope for the immortal reputation created by performing noble deeds.

Although Zeman's written text alters and omits elements of the original epic, her illustrations are based on careful research into the architecture and artistic styles of ancient Babylon. Her pen-and-ink and watercolour pictures not only create an atmosphere of the times in which the story was originally told, but also communicate the intense emotions of the hero as she interprets him. Zeman's depictions of the city of Uruk, based on archaeological research, serve as the background in 11 of the double-spreads in the three books. Initially built to 'make the people remember him forever', it is part of six of the illustrations in *Gilgamesh the King* in which his cruelty and pride are dominant. In an early scene, he is presented full-face in the foreground, a cruel gaze dominating his features, while behind him hundreds of slaves labour at building the city. However, in the penultimate illustration, he is a tiny figure in the background, watching a joyous procession of his subjects. The final double-spread contrasts with the opening one. Whereas, at the beginning, he had been the dominant figure, driving a chariot beside the river, a galley in the middle ground, and the city in the distance; now he is in the middle ground, a smaller figure on the boat, surrounded by friends. He has lost the arrogance that had isolated him from the rest of humanity.

The depictions of Uruk in *The Revenge of Ishtar* indicate the forces that will destroy the king's happiness. For example, as the angry goddess attacks, she is seen flying toward the city riding the Bull of Heaven. Uruk, pictured below her, is vulnerable. In the illustration showing Gilgamesh and Enkidu congratulating each other on slaying the bull, the angry goddess is in the foreground, the dominant figure in the picture. As in the first book, the final illustration includes the river and the city; however, instead of the three friends on the boat, it presents the spirit of the dead Enkidu and Shamhat flying to the afterworld. Gilgamesh alone, his body slumped forward in sadness, paddles a small boat. Interestingly, the king is pictured in the foreground in only two pictures. In the first, his profile reveals anger and dismay as Enkidu holds the dead body of Shamhat. Later, tears stream down his face as he embraces the dying Enkidu.

In *The Last Quest of Gilgamesh*, as the hero's humanization process is completed, Zeman foregrounds the king only twice. As he begins his perilous journey, he looks with determination on the landscape, his grim face presented in profile. When he finally arrives at the home of the wise old Utnapishtim, he sits humbly on the ground below his teacher. The harsh landscape dominates most of the illustrations; in them, Gilgamesh is a small figure whose body positions indicate the physical hardship and mental anguish he experiences. Uruk is seen only in the final illustration. Carried into the sky by the spirit of his dead friend, the small Gilgamesh looks down at the river and the magnificent city that ensures the immortality he sought at the beginning of the first book.

Zeman's art for her 'Gilgamesh Trilogy' reflects her work as a costume and set designer and painter of background scenes for her father, Czechoslovakian film maker Karel Zeman. The garments of her characters, which are altered as their circumstances change, assist in the presentation of action and characterization. The backgrounds are like movie backdrops designed to enhance the foreground figures. In addition, she uses a dominant color for each picture, evoking atmosphere in the way lighting affects a film.

Zeman has also written and illustrated a literary *pourquoi* folktale for younger readers: *The First Red Maple Leaf*, an account of Canada's seasonal cycles. Created in part as a tribute to her new country and a reflection of her interest in traditional Native narratives, it began as a fanciful answer to her children's questions about the red maple leaf on the Air Canada plane that brought them to Canada. At a time when Iceheart keeps the land in perpetual winter, a brave boy and a goose he has rescued travel to the south to find warm weather to bring to their homeland. The earlier illustrations are dominated by browns and whites; during the resolution of the conflict brighter colours appear. However, the continued presence of some whites and browns are reminders that winter will return.

In spite of her limited output, Ludmila Zeman has established herself as an important adaptor of traditional stories. Her 'Gilgamesh Trilogy' is an ambitious project that generally achieves its goal of reinterpreting the ancient narrative for a modern audience of older children. Although its text is limited, its illustrations communicate the psychological journey of Gilgamesh from cruel autocrat to humble, caring friend.

Appendix A:

English-Language Canadian Children's Book Awards

Canadian Library Association Book of the Year Award for Children

Since 1947, the Canadian Library Association has presented a bronze medal to the author of the best Canadian children's book. Because of a change in procedure, two awards were presented in 1966.

1947	Roderick Haig-Brown, *Starbuck Valley Winter*
1948	no award
1949	Mabel Dunham, *Kristli's Trees*
1950	Richard S. Lambert, *Franklin of the Arctic*
1951	no award
1952	Catherine Anthony Clark, *The Sun Horse*
1953	no award
1954	no award
1955	no award
1956	Louise Riley, *Train for Tiger Lily*
1957	Cyrus Macmillan, *Glooscap's Country and Other Indian Tales*
1958	Farley Mowat, *Lost in the Barrens*
1959	John F. Hayes, *The Dangerous Cove*
1960	Marius Barbeau and Michael Hornyansky, *The Golden Phoenix and Other French-Canadian Fairy Tales*
1961	William Toye, *The St. Lawrence*
1962	no award
1963	Sheila Burnford, *The Incredible Journey*
1964	Roderick Haig-Brown, *The Whale People*
1965	Dorothy M. Reid, *Tales of Nanabozho*
1966	James Houston, *Tikta'liktak: An Eskimo Legend* James McNeill, *The Double Knights: More Tales from Round the World*
1967	Christie Harris, *Raven's Cry*
1968	James Houston, *The White Archer: An Eskimo Legend*
1969	Kay Hill, *And Tomorrow the Stars: The Story of John Cabot*
1970	Edith Fowke, *Sally Go Round the Sun*

1971 William Toye, *Cartier Discovers the St. Lawrence*
1972 Ann Blades, *Mary of Mile* 18
1973 Ruth Nichols, *The Marrow of the World*
1974 Elizabeth Cleaver, *The Miraculous Hind*
1975 Dennis Lee, *Alligator Pie*
1976 Mordecai Richler, *Jacob Two-Two Meets the Hooded Fang*
1977 Christie Harris, *Mouse Woman and the Vanished Princesses*
1978 Dennis Lee, *Garbage Delight*
1979 Kevin Major, *Hold Fast*
1980 James Houston, *River Runners*
1981 Donn Kushner, *The Violin Maker's Gift*
1982 Janet Lunn, *The Root Cellar*
1983 Brian Doyle, *Up to Low*
1984 Jan Hudson, *Sweetgrass*
1985 Jean Little, *Mama's Going To Buy You a Mockingbird*
1986 Cora Taylor, *Julie*
1987 Janet Lunn, *Shadow in Hawthorn Bay*
1988 Kit Pearson, *A Handful of Time*
1989 Brian Doyle, *Easy Avenue*
1990 Kit Pearson, *The Sky is Falling*
1991 Michael Bedard, *Redwork*
1992 Kevin Major, *Eating Between the Lines*
1993 Celia Barker Lottridge, *Ticket to Curlew*
1994 Tim Wynne-Jones, *Some of the Kinder Planets*
1995 Cora Taylor, *Summer of the Mad Monk*
1996 Maxine Trottier, *The Tiny Kite of Eddie Wing*
1997 Brian Doyle, *Uncle Ronald*
1998 Kenneth Oppel, *Silverwing*
1999 Tim Wynne-Jones, *Stephen Fair*

Canadian Library Association Young Adult Canadian Book Award

Established by the Young Adult Caucus of the Saskatchewan Library Association, the Young Adult Canadian Book Award has been administered by the Canadian Library Association since 1989. It is presented annually to the author of an outstanding English-language book for young adults (ages 13–18). The winner must be a Canadian citizen or a landed immigrant, and the winning title must be published in Canada.

1981 Kevin Major, *Far from Shore*
1982 Jamie Brown, *Superbike!*
1983 Monica Hughes, *Hunter in the Dark*
1984 O.R. Melling, *The Druid's Tune*

1985 Mary-Ellen Lang Collura, *Winners*
1986 Marianne Brandis, *The Quarter-Pie Window*
1987 Janet Lunn, *Shadow in Hawthorn Bay*
1988 Margaret Buffie, *Who Is Frances Rain?*
1989 Helen Fogwell Porter, *January, February, June, or July*
1990 Diana Wieler, *Bad Boy*
1991 Budge Wilson, *The Leaving*
1992 Susan Lynn Reynolds, *Strandia*
1993 Karleen Bradford, *There Will Be Wolves*
1994 Sean Stewart, *Nobody's Son*
1995 Julie Johnston, *Adam and Eve and Pinch-Me*
1996 Tim Wynne-Jones, *The Maestro*
1997 R.P. MacIntyre, *Takes*
1998 Martha Brooks, *Bone Dance*
1999 Gayle Friesen, *Janey's Girl*

The Governor-General's Literary Awards for Juvenile Literature (1950-1959)

The Governor-General's Literary Awards for juvenile literature, which honoured books published the previous year, were discontinued after the 1959 presentation. Dates below indicate the publication years of the winners.

1949 R.S. Lambert, *Franklin of the Arctic*
1950 Donald Dickie, *The Great Adventure*
1951 John F. Hayes, *A Land Divided*
1952 Marie McPhedran, *Cargoes on the Great Lakes*
1953 John F. Hayes, *Rebels Ride at Night*
1954 Marjorie Wilkins Campbell, *The Nor'westers*
1955 Kerry Wood, *The Map-Maker*
1956 Farley Mowat, *Lost in the Barrens*
1957 Kerry Wood, *The Great Chief*
1958 Edith L. Sharp, *Nkwala*

The Canada Council Children's Literature Prizes for English-Language Writing (1975–1986)

In 1975, the Canada Council established English- and French-language prizes for the best books by Canadian writers and illustrators. Prizes in each category are not necessarily awarded each year. Beginning in 1978, awards were given for both text and illustration. These prizes were discontinued after 1986 and replaced by the revived Governor-General's Literary Awards in 1987.

1975 Bill Freeman, *Shantymen of Cache Lake*
1976 Myra Paperny, *The Wooden People*

1977 Jean Little, *Listen for the Singing*
1978 Text: Kevin Major, *Hold Fast*
Illustration: Ann Blades, *A Salmon for Simon*, text by Betty Waterton
1979 Text: Barbara Smucker, *Days of Terror*
Illustration: Laszlo Gal, *The Twelve Dancing Princesses*, text by Janet Lunn
1980 Text: Christie Harris, *The Trouble with Princesses*
Illustration: Elizabeth Cleaver, *Petrouchka*
1981 Text: Monica Hughes, *The Guardian of Isis*
Illustration: Heather Woodall, *Ytek and the Arctic Orchid*, text by Garnet Hewitt
1982 Text: Monica Hughes, *Hunter in the Dark*
Illustration: Vlasta van Kampen, *ABC, 123: The Canadian Alphabet and Counting Book*
1983 Text: sean o huigin, *The Ghost Horse of the Mounties*
Illustration: Laszlo Gal, *Hans Christian Andersen's The Little Mermaid*, text by Margaret Crawford Maloney
1984 Text: Jan Hudson, *Sweetgrass*
Illustration: Marie-Louise Gay, *Lizzy's Lion*, text by Dennis Lee
1985 Text: Cora Taylor, *Julie*
Illustration: Terry Gallagher, *Murdo's Story*, text by Murdo Scribe
1986 Text: Janet Lunn, *Shadow in Hawthorn Bay*
Illustration: Barbara Reid, *Have You Seen Birds?*, text by Joanne Oppenheim

Governor-General's Awards for Children's Literature (1987–)

Beginning in 1987, the Governor-General's Awards superseded the Canada Council Children's Literature Prizes. The intention in restoring the Governor-General's Awards was to accord to writers for children the same respect given to writers for adults. Administered by the Canada Council, these awards are presented to the best books by Canadian citizens, whether published in Canada or elsewhere.

1987 Text: Morgan Nyberg, *Galahad Schwartz and the Cockroach Army*
Illustration: Marie-Louise Gay, *Rainy Day Magic*
1988 Text: Welwyn Wilton Katz, *The Third Magic*
Illustration: Kim LaFave, *Amos's Sweater*, text by Janet Lunn
1989 Text: Diana Wieler, *Bad Boy*
Illustration: Robin Muller, *The Magic Paintbrush*
1990 Text: Michael Bedard, *Redwork*
Illustration: Paul Morin, *The Orphan Boy*, text by Tololwa M. Mollel
1991 Text: Sarah Ellis, *Pick-Up Sticks*
Illustration: Joanne Fitzgerald, *Doctor Kiss Says Yes*, text by Teddy Jam

1992 Text: Julie Johnston, *Hero of Lesser Causes*
Illustration: Ron Lightburn, *Waiting for the Whales*, text by Sheryl McFarlane

1993 Text: Tim Wynne-Jones, *Some of the Kinder Planets*
Illustration: Mireille Levert, *Sleep Tight, Mrs. Ming*, text by Sharon Jennings

1994 Text: Julie Johnston, *Adam and Eve and Pinch-Me*
Illustration: Murray Kimber, *Josepha: A Prairie Boy's Story*, text by Jim McGugan

1995 Text: Tim Wynne-Jones, *The Maestro*
Illustration: Ludmila Zeman, *The Last Quest of Gilgamesh*

1996 Text: Paul Yee, *Ghost Train*
Illustration: Eric Beddows, *The Rooster's Gift*, text by Pam Conrad

1997 Text: Kit Pearson, *Awake and Dreaming*
Illustration: Barbara Reid, *The Party*

1998 Text: Janet Lunn, *The Hollow Tree*
Illustration: Kady MacDonald Denton, *A Child's Treasury of Nursery Rhymes*

Mr Christie's Book Awards: English-Language Awards

To encourage the development and publishing of high-quality Canadian children's books and to foster an interest in them, Christie Brown & Co. annually sponsors awards in several categories for both English and French books. The categories have changed over the years. The list below indicates the year the winners were published; the awards are presented in the summer of the following year.

1989 Illustration: Ian Wallace, *The Name of the Tree*, text by Celia Lottridge
Text: Kit Pearson, *The Sky is Falling*

1990 Illustration: Kady Macdonald Denton, *The Story of Little Quack*, text by Betty Gibson
Text: Brian Doyle, *Covered Bridge*

1991 Illustration: Barbara Reid, *Zoe Board Books* (*Zoe's Rainy Day, Zoe's Snowy Day, Zoe's Windy Day, Zoe's Sunny Day*)
Text: Dennis Lee, *The Ice Cream Store*

1992 Illustration: Yvette Moore, *A Prairie Alphabet*, text by Jo Bannatyne-Cugnet
Text (Ages 8 and Under): Sheree Fitch, *There Were Monkeys in My Kitchen*
Text (Ages 9-14): Janet Lunn and Christopher Moore, *The Story of Canada*

1993 Ages 7 and under: Berny Lucas, *Brewster Rooster*
Ages 8–11: Song Nan Zhang, *A Little Tiger in the Chinese Night*, and Leo Yerxa, *Last Leaf First Snowflake to Fall*
Ages 12 and up: Diana Wieler, *RanVan the Defender*

1994 Ages 7 and under: W.D. Valgardson, author; Ange Zhang, illustrator, *Thor*
Ages 8–11: Barbara Greenwood, author; Heather Collins, illustrator, *A Pioneer Story*
Ages 12 and up: Sarah Ellis, *Out of the Blue*

1995 Ages 7 and under: Nan Gregory, author; Ron Lightburn, illustrator, *How Smudge Came*
Ages 8–11: Mordecai Richler, *Jacob Two-Two's First Spy Case*
Ages 12 and up: Joan Clark, *The Dream Carvers*

1996 Ages 7 and under: Don Gillmor, author; Marie-Louise Gay, illustrator, *The Fabulous Song*
Ages 8–11: Shelley Tanaka, *Discovering the Iceman: What Was It Like to Find a 5,300-Year Old Mummy?*, illus. Laurie McGaw
Ages 12 and up: Brian Doyle, *Uncle Ronald*

1997 Ages 7 and under: Barbara Nichol, author; Philippe Béha, illustrator, *Biscuits in the Cupboard*
Ages 8–11: Kevin Major, *The House of Wooden Santas*, illus. Imelda George (wood carvings) and Ned Pratt (photography)
Ages 12 and up: Kenneth Oppel, *Silverwing*

1998 Ages 7 and under: Marilyn Helmer and Paul Mombourquette, *Fog Cat*
Ages 8–11: Richard Scrimger, *The Nose from Jupiter*
Ages 12 and up: William Bell, *Zack*

IODE Violet Downey Book Award (National Chapter of Canada IODE)

Sponsored by the National Chapter of the Imperial Order of the Daughters of the Empire, this award goes to an outstanding English-language book for children 13 and under.

1985 Mary-Ellen Lang Collura, *Winners*
1986 Marianne Brandis, *The Quarter-Pie Window*
1987 Janet Lunn, *Shadow in Hawthorn Bay*
1988 Donn Kushner, *A Book Dragon*
1989 no award
1990 Paul Yee, *Tales from Gold Mountain*
1991 Barbara Smucker, *Incredible Jumbo*
Michael Bedard, *Redwork*
1992 Sheryl McFarlane and Ron Lightburn, *Waiting for the Whales*
1993 Julie Johnston, *Hero of Lesser Causes*
1994 Kit Pearson, *The Lights Go on Again*
1995 Sarah Ellis, *Out of the Blue*
1996 Jean Little, *His Banner Over Me*
1997 Janet McNaughton, *To Dance at the Palais Royale*

1998 Celia Barker Lottridge, *Wings to Fly*
1999 Gayle Friesen, *Janey's Girl*

IODE (Toronto) Children's Book Award

The Toronto Municipal Chapter of the Imperial Order of the Daughters of the Empire annually presents this award to a Toronto-area writer or illustrator of an outstanding Canadian-published book for children.

1974 Dennis Lee, *Alligator Pie*
1975 William Kurelek, *A Prairie Boy's Summer*
1976 Aviva Layton, *How the Kookaburra Got His Laugh*
1977 William Toye, *The Loon's Necklace*
1978 Laszlo Gal for illustration of three texts: *The Shirt of the Happy Man*, by Mariella Bertelli; *My Name Is Not Odessa Yarker*, by Marian Engel; and *Why the Man in the Moon Is Happy*, by Ronald Melzak
1979 Janet Lunn, *The Twelve Dancing Princesses*
1980 Olena Kassian for illustration of two texts: *The Hungry Time*, by Selwyn Dewdney; and *Afraid of the Dark*, by Barry Dickson
1981 Bernice Thurman Hunter, *That Scatterbrain Booky*
1982 Kathy Stinson, *Red Is Best*
1983 Tim Wynne-Jones, *Zoom at Sea*
1984 Ian Wallace, *Chin Chiang and the Dragon's Dance*
1985 Robin Muller, *The Sorcerer's Apprentice*
1986 Barbara Reid, *Have You Seen Birds?*, text by Joanne Oppenheim
1987 Caroline Parry, *Let's Celebrate! Canada's Special Days*
1988 Eric Beddows, *Night Cars*, text by Teddy Jam
1989 Brenda Clark, *Little Fingerling*, text by Monica Hughes
1990 David Booth, ed., *Voices of the Wind*
1991 Michael Bedard and Regolo Ricci, *The Nightingale*
1992 Janet Lunn, Christopher Moore, and Alan Daniel, *The Story of Canada*
1993 Celia Barker Lottridge, *Ten Small Tales*
1994 Joanne Findon (text) and Ted Nasmith (illustrations), *The Dream of Aengus*
1995 Linda Granfield (text) and Janet Wilson (illustrations), *In Flanders Fields: The Story of the Poem by John McCrae*
1996 David Booth (text) and Karen Reczuch (illustrations), *Dust Bowl*
1997 Ian Wallace, *A Winter's Tale*
1998 Marilyn Helmer (text) and Paul Mombourquette (illustrations), *Fog Cat*

Geoffrey Bilson Award for Historical Fiction

Established in memory of the respected historian and children's author Geoffrey Bilson, this annual prize is administered by the Canadian Children's Book Centre and is awarded to a Canadian author for an outstanding work of historical fiction for young people.

1988 Carol Matas, *Lisa*
1989 Martyn Godfrey, *Mystery in the Frozen Lands*, and Dorothy Perkyns, *Rachel's Revolution*
1990 Kit Pearson, *The Sky Is Falling*
1991 Marianne Brandis, *The Sign of the Scales*
1992 no award
1993 Celia Barker Lottridge, *Ticket to Curlew*
1994 Kit Pearson, *The Lights Go on Again*
1995 Joan Clark, *The Dream Carvers*
1996 Marianne Brandis, *The Rebellion: A Story of Upper Canada*
1997 Janet McNaughton, *To Dance at the Palais Royale*
1998 Irene Watts, *Good-bye Marianne*

Ann Connor Brimer Award

Awarded annually by the Nova Scotia Library Association for an outstanding book published in Canada by a resident of Atlantic Canada.

1991 Joyce Barkhouse, *Pit Pony*
1992 Kevin Major, *Eating Between the Lines*
1993 Budge Wilson, *Oliver's Wars*
1994 Lesley Choyce, *Good Idea Gone Bad*
1995 Sheree Fitch, *Mabel Murple*
1996 Don Aker, *Of Things Not Seen*
1997 Janet McNaughton, *To Dance at the Palais Royale*
1998 Kevin Major, *The House of Wooden Santas*
1999 Janet McNaughton, *Make or Break Spring*

The Elizabeth Mrazik-Cleaver Canadian Picture Book Award

Awarded in memory of author-illustrator Elizabeth Cleaver for the best Canadian picture book.

1986 Ann Blades, *By the Sea: An Alphabet Book*
1987 Barbara Reid, *Have You Seen Birds?*, text by Joanne Oppenheim
1988 Stéphane Poulin, *Can You Catch Josephine?*
1989 Eric Beddows, *Night Cars,* text by Teddy Jam
1990 Ian Wallace, *The Name of the Tree*, text by Celia Barker Lottridge
1991 Paul Morin, *The Orphan Boy*, text by Tololwa Mollel
1992 Ron Lightburn, *Waiting for the Whales*, text by Sheryl McFarlane
1993 Barbara Reid, *Two by Two*

1994 Leo Yerxa, *Last Leaf First Snowflake to Fall*
1995 Murray Kimber, *Josepha: A Prairie Boy's Story*, text by Jim McGugan
1996 Janet Wilson, *Selina and the Bear Paw Quilt*, text by Barbara Smucker
1997 Harvey Chan, *Ghost Train*, text by Paul Yee
1998 Pascal Milelli, *Rainbow Bay*, text by Stephen Hume

The Amelia Frances Howard-Gibbon Illustrator's Award

The Canadian Association of Children's Librarians annually presents a silver medal to the best illustrated children's book published in Canada by an illustrator who is a citizen or resident of Canada.

1971 Elizabeth Cleaver, *The Wind Has Wings*, compiled by Mary Alice Downie and Barbara Robertson
1972 Shizuye Takashima, *A Child in Prison Camp*
1973 Jacques de Roussan, *Au-delà du soleil/Beyond the Sun*
1974 William Kurelek, *A Prairie Boy's Winter*
1975 Carlo Italiano, *The Sleighs of My Childhood/Les Traineaux de Mon Enfance*
1976 William Kurelek, *A Prairie Boy's Summer*
1977 Pam Hall, *Down By Jim Long's Stage*, text by Al Pitman
1978 Elizabeth Cleaver, *The Loon's Necklace*, text by William Toye
1979 Ann Blades, *A Salmon for Simon*, text by Betty Waterton
1980 Laszlo Gal, *The Twelve Dancing Princesses*, text by Janet Lunn
1981 Douglas Tait, *The Trouble with Princesses*, text by Christie Harris
1982 Heather Woodall, *Ytek and the Arctic Orchid*, text by Garnet Hewitt
1983 Lindee Climo, *Chester's Barn*
1984 Ken Nutt, *Zoom at Sea*, text by Tim Wynne-Jones
1985 Ian Wallace, *Chin Chiang and the Dragon's Dance*
1986 Ken Nutt, *Zoom Away*, text by Tim Wynne-Jones
1987 Marie-Louise Gay, *Moonbeam on a Cat's Ear*
1988 Marie-Louise Gay, *Rainy Day Magic*
1989 Kim LaFave, *Amos's Sweater*, text by Janet Lunn
1990 Kady MacDonald Denton, *Til All the Stars Have Fallen: Canadian Poems for Children*, edited by David Booth
1991 Paul Morin, *The Orphan Boy*, text by Tololwa M. Mollel
1992 Ron Lightburn, *Waiting for the Whales*, text by Sheryl McFarlane
1993 Paul Morin, *The Dragon's Pearl*, text by Julie Lawson
1994 Leo Yerxa, *Last Leaf First Snowflake to Fall*
1995 Barbara Reid, *Gifts*, text by Jo Ellen Bogart
1996 Karen Reczuch, *Just Like New*, text by Ainslie Manson
1997 Harvey Chan, *Ghost Train*, text by Paul Yee
1998 Barbara Reid, *The Party*
1999 Kady MacDonald Denton, *A Child's Treasury of Nursery Rhymes*

The Vicky Metcalf Award

Presented annually by the Canadian Authors Association to a writer for a body of writing 'inspirational to Canadian youth'. No writer may win the award more than once.

1963	Kerry Wood
1964	John F. Hayes
1965	Roderick Haig-Brown
1966	Fred Swayze
1967	John Patrick Gillese
1968	Lorrie McLaughlin
1969	Audrey McKim
1970	Farley Mowat
1971	Kay Hill
1972	William E. Toye
1973	Christie Harris
1974	Jean Little
1975	Lyn Harrington
1976	Suzanne Martel
1977	James Houston
1978	Lyn Cook
1979	Cliff Faulknor
1980	John Craig
1981	Monica Hughes
1982	Janet Lunn
1983	Claire Mackay
1984	Bill Freeman
1985	Edith Fowke
1986	Dennis Lee
1987	Robert Munsch
1988	Barbara Smucker
1989	Stéphane Poulin
1990	Bernice Thurman Hunter
1991	Brian Doyle
1992	Kevin Major
1993	Phoebe Gilman
1994	Welwyn Wilton Katz
1995	Sarah Ellis
1996	Margaret Buffie
1997	Tim Wynne-Jones
1998	Kit Pearson

The Ruth Schwartz Children's Book Award

Established to honour Ruth Schwartz, a Toronto bookseller, these awards are selected by children from a short list compiled by booksellers. Since 1994 two awards have been given, one for a picture book and one for a young adult (fiction or non-fiction) title.

1976 Mordecai Richler, *Jacob Two-Two Meets the Hooded Fang*
1977 Robert Thomas Allen, *The Violin*
1978 Dennis Lee, *Garbage Delight*
1979 Kevin Major, *Hold Fast*
1980 Barbara Smucker, *Days of Terror*
1981 Suzanne Martel, *The King's Daughter*
1982 Marsha Hewitt and Claire Mackay, *One Proud Summer*
1983 Jan Truss, *Jasmin*
1984 Tim Wynne-Jones, *Zoom at Sea*
1985 Jean Little, *Mama's Going to Buy You a Mockingbird*
1986 Robert Munsch, *Thomas' Snowsuit*
1987 Barbara Reid, *Have You Seen Birds?*
1988 Cora Taylor, *The Doll*
1989 Janet Lunn, *Amos's Sweater*
1990 Diana Wieler, *Bad Boy*
1991 William Bell, *Forbidden City*
1992 Paul Yee, *Roses Sing on New Snow*
1993 Phoebe Gilman, *Something from Nothing*
1994 Picture Book: Michael Kusugak and Vladyana Krykorka, *Northern Lights: The Soccer Trails*
Young Adult: O.R. Melling, *The Hunter's Moon*
1995 Picture Book: Barbara Greenwood and Heather Collins, *A Pioneer Story: The Daily Life of a Canadian Family in* 1840
Young Adult: Julie Johnston, *Adam and Eve and Pinch-Me*
1996 Picture Book: Geoff Butler, *The Killick: A Newfoundland Story*
Young Adult: Welwyn Wilton Katz, *Out of the Dark*
1997 Picture Book: Paul Yee and Harvey Chan, *Ghost Train*
Young Adult: Kit Pearson, *Awake and Dreaming*
1998 Picture Book: Jo Ellen Bogart (text) and Laura Fernandes and Rick Jacobson (illustrations), *Jeremiah Learns to Read*
Young Adult: Martha Brooks, *Bone Dance*
1999 Picture Book: Celia Lottridge (text) and Harvey Chan (illustrations), *Music for the Tsar of the Sea*
Young Adult: Eric Walters, *War of the Eagles*

Appendix B:

Some Sources for Further Study

Introductions to the Criticism and Theory of Children's Literature

The following books offer a useful introduction to both traditional and newer methods of analysis. Because McGillis and Nodelman are Canadian academics, their guides occasionally refer to Canadian materials.

Lukens, Rebecca J. *A Critical Handbook of Children's Literature*, 6th edn (New York: Longman, 1999).

May, Jill P. *Children's Literature and Critical Theory* (New York: Oxford University Press, 1995).

McGillis, Roderick. *The Nimble Reader: Literary Theory and Children's Literature* (New York: Twayne, 1996).

Nodelman, Perry. *The Pleasures of Children's Literature*, 2nd edn (New York: Longman, 1996).

Surveys of Canadian Children's Literature

Both books below organize their discussions according to genres or topics. Egoff's pioneering study, updated with the assistance of Saltman, provides an excellent historical overview; Waterston's is less comprehensive, but it is a useful supplement.

Egoff, Sheila A., and Judith Saltman. *The New Republic of Childhood: A Critical Guide to Canadian Children's Literature in English* (Toronto: Oxford University Press, 1990).

Waterston, Elizabeth. *Children's Literature in Canada* (New York: Twayne, 1992).

Journals, Reviewing Sources, Reference Works, Internet Resources

Canadian Children's Literature (*CCL*) is the only academic journal devoted exclusively to the subject. Readers wishing more current reviews of new books should consult the journals we include in our list of abbreviations. We can note here, however, that both *Quill and Quire* and *CM: Canadian Materials*, which is now an electronic publication, provide first-rate starting points. *CM*'s Web site contains a search engine that offers access to both all issues of the electronic version of the magazine and an archive of reviews and features from the print version. *CCL*'s Web site contains a searchable database of past issues, but it does not provide on-line access to the articles and reviews themselves. Each annual volume of *Canadian Book Review Annual* (*CBRA*) and its *Canadian Children's Literature* (not to be confused with the journal of the same name) review large numbers of Canadian books. Most large libraries subscribe to *CBRA*, but readers can go to its Web site to find out about both publications. The Canadian Children's Book Centre promotes Canadian books and offers a number of publications, including *Our Choice*, a guide to good Canadian books and media. Its Web site is not updated frequently, but it does provide information about the Book Centre's services. The best Internet site to begin a search for information and authors' Web sites is based at the University of Calgary. David Brown's *CLWG: Children's Literature Web Guide* contains news about authors and awards, lists of books and awards, and numerous categorized links to other sites. Gale Research, which specializes in reference books for libraries, often includes discussions of Canadian children's writers in its publications. Consult the most recent volume of *Something About the Author* containing an index (some volumes do not include one) or the annual *Contemporary Authors: Cumulative Index* for a listing of entries in all of Gale's continuing series of reference books.

Canadian Book Review Annual
44 Charles Street West
Suite 3205
Toronto, Ontario M4Y 1R8
Telephone: (416) 961-8537
Fax: (416) 961-1855
http://www.interlog.com/~cbra/

Canadian Children's Book Centre
35 Spadina Road
Toronto, Ontario M5R 2S9
Telephone: (416) 975-0010
Fax: (416) 975-1839
http://www3.sympatico.ca/ccbc/mainpage.htm

Canadian Children's Literature
Department of English
University of Guelph
Guelph, Ontario N1G 2W1

Index